CHRIST IS COMING!

A Christ-centered Approach to Last-Day Events

Norman Gulley

REVIEW AND HERALD®
PUBLISHING ASSOCIATION
HAGERSTOWN, MD 21740

The author assumes full responsibility for the accuracy of all facts and quotations as cited in this book.

This book was
Edited by Gerald Wheeler
Copyedited by Eugene Lincoln
Jacket designed by Ron J. Pride
Cover photo/illustration: PhotoDisc/Ron J. Pride
Typeset: 11/12 Times

PRINTED IN U.S.A.

02 01 00 99 98 5 4 3 2 1

Library of Congress Cataloging in Publication Data

Gulley, Norman R.

Christ is coming! : a Christ-centered approach to last-day events /Norman Gulley.

p. cm.

Includes bibliographical references.

1. Seventh-day Adventists—Doctrines. 2. End of the world. 3. Second Advent. I. Title.

BX6154.G85 1998

236—dc21 98-23498

CIP

ISBN 0-8280-1335-7

"For more than 30 years Norman Gulley has been teaching and writing about the last things. His doctoral dissertation focused on Karl Barth's eschatology, and Gulley brings a depth of reflection and richness of research to this book. Christ Is Coming, *the pinnacle of his life's work, makes a major contribution to the Adventist Church and to Christian thought in general. What impresses me most about this book is Gulley's love for Christ and the assurance that He brings as we face the end-time."*

William G. Johnsson, Ph.D.
Executive Publisher and Editor
Adventist Review

"Seventh-day Adventists for too long have anticipated the end of this world with fear and trepidation. Norman Gulley successfully challenges that premise. He demonstrates that 'the real time of trouble is for those who hate God's people, and seek to eradicate them.' The author has given us a work that encompasses far more than predictions about last-day events. It summarizes the lifework of one who has taught systematic theology for almost 40 years."

Rose Otis
Vice President
North American Division

"At last a thorough treatment of the Adventist doctrine of eschatology with a solidly biblical and Christ-centered focus! Eschatology is treated wholistically, within the larger perspective of the biblical worldview and the major alternative worldviews and end-time movements. This book will be an invaluable guide to last-day events for college and seminary students as well as pastors and laypersons. I plan to use it as my textbook for my seminary class in biblical eschatology."

Richard M. Davidson, Ph.D.
Old Testament Department
Andrews University Theological Seminary
J. N. Andrews Professor of Old Testament Interpretation and Chair

"Gulley's book provides an exciting, positive picture of the Second Coming for those whose faith is in the Lord. It is well grounded in Scripture, written in an easy-to-grasp style, yet provides additional material for those who wish to dig deeper. A must read for every Adventist who believes and hopes for the soon return of our Lord."

Randall W. Younker, Ph.D.
Director, Ph.D./Th.D. programs
Andrews University Theological Seminary

"A comprehensive, sensible, thoroughly Adventist, thoroughly Christ-centered look at a doctrine of the end-times. This book fills a major gap in Adventist publication."

John Paulien, Ph.D.
Professor of New Testament Interpretation
Andrews University Theological Seminary

"Christ Is Coming! *is the most comprehensive volume on last-day events in the light of the great controversy that has ever been written. With its focus on Christ instead of the crisis, it brings hope to the heart and refreshes the soul."*

Jack J. Blanco, Th.D.
Dean, School of Religion
Southern Adventist University

Norman Gulley's book Christ Is Coming! *is a comprehensive, yet easy-to-read discussion of the major issues regarding salvation, the understanding of Scripture, and the end-time prophecies. Its evaluation of the deceptive end-time doctrines of our time is beneficial for every reader. Its greatest contribution is the consistent application of the everlasting gospel to the prophetic Word of God."*

Hans K. LaRondelle, Th.D.
Professor Emeritus of Theology
Andrews University Theological Seminary

Christ Is Coming! *is written to give the reader step- by-step instructions on how to prepare for the final events in the great controversy. Gulley takes complex contemporary themes and develops them into a simple, concise writing style for average people."*

Oliver J. McKinney
Ministerial Association Secretary
Southern Union Conference

"If you are serious about watching and working while awaiting the parousia of our Lord, Norm Gulley's thoroughgoing volume will help render the journey informed and expectant. I'll be keeping my copy close at hand."

Mervyn A. Warren, Ph.D., D.Min.
Chairman of Religion
Oakwood College

"The book is fragrant with hope, faith, and confidence in Christ's soon return, and I've been deeply moved by it. Those who know and love Norman Gulley as a teacher will hear his voice in every line, and if they listen carefully, they will hear Christ's voice as well."

Ed Christian, Ph.D.
Assistant Professor of English and Bible
Kutztown University of Pennsylvania

"One of the most popular religion classes at Southern Adventist University is Last-Day Events, taught by Norman R. Gulley. From years of experience and deep study he offers a unique textbook that is for all members of the church."

Leo Van Dolson, Ph.D.
Adjunct Professor of Religion and Health Evangelism
Southern Adventist University

"With the impressive thoroughness we've come to expect, Norm Gulley has done the Seventh-day Adventist Church and the Christian church in general a great service in preparing a textbook on last-day events. . . . It holds a wealth of immediately relevant information that every concerned and committed Christian will want to read." ***Warren Ashworth, Ph.D.***
Professor of Religion
Pacific Union College

"This comprehensive volume is a must for all who want to hear the present heartbeat of centrist Adventist eschatology." ***Arthur N. Patrick, D.Min., Ph.D.***
Visiting Associate Professor
Church History and Pastoral Ministry
La Sierra University

"A comprehensive and all-encompassing overview of where we are today in terms of last-day events. Dr. Gulley has written a book that all Seventh-day Adventists should read, whether they would agree with every point or not." ***Clifford Goldstein***
Editor, Liberty

Dedication

This book is dedicated to all my students, past, present, and future. What an inspiration and joy to have you in my classes! I dedicate the book to those I have had the privilege of presenting last-day events to at camp meetings, workers' meetings, and weekend seminars. You too were such a blessing to me! I look forward to more. I have learned from you. Last, I want to dedicate the book to each reader, that you may be encouraged to joyfully face final events.

Acknowledgments

I want to thank the Review and Herald® Publishing Association for undertaking to publish this volume. I salute you for sensing the church needs a textbook/sourcebook on last-day events. Special thanks are due Richard Coffen, vice president for editorial; Gerald Wheeler, assistant vice president; Jeannette Johnson, acquisitions editor; and Tim Crosby, editor-at-large. I am grateful to these persons and to all the team who worked so well on the project. As always, Gerald Wheeler did excellent work in editing.

I want to thank those who gave such kind and generous endorsements of this book. Their words are an encouragement. Above all, I want to thank my Saviour for the many ideas that came to me while looking at last-day events from His perspective. I have sensed His presence with me in the research and writing of this books, and worship and adore Him for His gracious leading during the many years of gathering and thinking through the data.

Grateful thanks to Peggy Bennett, director of libraries and her staff for obtaining interlibrary loan books and articles through the McKee Library at Southern Adventist University.

Foreword

The heartbeat of Adventism is succinctly expressed in the words of the Hymn, "We have this hope which burns within our hearts, hope in the coming of the Lord."

While early Adventists eagerly grasped the prophecies of the Second Coming, their focus centered not so much upon the doctrine per se as on Christ Himself. It was with tears of joy and eager anticipation that they looked forward to seeing their Saviour and Lord. That hope is still the spirit of Adventism today.

As the good news of salvation through Christ alone and His soon return is broadcast by satellite and shared with others by millions of Adventists around the world, the great controversy between Christ and Satan is intensifying. Planet Earth, filled with people for whom Christ died, hurtles through the pre-Advent time zone with comparatively few aware that they are heading toward the end of human history. The faster we travel, the greater our need of the Holy Spirit to help us focus on Christ instead of the crisis while at the same time recognizing the hazards along the way.

Dr. Norman Gulley has provided a comprehensive, Christ-centered volume on end-time events, movements, and scriptural teachings crucial to our understanding and safety. Postmodern thinking, which holds opposite values to be equally true; spirituality without the authority of Scripture; theistic evolution without 24-hour days of creation and a weekly Sabbath; worship as entertainment; and apparitions of Mary with supposed messages from heaven are only a few of the hazards exposed.

While Dr. Gulley wrote *Christ Is Coming!* first as a textbook for Seventh-day Adventist young people, I recommend it to all of whatever age and Christian persuasion whose hope is the return of our Lord and Saviour Jesus Christ.

Robert S. Folkenberg

Contents

Introduction

Our planet rushes toward its rendezvous with destiny. Time is running out. Will we make it to the third millennium? One thing is certain. People around the world sense that something is coming. Never before have people around the world had so many angel encounters. Never before have there been so many apparitions of the virgin Mary. Never before have psychics become so widely accepted. Never before has spiritualism had such a worldwide impact, as seen in the New Age and charismatic movements. Never before has the Catholic Church had such global influence. Never before have Christians been in a position to dominate American politics as in the Christian Coalition. Something is going on behind the scenes.

Planet Earth moves like a plane on a transoceanic flight. It has been a long time since takeoff, and the trip has been bumpy at times. Yet look ahead. A dreary, dark, dense sky threatens. Black, surly storm clouds gather along the whole horizon. They begin to surround and shake the plane. No detour offers an escape around the storm. Planet Earth must move into it. The most stupendous crisis of all time is about to unfold. The early time of trouble, the great time of trouble, and the time of Jacob's trouble loom large ahead. Even now turbulence batters the planet as it enters the fringes of the coming storm.

Recently, near the beginning of the semester, I took a survey of some students at Southern Adventist University who were studying last-day events. The results showed that 49 percent worry about the present pre-advent judgment, 56 percent are scared of last-day events (in fact, 41 percent would rather die than go through last-day events), 37 percent believe they gain entrance to heaven through Christ's sacrifice plus their human efforts, 50 percent are not sure they would be saved if they died today, and yet 88 percent claimed they know Christ as a personal friend.

That is a stunning revelation, when you realize they represent a cross section of Seventh-day Adventist youth from all over the United States and other countries, studying a variety of majors. They are among the final generation, yet many do not want to be part of it. Something is radically wrong here. And who could say that the results would be any better if we researched older people?

To be afraid of last-day events is human. Who wants to exchange a comparatively normal existence for what is just ahead? Yet it will be our finest hour, one we'll speak about forever in eternity, as we shall see later. It is the time when Satan faces resounding defeat. He knows this and is out to take over not only the world but Christians too!

As never before, Christians need faith: a faith that keeps a steady gaze on the coming Christ beyond the crisis. Christ, and not the crisis, should occupy their minds. For not so much *what* is coming as *who* is coming should occupy the mind. The outcome of a football game is not over until the fourth quarter. Satan causes havoc in final events, but Christ will have the last word. But that's not all. Christ will be with His people through those final events. He promised, "Never will I leave you; never will I forsake you" (Heb. 13:5). His presence will mean everything to His followers. He will do for them what they could never do for themselves. Many people look at final events as if they have to go through them alone. No wonder they remain petrified! But Christ longs that His people look to Him. Jesus asked if when the Son of man returns, would He find faith in the earth? (see Luke 18:8). Perhaps here is the problem. Few will have the necessary faith. Faith in Him will make the decisive, determining difference for the journey through end-time turbulence.

In this book we will look frankly at the coming crisis, but not apart from the present and coming Christ. As we rapidly move toward the third millennium, it is time to let Christ liberate us from the shackles of fear. Do you long to hope again? Or even for the first time?

Since 1960 college and seminary students have taken my last-day events class. It has been a joy to proclaim the good news about final events through these classes and seminars in different parts of the world. My conviction is that many Christians are far too scared of final events. But when they hear of coming events in their Christ-centered context, fear falls away. "Then you will know the truth, and the truth will set you free" (John 8:32). For nearly 40 years I've rejoiced to see thousands of persons begin to hope again. I have written this book so that you too may stop fearing coming events. Satan is in the business of getting Christians fixated on what is coming instead of on Christ.

By the way, I surveyed those students at the end of the semester. Ninety-six percent had lost their fear of last-day events. What a dramatic change wrought by Christ! They gained freedom to rejoice in Him and now face final events as their privileged destiny. So can you! May God bless you and give you freedom too.

Norman R. Gulley, Ph.D.
Professor of Systematic Theology
Southern Adventist University

Preface

Bookshelves bulge with last-day-events books that claim to predict the events awaiting us. They speak about the new world order, the New Age movement, the secret rapture, the alleged role of Israel in the end-time, Armageddon, and the millennium. Other books supposedly tell us about life after death, with alleged reports from resuscitated human beings returning to speak about what they experienced. More books report on the coming one-world government, the millennial kingdom, and America's role in final events. Reconstructionists, dispensationalists, and historicists all have their own ideas.

We need to know what is out there and how to evaluate it. This book does some of that for you. Above all, we need to see what Satan's strategy is through such movements. He is using the New Age movement, the charismatic movement, spiritualism, channeling, the Christian Coalition, and dominionists to take over the planet. As Christ's followers, we need to know how the concept of process theology undermines final events.

This book also looks at ideas that have a definite bearing on final events. Satan will use Sunday sacredness and the state of the dead as two pillars in the end-time. We will evaluate them. Today many people question the concept of hell, the view of the immediate survival of the soul at death, and Darwinian evolution. As Christians, we need to know about such debates and the biblical answers to them. All of these impact on last-day events. The issues of death and hell will form a part of final events for most Christians. Catholics add purgatory to the controversy. The proponents of all three concepts present them as final events for the individual in a way that grabs the focus from coming global or cosmic final events. What does the Bible speak about them? We need to know, so that we have an answer to give our Christian friends as well as having protection for ourselves. In an unprecedented way in the end-time Satan will confront Christians with what seems to be their dead loved ones.

Evolution challenges the first

angel's message of the book of Revelation. Sunday directly attacks the third angel's message. Both messages play a central role in final events. We'll study their meaning and expose the counterfeits launched against them. And we will explore the real issue in the coming Sunday law and examine the deeper meaning of the Sabbath for survival through those final events. This book will consider the importance of the pre-Advent judgment. All these things are vital to a preparation for final events and to give us insight to face them unafraid.

After looking at how to interpret end-time events and evaluate end-time movements and end-time doctrines, we then take the journey through final events. If you want to skip to the journey and take that first, then come back to the other sections, that is fine. But much in the earlier material will help make the journey clearer and equip you for the real journey just ahead.

Unless otherwise stated, I have used the New International Version of Scripture throughout.

Part One

Information for the Journey

Chapter 1

Hope for Postmoderns

Today we're in the midst of a profound transition from what scholars call modernity to a new period they label as postmodernity. The human race has entered a new era that presents unprecedented challenges and opportunities to our study of end-time events.

Many have attempted to describe postmodernity. "A massive intellectual revolution is taking place," Diogenes Allen says, "that is perhaps as great as that which marked off the modern world from the Middle Ages. The foundations of the modern world are collapsing, and we are entering a postmodern world. The principles formed during the Enlightenment (c. 1600-1780), which formed the foundations of modern mentality, are crumbling."[1]

Leith Anderson says, "We are experiencing enormous structural change in our country and in the world—change that promises to be greater than the invention of the printing press, greater than the Industrial Revolution, and greater than the rise and demise of Communism. Our world is changing so quickly that we can barely keep track of what is happening, much less figure out how to respond."[2]

Defined

We begin with a simple fact: Postmodernity comes *after* modernity. The seventeenth-century Enlightenment, which dominated human quest for knowledge and understanding for 200 years, launched the intellectual period we call modernity. Scientific method brought multiplied technological benefits, but it also negatively affected global ecology as well as bringing the human race to the brink of a nuclear holocaust. As a result, its earlier belief in knowledge as inherently good came to a shattering end. Thus, early in the twentieth century thinkers began to challenge the modern worldview, and it continues to be questioned.

Postmodernity is also *anti*modernity. The modern worldview included the acceptance of humanity's inevitable progress, often based on evolutionary theory. We have now come to a generation that for the first time does not see any inevitable better future. The optimism of the Enlightenment, with its vaunted belief in human reason, has given way to pessimism and meaninglessness. It is as if the world has suddenly awakened to a reality check. Whereas scientific method, reason, and universal objectivity influenced the modern worldview, postmodernity rejects scientific method, reason, and universal objectivity. The collapse of a unified, rational, and meaningful worldview has thrown the human race into a period in which each person approaches reality from his or her own particular presuppositions and assumptions. No single worldview provides a meaningful assessment of reality. "Defining the idea of postmodernism," Gary Phillips writes, "is a bit like nailing down Jell-O."[3]

Differences Between Modernity and Postmodernity

When it comes to comparing modernity and postmodernity, a radical discontinuity overshadows the continuities we do find. First, let us look at an example of continuity. The modern antipathy to metaphysics and the transcendental continues in postmodernity. "While modernism categorically denies the transcendent and spends a great deal of time and effort attempting to prove that the transcendent does not exist," William E. Brown says, "Postmodernism confronts the transcendent with a yawn."[4]

Postmodernity especially champions liberation causes. If we have no transcendent God, then human beings themselves have to become revolutionaries to bring change in their own strength and in their own way. The new worldview defends the marginalized. Yet at the same time, as Carl F. H. Henry notes, "religion is marginalized and trivialized,"[5] and "Postmodernists have genuinely given up on the idea of absolute truth."[6] What a paradox—they have an absolute mission or right (to liberate), yet without an absolute mandate or truth, which leaves one wondering how even liberation can be an absolute truth for them!

Modernistic philosophy shut God out of our part of His universe. Its closed continuum worldview rejected any inbreaking of the supernatural within the normal operation of cause and effect. Huston Smith suggests that the modern mind thought that "seeing further in a horizontal direction would compensate for loss of the vertical." But modernistic philosophy failed to realize that human vision on the horizontal plane is still confined within a closed universe and is therefore trapped in its own subjectivity. Smith illustrates this vision with a line silhouetting the Himalayan range. Modernity grabbed both ends and pulled it into a straight line.[7]

Also modernity flaunted human reason as the savior of all human problems. Such extreme rationalism was not enlightened, although it was a product of the Enlightenment. Postmodernists rightly question such intellectual arrogance, but go too far by rejecting reason altogether.[8] The solution lies between the two extremes, employing a proper use of reason under the guidance of Scripture to arrive at solutions. After all, the God of all truth invited humanity, "Come now, let us reason together" (Isa. 1:18).

Hope for Postmoderns

Difficulties in Postmodernity for the Study of End-time Events

Postmodernism raises major difficulties when presenting end-time events. If we are to be relevant to our generation, we must pay full attention to the challenges that postmodernity poses. The first thing we must keep in mind is that we must think through end-time events in light of the current generation, not one that has already gone. We must present final events afresh for every generation. This does not change the content, but it may change the way we communicate it.

1. Opposed to System

How can one present a systematic presentation of the journey through end-time events when postmoderns reject the very concept of such systems? We must realize it's one thing to reject a system, and another thing to live a muddled life. Often the very ones rejecting such systems still organize their day, plan their vacations, and work in a routine manner, arriving at appointments on time. Modern life demands schedules, whether for travel, business, or listening to the evening news. We find an inbuilt orderliness in air flights (sometimes), television programs, and the publication of *Reader's Digest, National Geographic,* and *U.S. News and World Report,* to name a few examples.

Postmoderns oppose systems only on the theoretical level, not everyday life. Yet there is no advantage to reject something at the theoretical level that proves eminently workable in ordinary living. We can understand why postmoderns want to discard the strictures of modernity, the science that led to ecological and nuclear threats to the planet, but modernity has more to it than that. It has a good side that continues in postmodernity, because life is more orderly than the theory of postmodernity allows.

2. Opposed to a Center

Although postmoderns reject the idea of a center in every theory, they cannot live out the concept in practice. If God is not the center of a person's life, then someone or something else will be. The Ten Commandments deal with the problem up front. The very first commandment says, "I am the Lord your God, who brought you out of Egypt, out of the land of slavery. You shall have no other gods before me" (Ex. 20:2, 3). The Deuteronomy account repeats it (Deut. 5:6, 7).

Humans are incurably worshipers, an important fact to remember, because the end-time confrontation will involve worship, and all humanity will participate. The fact that human beings worship stems from their creation by God (Gen. 1:26-31; 2:7, 20-25). God made them for Himself. If they do not worship God, they will worship some other god or gods, which is why religion occurs in every culture, however primitive or advanced. Creation has programmed human beings to seek a center to their life, to give it meaning and security. Postmodernity has not lessened the number of die-hard football and baseball fans. Basketball still draws the crowds, as do tennis, golf, and car racing. People still seek after Hollywood stars and praise them on Oscar nights. And work is often central to those wanting to get ahead, whether in professional or business life. Thus workaholism didn't recede with the advent of postmodernity. The effects of Creation and modernity still live on in spite of postmodernism's decentering theory.

3. Opposed to Any Worldview

Unlike all prior ages, postmodernity has no overarching worldview. Yet we cannot possibly live up to this theoretical position. Postmodernity is a revolt expressed in many different ways. One way occurs through liberation theology, a quest for political power influenced by Marxism. But even liberation theology has a worldview, seeing God as in the business of liberating marginalized people. Thus the concept of liberation holds the center of this worldview. This is but one example of how a movement even within postmodernity does have a worldview in practice.

Modernity had both a center and a worldview. Postmodernity has neither. Yet, paradoxically, postmodernity finds itself in a shrinking world that thinks more in global terms, ranging from economy to ecology. At the very time when philosophy seeks to throw order to the winds, a global village has emerged, demanding even greater order. To this extent, in many areas of life, a worldview has been thrust upon the very revolution that abandoned all worldviews.

4. Relativism

By rejecting any system, center, or worldview, the only option left to postmodernity was relativism. But relativism means that every individual has a right to his or her own view. The local situation has replaced the broader context, situation ethics usurped the moral code, and personal preference pushed aside values. "If it feels good" substituted for an objective norm. Order gives way to chaos, hope to nihilism, and the future to the ever-present. Reality has no goal, purpose, or fulfillment. Humanity has become less than human.

Such dysfunctionality cannot sustain a viable human existence. We want meaning in our lives. Postmoderns are desperate for meaning and a future. More than ever, they need to know the good news about final events on Planet Earth.

Postmodern Theory Cannot Be Lived

Having already noticed that it is impossible to actually live out some postmodern theories, we now take a closer look at this fact. Friedrich Nietzsche (1844-1900), father of postmodernism, proclaimed God as dead and promoted nihilism, or meaninglessness. Yet he discovered meaning in a social movement of his time and promoted it with gusto, thus demonstrating that he could not practice his own theory. Jean-Paul Sartre's (1905-1980) world was one of meaninglessness, a world without morals. Yet he couldn't live up to his theory when he signed the Algerian Manifesto, "taking a position as though morals have real meaning."[9]

A. J. Ayer suggested that only mathematico-logical truths and empirical truths are meaningful. All other statements that we cannot verify by sense data are "nonsense." Thus all biblical statements are meaningless. Such a view immediately confines truth statements, or statements of meaning, to a very narrow slice of life. It forces us to renounce poetry, music, religion, and art. But how can anyone live in such a narrowly prescribed world? Furthermore, the theory could not stand under its own test for a truth statement. After all, how can we possibly test a theory of language that accepts only mathematico-logical and empirical statements by that standard?

René Descartes (1596-1650), the father of modernity, used the method of doubt. David Hume (1711-1776) took it to its ultimate conclusion, and it plunged him into utter skepticism. David K. Clark said that "Hume's philosophy left him completely in the dark about what to think, whom to trust, what cause to defend, or what activity to pursue. Given modern requirements, reason could not dispel his doubts. But he noticed that the company of friends put him in better spirits. So he turned to dining and backgammon to heal his epistemological depressions. His philosophy, however, proved utterly impotent to avoid skepticism."[10] Hume needed relief from his theory, for it simply could not be lived.

Jacques Derrida claims that "all interpretations are misinterpretation," and that a text has no clear meaning. But he jettisoned his theory once when he was misunderstood in a debate with John Searle. "Believing that Searle's exposition of his position had been unfair to him, Derrida could not resist saying, at several points in his reply, that Searle had misunderstood him and misstated his views, even adding at one point that what he, Derrida, had meant should have been clear enough and obvious to Searle. This is indeed a very far cry from the claim that Derrida's essential position cannot be stated as others can (or that a reader should not try to grasp the author's intent!). Derrida thus abandons this position, just as others do, when he feels the need to replace a misstatement of his view with an adequate statement of it."[11]

Stanley Fish is "one of the most influential literary theorists"[12] and "radical" reader-response theorists, focusing on meaning in the reading community rather than in the biblical text itself.[13] Reader-response is an important part of the postmodern scene. Fish goes so far as to maintain that "the text as a formal entity does not exist apart from the reader's interpretive act."[14] In fact, reader-response theorists believe that readers are coauthors with the biblical writers, and they give to the text the meaning it should have. That is, the text has no real meaning in and of itself.

How could life operate on Fish's theory? It would destroy any agreement on the American Constitution, for example, or any other document, so that every citizen could interpret it as he or she chose. It would put the very concept of governance in jeopardy. Traffic signs would have no standard meaning, and driving would be hazardous. Some may choose to drive on the opposite side of the road, others could agree that red traffic lights indicate that you should drive straight through the intersection and that stop signs would mean you have the right-of-way. Contracts would be impossible and would bring business to a grinding halt, for the same wording would imply different things to different people.

If a text has no meaning in itself,

but only in the mind of the reader, then no language would have meaning in and of itself either. It would exist only in the mind of the hearer. Life would simply break down hopelessly on these terms, for no one could ever be sure that he or she could communicate. How could one order from a catalog over the phone? How could any TV station present the evening news? What purpose would weather reports have? What would an emergency 911 call accomplish? What meaning would a doctor's diagnosis have? What would university teaching accomplish? The list is endless. It is simply impossible to accept Fish's reader-response theory and make sense out of life.

Limits to Pluralism

The pluralism of postmodernity also causes chaos. As Mortimer J. Adler reminds us in his book *Truth in Religion,* "a stable and peaceful society cannot exist under the domination of two or more competing governments unless one is subordinate to the other."[15] Adler shows that pluralism has always existed when it comes to matters of taste and is tolerable in that context, but not in the context of truth.[16] He notes that "anything that is transcultural is clearly in the sphere of truth." Thus the pluralism endemic in postmodernism cannot survive in practice in certain contexts.

Opportunities in Postmodernism for Truth

Despite all its problems, however, postmodernism does give opportunity for truth to regain what it lost to modernism. Too often the church capitulated to the threat from modernism instead of resisting. The modern worldview had more influence than the biblical worldview, and the church surrendered to it. The tragedy is now obvious as the modern worldview has itself retreated before that of postmodernism.

1. Christianity's Capitulation to Modernism

Postmodernism has called modernism into question. Yet it is the very modernism to which the church often surrendered to keep its intellectual respectability. Since the 1960s, in the post-Vietnam era, many people have turned away from the materialism of the West to the mysticism of the East. Some of them are seeking for what they sense is missing in the West. Turning to the East for fullness, they explore Hinduism and Buddhism. "Those dissatisfied with secular modernity most often turn to the East or to the distant mythic past," says William C. Platcher. "One reason seems to be that Christianity cannot criticize our culture very effectively if it has already accepted many of the assumptions of that culture as the price of intellectual respectability."[17]

The fact is, as Stanley Grenz reminds us, "most major Protestant denominations" "'defected' to 'modernism.'"[18] Unsure of their own biblical foundation, they caved in to science and to culture. But the collapse of modernism demonstrated the limitations of science. Science cannot deal with ultimate or existential meanings. "Theology need cater to our prevailing styles of thought only if it wishes to," says Huston Smith. "Nothing in the way of evidence requires that it do so."[19] With respect to culture, I concur with William C. Platcher that "Christianity cannot criticize our culture very effectively if it has already accepted many of the assumptions of that culture as the price of intellectual respectability."[20] Accommodation closely accompanies the desire for acceptance. To confine Scripture to a cultural artifact is a case in point. Then Scripture ceases to be the Word of God to culture. Culture judges Scripture instead of the reverse.

2. More Room for Religion

Modernism stifled religion by closing the door to the transcendent with its rejection of metaphysics. It confined the parameters of possible thought and study to a closed continuum of cause and effect, so that it in effect removed God from the realm of human history. Science limited reality to the observable, so that the religious dimension of human experience could occupy only an interior substitute for objective reality. Now the collapse of this modern worldview has radically questioned such strictures.

"In a way that has never been possible in modernity, one can find philosophical or rational space for 'giving an account for the hope that is in you,'" Don R. Stiver comments. "In other words, there is no philosophical hindrance that a priori calls such a response into question. And given the importance of reason in modernity, this renewed sense of the rationality of religion opens up a new social and cultural space for religion. In other words, if the opportunity can be seized, postmodernity allows conceptual space for religion's stretching its arms and walking about in a way not possible in the cramped quarters allowed for it since the onset of modernity. The danger is that it may continue to pace back and forth in its all-too-familiar constricted confines, not knowing that the surrounding bars have long ago rusted away."[21]

3. Intellectual Strength of Christianity

Diogenes Allen, in his book *Christian Belief in a Postmodern World: The Full Wealth of Conviction,* speaks of "a new openness for faith." He reminds us that Christianity has been on the defensive intellectually during modernism. During that period many have declared that the post-Christian age has dawned, "on the basis of physics, biology, philosophy, psychology, sociology, and anthropology."[22]

We are now in an age when philosophy and science, once used to attack Christianity, now find themselves under siege. During the reign of modernism, Christianity came under severe attack for the first time. This was a revolt against the authority found in church and Scripture. Human beings became their own authority, and human reason ruled supreme. The historical-critical methods of biblical study did their devastating work on the biblical documents. Evolutionary theory radically called into question the Genesis account of Creation, and geology doubted the universal Flood story. Human reason elevated itself above divine revelation, thus bringing God's Word captive to humanity. But this worldview is now collapsing.

As Allen notes: "No longer can

Christianity be put on the defensive, as it has been for the last three hundred years or so, because of the narrow view of reason and the reliance on classical science that are characteristic of the modern mentality." We have a new opportunity to reevaluate the viability of Christianity[23] and to present final events to a world in need.

4. Purpose in the Biblical Worldview

Postmodernism contains much meaninglessness and purposelessness. If there was ever a time for us to hear the clear purpose of the biblical worldview, it is now. Scripture tells us where we came from, why we are here, and where we are going, and thus answers the three basic philosophical questions that have interested humanity for millennia. The human race needs to hear this sure word about purpose today, something that has everything to do with end-time events. As George G. Hunter rightly notes: "We have the opportunity to reintroduce purpose to a secular world that, because of science's conditioning, is preoccupied with cause and effect and blind to the issues of purpose for human life and history."[24]

5. Foundation for Truth

Because biblical or any other texts have no meaning in themselves to postmoderns, because they have no authoritative word to them, and because this has left them in a morass of meaninglessness, postmoderns wander around aimlessly without purpose or goal. Yet God made them in His image, with a desire to worship. Thus they need to hear the certain Word of God from Scripture. Through the Holy Spirit it will meet their deepest needs.

Paradoxically this comes at the time when people are standing up for their rights in an unprecedented way. The various liberation movements are an integral part of postmodernity, whether the Black, unfranchised, or feminist movements. Yet these very movements reach beyond the relativism of culture to absolutes that belong to the biblical worldview. Gene Edward Veith, Jr., said it well: "Postmodernists, more than most people, complain about how various power structures are unfair, and they are always demanding sensitivity, tolerance, and justice. Do they not realize that they are appealing to transcendent, authoritative moral absolutes?"[25]

Here is still another demonstration that it is impossible to live postmodern theory in practice. Humanity has a reality that cannot be confined within any passing worldview out of sync with the biblical worldview. This fact gives Scripture a point of contact even with postmoderns.

The Gospel as Transcultural, Transgenerational

Although first given after the Fall (Gen. 3:15), the gospel is everlasting (Rev. 14:6) and consistently the same throughout Scripture. Christ commissioned His church to take this same gospel to the world (Matt. 28:18-20), "to every nation, tribe, language and people" (Rev. 14:6). Every human being needs to hear the good news about salvation. This presupposes that it is possible for all to hear it, whatever their culture or experience.

Scripture states that "since the creation of the world God's invisible qualities—his eternal power and divine nature—have been clearly seen, being understood from what has been made, so that men are without excuse" (Rom. 1:20). Paul speaks of the Gentiles as having "the law . . . written on their hearts, their consciences also bearing witness" (Rom. 2:15). And this includes postmoderns.

God made humanity in His image (Gen. 1:26, 27), thus offering Him a point of contact through which to communicate. Although the Fall (Gen. 3:1-7) and subsequent sins defaced this image, sin has not totally destroyed it. That is why Christ is still the light that illuminates everyone coming into the world (John 1:9). He, as Creator (John 1:1, 2; Heb 1:1, 2), chose to make humanity in such a way that after the Fall it would be still possible to reach the human race despite its degraded condition.

If Christ made all humanity in His image, this includes postmodern human beings. The longing for Himself that Christ put into the human mind still draws postmoderns. The conscience in which God speaks and His voice is heard still dwells in even those who espouse postmodernism. Yes, postmoderns have overthrown the unified worldview of modernism, may be awash in a seemingly meaningless sea of pluralism without chart or compass, have hectic, stress-filled, and often dysfunctional lives, yet still they bear the image of God and have a receiver on board to hear the good news of the gospel and end-time events. Their case may seem hopeless, but their very hopelessness makes them long for hope and be open to the only One who can bring them meaning out of chaos. As Augustine of Hippo said, "Our hearts are restless until they find their rest in Thee."

The X Generation and Truth

In their book *A Generation Alone: Xers Making a Place in the World,* William Mahedy and Janet Bernardi explain what the X generation is like. Members of the X generation were born between 1961 and 1981. Some sociologists have called it the X generation because they perceived that as a group the generation stood for nothing and believed in nothing.[26] A generation dominated by technology, half of its members are divorced, and one in three have been abused. Born in the time of President Nixon, they have never known American's earlier trust in leadership. For the first time in American history, it is the generation, for the most part, who will not have it better than their parents.[27]

Mahedy and Bernardi comment that "Einstein's relativity theories along with quantum mechanics and recent discoveries in astronomy have rendered all previously held positions obsolete. Reality is far more complex than we had imagined it to be."[28] While it may be too sweeping a statement, it's true that for some the new science has contributed to postmodernism's insecurity. But far more than a new way to look at reality (for example, light as both/either particle or wave) is the insecurity produced by nuclear science. The Xers have had a rough life and find themselves in a rough environment. Aloneness defines the generation. But this is not loneliness; rather it is a life of activity without "family and friends." Postmoderns struggle with "issues of abandonment, alienation, and aloneness." Their greatest need is for a cohesive family unit.[29]

The Xers are a very needy group. In fact, "Generation X has been spiritually starved, emotionally traumatized, educationally deprived, condemned to a bleak economic future and robbed of the hope that should characterize youth." They live in a time when the world has become a "global village," when the nightly news graphically displays major problems halfway around the world. In such a time "a great spiritual hunger has arisen around the world as we repudiate the moral and intellectual emptiness of modern life and resist the impersonal forces of vast and dehumanizing systems"[30] Such facts cry out for the spiritual energy that can come only from the Word of God as it addresses a humanity in need with a message of hope about the end-time!

Postmoderns, for the most part, lack the spiritual life that brings lasting fulfillment and peace. In spite of all the relativism and dislike of systems and objectivity, absolutes, and the transcendent, the needs of postmoderns cry out for the very things they have rejected. Here again we see that they cannot live out their own theories.

Perhaps the best way to get the attention of postmoderns is to proclaim the certainty of end-time events, to give them a goal for the future and a hope for the present. They need to know that Christ is coming for them, that He will give them that which they do not have and cannot get from the relativism and confusion of postmodernism. End-time events on Planet Earth can bring them the Christ who will set them free to live now and forever.

---

[1] Diogenes Allen, *Christian Belief in a Postmodern World: The Full Wealth of Conviction* (Louisville, Ky.: Westminster/John Knox, 1989), p. 2.

[2] Leith Anderson, *A Church for the 21st Century* (Minneapolis: Bethany, 1992), p. 17.

[3] Gary Phillips, "Religious Pluralism in a Postmodern World," in *The Challenge of Postmodernism: An Evangelical Engagement,* ed. David S. Dockery (Wheaton, Ill.: 1995), p. 254.

[4] William E. Brown, "Roots of Post-Modernism: Also Sprach Nietzsche" (professional paper read to the Evangelical Theological Society, Southern Evangelical Seminary, Charlotte, North Carolina, Mar. 10, 1995).

[5] Carl F. H. Henry, "Postmodernism: The New Spectre?" in *The Challenge of Postmodernism,* p. 41.

[6] David S. Dockery, "The Challenge of Postmodernism," in *The Challenge of Postmodernism,* p. 14.

[7] Huston Smith, *Beyond the Post-Modern Mind* (Wheaton, Ill.: Theosophical, 1989), pp. 6, 7.

[8] Gene Edward Veith, Jr., *Postmodern Times: A Christian Guide to Contemporary Thought and Culture* (Wheaton, Ill.: Crossway, 1994), p. 68.

[9] Francis Schaefer, *The Complete Works of Francis Schaefer: A Christian Worldview* (Westchester, Ill.: Crossway, 1982), vol. 1, p. 134.

[10] David K. Clark, "Narrative Theology and Apologetics," *Journal of the Evangelical Theological Society* 35, No. 4 (December 1993): p. 510.

[11] John M. Ellis, *Against Deconstructionism* (Princeton, N.J.: University Press, 1989), pp. 13, 14.

[12] Anthony C. Thiselton, *New Horizons in Hermeneutics* (Grand Rapids: Zondervan, 1992), p. 474.

[13] *Ibid.,* pp. 515, 516.

[14] Grant R. Osborne, *The Hermeneutical Spiral: A Comprehensive Introduction to Biblical Interpretation* (Downers Grove, Ill.: InterVarsity, 1991), p. 378.

[15] Mortimer J. Adler, *Truth in Religion: The Plurality of Religions and the Unity of Truth, an Essay in the*

Hope for Postmoderns

Philosophy of Religion (New York: Macmillan, 1990), p. 2.

[16] *Ibid.,* pp. 2-4.

[17] William C. Platcher, *Unapologetic Theology: A Christian Voice in a Pluralistic Conversation* (Louisville: Westminster/John Knox, 1989), p. 12.

[18] Stanley J. Grenz, *Revisioning Evangelical Theology,* p. 25.

[19] Smith, p. 146.

[20] Platcher, p. 12.

[21] Don R. Stiver, "Much Ado About Athens and Jerusalem: The Implications of Postmodernism for Faith," *Review and Expositor* (91, 1994): p. 94.

[22] Allen, p. 2.

[23] *Ibid.*

[24] George G. Hunter III, *How to Reach Secular People* (Nashville: Abingdon, 1992), p. 95.

[25] Veith, p. 62.

[26] William Mahedy and Janet Bernardi, *A Generation Alone: Xers Making a Place in the World* (Downers Grove, Ill.: InterVarsity, 1994), p. 10.

[27] *Ibid.,* pp. 14-18.

[28] *Ibid.,* p. 42.

[29] *Ibid.,* pp. 19, 21, 32.

[30] *Ibid.,* pp. 25, 43.

Chapter 2

The Larger Biblical Worldview

Ptolemy thought the universe revolved around the earth, Copernicus said that the universe revolves around the sun.

But Einstein trashed that in the twentieth century. His theories of relativity broke through to a whole universe in motion. The confined views of Ptolemy, believed for almost 1,400 years, and of Galileo and Copernicus, held for 400 years, are gone! Einstein's worldview burst through the limitations of both like a runaway rocket. Science will never be the same.

A vastly expanded universe with all things in relation to each other, moving in space, represents the present worldview. Although the universe itself has remained the same, the way scientists now look at it has changed. Because personal knowledge is theory-laden, it affects observation and needs to be corrected by what the universe is actually like in and of itself.

The same is true with the biblical worldview. Most Christians come to Scripture primarily for human salvation. They haven't looked beyond to the Bible's larger worldview. Yet the larger biblical worldview transcends the salvation worldview. As we face the third millennium, it is time for Christians to grasp the cosmic controversy worldview that's so vital to understanding end-time events.

The cosmic controversy is the context for all final events on Earth. If you're familiar with this controversy, skip down to the section "Looking Behind the Struggles of Jesus."

The Larger Worldview of Scripture

People for the past few years have had an amazing interest in angels, and later we'll look into the reason for this. But for now we want to see what Scripture tells us about angels and the cosmic controversy.

1. Satan and His Angels According to Scripture

Scripture tells us more than that God sent His Son to live and die for humanity. Although Christ's mission is central in the Bible, Scripture presents it within the context of a battle between good and the evil, of a struggle between God and Satan. Innumerable angels encircle the throne in heaven (see Rev. 5:11). These beings, made a little higher than human beings (see Ps. 8:4, 5), do God's bidding and obey His word (see Ps. 103:20) as "ministering spirits sent to serve those who will inherit salvation" (Heb. 1:14). Angels help God's followers. In fact, humans "have entertained angels without knowing it" (Heb. 13:1), an awesome thought.

2. Looking Behind the Fall of Adam and Eve

The salvation worldview of Scripture begins in the Garden of Eden after Adam and Eve succumbed to the tempter, when Christ gave them the first gospel promise (Gen. 3:15). But Scripture penetrates beyond that promise to the one who tempted Adam and Eve. We note that a serpent deceived Eve (see verse 13). Who was this serpent? Ezekiel mentions that there was in Eden, where Adam and Eve were tempted, an angel who came from the exalted position as the "anointed . . . guardian cherub" (Eze. 28:14). The passage says, "You were on the holy mount of God; you walked among the fiery stones, You were blameless in your ways from the day you were created till wickedness was found in you. Through your widespread trade you were filled with violence, and you sinned. So I drove you in disgrace from the mount of God, and I expelled you, O guardian cherub, from among the fiery stones. Your heart became proud on account of your beauty, and you corrupted your wisdom because of your splendor. So I threw you to the earth" (verses 14-17).

The passage depicts Satan as originally created perfect, given an exalted position at God's throne, and it says that he became proud and sinned in heaven until the day came that God had to throw him out. It does not mention the other angels who joined him and were also cast out, but John adds that fact (see Rev. 12:4, 12, 13). This fallen angel who appears in Eden (see Eze. 28:13) is identified with the serpent of Genesis 3:2, 13, 14. John concurs by speaking of the old serpent as the devil (see Rev. 20:2; 12:9). Having caused angels to rebel against God in heaven, Satan then came to earth to cause the human race to rebel.

3. Looking Behind the Struggles of Jesus

Scripture clearly pulls back the curtain and shows that the sin problem on earth is but a small part of a cosmic battle between Christ and Satan. This throws into clearer relief the meaning of the exorcisms during Christ's lifetime on earth. Rather than rejecting them as some Christians have, we find them integral to our understanding of a battle between demons and Christ, or the two sides of the cosmic controversy. Without such a cosmic conflict we would expect the life of Christ to have been far different from the struggle He had. But within the context of a war between good and evil we can understand why demons constantly dogged His footsteps. Mark says that Christ "traveled throughout Galilee, preaching in their synagogues and driving out demons" (Mark 1:39). When the Pharisees questioned if Jesus exorcised with the power of Satan, Jesus replied,

"If Satan drives out Satan, he is divided against himself. . . . But if I drive out demons by the Spirit of God, then the kingdom of God has come upon you" (Matt. 12:26-28). With reference to the miracles of the 72 who reported to Christ, "Lord, even the demons submit to us in your name," Jesus replied, "I saw Satan fall like lightning from heaven" (Luke 10:17, 18).

The Gospels report that Satan attacked Christ immediately following His baptism in the Jordan river. Evidently it was God's will that this take place, for "Jesus was led by the Spirit into the desert to be tempted by the devil" (Matt. 4:1). After Jesus had fasted for 40 days and 40 nights, "the tempter came to him and said, 'If you are the Son of God, tell these stones to become bread' " (verse 3). It was a powerful temptation both to a man at the point of death and to a God who had the power to perform the deed! "Then the devil took him to the holy city and had him stand on the highest point of the temple. 'If you are the Son of God,' he said, 'throw yourself down. For it is written: "He will command his angels concerning you, and they will lift you up in their hands, so that you will not strike your foot against a stone" ' " (verses 5, 6). When you are emaciated and at the point of death, and no one knows you for whom you really are, it could be a great temptation to test God, who had made the promise that Satan quoted.

"Again, the devil took him to a very high mountain and showed him all the kingdoms of the world and their splendor. 'All this will I give you,' he said,'if you will bow down and worship me' " (verses 8, 9). What a temptation it is to one who, at the point of death, knew that one day crucifixion would be even worse! He came to die to win back our world that Satan had usurped from Him in Eden when he tricked Adam and Eve into choosing him as their new leader. The temptation was this: "If you bow to me now, you can get these kingdoms and avoid the horrors of Calvary." This last temptation shows insight into what the cosmic controversy is all about—Satan seeks to be worshiped. In other words, he wants to take the place of God, who alone is worthy of worship.

4. Looking Behind the Fall of Satan

Isaiah gives further insight into Satan's desire. "How have you fallen from heaven, O morning star, son of the dawn! You have been cast down to the earth, you who once laid low the nations! You said in your heart, 'I will ascend to heaven; I will raise my throne above the stars of God; I will sit enthroned on the mount of assembly, on the utmost heights of the sacred mountain. I will ascend above the tops of the clouds; I will make myself like the Most High' " (Isa. 14:12-14). Satan's rebellion was an attempt to take God's place. He wanted to be worshiped. Had he forgotten that Christ created him? Now, in the wilderness temptations, he again wanted his Creator to worship him. But the devil and his angels had once been loyal angels.

Jude notes "the angels . . . did not keep their positions of authority but abandoned their own home" (Jude 6).

Their loyalty turned to rebellion, and they spurned their Creator, Christ, as Judas would do later on earth. Christ says of the devil, "He was a murderer from the beginning, not holding to the truth, for there is no truth in him. When he lies, he speaks his native language, for he is a liar and the father of lies" (John 8:44). To pretend to be worthy of worship was a great lie, specially when he asked his Maker to bow before him!

5. Looking Behind the Cross

We cannot understand the mission of Jesus if we ignore the concept of the cosmic controversy. Not only did Satan dog Christ with temptations throughout His time on earth, as illustrated by the wilderness temptations, but he also schemed through the religious leaders to crucify Him. John records: "The evening meal was being served, and the devil had already prompted Judas Iscariot, son of Simon, to betray Jesus" (John 13:2). We can only imagine how Satan goaded the Jewish leaders and the Romans to crucify Jesus. The amazing thing is that even the rabble cried out, "Crucify! Crucify!" (John 19:6), though He had healed their sick, raised their dead, and done great things in their midst. Why would they turn on Him so, unless they too had become demon possessed?

In the trials and crucifixion of Jesus we find the climax of the cosmic struggle between Christ and Satan. The destiny of the world hung in the balance at the cross. Although we can glimpse the temptations He endured while He hung on the cross, we will never fully understand them. Amidst the anguish and shame of crucifixion, carrying the crushing weight of the world's sin (see Isa. 53:6), He faced derision from the very ones for whom He was hanging there. Was it worth it? Should He give up? "The people stood watching, and the rulers even sneered at him. They said, 'He saved others; let him save himself if he is the Christ of God, the Chosen One'" (Luke 23:35). Everything was at stake now for Satan. If Christ died triumphant, Satan was doomed. But if he could make Christ leave the cross or sin in one iota, his future would be secure. More than we can ever imagine, Satan flung all his fury at Christ hanging on the cross.

6. The Cross as the Decisive Battle in the Cosmic Controversy

The earliest incident about angels mentioned in Scripture does not involve their helping humans, but their participation in a fight—not on earth, but in heaven.

"There was war in heaven. Michael and his angels fought against the dragon, and the dragon and his angels fought back. But he was not strong enough, and they lost their place in heaven. The great dragon was hurled down—that ancient serpent called the devil, and Satan, who leads the whole world astray. He was hurled to the earth, and his angels with him. Then I heard a loud voice in heaven say: 'Now have come the salvation and the power and the kingdom of our God, and the authority of his Christ. For the accuser of the brothers, who accuses them before our God day and night, has been hurled down. They overcame him by the blood of the Lamb and by the word of their testimony; they did not love their lives so much as to shrink from death. Therefore rejoice, you heavens and you who dwell in them! But woe to the earth and the sea, because the devil has gone down to you! He is filled with fury, because he knows that his time is short'" (Rev. 12:7-12).

The same chapter mentions that the red dragon's "tail swept a third of the stars out of the sky and flung them to the earth" (verse 4). The devil flings "stars" to the earth, and Michael and His angels hurl Satan and his followers out of heaven. What we have here are two moments in the battle between Michael (Christ) and Satan. In the beginning Satan caused the fall of a third of the angels (stars) in heaven, and later on Planet Earth Satan worked to destroy humans around the world. But at Calvary, through His death, Jesus defeated Satan and his angels, and this passage pictures Him as exiling them to the earth. No wonder the immediate response was to praise Christ for His saving death.

7. Pentecost and the Cosmic Battle

Jesus referred to Satan as "the prince of this world" (John 12:31), and Paul calls him "the god of this age" (2 Cor. 4:4). As prince and god of our world, he claimed the human race as his. Christ came to earth to win back the right to own it once more, for the usurper Satan had wrenched it from Him when Adam and Eve accepted Satan, instead of Christ, as their leader (Gen. 3:1-6). God has made all His creatures, angelic and human, free to choose. Because He had formed Adam and Eve in the divine image (see Gen. 1:26, 27), He could converse with them. God respects creaturely freedom, for He does not want us to serve Him from fear or as automatons. Unfortunately, the wrong exercise of their freedom led to the angels' rebellion.

So we cannot charge God with causing sin. "The sole cause," says Francis Turretin, "was the proper will of each devil by which individuals of their own accord turned from good to evil."[1] Augustine said that "the good and bad angels have arisen, not from a difference in their nature and origin, since God, the good Author and Creator of all essences, created them both, but from a difference in their wills."[2] So a third of the angels rebelled then, and Adam and Eve also. Respecting the creaturely freedom of both Adam and Eve and Satan, God partially withdrew His presence in response to their choice, for Adam and Eve took Satan as their leader in place of Christ. Satan was the first antichrist. The Greek *anti* means "in place of" as well as "against." Satan stood in the place of Christ as the god of our world.

Even though God withdrew His Spirit to a degree from the human race, a sufficient presence of the Holy Spirit has always remained to lead people to Him (cf. John 1:9), but less than before the Fall. Consequently the Holy Spirit "is naturally not so prominent in the Old Testament as in the New."[3] Only within the context of the cosmic battle can we really understand Pentecost. God made human beings to be temples for the Spirit's indwelling (see 1 Cor. 3:16). They needed the Pentecostal outpouring, but that would have to wait for millennia.

Why did the Spirit's fullness have to wait till Pentecost? The fullness of the Spirit had everything to do with the fulfilled work of Christ. Old Testament believers longed for the coming of two members of the Godhead: the Messiah, presented in Isaiah 53, and the Holy Spirit promised in Joel 2:28. Apparently the fullness of the Spirit was not just a return to that of the pre-Fall situation but also had to do with bringing the human Jesus to them. For never before had the Spirit brought the God-man to human beings. In the Incarnation the Spirit brought God to humanity. Then in Pentecost and its extension in history, the Spirit brings the God-man to willing recipients.

Evidence of this waiting for the Holy Spirit appears in Christ's mission on earth. John prophesied that Jesus would baptize with the Spirit (see Matt. 3:11), something never done before. Yet one looks in vain for even one fulfillment of this in His precrucifixion ministry. He never baptized with the Spirit. Not until after Calvary, after paying the price to win back the world from the usurper Satan, did Jesus begin to fulfill John's prophecy. Thus, after Calvary, Jesus said to His disciples "Receive the Holy Spirit" as He breathed on them a special blessing (John 20:22). It was a foretaste of what would come at Pentecost.

Not only was Calvary a prerequisite for the impartation of the Spirit, but Calvary's acceptance was also a condition for Pentecostal fullness. That acceptance had still to come after Christ's ascension to heaven, for "as yet the Spirit had not been given, because Jesus was not yet glorified" (John 7:39, RSV). He was glorified in His inauguration in heaven (see Rev. 4, 5). When Jesus sat down at God's right hand (see Heb. 1:3) and the Father officially accepted His sacrifice at Calvary, the Father (see John 14:16, 26) and He (see John 16:7) together sent the Spirit to humanity. Now the fullness of the Spirit came at Pentecost because of the finished work of Christ in defeating Satan at the cross (see John 19:30; Rev. 12:9-13), and the acceptance of it in heaven.

Christ had won back the right to send His Holy Spirit in fullness to willing recipients without violating the creaturely freedom of Satan, his angels, or that of human beings. At the same time the fallen angels lost the right to ownership of our world. Thus without violating His respect for creaturely freedom, Christ could bestow the fullness of the Spirit that He had partially withdrawn. Thus the cosmic controversy, in its ultimate battle at Calvary, opened the way for Pentecost.

Calvary reminds us that "our struggle is not against flesh and blood, but against the rulers, against the authorities, against the powers of this dark world and against the spiritual forces of evil in the heavenly realms" (Eph. 6:12). The ultimate cause for sin and all its misery lies beyond our world in the rebel Satan, just as its remedy lies beyond our world in the righteous Redeemer, Jesus Christ.

8. The Cosmic Influence of Calvary

Many view Calvary as Christ's dying for us so that we can go to heaven. It is that. But there is more. That more has to do with the larger cosmic worldview of Scripture. The book of Colossians documents that Christ created all things "in heaven and on earth" (Col. 1:16), and that "in him all things hold together" (verse 17). "For God was pleased to have all his fullness dwell in him, and through him to reconcile to himself all things, whether things on earth or things in heaven, by making peace through his blood, shed on the cross" (verses 19, 20). Therefore, Christ said about His death, "Now is the time for judgment on this world; now the prince of this world [Satan] will be driven out" (John 12:31). "The prince of this world [Satan] now stands condemned" (John 16:11).

In what way could Calvary reconcile things, or people, in heaven? Given that Satan was behind the death of Christ, it exposed him for what he really is—a devil. By contrast, because Christ allowed Himself to be crucified, the universe saw Him for who He really is—a God of love (see 1 John 4:8, 16). Calvary influenced the unfallen angels who remained in heaven and did not join in the rebellion. They perceived a deeper revelation of God's love on the cross as they witnessed Him who knew no sin becoming sin for the human race (see 2 Cor. 5:21). The good news of the cross changed cowardly disciples into mighty apostles.

The book of Acts documents the rapid spread of the news geographically on a horizontal plane. Ephesians speaks of the impact of the church on the vertical plane. The church became a witness to the universe of the kind of God all unfallen beings serve. God's "intent was that now, through the church, the manifold wisdom of God should be made known to the rulers and authorities in the heavenly realms, according to his eternal purpose which he accomplished in Christ Jesus our Lord" (Eph. 3:10, 11).

Calvary, and what it did to the church, became a lesson book that shapes the universe. Thus Calvary stands revealed as far more than the price for human salvation, and the church as far more than the company of the saved. Calvary and church have a far wider impact. What took place at the cross influences the whole universe. "It seems to me that God has put us apostles on display at the end of the procession, like men condemned to die in the arena. We have been made a spectacle to the whole universe, to angels as well as to men" (1 Cor. 4:9).

Final events on earth will play themselves out before the entire cosmos. Here is the larger biblical worldview that forms the context for end-time events. As we shall document later, this is the reason why Christians go through the final tribulation rather than being whisked away before it arrives.

---

[1] Francis Turretin, *Institutes of Elenctic Theology,* trans. George Musgrave Giger (Phillipsburg, N.J.: Presbyterian and Reformed, 1992), vol. 1, p. 603.

[2] Augustine, *The City of God,* ed. Philip Schaff, *The Nicene and Post-Nicene Fathers* (Grand Rapids: Eerdmans, 1988), vol. 2, p. 226 (12.1).

[3] W. H. Griffith Thomas, *The Holy Spirit of God* (Grand Rapids: Eerdmans, 1976), p. 9. Thomas notes 88 direct references to the Holy Spirit in the Old Testament.

Chapter 3

Christ Knows the Future

Have you seen all those ads lately telling you to dial your psychic, and he or she will tell you whether you have a man or woman coming into your life, whether you will win the jackpot, or whether you will get that job you have been wanting? Yet while people flock to psychic hot lines for a few bucks a minute, some Christians say God doesn't know the future! We live in a bizarre world.

Instead of the nonsense of psychics, postmoderns need to know that their struggles make sense as a part of a larger cosmic conflict, that Christ won the battle between good and evil at Calvary, making their future sure. Now it is just a matter of time till God makes the results of Calvary manifest. Postmoderns must grasp the fact that the Christ of Calvary knows the future and that He is coming again—soon!

The devil hates the fact that he lost the decisive battle at the cross. He has done all sorts of things to hide the fact, to make the cross of no effect. If he can get the world to misunderstand the cross, deny it, or just ignore it, he hopes to win the battle in the end. In other words, he cannot undo the fact that he lost there, but he can try to take everyone with him, so Christ's death will have been in vain.

One strategy afloat today is the belief that God does not know the future. Called process theology, it says that God is just as much in process or continual development as the rest of us and knows as little about the future as we do. Such a concept torpedoes our assurance and hope in a known future, and therefore in the results of Christ's victory at Calvary. It leaves us wondering if the God of process theology dials a psychic too.

Process Thinking

Process theology traces its immediate indebtedness back to philosophy in the person of A. N. Whitehead (1861-1947), a Harvard professor. Charles Hartshorne (1897-   ) took Whitehead's views and incorporated them into theology while at the University of Chicago. Many of the later leading process theologians received their training at Chicago.

A twentieth-century view of God, process theology rejects the thirteenth-century classical view of God as "unchanging" (not moved by human needs) as propounded by Thomas Aquinas (1225-1274). The classical view, it claims, sees God as the "unmoved Mover"—who created everything but remains aloof and unaffected by it. Process thinking has God down here with us in the process of change Himself. Given the complex problems engulfing postmoderns, process theology seems to introduce a welcome focus on a closer "god," one who is with us, in—and affected by—life's struggle. Process theology also rejects the Reformed (Calvinistic) view of God with His predestination overriding human freedom. In contrast to the latter view, the process "god" allows human freedom.

Process Theology as Threat to Christianity

Many regard process theology as one of the greatest current threats to Christianity. Nash's *Process Theology* cites Donald Bloesch, who considers it a "new adversary of historic Christian faith,"[1] for "process theology has mounted," Bruce Demarest says, "one of the most potent challenges to orthodox Christian truth in the second half of the twentieth century."[2] In fact, "a number of American liberal theologians," Carl Henry reports, "energetically support process-theory as the framework for expounding Christian beliefs."[3] But something even more sinister lurks. "There is a disturbing new trend among some evangelical theologians to deny the biblical doctrine of foreknowledge," says William Craig, "and to explain away scriptural passages asserting this doctrine, simply because the rational attack on it seems to them unanswerable."[4]

The *Evangelical Dictionary of Theology* warns: "Though process theology has not yet become a major force in the church pew, it is very influential in the intellectual world of the seminaries and graduate schools, and no doubt is the most viable form of neoliberal theology now in the United States."[5]

Why do many consider process theology so dangerous? Process theology jettisons several major biblical beliefs, such as the Trinity, God's omniscience, creation out of nothing, the divinity of Jesus, the Resurrection, God's ultimate triumph over evil, and the reality of the future eternal life. The foundation for most of the distinctive doctrines of process theology is its claim that the monopolar (timeless, unchanging, independent) idea of God found in Christian theism should be replaced by a dipolar (both changing and changeless) view of God.[6] The latter concept calls for comment.

The dipolar view of God (Hartshorne)[7] includes (1) His primordial (unchanging and separate) nature as transcendent[8] and (2) His consequent nature as contingent (changing and dependent).[9] In a way it looks as though their "god" is schizophrenic! Process theology focuses almost exclusively on God's consequent (immanent, or dependent on the world for bodily existence) nature.[10] Here is the danger. In its preoccupation with bringing God closer to humanity, process theology presents a being who is less than God. It views God as a mind with the world (cosmos) as His body (Hartshorne). Since the world changes endlessly, each change brings greater completeness and fullness to God. God is therefore contingent (close to and part of the cosmic process), or dependent upon the world forever.

But how can He be God if He is dependent upon the world?

He can't—and that's the problem. He is no longer the God of Scripture.

Although process theology claims to view God as more involved with the world than do classical views about God, it's questionable whether it really achieves this, as Millard Erickson concludes.[11] "The real problem with process thought," says R. G. Gruenler, ". . . is how God can possibly be *active* in the world, since his primordial or abstract nature has no personal activity except as 'it' passively receives concrete actuality *from* the world."[12]

The way process theology approaches God's dependence upon the world makes it impossible for its exponents to view God as Creator of the world out of nothing. Rather, His eternal existence seems indebted to the universe, the opposite of biblical "creation out of nothing" by God. As William Craig put it: "Process theologians diametrically oppose the biblical doctrine of creation."[13] "According to Hartshorne, God formed the present universe out of an earlier universe and its potentialities for transformation. But that world was similarly made from a previous world, and that one from a yet earlier one, *ad infinitum*. Thus, the present world order is but the most recent of an infinity of prior universes in a series stretching back in time without beginning."[14] Here we have evolutionary theory projected backward into infinity.

Because God is dependent on the world, according to process theology, He *does not know* the future—that is to say that He waits to see what will take place, just like the rest of us. Because He knows the present and past fully, He may have a better understanding of future possibilities, but His knowledge of future events is as dependent upon those events taking place as He is dependent upon the world (cosmos) for His body. As Whitehead put it: "The future is fully and radically open"[15]—it is not known or perfectly known to God. Thus the infinite has become finite, the Creator is contingent on Creation, and the omniscient One no longer knows the future.

The "god" of process theology is neither identified with the world (pantheism) nor removed from the world (deism). He has the world within his being, although the world does not exhaust his being (panentheism).[16]

As a result, the "god" of process theology is less than the God of the Bible, even though process theology believes its view of God is an advance over the classical concept of God. Here we see that process doesn't mean progress. It represents the opposite—a reductionism. Yet, paradoxically, this "making of God in our image" issues out of the evolutionary worldview of our time. As the *Encyclopedic Dictionary of Religion* puts it: "The central conviction of process thought is that scientific insistence on evolution."[17]

Having accepted as a basic presupposition that everything is evolving, including humanity, process thinkers read the concept onto God. He too must be evolving.[18] By accepting the nonbiblical evolutionary worldview, process theology ends up with a nonbiblical "god." If we consider evolution as process, change for the better, we actually end up with change for the worse because of their view of God. "Whatever else may be said about process-theology as a contemporary conceptuality of a theory of God," says Carl Henry, "its deity is certainly not the God of the Bible."[19]

The Issue of Personal Freedom

"Norm, I don't believe God knows the future," a doctoral student once argued with me at the University of Edinburgh in Scotland. "If He did, then I would not be free!"

"Why?" I responded.

"Because the moment I allow that God knows everything I will do throughout life, then I will have to do those things whether I want to or not. Then I'm not free."

This is a real concern with those pushing process thought. If postmoderns want anything, they desire freedom.

We talked for a long time. I've pondered our discussion more since. If God does not know the future, then can I really be free—free to trust in a certain goal, with assurance in a God who knows what He is doing? Even freedom for the future requires knowledge that can be depended upon.

"Perhaps no area of doctrine has been more consistently debated throughout the twenty centuries of Christianity's life than that of God's sovereignty and man's responsibility," D. A. Carson observes.[20] Process theology is simply the most recent example of the continuing discussion.

Process theologians claim that if God knows the future fully, then the concept of human freedom is meaningless.[21] They believe that God's knowledge of the future (omniscience) and human freedom are mutually exclusive. Thus, either God knows all future details—including human decisions, or humans are truly free and God merely remains open to the future—waiting to see what human decisions will be.

To be fair to process thinkers, we should accept that they want to protect God from the problems of theodicy—that is, they do not want Him to know in advance that creaturely decisions will bring evil into the universe. They assume that if God did not know about such decisions, then creatures, and not God, are responsible for evil. Their point requires consideration.

A Deeper Dimension

There is, however, another deeper dimension involved. For process thinkers are really saying, "If God must be freed from responsibility for evil, *then humans must be freed from the restrictions of divine omniscience."* Apparently, for some at least, the driving force for the first derives from the second. A desire or need for personal freedom fuels their quest. They are more interested in personal freedom than anything else. "Although it tries to offer a solution to the problem of evil by limiting the power of God," R. G. Gruenler says, "its real motive, I am convinced, is to protect human freedom against the threat of a Sovereign God."[22]

The idea that human freedom is meaningless if God knows the future fully is no better logic than that of Jean-Paul Sartre, who exclaimed, "If God exists, then the future is determined and I am not free; I am free, therefore, God does not exist."[23] Or why not accept the logic of Jonathan Edwards' position: "If every event has a cause, then so do free human choices; God is the First Cause of everything, therefore, God must be the cause of our free choices"?[24] Clearly logic alone is not sufficient. Logic informed by Scripture provides the only safe pathway to knowledge.

Faulty Idea of Freedom

The crux of the matter may lie in a faulty understanding of freedom. The premise "If God isn't open (nonomniscient), then I am not free" presupposes that freedom includes "freedom *from* God." Yet Scripture is clear that "where the Spirit of the Lord is, there is freedom" (2 Cor. 3:16). Paradoxically, freedom comes not to those who seek it (as process theologians seem to believe) but to those who seek it not; for "whoever wishes to save his life shall lose it; but whoever loses his life for My sake and the gospel's shall save it" (Mark 8:35, NASB). As Gruenler put it: "Freedom is not defined as autonomous power apart from God, but rather as the creature's willingness to be faithful and selfless in service to God and to Jesus Christ"[25]

True Freedom

Scripture portrays freedom as a gift given by Christ. In fact, the gift comes with the Giver or the Giver with the gift. No freedom exists apart from Jesus Christ. Jesus said, "If the Son sets you free, you will be free indeed" (John 8:36). He left heaven for that purpose. Salvation is not merely a message sent but a Saviour present. Christ came to set the captives free (Isa. 61:1; Luke 4:18). Our Saviour calls people to Himself: "Come to me, all you who are weary and burdened, and I will give you rest" (Matt. 11:28). And He invites them to dwell with Him: "Remain in me. . . . Apart from me you can do nothing" (John 15:4). It is a gentle, *uncoercive* invitation. In accepting it we find we have nothing to lose and everything to gain.

Relationship with Christ proves that the deepest freedom in the world results from being His slave. When the truth is known, it makes one free (see John 8:32). We discover that "great peace have they who love your law, and nothing can make them stumble" (Ps. 119:165). Through an experience in Christ we learn that "neither death nor life, neither angels nor demons, neither the present nor the future, nor any powers, neither height nor depth, nor anything else in all creation, will be able to separate us from the love of God that is in Christ Jesus our Lord" (Rom. 8:38, 39).

The Truth About God

The truth that sets us free is the truth about God. Scripture does not present God as an unsympathetic sovereign, overriding human freedom. In fact, although anthropomorphic, it can even speak of God as *"repenting"* (cf. Gen. 6:6, KJV; 1 Sam. 15:10, 35, KJV; Amos 7:3, 6, KJV). "Such language," notes Carson, "applied so regularly to Deity, stands without close parallel in the literature of the Near East."[26]

Furthermore, among the characteristics ascribed to God, Scripture mentions "long-suffering, gentleness, . . . meekness" (Gal. 5:22, 23, KJV)—hardly terms that define an arbitrary sovereign.

Christ as Revelation of God

The clearest, most authentic, revelation of God occurs in Jesus Christ. He could rightly say, "He that hath seen me hath seen the Father" (John 14:9, KJV). We'll explore the following facets of this revelation: (1) eternal plan and prophecies; (2) the changing God; (3) the life of Christ; and (4) the cross.

1. Eternal Plan and Prophecies

Jesus met in counsel with the Father to become humanity's Saviour before its Fall (see Zech. 6:13). Scripture speaks also of Christ as "the Lamb slain from the foundation of the world" (Rev. 13:8, KJV). Old Testament prophecies demonstrate God's omniscience by foretelling specific details that will happen to the Messiah Jesus—both in life and in death (see Ps. 22; Isa. 53, 61).

2. The Changing God

The incarnation of God into human history shatters the straw man of process theology. For Jesus as Immanuel, God with us, contradicts any idea of an impassive God—one uninvolved with humanity. In fact, Scripture speaks of God in terms of *becoming.* For "The Word was God." "The Word *became* flesh and made his dwelling among us" (John 1:1, 14). It's this *becoming,* found at the very heart of the gospel, the very center of the good news in Scripture, that process theologians need to take seriously. Failing to think through this *becoming,* they have taken a leap into the dark in the *becoming* of Whiteheadian philosophy. Why substitute a human-conceived *becoming* for the *becoming* of Scripture?

Furthermore, the *becoming of process thought is diametrically opposed to the becoming of Scripture.* For the process "god" such becoming is one of necessity, because his dependence upon the world is essential to his own fulfillment. As the world supposedly becomes (by evolution) better, so the process "god" shares in this benefit. Not so with Christ. As God, He came voluntarily for the good of others and not for His own necessity (see 2 Cor. 5:18). The very *becoming* of process and incarnational thought are worlds apart from each other! The becoming of process thought is one of *growth,* whereas the becoming of the Incarnation involved *loss.*

Being in the form of God, Christ took the form of humanity (see Phil. 2:5-7). It means the omnipresent God (see Ps. 139:7; Jer. 23:23, 24; Acts 17:27, 28) became localized into one finite human body (see Heb. 10:5). Can there be any greater spatial condescension than that?

Unlike the *limited god* of process thought, the Incarnation involved a *self-limiting* (relinquishing of His omnipresence, and rarely using other divine attributes). Here we discern the deepest distinction between process *growth* and incarnational *change.* For while becoming human, Christ did not cease to be God. From within this new human form He was able to reveal what God is like. Through this change He was now able to portray the unchanging God.

By contrast, the "endlessly growing god" of process thought can never give a meaningful self-revelation, for any manifestation would be out-of-date the very next moment. Process thinking has no incarnation and hence grasps at some connection of God with humanity by having the world as his body. How much better the true Incarnation, in which genuine change involved God becoming what He had never been before (human), while remaining fully God. In this way, God came to relate to humanity from within human history. He became the God-man, one of us. You just can't get any more relevant than that!

3. The Life of Christ

Scripture reveals God living among human beings in Jesus Christ. And the picture it gives is not of some arbitrary sovereign, but of One who genuinely respects creaturely freedom. In fact, His people had lost genuine freedom, not just because they were bound under Roman rule but because they were slaves of human-made doctrines (just as human-made as much process thought).

So Christ launched His public ministry with the ringing words: "The Spirit of the Lord is on me, because he has anointed me to preach good news to the poor. He has sent me to proclaim freedom for the prisoners and recovery of sight for the blind, to release the oppressed" (Luke 4:18). He read from Isaiah 61:1, written some 700 years before. Jesus then concluded, "Today this scripture is fulfilled in your hearing" (Luke 4:21). And free the prisoners He did—through proclaiming the truth that sets one free (see John 8:32), forgiving sin, healing the sick, and resurrecting the dead.

Everything Christ did was for human benefit. He lived for others. His life never reflects that of an arbitrary sovereign overriding human freedom. See His gentle patience as He forgives the adulterous woman coming to Him for the seventh time (see Luke 8:2; Mark 16:9). He truly practiced what He taught Peter—to forgive seventy times seven (see Matt. 18:22). How many totally innocent, yet condemned, people could pray for those crucifying them, "Father, forgive them" (Luke 23:34) as He did?

4. The Cross

At the cross we have reached the deepest level from which we can gain an authentic understanding of God. Here, at Calvary, process theology receives its death blow.

Christ did not die to save human beings from the *sovereignty of God* but from the *slavery of Satan*. Ultimately at Calvary He set the prisoners free. Through His death He brought life. The cross liberated the world from the usurper Satan. Here He cried out, "My God, my God, why hast thou forsaken me?" (Matt. 27:46, KJV)—precisely because He had not forsaken humanity. He was willing to plunge into the abyss in order to bridge the chasm between God and humanity.

Obviously, each member of the Trinity suffered in this separation struggle—as only the perfect, eternal love of Each for the Others could comprehend. Who else had perfect love for others, who else had so loved forever? The everlasting "God is love" (1 John 4:16). When it dawns on us that God suffered to that extent to win human freedom, any idea that a sovereign God destroys human freedom stands exposed as false. Calvary defines divine sovereignty as an utter unselfish giving of oneself to win freedom for others, irrespective of the cost to self. Aulen calls such sovereignty "sovereign love."

Crossless Theology

The cross was foolishness to the Greeks (see 1 Cor. 1:22-24), and it is inconsequential to process theology. "Process theologians devote relatively little attention to the Cross," Bruce Demarest notes, "believing that the focus of Jesus' accomplishment resides in His life rather than in His death." Process thought doesn't take sin seriously, doesn't consider an afterlife, and doesn't regard Jesus as divine. No wonder their theology is crossless!

As Gunton observed, "Hartshorne's theology is irretrievably anthropomorphic."[27] Process theology ignores the fact that truth about God is *clearest at Calvary* rather than *in the Christian.* Such a focus would change their anthropology into authentic theology.

Process theology fails to realize how cross-centered Scripture is. For example, the Old Testament messianic prophecies, sanctuary sacrifices, and services all look forward to the cross. Each annual Passover celebration typified Calvary, pointing to the coming gift, and thereby shared in the gift itself. When someone promises to marry, those promises come with the same love given on the wedding day. Likewise, we can rightly understand prophecy only in the light of Calvary—for God's foreknowledge, given in prophecies, is just as much for the benefit of genuine human freedom as was Christ's death—to which they pointed. Thus sovereign omniscience is no more arbitrary than Calvary.

The New Testament speaks of a changed world after the cross. Calvary has made a decisive difference to human history. The world is no longer Satan's world. Christ has won back the right to govern it. It is His world. As such, our world moves toward the full visible realization of Calvary in the physical change to take place. In the meantime, prophecies concerning Christ's second return and the new world after the millennium are the very heartbeat of the New Testament.

In the time between Calvary and His coming advent, Christ comes to be with us through the Spirit and thereby continues to be the relevant God among us. For He dwells among us to bring change. This biblical picture of God among humans far surpasses the process "god" limited to this world.

So the category of "change" is biblical. But "change," as defined by process thought, is too narrow when applied to both God and humans. For in the end-time "we will all be changed" (1 Cor. 15:51, 52; see also 2 Cor. 3:18).

Conclusion

Although I am sympathetic with any attempt to gain a correct understanding of God, and hence question aspects of the unchanging God of Thomas Aquinas and reject the predestinating God of John Calvin, process theology presents an equally incorrect view of God. We need to judge all three views of God in the light of Christ's revelation of God. He became human (vs. unchanging); He came for all humanity (vs. predestination), and He, as God, came to redeem man, fulfilling Bible prophecy; and He will return to give eternal life to those responding to Him (vs. process theology).

In Jesus Christ we discover God, who also became human—a God who came that close to humanity. In Christ we find evidence that God did know the future when He prophesied of His first advent. And we can rest assured that He knows the future about His second advent too.

[1] Ronald H. Nash, ed., *Process Theology* (Grand Rapids: Baker, 1987), p. 49.

[2] *Ibid.,* p. 63. Demarest notes that "some younger evangelicals, particularly within the Arminian tradition, have bought into aspects of process theology" (p. 64). Gruenler calls this "the halfway house of conservative process theism." [R. G. Gruenler, *The Inexhaustible God, Biblical Faith and the Challenge of Process Theism* (Grand Rapids: Baker, 1983), p. 44].

[3] Carl F. H. Henry, "A Critique of Process-Theology," in *Readings in Christian Theology: The Living God,* ed. M. K. Erickson (Grand Rapids: Baker, 1985), vol. 1, p. 400.

[4] William L. Craig, *The Only Wise God; The Compatibility of Divine Foreknowledge and Human Freedom* (Grand Rapids: Baker, 1987), p. 12.

[5] Walter A. Elwell, ed., *Evangelical Dictionary of Theology* (Grand Rapids: Baker, 1984), p. 884.

[6] See Nash, p. 19.

[7] Charles Hartshorne, *A Natural Theology for Our Time* (La Salle, Ill.: Open Court, 1967), p. 128. Hartshorne wrote concerning God: "He is finite and infinite, eternal and temporal, necessary and contingent." On his dipolar view of God as primordial and consequent, see page 278.

[8] The primordial nature includes the following characteristics: abstract, necessary, transcendent, eternal, potential, one, infinite, cause, absolute, and immutable.

[9] His consequent nature includes the following characteristics: concrete, contingent, immanent, temporal, actual, many, finite, effect, relative, and mutable. For these, and those of note 1, see Nash, p. 19.

[10] Process theology considers change as related only to the consequent nature of God. The primordial nature is changeless, absolute, and eternal, whereas the consequent is changing, relative, and temporal.

[11] Millard J. Erickson, *Christian Theology* (Grand Rapids: Baker, 1985), p. 281. "Although process theology purports to view God as a personal being, unlike the impersonal unmoved mover of Greek metaphysics [philosophical concern with ultimate reality], it is questionable whether this is really the case. God seems to be little more than an aspect of reality. In what sense He is a personal, acting being is not made clear."

[12] Gruenler, p. 124.

[13] Nash, p. 145.

[14] *Ibid.,* p. 147.

[15] In John B. Cobb, Jr., and David R. Griffin, *Process Theology: An Introductory Exposition* (Philadelphia: Westminster, 1976), p. 112.

[16] See Van A. Harvey, *A Handbook of Theological Terms* (London: George Allen & Unwin, Ltd., 1966), pp. 147f.

[17] Paul K. Meagher, T. C. O'Brien, and C. M. Aberne, eds., *Encyclopedic Dictionary of Religion* (Washington, D.C.: Corpus, 1979) vol. 3, p. 2893.

[18] Henry, *Readings in Christian Theology: The Living God,* p. 401.

[19] *Ibid.,* p. 414.

[20] D. A. Carson, *Divine Sovereignty and Human Responsibility* (Atlanta: John Knox, 1987), p. 219.

[21] Even the most conservative theologians who have accepted a modified version of process theology main-

tain this claim. By definition a Seventh-day Adventist believes in eschatology—final events. The openness of God, not knowing the future, destroys the fullness of biblical eschatology, removing assurance, certainty, and a sense of urgency. It torpedoes the unique Adventist prophetic message and mission.

[22] Gruenler, pp. 7f.

[23] In Avid and Randall Basinger, *Predestination and Free Will* (Downers Grove, Ill.: InterVarsity, 1986), p. 63.

[24] *Ibid.*

[25] Gruenler, p. 39.

[26] Carson, p. 35.

[27] Colin E. Gunton, *Becoming and Being, the Doctrine of God in Charles Hartshorne and Karl Barth,* p. 222.

Chapter 4

Christ in Control of Final Events

The Japan Airlines jumbo jet whined as it sped across the sky. My wife and I, with our four children, looked around the huge plane. We had never been on one before. Having left Tokyo, Japan, hours before, we were now crossing India. Suddenly, without warning, the giant plane hit an air pocket and dropped several thousand feet over Delhi.

Plates flew off trays. The aircraft pulled out of the plunge. You could feel the wrenching of the giant wings as it slowly regained altitude. Then it happened. A monsoon storm smashed into the plane. Lightning flashed on all sides. Rain pelted down. The aircraft shuddered and shook. Leona, my wife, and I held hands as we sang softly together and prayed. It took a long hour to pass through the storm. Again and again I repeated: "The eternal God is your refuge, and underneath are the everlasting arms" (Deut. 33:27). Even underneath the strained wings of a jumbo jet, God had His everlasting arms. He was in control.

Escape From Egypt

Israel's escape through the Red Sea gives insight into the journey that awaits us through end-time events. Just as plagues pummeled Egypt (Ex. 8-11), so they will be poured out upon a whole world (Rev. 16). As Christ brought His people through the Red Sea to deliver them and destroy their enemies, so it will happen again on a global scale in final events. Christ promised, "I am the Lord, and I will bring you out from under the yoke of the Egyptians. I will free you from being slaves to them, and will redeem you with an outstretched arm and with mighty acts of judgment" (Ex. 6:6). In the end-time, spiritual Babylon will oppress God's people (see Rev. 13:12-15), but God will judge "her for the way she treated you" (Rev. 18:20; cf. Rev. 19:2).

God said to His ancient people, "You yourselves have seen what I did to Egypt, and how I carried you on eagles' wings and brought you to myself" (Ex. 19:4). In the New Testament we read the parable of the lost sheep. When Christ found the sheep, He did not say, "You good-for-nothing! Why did you leave the flock and cause me extra trouble?" No. "When he finds it, he joyfully puts it on his shoulders and goes home" (Luke 15:5, 6).

There you have it. Christ is in the business of leading His people all the way home to heaven just as He brought Israel out of Egypt and through the Red Sea, and just as He carries lost sheep all the way to the fold. It is urgent and vital that we get the picture. Christ is responsible for bringing us through final events on Planet Earth. Often we fear final events because we picture ourselves enduring them alone. Christ never asks us to do anything for Him without promising to be with us. When He said, "Go and make disciples of all nations," He added, "I am with you always, to the very end of the age" (Matt. 28:19, 20). As we face the storm ahead, Christ invites us, "Come to me, all you who are weary and burdened, and I will give you rest" (Matt. 11:28). "Never will I leave you; never will I forsake you" (Heb. 13:5). "Remain in me," for "apart from me you can do nothing" (John 15:4, 5).

We must always keep two facts together. First, Christ will not only be with us but will bring us through final events. Second, apart from Christ we can do nothing. So it's absolutely necessary that He be with us. Our responsibility is to be willing to be carried. He does the carrying.

Red Sea

There they were—trapped! The Red Sea seemed uncrossable, and the world's mightiest army stood poised to slaughter them at its shore. No escape was possible, humanly speaking. Terrified "they . . . cried out to the Lord" (Ex. 14:10). Back came the promise from Christ, "Do not be afraid. Stand firm and you will see the deliverance the Lord will bring you today. The Egyptians you see today you will never see again. The Lord will fight for you; you need only to be still" (verses 13, 14). Notice that Christ would bring deliverance. No human hand could hold the water back for Israel to cross on dry ground. Nor could any human hand release that same water to drown the Egyptian army. That was God's department. Israel had only to trust in Christ to do what He had promised and walk across.

How small their part was compared to His! Would they be willing to let Him carry them through that great time of trouble? They could refuse and not step onto the seabed. Scared of their final events, believing death was imminent, they would, in fact, perish at the hands of the Egyptians. The crucial point is that, though circumstances told them that there was no escape, that it was their end, they trusted Christ more than the surrounding situation. They saw beyond the crisis to Him. Thus "by faith the people passed through the Red Sea as on dry land" (Heb. 11:29).

The psalmist describes the crossing. Evidently once Israel looked away from the Egyptian army to Christ, then Christ manifested His presence. "With your mighty arm you redeemed your people, the descendants of Jacob and Joseph. The waters saw you, O God, the waters saw you and writhed; the very depths were convulsed. The clouds poured down water, the skies resounded with thunder; your arrows flashed back and forth. Your thunder was heard in the whirlwind, your lightning lit up the world; the earth trembled and quaked. Your path led through the sea, your way through the mighty waters, though your footprints were not seen" (Ps. 77:15-19).

When the Israelites stopped being scared of their final events and looked to Christ instead, then they saw that the enemy itself had every reason to have fear. In our final events just ahead we too will see that the enemy again will have every reason to be fearful. Whose side would you rather have been on—helpless Israel or the greatest army of the then-known world? Clearly, circumstances are deceptive. Christ radically changes the perceived outcome.

Our Greatest Danger

Those who crossed over the Red Sea couldn't forget the awesome experience. Yet tragically they soon lost sight of the One who brought them through. At Sinai they built the golden calf. "Then they said, 'These are your gods, O Israel, who brought you up out of Egypt'" (Ex. 32:4). They crafted an idol from their own jewelry. Something of their creation they elevated to be their god, and they attributed their miraculous escape from the Egyptians to an object they had just then formed. Israel had yet to learn that even lambs representing the Lamb of God were no more than animals.

In worshiping the golden calf, the Israelites sought something that they could see and handle. But in doing so, they worshiped the work of their own hands. They needed to realize they were the creation of God, not the creators of gods. They needed only to realize their utter dependence upon their Creator for everyday living as well as in the Red Sea times.

Our danger is the same. We create gods still: the god of financial success. the god of position. the god called career. The list is endless. All fashioned by our hands. We worship our creations rather than our Creator. I believe God is trying to get His people to realize their own helplessness as they face final events. He does not want them to become scared and lose hope, but He does intend that they realize the enormity of the crisis ahead. God wants them to flee to Him in utter dependence, to know as never before that He alone is their Creator and Redeemer.

Go Possess the Land

The time came to possess the Promised Land. Spies explored it and brought reports back.

"It's a land flowing with milk and honey," Caleb said.

"But terrible giants occupy the land!" contested another.

"No, it is truly a wonderful country. We left Egypt to possess it. God will take care of the giants. Let's go!" Joshua urged.

"Don't listen to them." Several loud shouts echoed across the encampment. "Those giants are too big! We cannot prevail!"

Another yelled, "The giants will kill us. Who wants to die? The desert is safer. Let's stay here!"

So it is today.

"An international Sunday law will

make us hated by all the world," shouts one.

"The great time of trouble is terrible. There will be a death decree. We'll die," a frightened saint moans.

"We'll have to live without an intercessor," another wails.

"The Spirit will be withdrawn from the earth," a discouraged pilgrim cries.

"Jacob's trouble will be intense mental anguish," a worried Christian sighs.

We're no different from ancient Israel. Right?

Where was the God of the Red Sea? He hadn't abandoned His people. They'd left Him. It was the golden calf experience again—at least as far as losing sight of Christ was concerned. The central problem of Israel here and throughout much of its history has been a failure to keep the power of God ever before them. They didn't think of His presence or look beyond their intermittent crises to Him. If they had set the Lord before them, they wouldn't have been moved (see Ps. 16:8).

So it is with us. What crowds your mind when you think of last-day events? Do the events themselves overshadow all else? Does the prospect of trouble overwhelm you? Does the coming crisis leave room for Christ? Giants—that's what they are. But if you look to Christ, what do you see? Calvary, victory, the world and its events in His hands. He is in control. His face fills the mental screen. While the events still loom, He will take care of them.

The Other Giant

Israel looked out from their hill on the one occupied by the Philistines. A valley lay between them (see 1 Sam. 17:3). When would the battle begin? "For forty days . . . morning and evening" (verse 16), Goliath walked across the valley to chide Israel. Eighty times he shouted out, "This day I defy the ranks of Israel. Give me a man and let us fight each other" (verse 10). "The armies of Israel were depressed. Their courage failed."[1]

"David said to Saul, 'Let no one lose heart on account of this Philistine; your servant will go and fight him'" (verse 32). Saul objected that David was only a boy (see verse 33), but David wasn't comparing himself with the giant—he was comparing God with the giant.

The giant thought that any encounter between himself and the lad David would be no contest. But David believed it would be no contest between God and the giant.

The giant was "over nine feet tall" (verse 4), perhaps "equivalent to 9½ feet."[2] His "armor would have weighed nearly 126 pounds." The point of his spear alone "weighed between 15 and 16 pounds."[3] King Saul had been a giant for his day. He stood "a head taller than any of the others" (1 Sam. 9:2). But "Saul was destitute of those higher qualities that constitute true wisdom. He had not in youth learned to control his rash, impetuous passions; he had never felt the renewing power of divine grace."[4] Though young and smaller, David was a giant in the Lord.

The shepherd lad refused Saul's armor. He said, "The Lord who delivered me from the paw of the lion and the paw of the bear will deliver me from the hand of this Philistine" (1 Sam. 17:37).

When the Philistine giant saw an unarmed youth coming against him, he felt like the wicked will feel against God's people in the end-time. "Wipe him/them out!" "Get rid of him/them!" "The Philistine cursed David by his gods. 'Come here,' he said, 'and I'll give your flesh to the birds of the air and the beasts of the field!'" (verse 44). "Mincemeat! That's what I'll make of you!" Can you see Saul and his army trembling?

Not David. He shot right back, "You come against me with sword and spear and javelin, but I come against you in the name of the Lord Almighty, the God of the armies of Israel, who you have defied. This day the Lord will hand you over to me, and I'll strike you down and cut off your head. Today I will give the carcasses of the Philistine army to the birds of the air and the beasts of the earth, and the whole world will know that there is a God in Israel" (verses 45, 46).

You know the rest of the story. The giant was decapitated because David didn't think about the danger to himself and was indignant about the Philistine's challenge to God. Maybe we should become indignant that the whole world will wonder at and follow the beast (see Rev. 13:3). Indignant that America will lead the world to "worship the beast" (verses 12-14). Indignant that Satan will deceive the masses and establish a death decree (see verse 15). The final giant will loom large worldwide against a modern David. It was false worship then, and it will be false worship again. David was angry because he knew the true God and communed with Him daily. "The armies of Israel were in peril, and David had been directed by an angel to save his people."[5] We have a destiny in the end-time too, as we will see later.

Other Giants

Goliath came "from Gath" (1 Sam. 17:4). Later Israel battled in Gath, and "there was a huge man with six fingers on each hand and six toes on each foot—twenty-four in all." When he taunted Israel, as Goliath had, "Jonathan . . . killed him" (2 Sam. 21:20, 21). David and Jonathan, like Joshua and Caleb before them, were unafraid of giants. They believed in God, and He did for them what they could never have done for themselves. It's always that way. God's role is to destroy the giants. The part people play is to trust Him to do so and to keep their eyes on the One for whom no giant can exist. In this way they rise above surrounding circumstances and gaze on the giant from God's perspective. Victory is assured. So it must be in final events on planet Earth.

---

[1] Ellen G. White, *Patriarchs and Prophets* (Mountain View, Calif.: Pacific Press, 1890), p. 645.

[2] *The Seventh-day Adventist Bible Commentary,* ed. F. D. Nichol (Washington, D.C.: Review and Herald, 1954), vol. 2, p. 535.

[3] Ralph W. Klein, *Word Biblical Commentary* (Waco, Tex.: Word, 1983), vol. 10, pp. 175, 176.

[4] White, p. 608.

[5] *Ibid.,* p. 645.

Chapter 5

Sneak Preview Into Last-Day Events

Have you ever been lost and tried to ask directions? Once a learned professor found himself in such a predicament. Spotting a lad by the side of the road, he stopped and asked, "Do you know the name of this road?"

"Nope."

"Do you know the name of the nearest town?"

"Nope."

"Do you know how to get to the interstate?"

"Nope."

"You don't know much, do you?" The man glared disdainfully down at the boy.

"I'm not lost," the youth replied.

~

Even learned professors do not know everything, especially when it comes to Scripture. Have you ever felt lost in the Bible? Say in Daniel and Revelation? Did you know that the Protestant Reformers of the sixteenth century wouldn't have anything to do with the book of Revelation? John Calvin wouldn't write a commentary on it. Martin Luther thought it had nothing to do with Christ.

Importance of Daniel and Revelation

The books of Daniel and Revelation are essential to get a grasp of final events. "Great truths that have lain unheeded and unseen since the day of Pentecost, are to shine from God's word in their native purity. To those who truly love God the Holy Spirit will reveal truths that have faded from the mind, and will also reveal truths that are entirely new. Those who eat the flesh and drink the blood of the Son of God will bring from the books of Daniel and Revelation truth that is inspired by the Holy Spirit. They will start into action forces that cannot be repressed. The lips of children will be opened to proclaim the mysteries that have been hidden from the minds of men. The Lord has chosen the foolish things of this world to confound the wise, and the weak things of the world to confound the mighty."[1]

Let's unpack the statement.

1. Since Pentecost, Christians have not heeded great truths.

2. Since Pentecost, great truths have been buried but will come to light in the end-time.

3. Such truths will be entirely new.

4. Christ will reveal them to those who know Him.

5. These entirely new truths will have irrepressible influence.

6. God will even reveal these entirely new truths to children.

7. Believers will proclaim these entirely new truths.

What will happen then? "When the books of Daniel and Revelation are better understood, believers will have an entirely different religious experience. They will be given such glimpses of the open gates of heaven that heart and mind will be impressed with the character that all must develop in order to realize the blessedness which is to be the reward of the pure in heart."[2]

So the entirely new truths will lead to an entirely new religious experience. Isn't that what we need?

Entirely New Religious Experience

For a long time church leaders have challenged, "We need a revival and reformation." Sometimes the response consists of working on becoming revived and reformed. Mine did. When as a teenager I longed for a deeper Christian experience, I made two lists and stuck then up on my bedroom wall. The first list enumerated the qualities I wanted to receive in my life. The other list recorded things I needed to give up. I left space beside each item for each day of the week. The idea was to chart my progress. Unfortunately, I often recorded defeat instead of victory.

Not until I shifted my focus from myself to Christ did I notice any difference. Scripture gives a simple principle: By beholding we become changed (see 2 Cor. 3:18). Through a steady gaze on Christ—wonder of wonders—we become like the One we admire the most. You see, my wall chart method was merely gazing at myself, and therefore I became ever more like myself—and that is no good, no use if you want change. Only beholding brings change. This is the principle all God's saints have mastered.

David did. That's why he defeated the giant. Giants also lurk within, and they are the hardest to beat. This is where Daniel and Revelation come in. A proper study of them will lead to an entirely new religious experience. Giants will tumble, and Christ will be supreme—within.

The Book of Daniel

First let us look at the book's author. He shared many traits with David. Both worked with royalty when young. Both knew God. Both became prophets. And both looked beyond external circumstances to God. A giant faced Daniel and mocked him just as verily as Goliath did to David. "You keep praying to God and to the lions you go!" King Darius had issued the decree. Daniel knew what it meant (see Dan. 6:6-9).

"Now when Daniel learned that the decree had been published, he went home to his upstairs room where the windows opened toward Jerusalem. Three times a day he got down on his knees and prayed, giving thanks to God, just as he had done before" (verse 10). Could he not pray in private? At least until the decree ended in 30 days? He could have. But that would be giving in partially to the giant. So he flung wide his window and prayed without fear. When the king's guards threw the prophet to the lions, Christ's angel shut their mouths (see verse 21). God delivered him just as publicly as his prayer commitment to God. Final events will be even more public. The international Sunday law against the Sabbath will be as public as you can get. All will watch modern Daniels. Their Sabbath worship will be public. More of that in a moment.

1. The Structure of the Book

Daniel is organized in a way that gives insight into final events. The first six chapters depict history and the last six, final events. The historical events give a sneak preview into future global events. The historical chapters contain a number of death decrees. Nebuchadnezzar passed one against his astrologers when they could not tell him his forgotten dream (see Dan. 2:5, 6). The second death decree was his "bow or burn" ultimatum (see Dan. 3:6). The third was the decree of Darius that all worship him for 30 days or go to the lions (see Dan. 6:6-9).

The fiery furnace and the lions' den death decrees had to do with worship. They portrayed the state legislating a form of worship upon its citizens, precisely what's coming in the end-time. "Worship the beast or die" will be the orders then (see Rev. 13:12-15). The good news is that none of the death decrees brought death to God's people in the past. Nor will the death decree in the future. We will study the reason for this later.

2. The Theme of the Book

The theme of deliverance holds the book together. In each of the three death decrees God provided deliverance. He revealed to Daniel the forgotten dream of Nebuchadnezzar, preventing the implementation of the death decree and delivering the astrologers (see Dan. 2:17-49). Then He protected the three Hebrew exiles thrown into the fiery furnace (see Dan. 3:16-28), as He did Daniel in the lions' den (see Dan. 6:21, 22). The historical deliverances move through the book, pointing to an eschatological deliverance in the end-time. "At that time Michael, the great prince who protects your people, will arise. There will be a time of distress such as has not happened from the beginning of nations until then. But at that time your people—everyone whose name is found written in the book—will be delivered" (Dan. 12:1). The book advances from local times of trouble to the greatest time of trouble ever. If the local deliverances were great, how much greater will be the coming global deliverance!

That is the point. The fact that the book records historical deliverances gives certainty to the coming deliverance. God's people often look at the greatest time of trouble and forget the greater deliverance that accompanies it. Again, focus is everything. The stories of deliverance are purposely placed in Daniel to show that there is more than a fiery furnace and a lion's den. There was deliverance from both! While a great time of trouble will come, the deliverance that closes it will be all the more remarkable.

3. God Is in Control

Closely associated with the theme of deliverance is that of God's control of human events. It assures the deliverance. Throughout the historical section we find reiterated "He sets up kings and deposes them" (Dan. 2:21), He gives dominion (see verse 37), and He extends kingdoms to anyone He wishes (see Dan. 4:17, 25, 32; 5:21). History moves to the time when "the God of heaven will set up a kingdom" (Dan. 2:44). "His kingdom is an eternal kingdom; his dominion endures" (Dan. 4:3; see also verse 34; Dan. 6:26).

This is why God's saints do not fear the enemy. "O Nebuchadnezzar, we do not need to defend ourselves before you in this matter. If we are thrown into the blazing furnace, the God we serve is able to save us from it, and he will rescue us from your hand, O king" (Dan. 3:16, 17). God longs for His people to trust Him the same way during the end-time. He desires for them to look beyond the trouble to the deliverance. Such a focus on the power of Christ brings an entirely new religious experience.

4. The Bow or Burn Decree

Here is a public decree about worship. At the sound of music all must bow and worship the statue on the plain of Dura. The image of solid gold counterfeited the one God had given to Nebuchadnezzar in his dream. The king didn't like the fact that he was only the head of gold, and that after him would come other kingdoms, represented by other metals in decreasing value. So he made a statue of solid gold. It really shouted, "My kingdom will last forever! So worship the symbol of this fact!"

"Bow or burn!" Worship this image or die in the fiery furnace. So it will happen on the modern plain of Dura around the world. An image to the beast will call for worship or death (see Rev. 13:12-15). O for the courage of those three exiles! They stood unafraid, just as did Joshua and Caleb before the giants, David before Goliath, Jonathan before the giant of Gath, or Daniel before the lions. All had one thing in common: They knew the power of God. When you have spent time with the King of kings, earthly potentates will cease to impress you. By beholding, these Bible heroes had become changed.

The Book of Revelation

Revelation divides into two sections, just as Daniel. It has a historical section (chapters 1-11) and a section on last-day events (chapters 13-22). Chapter 12, the apex joining the two, offers an overview of the great controversy from its inception until the Second Coming. Events in the historical section often go from John's day to the Second Advent (for example, the history of the seven churches [chapters 2, 3], the seven seals [chapters 6:1-8:5], and the seven trumpets [chapters 8:6-11:19]). The beast in the last-day events section has roots also in the historical period (chapter 13:1, 2). Except for them, the historical events are for us today mainly in the past, and reach into last-day-events only in either the sixth (chapters 3:14-22; 6:12-17) or seventh stages (chapter 11:15). The multiple sevens given in Revelation trace history throughout the sweep of the Christian age, including final times.

The book of Revelation takes in the whole Christian age. But unfortunately, many interpreters do not recognize this fact. Here are the main views.

1. Preterism

Preterism regards all of Revelation as confined to the first century. John wrote the book for his time, and it has no relevance for subsequent history or end events.

2. Futurism

Futurism takes the opposite view. It says most of Revelation lies in the future, beyond our times. Back in the sixteenth century the Reformers said the antichrist of Scripture was the Roman Catholic Church. In order to protect the church from their onslaught, Catholic scholars responded with the theories of Preterism and Futurism. Both schools of interpretation take the spotlight off the church in the present.

3. Historicism

Seventh-day Adventists reject preterism and futurism and accept historicism, for Revelation carries the reader throughout the whole sweep of the Christian age. In taking this position, Seventh-day Adventists stand alone. Much of Protestantism has bought into futurism, as best seen in dispensationalism (see next chapter). The fact that God gave the image dream to Nebuchadnezzar, which traced the nations from Babylon, Medo-Persia, Greece, Rome, the divided kingdoms, and to the kingdom of God, shows that the book of Daniel covers a much larger sweep of history than Revelation. But both books are historical throughout, divided into past and final-events history.

Another Major Division in Revelation[3]

Besides the history/final events overall structure, Revelation has eight separate parts. A vision of the throne room introduces seven of them (chapters 4; 5; 8:2-6; 11:19; 15:1-8; 16:18; 17:3; 19:1-10; 21:5-11). An important reason exists for this arrangement. Before looking at events transpiring on earth, our gaze should go first to heaven. There at the throne we see God and Christ as the slain Lamb. There we witness Calvary, where Christ defeated Satan. That qualifies Him for any further skirmishes on earth. Looking at the throne room reminds us that Christ is in control of final events. John depicts humans at the throne room (e.g., the 24 elders of Rev. 4, 5), reminding us that it's only a matter of time until the redeemed will be there too.

Therefore, throne-room scenes introduce each of the seven sections to give the reader courage. Christ-centered and cross-centered, they shout out, "Human victory is assured, because Jesus has already gained the victory." In just a matter of time we will witness the results of Calvary in end-time events.

Two Further Structures in Revelation

I used to think that John had not put his book together very well. It seemed to lack a chronological sequence. That's still true. For example, Revelation 14:1 has the 144,000 on Mount Zion with the Lamb before the three angels' messages. This means we see them in the millennium and new earth (see Heb. 12:22, 23) before the giving of the end-time messages (see Rev. 14:6-13) and the Second Advent takes place (see verses 14-20). There's a reason for this, though, as we'll see in a future chapter. It should give pause to those who try to make the text sequential. For example, Revelation 13:3 states that all the world will wonder after the beast and then goes on to speak of the 42-month persecution under the beast (verses 5-8). Some assume this persecution is still future. The 42 months are the same as 1,260 days, and Revelation 12:6 places those days in the past, during the time the church endured persecution (A.D. 538-1798), the time also referred to as "a time, times and half a time" (Rev. 12:14). Here we observe three ways of describing the same past persecution, and John presents a past persecution after one yet future. So Revelation isn't always chronological.

Further corroboration of this appears in the fact that all the world wonders after the beast in Revelation 13:3, and yet the beginning of American history does not get mentioned until verse 11. And America draws the world's attention to the beast (verse 12). So as we examine Revelation 13 and 14 we see that John can take a look into the future, and then return to earlier historical details. It is similar to his going to the throne room scene before considering history on earth.

This gives reason to the otherwise nonsequential presentation. Further evidence of the well-organized structure of Revelation occurs in two methods John employs to organize the book. We speak of the book unfolded over against the sanctuary structure on the one hand, and then also unfolded sequentially through the Jewish year, following the five major feasts on the other.

1. The Sanctuary Structure

I believe the Holy Spirit guided the structure of the book. He led John to write the visions in a sequence that matched a walk through the sanctuary. The earthly sanctuary had a courtyard with an altar of burnt offering and laver. Then the priests entered the holy place, and once a year the high priest went into the Most Holy Place. The two holy places represented the heavenly sanctuary ministry of Christ.

So the walk through the sanctuary in heaven begins on earth, in the courtyard. There we find Christ pictured with the seven churches (see Rev. 1:12-20). Then we enter the heavenly sanctuary and witness the inauguration of Christ into His heavenly sanctuary ministry (chapters 4; 5). Next we follow Christ in His intercession in the holy place (chapter 8:3-5) until John pulls the curtain back so we can peer into the Most Holy Place (chapter 11:19). This is precisely where the historical section of the book ends. The view into the Second Apartment indicates that Christ is about to go into the Second Apartment in 1844 and that chapters 13-22 will be about final events since 1844. Christ enters His investigative judgment work until its cessation (chapter 15:5-8). At His second advent He leaves the heavenly sanctuary (chapter 19:14-21). After the millennium (chapter 20) Christ returns to the new earth (chapters 21; 22).

John follows Christ in His heavenly sanctuary ministry, and divides the two sections of the book precisely where the historical ends and the eschatological begins. So the book is truly a revelation of Jesus Christ (see Rev. 1:1). Notice that Christ occupies the center of focus. Revelation is about Him far more than it is about times of trouble and the enemy. The fact that the heavenly sanctuary ministry forms the structure for the unfolding of the book reminds the reader that it is the Victor of Calvary, the One who has already triumphed over Satan, the One who has a sacrifice to minister (see Heb. 8:1-6; 9:23-28), who is central. In this way the whole book centers on the ministry of the victorious Christ. Thus, all the book, and not just the seven throne-room scenes, calls for the reader to behold Christ, and by beholding Him to become changed from scared saints facing final events to free saints rejoicing in a sure victory to come because of a finished victory already accomplished at Calvary.

Properly understood, final events on Planet Earth are more Calvary-centered than crisis-centered. When we allow the victory of Calvary to determine the meaning of final events, they take on an altogether different appearance. Satan cannot undo Calvary anymore than He can undo the Incarnation. It's the incarnate God, the One who also became a man, who'll be with us through final events. He'll give us the victory of Calvary to carry us through.

2. The Jewish Festival Year

The Holy Spirit led John to unfold his book by following Christ through His heavenly sanctuary ministry. But He also prompted the author to structure the book around the five major Jewish festivals in their calendar year. The book begins with the first feast of the year, and then goes on through to the final feast. The feasts all illustrate some feature of the plan of redemption and are Christ-centered.

The first feast, Passover, commemorates Calvary. John proclaims the One "who loves us and has freed us from our sins by his blood" (Rev. 1:5), thus mentioning Calvary in the beginning of his book. Fifty days later Pentecost, the outpouring of the Spirit, took place. It's interesting that after the Passover Israel finally came to Mount Sinai at the same time of the year that the later Pentecost took place. At Sinai Moses ascended the mount to receive the Ten Commandments from Christ (see Ex. 31:18). During Pentecost the ascended Christ received the sealed scroll from the Father (see Rev. 4; 5). Pentecost gave evidence that the sacrifice of Christ had been accepted. He could pour out the Spirit. The Spirit-outpouring has its basis in Calvary and will occur again in the latter rain.

The third feast was Trumpets, blown ten days before the Day of Atonement (see Lev. 23:23-27). Revelation 8-11 presents the trumpets. Then the next feast was the Day of Atonement (see Rev. 13-20). Notice how this agrees with the major divisions of the book. The trumpets announce the Day of Atonement and are completed by chapter 11 in the historical section.

SNEAK PREVIEW INTO LAST-DAY EVENTS

Then the Day of Atonement, beginning in 1844, occurs in Revelation 13-20, with the sneak preview into the Second Apartment in the last verse of chapter 11. So again the Day of Atonement feast comes in the last-day-events section. Thus the sanctuary and feast days both support the historical and final events division of the book. The final feast of the year was the Feast of Tabernacles, and it appears in chapter 21, in which God comes to the tabernacle with humanity on the new earth.

Both journeys in the sanctuary and the festival year begin at Calvary. The cross is the basis of both the heavenly sanctuary ministry and of the types of that ministry given in the major feasts. Calvary has a crucial place in the book of Revelation. In fact, as you come to the apex of the book in chapter 12, where both the history and last-day events join, a verse near the center of the book speaks of Calvary as the place that spelled the death knell for Satan, who is pictured as fallen to the earth because of it (Rev. 12:9-11).

The Great Controversy

Ellen G. White's *The Great Controversy* is a remarkable book for studying last-day events. Although she did not usually write an introduction to her books, she did for this one. She must have had an important reason why. "It is not so much the object of this book to present new truths concerning the struggles of former times," she says, "as to bring out facts and principles which have a bearing on coming events."[5]

While it's another history book, much more than that it presents *facts and principles* as insight into final events—facts and principles that will repeat themselves. You see, this book, like Daniel and Revelation, also divides between history (chapters 1-35) and last-day events (chapters 36-42). Principles and facts in the historical section give a sneak preview of facts and events yet to come. It's interesting that God inspired the structure of all three books in the same way. He must want us to learn from history what He will do for us in the future.

The Great Controversy begins with the destruction of the old city of Jerusalem and ends with the New Jerusalem in the new earth. With apologies to Charles Dickens, I see the book as "The Tale Between Two Cities." I recommend that chapters 36-42 be read first so that final events are clearly in mind, and then chapters 1-35. The earlier chapters will present events and principles that will remind you of what you read in the final-events section.

For example, a principle appears in how the Middle Ages' union of church and state led to persecution of others. So in the end-time the union of church and state in America will lead to the Sunday law and death decree (see Rev. 13:11-15). For an event, consider Luther. He felt the brunt of this church-state union and stood firm, calling God to help him. So will Sabbathkeepers in the end-time. I could offer many more examples. Many past local events provide insight into what will be played out on a global scale in the end-time. Have you ever read *The Great Controversy* this way? It opens your eyes. Try it.

Christ Is Coming!

[1] Ellen G. White, *Fundamentals of Christian Education* (Nashville: Southern Pub. Assn., 1923), p. 473.

[2] White, *Testimonies to Ministers and Gospel Workers* (Mountain View, Calif.: Pacific Press, 1944), p. 114.

[3] See Kenneth A. Strand in *Symposium on Revelation* (BRI, 1992), vol. 1, pp. 35-72, where eight visions are given.

[4] See Richard M. Davidson in *Symposium on Revelation,* vol. 1, pp. 99-130. I have found the *Symposium on Daniel* and the *Symposium on Revelation,* volumes 1 and 2, to be very helpful. I highly recommend them for further study.

[5] White, *The Great Controversy* (Mountain View, Calif.: Pacific Press, 1911), p. xii.

Chapter 6

Dispensational Final Events

John F. Walvoord, president of Dallas Theological Seminary, taught dispensational ideas on last-day events for years. He wrote many books. One of them[1] sold more than 1 million copies (1974-1976). When the Gulf War broke out, Walvoord put out a revised edition, and the White House ordered a number of copies.

People hunger to know what is coming. Have you ever heard of the secret rapture? The role of Israel in the final seven years? The rebuilding of the Jewish Temple in Jerusalem? The invasion of Israel by Russia and God's miraculous intervention? The conversion of the Jews in gratitude? The mission of the Jews to take the gospel to the world when the church is in heaven?

Many American Christians hold such views. To them these will be the final events on earth. But are they biblical? These views, and others, come from dispensationalists. Because the views are so all-pervasive in the United States, the chances are that your Christian friends espouse them. Therefore, it is vital that Seventh-day Adventists and other committed Christians be able to evaluate such claims by Scripture.

Jesus asked, "When the Son of Man comes, will he find faith in the earth?" (Luke 18:8). Christ said that those heeding His Word will survive tempests for they are on a solid foundation, whereas those who do not heed His words will not make it (see Matt. 7:24-27). The end-time tempests will be so severe that "none but those who have fortified the mind with the truths of the Bible will stand through the last great conflict."[2] Therefore, God's end-time sealing (Rev. 7:1-3) is a "settling into the truth, both intellectually and spiritually, so . . . [we] cannot be moved."[3] Our eternal destiny depends upon our relationship to biblical truth; hence the importance of biblical interpretation.[4]

System of Biblical Interpretation

Dispensationalism is a system of biblical interpretation that has "infiltrated almost every branch of Protestantism"[5] and has "considerable influence within conservative circles,"[6] as demonstrated by the *Scofield Reference Bible* (1909, 1917) and the *New Scofield Study Bible* (1967). It is therefore vital that all Christians be aware of dispensational interpretations and avoid a similar focus on biblical distinctions and preoccupation with the role of Israel and the Middle East in final events.[7] We'll see why as we get into the topic.

The Roots of the Movement[8]

John Nelson Darby (1800-1882) and C. I. Scofield (1843-1921), the principal pioneer contributors to dispensationalism, were lawyers who later became ministers, Darby in Britain and Scofield in America. The story begins in Britain. Darby, ordained a deacon in the Church of England (1825), became disenchanted with the politically dominated church and left it in 1827. Therefore, "it should be carefully noted that Darby's first and basic dissent was not on the question of eschatology [final events], but on the doctrine of the church."[9]

He had "doubts as to the scriptural authority for church establishments."[10] Add to this the fact that he failed miserably to keep God's law for seven years, and found relief only when he discovered in Ephesians 3 that the church is seated with Christ in heavenly places. He took the passage to mean that Christians are above the law and that the law applies merely to the former dispensation, to Israel. This led him "to compartmentalize Israel and the church as distinct objects of God's separate purposes."[11]

His personal experience influenced the way he understood the Bible. It led him to divide Scripture up into seven dispensations. During the years 1862-1868 he came to America and Canada on speaking tours, staying an aggregate of six years,[12] and through his contact with C. I. Scofield, and the Scofield Study Bible, the ideas of dispensationalism spread across the United States.

Dispensational Hermeneutics

1. Dispensations

We need to understand the term "dispensation." Scofield says "a dispensation is a period of time during which man is tested in respect of obedience to some *specific* revelation of the will of God."[13] The word "dispensation" means somewhat the same as the Greek word *oikonomia* and is perhaps referred to as a time period only in Ephesians 1:10.[14] Its usual meaning is stewardship, rather than a time period. Yet dispensationalism denotes the dividing of salvation history into distinct time periods, seven for Darby[15] and Scofield,[16] eight,[17] or even 10[18] or 12[19] for others, and three for the Dallas Theological Seminary.[20]

Dispensationalists admit that "the number of dispensations in a dispensational scheme, and even the names of the dispensations, are relatively minor matters." For "the essence of dispensationalism is (1) the recognition of a distinction between Israel and the Church, (2) a consistently literal principle of interpretation, and (3) a basic and working conception of the purpose of God as His own glory rather than as a single purpose of salvation."[21]

Daniel P. Fuller correctly concludes that dispensationalists "must, however, insist on at least three dispensations in order to assert the idea of the Church as a parenthesis between God's dealings with Israel."[22] Dispensationalists believe that God's program for Israel is merely on hold during the present "church age," to be resumed at the rapture of the church, with the ultimate fulfillment of all the covenantal promises to Israel during the millennial kingdom. So it requires a minimum of three dispensations.[23]

2. The Israel/Church Dichotomy

Ryrie's list (above) places the distinction between Israel and the church as the first essence of dispensationalism. In fact, it drives the entire system. Remove this distinction and dispensationalism would cease to exist. For the Israel/church dichotomy is basic to dispensational biblical interpretation.[24] Keep this basic distinction, and it multiplies numerous other distinctions—even beyond the various dispensations—in order to maintain the basic Israel/church contrast or separation.[25] Dispensationalists unite on the Israel/church dichotomy, even if they have four different views for when the "church-age" began,[26] and three views for when it will close.[27]

Scofield wrote a book entitled *Rightly Dividing the Word of Truth,*[28] based upon 2 Timothy 2:15. In commenting on "rightly dividing the Word," he said, "The Word of truth, then, has right divisions, and it must be evident that, as one cannot be 'a workman that needeth not to be ashamed' without observing them, so *any study* of the Word which ignores divisions must be in large measure profitless and confusing."[29] In other words, we must keep Israel and the church separate, as well as each dispensation. However, the biblical word "dividing" does not mean "divisions." The Greek word *orthotomeo* comes from *orthos:* "right" or "honest" and *stemno,* "to cut." "The renowned Syrian exegete Theodoret (c. 393-c. 458) applied the verb to 'a plowman who drives a straight furrow.' "[30]

Orthotomeo occurs only in 2 Timothy 2:15 in the New Testament, and only twice in the Greek Septuagint (or LXX) Old Testament (Prov. 3:6; 11:5). Many consider this compound verb to have "probably lost the meaning from which it was derived and . . . acquired the more general sense of right handling (RV, RSV). From this sense the derived noun came later to denote orthodoxy."[31] Orthodoxy says rightly dividing allows any part to be interpreted by the whole *(sola scriptura).* It means the New Testament will interpret the Old Testament, a premise anathema to dispensational divisions. "What God has joined together [whole Bible], let man not separate" (Mark 10:9) is good hermeneutical (interpretational) practice as well as marital advice.[32]

3. Consistent Literalism Claimed as the Dispensational Principle of Interpretation

Dispensationalists claim to use a literal "interpretation consistently in *all* . . . study of the Bible." They charge nondispensationalists "with allegorizing or spiritualizing when it comes to the interpretation of prophecy."[33] Claiming to be the only consistent literalists because they also give prophecy a literal interpretation,[34] they oppose "spiritualizing" in defense of biblical authority,[35] and against liberals.[36] But they especially reject a spiritual kingdom now rather than a literal Messianic kingdom later, thus ignoring the New Testament present fulfillment.[37] Paradoxically, they transform the ascension of the church into a rapture, claiming biblical authority when they have none,[38] and so do employ spiritualization in prophetic interpretation anyway![39]

The New Testament spiritualizes Old Testament passages and shows that the literalists in prophetic interpretation crucified Christ (see Matt. 23:13-39; Mark 12:1-12; Luke 12:56; John 11:45-57).[40] Unlike His contemporary Israel, Christ interpreted the kingdom as already in their midst (see Matt. 10:7; 12:28; more of this later). The entire book of Hebrews rests on the fact that the new covenant promised to Israel and Judah (see Jer. 31:31) is not some literal event in a future Messianic kingdom, but is already inaugurated in Christ for spiritual Israel, the church (see Heb. 8:6-13).

The question is not literal versus spiritual interpretation. The New Testament speaks of Christ as "the Lamb that was slain from the creation of the world" (Rev. 13:8), and as coming in the Second Advent on either "a white cloud" (Rev. 14:14) or "a white horse" (Rev. 19:11). Here we have a spiritual truth (His death atoning for humanity from the beginning), a literal truth (His return), and symbolic expressions (cloud/horse) all intermingled. Walvoord concedes the problems of using only literal interpretation,[41] but dispensationalists never apply this to the Israel/church relationship as does the New Testament. George Ladd rightly comments, "Our point of departure must be the way the New Testament interprets the Old Testament."[42]

We need to define *literal.* Literal, to dispensationalists, means obvious or clear meaning. It assumes that the words and the passage are transparent. Dispensationalists refer to their hermeneutic of literalism as "its plain interpretation,"[43] "normal" "ordinary" or "customary" meaning, the "grammatical-historical method,"[44] or the "plain grammatical sense."[45] But is the meaning of the Bible so transparent, particularly the prophetic passages? Even dispensationalists recognize that "almost complete confusion reigns in the interpretation of prophecy,"[46] and that "acquiring the knowledge of the spiritual [note the word] content of the Bible is a life task."[47] Why so long and why so many different interpretations if the meaning is so obvious? Why does Scripture warn that spiritual things "are spiritually discerned" (1 Cor. 2:14)? If the normal understanding of language is sufficient to grasp biblical truth, then would not the unspiritual also understand?

4. Evidence Opposing Consistent Literalism

Old Testament prophecies are the playground of dispensationalists, who project their fulfillment onto a future earthly kingdom. We need to weigh two facts against "consistent literalism," or the "transparent understanding" thesis. (1) Most Old Testament prophecies were written in the Hebrew language. Hebrew has a small vocabulary and is not as technically precise as New Testament Greek. "In literary form, written Hebrew is full of metaphors, elastic and vague; sometimes indeed it is capable of more than one meaning."[48] (2) "The authors of the various New Testament books did not introduce and apply the quotations from the Old Testament in a scientific manner, with literary accuracy characteristic of our day. Rather the OT passages were embodied in the Gospels, in the Epistles, in the Acts, and in the Apocalypse in order to bear witness to the fulfillment of the Old Covenant in the New."[49] This does not mean that New Testament writers misconstrue the Old Testament in their quotations. Rather, they bring out their true meaning and their fuller importance.

As C. Norman Kraus put it, "dispensationalist interpretation is built on an inadequate concept of the nature of language and its use. In seeking to uphold the supernatural quality of the biblical narrative, it has assumed that the biblical language is like the language of a science textbook; that is, its terms have a fixed meaning from beginning to end."[50]

5. A Literal Fulfillment of Prophecies Does Not Support Consistent Literalism

Not only do dispensationalists confine their focus to an alleged transparency of language, but they cite the literal fulfillment of prophecy to prove literalism.[51] They say "there is no nonliteral fulfillment of these prophecies in the New Testament. This argues strongly for the literal method."[52] Let us apply this hermeneutic to Christ to see if it works or not. Granted He was born in Bethlehem (see Micah 5:2; Matt. 2:4, 5), came out of Egypt (see Hosea 11:1; Matt. 2:14, 15), was crucified (see Isa. 53:7-12; John 18:1-19:37), and rose again (see Hosea 6:1, 2; 1 Cor. 15:3, 4)—all literal fulfillments of prophecy (note qualification[53]), but is this all He fulfilled? Is it not also true that through this One Israelite, Jesus Christ, the Abrahamic promise was fulfilled—the promise that "all peoples on the earth will be blessed through you" (Gen. 12:3)? Is it not true that "no matter how many promises God has made, they are 'Yes' in Christ" (2 Cor. 1:20)? And is it also not true that Christ has broken down the wall between Jew and Gentile (see Eph. 2:11-22), a concept that denies the dispensational Israel/church dichotomy?

Thus consistent literalism makes a selective use of Christ's fulfillment of Old Testament prophecy and hence is an inconsistent interpretation of prophecy.

6. Typological Interpretation Calls Into Question Consistent Literalism

Dispensational systematic theologian L. S. Chafer says: "Almost every important truth of the New Testament was typified and foreshadowed in the Old Testament,"[54] and that "the antitype serves to lift its type out of the commonplace into that which is inexhaustible and to invest it with riches and treasures hitherto unrevealed."[55] His insights are correct, and they agree with the New Testament interpretation of the Old Testament. If they had guided Chafer's theological system, it would have transcended the confining strictures of literalism. But other statements in dispensational writings like Chafer's are seminal for a totally different biblical interpretation.[56]

The New Scofield Study Bible disproves the dispensational claim to use a consistent literal interpretation. In its study notes it has Old Testament people and things not only receiving a literal interpretation but also functioning as types of antitypes in the New Testament. Thus historical persons or things are both literal and typical. Many typify Christ[57]—the study Bible interprets them christologically. Others typify the church—they are ecclesiologically interpreted. The introduction to the Song of Solomon offers a threefold interpretation: (1) literal (Solomon's love for Shulamite girl), (2) figurative (revelation of God's love to Israel), and (3) allegorical (Christ's love for the church).[58]

Although dispensationalists claim that the Old Testament doesn't even conceive of the church,[59] yet surprisingly it finds the whole Song of Solomon to be an "allegory" of the church "in spite of the fact that the book says nothing about either Christ or the church."[60] *The New Scofield Study Bible* also finds in the Old Testament numerous types for the church, including Eve,[61] Isaac,[62] Rebekah,[63] the tabernacle,[64] Aaron and sons,[65] the wave loaves,[66] and the Shulamite maiden.[67] But nowhere is Israel a type of the church, even though its claim to such an interpretation is far greater than any of the other choices. In fact, dispensationalists specifically state that Israel is not a type of the church.[68] This demonstrates the inconsistency of dispensational typological interpretation when it encounters their Israel/church dichotomy.

Moreover, *The New Scofield Study Bible* cites many types, even some extreme ones. As O. T. Allis concludes:[69] "While dispensationalists are extreme literalists, they are very inconsistent ones. They are literalists in interpreting prophecy. But in the interpreting of history, they carry the principle of typical interpretation to an extreme which has rarely been exceeded even by the most ardent of allegorizers."[70] So dispensationalists get criticized for something they accuse others of—allegorization.[71]

Many scholars recognize typology as an important hermeneutical key in biblical interpretation.[72]

7. The Principle of the Bible's Self-Interpretation *(Sola Scriptura)* Opposes Consistent Literalism and Alone Does Justice to the Biblical Worldview

Dispensational literal interpretation is actually too confining. It limits meaning to only the normal coinage of a given word, with no proper openness to the Protestant principle of the Bible's self-interpretation *(sola scriptura)*. Such a broader approach to Scripture would seem consistent with the dispensational claim to have a broader worldview—God's glory rather than just human salvation.

a. Divine Truth Greater Than Human Words

Divine truth is always far greater than the ability of human words to communicate it, even as God's divine Son was far greater than His manifestation in human flesh. Both the written and living words of God contain divine content that transcends the limited vehicle of the human. Literalism limits the meaning of words to the immediate context rather than allowing the theological context of the whole Bible to inform the interpretation. This means that dispensationalist interpreters confine Old Testament words to Old Testament times and cut them off from the continual unfolding of the plan of salvation, from typological fulfillment, and from meeting their fulfillment in Christ.

b. New Testament Fulfillment Transcends Old Testament

Looking to future fulfillment of Old Testament prophecy to Israel in Palestine ignores the fact that the New Testament fulfillment is (1) christological and (2) has escalated from a local to a global fulfillment. Here, briefly, are some of the biblical facts. Christ recognized that Old Testament people/institutions were types of Himself. True to type/antitype correspondence, He is "greater than Jonah" (Matt. 12:41), "greater than Solomon" (Luke 11:31), greater than David (Mark 2:25-28), and "greater than the temple" (Matt. 12:6). Just as lambs typified the Lamb of God (see John 1:29; Rev. 5:12, 13; 13:8), so prophets, priests, and kings were supposed to typify Christ's prophetic, priestly, and kingly ministries. In each, Christ transcended the type. So His was a better ministry (Heb. 8:6), a better sacrifice (Heb. 9:26), with a better covenant and "better promises" (Heb. 8:6), and consistency requires a better throne. For David's throne is transferred from Palestine (Jerusalem) to Christ's throne in heaven (Acts 2:34, 35; Heb. 1:3, 13; 8:1; 10:12; Rev. 3:21).

Therefore, says the New Testament, "what God promised our fathers he has fulfilled for us, their children, by raising up Jesus. . . . The fact that God raised him from the dead, never to decay, is stated in these words: 'I will give you the holy and sure blessings promised to David'" (Acts 13:32-34). So the ancient promises to Israel found their fulfillment in Christ. What is involved in this fact? "The promises were spoken to Abraham and to his seed. The Scripture does not say 'and to seeds,' meaning many people, but 'and to your seed,' meaning one person, who is Christ" (Gal. 3:16).

Paul here refers to Genesis 12:7, 13:15, and 24:7, in which God promises possession of the land. In the type/antitype correspondence, with its escalated fulfillment, Abraham becomes "heir of the world" (Rom. 4:13), not just of Israel. His heirs are "as numerous as the stars in the sky and as countless as the sand on the seashore" (Heb. 11:11, 12). He is the "father of many nations" (Rom. 4:16, 17). Yet even the original promise included being "a father of many nations" (see Gen. 17:5), with heirs as countless as stars and sand (Gen. 22:17). Not only is Abraham the father of many nations and heir of the world, transcending race (Israelites) and region (Palestine), but in his one seed Christ the distinction between Israel and other nations has been removed (see Eph. 2:13, 14), so that they have become "one new man" (verse 15), "one body" (Eph. 3:6), and "a holy temple" (Eph. 2:21). Translated literally, the Greek of Ephesians 3:6 says: "the nations are joint heirs *(sugkleronoma)* and a joint body *(sussoma)* and joint sharers *(summetocha)* of the promise of Him in Christ."

c. Christ Fulfills Promises Made to Abraham

So the promise made to Abraham has received its fulfillment in Christ. God called Abraham out so that through him He could bless all nations of the world (Gen. 18:18; 22:18; 26:4; 28:14). These references and their context indicate that many nations would arise from Jacob/Israel (Gen. 35:11), that his seed would be as the sands of the sea, and through them God desired to bless the world. So already the type reveals God's desired future that transcends race (Israelites) and region (Palestine). That mission depended upon Israel's remaining faithful to God. The promises God made to Israel were conditional (Deut. 28). Israel's unfaithfulness brought captivity (Assyrian and Babylonian) as He predicted (Deut. 28:32-68).

So where the seeds of Abraham (Israel) failed, there the seed Christ (Gal. 3:16) succeeded. Their failed mission to bless the world (Gen. 12:3) Christ accomplished (John 3:16). In Christ's history He recapitulated the history of Israel. Indeed, He was the new Israel (as the head of His body the church [Eph. 3:6; 5:19, 20; Col. 1:18]). He came out of Egypt (Matt. 2:15; cf. Hosea 11:1) and spent 40 days in the desert (Matt. 4:1; cf. 40 years, Deut. 8:2). Realizing the type/antitype correspondence, Christ's three quotations of Scripture in answer to Satan's wilderness temptations all came from Deuteronomy and the experience of Israel in the wilderness (see Matt. 4:4, cf. Deut. 8:3; Matt. 4:7, cf. Deut. 6:16; Matt. 4:10, cf. Deut. 6:13). His betrayal was typified by David's (see Luke 22:48, cf. Ps. 41:9), and His death and resurrection after three days was typified by Israel's restoration after three days (see 1 Cor. 15:3, 4, cf. Hosea 6:1, 2). Christ is now on David's throne (see Luke 1:32, 33; Heb. 1:3, 8, 13), from which He guides in the present building of the temple made up of Jew and Gentile Christians (see Eph. 2:20; 1 Peter 2:4, 5).

Although the cosmic nature of the promises and mission given to Abraham had a partial revelation in the Old Testament, true to the type/antitype escalation, the surprise of the New Testament is their fulfillment in and through Christ, who became the head (see Col. 1:18) of the new body (see Eph. 3:6), Jew and Gentile, that comprises the new "Israel of God" (Gal. 6:16). The promise transcends the Promised Land (Palestine) to the promised world (see Gen. 26:3, 4) and even to the heavenly inheritance (see 2 Tim. 4:18; Heb. 11:13-16; 1 Peter 1:4; 2 Peter 3:13). The heavenly is a surprising dimension of the inheritance not revealed in the Old Testament. Equally startling is the fact that this inheritance is not only future but already present "in Christ." For "God raised us up with Christ and seated us with him in the heavenly realms in Christ Jesus" (Eph. 2:6). Far transcending the dispensational focus on Palestine and Jerusalem, God says that His new Israel of God "have come to Mount Zion, to the heavenly Jerusalem, the city of the living God. . . . You have come . . . to Jesus the mediator of a new covenant" (Heb. 12:22-24). And the next surprise is the escalated mission. The Israel of God does have a mission to the world (see Matt. 28:19), as did ancient Israel (see Gen. 12:3), but "now, through the church, the manifold wisdom of God should be made known to the rulers and authorities in the heavenly realms" (Eph. 3:10).

d. Old Testament Promises Are Conditional

A covenant relationship with God was prerequisite to being true Israel and receiving the covenant promises in the Old Testament (see Gen. 17:8, 9; 22:18; 26:4, 5; Deut. 28:1-14). So in the New Testament the children of promise, not necessarily the natural children, are Abraham's offspring (see Rom. 9:2, 3). For "not all . . . Israel are Israel" (verses 6, 7), but only those who are inwardly (see Rom. 2:28, 29), that is, those who belong to Christ (see Gal. 3:27-29; cf. receive Christ, John 1:12) "believe" (Gal. 3:6-9; Matt. 3:9, 10). Christ said that Abraham's children are those who do the works of Abraham (see John 8:38-40). The present secular state of Israel fails to meet Christ's definition of the "Israel of God." Peter calls Gentiles in the new Israel of God "a chosen people, a royal priesthood, a holy nation, a people belonging to God" (1 Peter 2:9), because they have taken the role of Old Testament physical Israel.

e. The New Testament Focus on Christ, Not on Land

The New Testament, therefore, speaks about "the mystery that has been kept hidden for ages and generations, but is now disclosed to the saints," which is "Christ in you, the hope of glory" (Col. 1:26). Paul says, "We proclaim him" (verse 28), and considered his Jewish heritage as nothing compared to gaining "Christ and be found in him" (Phil. 3:8, 9). W. D. Davies rightly observed that "Paul ignores completely the territorial aspect of the promise. The land is not within his purview. . . . By personalizing the promise 'in Christ' Paul universalized it."[73]

Anthony Thiselton concludes that "the New Testament writers see Christ as an interpretive key for the interpretation and understanding of the Old Testament."[74] Nowhere does the New Testament promise the land of Palestine to the new Israel, the church. Christ, not Palestine, is the focus of the New Testament. Paul sums it up succinctly: "For no matter how many promises God has made, they are 'Yes' in Christ" (2 Cor. 1:20).

8. Dispensational Interpretation of the Seventieth Week of Daniel 9:24-27 Is Opposed to Consistent Literalism

If dispensationalists really believe in a literal interpretation, on what basis do they remove the seventieth week from the other 69 in the 70 weeks prophecy of Daniel 9:24-27? They detach the seventieth week from the other 69 and jump over 2,000 years of church history to give the last pre-Advent seven years to Israel, after the alleged church rapture. Here again the need to keep Israel and the church separate drives their quest. Such an interpretation of a time prophecy is anything but normal or usual. As Payne notes, it has distinct problems.[75]

No other time prophecy in Scripture gets interpreted in such a strange way. It seems to me that an authentic literal or normal interpretation would mandate that the seventieth week follow the other 69. As one scholar asked, "Is it credible that this prophecy, which speaks so definitely of 70 weeks and then subdivides the 70 into 7 and 62 and 1, should require for its correct interpretation that an interval be discovered between the last two of the weeks far longer than the entire period covered by the prophecy itself?"[76]

9. Some Books Critiquing Consistent Literalism

Since 1945 a number of significant books have critiqued dispensational hermeneutics (directly or indirectly). They include (listed chronologically by publication date) *Prophecy and the Church* (O. T. Allis, 1945),[77] *The Seed of Abraham* (A. Pieters, 1950),[78] *Crucial Questions About the Kingdom of God* (G. E. Ladd, 1952),[79] *The Kingdom of God* (J. Bright, 1953),[80] *The Gospel of the Kingdom* (G. E. Ladd, 1959),[81] *Jesus and the Kingdom: The Eschatology of Biblical Realism* (G. E. Ladd),[82] *The Gospel and the Land: Early Christianity and Jewish Territory Doctrine* (W. D. Davies, 1974), *The Bible and the Future* (Anthony A. Hoekema, 1979), *Gospel and Law: Contrast or Continuum? The Hermeneutics of Dispensationalism and Covenant Theology* (D. P. Fuller, 1980),[83] *The Israel of God in Prophecy: Principles of Prophetic Interpretation* (H. K. LaRondelle, 1983),[84] *The Covenants of Promise: A Theology of the Old Testament Covenants* (T. E. McComiskey, 1985).[85]

Bruce K. Waltke, Old Testament professor of Regent University, recently said: "In my opinion, the works by LaRondelle and Hoekema remain the best on the topic."[86] He says LaRondelle's work is a "superb book."[87] (I agree with his evaluation.)[88]

The cumulative evidence, given above, lays out the inconsistency of "consistent literalism" and finds it has problems that need addressing. For example: (1) the alleged unconditionality of the Abrahamic covenant; (2) the alleged belief that Israel can return in unbelief as a religious/political state to Palestine; (3) the alleged idea that Christ came to Israel to establish an earthly kingdom, which is only postponed; and (4) the alleged absence of the church in the purview of the Old Testament. The Israel/church dichotomy lies behind all four, producing continuing inconsistencies. Space limitations permit consideration of only the second one.

Is the Present Return of Israel Prophetic?[89]

Ever since the modern state of Israel began May 1948, dispensationalists have rejoiced in it as *the* sign of the nearness of Christ's return.[90] They believe that soon God is going to fulfill all the Old Testament promises to Israel because of the unconditional Abrahamic Covenant. God's faithfulness, not the faithfulness of Israel, will bring it about, so apparently it is no problem for dispensationalists to look at the modern state of Israel as fulfilling covenantal promises, even though Israel is highly secular and the vast majority have returned in religious unbelief.[91] It is interesting that even *The New Scofield Study Bible* can speak of restoration dependent on repentance[92] although it is an exception to the normal presentation.[93] Has God covenanted to Israel the land without any strings attached?

1. Loss of Land Because of Unbelief

Much more exists to the biblical covenant than a merely formal deed or legal transaction on paper, with no personal involvement. Without belief there can be no covenant experience. That the covenant is not unconditional is evidenced by the fact that it can be violated (Joshua 23:16; Judges 2:20, 21) or abandoned (Deut. 29:25, 26; Jer. 22:9). Moreover, the captivities of Israel to Assyria (2 Kings 15:29-17:24) and Judah to Babylon (2 Kings 18:17-19:36; Dan. 1:1-3) resulted from unbelief. The people had turned from God to serve other gods. Their covenant unfaithfulness did make a difference (Deut. 28:15-68). Each exile argues against the idea of an unconditional covenant or possession of the land as an inherited right.

2. Loss of Land Can Be Eternal

If covenantal experience is decisive to covenant permanence, then what did God mean when He said to David, "Your throne will be established forever" (2 Sam. 7:16; see also 1 Chron. 22:10; Ps. 89:4), and that Israel is God's "forever" (2 Sam. 7:24)? We must remember that God also said Judah "will lose the inheritance I gave you. . . . You have kindled my anger, and it will burn forever" (Jer. 17:4; cf. Jer. 23:40; 24:9). An eternal throne or an eternal disinheritance are two mutually exclusive divine promises. Dispensational-ists argue for the one while ignoring the other. Yet both are biblical. So by defending the "irrevocability" of the one, they necessarily attest the revocability of the other since two opposite futures cannot be fulfilled at the same time. The fact that one will be fulfilled, and not the other, is meaningful only if we accept the concept of conditionality. Thus Scripture says: "if you are careful to obey me, declares the Lord," "this city will be inhabited forever" (Jer. 17:24, 25).[94]

It is obvious that if Israel's departure from Palestine came from unbelief, then a return without obeying the Old Testament stipulations of belief[95] does not fulfill any prophetic promise.[96] Modern Israel is clearly "a nation without prophetic significance."[97] God said, "When you and your children return to the Lord your God and obey him with all your heart and with all your soul according to everything I command you today, then the Lord your God will restore your fortunes and have compassion on you and gather you again from all the nations where he scattered you" (Deut. 30:2, 3; cf. 2 Chron. 6:24, 25; and God's response, 2 Chron. 7:11-22).

When faced with this biblical evidence, John Walvoord admits the conditionality involved.[98] This makes the present state of Israel insignificant in the context of Old Testament prophecy. Nevertheless, Walvoord believes that the return is "one of the greatest miracles of world history"[99] and "scriptures make clear that the regathering will continue until consummated after [note the time] the second advent of Christ."[100] He conveniently gives no proof for his assertion (there is none). Here we see the length to which literalism goes to defend the Israel/church dichotomy.

3. Return to Location Not a Substitute for Return to Loyalty

Alexander Wachtel, at the Jerusalem Conference on Biblical Prophecy, said, "If we who believe in Jesus Christ as Son of God and Savior of the world cannot find some divine purpose in the return of the Jews, then we are embarked on a course that will undermine the unique claim of our gospel. . . . We must find the divine purpose in the return of Israel. If we cannot, then Christ is not the only way."[101] Here Wachtel misses the fundamental nature of the covenant as a relationship. No return to location can substitute for a return to loyalty.[102]

4. Is Israel's Original Entrance to the Land a Type for Its Present Situation?

The question could be raised, Is the present return of Israel a parallel with the original entrance into the land? Concerning that first event, God said, "It is not because of your righteousness or your integrity that you are going in to take possession of their land; but on account of the wickedness of these nations, the Lord your God will drive them out before you, to accomplish what he swore to your fathers, to Abraham, Isaac and Jacob" (Deut. 9:5). Did God bring Israel into Palestine because of His covenant promise to Abraham rather than because of Israel's faithfulness? If so, it would be the same as the dispensational argument about Israel's present occupation of the land.

To answer this question, we must first note that Deuteronomy 9:5 and 30:2, 3 both deserve equal attention. They are not mutually exclusive, nor is one more normative than the other. Rather, chapter 9 witnesses to the fact that no one is worthy of God's grace. The entrance into Canaan by Israel is a type of entrance into the heavenly Canaan by the redeemed. Not one of the redeemed will be worthy of it. Grace is the reason for both entrances. By contrast, in chapter 30, the writer says regaining the land is not possible without a return to God. Where is grace? Without denying the operation of grace (chapter 9), here Scripture reminds the reader that grace can be spurned. Whereas no human works earned entrance to Palestine (chapter 9), no return to Palestine will come without a return to God (chapter 30). Both biblical truths must receive their literal meaning.

As Duane L. Christensen put it: "If the gift of the land were contingent on the righteousness of the people, it would never be received. It was a gift, graciously given, not a reward. Nonetheless, . . . continued possession of the gift of the land is contingent on obedience. Disobedience of the covenant will lead to forfeiture of the land."[103] Nowhere in Scripture do we find any promise of Israel's return to the land while in a condition of unbelief.

5. The New Testament Contains No Promise of a Return to Palestine

Nowhere in the New Testament do we find a land promise given to Israel. Not even Romans 9-11 mentions land. In fact, the New Testament does not present Palestine as the goal for Abraham and his descendants. Instead, "he was looking forward to the city with foundations, whose architect and builder is God" (Heb. 11:9, 10). The book of Hebrews speaks of Israel as "longing for a better country—a heavenly one" (verse 16). The New Jerusalem witnesses to the union of Israel and the church with the names of the 12 patriarchs and 12 apostles inscribed on the gates and foundations respectively (Rev. 21:12-14).

Evidently the land of Canaan was but a type of the heavenly Canaan, the old Jerusalem but a type of the New Jerusalem, the land of promise but a type of the earth made new. A reductive literalism, ignoring the New Testament, completely misses the magnitude of the promise, for the normal understanding of biblical typology involves escalation. *The New Scofield Bible,* which finds so many different types in Scripture, never sees Palestine as a type of the new earth, nor does it comment on this vastly expanded interpretation of the land promise in Hebrews 11.[104]

6. Christ's Kingdom as His Reign, or Rule

"The majority of exegetes have recognized that the central meaning of *basileia,* as of the Hebrew word *malkuth,* is the abstract or dynamic idea of reign, rule, or dominion rather than the concrete idea of realm."[105] For "the Kingdom is not a realm or a people but God's reign."[106] George Ladd argues persuasively that the kingdom Christ offered Israel was His rule in their midst. Christ's "authority in deeds and words was nothing less than the presence of the Kingdom of God."[107]

Whereas God had sent many prophets to call them back to Him, now Christ was Himself in their presence, pleading, "Come to me, all you who are weary and burdened, and I will give you rest" (Matt. 11:28). Here was His gracious rule—to set them free in covenant relationship (Luke 4:18; cf. Isa. 61:1). He stands between the two Testaments, the embodiment of that covenant—humanity joined to God. To Him the promise of the Old Testament meets the fulfillment of the New, for in both "is the dynamic concept of the rule of God."[108] He came to give them the essence of that covenant—a relationship of resting in His gracious rule.

But "He was despised and rejected by men" (Isa. 53:3). Israel's leadership did nothing to help Him when the hated Romans went "up to him again and again, saying, 'Hail, king of the Jews' " (John 19:2, 3). Finally Pilate said to them, "Here is your king." In response the mob shouted, "Take him away! Take him away! Crucify him!" (verses 14, 15). The leadership rejected Christ's reign, not the realm.

Calvary as Christ's Last Word About Israel[109]

Christ spoke of this rejection as a fulfillment of prophecy (Ps. 118:22, 23), concluding, contrary to dispensationalists,[110] "Therefore I tell you that the kingdom of God will be taken away from you and given to a people who will produce its fruit" (Matt. 21:42, 43). So the church takes the place (functionally) of Israel, and is called "a holy nation" (1 Peter 2:9). "Israel's day as a nation favored and blessed of God . . . ended."[111] The 12 patriarchs of Israel gave way to the 12 disciples of the church, as Christ continued His saving mission through the "Israel of God" (Gal. 6:16). Not Old Testament literalism but the "It is finished" (John 19:30) from the cross is the last word concerning Israel. The Temple veil, rent from top to bottom by a divine hand,[112] declared that the place was holy no more, the covenant was broken, and God had gone from their midst.[113]

Hanging on the cross, Christ is the last Word over all Old Testament prophecy. Here is the Prophet, Priest, and King to whom they pointed. The Word made "flesh" (John 1:14), God united with man, the at-one-ment, He dies as man's substitute. The embodiment of the covenant, He is the law and the plan of salvation as well as the recapitulated history of Israel. As the Passover lamb saved the firstborn in the Exodus (type), so the greater exodus from earth to the heavenly Canaan is possible through the Lamb of God slain at Calvary (antitype). In Christ Israel and the church meet. The confined language of the Old Testament breaks forth as the Word, the ultimate revelation of God's promise to Abraham and all the families of the world. In the light of the cross and its subsequent "resurrection-ascension-intercession-return" we see the Word unfolded in a progressive revelation that bursts beyond all the restrictions of prophetic language. Speaking authoritatively about His kingdom rule, already in process, the New Testament has Christ moving toward a realm that embraces a new Jerusalem in a new heaven and a new earth.

The present return of Jews to Israel is therefore a purely secular event that has nothing to do with the Abrahamic promise or with salvation history. "For no matter how many promises God has made, they are 'Yes' in Christ" (2 Cor. 1:20). He has not merely brought fulfillment to the Abrahamic promise, He *is* the fulfillment. Through Him all the nations of the world are being blessed (Matt. 28:20; John 1:9).

The Future

Having examined dispensationalism of the past, we must now look at an epochal book released by Zondervan *(Dispensationalism, Israel and the Church: The Search for Definition,* cited afterward as *DIAC),*[114] which gives insight into the changes taking place in dispensationalism, allegedly subscribed to by a majority of dispensationalists today.[115] Because of space limitations I will give only a summary overview, with suggestions for future dialogue with dispensationalists.

Dispensationalism has experienced four dispensations of its own: i.e., Pre-Scofieldian, Scofieldian, Essentialist, and Progressive.[116] The fourth era issues out of an attempt to be "more accurate biblically"[117] and "to re-examine biblically the distinction between Israel and the church."[118] Ten younger dispensational scholars wrote *DIAC* to present a progressive theological hermeneutic beyond that found in the other three eras of dispensationalism. Their advance over previous dispensational contributions moves the dialogue with dispensationalism to a new level, as they have (1) critiqued some of the old positions that nondispensationalists also questioned as well as (2) accepted a new Christological hermeneutic absent in previous dispensational material.

The changes from their predecessors include: (1) Accepting a progressive fulfillment of Old Testament prophecies/promises in the church age, and thus a rejection of traditional futurism.[119] (2) Accepting the church as implicit in the Old Testament, and the moral law and the Sermon on the Mount as applicable in the church age rather than relegated to Israel in the millennium.[120] (3) Accepting that Old Testament prophecy, such as Joel 2 at Pentecost (Acts 2) and in the future, can have multiple fulfillments in the church age.[121] (4) Accepting that progressive fulfillment involves an inaugurated eschatology,[122] and a rejection of the church age as a parenthesis between Israel in the Old Testament and Israel during the millennium. (5) Rejecting a postponed kingdom and rule of Christ and focusing on His present rule from heaven's throne over all on earth.[123] (6) Rejecting the two new covenants for Israel and the church,[124] that is, finding the one new covenant sequentially fulfilled—spiritually in the church age and physically to Israel in the millennium.[125] (7) Rejecting the final difference between the earthly people of God (Israel) and the heavenly people of God (church), opting rather for a dwelling together in the new earth.[126]

Their theological advances are substantial, and clearly separate progressive dispensationalists from the other three varieties. Progressive dispensationalism has taken more seriously the fact of Christ's fulfilling Old Testament prophecies/promises. It has come a long way to respond positively to the biblical type/antitype interpretation with its inherent escalation in the New Testament fulfillment.

The ten dispensationalists who wrote the book have gone beyond futurism to include a fulfillment of promises and prophecies in Christ. They have transcended the simplistic literal/spiritual dualism and have done better justice to the principle of the Bible interpreting itself. Their work, a welcome development over their predecessors, advances beyond previous dispensational hermeneutics. We need to congratulate them.

However, the bottom line shared by the other three stages of dispensational development is still the distinction between Israel and the church, even though the book speaks of a "softening" of the dichotomy.[127] Progressive fulfillment presents the kingdom as (1) preliminary during the present interadvent period, (2) intermediate during the millennium, and (3) eternal after the millennium. Along this progressive unfolding of the kingdom (fulfillment) the parenthesis (of older dispensationalism) simply shifts from the church age to the millennium.

Conclusion

Walter Kaiser, Jr., suggests that in the next few years another book should be written titled *Dispensationalism Tomorrow*.[128] Craig Blaising and Darrell

Bock, editors of *DIAC,* suggest that "future publications need to carry the dialogue forward."[129] Elsewhere I have suggested what steps the next book could take.[130]

Progressive dispensationalists have moved the dialogue to a new height by doing better justice to biblical-inaugurated eschatology (how Christ fulfilled Old Testament promises/prophecies). The next step forward is to do justice to biblical consummated eschatology and thus to Christ's part in the fulfillment of end-time promises and prophecies. Dispensationalism's continuing focus on Israel and Palestine more than on Christ in last-day events has no biblical support.

---

[1] John F. Walvoord, *Armageddon, Oil and the Middle East Crisis* (Grand Rapids: Zondervan, 1990).

[2] E. G. White, *The Great Controversy,* pp. 593, 594.

[3] *The Seventh-day Adventist Bible Commentary,* Ellen G. White Comments (Washington, D.C.: Review and Herald, 1955), vol. 4, p. 1161.

[4] And also to the One who is the truth (see John 17:3).

[5] Thus Oswald T. Allis could say in 1945: "Dispensationalism as such, has made dispensationalism an issue of greater or lesser importance in practically all evangelical denominations at the present time" *(Prophecy and the Church* [The Presbyterian and Reformed, 1945], pp. 12, 13). By 1958 it was reported that "dispensationalists have infiltrated almost every branch of Protestantism" (Arnold B. Rhodes, ed.; F. H. Caldwell and L. C. Rudolph, assoc. eds., *The Church Faces the Isms: The Members of the Faculty of the Louisville Presbyterian Theological Seminary, Louisville, Kentucky* ([Nashville: Abingdon, 1958], p. 109).

[6] M. J. Erickson, *Christian Theology,* p. 1162.

[7] For example, see R. A. Anderson and J. M. Hoffmann, *All Eyes on Israel* (Fort Worth, Tex.: Harvest, 1977). See Ellen G. White, *Testimonies for the Church* (Mountain View, Calif.: Pacific Press, 1948), vol. 4, pp. 115, 116, relative to Jerusalem and conditionality.

[8] George M. Marsden compares dispensationalism to Marxism and catastrophism, which both divide history into periods brought to an end in judgment as does dispensationalism. George M. Marsden, *Fundamentalism and American Culture, the Shaping of Twentieth-Century Evangelicalism: 1870-1925* (Oxford, Eng.: Oxford University, 1980), pp. 64, 65.

[9] C. Norman Kraus, *Dispensationalism in America: Its Rise and Development* (Richmond, Va.: John Knox, 1958), p. 27.

[10] John Wick Bowman, "The Bible and Modern Religions," *Interpretation: A Journal of Bible and Theology,* 10, No. 2 (April 1956): p. 170.

[11] Daniel Payton Fuller, "The Hermeneutics of Dispensationalism" (unpublished doctoral dissertation, Northern Baptist Theological Seminary, Chicago, May 1957), pp. 183, 184.

[12] *Ibid.,* p. 68.

[13] C. I. Scofield, *The New Scofield Study Bible* (afterward *NSB)* (New York: Oxford University, 1967), p. 3, footnote on heading for Genesis 1:28.

[14] Rhodes, p. 104.

[15] His seven dispensations are as follows: (1) (Paradisiacal state) to the Flood, (2) Noah, (3) Abraham, (4) Israel, (5) Gentiles, (6) the Spirit, and (7) the Millennium. See Kraus, p. 29.

[16] His seven dispensations are (1) Innocence, (2) Conscience or Moral Responsibility, (3) Human Government, (4) Promise, (5) Law, (6) Church, and (7) Kingdom *(NSB),* pp. 3, 4.

[17] Charles C. Ryrie, *Dispensationalism Today* (Chicago: Moody, 1973), p. 50.

[18] Kraus, p. 26.

[19] See Charles F. Baker, *A Dispensational Theology* (Grand Rapids: Grace Bible College, 1972), p. 3.

[20] These three dispensations are the Mosaic law, the present dispensation of Grace, and the future millennial kingdom. See Ryrie, p. 50.

[21] Ryrie, p. 48.

Dispensational Final Events

[22] Daniel P. Fuller, *Gospel and Law: Contrast or Continuum? The Hermeneutics of Dispensationalism* (Grand Rapids: Eerdmans, 1980), p. 12.

[23] Lewis Chafer calls these three "law," "grace," and "kingdom." *Systematic Theology* (Dallas: Seminary Press, 1948), Vol. IV, p. 183.

[24] Louis A. DeCaro rightly notes that "without this basic dichotomy in its hermeneutics, dispensationalism could not endure as a distinct system of biblical interpretation. The whole system turns on this alleged division existing between Israel and the Church." *Israel Today: Fulfillment of Prophecy?* (Presbyterian and Reformed, 1976), p. 26.

[25] Here are some of these divisions: 1. The church founded by Paul is different from the church founded by Peter; the first is a genuine church, the second a counterfeit (Allis, pp. 102, 103). 2. The Scofield Bible gives seven different judgments *(NSB,* p. 1384). 3. Although "all Scripture" is profitable (2 Tim. 3:16), "all Scripture is not addressed to the Jew, nor is it all addressed to the Christian" (Lewis S. Chafer, "Dispensationalism," *Bibliotheca Sacra* 93 [October 1936], p. 417). Thus, the Sermon on the Mount is not for the church (Ryrie, p. 108), nor is the Lord's Prayer (Chafer, *Systematic Theology,* Vol. IV, pp. 221, 222). Others make additional divisions in the New Testament. 4. Contrast between the kingdom of heaven and the kingdom of God (John F. Walvoord, *The Church in Prophecy* [Grand Rapids: Zondervan, 1976], p. 25). 5. There is a spiritual as well as a natural seed of Abraham (John F. Walvoord, *The Millennial Kingdom* [Grand Rapids: Dunham, 1966], p. 144). 6. Both Israel and the church have new covenants *(ibid.,* p. 210). It is understandable that dispensationalists divide the Second Coming into two, a secret rapture for the church and the Second Coming to earth to reign over Israel.

[26] The four options for beginning the church age are Acts 2 (Scofield, Ryrie), Acts 13 (moderate ultradispensationalists), Acts 28 (extreme ultradispensationalists), and with Paul, before writing his first Epistle (Baker). See Baker, pp. 4-6.

[27] The three views are pretribulation, midtribulation, and posttribulation, with the majority of dispensationalists supportive of the first view.

[28] C. I. Scofield, *Rightly Dividing the Word of Truth* (Neptune, N.J.: Loizeaux, 1896).

[29] *Ibid.,* p. 5.

[30] Ralph Earle, *The Expositor's Bible Commentary,* Frank E. Gaebelein, gen. ed. (Grand Rapids: Zondervan, 1978), vol. 11, p. 402.

[31] Donald Guthrie, *Tyndale New Testament Commentaries, the Pastoral Epistles* (Leicester, England: InterVarsity, 1988), p. 148.

[32] "The truths of the Bible must be rightly interpreted so that no part of the Scriptures will be set in opposition to the picture presented by the Bible as a whole." *The Seventh-day Adventist Bible Commentary* (Washington, D.C.: Review and Herald, 1957), vol. 7, p. 336.

[33] Ryrie, p. 89; Chafer, "Dispensationalism," p. 400; John F. Walvoord, *The Blessed Hope and the Tribulation* (Grand Rapids: Zondervan, 1977), p. 28.

[34] The only exception they grant is the obvious use of symbols. See Walvoord, *The Millennial Kingdom,* p. 130.

[35] They claim that "a method of interpretation which is free to spiritualize or overlook important revelations in doctrine has led the way for others to deny the authority of Scripture" (Lewis Chafer, *Systematic Theology,* Vol. IV, p. 267).

[36] Chafer says, "The liberal theologian spiritualizes both the virgin birth and the Davidic throne" ("Dispensationalism," p. 400). He is right in the first, but overlooks the fact that the New Testament does the second (see Acts 2:33-36; 13:22-37; 15:13-19; Rev. 3:7).

[37] "The prophecies concerning the King and His earthly kingdom remain unfulfilled to this hour. They are not forgotten or abandoned. Neither are they receiving a *spiritual* fulfillment. They are yet to be fulfilled when the King returns to the earth" (Chafer, *Systematic Theology,* Vol. IV, p. 176). He overlooks the present fulfillment in the reign of Christ at the throne of God, which is an important spiritual interpretation of the New Testament (Acts 2:25, 33, 34; 5:31; 7:55, 56; Rom. 8:34; Eph. 1:20; Col. 3:1; Heb. 1:3, 13; 8:1; 10:12; 12:2; and 1 Peter 3:22).

[38] A literal interpretation of 1 Thessalonians 4:1-18 places the ascension of the church at the time of Christ's descent, to meet Him in the air. Clearly it is a Second Advent passage, not some prior rapture built partially upon a seventieth week taken out of its literal context (see Dan. 9:24-27). Against this biblical view of the two simultaneous events, Walvoord dubs the interpretation of the rapture and Second Advent together as "spiritualization"

(The Church in Prophecy, p. 116).

[39] John F. Walvoord, *The Rapture Question* (Grand Rapids: Zondervan, 1976), p. 8.

[40] "All of the apostles give spiritual interpretation of the Old Testament prophecies, and literalists do not find fault with them for that. It is universally agreed that the chief cornerstone laid in Zion is to be interpreted as Jesus Christ. Peter likens Christians to living stones built up into a spiritual temple. The apostle Paul, speaking of the experiences of Israel in the wilderness, says, 'And did all eat the same spiritual meat; and did all drink the same spiritual drink; for they drank of that spiritual Rock that followed them: and that Rock was Christ' (1 Cor. 10:3, 4)" (George L. Murray, *Millennial Studies, a Search for Truth* [Grand Rapids: Baker, 1948]), p. 40.

[41] Walvoord, *The Millennial Kingdom,* p. 130.

[42] George E. Ladd, *Crucial Questions About the Kingdom of God* (Grand Rapids: Eerdmans, 1968), p. 139; see pp. 135-141.

[43] Ryrie, p. 10.

[44] J. Dwight Pentecost, *Things to Come, a Study in Biblical Eschatology* (Grand Rapids: Zondervan, 1978), p. 9.

[45] George N. H. Peters, *The Theocratic Kingdom of Our Lord Jesus, the Christ, as Covenanted in the Old Testament and Presented in the New Testament* (Grand Rapids: Kregel, 1952), vol. 1, p. 192.

[46] Walvoord, *The Blessed Hope and the Tribulation,* p. 7. A Spirit-led study of Scripture brings the student to the unifying truth that unites all prophecy in a harmonious whole.

[47] Chafer, *Systematic Theology,* Vol. I, p. vi.

[48] Raymond E. Brown, *The Sensus Plenior of Sacred Scripture* (published doctoral dissertation, St. Mary's University, Baltimore, Maryland, 1955), p. 125.

[49] Simon Kistemaker, *The Psalm Citations in the Epistle to the Hebrews* (University of Amsterdam, 1961), p. 13.

[50] Kraus, p. 132.

[51] Note Pentecost claims: "In the field of fulfilled prophecy it is not possible to point to any prophecy that has been fulfilled in any way other than literally" *(Things to Come, a Study in Biblical Eschatology,* p. 61).

[52] Ryrie, p. 88.

[53] Certain details can differ in fulfillments. For example, the weeping in Jeremiah 31:15 was in Ramah (north of Jerusalem), whereas in Matthew 2:17, 18 the weeping occurs in Bethlehem (south of Jerusalem).

[54] Chafer, *Systematic Theology,* Vol. IV, p. 204.

[55] *Ibid.,* Vol. I, p. xxx.

[56] Walvoord says, "It is a major error to make the word *kingdom,* which is a common term, always mean the same in all its uses. Rather, it must be interpreted by its context" *(The Church in Prophecy,* p. 26). He should have applied this to the word Israel as well. Also Walvoord says, "The study of prophecy in any area necessarily has to be subject to the context of the entire revelation of the Word of God" ("Christ's Olivet Discourse on the End of the Age," *Bibliotheca Sacra* 128 [April 1971]: 113). Again this would remove the Israel/church dichotomy. Walvoord again: "It is therefore not too much to say that the rapture question is determined more by ecclesiology than eschatology" *(The Rapture Question,* p. 16). Here he admits the Israel/church presupposition behind the rapture does not have its roots in eschatology. Elsewhere Walvoord says that "prophecy should be interpreted literally unless there is good evidence to the contrary" ("The Resurrection of Israel," *Bibliotheca Sacra* 124 [January 1967]: 5). This opens up the possibility of transcending literalism. In another place Walvoord says, "the partial-rapture theory is also objectionable because it divides the body of Christ and ignores plain teaching of Scripture . . ." *(The Millennial Kingdom,* p. 251). Apply this to the Israel/church dichotomy, for the same reason, and dispensationalism ceases to exist. Pentecost comments that "the central theme of all prophecy is the Lord Jesus Christ" *(Things to Come,* p. 63). This insight would also radically change dispensationalism.

[57] In my research in the *NSB,* I discovered the following 30 types of Christ, and there may well be more: (1) skins of Genesis 3:21 (8), (2) Lamb (8), (3) Adam (10), (4) ark (11), (5) Melchizedek (22), (6) Isaac (32), (7) ram (32), (8) Joseph (53), (8) Benjamin (62), (9) Moses (72), (10) Passover (84), manna (91), (11) Rock of Exodus 17:6 (92), (12) shewbread (103), (13) lampstand (103), (14) acacia wood (104), (15) inner veil of Exodus 26:31 (105), (16) Aaron and sons (106), (17) altar of incense (111), (18) laver (112), (19) burnt offering (127), (20) bullock/ox (127), (21) sweet savor offering (128), (22) meal offering (128), (23) peace offering (129), (24) sin offering (130), (25) slain live bird of Leviticus 14:4 (144), (26) earthen vessel of Leviticus 14:5 (144), (27) living goat of Leviticus 16:5 (147), (28) Feast of First Fruits of Leviticus 23:10 (157), (29) Boaz (161), and (30) Nazarite (175).

[58] *NSB,* p. 705.

[59] They consider the church a "parenthesis," "an unforseen age," not even within the purview of the Old Testament. Walvoord, *Millennial Kingdom,* pp. 231, 247; Chafer, "Dispensationalism," p. 404.

[60] Erickson, p. 1163.

[61] *NSB,* Gen. 2:23, p. 6.

[62] *NSB,* Gen. 21:3, p. 30.

[63] *NSB,* Gen. 24:1, p. 34.

[64] NSB, Ex. 25:9, p. 101.

[65] *NSB,* Ex. 28:1, p. 106.

[66] *NSB,* Lev. 23:17, p. 157.

[67] *NSB,* S. of Sol. 2:14, p. 706.

[68] George N. H. Peters, *The Theocratic Kingdom* (Grand Rapids: Kregel, 1952), vol. 1, p. 212.

[69] A few examples include Sarah as a type of grace (30), unnamed servant (Gen. 24:1) as a type of the Holy Spirit (34), Asenath (Gen. 41:45) as a type of the church (59), rods becoming serpents as symbols of Satan (78, 79), and manna as a type of Christ's humiliation, giving His flesh that believers may have life (91).

[70] Allis, *Prophecy and the Church,* p. 21.

[71] We have already noted how one of the three methods of interpreting the Song of Solomon is allegorical and that Ryrie opposed the allegorical method.

[72] See Leonhard Goppelt, *Theological Dictionary of the New Testament,* Gerhard Kittel and Gerhard Friedrich, eds., Geoffrey W. Bromiley, trans. and ed. (Grand Rapids: Eerdmans), vol. 8, pp. 246-259; Richard M. Davidson, *Typology in Scripture, a study of hermeneutical tupos structures* (Berrien Springs, Mich.: Andrews University Press, 1981), pp. 15-111; John E. Alsup, "Typology," *The Anchor Bible Dictionary,* David Noel Freedman, ed. (New York: Doubleday, 1992), vol. 6, pp. 682-685; Hans K. LaRondelle, *The Israel of God in Prophecy: Principles of Prophetic Interpretation* (Berrien Springs, Mich.: Andrews University Press, 1983), pp. 35-59; and Anthony C. Thiselton, New Horizons in Hermeneutics, pp. 163, 164.

[73] W. D. Davies, *The Gospel of the Land, Early Christianity and Jewish Territorial Doctrine* (London: University of California, 1974), pp. 178, 179.

[74] Thiselton, p. 27.

[75] "Dispensational writers commonly take Daniel 9:27 as separated from, and subsequent to, verse 26 rather than as an explanation of it; and the subject who confirms the testament (or covenant) is held to be the prince of verse 26, meaning the antichrist. Serious problems, however, beset such a reconstruction" (J. Barton Payne, *Encyclopedia of Biblical Prophecy, the Complete Guide to Scriptural Predictions and Their Fulfillment* [New York: Harper and Row, 1973], p. 388). The problems include: (1) Scripture hints at no interval between the 69 and 1; (2) "it assumes an unprecedented covenant-making by the antichrist" with no hint of such a thing in Scripture; and (3) "it transforms a past prince of Rome into a future deputy of the devil" (p. 389).

[76] Allis, p. 118.

[77] Philadelphia: Presbyterian and Reformed, 1945.

[78] Grand Rapids: Eerdmans.

[79] *Ibid.*

[80] Nashville: Abingdon-Cokesbury.

[81] Grand Rapids: Eerdmans.

[82] London: S.P.C.K.

[83] Grand Rapids: Eerdmans.

[84] Berrien Springs, Mich.: Andrews University Press.

[85] Grand Rapids: Baker.

[86] Bruce K. Waltke, in *Dispensationalism, Israel and the Church: The Search for Definition,* Craig A. Blaising and Darrell L. Bock, eds. (Grand Rapids: Zondervan, 1992), p. 353.

[87] *Ibid.*

[88] I have studied through LaRondelle's book more than once and gained many insights behind some ideas presented in this chapter. The book helped launch me some time ago into an in-depth study into biblical and dispensational and nondispensational sources relative to the topic.

[89] For further reading on this question, see Gerhard F. Hasel, "Israel in Bible Prophecy," *JATS3,* No. 1, pp. 120-155.

[90] They have considered modern Israel "the great sign" (Alexander Wachtel, "Why Did the Jews Have to Return to Israel," in *Prophecy in the Making,* Carl F. H. Henry, ed. [Carol Stream, Ill.: Creation House, 1971], p. 158); "God's principal sign" (Walvoord, *Millennial Kingdom,* p. 341), or the "paramount prophetic sign" and "most important prophetic sign" of Christ's imminent return (Hal Lindsey, with C. C. Carlson, *The Great Late Planet Earth* [Grand Rapids: Zondervan, 1974], pp. 43, 57 respectively).

[91] Robert L. Evans, *The Jew in the Plan of God* (New York: Loizeaux, 1950), p. 176.

[92] *NSB,* Deut. 30:3, p. 251.

[93] For example, the following: "restored [to land] and converted" (p. 716, see also pp. 747, 974); "a partial restoration of Israel to the land in unbelief has already taken place in accordance with prophecy" (p. 446). The notes give no biblical evidence, because there is none. See Deuteronomy 28.

[94] Cf. Ellen G. White, *The Desire of Ages* (Mountain View, Calif.: Pacific Press, 1898), p. 577; *The Great Controversy,* p. 19.

[95] I agree with DeCaro that "any return to the land would be predicated upon the same conditions necessary to retain possession of the land—faith, obedience, and covenant renewal" *(Israel Today: Fulfillment of Prophecy?* p. 21).

[96] "The return in unbelief notion was not in the theology of the prophets, neither is it consistent with the whole of the biblical context" (DeCaro, p. 32). Alexander Wachtel misses this fact when he claims that the return in Deuteronomy "is precipitated by repentance. . . . In Isaiah, Jeremiah and Ezekiel the return is precipitated by the pardoning act of God" *(Prophecy in the Making,* p. 152).

[97] DeCaro, p. 35.

[98] Walvoord, *The Millennial Kingdom,* p. 177.

[99] Walvoord considers the return of Israel to Palestine as "one of the greatest miracles of world history" *(Armageddon, Oil and the Middle East Crisis,* p. 66). He further believes that "the history of Israel since 1948 is a remarkable record of divine providence as God has miraculously preserved Israel, in spite of her unbelief in Christ" (p. 32). Such a preservation in unbelief is contrary to the biblical history of the relationship between God and Israel in the Old Testament. Walvoord is inconsistent in holding to the conditions (repentance, Deut. 30:2, 3; see footnote 106) for returning to the land with the unconditional land promise (p. 69). Such positions are mutually exclusive.

[100] Walvoord, *The Millennial Kingdom,* p. 182.

[101] Wachtel, "Why Did the Jews Have to Return to Israel?" pp. 157, 158.

[102] John Walvoord turns the biblical data upside down, and calls this a literal interpretation. For example, instead of the condition for the return of the land to be a return to God, he says, "The fulfillment of the new covenant is conditioned on the regathering of Israel from their worldwide dispersion" *([Bibliotheca Sacra,* p. 103]: 1946, p. 21).

[103] Duane L. *Christensen, Word Biblical Commentary,* vol. 6A (Dallas: Word, 1991), p. 184.

[104] See *NSB,* p. 1322. Commenting on Revelation 21:2, it says: "The new Jerusalem is the dwelling place throughout eternity for the saints of all ages and fulfills the hope of Abraham for the heavenly city (Heb. 11:10-16; cf. Heb. 12:22-24)" *(NSB,* p. 1375). The implications of this fact are never spelled out or taken seriously.

[105] George E. Ladd, *Jesus and the Kingdom, the Eschatology of Biblical Realism* (S.P.C.K., 1966), p. 126.

[106] *Ibid.,* p. 21.

[107] *Ibid.,* p. 162.

[108] John Bright, *The Kingdom of God: the Biblical Concept and Its Meaning for the Church* (New York: Abingdon-Cokesbury, 1953), p. 197.

[109] Calvary is Christ's last word about Israel in His human history, although the Holy Spirit spoke for Him later in the New Testament (see John 16:12-14).

[110] Lewis Chafer says that "the rejection of the divine offer at Kadesh corresponds to the rejection of the King." He concludes that just as Israel entered the land 40 years later, so "Israel will yet be regathered into her own land . . ." ("Dispensationalism," p. 403).

[111] "When Christ should hang upon the cross of Calvary, Israel's day as a nation favored and blessed of God would be ended" (E. G. White, *The Great Controversy,* p. 21).

[112] For those believing the church is a continuation of Israel, Chafer asks a series of questions, including "Why the rent veil?" (Chafer, *Systematic Theology,* Vol. I, p. xix). It reveals that Chafer did not understand the significance of the event.

[113] E. G. White, *The Desire of Ages,* pp. 756, 757.

[114] Craig A. Blaising and Darrell L. Bock, eds., *Dispensationalism, Israel and the Church: The Search for Definition* (Grand Rapids: Zondervan Publishing House, 1992).

[115] According to a report given to this writer by Darrell Bock, one of the editors of *DIAC,* after presenting my paper at the Evangelical Theological Society/Adventist Theological Society meeting, November 20, 1992, Airport Hilton, San Francisco. However, I asked Bock if they ever planned to put out a revised edition of the popular *New Scofield Study Bible* incorporating the advance positions taken in their book. He did not believe they would. If dispensationalists continue to look to the NSB as their Bible, one wonders what impact progressive dispensationalists will have on them in the long run. It is significant that John F. Walvoord updated his *Armageddon, Oil and the Middle East Crisis* (1974, 1976) in 1990 at the time of the Gulf War without changing any of the traditional dispensational views. The cover claims that over one million copies are in print. One wonders how many of these readers have been affected by progressive dispensationalism? This is why I have presented traditional dispensational thinking in this article, as it may still remain a formidable challenge despite the good work of progressive dispensationalists.

[116] *DIAC,* p. 379; cf. p. 15.

[117] *Ibid.,* p. 15

[118] *Ibid.,* p. 33.

[119] *Ibid.,* pp. 46-51, 224.

[120] *Ibid.,* pp. 253, 254.

[121] *Ibid.,* p. 58.

[122] *Ibid.,* pp. 39-43.

[123] *Ibid.,* pp. 46-55.

[124] *Ibid.,* p. 91.

[125] *Ibid.,* pp. 93-97.

[126] *Ibid.,* p. 303.

[127] *Ibid.,* p. 224.

[128] *Ibid.,* p. 373.

[129] *Ibid.,* p. 385.

[130] Norman R. Gulley, "Progressive Dispensationalism: A Review of a Recent Publication," *Andrews University Seminary Studies* 32 (Spring 1994).

Chapter 7

Other Views on Final Events

The nineteenth century saw the birth of the Seventh-day Adventist Church, the beginning of Darwinian evolution, the entrenchment of the historico-critical methodology in biblical study, and a widespread rejection of eschatology. When the time came for God to launch His end-time church, the enemy had his end-time tools to attempt to thwart the mission of that church.

It's incumbent upon Seventh-day Adventists to remember that belief in human beings' innate ability to evolve (evolution), the use of human judgment over God's Word (historico-criticism), and the jettisoning of Christ's advent in many religious circles find a common source in Satan's final attack against God's church (cf. Rev. 12:17). Each one places human thought above a "thus saith the Lord." In each case human beings look to their own supposed powers to develop, interpret, or bring utopia, rather than looking to Christ as Creator, interpreter, and coming Lord.

Each concept involves the relationship that human beings sustain to Christ. Is Christ Lord over humanity or humanity lord over Christ? The former portrays the nature of the end-time church. The latter reveals the nature of Satan's end-time attack against the church.

Evidently Satan knew the 2300-year prophecy (see Dan. 8:14) well and schemed to thwart God's end-time movement, scheduled to begin in 1844, by raising up counterfeits such as Joseph Smith and Mormonism, Mary Baker Eddy and Christian Science, Margaret MacDonald and dispensationalism, the Fox sisters and modern spiritualism, and Helena Blavatsky and the Theosophical Society—to name a few examples. All of them, in different ways, claimed either the prophetic gift or served as channels for messages from Satan. And all were a counterfeit revelation for a genuine end-time prophetic gift (see Rev. 12:17; 19:20), fulfilled by Ellen G. White.

Nineteenth-Century Ideas About the End

1. Schleiermacher as Judge Over God's Word

Other Views on Final Events

Within this context, we need to briefly consider the two leading theologians of the nineteenth century,[1] Friederich Schleiermacher[2] and Albrecht Ritschl,[3] who both gave up a belief in eschatology. Schleiermacher longed to communicate with his cultured university students who despised Christianity. How could he reach them? His motive was good—but not his method. He decided that to reach these people and convince them to accept Christianity, he would meet them where they were and begin the study of God through a study of humanity. In fact, he believed that by looking within human experience he could prove to them that God did exist. Although he attempted to avoid the critiques of Hume and Kant,[4] in the process he became unwittingly as critical himself.

For example, his basic thesis posited that God exists because humans have a feeling of absolute dependence upon Him.[5] We may question his thesis,[6] but let us proceed. What was Schleiermacher really saying? That human feeling, and not God's Word, is authoritative. In fact, we must judge the Word of God by human feelings, and not the other way round (as it should be).[7] As a result, many jettisoned truths if their feelings could not accept them. So Schleiermacher rejected the Trinity because he could not feel three Gods. How could anyone feel three?[8] Nor could Schleiermacher sense the Second Advent, so he dismissed it.[9] But how can one experience something that has not yet arrived?

Does this sound strange? Lest we forget, we are talking about the leading theologian of the nineteenth century. Karl Barth even considered that Schleiermacher, in his *Christian Faith* (1884), went beyond Augustine, Aquinas, Melanchthon, Zwingli, and Calvin.[10] Scholars categorize theology as before and after Schleiermacher as in philosophy they speak of before and after Kant[11] and science classifies before and after Darwin.

As Richmond observed, theologically he "initiated" and "dominated" the nineteenth century.[12] He is a classic example of a human being sitting as judge over God's Word—and with disastrous results. Subjective feelings reigned supreme over God's objective revelation. No wonder God warned against the danger of judging things by feelings in messages He gave through Ellen White.[13] She said a person "is to base his faith not on feeling but upon the evidence and the Word of God."[14]

2. Ritschl as Judge Over God's Word

Albrecht Ritschl was the second leading theologian of the nineteenth century. Many considered his *The Christian Doctrine of Justification and Reconciliation* (1888) the greatest dogmatic treatise since Schleiermacher's *Christian Faith.*[15] He also looked within, but broadened his gaze to focus on the kingdom as a result of human moral effort.[16] Speaking of the future kingdom, Ritschl said, "Hitherto we have been accustomed to regard the early Christian expectation of the nearness of the world's end as belonging to the shell and not to the kernel. And there the matter will rest, for that anticipation has not acted prejudicially on any of the positive social duties which follow from Christianity."[17]

Such disposable, time-related words or ideas as those within the category of the "shell" were the very materials Bultmann later demythologized. Truth, to Ritschl and Bultmann, was like an onion core. The outer skins were the mere form that we needed to peal off in order to get to the real thing. But all that was left in this case, as Mackintosh notes, is "a purely present and mundane commonwealth" and not a coming kingdom.[18]

Neither the immanental kingdom of Schleiermacher nor the moral kingdom of Ritschl represent the biblical view of Christ's coming kingdom. Both men were too preoccupied with the human rather than with Christ, so they focused on the kingdom *in man* (Schleiermacher) or *by man* (Ritschl) instead of the kingdom *to man* as in the Bible. Both threw out belief in a coming kingdom because they had placed their judgment above the Word of God.

Twentieth-Century Ideas About the End

Albert Schweitzer (1906) and Karl Barth (1918) wrote books that caused theologians to rediscover eschatology.[19] Yet neither of those two books, *Quest of the Historical Jesus* and *Romans,* really accepted the biblical view of the world's end. Both still clung to human judgment over the Word of God.

1. Albert Schweitzer

Schweitzer believed that Christ promised that the Son of Man would return before the disciples had finished going to all the cities of Israel on their first missionary journey (Matt. 10:23), and that His disciples would see Him coming in His kingdom (Matt. 16:28)—both which have reasonable biblical explanations.[20] But Schweitzer, in his several editions of *The Quest of the Historical Jesus,* never gave up his belief that Jesus made a promise that He did not keep.[21] In fact, Schweitzer sees Christ going to the cross with a last desperate attempt to fulfill His promises.

"There is silence all around. The Baptist appears, and cries: 'Repent, for the kingdom of heaven is at hand.' Soon after that comes Jesus, and in the knowledge that He is the coming Son of Man lays hold of the wheel of the world to set it moving on that last revolution which is to bring all ordinary history to a close. It refuses to turn, and He throws Himself upon it. Then it does turn; and crushes Him. Instead of bringing in the eschatological conditions, He has destroyed them. The wheel rolls onward, and the mangled body of the one immeasurably great Man, who was strong enough to think of Himself as the spiritual ruler of mankind and to bend history to His purpose, is hanging up it still. That is His victory and His reign."[22]

Schweitzer's judgment of the written Word led him to give up belief in the living Word. Merely considering Jesus a deluded man, he gave up Christianity and accepted a reverence for life philosophy instead. This "missionary" to Africa had no message to give. So the man who caused scholars to rediscover eschatology actually gave it up himself.

2. Karl Barth

Barth's *Romans* fell as a bombshell

on the theological world and shook up the nineteenth-century rejection of eschatology. Yet it did not have a grasp of the biblical picture. Barth could not accept that Jesus, the living Word, entered human history in His incarnation, so he also rejected the view that the Second Advent would be an event in history.[23]

He came to the Bible with presuppositions from Plato, Overbeck, and Kierkegaard,[24] so the eternal God was distanced by an infinite gulf from humanity in time. Once more, the human was very much in charge—judging God's Word. So both men, although they caused other scholars to rediscover eschatology, actually did not have an eschatology themselves. They both, in different ways, allowed human wisdom to sit in judgment of God's Word, resulting in a too-human Jesus for Schweitzer and a too-divine Christ for Barth.

3. Three One-sided Eschatologies

The twentieth century spawned a number of eschatological schools.[25] We will briefly consider three, all of which grew out of a human-oriented judging of the Word of God. C. H. Dodd's "realized eschatology" (1936) reduced salvation-history to the life-death of Jesus Christ, so the goal of history had already been realized in Christ, and that was all there would ever be. Dodd's concept has no present or future advent.[26]

Rudolf Bultmann's "existential," or "timeless," eschatology viewed the Advent as taking place in the everlasting present as the Holy Spirit comes in repeated encounters to the Christian.[27] This yo-yo like repetition is all the Second Advent there will ever be. Whereas Dodd's approach was a one-sided focus on the past, Bultmann's had a one-sided focus on the present. Both had no place for a second coming of Christ.

Jürgen Moltmann's "proleptic eschatology," in his *Theology of Hope,* appears, on the surface, to be a real belief in the Second Advent. At least it is forward-looking. But it is equally one-sided in that its future focus lacks proper reference to the present and past.[28] Apparently Moltmann believes he champions the sovereignty of God. To do this he seems to assume that God is free to do anything He desires in future events and is apparently not bound even by the Bible.

Here we have a subtle twist. For was not God sovereign and free when He predicted what He would do in future events in the Bible? How valuable is any defense of God's future sovereignty if it destroys His past sovereignty? Moltmann's judgment puts itself above the revelation God has made of end events. He even goes to the length of telling us we must be open to the "startlingly new,"[29] which seems to lay him wide open, without protection, to the final delusion when Satan pretends to be Christ—meeting people on the earth instead of in the air as the Bible warns.[30]

So we can see that Satan's strategy has sought to place human judgment above the Word of God, to make human beings unready for the advent of Christ, while receptive for a false advent. In view of this fact, Seventh-day Adventists should reassess the method of biblical interpretation called historical-criticism, which places human judgment above God's Word.

Danger of Historical Criticism of Scripture

Others have reassessed this method, even though they once taught it. For example, Michael Green, rector of St. Aldergate's in Oxford, once used the historical-critical method in his teaching. He discovered that it caused those in training for the ministry to lose their faith.[31] He writes that, unlike modern critics of the New Testament, ancient historians "almost to a man have a high regard for the New Testament material."

"I see a bondage to the historical-critical method, which very properly seeks to get back to the original text, the original setting and the original meaning. All too often when this is done, the possibility of inspiration is totally discounted. The biblical writers are treated as if they made no claim to inspiration, and displayed no mark of it."[32]

Walker Wink of Union Theological Seminary, New York, said, "Historical biblical criticism is bankrupt."[33] Gerhard Maier wrote a book entitled *The End of the Historical-Critical Method,*[34] noting that "the subtle net woven by the higher-critical method resulted in a new Babylonian captivity of the church."[35] Commenting on Maier, Carl F. H. Henry concludes: "Maier declares rightly that recent applications of the historical-critical method have brought biblical studies to an intolerable impasse through the vast array of conflicting verdicts for which its sanction is claimed. The proper response to divine revelation, he contends, is obedience rather than criticism, which elevates human reason into a judge over revelation."[36]

Karl Barth compared the historical-critical method with the teaching office of the Catholic Church, because both replace the divine authority of Scripture with human authority. "All exegesis may become predominantly an imposition instead of an exposition," he said, "and to that extent deteriorate into a dialogue of the Church with itself. And we shall not banish this danger, but only really begin to conjure it up and render it acute, by making right exposition depend on the verdict of an ultimately decisive Church teaching office, or on the verdict of an historical and critical science, comporting itself with an equal infallibility."[37]

C. S. Lewis, of Cambridge University, called into radical question the criticism of the critics. He said, "Whatever these men may be as Biblical critics, I distrust them as critics. They seem to me to lack literary judgment, to be imperceptive about the very quality of the texts they are reading. . . . If he tells me that something in a Gospel is legend or romance, I want to know how many legends and romances he has read, how well his palate is trained in detecting them by the flavor; not how many years he has spent on that Gospel."[38] Lewis had studied different types of literature and could tell that the biblical critics had not.

Elsewhere in *Fern-seed and Elephants* he comments, "I have been reading poems, romances, vision-literature, legends, myths all my life. I know what they are like. I know that not one of them is like this."[39] "These men," he continues, "ask me to believe they can read between the lines of the old texts; the evidence is their obvious inability to read (in any sense worth discussing) the lines themselves. They claim to see fern-seed and can't see an elephant ten yards away in broad daylight."[40]

Lewis observes how the critics try to reconstruct Scripture the way they think it should be and retorts, "What forearms me against all these reconstructions is the fact that I have seen it all from the other end of the stick. I have watched reviewers reconstructing the genesis of my own books in just this way." And they were wrong.[41] He said that the same types of criticism have gone the rounds in nonbiblical literature. Scholars used to cut up Shakespeare's three-part play *King Henry VI* into a half dozen authors, but no more. Homer was once a legend, but no longer. People can believe in a historical Arthur now too. Lewis concludes, "Everywhere, except in theology, there has been a vigorous growth of skepticism about skepticism itself."[42]

In *The Challenge of Postmodernism: An Evangelical Engagement,* I have written a chapter entitled "Reader-Response Theories in Postmodern Hermeneutics: A Challenge to Evangelical Theology."[43] It unfolds the changing paradigms that have appeared in recent years. Each new paradigm questions the one preceding it, so the historical paradigm gave way to the literary paradigm, and that to the cultural paradigm. Who knows what will come next? All of them are human attempts to maintain control over scriptural interpretation. But the Bible is its own best interpreter.

Biblical Eschatology Is Three-dimensional

The only safe ground is to take the Bible as it reads and allow it to be the only basis of belief.[44] Seventh-day Adventist eschatology rests upon the solid revelation of the Word of God, and is only secondarily corroborated by the writings of Ellen G. White.

Whereas some eschatologies of the twentieth century have been one-sided, focusing primarily on the past (Dodd's "realized eschatology"), the present (Bultmann's "existential eschatology"), or the future (Moltmann's "proleptic eschatology"), the biblical view is three-dimensional, for "Jesus Christ is the same yesterday and today and forever" (Heb. 13:8). He has fulfilled His promise to return in the past and the present and it waits fulfillment only in the future.

Look at it this way. He said He would rise again from the dead (see Matt. 27:63; Mark 8:31; Luke 18:33). Resurrection morning He did it (see Luke 24:1-8). Christ promised to send the Comforter (see John 16:7-16), and through Him, to be present with His people (see John 14:15-18) even to the end of the world (see Matt. 28:20; Heb. 13:5). At Pentecost, and its extension through history He has been fulfilling His promise (see Acts 2:1-4). We therefore have two historical fulfillments back of the final coming again in the Second Advent.

Add to this the fact that the promises of the Messiah's coming in the Old Testament (e.g., Isa. 7:14) met their fulfillment in the Incarnation (see Matt. 1:18-25), and we see that the New Testament already has three fulfillments concerning Christ's first advent. They give credibility to His final return. He has already proven Himself reliable in three events that all brought Him to the human race.

Christological Eschatology

The study of end-events begins with Christ and not with end-events. We must not begin in the future and read back into the past, starting with events and fitting Christ into them. Rather, we must begin with Christ, and out of an understanding of who He is, spell out final events. That is precisely where Schweitzer and the early Barth went wrong. Both began with their idea of final events and then fitted Christ into that view, so that Schweitzer had a too-human Jesus and Barth a too-divine Christ. They arrived at opposite ideas of Jesus Christ because they began with end-events. Theirs was an eschatological Christology, but the Bible presents a Christological eschatology. We can do the same with questions of "hast-delay"[45] or of "the final demonstration."[46]

What do we mean by the term Christological eschatology? That the study of final events should be more concerned with who is coming than with what is coming. The biblical focus is Christ-centered rather than crisis-centered. As Carl F. H. Henry put it: "Not dates and places but Christ stands at the center of the Bible and of biblical eschatology."[47] Even in the Old Testament, G. E. Ladd reminds us, "their hope was not in the future but in God."[48] It is much more the case in the New Testament. For, as Oscar Cullmann noted, "the 'end' as the meaning of redemptive history, however, is Jesus Christ, who has already appeared."[49]

---

[1] Theologians have variously called nineteenth century the "greatest century in theology since the fourth" (H. R. Mackintosh, *Types of Modern Theology* [London: Collins, 1964], p. 183); "the century of religious experience" (J. Richmond, *Faith and Philosophy* [London: Hodder and Stoughton, 1966], p. 54); a century of "secularization" (R. Niebuhr, *Faith and History* [London: Nisbet, 1947], p. 15); and the "Century of Hope" (F. S. Marvin, *A Century of Hope* [Oxford: Clarendon, 1919]). Two historians have referred to it as the "Revolutionary Age" (K. S. Latourette, *Christianity in a Revolutionary Age,* vols. 1-5 [London: Eyre and Spottis Woode, 1959-1963]; and A. R. Vidler, *The Church in an Age of Revolution* [London: Penguin Books, Harmand's Worth, 1961]). Barth noted two lines of theological thought in the nineteenth century, stressing respectively, reason and feeling *(From Rousseau to Ritschl* [London: SCM, 1959], p. 190); whereas K. Heim saw three main lines of development, the moral autonomy of the individual, speculative theology, and that of religious feeling *(Expository Times* 48, October 1936-September 1937): pp. 55-58; pp. 132-135). From whichever of these standpoints we view it, it appears as the century of anthropocentricism, and theologically speaking, Barth considered that lines from everywhere, both positive and negative, led to Schleiermacher—for it was "his century" *(Die Protestantische Theologie im 19. Jahrhundert* [Zürich: EVZ, 1947], pp. 377, 381).

[2] In 1889 Schleiermacher was considered as having "almost unequaled veneration" (F. Lichtenberger, *History of German Theology in the Nineteenth Century* [Edinburgh: T & T Clark, 1889], pp. 47, 48), was studied and honored more in 1910 than in 1830 (K. Barth, *From Rousseau to Ritschl* [London: SCM, 1959], pp. 306, 307), and studied with closer application in continental circles than anyone except Luther from 1887-1937 (H. R. Mackintosh, *Types of Modern Theology* [London: Collins, 1964], p. 36). He was the pioneer of Christian humanism as far as a thorough going method is concerned (E. Brunner, *Die Mystik und das Wort* [Tübingen: Verlag von J.C.B. Mohr, Paul Sibeck, 1924], p. 8). Some have called him the "father of modern Protestantism" (J. Richmond, *Faith and Philosophy* [London: Hodder and Stoughton, 1966], p. 66) and "the father of modern theology" (C. Van Til, *The New Modernism* [London: J. Clarke, 1946], vol. 1, p. 365). Brunner referred to him as the greatest theologian of the nineteenth century (Brunner, p. 8). Barth said of him, "the first place in the history of theology of

the most recent times belongs and will always belong to Schleiermacher and he has no rival" (p. 306).

[3] In the editors' preface to the English translation of Ritschl's book, H. R. Mackintosh and A. B. Macaulay not only pointed to it as his monumental work, but as the greatest dogmatic treatise since Schleiermacher's *The Christian Faith* (A. Ritschl, *The Christian Doctrine of Justification and Reconciliation* [T & T Clark, 1900]).

[4] The so-called objective classical evidences for God include the cosmological (cause) and teleological (design). Hume and Kant called both into question because a person cannot now see God at work creating. Kant turned to the subjective, or human morality, as evidence. Schleiermacher also followed suit, looking within in an attempt to escape the critique on the objective evidences.

[5] Rather than the rational or moral proofs for God's existence, he maintained that God is given in, and with, the feeling of absolute dependence *(The Christian Faith,* pp. 133, 134).

[6] Only a person under the influence of the Holy Spirit, and not necessarily the cultured antagonists of Christianity that Schleiermacher longed to convert, could really so feel God.

[7] To discover doctrines, Schleiermacher looked within human nature rather than in God's Word. Note the following insights from his *Christian Faith.* The starting point in dogmatics is the self-consciousness of the individual (p. 501), which is the God-consciousness of the redeemed person (pp. 541, 542), or the religious self-consciousness (pp. 231, 232). Thus, dogmatics is an examination and articulation of the sphere of the inner life of Christian piety (pp. 428, 485), a fruitful self-analysis (p. 554) because doctrines are but religious affections set forth in speech (pp. 66, 67, 76, 91, 92, 127, 132, 141, 142). It is this feeling of absolute dependence that dogmatics explains (p. 198) as it argues from the redeemed to the Redeemer (p. 65).

[8] *Ibid.,* p. 144.

[9] Affirmation of the self-consciousness relative to the consummation of the church are, he says, "most unreliable" *(ibid.,* p. 529), for the Christian consciousness has nothing to say regarding a "condition so entirely outside our ken" (p. 697).

[10] Unlike their articulated chapters, articles or loci, Schleiermacher's was "a single astonishingly coherent view of the separate parts *(disjecta membra)* of the historical Christian faith" (Kart Barth, *Theology and Church* [London: SCM, 1962], p. 181).

[11] Brunner, p. 8.

[12] J. Richmond, *Faith and Philosophy* (London: Hodder and Stoughton, 1966), pp. 54, 55.

[13] Ellen G. White notes that one can strengthen "unbelief by dwelling upon poor feeling" *(Testimonies,* vol. 3, p. 108) Feelings "are not safe guides" *(ibid.,* vol. 1, p. 413). "Feeling must not be the criterion" *(ibid.,* vol. 5, p. 298). "It is not safe for you to trust to impressions and feelings" *(ibid.,* vol. 3, p. 418).

[14] *The Seventh-day Adventist Bible Commentary,* Ellen G. White Comments, vol. 7, p. 928.

[15] A. Ritschl, *Justification and Reconciliation,* introduction by editors H. R. Mackintosh and A. B. Macaulay (Edinburgh: T & T Clark, 1900), p. v.

[16] *Ibid.,* p. 11.

[17] *Ibid.,* p. 613.

[18] H. R. Mackintosh, *Types of Modern Theology* (London: Collins, 1964), p. 149.

[19] Schweitzer forced the world of New Testament scholarship to consider the problem of the kingdom of God in the teaching of Jesus Christ (N. Perrin, *The Kingdom of God in the Teaching of Jesus* [London: SCM, 1963], p. 28) and deserves the merit of drawing attention to the fact that Jesus and early Christianity expected the appearance of the Messiah in glory and the consequent end of our world in the very near future (E. Brunner, *Eternal Hope* [London: Lutterworth, 1954], p. 127). This discovery of the central significance of eschatology was one of the most important events in recent Protestant theology (J. Moltmann, *Theology of Hope* [London: SCM, 1967], p. 37), marking a turning point in biblical criticism (G. E. Ladd, *Jesus and the Kingdom* [London: SPCK, 1966], p. 4). Barth's commentary marks the great turning point in the modern understanding of eschatology after Schweitzer (T. F. Torrance, *Karl Barth: An Introduction to His Early Theology, 1910-1931* [London: SCM, 1962], p. 78), with its rediscovery of the eschatological nature of the kingdom of God (J. P. Martin, *The Last Judgment in Protestant Theology From Orthodoxy to Ritschl* [Edinburgh: Oliver and Boyd, 1963], p. 208).

[20] The Son of Man, proleptically, had come into His kingdom when God became human. In Christ the kingdom had drawn near. Yet Matthew 10:23 puts the coming into the future. "Possibly Jesus is here speaking in general terms to all Christians, indicating that there will be places in which to labor and people ready to receive the message until the 'gospel of the kingdom shall be preached in all the world'" *(The SDA Bible Commentary,* vol. 5, p. 378). See

Matthew 24:14. "And Christ declares: 'Ye shall not have gone over the cities of Israel, till the Son of man be come' (Matt. 10:23). Until in heaven is spoken the word, 'It is finished,' there will always be places for labor, and hearts to receive the message" (E. G. White, *Testimonies,* vol. 6, p. 478). The second prediction was fulfilled six days later when Peter, James, and John saw Christ glorified on the Mount of Transfiguration (Matt. 17:1, 2).

[21] "The whole history of 'Christianity' down to the present day, that is to say, the real inner history of it, is based on the delay of the Parousia, the nonoccurrence of the Parousia, the abandonment of eschatology, the progress and completion of the 'de-eschatologisating' of religion which had been connected therewith. It should be noted that the non-fulfillment of Matt. 10:23 is the first postponement of the Parousia. We have therefore here the first significant date in the 'history of Christianity;' it gives to the work of Jesus a new direction, otherwise inexplicable" (A. Schweitzer, *The Quest of the Historical Jesus* [London: Adam and Charles Black, 1954], p. 358).

[22] *Ibid.,* pp. 368, 369.

[23] Barth was revolting against the immanentism of Schleiermacher (God in man), but went to the other extreme of positing a "wholly other" God *(Ganz Anderer).* As the introduction to his *Romans* mentions, Plato and Overbeck influenced him. He was also indebted to Kierkegaard. He said, "If I have a system, it is limited to a recognition of what Kierkegaard called the 'infinite qualitative distinction' between time and eternity, and to my regarding this as possessing negative as well as positive significance: 'God is in heaven, and thou art on earth' " *(Romans* [London: Oxford University, 1933], p. 10).

[24] Barth gives credit also to Overbeck, Kant, Kierkegaard, and Dostoevsky *(The Epistle to the Romans,* translated from the sixth edition by E. C. Hoskyns [London: Oxford University Press, 1965], preface to the second edition, pp. 3, 4).

[25] They include Schweitzer's "Thorough-Going Eschatology," C. H. Dodd's "Realized Eschatology," J.A.T. Robinson's "Fully Inaugurated Eschatology," W. Manson's "Spiritualized Apocalyptic Eschatology," R. Bultmann's "Existential Eschatology," and J. Moltmann's "Proleptic Eschatology."

[26] Dodd believed that we must understand the parables of Christ in the context of the life situation of Jesus *(Sitzen leben Jesu).* He therefore argued that with the ministry, death, and resurrection of Jesus we have the eschatological event, the climax of all history, the coming of the kingdom—in the absolute and not provisional sense—so that the new age is inaugurated *(The Apostolic Preaching and Its Developments* [London: Hodder and Stoughton, 1936], pp. 7, 28, 38, 39, 46, 63, 93, 128, 232).

[27] Bultmann, in his 1955 Gifford lectures at the University of Edinburgh, said, "The problem of eschatology grew out of the fact that the expected end of the world failed to arrive, that the 'Son of Man' did not appear in the clouds of heaven, that history went on, and that the eschatological community could not fail to recognize that it had become a historical phenomenon and that the Christian faith had taken on the shape of a new religion" *(History and Eschatology* [Edinburgh University, 1957], p. 38). In this context he suggests that "the meaning of history lies always in the present, and when the present is conceived as the eschatological present by Christian faith the meaning in history is realized. . . . In every moment slumbers the possibility of being the eschatological moment. You must awaken to it" *(ibid.,* p. 155).

[28] Moltmann can say, "From first to last, and not merely in the epilogue, Christianity is eschatology" *(Theology of Hope* [London: SCM, 1967], p. 16). Theology begins with eschatology, so that everything is thought out from that future *(ibid.).* In fact, the medium of theology is eschatology (p. 41). Future focus overlooks the past and present (pp. 282-288).

[29] "If, however, the future were to bring something startlingly new, we have nothing to say of that, and nothing meaningful can be said of it either . . ." *(Theology of Hope,* p. 17). He refers to "hope for the unexpected" and "future novelty" (p. 25). "If the promise is not regarded abstractly apart from the God who promises, but its fulfillment is entrusted directly to God in his freedom and faithfulness, then there can be no burning interest in constructing a hard and fast juridical system of historic necessities according to a schema of promise and fulfillment—neither by demonstrating the functioning of such a schema in the past nor by making calculations for the future. Rather, the fulfillments can very well contain an element of newness and surprise over against the promise as it was conceived. That is why the promise does not fall to pieces along with the historical circumstances or the historical thought forms in which is was received, but can transform itself—by interpretation—without losing its character of certainty, of expectation and of movement. If they are God's promises, then God must also be regarded as the subject of their fulfillment" *(ibid.,* p. 104). "Now it has also been observed that very many of the prophets' words about the future, especially their political predictions, did not come to pass in the way they

were originally meant, and that history has thus outrun, and thereby antiquated, many words of promise. And this has been made a reason for no longer understanding history from the standpoint of promise but seeing in history a reality which overreaches these words of promise" ("History Has Outrun the Words," pp. 110, 111).

[30] Moltmann may deny that he has gone this far, but reading through his book *Theology of Hope* one sees an openness to something new from the future that seems to transcend that given in divine revelation.

[31] "It is not infrequently the case that after studying theology a man loses his faith, which was once radiant. And it is all too possible for the modern professor, like the scribes, to take away the key of knowledge of God in the course of theological education: 'you did not enter yourselves, and you hindered those who were entering' (Luke 11:52). I know that this is easily done as a theological teacher. To my shame, I have done it myself" (Michael Green, *The Empty Cross of Jesus* [Downers Grove, Ill.: InterVarsity Press, 1984], p. 158).

[32] *Ibid.,* p. 157.

[33] Walter Wink, *The Bible in Human Transformation: Toward a New Paradigm for Biblical Study* (Philadelphia: Fortress, 1973), p. 1.

[34] Gerhard Maier, *The End of the Historical-Critical Method,* trans. E. W. Leverenz and R. F. Norden (St. Louis: Concordia, 1977).

[35] *Ibid.,* p. 48.

[36] Carl F. H. Henry, *God, Revelation and Authority* (Waco, Tex.: Word, 1979), vol. 4, p. 387. Henry also notes that Maier has returned to the doctrine of verbal inspiration, which seems a swing of the pendulum to another extreme—the opposite of the historical-critical method.

[37] Karl Barth, *Church Dogmatics,* trans. G. T. Thomson (Edinburgh: T & T Clark, 1963), vol. 1, p. 119. In citing Barth we do not support his equally devastating use of Scripture through theological presuppositions that impose on the objective Word.

[38] C. S. Lewis, *Fern-seed and Elephants,* p. 106, 107.

[39] *Ibid.,* p. 108.

[40] *Ibid.,* p. 111.

[41] *Ibid.,* p. 114.

[42] *Ibid.,* p. 119.

[43] David S. Dockery, *The Challenge of Postmodernism: An Evangelical Engagement* (Wheaton, Ill.: Victor Books, 1995), pp. 208-238.

[44] Ellen G. White, *Selected Messages* (Washington, D.C.: Review and Herald, 1958), book 1, p. 416.

[45] We can give only a few brief strokes here, some hermeneutical principles about the haste-delay problem. If man can delay or hasten Christ's coming then are human beings actually in charge? Or if God has set the day of His return, is this arbitrary? We can look at the haste-delay question solely from the human perspective, but to do so will lose the holistic view of Scripture. Men do hasten or delay Christ's return, but not in the absolute sense, or His coming would be in human hands. The other side is the fact that God is in control of human history and knows the end from the beginning, and so knows the date of Christ's return. These two levels are missiological and theological. The missiological speaks from a human perspective—of hastening or delaying Christ's return. The purpose is to get Christians into mission for others. The theological speaks from the perspective of God, of His foreknowledge. The purpose is to assure us that He is in control, so we can be secure. The missiological, by itself, may find the Advent nebulous when left to human response. The theological, by itself, may consider the Advent capricious—ready or not, here I come. We find the balance by holding the two together—God knows everything about the future, including humanity's hastening and delaying, and has simply fed that into His computer to get the best printout date for His return (an anthropocentric description). Instead of studying either the theological or the missiological strands in a vacuum by themselves, we approach them in reference to each other.

In short, we must not begin this study with the missiological level, but with the theological. To begin with the missiological is similar to an eschatological Christology, whereas to begin with the theological parallels a Christological eschatology.

[46] The focus must be on Christ and not on Christians, on what He wants to do through us, rather than what we need to do, and on what He will do for us rather than on what we will do for Him.

[47] Henry, vol. 6, p. 498.

[48] Ladd, *Jesus and the Kingdom,* p. 61.

[49] Oscar Cullmann, *Christ and Time,* trans. F. V. Filson (London: SMC, 1967), p. 140.

Chapter 8

The Role of the Catholic Church

It doesn't even have an extensive doctrine of final events, yet it plays a central role in the last days. Look in Augustine's *The City of God,* Thomas Aquinas's *Summa Theologica, The Documents of Vatican II* (1963-1965), or the latest *Catechism of the Catholic Church* (1994), and you will not find any outline of end-time events before the Second Advent in Catholic thinking. Thus, despite the fact that it does not focus on final events, the Catholic Church will still itself be a major player in them.

Earmarks of the Counterfeit

Although we'll look at some negative facts about the Catholic Church, let it be clearly stated: Many of God's children are Catholics. I respect them. They will gladly respond to the final call to join Christ's followers (see Rev. 18:1-4). But the ecclesiastical and theological system itself has problems—problems that we must carefully consider; problems that can destroy any church in a multitude of ways.

Paul warned about these kinds of problems already in the first century. "The secret power of lawlessness is already at work" (2 Thess. 2:7). Influences opposed to Christ's church infiltrated it from the very beginning. Could you expect otherwise? Immediately after Calvary Satan attacked Christ's followers. Defeated by the events of Calvary, he hoped to nullify them by robbing all human beings of the cross's benefits. Although he knew he couldn't change the victory of Calvary, he hoped to make it of no effect for everyone. He had the world. Israel he had defeated. Now he must get the church. "When the dragon saw that he had been hurled to the earth, he pursued the woman [church] who had given birth to the male child" (Rev. 12:13).

At Ephesus Paul admonished the elders: "Keep watch over yourselves and all the flock of which the Holy Spirit has made you overseers. Be shepherds of the church of God, which he bought with his own blood. I know that after I leave, savage wolves will come in among you and will not spare the flock. Even from your own number men will arise and distort the truth in order to draw away disciples after them" (Acts 20:28-30).

Even Seventh-day Adventists have not appreciated the fact that Satan was introducing error into the church even during the lives of the apostles. The New Testament epistles were written to combat error already spreading among Christ's followers. To read even the earliest extrabiblical church writings is to find a church full of strange ideas and doctrines.

Through the centuries, with cunning craft, Satan worked among all Christians. In the end-time, prophecy tells us, "The dragon was enraged at the woman and went off to make war against the rest of her offspring—those who obey God's commandments and hold to the testimony of Jesus" (Rev. 12:17). Satan hates the truth. Cowering under the truth about Calvary, he rejects commandments and Scripture and opposes the end-time manifestation of the prophetic gift ("The testimony of Jesus is the spirit of prophecy" [Rev. 19:10]).

How Satan Has Made a Counterfeit

We have far more to fear from within Christendom than from outside. A trojan horse does more to defeat truth than the forces of the world outside can ever do. Prophecy tells us that the world is not the final power in the end-time, but corrupt religion itself. Consider the evidence of how error has used and manipulated the Christian church through the centuries.

1. Opposition to Calvary

Vatican II (1963-1965) claims that Christ handed over the church to Peter to shepherd,[1] and then "the apostles left bishops as their successors, 'handing over their own teaching role' to them."[2] In this way bishops preside "in place of God over the flock."[3] Thus "the bishop is to be considered the high priest of his flock. In a certain sense it is from him that the faithful who are under his care derive and maintain their life in Christ."[4] Even belief in Christ comes "through the Church."[5] Perhaps these citations from the official Vatican II Council are sufficient to see that the Catholic Church can come between the believer and Christ, as Paul warned.

Now we're ready to look at the Lord's Supper (called Eucharist, or Mass). Catholic theology argues that no Christian community can exist "unless it has its basis and center in the celebration of the most Holy Eucharist."[6] Christ should be its basis and center. Furthermore, "the Eucharist shows itself to be the source and the apex of the whole work of preaching the gospel."[7] "Priests fulfill their chief duty in the mystery of the Eucharistic Sacrifice. In it the work of our redemption continues to be carried out."[8] Therefore, "the Eucharistic Sacrifice" is "the center and root of the whole priestly life."[9]

Sadly, in practice and popular thought the Eucharist can usurp the place of Christ. Through the Eucharist "grace is channeled to us."[10] "The purpose of the sacraments is to sanctify men . . ."[11] It's by the Eucharist that "the Church constantly lives and grows."[12] "For the most blessed Eucharist contains the Church's entire spiritual wealth."[13] "In brief, the Eucharist is the sum and summary of our faith,"[14] because "life in Christ has its foundation in the Eucharistic banquet."[15]

The Eucharist is a sacrifice of Christ. First the priest claims to create Christ from the wafer and wine (through a process called transubstantiation) and offers His sacrifice through it every time there is a Mass. That happens daily in a million places. In a way, we could regard Christ as coming under the control of the officiating priest. Protestants see the whole process as contradicting the fact that "Christ was sacrificed once" (Heb. 9:23-28) and that His death is as unrepeatable as His incarnation or second coming. *The Catechism of the Catholic Church* recognizes this perception when it says, "The Paschal mystery of Christ is celebrated, not repeated."[16]

The Catholic Church is clearly eucharistic-centered and not Calvary-centered. "The Eucharist cannot unite us to Christ without at the same time cleansing us from past sins and preserving us from future sins."[17] "As bodily nourishment restores lost strength, so the Eucharist strengthens our charity, which tends to be weakened in daily life."[18] Such theology points the believer to the Eucharist to receive spiritual nourishment, Christ, grace, and victory. Thus, in many ways the Catholic Church gathers around a human-made altar rather than around the cross, even though they claim "the sacrifice of Christ and the sacrifice of the Eucharist are *one single sacrifice:* 'The victim is one and the same: the same now offers through the ministry of priests, who then offered himself on the cross; only the manner of offering is different.'"[19]

Such countless repetitions of the "sacrifice" of the Eucharist can only blur the Crucifixion in the mind of believers, robbing them of their sense of the one and only Calvary.

2. Opposition to Commandments

Christ summed up all His commands as love to God and love to other human beings (Matt. 22:37-40).

The first commandment says, "You shall not make for yourself an idol" (Ex. 20:4). Yet popular tradition has let the Communion bread and wine emblems become an idol. The *Catechism* states: "The Catholic Church has always offered and still offers to the sacrament of the Eucharist the cult of adoration, not only during Mass, but also outside of it, reserving the consecrated hosts with the utmost care, exposing them to the solemn veneration of the faithful, and carrying them in procession."[20] Such practices, as well as relics and statues of saints and the veneration of Mary, have blurred the clear image of Christ and drawn attention away from Him. If we cannot see God clearly, we cannot love Him as much.

As the Catholic Church has increasingly acknowledged, the Inquisition in Europe and church crusades against Muslims and Jews have obscured Christ's command to love others. It has also stood silently by when it should have intervened in the suffering of others, as in the case of the Jewish Holocaust.

Paul echoed Christ when he said, "The entire law is summed up in a single command: 'Love your neighbor as yourself'" (Gal. 5:14). The Catholic Church failed when it violated the very essence of the whole law in the way it caused the death of innocent people, reflecting how Daniel was shown the little horn "waging war against the saints" (Dan. 7:21).

3. Opposition to Scripture

Too often Catholicism has placed tradition above Scripture. As reported in the *Documents of Vatican Council II,* "in order to keep the gospel forever whole and live within the Church, the apostles left bishops as their successors, 'handing over their own teaching role' to them."[21] Tradition claims that the apostles bequeathed to the leaders of what would become the Catholic Church their own apostolic teaching office. This is why the 1994 *Catechism of the Catholic Church* carries the title "Apostolic Constitution *Fidei Depositum,"* which means it represents the faith deposited through apostolic authority. Repeatedly Vatican II spoke of "sacred tradition and sacred scripture," and in that order.[22] Tradition is not only apostolic, but is the latest apostolic revelation, and hence has precedence. It thrusts Scripture from its role of preeminence.

"Sacred tradition and sacred Scripture form one sacred deposit of the word of God, which is committed to the Church."[23] As when two streams merge to form one river, so Catholics see no real difference between them. Catholics believe they both come from the Holy Spirit. "The Father's self-communication made through his Word in the Holy Spirit, remains present and active in the Church: 'God, who spoke in the past, continues to converse with the Spouse of his beloved Son.'"[24] This means that revelation continues in and through the church as it did through the apostles. Although the *Catechism* says "this Magesterium [teaching office] is not superior to the Word of God, but is its servant," it also comments, "The way of interpreting Scripture is subject finally to the judgment of the Church."[25]

Sadly, though the church rightly teaches and emphasizes Christ, its practice sometimes places itself above Christ. The Mass ignores His completed sacrifice and in a way replaces Calvary. Catholicism's claim of apostolic authority for its tradition removes Scripture as the unique revelation of God to humanity and substitutes a human final authority of continuing revelation through the church. Thus many Catholics find themselves going to Calvary through the Mass and to Scripture through tradition. A human leadership interposes itself between the members and Calvary and the members and Scripture. That very interposition can confine Catholics at a distance from both the death of Christ for them and the Scriptures that testify about Him.

Anything that keeps Christians from the cross and Scripture is doing the exact opposite of what both are intended to be—a very personal encouragement to each follower of Christ. And anything that weakens the relationship between Christ and the believer can be distorted by Satan.

4. Antichrist

The Catholic Church presents itself as the continuation of the intercessory ministry of Christ; yet, as we have seen, it places gulfs between Christ and the believer. To overcome them, it encourages Catholics to pray to saints or approach Christ through their priest instead of going directly to Him. On the other hand, it says that all of heaven's blessings reach the believer through itself instead of directly from Christ. Many see the church as a mediator for Christ the Mediator. It's as if Christ cannot do it by Himself.

One way this becomes noticeable is the way the church reveres Mary, the mother of Christ. Singling her out as different from any other human being, they believe she was born without original sin so that Christ could Himself be born without original sin. If she could receive that gift, why not everyone else? And if anyone could receive that gift, why do we need a Saviour? Vatican II declared that "she conceived, brought forth, and nourished Christ. She presented Him to the Father in the temple, and was united with Him in suffering as He died on the cross. In an utterly singular way she cooperated by her obedience, faith, hope, and burning charity in the Savior's work of restoring supernatural life to souls. For this reason she is mother to us in the order of grace."[26]

Official Catholic theology presents her as "model of the Church." In fact, "in the most holy Virgin the Church has already reached that perfection whereby she exists without spot or wrinkle." And "devotedly meditating on her and contemplating her in the light of the Word made man, the Church with reverence enters more intimately into the supreme mystery of the Incarnation and becomes ever increasingly like her Spouse."[27]

Mary holds a prominent place in Catholic thinking. It views her as "Queen over all things" and "Mother of her Lord and as her [the church's] own mother." So Catholics say, "We believe that the Holy Mother of God, the new Eve, Mother of the Church, continues in heaven to exercise her maternal role on behalf of the members of Christ."[28] Such views again blur the role of Christ in salvation that is His alone.

Catholicism in the End-time

1. New Focus in Vatican II

Between A.D. 325 and 1965 Catholic delegates from around the world gathered in 21 ecumenical councils. The first one was in Nicea and the last was Vatican II (1963-1965). For the first time in the history of such councils, Vatican II went beyond the in-house business for the church. It reached out beyond itself to all the major religions of the world, including non-Christian and Jewish.[29]

The Catholic Church also addressed other Christian denominations, calling them "separated Churches." By "separated" they mean that the other Christian denominations had left them. "For the Spirit of Christ has not refrained from using them as a means of salvation which derive their efficacy from the very fullness of grace and truth entrusted to the Catholic Church." "For it is through Christ's Catholic Church alone, which is the all-embracing means of salvation, that the fullness of the means of salvation can be obtained. It was to the apostolic college alone, of which Peter is the head, that we believe our Lord entrusted all the blessings of the New Covenant, in order to establish on earth the one Body of Christ into which all those should be fully incorporated who already belong in any way to God's People."[30] By addressing the statement to "separated brethren,"[31] the writers clearly show that they view the unity of all churches as possible only within the Catholic Church.

This includes the Eastern Orthodox Church, which split from the Catholic Church in 1054, and the Protestant churches that derive from Luther's break with the Catholic Church in 1517. To all of them the Vatican II document presents the pope as "the divinely appointed successor of St. Peter in supreme governance over the universal Church."[32]

Already through *The Documents of Vatican II* the Catholic Church has positioned itself to unite all non-Christian religions, Jews, and all Christian denominations to itself. We now turn to consider some happenings in the life of Pope John Paul II that has moved this plan forward.

2. The Pope's Sense of Destiny

Pope John Paul II has a strong sense of destiny. Reportedly he considers his election on October 16, 1978, as pope a direct work of Mary, the mother of God.[33] This has its roots in an event on August 26, 1956, when he was among the millions of Polish Catholics who dedicated themselves "in submission to Mary as her nation of slaves."[34] Wojtyla and Wyzynski, Catholic leaders in Poland, believed that such a consecration to Mary was a geopolitical move to free Poland from Russian influence.

a. Saved and Contacted by Mary

On May 13, 1981, Mehmet Ali Agca fired two bullets at the pope's head in St. Peter's Square. Approximately 75,000 people in the square and about 3.5 million on television watched the attempted assassination. The pontiff was standing on the "popemobile" and just at that moment bent to greet a little girl who had a picture of Mary pinned to her blouse. It saved his life.

While convalescing that summer in the Policlinico, the pope reflected on the way he had been spared and attributed it to Mary. The attempted assassination had occurred on the day of the official feast of Mary as Our Lady of Fatima. "It was in this mode of prayer and this mood of total trust in Mary that Pope John Paul II had what has been, as far as is publicly known, his only supernatural vision of things to come. . . . It came as an exact repetition of a miraculous happening recorded sixty-four years before at the hamlet of Fatima, in Portugal. It was just as if he had been present at Fatima around midday, October 13, 1917." An apparition of Mary visited the pope "in the luminous skies of Latio above the Seven Hills of Rome, in August 1981."[35]

b. The Fatima Vision

Three peasant children, Francisco Marto (9 years old), Jacinta Marto (7 years old), and their cousin Lucia dos Santos (10 years old), the first two illiterate, and Lucia only barely able to read and write, encountered the alleged Mary on May 13, 1917, in the fields of Coca da Iria. "She told them she had an important message for all the nations and all men and women; and that, after coming to see them each thirteenth day of the coming months, on October 13 she would by the power of God perform a miracle in order to substantiate the authenticity and vital importance of her message."[36]

Word spread around the world about the event, and many people came to observe what might happen. Rain and clouds blanketed Fatima on October 13. But at midday, the rain stopped suddenly, clouds rolled back, and the sun came shining through. "The sun they now clearly saw was the same sun John Paul II later saw in August 1981." "This sun was a fast-spinning plate of brightly shining silver, a giant pinwheel turning on its own axis, casting off beams of colored lights—red, orange, yellow, green, blue, indigo and violet—that tinted faces, clothes, cars, carts, umbrellas, animals, ponds, grass, mountaintop and horizon in all the successive hues of the rainbow. Everyone was able to stare fixedly at this brilliant disk, but yet without pain and without being blinded."[37]

The blazing disk then roamed in and out of the clouds, stopping occasionally to spin and throw out rainbow colors. Then the great mass zigzagged down toward earth, causing great fear and cries of "It's the end of the world." Malachi Martin reports that after the disk vanished, all realized that the ground and their clothes were dry. A wind came up, yet the tree branches stood still.[38] No one could doubt the unusual occurrences. They supported the claims of the three peasant children.

c. The Messages of Fatima

Two of the messages given on May 13, 1917, became public knowledge. The apparition of Mary asked that the third be sealed for a later revelation. The first said that many in the world are on their way to hell. The second predicted "the outbreak of World War II." "Mary also spoke about Russia and asked that the Pope and all the bishops of the Church consecrate it in an especially solemn manner to her. If this was not done, the children reported Mary as saying, Russia would spread error and evil throughout the world; many human beings would suffer and die as a consequence."[39]

When the third secret message finally became known, it said that the church should consecrate Russia to Mary or face dire consequences, and that the nations will be punished. The pope was to open the sealed envelope with the third message in 1960. Pope John XXIII opened it, and did not act. Neither did his successors Paul VI and John Paul I.[40] By contrast, Pope John Paul II is devoted to Mary and wants to fulfill the third message at Fatima. He believes Mary will bring the world under the Catholic Church as a fulfillment of the third message of Fatima.

3. All the World Wondered

Never before has a pope traveled so widely as John Paul II. Crowds turn out to see him in all parts of the world. And never before has the prestige of the church had such global dimensions. In a world with a vacuum of values, the church seems to be the great defender of morals, as in its stand against abortion and euthanasia. In fact, Billy Graham called the pope "the moral leader of the world."

Other denominations are offering unprecedented support for Catholicism. One factor feeding it is the charismatic movement. It entered Protestant churches in the early 1960s, when the Vatican II Council convened. Later that decade the charismatic movement penetrated Catholicism and spread quickly through much of the church in just 10 years. The most tangible evidence of the charismatic movement is speaking in tongues. When Catholics received it as did Protestants, then observers took it as an evidence that God accepted both. (We will take a careful look at the movement in a later chapter.)

Scripture declares that "the whole world was astonished and followed the beast" (Rev. 13:3). In fact, the whole earth will "worship" the Papacy (Rev. 13:12). It involves political enmeshment with every nation as a geopolitical power. The church offers a religious veneer that many nations believe will bring them blessings in their struggles to survive. Miracles will also seem to support the church. There will be "great and miraculous signs, even causing fire to come down from heaven to earth in full view of men. Because of the signs he was given power to do on behalf of the first beast, he deceived the inhabitants of the earth" (Rev. 13:13, 14).

Revelation 16 tells of "spirits of demons performing miraculous signs, and they go out to the kings of the whole world, to gather them for the battle on the great day of God Almighty" (verse 14). We will look further at these miracles in another chapter. For now it is clear that demons perform miracles to unite the world under a religious power.

4. The Final Showdown Between Christ and the Counterfeit

The Catholic Church and the Seventh-day Adventist Church are the most widespread churches on earth. Most other churches either do not have as extensive a global presence or consist of a system of national churches held together rather loosely. Scripture describes the confrontation in the end-time is between two global churches.

The central difference between the two churches has to do with their relationship to Christ. The Catholic Church is *anti*christ in that it is *against* Christ, because it acts *in place of* Christ. The Mass substitutes for Calvary, priests replace Christ's role in His present ministry, and Mary replaces Christ in the end-time geopolitical scheme to take over the world.

a. The Mission of the Seventh-day Adventist Church

By contrast with the Catholic Church, "the sacrifice of Christ as an atonement for sin is the great truth around which all other truths cluster. In order to be rightly understood and appreciated, every truth in the word of God, from Genesis to Revelation, must be studied in the light that streams from the cross of Calvary."[41] God's end-time church will present every fundamental belief in the light of Calvary. In fact, Ellen White compares the presentation of truths without the cross to Cain's offering without the lamb. She urges, "Of all professing Christians, Seventh-day Adventists should be foremost in uplifting Christ before the world."[42]

Whereas the Catholic Church is Mass-centered, the Seventh-day Adventist Church in the end-time seeks to be Calvary-centered. The mark of God's end-time church is not only Sabbath versus Sunday, but Calvary versus the Mass. Christ must be the all-encompassing focus of Seventh-day Adventists.

The first vision given to Ellen G. White showed God's people on their way to heaven.[43] They traveled a narrow path. Those who kept their eyes upon Jesus made it safely. The others didn't and fell to the world below. Satan's studied strategy during the end-time is to remove the focus of Christians away from Christ to anything that will effectively keep Him hidden. It can be absorption in the affairs of living, earning a livelihood, even in doing good. Anything that comes between the Christian and Christ is antichrist, because it substitutes something else for His rightful role.

Christ warned about the shock to come at the Second Advent. "Many will say to me on that day, 'Lord, Lord, did we not prophesy in your name, and in your name drive out demons and perform many miracles?' Then I will tell them plainly, 'I never knew you. Away from me, you evildoers'" (Matt. 7:22, 23). Having prophesied and performed miracles, they thought what they did was authentic. They assumed such events proved that they were on Christ's side. Yet they lacked the only evidence that counts—they did not really know Christ, whom to know is life eternal (see John 17:3). Something, whether it be the Mass, tradition, priests, Mary, saints, or countless other things—all hid Christ from them.

It can also happen in God's end-time church. Laodicea claimed, "I am rich; I have acquired wealth and do not need a thing." Christ replied, "But you do not realize that you are wretched, pitiful, poor, blind and naked" (Rev. 3:17). Christ stands outside each of our lives and churches, hoping to enter (see Rev. 3:20). Laodicea was a church filled with all you could imagine, but devoid of Christ. Modern churches substitute other things for Christ, but to do so is to put the human in place of Christ. The end-time showdown will be a church filled with Christ facing a church filled with the human.

---

1 *The Documents of Vatican II* (London: Chapman, 1967), p. 23.
2 *Ibid.*, p. 115.
3 *Ibid.*, p. 40.
4 *Ibid.*, p. 152.
5 *Ibid.*, p. 600.
6 *Ibid.*, p. 545.
7 *Ibid.*, p.542.
8 *Ibid.*, p. 560.
9 *Ibid.*, p. 563.
10 *Ibid.*, p. 142.
11 *Ibid.*, p. 158.
12 *Ibid.*, p. 50.
13 *Ibid.*, p. 541.
14 *The Catechism of the Catholic Church* (Liguori, Mo.: Liguori, 1994), p. 334.
15 *Ibid.*, p. 351.
16 *Ibid.*, p. 287.
17 *Ibid.*, p. 351.

The Role of the Catholic Church

[18] *Ibid.,* p. 352.
[19] *Ibid.,* p. 344.
[20] *Ibid.,* p. 347.
[21] *Documents of Vatican II,* p. 115.
[22] *Ibid.,* p. 117.
[23] *Ibid.*
[24] *Catechism of the Catholic Church,* p. 25.
[25] *Documents of Vatican II,* p. 121.
[26] *Ibid.,* p. 91.
[27] *Ibid.,* pp. 92, 93.
[28] *Ibid.,* pp. 252-254.
[29] *Ibid.,* pp. 660-668.
[30] *Ibid.,* p. 347.
[31] *Ibid.,* p. 351.
[32] *Ibid.,* p. 374.
[33] Malachi Martin, *The Keys of This Blood: The Struggle for World Domination Between Pope John Paul II, Mikhail Gorbachev and the Capitalist West* (New York: Simon and Schuster, 1990), pp. 616, 617.
[34] *Ibid.,* p. 621.
[35] *Ibid.,* p. 627.
[36] *Ibid.*
[37] *Ibid.,* p. 628.
[38] *Ibid.,* pp. 628, 629.
[39] *Ibid.,* p. 630.
[40] *Ibid.,* pp. 628-634.
[41] Ellen G. White, *Gospel Workers,* (Washington, D.C.: Review and Herald, 1948), p. 315.
[42] Ellen G. White, *Evangelism,* (Washington, D.C.: Review and Herald, 1946), p. 188.
[43] Ellen G. White, *Early Writings,* (Washington, D.C.: Review and Herald, 1945), pp. 14, 15.

Chapter 9

The Ecumenical Movement

Ecumenism comes from the Greek word *oikoumene,* meaning "the entire inhabited earth" (see Acts 17:6, 7; Matt. 24:14; Heb. 2:25). More precisely, it's an attempt to unite all Christians.[1] But prophecy tells us that it will go beyond Christianity and will involve the whole world (see Rev. 13:3, 4), thus spreading to other religions.

Christ prayed "that all of them may be one, Father, just as you are in me and I am in you" (John 17:21). Proponents say Paul also urged it: "Make every effort to keep the unity of the Spirit through the bond of peace. There is one body and one Spirit—just as you were called to one hope when you were called—one Lord, one faith, one baptism; one God and Father of all, who is over all and through all and in all" (Eph. 4:3-6). In his ministry Paul wrestled against forces seeking to divide the church. As T. B. Weber observed: "Throughout his ministry, the apostle worked to maintain the unity of the church in the face of theological deviation (Galatians and Colossians) and internal division (1 and 2 Corinthians)."[2] As we'll see, that's a whole different story from today's ecumenical movement.

1. Historical Overview

Often people study ecumenism in light of such schisms from the Roman Catholic Church as those in ancient times (Syrian and Egyptian), in 1054 (Eastern Orthodox), and from 1517 onward (Protestants). Many assume that Christ and Peter established the Catholic Church, and the Catholic Church remains authentic through apostolic succession, so that ecumenical means a return to the one Church (Catholic) of Christ. However, we should keep in mind that the Catholic Church as we know it in today's form and structure actually began in the fourth century A.D., not in the time of the apostles. It is significant that the Anglican-Roman Catholic International Commission (ARCIC), in its final report in 1982, said that "the New Testament contains no explicit record of a transmission of Peter's leadership; nor is the transmission of apostolic authority in general very clear."[3]

THE ECUMENICAL MOVEMENT

Here is an overview of ecumenical endeavors:

1. 325: The Nicene Creed affirmed belief in the "one holy, catholic, and apostolic church."

2. 1054: Eastern Orthodox churches split from the Western Catholic Church.

3. 1517: Protestant churches began to leave the Catholic Church.

4. 1846: Evangelical Alliance formed from more than 50 denominations in Britain and America.

5. 1908: Federal Council of Churches formed from 31 American Protestant churches.

6. 1910: International Missionary Council at Edinburgh.

7. 1921: International Missionary Council, Lake Mohonk, New York. Tried to get Protestant missionary agencies to cooperate with each other.

8. 1925: Conference on Life and Work, Stockholm. Sought unity among churches in solving social, political, and economic problems.

9. 1927: Conference on Faith and Order, Lausanne. Looked at the theological basis for unity.

10. 1948: World Council of Churches (WCC) formed at Amsterdam with 147 denominations from 44 countries.

11. 1954: WCC at Evanston, Illinois.

12. 1961: WCC at New Delhi, India.

13. 1964: (Nov. 21). Vatican Council II, Decree on Religious Freedom and Decree on Ecumenism.

14. 1964: (Nov. 21). Pope Paul VI's Decree on Ecumenism *(Unitatis Redintegratio).*

15. 1965: (Dec. 7). Pope John XXIII and Patriarch of Constantinople lifted the excommunication that Pope Leo IX and Patriarch Michael Caerularius imposed on each other in 1054.

16. 1968: WCC at Uppsala, Sweden.

17. 1975: WCC at Nairobi, Kenya.

18. 1983: WCC at Vancouver, British Columbia.

19. 1995: (May 25). Pope John Paul II's Encyclical on Ecumenism *(Ut Unum Sint).*

This list gives a quick overview of ecumenical landmarks. The *Roman* Catholic Church attempted to win, or force, back the Eastern Orthodox Church after the two groups had split. But no effort for unity of the churches occurred for three centuries (seventeenth through the nineteenth). In fact, the Protestant churches continued to divide all the time until today hundreds of different denominations exist. Not until the twentieth century did ecumenism become a driving force among many churches. For much of the first half of the century Protestant churches promoted any ecumenical efforts. Concerning the 1910 Edinburgh Ecumenical Conference, August B. Hasler reports: "The Roman Catholic Church was not represented, but Orthodox Churches assured the organizers of their support."[4]

In his book *Roman Catholicism: A Contemporary Evangelical Perspective,* Paul G. Schrotenboer notes four facts drawing the churches together today: 1. "The growth and spread of secularism and antichristian ideologies in an increasingly hostile world."

2. The use of mass media by the Catholic Church and the gifts of Pope John Paul II have "projected to the world a completely new image of the Roman Catholic Church as an institution that is very attractive." 3. The formidable growth of Protestant independent churches that "are not clearly conscious of the doctrinal heritage of the Reformation and consequently of the sharp doctrinal differences between Roman Catholics and evangelicals." 4. "The clear anti-Marxist stance of the present pope has provided Catholicism with a new ground for acceptance even among Protestant or evangelical persons in North America and Europe. This acceptance on ideological grounds often does not take into account the demands of evangelical truth."[5]

2. Vatican Council II

Not until the pontificate of Pope John XXIII did the Catholic Church begin to really take a leadership role in ecumenism. On January 25, 1959, he called for an ecumenical council that invited "separated communities" to attend as observers. He also established a Secretariat for Promoting Christian Unity, with scholar Austin Cardinal Bea at its head. Vatican II Council was a purposeful outreach to "separated brothers," to those who had left her, such as the Eastern Orthodox and the original Reformation Protestants. As Walter M. Abbott, S.J., affirmed, "the Decree on Ecumenism marks the full entry of the Roman Catholic Church into the ecumenical movement."[6] Vatican II went further than Protestant ecumenism in reaching out to Jews and to all non-Christian religions. In Vatican II the Catholic Church launched a mission to bring the world into its fold. Its vision was universal union, not just Christian unity.

Vatican II is the twenty-first ecumenical council. The first eight involved the Christian church worldwide, but after the Eastern Orthodox schism in 1054, the later councils were Western ones. The first six defended important biblical truths, including Christ (against Arius, Nestorius, Eutyches, and Monothelitism) and the Holy Spirit. But unbiblical doctrines also developed in them, such as Mary being exalted to *Theotokos,* "bearer of God" (A.D. 431); veneration of images (787); compulsory clerical celibacy (1139); transubstantiation in the Mass (1215); condemnation of Protestant biblical beliefs (1545-1563); and papal infallibility (1869-1870).[7]

The documents of Vatican II describe the Catholic Church as "God's only flock."[8] What about the "separated brethren"? The decree states that: "For men who believe in Christ and have been properly baptized are brought into a certain, though imperfect, communion with the Catholic Church."[9] The "separated churches" "derive their efficacy from the very fullness of grace and truth entrusted to the Catholic Church."[10] Clearly the Vatican considers ecumenism no mere unity of churches, but a return to the Catholic Church itself. So Vatican II hopes that "all Christians will be gathered, in a common celebration of the Eucharist, into that unity of the one and only Church which Christ bestowed on His Church from the beginning. This unity, we believe, dwells in the

Catholic Church as something she can never lose, and we hope that it will continue to increase until the end of time."[11] "For it is through Christ's Catholic Church alone, which is the all-embracing means of salvation, that the fullness of the means of salvation can be obtained."[12] In this way the church replaces Christ as the means of salvation. Union is church-centered rather than Christ-centered. Here, yet again, we see Satan's studied strategy to shove Christ from view and replace Him with something else.

Many people focus on the terms "separated brethren" and "separated churches," and they rejoice in what appears to be a change in the Catholic Church. But what has not altered is the Catholic doctrines that brought about the separations from the Catholic Church in the first place. They remain the same. The documents call them "weighty differences," and they include the work of redemption, the mystery and ministry of the church, and the role of Mary in salvation. Vatican II expects the "separated brethren" to come back and celebrate the Eucharist together in visible union, yet the Eucharist itself is one of the key causes for division among them.[13] In fact, Vatican II states that "in His Church He instituted the wonderful sacrament of the Eucharist by which the unity of the Church is both signified and brought about."[14] Evidently the "separated brethren" must make all the change in doctrine. Vatican II did not alter a single Catholic doctrine, a pattern that has occurred throughout the history of Catholic theology. Traditions handed down by the church remain unchanged. As Pope Paul VI said in his *De Ecclesia* (1964), "nothing really changes in the traditional doctrine."

A uniting on points of common concern is under way, a union that seems to override doctrinal differences. Catholic theologian Karl Rahner says that Christians "have more in common than separates them and possess a common task in regard to the 'world.'"[15] Some of the common goals are social, having to do with family values and the sacredness of life (versus abortion). The forces at work against such values represent a common enemy for all Christians. This common enemy drives the churches together, very much as citizens of all persuasions come together in wartime. In fact, "the study of theology has become, in the second half of the twentieth century, increasingly an ecumenical activity, with cooperation and interaction between scholars of different traditions so . . . that confessional distinctives have steadily diminished." There has been a "quest for consensus rather than truth," which includes "taking the churches' standpoints rather than the Bible as its basis."[16]

"It is hard to imagine any of the major Protestant churches embarking on doctrinal definition in the present theological climate," says Gerald L. Bray. He believes "all the emphasis is on unbridled pluralism and the tolerance of any kind of faith or unbelief."[17] Concerning Protestant and Catholic churches, Karl Lehmann and Wolfhart Pannenberg note, "Today the churches share a largely common, supradenominational interpretation of Scripture, and a common awareness of the historical contingency of theological formulations. And on this basis new convergencies have grown up in our understanding of the content of faith. In this process, one-sided emphases have been corrected, emphases which were partly the cause of the division but which partly grew up as its consequence, and in the wake of the controversial theology that developed out of the separation."[18]

Protestantism is willing to change its doctrines to meet the common enemy, but not the Catholic Church. Speaking about evangelicals and Catholics, Michael Horton observes, "If it is not Rome that has altered its position in favor of the gospel, then it must be the other partner that has moved from its earlier position."[19] James R. White asks: "What has led to the 'de-protestantization' of much of Protestantism today?" He answers: "The Reformers knew the key to resisting the onslaught of Rome in their day, but many today seem to have forgotten what it is. The Bible. The Bible alone, and all of the Bible. *Sola Scriptura* is just as important today as it was for a Luther or a Zwingli or a Calvin at the time of the Reformation."[20]

While many overlook biblical truth in the quest for unity on common points of doctrine, they do not see the Catholic Church for what it really is, and its eschatological mission remains uncomprehended. As long as Roman Catholicism holds true to its doctrinal beliefs, it must advance the view that it alone is the real body of Christ on earth. As Ansgar Ahlbrecht noted: "The Catholic Church does not regard itself as a confession, that is, as one denomination among others, but as the one Church of Christ."[21]

Consider this "de-protestantization." Protestant and Anglican churches sought union beyond truth, "suggesting that the question of truth did not matter." Hence, "the slogan used in those days was doctrine divides while service unites."[22] Today, ecumenism still has its common points of agreement high on the agenda, letting distinct doctrines slip from the gaze (in non-Catholic churches), whereas the Catholic Church remains insistent on her unique doctrines. Vatican II states: "Nothing is so foreign to the spirit of ecumenism as a false conciliatory approach which harms the purity of Catholic doctrine and obscures its assured genuine meaning."[23]

Timothy P. Weber notes two kinds of ecumenicism. 1. The World Congress on Evangelism (Berlin, 1966; Lausanne, 1974) declared that unity "is based on truth (adherence to the historic gospel)." Called the "cooperative model" of unity, in it conservative evangelicals "sought to restore evangelism to primary place in the church's mission in the hope that more visible kinds of unity would follow." 2. "The federation model of the World Council of Churches tended to downplay the necessity of doctrinal agreement and evangelism while stressing concerted social and political action in Christ's name."[24]

"Today, for good or bad, the lines that separate evangelicals and Roman Catholics are fading," says Davis Duggins. "More and more people from both sides are working together on common social causes, and many of them are describing their spiritual lives in similar language. Some evangelical leaders welcome the changing landscape. 'It's high time that all of us who are Christians come together regardless of the difference of our confessions and our traditions and make common cause to bring Christian values to bear in our society.' "[25] Johannes Brosseder speaks of an ecumenical theology. He calls it "a theology of fellowship, a theology which has discovered that what is common is proportionally much greater than the differences and divergences."[26] Charles Colson writes in the foreword of Keith Fournier's book, "When the barbarians are scaling the walls, there is no time for petty quarreling in the camp."[27]

But doctrinal issues do matter. And they are not minor compared to points of common agreement. The differences involve essentials of the gospel. Praying to Mary as coredeemer, for example, is not a peripheral difference. It radically calls into question the sole mediatorship of the one Redeemer, Jesus Christ. As J. Daryl Charles put it: "The profound theological differences, for example, that separate evangelicals and Catholics cannot be ignored or circumvented, nor can they be 'negotiated.' "[28] Commenting on the slogan "Doctrine divides, experience unites," John M. Frame says, "We cannot brush doctrine aside as a mere impediment to unity, as many users of that slogan would like to do. A doctrinally indifferent church is a church that does not care about the gospel message, for the gospel is precisely a doctrine, a teaching, a narrative of what God has done for our salvation."[29]

In *Evangelical Renewal in the Mainline Churches,* eight scholars present what is going on in various major denominations. James Heidinger II notes "doctrinal compromise and unbelief" as "the heart of United Methodism's tragic decline."[30] Waldo J. Werning comments: "The proper basis of such Lutheran fellowship lies in agreement in doctrine, not in human ceremonies, and in the recognition that Christian practice is the application of doctrine to life."[31] Homer Tricules says that "informed evangelicals reject the claim that doctrine divides while evangelism unites. . . . American Baptist laypeople need to be grounded in the essentials of sound doctrine."[32]

Genuine unity can come only from the whole truth. Only as churches accept all that Scripture has to say can they achieve Christ's prayer for unity. Uniting on common points of doctrine while ignoring distinct doctrines is an insufficient basis for union. George Carey speaks of a "common core of truths" that includes six beliefs: that Jesus Christ is Lord and Saviour; that God is Triune; that faith in Jesus and baptism into Him through the trinitarian confession constitute the new birth and the initiatory rite into the church; that through the Holy Spirit the Christian church is constituted and that it takes all ministries and gifts in the body to express the fullness of the catholic faith; that our faith is divinely revealed in Scripture and expressed in the ancient creeds of the church; and that Jesus Christ will come again in glory as Lord, Judge, and Saviour. He goes on to suggest that Protestants can accept the Catholic emphasis on Mary as long as it does not obscure Christ.[33]

Here we observe nonbiblical dogmas added to biblical truths. It not only introduces human traditions as equal to divine revelation, but these very traditions obscure the uniqueness of Christ. Any addition to God's divine revelation is a human work that divine revelation needs to call into question. The six beliefs cited by George Carey represent a minimalist basis for union, but major doctrines in the Catholic Church, such as human tradition being equal to divine revelation, the function of Mary in redemption, and human works needing to be added to the gift of salvation all undermine them. Human error never serves biblical truth. Human works can never add to Christ's gift of salvation.

It is an immense paradox that the Reformers, who stood so solidly for truth against error, through their heirs are seeking union with error at the expense of truth. At the same time, Roman Catholicism remains staunchly opposed to any change of its doctrines, despite its efforts to bring back the "separated brethren." What would Luther, Calvin, and Zwingli think? How would the martyrs react? All that they stood and fought for could be lost in a merger on common points of doctrine.

All efforts to unite churches will not see Roman Catholicism losing its uniqueness or dominance. As Richard John Neuhaus noted: "Even when, please God, all the churches are in full communion in the one Church Catholic, there will likely be a Roman Catholic Church. By virtue of its size, tradition, structure, charisms, and energies, the Roman Catholic Church will have a singular part in shaping the world-historical future of Christianity."[34]

It is from within Christendom that the final attack against Christ will come. A false Christianity will reject the true gospel. This false Christianity will have, by its very nature, joined the rest of the world—or as prophecy puts it, "The whole world was astonished and followed the beast. . . . They also worshiped the beast" (Rev 13:3, 4). H. B. Swete, in his *Commentary on the Apocalypse,* perceptively states: "Those who take note of the tendencies of modern civilization will not find it impossible to conceive that a time may come when throughout Christendom the spirit of Antichrist will, with the support of the state, make a final stand against a Christianity which is loyal to the person and teaching of Jesus."[35]

3. Controversial Document (March 29, 1994)

On March 29, 1994, thirteen persons,[36] both Catholic and evangelicals, issued a document entitled "Evangelicals and Catholics Together: The Christian Mission in the 3rd Millennium" *(ECT).* Twenty-five well-known Catholic and evangelical leaders endorsed it.[37] The document caused a furor in both Catholic and evangelical circles. Dave Hunt said, "The document in effect overturned the Reformation and will unquestionably have far-reaching repercussions throughout the Christian world for years to come."[38]

One of the key differences between Catholic and evangelical theology has to do with justification by faith alone through Christ alone. Martin Luther discovered in the book of Romans that "the righteous will live by faith" (Rom. 1:17). This truth became the heart of the Reformation. It rejected the Catholic notion that justification results through faith plus human works. Any human activity detracts from the one saving work of Jesus Christ. "The doctrine of Justification," wrote John Calvin, "is the principal ground on which religion must be supported."[39]

R. C. Sproul's book *Faith Alone: The Evangelical Doctrine of Justification* calls into question the *ECT* document. He rightly points out that Catholics and evangelicals understand justification differently. Even the Council of Trent taught justification by faith. But it was not by faith *alone*. That was the key issue of the Reformation. "The word *alone* was a solecism on which the entire Reformation doctrine of justification was erected. The absence of the word *alone* from *ECT's* joint affirmation is most distressing."[40]

The key word "alone" is missing throughout Catholic thinking. Evangelicals believe the gospel is justification through faith *alone* by Christ *alone* found in Scripture *alone*. By contrast Catholics see faith as a human work, so there is *no faith alone, Christ alone, nor in Scripture alone*. Catholic tradition adds human penance and purgatory to justification and to Christ's work just as the tradition of the Magesterium adds to Scripture. The human additions to the work of Christ in salvation and revelation deny the free gift of the gospel. Thus this "human addition" distinguishes Roman Catholicism from authentic evangelicals.

John MacArthur said that "despite all the recent dialogue among those desiring to reunite Rome and Protestantism, there has been no suggestion that Rome will ever repudiate its stance against justification by faith. For that reason, I believe the trend toward tolerance and cooperation is a destructive one because it blurs the distinction between biblical truth and a system of false teaching."[41]

4. The Council of Trent (1545-1563)

We need to look at this *ECT* document in the light of the Council of Trent. As one reads through the council's canons and decrees, it is obvious that the session reformed the church but not doctrine. In fact, it denied every unique doctrine of the Reformation with anathemas.[42] Real reform must be based upon biblical truth.

The Council of Trent rejected the Reformer's view on justification. Consider the following six canons:

"Can. 4. If anyone says that man's free will moved and aroused by God, by assenting to God's call and action, in no way cooperates toward disposing and preparing itself to obtain the grace of justification, that it cannot refuse its assent if it wishes, but that, as something inanimate, it does nothing whatever and is merely passive, let him be anathema."

"Can. 9. If anyone shall say that the sinner is justified by faith alone, meaning that nothing else is required to cooperate in order to obtain the grace of justification, and that it is not in any way necessary that he be prepared and disposed by the action of his own will—let him be anathema."

"Can. 11. If anyone shall say that men are justified either by the sole imputation of the righteousness of Christ or by the sole remission of sins, to the exclusion of the grace and charity that is poured forth in their hearts by the Holy Spirit and remains in them, or also that the grace by which we are justified is only the good will of God—let him be anathema."

"Can. 12. If anyone shall say that justifying faith is nothing else but confidence in divine mercy, which remits sins for Christ's sake, or that it is this confidence alone which justifies us—let him be anathema."

"Can. 24. If anyone shall say that the justice received is not preserved and also increased before God through good works, but that those works are merely the fruits and signs of justification obtained, but not the cause of increase—let him be anathema."

"Can. 32. If anyone says that the good works of the one justified are in such manner the gifts of God that they are not also the good merits of him justified; or that the one justified by the good works that he performs by the grace of God and the merit of Jesus Christ, whose living member he is, does not truly merit an increase of grace, eternal life, and in case he dies in grace, the attainment of eternal life itself and also an increase of glory, let him be anathema."[43]

Here human activity hides Christ's sole work for human salvation. Any addition to the gospel is not the gospel. Paul says: "Clearly no one is justified before God by the law, because, 'The righteous will live by faith'" (Gal. 3:11, cf. Gal. 2:16). Christians in Galatia accepted a doctrine of justification plus human efforts, just as Catholic theology does. The apostle called it "a different gospel—which is really no gospel at all" (Gal. 1:6, 7). Catholic theology has many human works, such as penance, intercession of saints, the role of Mary, and purgatory, that all deflect attention from Christ's saving work.

Christ plus anything for human salvation negates the gift, negates grace, and negates justification. So many see the Catholic "gospel" as identical to the evangelical gospel, but that is impossible. Although it is good for Christians to come together to unite against humanism in its many forms (abortion, declining moral values, antifamily issues), they need to realize that Christ plus anything human is also humanism. For wherever we link Christ to human works, the human works then take center stage and become the driving force in life. Humanism to earn salvation is no better than humanism in needless abortions. Both deny the proper place to Christ in human affairs.

The same thing holds true of the church as a corporate body. The Catholic Church regards salvation as based upon union with the church rather than union with Christ. The sacraments of the church save. The church interprets Scripture, which means interpreting the mission of Christ. And the church administers penance, last rights, and assists a person through purgatory. Catholic theology is church-centered rather than Christ-centered, even though it claims that the church is merely the channel through which Christ works. Tradition has made Catholic ecclesiology consist of Christ *plus* the church. As J. Daryl Charles rightly observed: "Genuine Christian unity will reflect a shift from a church-centered to Christ-centered focus."[44]

The Council of Trent emphasizes the place of human works in justification, and thus it contradicts the Reformers. Since neither Vatican Council I or Vatican Council II changed the positions taken at Trent, it is therefore still the official position of the Catholic Church. Even the 1994 *Catechism of the Catholic Church* still presents the human element of Trent. Thus justification "is granted us through Baptism" (2020). Sanctifying grace "is infused by the Holy Spirit" (2023). Merit is given "to man's collaboration" (2025), for "moved by the Holy Spirit, we can merit for ourselves and for others all the graces needed to attain eternal life, as well as necessary temporal goods" (2027). And "penance offers a new possibility to convert and to recover the grace of justification" (1446).[45]

Such alleged human contributions to salvation detract from the only Saviour, Jesus Christ. This makes Catholic teaching opposed to Scripture, even though it uses the words "justification by faith." Norman L. Geisler and Ralph E. MacKenzie note that the *ECT* "document overlooks the crucial disagreements concerning the nature and extent of justification: grace alone, through faith alone, based on Christ alone." Besides this, "questions concerning the idolatrous implications surrounding the worship of the consecrated host are not addressed. Evangelical concern over inappropriate attention involved in the veneration of saints, images, and especially Mary is not addressed."[46] Geisler and MacKenzie conclude that "in the eyes of historical Protestantism, it is a false gospel."[47]

Clothing the true gospel with garments of humanism robs it of its good news. It is not good news that penance, human works for merit, and purgatory on the one hand, and saints and Mary interceding on the other hand, need to be added to the free gift in Jesus Christ. The gospel is either a free gift or it is not—it cannot be both. No amount of gospel language on the part of Catholic theology can be married to human works and still leave the gospel gift intact. Anything that takes the place of Christ, makes Him secondary, or ignores His free gift of justification—is against Christ, is antichrist.

For a number of years I taught a class on Vatican II to graduate seminary students. Reading carefully through the 16 documents from it made it clear that any changes were superficial. For example, they addressed "separated brethren" but still in the context that the Catholic Church is the only Body of Christ. Although Vatican II allowed priests to say the Mass in the vernacular, the Mass is still the repetition of the sacrifice of Christ (even though unbloody), thus denying the uniqueness of Calvary. Vatican II continued the double focus of Trent by presenting change without any transformation of doctrine.

5. Pope John Paul II (May 25, 1995)

On May 25, 1995, Pope John Paul II released a 105-page Encyclical letter entitled *Ut Unum Sint* ("that they may all be one")—words from Christ's prayer (John 17:21, KJV). The pope said, "In our ecumenical age, marked by the Second Vatican Council, the mission of the Bishop of Rome is particularly directed to recalling the need for full communion among Christ's disciples." This is true "especially as the year 2000 approaches, a year which Christians will celebrate as a sacred Jubilee" commemorating the Incarnation.[48]

Concurring with Pope John XXIII,

Pope John Paul II says: "What unites us is much greater than what divides us."[49] In other words, seek unity on what the churches have in common. The pope assures his readers that "we are on the way toward full unity," for "truly the Lord has taken us by the hand and is guiding us."[50] John Paul II notes that "with increasing frequency Christians are working together to defend human dignity, to promote peace, to apply the Gospel to social life, to bring the Christian spirit to the world of science and of the arts. They find themselves ever more united in striving to meet the sufferings and the needs of our time: hunger, natural disasters and social injustice." In fact, "Christians are becoming ever more united in their rejection of violence, every kind of violence, from wars to social injustice."[51]

The pope is right in stating that the basis of unity is truth. "Love for the truth is the deepest dimension of any authentic quest for full communion between Christians. . . . Full communion of course will have to come about through the acceptance of the whole truth into which the Holy Spirit guides Christ's disciples."[52] The Spirit of Truth has manifested that truth in Scripture alone. But the pope believes the Spirit has also worked through "the great Tradition" and the "Church's living Magesterium."[53]

John Paul asks "how much further we must travel until that blessed day when full unity in faith will be attained and we can celebrate together in peace the Holy Eucharist of the Lord." He notes that "the obligation to respect the truth is absolute," and then enumerates those absolute truths as areas for fuller study. "(1) the relationship between Sacred Scripture, as the highest authority in matters of faith, and Sacred Tradition, as indispensable to the interpretation of the Word of God; (2) the Eucharist, as the Sacrament of the Body and Blood of Christ, an offering of praise to the Father, the sacrificial memorial and Real Presence of Christ and the sanctifying outpouring of the Holy Spirit; (3) Ordination, as a Sacrament, to the threefold ministry of the episcopate, presbyterate and diconate; (4) the Magesterium of the Church, entrusted to the Pope and the Bishops in communion with him, understood as a responsibility and an authority exercised in the name of Christ for teaching and safeguarding the faith; (5) the Virgin Mary, as Mother of God and Icon of the Church, the spiritual Mother who intercedes for Christ's disciples and for all humanity."[54] These nonbiblical doctrines remain unchanged in Catholic theology.

The pope turns to the common martyrology held by the churches. He states that "the communion between our Communities, even if still incomplete, is truly and solidly grounded in the full communion of the saints—those who, at the end of a life faithful to grace, are in communion with Christ in glory. These saints come from all the Churches and Ecclesial Communities which gave them entrance into the communion of salvation."[55] To ground union on the "full communion of the saints" is not biblical, as we will see in later chapters investigating the state of the dead. Scripture simply does not teach the fact of Mary, saints, and martyrs living in heaven in communion today. Even if it were in Scripture, communion in heaven cannot be the basis of communion on earth. Biblical truth is the product of the "Spirit of truth," and so doctrinal truth is the only basis of authentic unity under the Spirit of truth. For Jesus, speaking of His true successor, the Holy Spirit, and not Peter, said, "the Spirit of truth . . . will guide you into all truth" (John 16:13). "He will bring glory to me" (verse 14).

In his final exhortation, the pope refers to his Apostolic Letter *Tertio Millennio Adveniente,* sent on November 10, 1994. "In my recent Letter to the Bishops, clergy and faithful of the Catholic Church indicating the path to be followed toward the celebration of the *Great Jubilee of the Holy Year 2000,* I wrote that 'the best preparation for the new millennium can only be expressed in a renewed commitment to apply, as faithfully as possible, the teachings of Vatican II to the life of every individual and of the whole Church.' The Second Vatican Council is the great beginning—the Advent as it were—of the journey leading us to the threshold of the Third Millennium. Given the importance which the Council attributed to the work of rebuilding Christian unity, and in this our age of grace for ecumenism, I thought it necessary to reaffirm the fundamental convictions which the Council impressed upon the consciousness of the Catholic Church, recalling them in the light of the progress subsequently made toward the full communion of all the baptized. There is no doubt that the Holy Spirit is active in this endeavor and that he is leading the Church to the full realization of the Father's plan, in conformity with the will of Christ."[56]

Thus the pope credits the Holy Spirit with directing the reaffirmation of nonbiblical Catholic doctrines at Vatican II and considers faithfulness to the teachings of Vatican II will lead to true union. Jesus in His prayer for union pleaded to the Father "that they may be one as we are one" (John 17:22). The Father, Son, and Holy Spirit are united in truth. In this same prayer for unity among His disciples, Jesus asked the Father to "sanctify them by the truth: your word is truth" (verse 17). No true unity can exist among Christians apart from a unity over biblical truth. Nonbiblical doctrines, common social concerns, the fact of martyrs—none of them is the right basis for unity.

6. The Coming Great Church

In his book *Ecumenism and the Evangelical* Jacob Marcellus Kik has a chapter entitled "The Coming Great Church." Along with other postmillennialists, those who hold that Christ will come after the millennium of peace on earth, he believes that the churches will unite as one before the Second Advent. He finds the first hint of this in Genesis 3:15 where God said to the serpent, "I will put enmity between you and the woman, and between your offspring and hers; he will crush your head, and you will strike his heel." He rightly sees Christ as the One who brings Satan's defeat but wrongly believes that He works it out in history so that the millennium comes before the Second Advent, a view that we will evaluate in a later chapter.

It is pertinent to our discussion to

note that Roman Catholics interpret Genesis 3:15 differently. They follow the Latin Vulgate, which says "she," rather than "he," will crush Satan's head. The word "she" applies to Mary, in place of the "he" that refers to Christ. In Catholic theology it seems that Mary has become the great unifier of churches in the end-time. They see the unprecedented number of alleged apparitions of Mary today as possibly contributing to the uniting of churches.

In his 1987 (Marian year) encyclical *Redemptoris Mater* Pope John Paul II presented Mary as the one who can promote unity among Christian churches. "Why should we not all together look to her as *our common Mother,* who prays for the unity of God's family and who 'precedes' us all at the head of the long line of witnesses of faith in the one Lord, the Son of God, who was conceived in her virginal womb by the power of the Holy Spirit?"[57]

Imagine the push for unity when Satan comes as Christ and calls all to follow him in observing Sunday! It will be the final nonbiblical doctrine that unites the churches, a doctrine invented by error in the post-New Testament church. Then those who follow Christ and honor His Sabbath will leave these churches—along with a world that joins them. The important thing to focus on is this—the ecumenical movement is another example of Satan's attempts to hide Christ and His truth, and is an important part of final events on planet Earth.

Years ago God showed Ellen G. White the end-time. The insights He presented her are as up-to-date as the sources referred to in this chapter. She wrote that among Protestants, "the opinion is gaining ground that, after all, we do not differ so widely upon vital points as has been supposed, and that a little concession on our part will bring us into a better understanding with Rome."[58] But the fact is, "when the leading churches of the United States, uniting upon such points of doctrine as are held by them in common, shall influence the state to enforce their decrees and to sustain their institutions, then Protestant America will have formed an image of the Roman hierarchy, and the infliction of civil penalties upon dissenters will inevitably result."[59] Eventually "there will be a national apostasy which will end only in national ruin."[60] In fact, "every soul that is not fully surrendered to God . . . will form an alliance with Satan against heaven, and join in battle against the Ruler of the universe."[61]

The end-game is all the world wondering after and worshiping erroneous theology and practice and thus unwittingly the devil who works through them (Rev. 13:1-4). America will take the lead in this final union (verses 13:11-16). That's the universal destiny of the ecumenical movement.

---

[1] From an evangelical perspective, see David F. Wright in *New Dictionary of Theology,* eds. Sinclair B. Ferguson, David F. Wright, and J. I. Packer (Downers Grove, Ill.: InterVarsity, 1988), pp. 219-222. He gives perceptive critiques; and T. P. Weber in *Evangelical Dictionary of Theology,* ed. Walter A. Ellwell (Grand Rapids: Baker, 1987), pp. 340-342. From a Catholic perspective, see August B. Hasler, Victor Conzemius, and Karl Rahner in *Sacramentum Mundi,* ed. Karl Rahner (New York: Herder and Herder, n.p.d.), vol. 2, pp. 191-202. Other sources include: R. Rouse and S. C. Neill, eds., *A History of the Ecumenical Movement,* 1517-1948; H. Fey, ed.; *A History of the Ecumenical Movement,* 1948-1968; R. M. Brown, *The Ecumenical Revolution;* N. Goodall,

The Ecumenical Movement

The Ecumenical Movement and Ecumenical Progress: A Decade of Change in the Ecumenical Movement, 1961-1971; J. D. Douglas, ed., *Let the Earth Hear His Voice;* B. Leeming, *The Vatican Council and Christian Unity;* J. D. Murch, *Cooperation Without Compromise: A History of the National Association of Evangelicals.*

[2] Weber in *Evangelical Dictionary of Theology,* p. 341.

[3] *The Final Report* (London, 1982), p. 83, as quoted by David F. Wright in *New Dictionary of Theology,* pp. 219, 220.

[4] Hasler in *Sacramentum Mundi,* vol. 2, p. 193.

[5] Paul G. Schrotenboer, *Roman Catholicism: A Contemporary Evangelical Perspective* (Grand Rapids: Baker, 1987), pp. 18, 19.

[6] Walter M. Abbott, S.J. in Schrotenboer.

[7] For helpful insights, see Justo L. Gonzales, *The Story of Christianity* (San Francisco: Harper & Row, 1984), vol. 1, pp. 413, 414; and August B. Hasler, Victor Conzemius, Karl Rahner, Gotthold Hasenbuttl, Johannes Brosseder, Willehad P. Eckert, Eduard Stakemeir, and Angar Ahlbrecht in *Sacramentum Mundi* (New York: Herder and Herder), vol. 1, pp. 191-212.

[8] *The Documents of Vatican II,* p. 344.

[9] *Ibid.,* p. 345.

[10] *Ibid.,* p. 346.

[11] *Ibid.,* p. 348.

[12] *Ibid.,* p. 346.

[13] *Ibid.,* p. 362.

[14] *Ibid.,* p. 343.

[15] Karl Rahner in *Sacramentum Mundi,* vol. 2, p. 200.

[16] David F. Wright, in *New Dictionary of Theology,* pp. 219, 220.

[17] Gerald L. Bray, *Creeds, Councils and Christ* (Downers Grove, Ill.: InterVarsity, 1984), p. 32.

[18] Karl Lehmann and Wolfhart Pannenberg, eds., trans. Margaret Kohl, *The Condemnations of the Reformation Era: Do They Still Divide?* (Minneapolis: Fortress, 1989), p. 14.

[19] Michael Horton, foreword to R. C. Sproul, *Faith Alone: The Evangelical Doctrine of Justification* (Grand Rapids: Baker, 1995), p. 12.

[20] James R. White, *Answers to Catholic Claims: A Discussion of Biblical Authority* (Southbridge, Mass.: Crowne, 1990), p. iv.

[21] Ansgar Ahlbrecht, in *Sacramentum Mundi,* vol. 1, p. 211.

[22] Walter M. Abbott in *The Documents of Vatican II,* Introduction to the Decree on Ecumenism, p. 339.

[23] *Ibid.,* p. 354.

[24] Weber, p. 342.

[25] Davis Duggins, "Evangelicals and Catholics: Across the Divide: How Can We Relate to One Another in This Secular Age," *Moody Monthly,* November 1993, p. 12.

[26] Johannes Brosseder in *Sacramentum Mundi,* vol. 1, p. 207.

[27] Charles Colson in Keith A. Fournier, *Evangelical Catholics* (Nashville: Nelson, 1990), p. vi.

[28] J. Daryl Charles, "Evangelical-Catholic Dialogue: Basis, Boundaries, Benefits," *Pro ecclesia* 3, No. 3 (1994): p. 293.

[29] John M. Frame, *Evangelical Reunion: Denominations and the One Body of Christ* (Grand Rapids: Baker, 1991), p. 84.

[30] Ronald H. Nash, ed., *Evangelical Renewal in the Mainline Churches* (Westchester, Ill.: Crossway, 1987), p. 24.

[31] *Ibid.,* p. 76.

[32] *Ibid.,* p. 85.

[33] George Carey, *A Tale of Two Cities: Can Protestants and Catholics Get Together?* (Downers Grove, Ill.: InterVarsity, 1985), pp. 161, 162. In speaking of five common theological tenets that unite evangelicals, John Warwick Montgomery also takes a minimalist approach to unity, which fails to take into consideration doctrinal distinctives that are biblical. His essentials are: conviction that the Bible alone is God's objective inerrant revelation to humanity; subscription to the ecumenical confessions as expressing the trinitarian heart of biblical religion; belief that the Reformation confessions adequately convey the soteriological essence of the scriptural message, namely, salvation by grace alone through faith in the atoning death and resurrection of the God-man Jesus Christ;

stress upon personal, dynamic, living commitment to Christ and the resultant prophetic witness for Him to the unbelieving world; and a strong eschatological perspective. *Ecumenicity, Evangelicals, and Rome* (Grand Rapids: Zondervan, 1969), p. 17.

[34] Richard John Neuhaus, *The Catholic Moment: The Paradox of the Church in the Postmodern World* (San Francisco: Harper & Row, 1987), p. 287.

[35] H. B. Swete, *Commentary on the Apocalypse,* p. 257. Quoted by Wilbur M. Smith in "Armageddon, *Baker's Dictionary of Theology,* p. 64.

[36] Charles Colson (Prison Fellowship), Juan Diaz-Villar, S.J. (Catholic Hispanic Ministries), Avery Dulles, S.J. (Fordham University), Bishop Francis George (Diocese of Yakima, Washington), Kent Hill (Eastern Nazarene College), Jesse Miranda (Assemblies of God), Msgr. William Murphy (Chancellor of the Archdiocese of Boston), Richard John Neuhaus (Institute on Religion and Public Life), Brian O'Connell (World Evangelical Fellowship), Herbert Schlossberg, Archbishop Francis Stafford (Archdiocese of Denver), George Weigel (Ethics and Public Policy Center), and John White (Geneva College and the National Association of Evangelicals).

[37] William Abraham (Perkins School of Theology), Elizabeth Achtemeir (Union Theological Seminary—Virginia), William Bently Ball (Harrisburg, Pennsylvania), Bill Bright (Campus Crusade for Christ), Robert Destro (Catholic University of America), Augustine DiNoia, O.P. (Dominican House of Studies), Joseph P. Fitzpatrick, S.J. (Fordham University), Keith Fournier (American Center for Law and Justice), Bishop William Frey (Trinity Episcopal School for Ministry), Mary Ann Gledon (Harvard Law School), Os. Guinness (Trinity Forum), Nathan Hatch (University of Notre Dame), James Hitchcock (St. Louis University), Peter Kreeft (Boston College), Matthew Lamb (Boston College), Ralph Martin (Renewal Ministries), Richard Mouw (Fuller Theological Seminary), Mark Noll (Wheaton College), Michael Novak (American Enterprise Institute), Cardinal John Joseph O'Connor (Archdiocese of New York), Thomas Oden (Drew University), J. I. Packer (Regent College, British Columbia), Pat Robertson (Regent College), John Rodgers (Trinity Episcopal School of Ministry), and Bishop Carlos A. Sevilla, S.J. (Archdiocese of San Francisco).

[38] Dave Hunt, *A Woman Rides the Beast* (Eugene, Oreg.: Harvest House, 1994), p. 5.

[39] John Calvin, *Institutes of the Christian Religion* (London: James Clarke, 1962), vol. 2, p. 37.

[40] R. C. Sproul, *Faith Alone: The Evangelical Doctrine of Justification* (Grand Rapids: Baker Books, 1995), p. 36.

[41] John MacArthur, quoted by Davis Duggins, *Moody Monthly,* November 1993, p. 15.

[42] *The Canons and Decrees of the Council of Trent,* trans. H. J. Schroeder, O.P. (Rockford, Ill.: Tan Books, 1978).

[43] *Ibid.,* pp. 42-46. Thirty-three canons oppose the Reformation doctrine of justification by faith.

[44] J. Daryl Charles, "Evangelical-Catholic Dialogue: Basis, Boundaries, Benefits," *Pro Ecclesi.* 3, No. 2 (1994): 305. Charles is optimistic that unity can be achieved. He looks at matters shared by Catholics and non-Catholics but ignores the differences that mitigate against union.

[45] *Catechism of the Catholic Church,* pp. 363, 489, 490.

[46] Norman L. Geisler and Ralph E. MacKenzie, *Roman Catholics and Evangelicals,* p. 501.

[47] *Ibid.,* p. 502.

[48] John Paul II, *Ut Unum Sint* (Boston: Pauline, 1995), pp. 11-15.

[49] *Ibid.,* p. 32.

[50] *Ibid.,* pp. 35, 37.

[51] *Ibid.,* pp. 83-85.

[52] *Ibid.,* p. 46.

[53] *Ibid.,* p. 48.

[54] *Ibid.,* pp. 87-89.

[55] *Ibid.,* p. 93.

[56] *Ibid.,* p. 107.

[57] John Paul II, *The Encyclicals of John Paul II (Redemptoris Mater),* ed. J. Michael Miller, C.S.B. (Huntington, Ind.: Our Sunday Visitor, 1996), p. 386.

[58] E. G. White, *The Great Controversy,* p. 563.

[59] *Ibid.,* p. 445.

[60] *The Seventh-day Adventist Bible Commentary,* Ellen G. White Comments, vol. 7, p. 976.

[61] E. G. White, *Testimonies to Ministers,* p. 465.

Chapter 10

Modern Spiritualism

Spiritualism has many forms: séances, channeling, spirit-guides, delusive teachings, impersonations, signs and wonders, miracles, and more. It consists of any way that demons work to deceive and destroy. "They are spirits of demons performing miraculous signs, and they go out to the kings of the whole world, to gather them for the battle on the great day of God Almighty" (Rev. 16:14).

Involving the whole confederacy of evil united to take over the planet, it is a strategic part of final events on earth. When did it begin?

"The Spiritualist movement began in the United States at Hydesville, N.Y., in 1848. The mediums were two little sisters named Margaret and Katherine Fox. The story is that a man had been murdered in their house. The girls said the spirit of this man returned at night and rapped on the walls and furniture of their room. The children said the spirit agreed to answer questions by giving a certain number of raps for 'yes' and a different number for 'no.' The story about this spirit spread. The children were taken to Rochester, N.Y. According to the story, the spirit went along with them. More and more persons claimed to hear the spirit. Within a few months the rappings stirred interest in many countries. Soon other persons said they were mediums, and that spirits came to rap for them."[1]

In 1850 a young girl named Ellen G. White received a vision. "I saw the rapidity with which this delusion was spreading," she said afterward. "A train of cars was shown me, going with the speed of lightning. The angel bade me look carefully. I fixed my eyes upon the train. It seemed that the whole world was on board. Then he showed me the conductor, a fair, stately person, whom all the passengers looked up to and reverenced. I was perplexed and asked my attending angel who it was. He said, 'It is Satan. He is the conductor, in the form of an angel of light. He has taken the world captive. They are given over to strong delusions, to believe a lie that they may be damned. His agent, the highest in order next to him, is the engineer, and others of his agents are employed in different offices as he may need them, and they are all going with lightning speed to perdition.' "[2]

Here are two end-time forms of revelation—spiritualism and the last-days' gift of prophecy. Spiritualism bent on glorifying Satan, the gift of prophecy as the testimony of Jesus (Rev. 19:10). One reveals Satan, the other Christ.

The Pretense of Spiritualism

Spiritualism constantly adopts new disguises in the end-time. "While it formerly denounced Christ and the Bible, it now *professes* to accept both."[3] Yet "many will be confronted by the spirits of devils personating beloved relatives or friends and declaring the most dangerous heresies. These visitants will appeal to our tenderest sympathies and will work miracles to sustain their pretensions."[4] "Among the most successful agencies of the great deceiver are the delusive teachings and lying wonders of spiritualism."[5]

By 1893 spiritualism considered itself a church and initiated a program to convert the world. A year later, it claimed 60 million adherents and published 200 journals—an astounding accomplishment. In 1913 its adherents founded the Progressive Spiritual Church to establish spiritualism on a more religious basis. The *Encyclopedia Americana* defines spiritualism as "a religious sect or denomination, a form of Christianity."[6]

By 1972 three major churches existed: the International General Assembly of Spiritualists, with headquarters in Norfolk, Virginia; the National Spiritual Alliance of the United States of America, with headquarters in Lake Pleasant, Massachusetts; and The National Spiritualist Association of Churches, with headquarters in Milwaukee, Wisconsin.[7] "As the teachings of spiritualism are accepted by the churches, the restraint imposed upon the carnal heart is removed, and the profession of religion will become a cloak to conceal the basest iniquity. A belief in spiritual manifestations opens the door to seducing spirits and doctrines of devils, and thus the influence of evil angels will be felt in the churches."[8] And it's happening today in an unprecedented way.

No Protection in Churches Against Spiritualism

Satan plans to take over the world, which includes the churches. "Little by little he has prepared the way for his masterpiece of deception in the development of spiritualism. He has not yet reached the full accomplishment of his designs; but it will be reached in the last remnant of time."[9] According to Ellen White, it will be easy for Satan. "The popular ministry cannot successfully resist spiritualism. They have nothing wherewith to shield their flocks from its baleful influence. Much of the sad results of spiritualism will rest upon ministers of this age; for they have trampled the truth under their feet, and in its stead have preferred fables. The sermon which Satan preached to Eve upon the immortality of the soul—'Ye shall not surely die'—they have reiterated from the pulpit; and the people receive it as pure Bible truth. It is the foundation of spiritualism."[10]

Modern Spiritualism

The idea that the dead live on after death crept into Christianity from pagan sources and became a part of Catholic tradition as well as the teaching of most other denominations. This false doctrine has permeated not only most of Christianity but the non-Christian religions as well. So most of the world has no protection against Satan's use of spiritualism in the end-time.

Role of Spiritualism in the End-time

Scripture warns about the activity of spiritualism in the end-time. "The Spirit clearly says that in later times some will abandon the faith and follow deceiving spirits and things taught by demons" (1 Tim. 4:1). For indeed, "the coming of the lawless one will be in accordance with the work of Satan displayed in all kinds of counterfeit miracles, signs and wonders" (2 Thess. 2:9). Jesus warned that "false Christs and false prophets will appear and perform great signs and miracles to deceive even the very elect—if that be possible" (Matt. 24:24).

1. Spiritualism to Capture the World

Satan wages an all-out struggle during the end-time to conquer the world by taking human minds captive. Spiritualism provides the agency to implement his plan. Fallen angels seek to possess people just as they did in Christ's time. They may not now have such individuals writhing on the ground in traditional demon-possession, but they do take over and control the human mind nevertheless. Demons attempt to get people to believe in counterfeit revelations and thus nullify God's true revelation.

Revelation 16:13 says that spirits of demons will work through the dragon, the beast, and the false prophet. "They are spirits of demons performing miraculous signs, and they go out to the kings of the whole world, to gather them for the battle on the great day of God Almighty" (verse 14). It will be when spiritualism has the whole world on board, as Ellen White saw in her train vision.

The Old Testament does not mention fallen angels. "Old Testament history presents occasional mention of their existence and agency; but it was during the time when Christ was upon earth that evil spirits manifested their power in the most striking manner. Christ had come to enter upon the plan devised for man's redemption, and Satan determined to assert his right to control the world."[11] He will do the same again—just before Christ's second coming.

2. Worse Than We Can Imagine

"Spiritualism is about to take the world captive. There are many who think that spiritualism is upheld through trickery and imposture, but this is far from the truth. Superhuman power is working in a variety of ways, and few have any idea as to what will be the manifestations of spiritualism in the future."[12] Ellen G. White had a sneak preview of what's coming. "People know but little, yet, of the corrupting influence of spiritualism. The curtain was lifted, and much of its dreadful work was revealed to me. I was shown some who have had an experience in spiritualism, and have since renounced it, who shudder as they reflect upon how near they came to utter ruin. They had lost control of themselves, and Satan made them do that which they detested. But even they have but a faint idea of spiritualism as it is."[13]

The imagery of the collapse of Babylon in Revelation 18 describes how bad the results of spiritualism will be in most churches. "Fallen! Fallen is Babylon the Great! She has become a home for demons and a haunt for every evil spirit" (Rev. 18:2). The demonic will be in almost total control of Christianity. It will be the worst condition ever known throughout the history of the Christian church.

The tragedy is that demon-possessed Christians will be no more able to free themselves than the demoniacs in Christ's day. Worse still—they will feel no need for change. They think that God is working mightily in their midst through the miracles and the spiritualistic messages they receive. Paul warns: "See to it that no one takes you captive through hollow and deceptive philosophy, which depends on human tradition and the basic principles of this world rather than on Christ" (Col. 2:8). Commenting on this verse, Ellen G. White said: "I was directed to this Scripture as especially applying to modern spiritualism."[14]

3. Inward Focus of Spiritualism

The first revelation God gave to the end-time remnant through Ellen G. White was to keep their eyes on Christ. That continues to be the only safe way. Why? Because Satan seeks to wrench the gaze away from Christ to focus within human beings. Christ always calls Christians to look beyond themselves. Satan pulls the gaze within. If he can keep their attention on themselves, or within the church, he can push Christ out of view. He can get human beings absorbed within themselves. Then they either get proud or discouraged—either is self-centered and is spiritual slavery.

Consider what spiritualism's *Centennial Book* teaches. It claims that spiritualism is "to transform, if not, perhaps, in time, do away with theology, which has been maintained by a hierarchy, and to make *"the life of the Spirit* the all in all in religion, as it was the all in all with the founder of Christianity." According to this book, Jesus taught that "salvation comes from *within*, not from without. There could be no such thing, in the nature of things, as a vicarious atonement for the sins of the world. Man can be *at one* with the Universal Spirit only through his own spiritual vitality. That alone is Salvation."[15]

The idea that human beings don't need a Saviour is obviously an attack against Christ. It argues that salvation results from within, from human experience, not from Christ. But it thrusts humans back upon themselves and their supposed resources, and away from the only Saviour who can help them. "Satan is making the world believe that the Bible is a mere fiction, or at least a book suited to the infancy of the race, but now to be lightly regarded, or cast aside as obsolete. And to take the place of the word of God he holds out spiritual manifestations. Here is a channel wholly under his *control;* by this means he can make the world believe what he will."[16]

Much study today focuses on spirituality. "All major religions have spirituality," some claim. So how can Christianity claim to be the only true religion? When we study the charismatic movement, we'll see tongues promoted as a spiritual phenomena. Tongues make doctrinal differences obsolete. "It's not what you believe, but what you do that counts." Human tongues have silenced God's Word. The bottom line is simple. God is working through all religions, an idea popular today. Many roads lead to heaven. This uniting on experience, not doctrine, has its origin in spiritualism, as demons work through paganism as well as Christianity (see Rev. 16:13, 14).

Masterpiece of Deception

We noticed above that spiritualism is Satan's masterpiece of deception because it worked so well in Eden. Satan took the form of a beautiful creature called a serpent and, speaking through it, caused Eve to fall. His simple approach was "seeing is believing." She observed that even though the serpent ate the forbidden fruit, it still remained alive. Eve "saw that the fruit of the tree was good for food and pleasing to the eye, and also desirable for gaining wisdom" (Gen. 3:6), for the serpent could speak her language.

The fall of humanity came through an appeal to the senses, the trump card in Satan's arsenal for the end-time. Through miracles, messages, and his own impersonation as Christ, he'll take the world captive. The way he launched the struggle between good and evil on earth is the way it will conclude. But there'll be an enormous difference between a local happening in Eden and the global impact at the end-time. Imagine satellite television instantly flashing worldwide the counterfeit Christ's arrival on the planet. But the method is the same. "Seeing is believing" will work. The entire world will fall for the counterfeit—except those who have focused on the real Christ and the real Scriptures. Spiritualism provides Satan's groundwork for that final delusion.

[1] *World Book Encyclopedia* (1972), vol. 18, p. 621.
[2] Ellen G. White, *Early Writings,* p. 263.
[3] E. G. White, *The Great Controversy,* p. 558.
[4] *Ibid.,* p. 560.
[5] *Ibid.,* p. 524.
[6] *Encyclopedia Americana* (1985), vol. 25, p. 514.
[7] *World Book Encyclopedia,* vol. 18, p. 621.
[8] E. G. White, *The Great Controversy,* pp. 603, 604.
[9] E. G. White, *Maranatha* (Washington, D.C.: Review and Herald, 1976), p. 166.
[10] E. G. White, *Testimonies for the Church,* vol. 1, p. 344.
[11] E. G. White, *The Great Controversy,* pp. 513, 514.
[12] E. G. White, *Evangelism,* pp. 602, 603.
[13] Ellen G. White, *Spiritual Gifts* (Battle Creek, Mich.: SDA Pub. Assn., 1864), vol. 4b, p. 102.
[14] *Ibid.,* p. 87.
[15] *Spiritualism's Centennial Book,* p. 50, quoted in LeRoy Edwin Froom, *Spiritualism Today* (Washington, D.C.: Review and Herald, 1963), p. 23.
[16] E. G. White, *The Great Controversy,* p. 557. (Italics supplied.)

Chapter 11

The Charismatic Movement

So spiritualism is Satan's trump card. Spirits employ all possible religious avenues. It's popular today to say God is working though all religions, but often it's really Satan. What, for example, about the charismatic movement, found in nearly all churches?

Because the charismatic movement is such an important part of Satan's final push to take the world captive, because it is one important manifestation of spiritualism in the end-time, we must carefully evaluate this contemporary phenomenon.

Challenge to End-time Christians

I once pastored the Fatherland Seventh-day Adventist Church in downtown Nashville, Tennessee. Another denomination used the building on Sundays. One day I decided to attend the Sunday service. Walking down the road approaching the church, I heard bedlam from within. Arriving at the church, I had just begun to climb the stairs when someone shrieked. "He's received the Spirit!" "Glory! Hallelujah," people shouted. Because no one had seen me, I turned and got out of there as quickly as I could.

Years ago some Adventist youth tried speaking in tongues. Roland Hegstad's book *Rattling the Gates,* as well a series in *Insight* magazine, dealt with the problem. Dr. Lowe, a dentist and graduate from Loma Linda University, wrote of his experience of speaking in tongues in *The Full Gospel Businessmen's Fellowship* journal, a Pentecostal magazine that goes to different parts of the world. Splashed across the glossy front cover were the words "Seventh-day Adventist" and "Glossolalia" (i.e., tongues-speaking). Recently two Andrews University scholars wrote books on speaking in tongues, taking different positions on the phenomena: Gerhard F. Hasel, *Speaking in Tongues: Biblical Speaking in Tongues and Contemporary Glossolalia;*[1] and William E. Richardson, *Speaking in Tongues: Is It Still the Gift of the Spirit?*[2] Because speaking in tongues is an important part of Satan's end-time counterfeit, we will look at the phenomena with a degree of depth. Seventh-day Adventists need to understand what is involved so they can evaluate this movement and help their Christian friends to do the same.

Extensive Influence

The Pentecostal movement, with its phenomenal outburst of tongues, has swept across the Christian world.[3] Called the third force in Christendom,[4] it constitutes what some have seen as "a revolution comparable in importance" with the Protestant Reformation and the launching of the apostolic church.[5]

But it's more than a third force in Christianity, for it invaded Protestantism in the early 1960s and Catholicism in 1967.[6] Pope John XXIII prayed for a new Pentecost,[7] and his Vatican II Council encouraged charismatic gifts[8] —in answer to the pope's wishes.[9] But who could have predicted the powerful influence that one of those gifts would have? For just two years after Vatican II, tongues broke out in Catholicism and spread to Catholics in almost 100 countries in just 10 years![10] Today tongues-speech appears within every major denomination,[11] but not among many Seventh-day Adventists.[12] Never has a movement taken over the churches to such a degree.

At the Fifth Pentecostal World Conference in Toronto, Canada, in 1958, the keynote speaker observed: "They say Pentecost [i.e., the Pentecostal movement] is the *third* great force in Christendom. But it is really the *first* great force. . . . Who will deny that the first period of the Christian era was in every sense Pentecostal? . . . But the Church did not maintain its purity. . . . Hence, the necessity for the Reformation. . . . But this in turn . . . lacked completeness, lapsed into formality and dead ritualism, which led to the need for revival. Hence the great Wesleyan revival. . . . But all of this needed a new and greater dynamic. Hence, the Pentecostal revival came to ripen the grain and bring it to harvest."[13]

Compare this with the Seventh-day Adventist Church, also partly out of Wesleyan or Methodist roots.[14] Its mission is to restore apostolic truth (not tongues), to be the completion of the Reformation, and to have a prophetic remnant end-time mission. Pentecostals also have what they perceive as a prophetic mission.

Proponents of the tongues movement (whether in its classical Pentecostal form or in its neo, or charismatic movement development) believe tongues to be the fulfillment of Joel 2:28.[15] They view the phenomenal spread of tongues throughout all denominations as the promised latter rain just before the Second Advent. They see it as the outpouring of the Holy Spirit in a second Pentecost—a repetition of the Acts 2 gift of tongues. Seeking to repeat that Pentecost as the ultimate in Christian experience, they originated their name "Pentecostal."

Astonishing Growth

Actually, Pentecostalism didn't begin until the turn of the twentieth century, and yet by the year 2000 it is projected to be 300 million strong.[16] Many consider its spread the most remarkable in the Christian world.[17] Considered the "fastest-growing Christian group in the world"[18] and "the greatest spiritual renewal the church has known since the days of the apostles,"[19] it has had perhaps unparalleled impact on the churches.[20] Its "worldwide sweep"[21] has entrenched it even in Russia[22] and China.[23] On the American scene more than 3 million have spoken in tongues,[24] with one new charismatic church being built each day.[25] As R. G. Gromacki concludes: "This movement, with its emphasis upon glossolalia, is a force that must be reckoned with."[26]

Roots and Focus

The immediate roots of Pentecostalism occur in the holiness movement that developed out of Methodism. Each of them share a common focus on an additional experience beyond regeneration, or on a work of the Spirit beyond accepting Christ. (1) The Wesleys believed in the second work of sanctification beyond justification, (2) the holiness movement (including its Keswick expression)[27] believes in the second blessing of the Spirit beyond conversion, and (3) Pentecostals believe in the baptism of the Spirit beyond baptism into Christ.

Thus Pentecostals speak of the *full* gospel.[28] They insist that conversion comes short of obtaining the fullness. Tongues-speaking is the fullness. Then you know you have arrived, they say, because *conversion, plus tongues, constitutes the full gospel.*

Tongues-speakers claim that the believers *have to receive tongues before they can experience any other gift.*[29] Not only that, they hold that tongues are the entrance to all the spiritual *fruit* also.[30] How do nontongues-speaking committed Christians also exhibit such spiritual fruit? Some even propose that tongues are even the entrance to *doctrines.*[31] What does that mean? Tongues also serve as the gateway to another spiritual dimension[32] and maybe the only way to deeper levels of spirituality.[33] One gets the impression that, for them, tongues are more important than Christ. We'll look at this aspect later.

On the broader spectrum, a tongues recipient does not only become eligible for other gifts and fruit, but becomes a channel for gifts for others.[34] So whether for oneself or for others, Pentecostals consider tongues as an absolute prerequisite. No wonder the experience is so important to Pentecostals and charismatics.

Importance of Acts to Tongues-speakers

The book of Acts is the primary biblical book for Pentecostals and charismatics. Not only because of the day of Pentecost with its tongues-speech (Acts 2) but also because of chapters 8, 10, and 19. We'll briefly consider why. In Samaria some persons accepted the word of God (Acts 8:14), but Peter and John, when sent to them, discovered that they had not received the Holy Spirit (verse 16). So the apostles prayed and laid hands on them, and the people received the Holy Spirit (verse 17). Tongues-speakers believe this represents a Spirit baptism subsequent to conversion, or to hearing God's Word. And some believe those baptized here spoke in tongues because Simon the Sorcerer immediately wanted to buy the same power (verses 18, 19).

The next example concerns Peter's visit to the Gentile Cornelius. As Peter spoke the Holy Spirit was poured out, and the people responded in tongues (Acts 10:44-46). The final example concerns the Ephesians and Paul's encounter with them. They hadn't received the Holy Spirit, for they hadn't even heard of Him (Acts 19:1, 2). But they had accepted John's baptism (verse 3), and so were believers. Paul placed his hands on them, the Holy Spirit descended on them, and they spoke in tongues (verses 4-7).

Tongues-speakers present the day of Pentecost and the three later occasions as examples of a Spirit baptism subsequent to conversion. After all, the 12 disciples had been converted long before Pentecost—which was also true of those in Samaria, of Cornelius the Gentile, and of the 12 at Ephesus.

Tongues-speakers also note that Paul lists tongues as one of the gifts in 1 Corinthians. But when Paul judges tongues as the least of the gifts (1 Cor. 12:28), observing that not every one has the tongue gift (verse 29) and that it will one day cease (1 Cor. 13:8), then tongues-speakers make a distinction between tongues as a gift (1 Corinthians) and tongues as a sign (Acts).[35] *Tongues-speakers believe that tongues are the* most *important sign of the Spirit's baptism* (Acts) *even though they are the* least *of the gifts* (1 Corinthians).

The Debate on Tongues in Acts and Corinthians

Before evaluating the tongues-speaking claims, we need to look at the spectrum of interpretations regarding tongues in Acts and First Corinthians. We will next take note of the longer ending of Mark 16, in which we find the only Gospel reference to tongues. Then we'll enumerate the major views and give some examples of their exponents in the footnotes.

1. The tongues of Acts are real languages.[36]

2. The tongues of Acts are ecstatic sounds.[37]

3. The tongues of 1 Corinthians are real languages.[38]

4. The tongues of 1 Corinthians are ecstatic sounds.[39]

Obviously such interpretations directly oppose each other. Other variations also exist. For example: 1. Acts 2 includes both ecstatic sounds, followed by Peter's sermon as an interpretation.[40] 2. Peter's sermon, not tongues, made the converts.[41] 3. The tongues in Acts 2 were addressed to God and not to human beings.[42] 4. The tongues in Acts 2 were not for evangelism, even though foreign languages—they were a sign of the Holy Spirit.[43] 5. Acts 2 includes ecstatic sounds, which some listeners thought they recognized as foreign languages.[44] 6. Acts 2 was each disciple speaking every one of the foreign languages.[45] 7. Acts 2 were languages unknown as spoken but known as heard.[46] 8. Acts 2 was not the gift of tongues at all, but the gift of hearing,[47] for as Peter spoke all foreigners present heard his words in their own language.[48] 9. The tongues of Acts 2 were not languages, because Greek and Aramaic were known throughout the biblical world, making tongues as languages unnecessary.[49] 10. The languages of Acts 2 were not a gift to evangelize, but a sign of the Spirit's reception.[50] 11. In all the New Testament tongues are unknown foreign languages to the speakers.[51] 12. The tongues in 1 Corinthians were not a human language.[52] 13. First Corinthians reports an unlearned human language.[53]

The suggested possibilities are overwhelming! Those seeing a dissimilarity between the tongues of Acts 2 and 1 Corinthians point to Acts as being history compared to Corinthians as being doctrine,[54] and to Acts being history compared to the book of 1 Corinthians as being didactic.[55] However, those recognizing a similarity between the tongues of Acts 2 and that of 1 Corinthians suggest that we should study Corinthians in the light of Acts,[56] or Acts in the light of Corinthians[57]—thus making one or the other normative for both.

The longer ending of Mark 16, which mentions tongues, merits a few words. A majority of scholars reject the authenticity of verses 9-20, as the most reliable early manuscripts do not include them. Some consider that its tone and vocabulary is not Markan.[58] They suggest that it is definitely not first century[59] and is probably the work of an editor in the second century.[60] Others point out, however, that if this is true, then tongues-speaking continued beyond the first into that second-century church.[61] By contrast, Gerhard Hasel notes that "a careful verse-by-verse examination of all the words and phrases of Mark 16:9-20 reveals that the case for Markan authorship seems quite strong."[62] Some have suggested that Mark 16 teaches that all Christians should speak in tongues—yet neither history nor the present supports such a conclusion.[63] A number of tongues-speakers have no doubt concerning the authenticity of this passage,[64] while others consider it the great missionary Magna Carta.[65] Ellen G. White evidently accepts it,[66] as do some others.[67]

The longer Markan ending includes the divine commission with the following signs to accompany the preachers—exorcism: speaking in new tongues *(glossais lalesousin kainais,* verse 17), protection against snake's venom and drinking deadly poison (verse 18), and the promise of the ability to heal the sick (verse 19). Scholars point out that some of these things occur in other parts of the New Testament.[68] Tongues would be in this list. Interpreters understand the new tongues of Mark 16 as either languages[69] or as ecstatic sounds.[70]

Together with this plethora of

1. Akolalia	Speaker uses one language, hearer hears another.[71]
2. Babble	Never used of tongues.[72]
3. Cryptomnesia	Unknown tongue from hidden memory, perhaps from a previous life.[73]
4. Ekstasis	Predominance of the unconscious life.[74]
5. Existanto	Literally to stand outside of oneself.[75]
6. Ermeneglossia	Interpreting a tongue.[76]
7. Glossa	Ecstatic utterances,[77] languages,[78] never a natural language.[79]
8. Glossolalia	Unintelligible, noncognitive.[80]
9. Heteroglossolalia	Other speaks in their language—you hear in yours.[81]
10. Preincarnation language	Language from a supposed previous life.[82]
11. Xenolalia, Xenoglossy	Foreign language.[83]
12. Zenolalia	Foreign language.[84]

views on tongues in the Bible, one finds in the literature a number of key terms used by those who believe in tongues-speech:

With these views and terms before us, we are now ready to evaluate the tongues phenomenon from a biblical, sociological, and linguistic perspective.

Biblical Evaluation of Tongues

Some see in contemporary tongues a similarity or replication of biblical tongues.[85] Others consider them to be different.[86] Some are not sure.[87] First, we'll evaluate the claim that today's tongues are the same as biblical tongues.

Tongues-speakers consider tongues the outward sign of the inward baptism by the Holy Spirit.[88] They believe that God could have chosen any of the gifts to be this sign, yet tongues are consistently His choice in Acts.[89] Most, therefore, view tongues as *the* sign of Spirit baptism.[90] They also maintain that Spirit baptism gives them power, not purity.[91] Or as Paul Rabe, a German Pentecostal leader, put it at the 1955 Pentecostal World Conference: "By being born again we as individuals have been saved ourselves, but by the baptism of the Spirit we receive power, or shall we say power to save others. . . . By being born again we have become the children of God, but by the baptism in the Spirit we become the soldiers of Christ."[92] Thus, receiving Christ is only a beginning—to be filled with the Spirit is the full gospel, evidenced by tongues.

To carefully evaluate the tongues phenomenon we must (1) examine the two-baptism theory; (2) penetrate to the real sign value of tongues; (3) ask why Acts presents the reception of the Spirit following conversion in chapters 2, 8, 10, and 19; (4) discover the real meaning of the *full* gospel; (5) understand the function of the Spirit since Pentecost; and (6) discern what *the sign* of the Spirit's presence really is. We'll proceed in that order.

The Two-Baptism Theory

Tongues-speakers consider tongues a second baptism. Yet Jesus speaks of water and Spirit baptism as one event. To Nicodemus He said: "No one can enter the kingdom of God unless he is born of water and the Spirit" (John 3:5). Paul concurs when he writes of "one Lord, one faith, one baptism" (Eph. 4:6). The divine commission speaks of "baptizing" but never hints at a dual baptism (Matt. 28:18-20). In fact, no text in Scripture substantiates the two-baptism theory.

Tongues as a/the Sign

But the Bible does describe tongues as a sign. For Pentecostals and charismatics, tongues are a sign to *believers* of Spirit baptism. For Paul, "Tongues . . . are a sign, *not for believers but for unbelievers*" (1 Cor. 14:22). In the previous verse (verse 21) Paul quotes Isaiah 28:11, 12: "'Through men of strange tongues and through the lips of foreigners I will speak to this people, but even then they will not listen to me,' says the Lord."[93] Such tongues were "strange" because they were foreign languages. "God had spoken to His people in their own tongue through His messengers the prophets, but they did not listen. Now He would speak to them by other means, first the Assyrians and later the Babylonians, the Persians, and the Romans."[94]

Here tongues, or foreign languages, are a sign to God's people. *They were a sign of judgment—not of Spirit baptism, or full acceptance.*[95] Earlier God had predicted this when Israel stood at mounts Ebal and Gerazim prior to entering the Promised Land. God said, "The Lord will bring a nation against you from far away, from the ends of the earth, like an eagle swooping down, a nation whose language you will not understand" (Deut. 28:49). Jeremiah repeated the same thought (see Jer. 5:15).

Paul reminded the Corinthians of this function of tongues, because they seemed to glory in tongues-speaking—as if it were the ultimate in Christian experience. But, the apostle said, it could be the very opposite—the judgment of God. His message to the Corinthians is very relevant to Pentecostal/charismatic tongues-speakers today.[96]

Why Spirit Baptism After Conversion in Acts

Pentecost was a unique moment in salvation history, as singular and unrepeatable as the Incarnation and Second Advent. In fact, prophecy in the Old Testament spoke of the coming of Pentecost as it did that of the Messiah. Joel 2:28 pointed to that new day when the Spirit would be poured out upon all flesh, ushering in a new age—quite different from the old one.[97] "The epochal significance of Pentecost raises the whole course of salvation-history to a new plane," says James Dunn. "Pentecost can never be repeated—for the new age is here and cannot be ushered in again."[98]

Thus Pentecost is the inauguration of the church.[99] God celebrates this "birthday" by sending the wind and tongues of fire (Acts 2:2-4). Wind and fire do not accompany tongues in chapters 8, 10, or 19. Most tongues-speakers overlook this significant difference. As the same author wrote Luke and Acts, it is of interest to compare the two Spirit baptisms—of Jesus at the Jordan (Luke 3:21-23), and of His disciples at Pentecost (Acts 2:1-21). Both begin a new phase of salvation history that needs only to be launched once.[100] And both started a ministry. Just as Jesus began His public ministry after His Spirit baptism (Luke 3:23) so the disciples were told to go into the upper room until they were baptized with the Spirit's power (Luke 24:46-49), then to be sent forth to take the gospel to Jerusalem, Judea, Samaria, and to the uttermost parts of the earth (Acts 1:8).

The conduct of this divine commission has everything to do with the repeated Spirit baptisms in Acts 8, 10, and 19. For each new extension beyond Jerusalem and Judea to Samaria, to Cornelius and to the Ephesians, was an advance beyond the Jews to Gentiles. In its own way, each marked the launching of the gospel in a new area, and so the tongues aspect of Pentecost repeated itself in these three places.[101] *They constituted an extension of Pentecost to new peoples rather than its repetition.*

The Real Meaning of the *Full* Gospel

The "double seeking" prevalent today contradicts the biblical norm. We speak of (1) seeking tongues rather than the Holy Spirit, and (2) seeking a fullness of experience where it is not to be found. We'll take them up in that order.

Some Pentecostals say the seeking is after God rather than for tongues. For example, L. T. Holdcroft claims that "Pentecostals hold that speaking in tongues is not itself the Baptism, but only the sign or evidence. Seekers are not to seek tongues, but to seek God, and His Son, and the presence of the personal Holy Spirit. When the quest is successful, tongues are a sign both to the seeker and to those about him."[102]

But this raises questions. Do tongues-seekers really search for God more than the experience of glossolalia? Some spend months and years attempting to speak in tongues—have they not yet found God, even after becoming Christians? Doesn't the phenomenon overshadow the personal presence of God for such Christians? And what of Paul's warning to the Corinthian tongues-seekers that not all speak in tongues (1 Cor. 12:30), yet all are part of the Body of Christ (verse 27), endowed with spiritual gifts (verse 28), and hence recipients of the Spirit (verses 4-11)?

A basic problem lurks behind tongues-seeking—whether one couches it in a context of reaching out for God or not. For they seek for either tongues or the Spirit when they've already received the Spirit.[103] Tongues-seekers need to seriously ask themselves if the gift has become more important to them than the Giver.

This brings us to the purpose of their search. They yearn for a fuller experience—the *full* gospel. But can they find this fullness in glossolalia? Nowhere does the Bible urge Christians to seek to speak in tongues to experience the full gospel. We must remember that Peter, the Pentecostal preacher, nowhere invites Christians to speak in tongues, and Paul—with his nearly 100 chapters—mentions tongues in only three of them (1 Cor. 12-14), and then only as a warning against seeking such a gift. Jesus never spoke in tongues—and who could ever doubt the fullness of His experience! We need to take a long hard look at where we can find such fullness.

The Bible clearly says "you have been given fullness in Christ" (Col. 2:10)—the Christ in whom "all the fullness of the Deity lives in bodily form" (verse 9; cf. Col. 1:19). So fullness occurs in Christ, not in tongues. As F. D. Bruner rightly concludes: "It is the sustained doctrine of the Epistle to the Colossians that, according to the good pleasure of the Father, spiritual fullness is located for men in no other place—in no other be it ever so spiritual place—than in Jesus Christ."[104]

Scripture recognizes only one gospel—not two, one "ordinary" and the other "fuller." The gospel is Jesus Christ. Christ is "the Alpha and the Omega," the first and the last (Rev. 1:8). He's the One "in whom are hidden all the treasures of wisdom and knowledge" (Col. 2:3). The gospel includes "Christ in you, the hope of glory" (Col. 1:27). And when do we receive this fullness? "You are all sons of God through faith in Christ Jesus, for all of you who were baptized into Christ have clothed yourselves with Christ" (Gal. 3:26, 27). *We obtain the full gospel the moment we receive Christ.*

Therefore, any attempt to add to this fullness is not a search for a greater gospel—there is none. It's another, a counterfeit gospel. Paul faced this problem in Corinth, Collossae, and Galatia. He said to the Galatians: "I am astonished that you are so quickly deserting the one who called you by the grace of Christ and are turning to a different gospel—which is really no gospel at all. Evidently some people are throwing you into confusion and are trying to pervert the gospel of Christ" (Gal. 1:6, 7). Clearly any attempt to add to the fullness found in Christ is not the gospel.

But we need to penetrate to an even deeper dimension. If the fullness is not to be found in Christ but in the Spirit and tongues, then the Spirit offers us more than Christ, seriously questioning the fact that Christ is our only Saviour. It also presents Christ as inadequate to meet our needs. In addition, it also places a distinction in the Trinity, as if the One makes up for the lack of the Other. But it also raises doubt about the Spirit's ability. Seekers have to become good enough to receive the Spirit and tongues. But this gives to the seeker the very ability (to perfect himself) that Scripture credits the Spirit. "Without the filling of the Holy Spirit men are given the Herculean task of removing all known sin," says F. D. Bruner, "in order, finally to obtain this full Spirit. But if men can do all this *without* the full Spirit why is he necessary?"[105]

The "full gospel" of tongues-seekers attacks both the adequacy of Christ and the necessity of the Spirit. What kind of gospel is that?

The Function of the Spirit Since Pentecost

The role of the Spirit since Pentecost is not to be "another gospel" added to the only gospel. Even if tongues-seekers really seek the Giver, rather than the gift—for the Spirit rather than tongues—they still attempt to add to the fullness found in Christ. They also overlook the function of the Holy Spirit since Pentecost.

Since His bodily ascension to heaven's throne (Acts 2:32, 33), Christ sends the Spirit (John 16:7; cf. John 14:16, 26) and comes through the Spirit (John 14:18), to be with His people always to the end of the world (Heb. 13:5; Matt. 28:20). So the Spirit brings Christ. He has no mission to provide an added fullness beyond that found in Christ. That is why the New Testament refers to Him as "the Spirit of his Son" (Gal. 4:6), "the Spirit of Christ" (Rom. 8:9; 1 Peter 1:11), and "the Spirit of Jesus Christ" (Phil. 1:19).[106]

In the very renaming, Scripture makes the Spirit and Son indivisible in Their mission to humanity. That is precisely why Scripture recognizes only "one baptism" (Eph. 4:6)—into Christ through the Spirit. A baptized person has already arrived at the fullness and need seek no more. The theory that Spirit baptism comes sometime after baptism into Christ overlooks the indivisible relationship of the Spirit with the Son.

It's crucial to grasp the perspective of the New Testament. People don't become Christian until they receive the Holy Spirit (in a second-baptism sense) precisely because the Spirit brings Christ to them, thereby making them Christians. In fact, as Dunn observes: "It is not sufficiently realized that in NT times the possession of the Spirit was *the* hallmark of the Christian."[107]

"To become a Christian, in short, is to receive the Spirit of Christ, the Holy Spirit."[108] Therefore, "no Christian was without the Spirit, for only those who had [received] the Spirit were ipso facto Christians."[109]

Tongues-seekers who claim to be really seeking the Holy Spirit second baptism must pause to ask themselves if they are really Christian. For *"if anyone does not have the Spirit of Christ, he does not belong to Christ"* (Rom. 8:9). Here was Paul's urgent concern about the Corinthian tongues-seekers. As Robert M. Anderson put it, "Paul's argument against the Corinthian extremists was that every believer has the Spirit (Pneuma) and every believer has some gift of the Spirit (charisma). This surely implied that every believer was both a pneumatic and a charismatic despite the absence of any extraordinary visible manifestation."[110]

No conversion account in the New Testament speaks of a person coming to Christ without the Spirit, and thus needing Him later. For no one becomes a Christian without receiving the Spirit. It was true of Paul,[111] Cornelius, and the 12 at Ephesus.

The Sign of the Spirit's Presence

Paul reminded the Corinthians, who themselves were making too much of tongues, that they had been "all baptized by one Spirit into one body" (1 Cor. 12:13) even though not all of them spoke in tongues (verse 30). *So it's possible to be Spirit baptized and still not speak in tongues.*

Not only is this so, but Paul clearly speaks out about the real sign of Spirit baptism. It has nothing to do with spiritual gifts, for gifts can be counterfeited. It involves *spiritual fruit,* precisely because we cannot counterfeit them for a sustained duration. "The fruit of the Spirit is love, joy, peace, patience, kindness, goodness, faithfulness, gentleness and self-control" (Gal. 5:22, 23).

Spirit fruit is a universal test of Spirit gifts. Every Spirit-baptized person has all the fruit, even though he or she has only one or more of the gifts. No Christian has all the gifts, but every Christian has all the fruit. To be a valid gift of the Spirit, each gift comes with all the fruit (the reverse is never true). This opens up the deepest issue involved on the question of tongues—the recipient of the least gift has the fullness of the Giver, for no gift comes apart from the Giver. That is why each spiritual gift has all the spiritual fruit accompanying it. *So the fullness of the Spirit is realized in spiritual fruit and not in spiritual gifts, or else no one would ever experience the full gospel.*

Then the sign of Spirit baptism—of the full gospel—is the revelation of all the fruit of the Spirit rather than the exercise of all the gifts of the Spirit. By contrast, tongues-speech is only one gift, and the least one at that! How can the least gift reveal the fullness (full gospel) and be *the* sign of Spirit baptism? It obviously falls far short.

"The fruit of the Spirit is love. . . ." (Gal. 5:22). Jesus gave what He called a new commandment in the upper room just before His death. It was to "love one another" (John 13:34). Scripture says that "by this shall all men know that ye are my disciples, if ye have love one to another" (KJV). Those who receive the

"Spirit of Christ" will love as Christ did. Love, and not tongues, is the sign of a full Christian experience. That's precisely why Paul placed the "great love chapter" (1 Cor. 13) in the middle of the three chapters on tongues (1 Cor. 12-14). It's crucial to his argument[112]—we must seek the greatest gift (love) and not the least (tongues). Here, interestingly, Paul classifies love as a gift, whereas in Galatians 5 he refers to it as a fruit. The fact is that the fruit of the Spirit is from the Spirit, and hence a gift.

Furthermore, Paul considers the tongues-speakers at Corinth "babes in Christ" and "yet carnal" (1 Cor. 3:1, 3), the opposite to the idea "that the ability to speak with tongues is a sign of mature, full-grown Christianity."[113]

Tongues and the "Spirit of Truth"

But that is not all. If tongues are the sign of the Spirit, how come people of opposite doctrinal convictions receive the same gift? Or put another way, how can the "Spirit of truth" (John 14:17) give "the sign" of His baptism to those who oppose truth?

For example, Catholics who pray to Mary and implore saints to intercede on their behalf receive the tongues gift as readily as Protestants who look to Christ as their only intercessor. The whole spectrum of beliefs—and/or lack of them—occur among tongues-speakers, for they belong to every major denomination.[114] The charismatic movement "seems to exhibit none of the traditional boundaries that have marked so much of Protestantism in recent decades. Virtually every tradition is represented under the bulging umbrella of renewal."[115] A plethora of opposing views exists among tongues-speakers, and yet they each claim to get their gift from the same "Spirit of truth."

In fact, "tongues speaking occurs among liberals and others who deny the inspiration of the Scriptures, the virgin Birth, the substitutionary atonement, the doctrine of Creation, and other vital doctrines. One young man who spoke in tongues at Yale University later admitted that he was not a believer at all at the time. . . . Marcus Bach, a leading advocate of tongues, denies the personality of the Holy Spirit and teaches that 'all roads that lead to God are good.' . . . The United Pentecostal Church is so named because it denies the doctrine of the Trinity."[116]

The tongues movement is even "composed of both saved and unsaved."[117] Truth has become less important than speaking in tongues. The experience has transcended doctrinal differences. Never before has ecumenism been so successful—and so rapid in its realization. When truth gets denigrated below a gift—how can that gift come from the "Spirit of truth," who Jesus promised would come to "guide you into all truth" (John 16:13)? And the result? Some tongues-speaking has been deciphered as blasphemy against Christ[118]—the very opposite of the Spirit's mission to glorify Him (verse 14).

Tongues-speech appears throughout non-Christian religions and society, and so one cannot consider it "the sign" of the Spirit just because it takes place. As it is so universally present in a non-Christian setting, it can just as easily be the sign of unholy spirits as of the Holy Spirit. In fact, while being the least gift of the Spirit, it may now be the gift most counterfeited by other spirits.[119] We next consider non-Christian tongues.

Non-Christian Tongues-speaking

As John Bunn observed, "Many Christians would no doubt be surprised to learn that instances of frenzied speech predate the account of glossolalia in Acts by several hundred years. Although masses of contemporary Christians have been exposed to tongue-speaking, they seem to have little appreciation either for its ancestral heritage or its relatively modern expression in non-Western cultures."[120]

Mesopotamian religion from 2000 to 1500 B.C. gives examples of tongues-speech such as found in the Mari texts, the Egyptian cases of Wen-Amon and the cult of Osiris and Isis, the Thracian cult of Dionysius, the Syrian cult of Adonis, the Phyrgian cult of Attis and Cybele, the Persian cult of Mithras, the Arabic Kahin and dervish examples, Muslims in India citing the Quran in Arabic even though not knowing Arabic, sorcerers speaking incoherently in China while communing with spirits, the Grecian Delphic oracle and mystery religions, the records of Herodotus, Virgil's *Aeneid* and Plato's *Phaedo,* and the western shamans, to name some.[121] "And among such ecstatics, whether Mesopotamian, Egyptian, Israelite, Canaanite, Greek, or Muslim, there were those who, when possessed by the spirit of deity, delivered messages in strange tongues." Therefore, "no religion, ancient or modern, may claim exclusive rights to such a religious act."[122]

The reader should keep in mind that the Corinthians had come out of paganism and undoubtedly knew of, if not participated in, the ecstatic experiences of the Delphic oracle. In 1 Corinthians 12:2 Paul seems to be contrasting their past experience with the present: "You know that when you were pagans, somehow or other you were influenced and led astray to mute [KJV: "dumb"] idols." Scripture often terms the pagan gods as "dumb" in contrast to God, who "imparts to His followers spiritual gifts that enable them to speak in His name" (see Ps. 115:4, 5; 135:15-17; Hab. 2:18, 19).[123]

Possession by spirits or induced tongues recur often in non-Christian tongues-speech. Both happened at the Delphic oracle, not far from the Corinthians. "The oracles of the Delphi sibyl were delivered during a state of possession or ecstatic seizure. As such, the messages were very enigmatic and delivered in a language not akin to any known."[124] Likewise, in the context of Islam, "a dervish utilizes certain conditioning agents to achieve a state in which he will become the spokesman of Allah. Contemplation, repetition of the divine name, recitation of creeds, religious formulas, prayers, and passages from the Quran are effectively used to induce a state of ecstasy. Vocalization of the literature is, at first, slow and deliberate, but then the momentum increases at an alarming rate. Suddenly the recitations are punctuated again and again with the explosive syllable *hu*. As the tempo increases, so does bodily movement, and the climax is an ecstatic delirium. In this state prophecies are given. These are considered to be messages from the realm of the spirit. . . .

The messages are quite often delivered in no known language."[125]

As Anthony Hoekema has rightly observed, "The emotional stimulation which often gives rise to tongues in non-Christian circles could also cause tongues-speaking among Christians."[126] I believe the evidence supports his concern. We now turn to this danger.

"Christian Tongues" Induced

A "tarrying meeting" appears to be where "most Pentecostal baptisms occur."[127] Even those taking place in solitude perhaps always follow time spent in such a meeting.[128] So it is crucial to understand the psychology of such sessions. In "tarrying meetings," often attended for years,[129] those seeking the tongues-gift spend "long agonizing hours 'tarrying' for the Spirit."[130] This phenomenon is unique to the "gift" of tongues. Christians do not seek the other gifts of the Spirit in this way. For example, we do not read of long searches for the gift of healing, teaching, or preaching. Rather, recipients come to realize the gift and then pray for power to be used in the stewardship of the gift.

Not only do we find this unique difference, but we discover also that a priming, inducement, or conditioning usually precedes the reception of tongues—thereby raising a question about its quality as a *gift*. Again, such an "induction process"[131] is a human aid in the reception of the "gift" and is unheard of for receiving any other spiritual gift. Moreover, it is the usual process—for tongues do "not frequently occur spontaneously."[132]

This "induction process" has "led many investigators to interpret tongue speaking as psychologically conditioned."[133] Atmosphere is crucial. It includes others involved in tongues-speaking surrounding the seekers, fast hand clapping, and music with a tempo and decisive beat; and the service is characterized by *ardor* rather than *order,* and God being the "subject of action" rather than the "object of worship."[135]

Charismatics give careful instruction to the seekers. For example, the individual must (1) not question whether the experience is false; (2) "open his mouth wide and breathe as deeply as possible at the same time telling himself that he is receiving the Spirit now";[136] (3) repeat some foreign words or meaningless words[137] such as "Aish nay gum nay tao" to prime the pump, since tongues-speaking is a "learned skill";[138] and (4) repeat a phrase or words since to do so often induces tongues[139] (even repeating "the name of Jesus over and over with great rapidity until he begins to stammer"[140] induces tongues-speech); and (5) laying hands on the seeker by one, or by many, in the group surrounding him or her.[141]

Such human intervention, to induce the reception of a divine gift, raises questions about the Giver's ability to prepare the recipient Himself. Since when did God need such human help? Evangelicals are right when they question Catholic works for salvation, for that is God's department. He is the only Saviour. But they show remarkable inconsistency when, with Catholics, they seek for tongues. If tongues are a genuine gift of the Spirit, then they are precisely that—a gift. It needs no human inducement any more than human works can earn salvation. Tongues and salvation are both gifts of God. Human efforts are not only out of place, but are only "a human effort to reproduce a Biblical phenomenon."[142] They are comparable to the snakes produced by the Egyptian magicians—a counterfeit for the genuine snake God made for Moses (Ex. 4:2-5; 7:9-12).

Focusing on the repetition of words or a phrase reminds me of my visit to the headquarters of the Soka Gakkai "new religion" in Tokyo, Japan. They date their Buddhist religion to Nichiren of the thirteenth century, and together with the Risho Kosekai movement have had phenomenal growth in post-war Japan. Devotees in quest of enlightenment repeat the words "Nam Myo Renge Kyo" ad infinitum until they experience the moment of enlightenment it induces. Here we have Buddhists and Christians seeking for a psychological "high"—enlightenment or tongues—and both get there by the same method. Endless repetitions override the conscious mind just like the hypnotic beat of music, often used for the same effect.

Bypassing the Conscious Mind

We must be careful here, for the path of truth and counterfeit lie close together. Paul, speaking of the genuine tongues gift says, "If I pray in a tongue, my spirit prays, but my mind is unfruitful"[143] (1 Cor. 14:14), reminiscent of the Spirit's prayer when He "intercedes for us with groans that words cannot express" (Rom. 8:26). This makes the phenomenon easier to counterfeit, and is another reason why it is a poor choice as the sign of Spirit baptism. No wonder Scripture never speaks of tongues as a sign, and Paul decides "I will also pray with my mind" (1 Cor. 14:15).

We come to a basic principle of biblical interpretation. Every spiritual gift must be as rational as the Spirit who gives it. None of the gifts mentioned in Romans 8:6-8, 1 Corinthians 12:7-11, 28-31, and Ephesians 4:11-13 is irrational. God invited human beings to reason with Him (Isa. 1:18), and Scripture designates the Holy Spirit as the One to guide humans "into all truth" (John 16:13), teaching them "all things" (John 14:26), and revealing Christ to them (John 15:26). Christ concurred that loving God included "with all your mind" (Luke 10:27, 28). Any bypassing of the conscious mind would seem to be out of harmony with God's rational, revelatory mission. When the Spirit "intercedes for us with groans that words cannot express," this does not mean He is speaking in an unknown tongue to Him (He is omniscient, e.g., Ps. 147:5), but that our human language and comprehension fall short of doing justice to what He says.

By contrast with the genuine gift of tongues, the contemporary manifestation seems to bypass the conscious mind to a degree never intended by the biblical gift. It also has a long and carefully documented history. "Since at least the time of Plato, speaking in tongues has been recognized as ecstatic speech; speech that is dissociated from thought and flows forth involuntarily and automatically. The conclusion that the tongues-speaker is in an altered state of consciousness is supported by the consensus of those historians, sociologists, anthropologists, theologians, psychologists, psychiatrists, and neurophysiologists who have studied the phenomenon."[144]

One tongues-speaker tells his experience. "While I was praying one of the workers got hold of me and said: 'Holy Ghost, we command thee to go into this soul.' The workers were jabbering and shaking their hands over me, and a *hypnotic power* (as I know now) took possession of me, and I fell among the people on the floor and knew nothing for ten hours. When I came to my senses I was weak and my jaws were so tired they ached."[145]

John Kildahl, in his psychological observations of tongues-speakers, notes that "the capability of being hypnotized and the capability of speaking in tongues are closely related."[146] In his book, *The Psychology of Speaking in Tongues,* Kildahl compares his hypnotic work with that of those leading tongues-seekers. "When I hypnotize someone, I begin by saying to my subject, 'Lie back, . . . shut your eyes, . . . relax, . . . breathe deeply, . . . and listen to the sounds of your breathing. As you relax, you can feel yourself getting tired and drowsy. . . .' In the dimly lit fireside room of the First Presbyterian Church, a small circle of members quietly listened to their pastor say, 'The Lord is in your presence. . . . He is with you now. . . . Open yourself to Him. . . . Empty yourself of all your thoughts. . . . Wait on Him. . . . Let all your anxieties flow out of you. . . . The Lord wants to give you the gift of His Holy Spirit. . . . Open your mouth, and He will give you utterance.' "[147]

He concludes: "It is our thesis that hypnotizability constitutes the *sine qua non* of the glossolalia experience. If one can be hypnotized, then one is able under proper conditions to learn to speak in tongues. While glossolalia is not the same as hypnosis, it is similar to it and has the same roots in the relationship of the subject to the authority figure."[148]

L. T. Holdcroft observes that "the realm in which the gift of tongues operates is not the human mind, but the human organs of speech. The mind is primarily a spectator to the events, and it neither frames the utterances, nor does it premeditate or prearrange them."[149] Such a "takeover by the subconscious is similar to that manifested in automatic writing."[150] Clinical psychiatric data informs us that tongues-speech is "a form of dissociation within the personality, in which a set of voluntary muscles respond to control centers other than those associated with consciousness."[151]

Psychiatrist Jung believed the deeper levels of the unconscious take over from the ego to control.[152] Some consider this power to be the Holy Spirit,[153] others attribute it to demon-possession.[154] By contrast with much contemporary tongues-speech, 1 Corinthians portrays the tongues-speaker as in control, for Paul limited them to two or three individuals at any meeting, and they must speak one at a time and only with an interpreter present (see 1 Cor. 14:26-28). As Leon Morris observed: "This shows us that we must not think of 'tongues' as being the result of an irresistible impulse of the Spirit, driving the man willy-nilly into ecstatic speech."[155]

So the genuine gift of tongues in 1 Corinthians differs from that of Acts 2, because the individual directs it to God and not to human beings (in praise rather than proclamation) and it is in a tongue unknown to the speaker rather than a foreign language gifted to the speaker. Such a gift exercised in an orderly manner seems far different from much of contemporary tongues-speech. As Kelsey commented on the present expression: "Tongue speaking seems to be a deliberate attempt to abandon one's self to the irrational, unknown forces which lie beyond consciousness. It strikes at the very center of our culture's rational meaning. It is an observable denial of the very genius which has rescued Western civilization from the chaos of the Dark Ages and unconsciousness."[156]

We need only to remind ourselves that a similar transcending of intellectual categories and human logic occurs in Eastern mysticism[157] and the New Age movement. Is the source not the same for all of them? Robert Gromacki believes that all modern glossolalia can be produced "satanically, psychologically, and artificially" and that none of it comes from God.[158] Psychiatrists have documented that tongues-speaking is not a "spiritual phenomenon" and is easy to produce.[159]

Linguistic Analysis of Tongues

If the phenomenon involves bypassing the conscious mind, we would assume that the resulting tongues-speech would give evidence of that fact. It does. We will confine ourselves to just a few comments from linguists.

William Welmes, professor of African languages at UCLA, considered tongues to be a "linguistic fraud and monstrosity."[160] During two investigations of interpretation of tongues researchers privately played the same tape of tongues-speech to different interpreters, and not once did they give the same translation. They interpreted the tape as (1) the speaker seeking guidance about a new job and (2) a prayer of thanksgiving for health after recent sickness. The test subjects interpreted another tape as (1) the speaker praying for children's health and (2) an expression of gratitude to God for a recent successful church fund-raising effort.[161] A son of missionary parents, attending a tongues meeting, rose and spoke the Lord's Prayer in an African dialect. Those present interpreted it as a message concerning the imminent return of Christ.an [162]

If tongues are easy to produce, then it seems that their interpretations are just as easy. Both leave questions about their authenticity.

Why Tongues?

Why has the phenomena erupted in the Christian church and taken it over? A whole range of stated reasons appear in the literature on the topic, and we will mention some of them now. They include such things as responses to (1) an essentially godless society,[163] (2) a superficial and impersonal religion,[164] (3) hyperintellectualism and formal worship,[165] (4) social discontent,[166] and (5) dislocation.[167] Tongues therefore constitute a release from tension and anxiety,[168] freeing the mind from extreme rationalism[169] and providing a religious high.[170]

Pentecostalism began among those who were *economically deprived,*[171] and in its charismatic form since the 1960s it has arisen among those who are scholars, professionals, the higher classes, and the financially successful, but who are *emotionally deprived*.[172] Besides these factors, Pentecostalism began as a reaction to liberalism and higher criticism.[173] Robert Anderson observed: “Holiness people were repelled, too, by the currents of theological liberalism in the denominations. The ‘Higher Criticism’ of Scripture undermined the authority of the Bible; the comparative study of religion, by placing Christianity in a relativistic framework, deprived it of its unique and absolute character; and evolutionary theory in both its biological and social applications detracted from the supernatural and personal attributes of the Deity—so it seemed, at least, to many Holiness believers.”[174]

If only the tongues-seekers had sought to understand the Bible more than to seek tongues and had placed the Word as central rather than a gift. In short, if only they had understood the function of the Holy Spirit since Pentecost, the tongues movement would never have erupted. We come to a basic principle—that wherever a vacuum exists, it provides opportunity for a counterfeit to fill it. Tongues fill a void in theology as well as in life. For, as J. R. Williams reminds us, “our single greatest neglect (especially in Western theology) has been in the area of the Holy Spirit.”[175]

Tongues Movement as Fulfillment of Prophecy

The contemporary tongues movement seems to be fulfilling two prophecies: the predicted (1) union of churches[176] and the predicted (2) false Pentecost, or false latter rain.[177] We will consider them in that order.

Religious declension leads churches to unite on common points of doctrine.[178] Spiritualism, Protestantism, and Catholicism join together—and do so because spiritualism, through a Christian guise, performs miracles that have convincing power, and thereby takes over the Christian churches.[179] One aspect of the final counterfeit concerns the *method* Satan employs to unite the churches. The “apparently Christian miracle” gift of tongues could be involved in this.

The other aspect concerns the *purpose* for Satan’s working through the churches in the end-time. Many consider the outpouring of power for apparent healing[180] and for tongues-speech the promised latter rain to come just before the second advent of Christ.

The charismatic literature suggests three dimensions of this latter rain outpouring. That is, in the *past* (it began in 1889, but really became a downpour with tongues-speech at Topeka, Kansas, January 1, 1901, at Azusa Street in 1906, and a cloudburst in the charismatic movement of the 1950s);[181] in the *present* (the tongues movement exploding throughout Christendom);[182] and in the *future* (we are on the verge of the climax of this final outpouring to evangelize the world).[183]

We focus on the present and immediate future dimensions. “Pentecostals believe that their movement is really the *latter rain,* i.e., the prelude to the end.”[184] And “neo-Pentecostals believe that the Church is on the verge of a great spiritual awakening—a sort of a ‘Latter Rain’ before the ‘final harvest.’ ”[185] The fact that we are witnessing the greatest uniting of churches and outpouring of power for what so many perceive as healing and tongues-speech gives the appearance that it is indeed the promised latter rain (see Deut. 11:14; Joel 2:25-28; Zech. 10:1; and James 5:7). But is it?

Ellen White warns against a counterfeit latter rain that operates under a Christian guise just before the genuine Pentecost. "Notwithstanding the widespread declension of faith and piety, there are true followers of Christ in these churches. Before the final visitation of God's judgments upon the earth there will be among the people of the Lord such a revival of primitive godliness as has not been witnessed since apostolic times. The Spirit and power of God will be poured out upon His children. At that time many will separate themselves from those churches in which the love of this world has supplanted love for God and His word. Many, both of ministers and people, will gladly accept those great truths which God has caused to be proclaimed at this time to prepare a people for the Lord's second coming. The enemy of souls decides to hinder this work; and *before the time for such a movement shall come, he will endeavor to prevent it by introducing a counterfeit.* In those churches which he can bring under his deceptive power he will make it appear that God's special blessing is poured out; there will be manifest what is thought to be great religious interest. Multitudes will exult that God is working marvelously for them, when *the work is that of another spirit. Under a religious guise, Satan will seek to extend his influence over the Christian world.*"[186]

Conclusion

Therefore, far from being *the sign of Spirit baptism, tongues may well be the sign of the counterfeit Spirit baptism.*[187] Only one biblical book, 1 Corinthians, mentions tongues as a gift of the Spirit. Romans and Ephesians do not include tongues as one of the gifts. This is significant because some evidence suggests that Paul wrote Romans in the winter of A.D. 57-58 and Ephesians in A.D. 62—both after 1 Corinthians, concluded in the spring of A.D. 57.[188] Hence, not only are tongues the least gift in 1 Corinthians (chapter 12:8-10, 28-30)[189] but they are not even mentioned in subsequent passages on the gifts (Rom. 12:6-8; Eph. 4:7-13) even though Paul wrote all three books.

As the four listings (two in 1 Corinthians) are not exhaustive,[190] one would expect to find some gifts mentioned only once. Actually, only one gift appears in all four. It's not tongues, but prophecy! So, if a gift could function as *the* sign for Spirit baptism, then mathematically prophecy would have it over tongues, and furthermore, Paul also lists prophecy as second in importance and places tongues and their interpretation last (1 Cor. 12:28).[191] Even the best biblical perspective on tongues removes it from its pinnacle position, for Paul said: "I would like every one of you to speak in tongues, but I would rather have you prophesy" (1 Cor. 14:5). Pentecostals and charismatics need to remember that tongues were a problem in Corinth. Paul wrote to correct the problem and not to promote it.

Without the problem being present, he may never have included tongues in 1 Corinthians at all, or because of its marked presence in Corinth he purposely omitted it from his listing in Romans and Ephesians. Moreover, if he mentions it only once, and even then as the least of all Spirit gifts, it opposes the contemporary emphasis on it as the chief of all gifts, *the* sign of Spirit baptism. Furthermore, because no one has all the gifts and all have different gifts, then gifts by definition cannot be a sign, let alone *the* sign of Spirit baptism. No wonder Paul points to the fruit of the Spirit rather than the gifts of the Spirit as revealing the Spirit's presence. Also, gifts can be counterfeited but not fruit, over the long haul.

Why is the charismatic movement sweeping the Christian world? I believe it is the predicted counterfeit Pentecost to precede the genuine one and that it attempts to nullify God's authentic latter rain. Christians find themselves caught up in an experience opposed by, and beyond, the safety of God's Word. They search (1) for gifts more than the Giver, (2) for the spectacular (least) gift more than the others, and (3) for an experience of the Spirit supposedly beyond their experience in Christ. In doing so they overlook the biblical fact that anything beyond Christ is not Christian.[192] No *full* gospel beyond Christ can possibly exist, for the fullness is found only in Him (see Col. 2:9, 10).

[1] Gerhard F. Hasel, "Speaking in Tongues," *Adventist Theological Society Monographs,* vol. 1 (Berrien Springs, Mich.: Adventist Theological Society, 1991).

[2] William E. Richardson, *Speaking in Tongues* (Hagerstown, Md.: Review and Herald, 1994).

[3] "One of the distinctive charismatic characteristics is glossolalia—the gift of speaking in tongues. Certainly it is the single most controversial aspect in the Pentecostal sweep of the Christian community" *(Speaking in Tongues: Let's Talk About It,* Watson E. Mills, ed. [Waco, Tex.: Word, 1973], p. 13; cf. *Perspectives on the New Pentecostalism,* Russell P. Spittler, ed. [Grand Rapids: Baker, 1976], p. 205, in which Clark H. Pinnock says, "For I recognize it as a sweep. I recognize it as an upsurge of the Spirit").

[4] Perhaps called "third force" first by Henry P. Van Dusen, president of Princeton Theological Seminary, in his article "Third Force in Christendom," *(Life,* June 9, 1958, pp. 113-124). Van Dusen's "third force includes, in addition to the various types of Pentecostals, the Churches of Christ, the Seventh-day Adventists, Nazarenes, Jehovah's Witnesses, and Christian and Missionary Alliance." See Frederick D. Bruner, *A Theology of the Holy Spirit* (Grand Rapids: Eerdmans, 1970), p. 29, footnote 25.

But subsequently the literature seems to narrow the term to Pentecostalism. Thus "Pentecostalism has now become a movement of worldwide importance, reckoned as 'a third force in Christendom' (alongside Catholicism and Protestantism) by not a few leading churchmen" (James D. G. Dunn, *Baptism in the Holy Spirit: A Re-examination of the New Testament Teaching on the Gift of the Spirit in Relation to Pentecostalism Today,* Studies in Biblical Theology, Second Series, No. 15 [SCM, 1970], p. 2; cf. Cyril G. Williams, *Tongues of the Spirit: A Study of Pentecostal Glossolalia and Related Phenomena* [Cardiff: University of Wales, 1981], p. 46; cf. Gordon F. Atter, The Third Force [Ontario, Canada: The College Press, n.p.d.].

[5] Henry P. Van Dusen, quoted in Watson E. Mills, *Speaking in Tongues: A Guide to Research in Glossolalia* (Grand Rapids: Eerdmans, 1986), p. 340.

[6] Richard Quebedeaux, *The New Charismatics* (San Francisco: Harper & Row, 1983), vol. 2, p. 215.

[7] "May there be repeated thus in the Christian families the spectacle of the apostles gathered together in Jerusalem after the Ascension of Jesus to heaven, when the newborn Church was completely united in communion of thought and prayer. . . . And may the Divine Spirit deign to answer in a most comforting manner the prayer that rises daily to Him from every corner of the earth: 'Renew your wonders in our time, as though for a new Pentecost.'" (quoted in Richard Quebedeaux, *The New Charismatics: The Origins, Development, and Significance of Neo-Pentecostalism* [New York: Doubleday, 1976], p. 177).

[8] "These charismatic gifts, whether they be the most outstanding or the more simple and widely diffused, are

to be received with thanksgiving and consolation, for they are exceedingly suitable and useful for the needs of the Church" *(The Documents of Vatican II,* Walter M. Abbott, gen. ed. [London: Geoffrey Chapman, 1967], p. 30.

[9] Richard Quebedeaux, *The New Charismatics 11,* pp. 213, 214.

[10] Rene Laurentin, "The Birth of Catholic Pentecostalism," *Catholic Pentecostalism* (Doubleday, 1977), reprinted in *Speaking in Tongues: A Guide to Research on Glossolalia,* Watson E. Mills, ed. (Grand Rapids: Eerdmans, 1986), p. 235.

[11] Dr. Robert G. Gromacki could say in 1967 that "practically all of the major historic denominations have been permeated and influenced by the new charismatic revival" *(The Modern Tongues Movement* [Pennsylvania: Presbyterian and Reformed, 1967], p. 34). "Practically all of the major historic denominations now have tongues-speakers within their ranks, both among the clergy and the laity" (p. 50). Synan observed that by 1980 "the charismatic movement had entered all the traditional churches of Christendom" (Vinson Synan, *The Twentieth-Century Pentecostal Explosion* [Altamonte Springs, Fla.: Creation, 1987], p. 11).

[12] See the 12 articles written by Arthur L. White, *Review and Herald,* August 4, 10, 17, 24, 1972, March 8, 15, 22, 29, April 5, 12, 19, 26, and August 9, 1973. They present the ecstatic experiences that took place in the Seventh-day Adventist Church during the lifetime of Ellen White. "Tongues in Early SDA History," March 15, 1973, presents four instances of tongues, with Ellen White present for three of them. She never condoned tongues, but does warn against ecstatic experiences as these articles document. The tongues movement knocked at the Adventist Church door in the 1950s; see Roland Hegstad's *Rattling the Gates* (Washington, D.C.: Review and Herald, 1974), p. 74.

[13] Frederick Dale Bruner, *A Theology of the Holy Spirit* (Grand Rapids: Eerdmans, 1970), pp. 27, 28.

[14] Anderson believes that those from Wesleyan roots became Pentecostal by accepting Keswick (Robert M. Anderson, *Vision of the Disinherited: The Making of American Pentecostalism* [Oxford: Oxford University, 1979], p. 43).

[15] In 1936 Smith Wigglesworth, Pentecostal evangelist of Yorkshire, England, claimed to have a prophecy for David John du Plessis. He said to Du Plessis, "There is a revival coming that at present the world knows nothing about. It will come through the churches. It will come in a fresh way. When you see what God does in this revival, you will then have to admit that all that you have seen previously is a mere nothing in comparison with what is to come. It will eclipse anything that has been known in history. . . . The Lord intends to use you in this revival" (Peter Hocken, *Streams of Renewal: The Origins and Early Development of the Charismatic Movement in Great Britain* [Paternoster, 1986], p. 19). Du Plessis told few about it during a 25-year period, and went on to become the leading instrument to take Pentecostalism into the churches. He served on the World Council of Churches. Pentecostals believe that the tongues movement not only fulfills Wigglesworth's prophecy, but that of Joel 2:28. For example, as Bruner noted: "As the apostolic church represented the former rain bringing the first-fruits, Pentecostals believe that their movement is God's ordained latter rain bringing in the last fruits of the great harvest, the immediate prophase to the second advent" (F. D. Bruner, *A Theology of the Holy Spirit,* p. 28).

[16] Based on the *World Christian Encyclopedia,* David Barrett, ed., as presented in Vinson Synan, *The Twentieth-Century Pentecostal Explosion,* pp. 11, 12.

[17] "The resurgence of Pentecostalism . . . is one of the most, if not the most, remarkable phenomenon in the Christian world at this present time" (Cyril G. Williams, *Tongues of the Spirit,* p. 94).

[18] Hector Camacho, *A Critical Examination of Glossolalia in American Christianity* (thesis, graduate school, Trinity University, 1971), p. 47.

[19] Vinson Synan, *In the Latter Days: The Outpouring of the Holy Spirit in the Twentieth Century* (Ann Arbor, Mich.: Servant, 1984), pp. 3, 4.

[20] "The charismatic movement has made an impact on the church possibly unparalleled in history" (John F. MacArthur, Jr., *The Charismatics* [Grand Rapids: Zondervan, 1978], p. 130).

[21] Bruner, *A Theology of the Holy Spirit,* p. 23.

[22] "Pentecostalism has become firmly established in the USSR" (William C. Fletcher, *Soviet Charismatics: The Pentecostalism in the USSR,* American University Studies, Series VII, Theology and Religion [New York: Peter Lang, 1985], vol. 9, p. 149).

[23] Both in Russia and China, Pentecostals are the fastest-growing Christian groups (Bruner, p. 24).

[24] "During this century some two or three million, and perhaps a great many more, Americans have had a strange personal experience of religion known as speaking in tongues" (Morton T. Kelsey, *Tongue Speaking: An Experiment in Spiritual Experience* [New York: Waymark, Doubleday, 1964], p. 1).

[25] Assemblies of God are "reported to be building one new church a day in America" (Bruner, p. 25).

[26] Gromacki, p.29.

[27] Torrey and Moody were inspired by the Keswick movement and spoke of a personal baptism, a second work, that each person must experience. This influenced Pentecostalism (Synan, pp. 38-42).

[28] Hence the name "Full Gospel Businessmen's Fellowship" given to a group of business-oriented Pentecostals inspired by Oral Roberts who were largely instrumental in the rapid progress of the charismatic movement.

[29] Synan, p. 26.

[30] "The Christian who receives spiritual baptism and speaks in tongues then enters into a charismatic life in which he is open to receive all of the other gifts of the Spirit. . . . The fruits of love and compassion and brotherhood also flow from the Spirit as one receives it in an experience of tongues" (Kelsey, pp. 78, 79).

[31] "For the Pentecostals glossolalia is not the kingpin of a network of charisma but a way into the whole of Christian doctrine" (Simon Tugwell, Peter Hocken, George Enery, John O. Mills, *New Heaven? New Earth? An Encounter With Pentecostalism* [Springfield, Ill.: Templegate, 1976], p. 124).

[32] J. Massynbaerde Ford, "Towards a Theology of Speaking in Tongues." *Theological Studies* 32 (1971): 3-29, reprinted in *Speaking in Tongues: A Guide to Research on Glossolalia,* p. 289.

[33] Kelsey, p. 231.

[34] Steve Durasoff, *Bright Wind of the Spirit: Pentecostalism Today* (New Jersey: Prentice-Hall, 1972), p. 5.

[35] For example, the minutes of the Thirty-fifth General Council of the Assemblies of God Article 8, (1973) say, "The baptism of believers in the Holy Ghost is witnessed by the initial physical sign of speaking with other tongues as the Spirit of God gives them utterance (Acts 2:4). The speaking in tongues in this instance is the same in essence as the gift of tongues (1 Cor. 12:4-10, 28), but different in purpose and use" *(Perspectives on the New Pentecostalism,* Russell P. Spittler, ed., p. 120). "There is likewise an apparent distinction between speaking in tongues as *evidence* that the Holy Spirit has come and the manifestation of tongues as a *gift* of the Spirit" *(The Glossolalia Phenomenon,* pp. 37, 38). "The Pentecostal position is that the tongues in Acts were a *sign,* but the tongues at Corinth were a *gift.* The *sign* of tongues, they maintain, is the unique seal and proof of the baptism with the Spirit. All Christians, they assert, should seek and expect the *sign,* but not all should expect to receive the *gift"* (Charles R. Smith, *Tongues in Biblical Perspective: A Summary of Biblical Conclusions Concerning Tongues* [Indiana: BMH, 1973], p. 53). "The 'sign' requires no interpretation where the 'gift' always requires interpretation *when exercised publicly"* (Joe E. Campbell, *Warning! Do Not Seek for Tongues: An Exposé of the Devil's Counterfeit Offer Attempting to Popularize Pentecost* [Raleigh, N.C.: World Outlook, 1917], pp. 79-81, 85]; cf. C. G. Williams, *Tongues of the Spirit: A Study of Pentecostal Glossolalia in Related Phenomena,* p. 77); Morton T. Kelsey, *Tongue Speaking: An Experiment in Spiritual Experience,* pp. 78, 152). "Both in Pentecostalism and in the Charismatic Renewal, tongues are regarded as one of the gifts of the Holy Spirit, but Pentecostals have distinguished tongues as a 'sign' of the individual's initial baptism in the spirit . . . and subsequent manifestations in which the 'gift' of the Spirit is at work" *(Strange Gifts: A Guide to Charismatic Renewal,* David Martin and Peter Mullen, eds., pp. 73, 74).

[36] "Pentecost had made good the promise, and had shown as the firstfruits of the harvest the recovery of the world's languages to the service of Christianity" *(The Pulpit Commentary,* H. M. Spence and J. S. Exell, eds., *1 Corinthians* [Chicago, Ill.: Wilcox and Follett, n.p.d.), p. 402). The disciples spoke at least 15 languages: *(The Glossolalia Phenomenon,* W. H. Horton, gen. ed. [Cleveland, Tenn..: Pathway], p. 43; Henry Alford and E. F. Harrison, *The Greek Testament,* vol. 2, *Acts, Romans, Corinthians* [Chicago: Moody, 1968], pp. 15, 16; Robert Jamieson, A. R. Fausset, D. Brown, *A Commentary, Critical, Experimental and Practical on the Old and New Testaments,* vol. 3 [Grand Rapids: Eerdmans, 1984], part 2, p. 8; *Barnes Notes on the New Testament,* R. Frew, ed. [Grand Rapids: Baker, 1983], p. 23; John Peter Lange, *Commentary on the Holy Scriptures, Critical, Doctrinal and Homiletical* [Grand Rapids: Zondervan, 1866], Acts, p. 31; *The Broadman Bible Commentary,* C. J. Allen, gen. ed., vol. 10, Acts-1 Corinthians, [Broadman, 1970], p. 25).

[37] *Strange Gifts: A Guide to Charismatic Renewal,* David Martin and Peter Mullen, eds. (Basil Blackwell, 1984), p. 79; James D. G. Dunn, *Jesus and the Spirit: A Study of the Religious and Charismatic Experience of Jesus and the First Christians as Reflected in the New Testament* (Philadelphia: Westminster, 1975), p. 152; Smith's *Dictionary of the Bible,* revised by H. B. Hackett, Vol. IV (Grand Rapids: Baker, 1981), pp. 3307, 3308; W. E. Mills, *Speaking in Tongues,* pp. 52, 53, 55; C. G. Williams, *Tongues of the Spirit,* pp. 31-36, 213; John P. Kildahl, *The Psychology of Speaking in Tongues* (New York: Harper & Row, 1972), p. 23.

[38] John Calvin, *Commentary on the Epistles of Paul the Apostle,* trans. J. Pringle (Grand Rapids: Eerdmans, 1948), vol. 1, pp. 89, 435; Charles Hodge, *An Exposition of the First Epistle to the Corinthians* (Grand Rapids: Eerdmans, n.p.d.), pp. 266, 277, 280; Robert Jamieson, A. R. Fausset, D. Brown, vol. 3, part 3 (Grand Rapids: Eerdmans, 1984), p. 323; *Barnes Notes on the New Testament,* R. Frew, ed. (Grand Rapids: Baker, 1983), l Corinthians, pp. 260, 261; tongues as "an ability conferred by the Spirit to utter thoughts and feelings . . . peculiar to the individual . . . [in] his tongue" (Lange, 1 Corinthians pp. 289, 290); *The Expositor's Biblical Commentary,* vol. 10 (Grand Rapids: Zondervan, 1976), p. 273; L. Thomas Holdcroft, *The Holy Spirit: A Pentecostal Interpretation* (Springfield, Mo.: Gospel, 1979), pp. 121, 160; George B. Cutten, *Speaking with Tongues: Historically and Psychologically Considered* (New Haven, Conn.: Yale University, 1927), p. 30; Anthony A. Hoekema, *What About Tongue-Speaking?* (Grand Rapids: Eerdmans, 1966), pp. 43, 83; Anthony D. Palma, *Tongues and Prophecy—A Comparative Study in Charismata* (Thesis, Concordia Seminary, 1966), p. 46.

[39] *The New International Commentary on the New Testament,* F. F. Bruce, ed. (Grand Rapids: Eerdmans, 1987), 1 Corinthians, pp. 571, 598; "Glossolalia is not the speaking of a foreign language, for nobody needs a charisma to understand that sort of language" (F. W. Grosheide, *Commentary on the First Epistle to the Corinthians* [Grand Rapids: Eerdmans, 1972], p. 300; William Barclay, *The Letters to the Corinthians* [Philadelphia: Westminster, 1956], p. 124; Leon Morris, *The First Epistle of Paul to the Corinthians* [Leicester, England: InterVarsity, 1983], pp. 172f; *The International Standard Bible Encyclopedia,* James Orr, ed., vol. 4 [Grand Rapids: Eerdmans, 1984], p. 2296; R. M. Anderson, *Vision of the Disinherited: The Making of American Pentecostalism* [Oxford: Oxford University, 1979], p. 22; C. G. Williams, *Tongues of the Spirit,* p. 25; M. T. Kelsey, *Tongue Speaking,* p. 157; G. T. Montague, *The Holy Spirit, Growth of a Biblical Tradition* [New York: Paulist, 1976], p. 155; T. C. Edwards, *A Commentary on the First Epistle to the Corinthians* [Minnesota: Klock and Klock Christian, 1979], p. 320; A. A. Hoekema, *What About Tongue-Speaking?* [Grand Rapids: Eerdmans, 1966], p. 85).

[40] Mills, *Speaking in Tongues: A Guide to Research on Glossolalia,* p. 331.

[41] Charles R. Smith, *Tongues in Biblical Perspective: A Summary of Biblical Conclusions Concerning Tongues,* p. 42.

[42] David du Plessis, *Simple and Profound* (Orleans, Mass.: Paraclete, 1986), p. 28.

[43] *The Glossolalia Phenomenon,* pp. 43, 44.

[44] James D. G. Dunn, *Jesus and the Spirit: A Study of the Religious and Charismatic Experience of Jesus and the First Christians as Reflected in the New Testament* (Philadelphia: Westminster, 1975), p. 52.

[45] For example, Augustine, in *De Verb. Apost,* clxxv. 3 referenced in *Smith's Dictionary of the Bible,* rev. by H. B. Hackett, vol. 4 (Grand Rapids: Baker, 1981), p. 3306.

[46] Harold Horton, *What Is the Good of Speaking With Tongues? An Enthusiastic Vindication of Supernatural Endowment* (London: Assemblies of God), p. 25.

[47] This was suggested and rejected as early as A.D. 350 by Gregory of Nazianzen; see Kelsey, p. 150; Gregory of Nyssa accepted it as a gift of hearing, see *Smith's Dictionary of the Bible,* vol. 4, p. 3306; Venerable Bede considered it to be a gift of hearing, see *Perspectives on the New Pentecostalism,* Russell P. Spittler, ed., p. 4.

[48] G. Campbell Morgan, *The Corinthian Letters of Paul, an Exposition of 1 and 2 Corinthians* (New Jersey: Fleming H. Revell, 1946), pp. 170, 171.

[49] *The Pulpit Commentary,* H.H.M. Spence and J. S. Exell, eds., 1 Corinthians (Chicago: Wilcox and Follett, n.p.d.), p. 398.

[50] *The Glossolalia Phenomenon,* p. 44.

[51] A. D. Palma, *Tongues and Prophecy: A Comparative Study in Charismata* (thesis, Concordia Seminary, 1966), p. 51.

[52] Robert M. Anderson, *Vision of the Disinherited: The Making of American Pentecostalism* (Oxford: Oxford University, 1979), p. 22.

[53] Hector Camacho, *A Critical Examination of Glossolalia in American Christianity* (thesis, graduate school, Trinity University, 1971), p. 9.

[54] Anthony A. Hoekema, *What About Tongue-Speaking?* (Grand Rapids: Eerdmans, 1966), pp. 97, 98.

[55] *Perspectives on the New Pentecostalism,* Russell P. Spittler, ed., pp. 121, 125.

[56] For example, Henry Alford, rev. by E. F. Harrison, *The Greek Testament* (Chicago: Moody, 1968), p. 16.

[57] Roy A. Harrisville, "Speaking in Tongues: A Lexicographical Study," *Catholic Biblical Quarterly* 38, No. 1

(January 1976): 35-48; Ernest Best, "The Interpretation of Tongues," *Scottish Journal of Theology* 28, No. 1 (1975): 45-62; both articles were republished in Mills, *Speaking in Tongues: A Guide to Research on Glossolalia,* pp. 38, 305 respectively.

[58] *The Anchor Bible, Mark,* William F. Albright and David N. Freedman, eds. (New York: Doubleday, 1986), p. 673.

[59] Mills, *Speaking in Tongues: A Guide to Research on Glossolalia,* p. 57.

[60] "The passage is not found in any Greek manuscript earlier than the fifth century, and is not mentioned by any writer earlier than Eusebius, the fourth-century bishop and church historian. It may have been composed and added to some manuscripts of the gospel some time in the second century" (Frank W. Beare, "Speaking With Tongues: A Critical Survey of the New Testament Evidence," *Journal of Biblical Literature* 83 [September 1964]: 229-246; reprinted in *Speaking in Tongues: A Guide to Research on Glossolalia,* p. 108. "We do not know when and where the longer ending was appended" (M. Robert Mansfield, *Spirit and Gospel in Mark* [Peabody, Mass.: Hendrickson, 1987], p. 140).

[61] "Though it may be doubtful that these were the direct words of Jesus, this passage certainly represents the experience and expectation of the early church. In fact, the very probability that it comes from the second century makes it all the more significant. It then becomes a primary indication that the practice of tongues was not confined to the first days of the church" (Morton T. Kelsey, *Tongue Speaking, an Experiment Spiritual Experience,* p. 25).

[62] Gerhard F. Hasel, *Understanding the Living Word of God* (Mountain View, Calif.: Pacific Press, 1980), p. 99.

[63] R. G. Gromacki, p. 140.

[64] "The passage's authenticity is not, with Pentecostals, in question" (Bruner, p. 81); cf. "Virtually all scholars, including Pentecostals, agree that the reference to tongues in Mark 16:17 is spurious" (Mills, *Speaking in Tongues: A Guide to Research on Glossolalia,* p. 14).

[65] R.C.H. Lenski, *The Interpretation of St. Mark's Gospel* (Columbiana, Ohio: Wartburg, 1946), p. 764.

[66] E. G. White, *The Desire of Ages,* pp. 818, 821.

[67] "William F. Farmer shows that there is evidence for a deliberate omission of Mark 16:9-20, which favors the original inclusion and thus authenticity of these verses. He also argues that if this ending were not original, it would be most difficult to explain the widespread early knowledge in Irenaeus, Tatian, the Old Latin and Coptic versions" (Gerhard F. Hasel, *Understanding the Living Word of God,* p. 98). Hasel supports the Markan authorship *(ibid.,* p. 98, 99).

[68] R.C.H. Lenski, *The Interpretation of St. Mark's Gospel,* pp. 768-770; Paul B. Smith, *The Church on the Brink* (Wheaton, Ill.: Tyndale, 1977), p. 97.

[69] *Ibid.,* p. 769.

[70] C. R. Smith, *Tongues in Biblical Perspective: A Summary of Biblical Conclusions Concerning Tongues,* pp. 29, 30.

[71] Harold Hunter, *Spirit-Baptism: A Pentecostal Alternative* (New York: University Press of America, 1983), p. 15.

[72] *Speaking in Tongues: Let's Talk About It,* p. 84.

[73] *Ibid.,* p. 132; Robert M. Anderson, *Vision of the Disinherited: The Making of American Pentecostalism,* pp. 18, 19.

[74] L. T. Holdcroft, *The Holy Spirit: A Pentecostal Interpretation,* p. 109; Kelsey, p. 197.

[75] William G. MacDonald, "Glossolalia in the New Testament," *Bulletin of Evangelical Theological Society* 7 (1964): pp. 59-68, republished in *Speaking in Tongues: A Guide to Research on Glossolalia,* p. 129.

[76] H. N. Malony, A. A. Lovekin, *Glossolalia: Behavioral Science Perspectives on Speaking in Tongues* (Oxford: Oxford University, 1985), p. 254; L. C. May, "A Survey of Glossolalia and Related Phenomena in Non-Christian Religions," *American Anthropologist* 58, No. 1 (1956): 75-96, republished in *Speaking in Tongues: A Guide to Research in Glossolalia,* p. 58.

[77] C. R. Smith, *Tongues in Biblical Perspective: A Summary of Biblical Conclusions Concerning Tongues,* p. 28.

[78] George B. Cutten, *Speaking With Tongues: Historically and Psychologically Considered* (Hartford, Conn: Yale, 1927), p. 30.

[79] William J. Samarin, "Glossolalia as a Vocal Phenomenon," *Speaking in Tongues: Let's Talk About It,* p. 131.

[80] C. G. Williams, *Tongues of the Spirit: A Study of Pentecostal Glossolalia and Related Phenomena,* p. 25.

[81] *Perspectives on the New Pentecostalism,* p. 19; William G. MacDonald, "Glossolalia in the New Testament,"

Bulletin of Evangelical Theological Society 7 (1964): 59-68, republished in *Speaking in Tongues: A Guide to Research on Glossolalia,* pp. 127, 128.

[82] *Speaking in Tongues: Let's Talk About It,* p. 135; Cutten, p. 151.

[83] Robert M. Anderson, *Vision of the Disinherited: The Making of American Pentecostalism,* p. 22.

[84] *Speaking in Tongues: A Guide to Research on Glossolalia,* p. 2.

[85] Robert M. Anderson, *Vision of the Disinherited: The Making of American Pentecostalism,* p. 92; Harold Horton, *What Is the Good of Speaking With Tongues? An Enthusiastic Vindication of Supernatural Endowment,* p. 33; *Strange Gifts: A Guide to Charismatic Renewal,* pp. 72, 81; NT phenomenon "close enough" to today's tongues (J.P.M. Sweet, "A Sign for Unbelievers: Paul's Attitude to Glossolalia," *New Testament Studies* 13 [April 1967]: 240-257), reprinted in *Speaking in Tongues,* p. 142.

[86] Tongues ceased in the first century: Gromacki, pp. 28, 115, 118, 119, 125-127, 128, 131; L. T. Holdcroft, *The Holy Spirit: A Pentecostal Interpretation,* p. 98; C. R. Smith, *Tongues in Biblical Perspective: A Summary of Biblical Conclusions Concerning Tongues,* pp. 57, 59, 69, 70, 129; John F. MacArthur, *The Charismatics, a Doctrinal Perspective* (Grand Rapids: Zondervan, 1978), p. 162.

[87] "The degree of similarity between the New Testament phenomenon of glossolalia and later manifestations (e.g., current ones) is uncertain." Hector Camacho, *A Critical Examination of Glossolalia in American Christianity* (thesis), p. 119; Concerning the words "glossais lalein," "it cannot be determined . . . whether the New Testament phrase can be used appropriately to describe current 'speaking in tongues' phenomena." Stuart D. Currie, "Speaking in Tongues: Early Evidence Outside the New Testament Bearing on Glossais Lalein," *Interpretation* 19 (1965): 274-294, reprinted in *Speaking in Tongues, a Guide to Research on Glossolalia,* p. 105.

[88] The Church of God, for example, has the following declaration, which is typical. "We believe in the Baptism with the Holy Ghost subsequent to cleansing—the endowment of power for service" (Matt. 3:11; Luke 24:49-53; Acts 1:4-8). "We believe in the speaking in tongues as the Spirit gives utterance, as the initial evidence of the Baptism of the Holy Ghost" (John 15:26; Acts 2:4; 10:44-46; 19:1-7). "Declaration of Faith of the Church of God," *Book of the Minutes General Assemblies Churches of God* (1948) quoted by Hector Camacho, *A Critical Examination of Glossolalia in American Christianity* (thesis), p. 26.

[89] For example, William G. MacDonald, "Glossolalia in the New Testament," *Bulletin of Evangelical Theological Society* 7 (1964): 59-68, reprinted in *Speaking in Tongues: A Guide to Research on Glossolalia,* p. 139.

[90] "Although this is the majority opinion of the modern tongues movement, some Full Gospel people do not accept tongues as the only or necessary sign" (Gromacki, p. 98).

[91] Harold D. Hunter, *Spirit-Baptism: A Pentecostal Alternative* (New York: University Press of America, 1983), pp. 4, 8. For tongues-speakers this baptism "shifted from the idea of sanctification and holiness . . . to that of empowering for service" (James D. G. Bruner, *Baptism in the Holy Spirit,* p. 2).

[92] Quoted by Bruner, p. 74.

[93] Cf. "In my opinion, it is quite incongruous to infer that the Isaiah passage has a bearing upon charismatic conditions in the Christian church in general, or upon speaking in tongues in particular" (Cyril G. Williams, *Tongues of the Spirit: A Study of Pentecostal Glossolalia and Related Phenomena,* p. 77).

[94] *The Seventh-day Adventist Bible Commentary,* vol. 4, p. 210.

[95] "Because of Judah's constant unbelief and departure from the faith, God was going to bring judgment upon her—a judgment signaled by languages—other tongues" (John F. MacArthur, Jr., *The Charismatics,* p. 167).

[96] "Paul warns the Corinthians that according to Scripture tongues are meant as a sign for (= against!) those who reject God's simple message, not as the Corinthians assume, as a sign for the benefit of believers . . ." (William G. MacDonald, *Glossolalia in the New Testament,* p. 144).

[97] For further evidence on this, "The Christ-centered Ministry of the Spirit," see *Adventist Perspectives* 2, No. 1 (1988): 51-56.

[98] James D. G. Dunn, *Baptism in the Holy Spirit,* p. 53.

[99] *Ibid.,* p. 49.

[100] "When we look at Pentecost in the context of Luke-Acts it becomes evident that Pentecostal and Catholic alike have again missed the principal significance of the story. For once again we stand at a watershed in salvation-history, the beginning of the new age and new covenant, not for Jesus this time, but now for his disciples. What Jordan was to Jesus, Pentecost was to the disciples" (Dunn, p. 40).

[101] Although Acts 8 does not speak of tongues, we include it here as so many tongues-speakers include it with

chapters 10 and 19. To put it another way, wherever the book of Acts mentions tongues subsequent to Acts 2, it is not a repetition of Pentecost but an extension of the unrepeatable Pentecost.

[102] L. T. Holdcroft, *The Holy Spirit: A Pentecostal Interpretation,* p. 122.

[103] This is not to suggest that one should not seek for a new baptism of the Spirit each day. This we should. But it does hold that seekers after tongues are often searching for the gift rather than the Giver.

[104] F. D. Bruner, *A Theology of the Holy Spirit,* p. 241.

[105] *Ibid.,* p. 235.

[106] See *Adventist Perspectives* 2, No. 1: 51-56.

[107] Dunn, p. 66.

[108] *Ibid.,* p. 96.

[109] *Ibid.,* p. 228.

[110] Robert M. Anderson, *Vision of the Disinherited: The Making of American Pentecostalism* (Oxford: Oxford University, 1979), p. 24.

[111] "The view that Paul's conversion was instantaneous and that he was only later filled with the Spirit is very common, but it is one which must be sharply questioned. . . . Paul's conversion was only completed when he called on Jesus as Lord, was filled with the Spirit and had his sins washed away; then, and only then, can he be called a Christian" (Dunn, pp. 73, 78).

[112] "Chapter 13 is not to be regarded as interrupting the discourse concerning the charismata. On the contrary, it is a necessary link in the argument which has as its purpose to assign to the glossolalia its rightful place" (F. W. Grosheide, *Commentary on the First Epistle to the Corinthians: The English Text With Introduction, Exposition and Notes* [Grand Rapids: Eerdmans, 1972], p. 303).

[113] Anthony A. Hoekema, *What About Tongue-Speaking?* p. 97.

[114] Charles R. Smith, *Tongues in Biblical Perspective,* p. 20; Robert G. Gromacki, *The Modern Tongues Movement,* p. 50.

[115] *Speaking in Tongues: Let's Talk About It,* p. 13.

[116] Charles R. Smith, *Tongues in Biblical Perspective,* p. 22.

[117] Robert G. Gromacki, *The Modern Tongues Movement,* p. 50.

[118] Smith, p. 22.

[119] Along with the gift of healing, also much prized by Pentecostals and charismatics.

[120] John T. Bunn, "Glossolalia in Historical Perspective" *Speaking in Tongues: Let's Talk About It,* p. 36.

[121] *Ibid.,* pp. 36-47; William J. Samarin, "Glossolalia as Vocal Phenomenon," p. 130; *Speaking in Tongues: A Guide to Research on Glossolalia,* p. 54; L. C. May, "A Survey of Glossolalia and Related Phenomena in Non-Christian Religions," *American Anthropologist;* Robert M. Anderson, *Vision of the Disinherited,* p. 20.

[122] *Speaking in Tongues, Let's Talk About It,* p. 46.

[123] *The Seventh-day Adventist Bible Commentary,* vol. 6, p. 769.

[124] Bunn, "Glossolalia in Historical Perspective," P. 43.

[125] *Ibid.*

[126] Anthony A. Hoekema, *What About Tongue-Speaking?* p. 130.

[127] Frederick D. Bruner, *A Theology of the Holy Spirit,* p. 103.

[128] "It is also possible for tongue-speech to occur apart from any group" (Morton E. Kelsey, Tongue Speaking, p. 13); Du Plessis said of his own baptism, "I refused to let anyone lay hands on me . . . I went off by myself and knelt alone in a corner, away from the rest, and asked the Lord to help me, and to baptize me" *(Simple and Profound,* p. 22). Note: He had evidently been in the meeting..

[129] "Sometimes people agonize for years to receive this gift." One example is given of a person who sought for the gift for 10 years. "I have read of instances where people have become mentally ill because they failed to 're-ceive'" (Anthony A. Hoekema, *What About Tongue-Speaking?* p. 58).

[130] Hector Camacho, *A Critical Examination of Glossolalia in American Christianity,* p. 52.

[131] Term used by John P. Kildahl, "Psychological Observations," *The Charismatic Movement,* Michael P. Hamilton, ed. (Grand Rapids: Eerdmans, 1975), pp. 124-142; reprinted in *Speaking in Tongues,* Watson E. Mills, ed., p. 353.

[132] Robert G. Gromacki, *The Modern Tongues Movement,* p. 50.

[133] Hector Camacho, *A Critical Examination of Glossolalia in American Christianity,* p. 53.

THE CHARISMATIC MOVEMENT

[134] *Ibid.;* Frederick D. Bruner, *A Theology of the Holy Spirit,* p. 133.

[135] Bruner, pp. 137, 138.

[136] Robert G. Gromacki, *The Modern Tongues Movement,* p. 100. Gromacki gives seven instructions that he calls "auto-suggestions" (pp. 99, 100).

[137] *Speaking in Tongues,* Watson E. Mills, ed., p. 339.

[138] John P. Kildahl, *The Psychology of Speaking in Tongues,* p. 3; "Tongue speakers have had to be coached, coaxed, and forced into their utterances" (Charles R. Smith, *Tongues in Biblical Perspective,* p. 96).

[139] Some tongues seekers are "told to breathe deeply and say 'cha-cha,' 'cha-cha,' 'cha-cha' in the same manner until the Holy Spirit takes over and they speak in tongues" (Joe E. Campbell, *Warning! Do Not Seek for Tongues,* p. 30).

[140] *Speaking in Tongues,* p. 339.

[141] Bruner, p. 113.

[142] Robert G. Gromacki, *The Modern Tongues Movement,* p. 100.

[143] Concerning "Unfruitful," "This has been understood in two ways: (1) The prayer is unfruitful because it is not understood by the hearers and consequently imparts no benefit. (2) The conscious mind is largely if not entirely inoperative during the exercise of the gift, as in the case of a prophet in vision" *(The Seventh-day Adventist Bible Commentary,* vol. 6, p. 789).

[144] Robert M. Anderson, *Vision of the Disinherited,* p. 11.

[145] George B. Cutten, *Speaking With Tongues: Historically and Psychologically Considered,* p. 131.

[146] John P. Kildahl, "Psychological Observations," *The Charismatic Movement,* p. 355.

[147] John P. Kildahl, *The Psychology of Speaking in Tongues* (New York: Harper & Row, 1972), p. 37.

[148] *Ibid.,* pp. 54, 55.

[149] L. T. Holdcroft, *The Holy Spirit: A Pentecostal Interpretation,* p. 161.

[150] John P. Kildahl, *The Psychology of Speaking in Tongues,* p. 25.

[151] Frank Stagg, E. G. Hinson, Wayne E. Oates, Glossolalia: *Tongue Speaking in Biblical, Historical, and Psychological Perspective* (Nashville: Abingdon, 1967), p. 93.

[152] *Speaking in Tongues: A Guide to Research and Glossolalia,* p. 435; Morton T. Kelsey, *Tongue Speaking,* p. 7.

[153] Stuart D. Currie, "Speaking in Tongues: Early Evidence Outside the New Testament Bearing on Glossais Lalein," *Interpretation,* XIX (1965), pp. 274-294; reprinted in *Speaking in Tongues,* Watson E. Mills, p. 98.

[154] Morton T. Kelsey, *Tongue Speaking,* pp. 138-140, cf. pp. 144, 146, 147.

[155] Leon Morris, *The First Epistle of Paul to the Corinthians: An Introduction and Commentary,* pp. 199, 200.

[156] Morton T. Kelsey, *Tongue Speaking: An Experiment in Spiritual Experience,* p. 222.

[157] Cyril G. Williams, *Tongues of the Spirit: A Study of Pentecostal Glossolalia and Related Phenomena,* p. 83.

[158] Robert G. Gromacki, *The Modern Tongues Movement,* pp. 49, 50.

[159] For example, George B. Cutten: "As far as I know there is no case of speaking in strange tongues which has been strictly and scientifically investigated that cannot be explained by recognized psychological laws" (*Speaking With Tongues,* p. 181); Psychiatrist Stuart Bergsman: "All these [experiences] have left me with the conviction that glossolalia especially can be psychologically explained and is not, in general, a 'spiritual' phenomenon" (Anthony A. Hoekema, *What About Tongue-Speaking?* p. 129). Psychiatrist E. Mansell Pattison: "As a psychological phenomenon, glossolalia is easy to produce and readily understandable" *(ibid.).*

[160] Robert G. Gromacki, *The Modern Tongues Movement,* p. 66.

[161] *Speaking in Tongues: A Guide to Research on Glossolalia,* p. 361; cf. John P. Kildahl, *The Psychology of Speaking in Tongues,* p. 63.

[162] *Speaking in Tongues: A Guide to Research on Glossolalia,* p. 362.

[163] John P. Kildahl, *The Psychology of Speaking in Tongues,* p. 34.

[164] Frank Stagg, E. G. Hinson, Wayne E. Oates, *Glossolalia,* p. 84.

[165] Hector Camacho, *A Critical Examination of Glossolalia in American Christianity,* p. 81.

[166] Robert M. Anderson, *Vision of the Disinherited,* p. 240.

[167] *Speaking in Tongues: Let's Talk About It,* Watson E. Mills, ed., p. 31.

[168] Cyril G. Williams, *Tongues of the Spirit,* p. 166.

[169] Morton T. Kelsey, *Tongue Speaking,* p. 222.

[170] John F. MacArthur, *The Charismatics,* pp. 156, 157.

[171] One researcher suggests that in 1927 Pentecostals were nearly all from those of low mental ability (George B. Cutten, *Speaking With Tongues,* pp. 6, 168); early tongues-speakers were from rural areas and lower classes (Hector Camacho, *A Critical Examination of Glossolalia in American Christianity,* p. 19).

[172] Tongues entered higher classes after World War I *(Perspectives on the New Pentecostalism,* p. 259); Neo-Pentecostals are scholars, professionals (Robert G. Gromacki, *The Modern Tongues Movement,* p. 50; Hector Camacho, *A Critical Examination of Glossolalia in American Christianity,* p. 59; Wealthy, *Speaking in Tongues: A Guide to Research and Glossolalia,* p. 302; Richard Quebedeaux, *The New Charismatics: The Origins, Development, and Significance of Neo-Pentecostalism* [New York: Doubleday, 1976], p. 201).

[173] The Holiness movement opposed (1) Darwin's evolutionism, (2) higher criticism, and (3) Horace Bushnell's aversion to Christian conversion (Morton T. Kelsey, *Tongue Speaking,* pp. 70-73).

[174] Robert M. Anderson, *Vision of the Disinherited,* p. 31.

[175] J. R. Williams, "Pentecostal Theology: A Neo-Pentecostal Viewpoint," in *Perspectives on the New Pentecostalism,* Russell P. Spittler, ed., p. 85.

[176] "All the world wondered after the beast" (Rev. 13:3, KJV), so that means the churches will unite.

[177] E. G. White, *The Great Controversy,* p. 464.

[178] *Ibid.,* pp. 444, 445.

[179] *Ibid.,* p. 588.

[180] The faith-healing movement is an important dimension of the counterfeit latter rain and Pentecostal movements, which would take a separate chapter to develop. For example, Oral Roberts inspired the formation of the Full Gospel Businessmen's Fellowship, which did much to take the tongues movement worldwide.

[181] W. H. Turner, *Pentecost and Tongues* (Franklin Springs, Ga.: Advocate, 1968), p. 99; Anthony A. Hoekema, *What About Tongue-Speaking?* p. 62; Pneuma, *The Journal of the Society of Pentecostal Studies,* No. 2 (Fall 1980); L. T. Holdcroft, *The New Order of the Latter Rain,* pp. 46-64; Pneuma, *The Journal of the Society of Pentecostal Studies* 4, No. 1: Richard Riss, *The Latter Rain Movement of 1948,* pp. 32-45; Frank Bartleman, *Azusa Street* (Plainfield, N.J.: Logos International, 1980), p. v.; Frank Stagg, E. G. Hinson, Wayne E. Oates, *Glossolalia,* pp. 67-69; Joe E. Campbell, *Warning! Do Not Seek for Tongues,* pp. 3, 4; Morton T. Kelsey, *Tongue Speaking,* p. 77; Vinson Synan, *In the Latter Days: The Outpouring of the Holy Spirit in the Twentieth Century* (Michigan: Servant Books, 1988), pp. 38-42; Robert M. Anderson, *Vision of the Disinherited,* pp. 40-45; John F. MacArthur, *The Charismatics,* p. 171.

[182] Bruner, p. 28.

[183] Hector Camacho, *A Critical Examination of Glossolalia in American Christianity,* p. 61.

[184] Bruner, p. 28.

[185] Hector Camacho, *A Critical Examination of Glossolalia in American Christianity,* p. 61.

[186] E. G. White, *The Great Controversy,* p. 464.

[187] Miracles are a comparable sign today, and are also a part of the Pentecostal-Charismatic-faith healing movement (Rev. 16:13-16).

[188] *The Seventh-day Adventist Bible Commentary,* vol. 6, pp. 467, 655, 994.

[189] Interpreters generally recognize verses 28-30 as a prioritization of the first, second, and third gifts. Tongues and their interpretation comprise the last two.

[190] The four lists of gifts vary quite considerably and are not exhaustive. For example, they do not include the gifts of music, creativity, and writing. Evidently Paul was concerned with the Spirit gifts required to build up the infant church, yet undoubtedly did not mention all because music must have been an important part of that ministry.

[191] In fact, if tongues-seekers need to select a gift as *the* sign of Spirit baptism, then the gift of apostleship, placed first by Paul (1 Cor. 12:28), would seemingly have priority over the rest.

[192] See *Adventist Perspectives* 2, No. 1 (1988), pp. 51-56.

Chapter 12

Theosophy: Roots of the New Age Movement

London is a big city. It's easy for little kids to get lost in it. Bigger people too! One of the reference points in London is Charring Cross. Located near the center of the city, it has helped many stranded people find their way. One day a little girl found herself lost. She sobbed her heart out, not knowing where she was. A kind English bobby (policeman) found her.

"Are you lost?"

"Yes." She looked up at him through her tears.

"Do you know the address where you live?"

"No." She sniffled.

"Do you know your telephone number?"

"No, no," she sobbed.

"So what do you know about the place where you live?" he asked.

Silence. Then her face brightened. "I know the cross," she said. "Show me the cross, and I can find my way home from there."[1]

Satan hates the cross and seeks to provide all sorts of other road maps for people to try to find their way spiritually home. One such road map, called theosophy, is actually a major detour away from Calvary. It's a forerunner of another popular road map today called the New Age movement. Because the New Age movement is an important part of end-time events, we need to look at its roots carefully. Theosophical literature includes ideas from fallen angels speaking through its leaders.

Where We've Come So Far

We've seen that Satan gathers the world to his camp. The showdown will be Armageddon (see chapters 42 and 44). He must really think he can win. The masses have flocked to his side. Also we discovered that many believe that all religions will get them home. "It doesn't matter which path you take, as long as you take one," they say. "All lead to the same destination." That's just what Satan wants lost people to swallow. Then when the masses march in the wrong direction, he gloats over them with glee. As long as they keep wandering and don't think of the reference point—the cross—he has them. So a return to Rome, ecumenism, and spirituality take the place of doctrine. It's like the preacher who wrote in his sermon notes: "Weak argument here, so pound the desk. Speak loudly." As if noise will make the difference. Modern religion has much noise in it. Music will do it. Shouting in tongues will work. Anything that makes emotions rule the mind suits the enemy well.

We've seen how spiritualism uses miracles. Have you watched those TV faith healers? There you have noise. A shove helps too. You've seen the sick fall back down after a push on the forehead. But Jesus healed quietly and without a show. Talk about tongues being a sign of the Spirit. Which spirit? God's Spirit has His own reputation. As we have seen, the Bible says: "The fruit of the Spirit is love, joy, peace, patience, kindness, goodness, faithfulness, gentleness and self-control" (Gal. 5:22, 23). That's it—"gentleness!" Does that characterize the noise of tongues-speech and the shoving of faith healers? Hardly.

So spiritualism remains Satan's trump card. With cunning and craft he plays it. He works through it to appeal to the senses just as he did in Eden. It worked then, and it's succeeding now. Spiritualism operates through the charismatic movement as it convinces people to seek tongues and not the Saviour, works rather than Christ. A purposeful diversion, it gets people off the right road that leads home. "Here's the way"—but it's going in the opposite direction.

Spiritualism in the end-time operates through the charismatic movement in the churches and through the New Age movement in the world at large. Through both, Satan seeks to take over the world. At work in both are "spirits of demons performing miraculous signs" as "they go out to the kings of the whole world, to gather them for the battle on the great day of God Almighty" (Rev. 16:14).

When the charismatic movement began to infiltrate almost all Christian denominations, the New Age movement began to grab the unchurched and even some of the churched. It seems as if Satan launched his final push for world domination in the 1960s.

Both have ancient roots too. Spiritualism got its modern start at the same time the Seventh-day Adventist Church began. The New Age movement has roots that go back to Buddha, about 500 B.C. In reality, though, spiritualism and the New Age movement trace back to Eden, in which Satan lied, "You will not surely die," and "you will be like God" (Gen. 3:1-5).

The End-time Plan

Blending other religions with Christianity will not advance the cause of Christ. Yet such an attempted mixing is at the heart of the New Age movement and its end-of-the-age plan. What is this plan especially championed by H. P. Blavatsky and Alice Bailey?[2] It claims that all religions come from the same source.[3] Such a belief alleges that doctrines, dogmas, and creeds not only divide their adherents but distance them from their source in mysticism,[4] the original mysteries[5]—viewed as the immanent God/Christ,[6] a synthesizing of "tension between spirit and matter."[7] The New Age plan is to restore this spiritual dimension by evolving human consciousness[8] into a return to the spirit[9] by going beyond belief to experience. It wants us to realize that we are divine entities with a global destiny having a unique New Age plan for eschatological things.

I will let the leaders of Theosophy speak for themselves. Some may ask, "Why in the world do we have to read about Theosophy?" Good question. We're looking behind the present New Age movement to see what its precursor did, searching for Satan's plan to get all the world into his camp. Remember he will come as Christ (c.f. 2 Cor. 11:14). How will that influence a mostly non-Christian world? How does this contribute to all the world worshiping Satan (Rev. 13:4)? We'll see that the names of Jesus and Christ appear in this older theosophical literature, as it does in the current New Age movement publications. But it demotes Christ to just one of many religious leaders. Yet, paradoxically in some passages, He's also the leader in realms above. But that's only when it suits Satan.

Satan will come not as Buddha or Muhammad but as Christ. But the demoting of Christ seems Satan's favorite approach. When he wanted to take Christ's place, it didn't work. So now he vicariously grabs that position by demoting Christ. In this way Satan makes room for other religions to have equal place in the public square. He claims that all religions lead home. Human beings have many points of reference—not just the cross. But look at what he does to the cross. Consider the way spirituality dominates the discussion and how doctrinal differences get thrown on the trash heap.

We know Catholics and Protestants are getting closer today. We'll study this in the chapter on the Christian Coalition. Christians of all denominations push a common moral agenda, like the right to life for the unborn. But they trash the right of doctrines to show the way. Their moral crusade combats a disintegrating culture, yet their doctrines, which make them different from that culture, lay in shreds as the mad moral dash rides roughshod over all else. That's what's happening in all religions. Forget the differences. Concentrate on the one fact shared in common—spirituality. That's what it is. And spirituality is just another name for spiritualism. Demons work through non-Christian religions as well as Christian denominations. They throw truth to the winds in the cause of a lie. The final coming of Satan as Christ—that's the lie. All we read about in these chapters on Theosophy and the New Age movement have one common goal—to prepare the world for Satan's coming as the false Christ.

So we will take a look at this aspect of Satan's end-time strategy. If you want to skip this and the next chapter, that's fine. It documents the strategy, so you can see that it's not just in my imagination. Here you'll find the evidence. But you've got the game plan now. Don't miss chapter 14, which shows how Satan attacks Christ in New Age Bibles, even though he plans to come as Christ. In these chapters you'll see how Satan hates Christ and the cross, yet he pretends to come as Christ! He pretends to be the One whom he hates the most! He does that because he wants to derail spiritual travelers from the only road that goes home. Jesus said, "I am the way and the truth and the life. No one comes to the Father except through me" (John 14:6). Satan will do everything possible to hide Christ and the cross that gets human beings to Him. That's what it's all about.

New Age of Synthesis

The coming New Age has been variously named "Age of Aquarius,"[10] "Age of the Group,"[11] "Age of God the Holy Spirit,"[12] and "New Age of Synthesis."[13] Each title speaks of a time when a New Age "global consciousness" will result from a recognition of a single source for all religions.[14]

Some believe that "Christ is the essence of all evolving life."[15] He is "the Cosmic Christ who lives and breathes in Jesus and in *all* God's children, in all the prophets of religions everywhere, in all creatures of the universe."[16] Matthew Fox sees this pantheistic mysticism of the Cosmic Christ as the key to global unity—the ultimate synthesis. "The Cosmic Christ and the living cosmology that the Cosmic Christ ushers into society and psyche have the power to launch an era of what I call deep ecumenism. Deep ecumenism is the movement that will unleash the wisdom of *all* world religions—Hinduism and Buddhism, Islam and Judaism, Taoism and Shintoism, Christianity in all its forms, and native religions and goddess religions throughout the world. This unleashing of wisdom holds the last hope for the survival of the planet we call home."[17]

His "Cosmic Christ" concept regards Christ as much in everyone as in the man Jesus. "Does the fact that the Christ became incarnate in Jesus exclude the Christ's becoming incarnate in others—Lao-tzu or Buddha or Moses or Sarah or Sojourner Truth or Gandhi or me or you? Just the opposite is the case."[18] "Divinity wants to birth the Cosmic Christ in each and every individual."[19] Here synthesis has overthrown the uniqueness of Christ (His unrepeatable incarnation) in Scripture.

Brief Overview of Roots

Before looking at the roots of the New Age movement, we need to remember that the writings of Helenova Blavatsky and Alice Bailey all had their origin in fallen angels. Through such documents we see what fallen angels are saying about matters that prepare the world for Satan's final takeover bid.

The New Age movement focuses chiefly on an age to come, an eschatological movement that points to an achievable goal for humanity. Post-Vietnam America was antiestablishment, antimaterialism, and pro-spirit, seeking to transcend humanistic materialism and inaugurate a new age. It was a form of escapism preoccupied with humanity's place in the universe, its evolution to divinity, and therefore its shared place within the pantheistic presence called "god." Meditation, introspection, and mantra-chanting became hallmarks of those seeking to transcend the present through enlightenment. "Global consciousness" held out hope for the planet. But "most contemporary New Agers were probably never a part of the sixties counterculture."[20]

This revolt of the 1960s goes back to several sources that fed into the emerging

New Age movement.[21] We'll briefly consider the thinking of: (1) Pierre Teilhard de Chardin, (2) Helena P. Blavatsky, and (3) Alice A. Bailey as sources for New Age eschatology. All three believed in evolution and in humanity's transcending present conditions. Extrabiblical sources guided all three.

Pierre Teilhard de Chardin

Although the Catholic Church opposed the priest/paleontologist Teilhard's writings, Vatican II stressed freedom for Catholic scientists to accept evolutionary theory, the concept basic to Teilhard's eschatology.[22] It was the first of the 21 ecumenical councils to address world religions.[23] When we consider that Pope John Paul II admonished Catholics "to look to the East for inspiration,"[24] then, truly, "the Roman Catholic Church has also been fertile soil for New Age-associated theology and suppositions."[25]

Teilhard makes up his own dictionary of words. You'll see them in the following paragraph. The whole idea is that evolution ends in a humanity lumped into one collective consciousness.

In *The Future of Man* Pierre Teilhard de Chardin writes of the "progressive genesis of the Universe"[26] in which the "*human spirit* is still in process of evolution."[27] This is an "anthropogenesis"[28] within a "cosmogenesis,"[29] for both the cosmos and consciousness are evolving. Teilhard, in speaking of the "highest state of consciousness"[30] and the "growth of consciousness,"[31] focuses on a "super-consciousness" and its connection with a "new age."[32] The paleontologist looked for a "universal unification"[33] of humanity, its "socialization,"[34] "collectivisation,"[35] "totalization,"[36] or "planetisation."[37] He believed humanity now faces a cosmic choice.[38] The human race is at the "critical point" in evolution. "We can progress only by uniting."[39]

Teilhard compared what he saw as the contemporary critical moment with that faced by Copernicus with his revolutionary cosmology in the sixteenth century.[40] Copernicus discovered a world in motion. Teilhard perceived a cosmos and humanity in process moving toward "superhumanization,"[41] to the "emergence of the 'Ultra-Human.'"[42] This "one single consciousness," or culmination of anthropogenesis, is the human precondition for the end of the world.[43] "It is then, we may be sure, that the Parousia will be realized in a creation that has been taken to the climax of its capacity for union."[44] In other words, human beings hold the key to bring the Second Advent.

Theosophical Preparation for the New Age

So the world's end depends upon human progress and, as we shall see, human action. One might call Teilhard's approach an anthropocentric eschatology. It is compatible with Theosophy, in which human works are central. Theosophic, esoteric secrets, allegedly passed on through the centuries, today influence New Age philosophy. Through its teaching it aims that "the West will learn to understand and appreciate the East at its true value."[45]

Ellen G. White warns against Theosophy. "There is danger in having the least connection with Theosophy, or spiritualism. It is spiritualism in essence, and will always lead in the same path as spiritualism. These are the doctrines that seduce the people whom Christ has purchased with His own blood. You cannot break this spell."[46]

Esotericist Benjamin Creme, spokesperson for the coming Meitreya (supposed "Christ"), summed up the contribution of theosophical leaders Blavatsky and Bailey to the New Age movement as follows: "From the Hierarchical point of view, the *Secret Doctrine* of Madame Blavatsky, the founder of the Theosophical Society, represents the preparatory phase of the Teaching given out to the world for this new age. The Teaching embodied in the *Alice Bailey Teachings* represents the intermediate phase of this Teaching. . . . The next stage, the Revelatory Phase, we are told, will emerge, worldwide, through the medium of the radio, after 1975. That is because the Masters and the Christ will soon be in the world, and the Revelations will take place through the medium of the radio (and television)."[47]

The idea of a Hierarchy of Masters allegedly guiding our planet and sending messages to humanity first came from Blavatsky in 1875 and in much greater detail by Bailey from 1919 to 1949.[48] *Isis Unveiled* and *The Secret Doctrine* by Blavatsky "laid the foundation for the modern New Age belief system."[49] Blavatsky and Bailey—the latter with her own 25 books—became an influential force behind the development of New Age eschatology.[50] The books reveal Satan's scheme and strategy for the end-time.

Helena P. Blavatsky (1831-1891)

Blavatsky, in *The Secret Doctrine*, claims that the teachings belong neither to the Hindu, the Zoroastrian, the Chaldean, nor the Egyptian religions, and neither to Buddhism, Islam, Judaism, nor Christianity exclusively. *The Secret Doctrine* contains the essence of all the religions. The various religious schemes are now made to merge back into their original element, out of which every mystery and dogma has grown, developed, and became materialized.[51]

Not only is syncretism apparent here, but the materialized doctrines, dogmas, or creeds seem to go back to a single spiritual source.[52] Later we'll see the claim that Christ will finally restore the mysteries, and this in the context of a focus on the spiritual. The first volume of *The Secret Doctrine* is entitled "Cosmogenesis," and the second volume, *Anthropogenesis*—the same two aspects of evolution perceived by Teilhard de Chardin. The interesting fact is that the Catholic De Chardin and the Theosophist Blavatsky (and later Bailey) all held a process world view for both cosmos and creatures (see chapter 3).

Blavatsky said she wrote her *Isis Unveiled* under supernatural orders,[53] channeled to her through dictation[54] or through "visible" quotations.[55] She stated that "every word of information found in this work or in my later writings, comes from the teachings of our Eastern Masters."[56] In this setting, it's important to note her syncretism of Christianity with other religions. Thus Blavatsky believed that Christ taught the mysteries,[57] that "Jesus was a kabalist" who hinted "that John was the *revolutio,* or transmigration of Elias,"[58] and that He received His education from Essene priests in Egypt or Judea.[59] She said the supposedly true gospels were determined through magic,[60] and that "the true spirit of Christianity can alone be fully found in Buddhism."[61]

Established in 1875 by Blavatsky, the Theosophical Society adopted several major goals that have remained worded the same since 1896. They are: "(1) To form the nucleus of a Universal Brotherhood of Humanity without distinction of race," creed, sex, caste, or color. (2) To encourage the study of comparative religion, philosophy, and science. (3) To investigate unexplained laws of nature and the powers latent in humanity.[62] It follows that "the Fellows may be Christians or Mussulmen, Jews or Parsees, Buddhists or Brahmins, Spiritualists or Materialists, it does not matter."[63]

Theosophy is an occult movement whose Fellows devote themselves to the esoteric study of the secrets of wisdom handed down through the ages.[64] To them, the material universe is a temporary illusion that has come into existence through evolution.[65] Theosophy teaches "as there are seven fundamental forces in nature, and seven planes of being, so there are seven states of consciousness."[66]

Humanity is an emanation from divinity. At an advanced point upon the path, those who have spent several incarnations to its achievement reach adeptship. Nobody has ever reached adeptship in the Secret Sciences in one life. It requires many incarnations.[67] (And this included the man Jesus too!). Here again we see the ancient lie: "You will be like God" (Gen. 3:5). It is not ancient wisdom at all, but what got us into all the mess in the first place.

Theosophy decidedly rejects resurrection in favor of reincarnation.[68] It considers the body an illusion. Only the human spirit is real.[69] The whole system is one of human works, through various lives, to rid one of karma—the bad from previous lives that allegedly causes the inequality people experience.[70] Therefore it rejects Calvary. "The faintest glimmering sense of Justice revolts against this Vicarious Atonement! . . . That the spilling of one blood washes out the other blood spilt—this is preposterous!"[71]

Against this background we better understand the theosophical eschatology imbibed by the New Age movement. Theosophy believes that during the last quarter of every hundred years "Masters" attempt to help humanity's spiritual progress in a marked and definite way. Toward the close of each century you will invariably find that an outpouring or upheaval of spirituality—or call it mysticism, if you prefer—has taken place. People have appeared in the world as the Masters' agents, presenting occult knowledge and teaching.[72] That means there's more demonic energy pouring out as we end this century. The fact is that the end-time will indeed witness unprecedented energy—from Satan and from the latter rain Holy Spirit poured out from heaven.

Blavatsky sums up the purpose of the Theosophical Society as preparing the world for the coming of a "new torch-bearer of Truth." Thus, "if the Theosophical Society survives and lives true to its mission, to its original impulses through the next hundred years, . . . will be a heaven in the twenty-first century in comparison with what it is now!"[73] Note that theosophists expect a teacher to appear before the turn of the century, who will bring "new truths," and that they will have prepared the way for his arrival.

Alice A. Bailey

Alice A. Bailey, Blavatsky's successor, may well have been the first to use the term "new age." She employs it at least six times in *The Externalization of the Hierarchy,* and as early as 1919.[74] An alleged ascended Master D. K. provided insights into final events on earth to Blavatsky and Bailey, speaking of it as the "Plan."[75]

We'll look at facets of this plan. Three centers—Shamballa (source of highest energies), the hierarchy, and humanity—occupy center stage in the book. The hierarchy consists of ascended Masters (human beings who attained fifth initiation), who are allegedly assigned to guide human evolution.[76] They originally stood between Shamballa and humanity, until a new direct alignment between Shamballa and humanity was achieved in May 1946.[77] Since then, energy has been flooding our planet as a part of the preparatory process for final events. This pantheistic and mystical energy "will change the mode of human living and inaugurate the new age"[78] as a kind of counterfeit latter-rain Holy Spirit, for energies in New Age eschatology are nonpersonal.[79]

Let us look at what such energies supposedly do in final events. For one thing, they change human consciousness. The hierarchy's "emphasis is solely on *the consciousness aspect,*"[80] partly because peace must precede the reappearance of Christ,[81] and "these energies bring about . . . the 'events' of the day."[82] But members of the hierarchy have also been coming to live on earth since 1860,[83] with many of their disciples "today actively functioning in human affairs . . . to change the trend of human thinking from a frank materialism to a genuine spiritual aspiration."[84]

Creme reports that in 1976 five Masters came[85] to New York, London, Geneva, Darjeeling, and Tokyo—the five centers serving as exits for energy through which, Bailey claims, the "rebuilding and reorganizing of the world" will take place.[86] Psychic Ruth Montgomery speaks of "Walk-ins" from Sirius who come "in and out of earth lives quite easily" and find ways "that may help us develop beyond our present limitations."[87] You might say a lot of advents take place before the Second Advent. At least that's the theory fallen angels are dictating for consumption by the masses.

Bailey says the Hierarchy, Christ, and Masters of Wisdom will all visit Planet Earth. The process has taken a long time due to human unreadiness and hierarchical difficulty in reentering physical manifestation. The externalization process actually began in the year 1425.[88] The externalization (reentering the physical plane) supposedly occurs in three stages: (1) The coming of junior members of the hierarchy to become leaders on the planet.[89] The "real Builders of the new world," they will take over the control "subjectively as well as objectively—of the direction of human affairs."[90] (2) The senior members of the hierarchy "will take over from them, and theirs will be the task of instituting a more unified preparation for the return of the Christ. The first group prepares humanity for the possibility; the second group definitely prepares for the return itself. . . . This second group will implement the new religion."[91] (3) Then Christ and the Masters of Wisdom will arrive.[92]

Reappearance of Christ

In 1935 Bailey spoke of a transitional period between the Piscean Age and the Aquarian Age.[93] Christ's reappearance will "inaugurate the new age and so complete the work He began in Palestine two thousand years ago."[94] We must understand this within its evolutionary context, for humans, angels, and Christ are all evolving.[95] Human evolution is "the steady growth of divinity."[96] In fact, humanity will be so spiritual at the time of Christ's appearance that inexplicably it will "call forth a degree of holiness on His part which would negate His appropriation of a physical body of a caliber which would enable Him to manifest among men. This was *not* the case two thousand years ago; it is, however, the case today, so great is human advancement and the success of the evolutionary process."[97]

Yet, paradoxically, "to enable Him today to walk among men requires a world which will have in it enough effective workers and spiritually-minded people to change the atmosphere of our planet; then and only then, the Christ can, and will, come."[98] The first time Christ showed humanity that God was near or immanent in the man Jesus.[99] He revealed divinity in all human beings. For example, "at the Transfiguration, Christ revealed the glory which is innate in all men."[100] Yet "His work [is] unfinished."[101] Christ returns to complete His mission. And what does that involve? A greater work, because He has evolved together with the human race during the intervening 2,000 years.[102] Now He will "bring a new salvation to humanity."[103]

Such New Agers present Christ in process in a manner similar to process theology. Human beings seek divinity within as well as growth into divinity. The transformed consciousness results from the energies flowing from the hierarchy to humanity. Changed consciousness also alters human perception of biblical truths. For example, "humanity itself will be the world-savior."[104] Logically, "Good Friday will fade out of the consciousness of humanity in due time."[105] Who needs the cross when he or she is divine? Now Christ prepares for "His true mission," no longer to emphasize "the existence of a wrathful God, needing to be placated by death" but "in preparation for His instituting a new and more correct presentation of divine truth."[106]

Among other endeavors, Christ allegedly is getting ready "for a revelation which will inaugurate the new era and set the note for the new world religion."[107] What is this new world religion? That Christ is only one of many world saviors (as teacher).[108] Buddha was the first and the most prominent, with Christ. Buddha and Christ work together.[109] Spangler considers both as bridges but in different ways.[110] Buddha operates on the intuitional plane.[111] His final work for humanity involves helping in the externalization of the hierarchy[112] (i.e., coming in bodily form to earth again). He also sends disciples to reform Buddhism in the second stage of externalization—to form the one new religion.[113]

If human beings, angels, the hierarchy, and even Christ are all evolving, then so are religions toward a one universal religion. This involves Christ's coming "to restore the ancient spiritual landmarks . . . in preparation for the restoration of the Mysteries. These Mysteries, when restored, will unify all faiths."[114] So evolution turns everything upside down. No biblical truths are sufficient, because they are constantly evolving. Hence the need to get the latest form of them through fallen angels channeling messages. Even Christ's teachings are outdated, since He is even more evolved now. There's no end to it. It's a devastating undermining of Christ and biblical truth.

Everything is up for grabs. One thing is certain. Calvary has been tossed on the garbage heap. Look at this alleged supernatural message. "It must be remembered that it is the teaching given by the Christ which saves humanity—not any symbolic death upon a cross. *Men must save themselves by their reaction and their response to the teaching given in its purity by the Christ.*"[115] The bottom line is that only the present teaching of the Christ saves. The biblical teachings of Christ are no better than Calvary. So human beings are supposedly to evolve beyond perceiving Jesus as a substitute, crucified Saviour to being an example of a man with divinity within. What Jesus was, all human beings are to become. Jesus came to teach us that we too can become divine.[116]

Look how far they take their dumping of biblical truths relative to the end-time. In fact, there is no real Second Advent, for "at no time has He [Christ] ever left the earth."[117] He is in central Asia.[118] What's He doing there? He guides humanity from a mountain retreat.[119] So reappearance, or externalization, describes His appearing more than Second Advent or return.[120]

Bailey jettisons biblical views of the Advent. For example, she claims that "the generally accepted idea that He will return as a triumphant warrior, omnipotent and irresistible, has surely no basis in fact"[121] (cf. Rev. 19:11-21). In fact, He works to avert a final war. No Armageddon here.[122] According to Bailey, world peace is prerequisite for Christ's reappearance.[123] What about the crucial manner of Christ's return, that which inspiration says cannot be counterfeited[124]—the coming in the clouds rather than being found on earth (cf. Matt. 24:26, 27; 1 Thess. 4:16-18)? That's dumped because Christ is allegedly on the planet already. However, we'll see another version when we examine the New Age movement.

"How He will come, in what manner, I may not and should not say," Bailey continues. "The exact moment has not yet arrived, nor has the method of His appearance been determined. The factual nature of the two earlier and preparatory moves, already made by the Hierarchy under His direction, are the guarantee that He *will* come and that—when He does—mankind will be ready."[125] In total disagreement, Christ emphasized the importance of the manner of His coming. Interpreters often call Matthew 24 the "signs chapter," but the question raised by the disciples was

"What will be the sign of your coming and of the end of the age?" (Matt. 24:3, NIV). The word "sign" (Greek, *semeion)* is in the singular, not plural.

Beside warning against false christs roaming around on the planet (verses 4, 23-27), Jesus specifically answers the question by stating, "At that time the sign *[semeion,* singular] of the Son of Man will appear in the sky" (verse 30). The sign of the genuine Christ rests on where you meet Him. The counterfeits move on the ground. We meet the genuine One in the sky. Paul echoed the same perspective: "For the Lord himself will come down from heaven, . . . and the dead in Christ will rise first. After that, we who are still alive and are left will be caught up with them in the clouds to meet the Lord in the air" (1 Thess. 4:16, 17).

Here's the issue—rejecting the uniqueness of Scripture, the written Word, parallels rejection of Christ the unique living Word (John 1:1, 14). In place of prophecy we find astrology, in place of salvation is evolution, and in place of God's revelation is the supposed fact that "the circumstances of His return are only symbolically related in the world Scriptures;" and hence "this may produce a vital change in the preconceived ideas of humanity."[126] No scripture remains to protect the human race from the counterfeit coming of Satan as Christ walking on our planet. That's Satan's strategy. "Any idea of meeting Christ in the air is old hat," claim fallen angels. "Truth has evolved. That we will meet him on the ground is the latest revelation."

In this context, interestingly but not surprisingly, "the Christ Who will return will not be like the Christ Who (apparently) departed."[127] Bailey lists several reasons. We choose one. "He has been for two thousand years the supreme Head of the Church Invisible, the spiritual Hierarchy, composed of disciples of all faiths. [Note he is chief above all other religious leaders.] He recognizes and loves those who are not Christian but who retain their allegiance to their Founders—the Buddha, Muhammad, and others. He cares not what the faith is, if the objective is love of God and of humanity. If men look for the Christ Who left His disciples centuries ago, they will fail to recognize the Christ Who is in process of returning."[128]

What we have here is a liberal openness to all religious devotion but an intolerance towards devotion to Christ. When the New Age Christ looks for those to use, to prepare for His appearance, He will not select those devoted to Him but those who are open to His "thought currents."[129] Yet, paradoxically, the Second Advent is not personal, for "the outpouring of the Christ principle" is "the true second Coming."[130] The ascended Master warns, "I would ask all of you who read these words anent the second Coming, to reserve opinion as to the exact nature of that event. Keep the concept *impersonal* and link not that appearance to a personality or to an individual."[131]

Yet Christ comes from the mountains, by a plane, to inaugurate a new age and restore the Mysteries.[132] How can He be both literal/physical and yet so impersonal? Other contradictions surface in Bailey's presentation. For example: (1) If *"evolution proceeds by choice, not by chance,"*[133] do not human beings control the reappearance date of Christ? (2) If planets decide the passing from the Piscean to the New Age of Aquarius, do humans really have any choice after all?[134] (3) If those living today have lived before (reincarnation, and thus continually evolving) and for the first time now assist their own evolution,[135] and some deliberately make their appearance at this time[136]—together with ascended Masters[137]—to help bring in the New Age, how is the world getting worse, as in the days of Noah (Matt. 24:37-40)?

Whereas more recent New Age-channeled gospels distinguish between the man Jesus and the cosmic Christ,[138] Bailey confuses them. She apparently relegates Christ to a lesser place and power than God,[139] and speaks of a termination of His relationship with humanity.[140] "Master K. H. will assume the role of World Teacher in the distant future when the Christ moves on to higher and more important work than dealing with the consciousness of humanity." It's this limited role as Teacher for humanity that we keep in mind as we now return to Bailey's book *The Reappearance of the Christ,* a volume that repeats many of the same ideas presented in *The Externalization of the Hierarchy.*

The Coming Teacher

Bailey presents the coming Teacher as an Avatar who typically reveals the next evolutionary step of humanity's unrealized divinity.[141] Although "we are all Gods,"[142] our consciousness is developing. Despite the fact that God's transcendence is universally recognized, "slowly, there is dawning upon the awakening consciousness of humanity, the great paralleling truth of God Immanent."[143] God's immanence "is the clue to the evolutionary process."[144] Christianity is *"an expression—in essence, if not yet entirely factual—of the love of God, immanent in His created universe."*[145]

In fact, God is immanent in all faiths,[146] and works through all religions.[147] Humanity's progress, its improving consciousness, is merely the discovery of this fact. We are only realizing our inherent divinity. Hence evolution has everything to do with perception—perhaps it's more a discovery than a development. Such a discovery, Bailey claims, reveals a basic Christian error—"the vicarious at-one-ment has been substituted for the reliance which Christ Himself enjoined us to place upon our own divinity."[148] The coming of Avatars aids in this revelation.

Avatars are humans who have "achieved perfection," which means that being divine needs to be qualified with at least earning the discovery of personal divinity. Such individuals become "channels" for the transmission of certain qualities to humanity.[149] Buddha and Christ are avatars of the East and West respectively.[150] In fact, she considers Hermes, Buddha, and the Christ as "World Saviors."[151]

Such teaching effectively reduces Jesus to merely one of many and considers allegiance to any religious leader of equal importance as allegiance to Him. The coming Christ is not unique, but only a part of the long series of avatar revelations.[152] Moreover, the coming Christ has "evolved," allegedly going beyond what He was during the

First Advent. It will enable Him to teach "new truths," such as reincarnation.[153] So the Second Coming is merely a part of a whole series of second comings. In fact, reincarnations can involve more than 500 comings to earth for new earth lives, as Buddha allegedly experienced.

Another change she sees in Christ concerns the purpose for His reappearance. Bailey speaks of three different aspects of God being revealed. Buddha and Christ revealed two aspects, light and love. The coming Christ will embody the will of God.[154] "It remains now for the highest of the divine aspects, the will of God, to receive embodiment and for this the Christ is preparing."[155] Christ may return as "a Christian or a Hindu by faith, a Buddhist or of no particular faith at all; He will not come as the restorer of any of the ancient religions, including Christianity, but He will come to restore man's faith in the Father's love, in the fact of the livingness of the Christ and in the close, subjective and unbreakable relationship of all men everywhere."[156]

No wonder, then, the coming Christ will establish a new world religion.[157] This is all included in the "new expansion of consciousness" messages received by Bailey.[158] Masters of wisdom work to "expand" consciousness.[159] "Change" would be a better word. New Agers focus on a "global consciousness" that is essentially the same. Bailey calls this "group consciousness." Christ will bring about such global unity.[160] Clearly, she makes experience of the Father's love and interpersonal relationships as everything at the expense of objective truth.

According to Bailey, in 1945 Christ announced to the spiritual Hierarchy and to His disciples on earth that "He had decided to emerge again in physical contact with humanity, *if* they would bring about the initial stages of establishing right human relations." Ever since then Christ has been channeling energy, making the world better.[161] So both humans and Christ have works to do that are preconditions to His reappearance. Christ's "Aquarian work began, and it will continue for two thousand five hundred years."[162] When He arrives, Bailey believes, Christ will assume the astral body and mind of Buddha, and significantly "the Avatar of Synthesis has become, for the time being, His close Associate. . . . The Avatar of Synthesis will fortify Him, and He will be buttressed by this 'Silent Avatar,' Who (to speak symbolically) will 'keep His eye upon Him, His hand beneath Him and His heart in unison with His.'"[163]

We see two major delusions here. The first catapults the Second Advent into the distant future. The second radically reduces Christ from being the unique Saviour of the world to Someone who needs another avatar to lean on to enable Him to function. The One who is the Truth (John 14:6) depends upon one who represents a synthesis. Then, it is claimed, the ancient mysteries, preserved by Masonry, will be revealed at Christ's coming. They "contain the entire clue to the evolutionary process."[164] So Christ merely reappears to bring to light the supposed fountain from which all religions have flowed. He establishes a universal religion and inaugurates the New Age.

Conclusion

Martin Katchen and Russell Chandler believe that the New Age movement, flowing out of the roots considered above, "is a logical continuation of trends existent in American liberalism since the 1830s."[165]

Such occult literature, though not easy reading, is a threat to the idly curious. The plan Blavatsky and Bailey describe attempts to infuse optimism into a humanity faced with Armageddon. Human works replace Calvary, energy replaces the Holy Spirit. An evolving Christ in the Asiatic mountains substitutes for Christ's intercession at God's right hand. Devotion to Christ vanishes before His controlling "thought currents." "Global consciousness" overwhelms individual loyalty to truth. Astrology takes the place of prophecy. The divinity of humanity nullifies the uniqueness of Christ. Human evolution erases God's redemption—all because spirit-guide writings have usurped God's revelation in Scripture.

As the late Walter Martin, a leading authority on cults, stated: "Today some 35 to 50 million people are involved in some form of cultic organization throughout America and on foreign mission fields. Almost 60 million dabble in some New Age practice or occultic thinking."[166] John the revelator warned: "I saw three evil spirits . . . ; they came out of the mouth of the dragon, out of the mouth of the beast and out of the mouth of the false prophet. They are spirits of demons performing miraculous signs, and they go out to the kings of the whole world, to gather them for the battle on the great day of God Almighty. Behold, I come like a thief! Blessed is he who stays awake" (Rev. 16:13-15).

Spirits of devils—energies from beneath—are using philosophy and signs to capture our planet for Satan, to prepare it for his false appearing as Christ. "It is true that spiritualism is now changing its form and, veiling some of its more objectionable features, is assuming a Christian guise. But its utterances from the platform and the press have been before the public for many years, and in these its real character stands revealed. . . . Even in its present form, so far from being more worthy of toleration than formerly, it is really a more dangerous, because a more subtle, deception. While it formerly denounced Christ and the Bible, it now *professes* to accept both. But the Bible is interpreted in a manner that is pleasing to the unrenewed heart, while its solemn and vital truths are made of no effect."[167]

Syncretism, synthesis, the mixing of truth and error, lie at the heart of these roots to New Age eschatology, and herein we see its danger. Historian Arnold Toynbee "predicted that the most significant development of the age would be the influence of the Eastern spiritual perspective on the West."[168] "C. S. Lewis saw the battle lines clearly drawn. He noted that in the final conflict between religions, Hinduism and Christianity would offer the only viable options, because Hinduism absorbs all religious systems, and Christianity excludes all others, maintaining the supremacy of the claims of Jesus Christ."[169]

Just before us is "the hour of temptation, which shall come upon all the world, to try them that dwell upon the earth" (Rev. 3:10, KJV). All whose faith does not firmly rest upon the Word of God will find themselves deceived and overcome. Satan works "with all deceivableness of unrighteousness" (2 Thess. 2:10, KJV) to gain control of the human race, and his deceptions will continually increase. But he can gain his object only as human beings voluntarily yield to his temptations. Those who seek a knowledge of the truth and strive to purify their souls through obedience, thus doing what they can to prepare for the conflict, will find, in the God of truth, a sure defense. "Because thou hast kept the word of my patience, I also will keep thee" (Rev. 3:10), the Saviour promises. "He would sooner send every angel out of heaven to protect His people than leave one soul that trusts in Him to be overcome by Satan."[170]

---

[1] Based upon Max Lucado, *And the Angels Were Silent* (Sisters, Oreg.: Multnomah, 1992), p. 43.

[2] "I discovered, first of all, that there is a great and divine Plan. I found that this universe of ours is not a 'fortuitous concurrence of atoms' but that it is the working out of a great design or pattern which will be all to the glory of God. I found that race after race of human beings had appeared and disappeared upon our planet and that each civilization and culture had seen humanity step forward a little further upon the path of return to God. I discovered, for the second thing, that there are Those Who are responsible for the working out of that Plan and Who, step by step and stage by stage, have led mankind on down the centuries. I made the amazing discovery, amazing to me because I knew so little, that the teaching about this Path or this Plan was uniform, whether it was presented in the Occident or in the Orient, or whether it had emerged prior to the coming of Christ or afterwards. I found that the Head of this Hierarchy of spiritual Leaders was the Christ" (Alice A. Bailey, *The Unfinished Autobiography of Alice A. Bailey* [New York: Lucis, 1979], p. 139).

[3] "Our examination of the multitudinous religious faiths that mankind, early and late, have professed, most assuredly indicates that they have all been derived from one primitive source. It would seem as if they were all but different modes of expressing the yearning of the imprisoned human soul for intercourse with supernal spheres" (H. P. Blavatsky, *Isis Unveiled* [Wheaton, Ill.: Theosophical, 1972] vol. 2, p. 639). This "single source, . . . is the Brotherhood of the White Lodge, the Hierarchy of Adepts who watch over and guide the evolution of humanity, and who have preserved these truths unimpaired; from time to time, as necessity arose, reasserting them in the ears of men" (Annie Besant, *The Ancient Wisdom* [Madras: Theosophical, 1959], p. 41).

[4] "Part of the demand we must make on our own tradition consists in challenging the Protestant traditions to let go of their fear of mysticism and to reclaim from the spirit of their founders a living mysticism" (Matthew Fox, *The Coming of the Cosmic Christ* [San Francisco: Harper & Row, 1988], p. 236).

[5] "The mysteries have consistently proclaimed that there is no gulf, no gap between matter as we experience it in our third-dimensional bodies and spirit" (David Spangler, *Reflection on the Christ* [Findhorn: Lecture Series, 1977], pp. 46, 47).

[6] "God is the evolutionary drive of consciousness in the universe" (Marilyn Ferguson, *The Aquarian Conspiracy: Personal and Social Transformation in the 1980s* [Boston: Houghton Mifflin, 1976], p. 49). "The Christ is the basic evolutionary force within creation" (David Spangler, *Reflection on Christ,* pp. 8, 13).

[7] "There is a fundamental tension that we must reduce if we are to become the builders and the architects of the New Age. . . . It is the tension between spirit and matter. . . . There is a definite necessity to blend them, to synthesize them" *(ibid.,* p. 51).

[8] Erich Jantsch, *The Self-organizing Universe: Scientific and Human Implications of the Emerging Paradigm of Evolution* (Oxford: Pergamon, 1980), p. 307.

[9] "Evolution, then, is a labored return toward Spirit, toward Source" (Russell Chandler, *Understanding the New Age* [Dallas: Word, 1988], p. 275).

[10] "Theosophical theory presupposes seven ages of man in cyclic succession" (Viva Emmons, *The Roots of Peace: A Study of Human Potential in Relation to Peace* [Wheaton, Ill.: Theosophical, 1969], p. 108). Six of them are Gemini, Taurus, Aries, Pisces, Aquarius, and Capricorn. Cf. Alice A. Bailey, *The Reappearance of the Christ* (New York: Lucis, 1948), pp. 121-128.

[11] Benjamin Creme, *The Reappearance of the Christ and the Masters of Wisdom* (London: Tara), p. 202.

[12] Ursula Burton and Janice Dolley, *Christian Evolution: Moving Towards a Global Spirituality* (Northamptonshire: Turnstone, 1984), p. 101.

[13] Creme, p. 202.

[14] Besant, p. 4.

[15] David Spangler, *Revelation: The Birth of a New Age* (San Francisco: Rainbow Bridge, 1976), p. 117.

[16] Matthew Fox, *The Coming of the Cosmic Christ,* p. 7.

[17] *Ibid.,* p. 228.

[18] *Ibid.,* p. 235.

[19] *Ibid.,* p. 122.

[20] Elliot Miller, *A Crash Course on the New Age Movement: Describing and Evaluating a Growing Social Force* (Grand Rapids: Baker, 1989), p. 24.

[21] They include Teilhard de Chardin's cosmogenesis and anthropogenesis, Helena Blavatsky and Alice Bailey's theosophical eschatology, Darwin's evolutionary philosophy, and the worldview of Eastern religions. In essence, the New Age movement is not only a revolt against the establishment, but also against Christianity. We should keep in mind that philosophers such as Spinoza and Hegel prepared the Western mind to accept spiritual monism.

And even Christianity has generated compatible mutations. Christian Science is one example. Those who wish to synthesize Christianity with the New Age often appeal to Teilhard de Chardin, a Roman Catholic priest. Themes in the process theologies of Whitehead and Hartshorne are conducive to synthesis. The New Age movement includes both people who are religious—Christians, Hindus, and animists—and many who do not identify with a religious tradition.

Some of the other predecessors include transcendentalism, spiritualism, the new thought of Swedenborg/Mesmer, psychoanalysis, and Carl Jung's theory of collective unconsciousness. Another aspect is a paradigm-shift debate relative to the spiritual vacuum caused by the mechanistic worldview of Descartes and Newton, and the rise of the new physics championed by Fritjof Capra.

[22] Vatican II commented on the freedom of scientific study, including the acceptance of its basic world view ("evolution") as follows: "This sacred Synod, therefore, recalling the teaching of the first Vatican Council, declares that there are 'two orders of knowledge' which are distinct, namely, faith and reason. It declares that the Church does not indeed forbid that 'when the human arts and sciences are practiced they use their own principles and their proper method, each in its own domain.' Hence, 'acknowledging this just liberty,' this sacred Synod affirms the legitimate autonomy of human culture and especially of the sciences" *(The Documents of Vatican II,* gen. ed. Walter M. Abbott, S.J., trans. ed. Very Rev. Msgr. Joseph Gallagher [London: Geoffrey Chapman, 1967], p. 265; cf. "the rightful independence of science," p. 234.

[23] Abbott, pp. 660-671. It was also the first time an ecumenical council addressed other Christian churches as well as pagans and Jews. The statement "For all peoples comprise a single community" (p. 660), gives insight into the global focus of modern Catholicism, a position similar to that found in the New Age movement.

[24] Los Angeles *Times,* Jan. 25, 1987.

[25] Russell Chandler, *Understanding the New Age* (Dallas: Word, 1988), p. 208. Another example of a Catholic priest, like De Chardin, going beyond Scripture in "New Age" ideas is Matthew Fox (cf. note 16). Fox is director of the Institute in Culture and Creation Spirituality at Holy Names College, Oakland, California.

[26] Pierre Teilhard de Chardin, *The Future of Man,* Norman Denny, trans. (London: William Collins, 1969), p. 13.

[27] *Ibid.,* p. 15.

[28] *Ibid.,* p. 280.

[29] *Ibid.,* pp. 273, 274.

[30] *Ibid.,* p. 15.

[31] *Ibid.,* p. 67.

[32] *Ibid.,* p. 84.

[33] *Ibid.,* p. 323.

[34] *Ibid.,* p. 129.

[35] *Ibid.,* p. 131.

[36] *Ibid.,* p. 265.

Theosophy: Roots of the New Age Movement

[37] *Ibid.*, p. 129.
[38] *Ibid.*, p. 77.
[39] *Ibid.*
[40] *Ibid.*, pp. 269-271.
[41] *Ibid.*, p. 117.
[42] *Ibid.*, pp. 273, 274.
[43] *Ibid.*, pp. 321-323.
[44] *Ibid.*, p. 322.
[45] H. P. Blavatsky, *The Key to Theosophy: An Abridgement,* Joy Mills, ed. (Wheaton, Ill.: Theosophical, n.p.d.), p. 167.
[46] *Ellen G. White Manuscript Releases,* vol. 13, p. 1.
[47] Benjamin Creme, *The Reappearance of the Christ and the Masters of Wisdom,* pp. 199, 200.
[48] *Share International* 4, No. 6: last page. Cf. e.n., p. 47.
[49] Elliot Miller, *A Crash Course on the New Age Movement,* p. 146.
[50] "The Theosophical Society did fuel the emerging New Age movement" (Walter Martin, *The New Age Cult* [Minneapolis: Bethany House, 1989], p. 17).
[51] H. P. Blavatsky, *An Abridgement of the Secret Doctrine,* Elizabeth Preston and Christmas Humphreys, eds. (London: Theosophical, 1966), p. xx.
[52] Cf. H. P. Blavatsky, *An Abridgement of the Secret Doctrine,* p. xxxii.
[53] H. P. Blavatsky, *Collected Writings 1877: Isis Unveiled* (Wheaton, Ill.: Theosophical, 1972), vol. 1, p. 4.
[54] "Portions of this work were written by the ordinary conscious mind of its acknowledged author. Others were dictated to her by one or another Initiate, for whom she served as an amanuensis, along lines of clairaudient communication. Still other portions of her manuscript were written when one or another of these Initiates temporarily overshadowed her outer form and used it. And there were also portions which were precipitated for her, in *her own handwriting,* while she was asleep" (H. P. Blavatsky, *Collected Writings 1877: Isis Unveiled,* p. 11).
[55] *Ibid.*, p. 17.
[56] *Ibid.*, p. 37.
[57] H.P. Blavatsky, vol. 2, p. 145. Cf.: "There was a secret doctrine preached by Jesus to the few who were deemed worthy to become its recipients and custodians" *(Collected Writings 1877: Isis Unveiled,* vol. 2, p. 191).
[58] *Ibid.*, p. 152.
[59] *Ibid.*, p. 305.
[60] *Ibid.*, p. 251.
[61] *Ibid.*, p. 240.
[62] H. P. Blavatsky, *The Key to Theosophy: An Abridgement,* p. 24.
[63] *Ibid.*, p. 13.
[64] *Ibid.*, pp. 14, 15.
[65] *Ibid.*, p. 51.
[66] *Ibid.*, p. 54.
[67] *Ibid.*, p. 127.
[68] *Ibid.*, p. 57.
[69] *Ibid.*, p. 128.
[70] *Ibid.*, p. 122.
[71] *Ibid.*, p. 131.
[72] *Ibid.*, pp. 167, 168.
[73] *Ibid.*, p. 168.
[74] Alice A. Bailey, *The Externalization of the Hierarchy* (New York: Lucis, 1957), pp. 3, 7, 62, 502, 641, 653.
[75] "H. P. Blavatsky gave the background of the Plan, under impression from me; the more detailed structure and the sweep of the hierarchical intention have been given by me in the books which A.A.B. has introduced under her own name to the public (in so doing acting under my instructions)" (Alice A. Bailey, *The Externalization of the Hierarchy,* p. 685); Cf.: "and myself, the so-called Master D. K." (Alice A. Bailey, *The Externalization of the Hierarchy,* p. 659). "Now we come to the work which I (D. K.), a second ray Master, am attempting to do"

(Bailey, p. 669). Bailey mentions the plan at least 10 times in this volume, for example, on pages 21, 505, 520, 525, 589, 664, 670, 672, 685, and 693. It would seem that the alleged Master D. K. revealed the plan to Blavatsky and continued to unfold it to Bailey.

[76] *Ibid.,* p. 510.

[77] *Ibid.,* p. 519.

[78] *Ibid.,* p. 548.

[79] A pantheistic and mystical energy pours into the planet rather than the person of the Holy Spirit as in the latter rain. The book frequently speaks of energies coming to humanity. For example, see pages 7, 8, 525, 536, 540.

[80] *Ibid.,* p. 526.

[81] *Ibid.,* p. 616.

[82] *Ibid.,* p. 673. Human freedom can limit the foreknowledge of the hierarchy, so human freedom is a factor mentioned *(ibid.,* pp. 61, 62).

[83] *Ibid.,* p. 697.

[84] *Ibid.,* p. 698.

[85] Creme, p. 97.

[86] Alice A. Bailey, *The Externalization of the Hierarchy,* p. 675.

[87] Ruth Montgomery, *Aliens Among Us* (New York: G. P. Putnam's Sons, 1985), pp. 89, 92.

[88] Alice A. Bailey, *The Externalization of the Hierarchy,* p. 568.

[89] "They will appear in office of some kind or another; they will be the current politicians, businessmen, financiers, religious teachers or churchmen; they will be scientists and philosophers, college professors and educators; they will be the mayors of cities and the custodians of all public ethical movements" *(ibid.,* pp. 570, 571).

[90] *Ibid.,* p. 572.

[91] *Ibid.,* pp. 572, 573.

[92] *Ibid.,* pp. 573, 574.

[93] *Ibid.,* p. 3.

[94] *Ibid.,* p. 508.

[95] *Ibid.,* pp. 503, 663.

[96] *Ibid.,* p. 589.

[97] *Ibid.,* p. 617.

[98] *Ibid.*

[99] *Ibid.,* p. 592.

[100] *Ibid.,* p. 604.

[101] *Ibid.,* p. 595.

[102] *Ibid.,* p. 663.

[103] *Ibid.*

[104] *Ibid.,* p. 539.

[105] *Ibid.,* p. 542.

[106] *Ibid.,* pp. 542, 543.

[107] *Ibid.,* p. 545.

[108] *Ibid.,* p. 635.

[109] *Ibid.,* p. 661.

[110] David Spangler, *Reflections on Christ,* p. 87.

[111] Alice A. Bailey, *The Externalization of the Hierarchy,* p. 683.

[112] *Ibid.,* p. 546.

[113] *Ibid.,* p. 573.

[114] *Ibid.*

[115] *Ibid.,* p. 635.

[116] *Ibid.,* pp. 607, 608.

[117] *Ibid.,* pp. 589, 597.

[118] *Ibid.,* p. 590.

[119] *Ibid.,* p. 620.

[120] Cf. *ibid.*, p. 607.

[121] *Ibid.*, p. 609.

[122] *Ibid.*, p. 546.

[123] "It will be the masses everywhere who will slowly unite to bring about the conditions needed for the reappearance of the Prince of Peace, bringing with Him the potency and the benediction of the Avatar of Synthesis" (*ibid.*, p. 650).

[124] E. G. White, *The Great Controversy*, p. 625.

[125] Bailey, p. 602. "His coming in the air might be interpreted literally to mean that at the right time He will come by plane from the place on earth where He has been for many generations" *(ibid.*, pp. 575, 576).

[126] *Ibid.*, p. 611.

[127] *Ibid.*, p. 612.

[128] *Ibid.*

[129] *Ibid.*, pp. 695, 696. "It is a unified group endeavor, generated in each ashram and fostered by all alike, to bring the entire group—as a band of world servers—into the aura of the thought currents of the Christ, as He formulates His ideas, creates the thought-form needed prior to manifestation, and makes His arrangements for His reappearing" *(ibid.*, p. 680).

[130] *Ibid.*, p. 510.

[131] *Ibid.*, p. 504.

[132] *Ibid.*, pp. 575, 576.

[133] Barbara Marx Hubbard, *Happy Birthday Planet Earth: The Instant of Cooperation* (Santa Fe, N.Mex.: Ocean Tree Books, 1986), p. 16. If the reappearance was predicted as near in 1919, how could its first stage be predicted to be announced in 2020—more than 100 years later? cf. p. 530.

[134] *Ibid.*, pp. 561, 562.

[135] "The present can also be seen, indicating the way of the future and revealing clearly the Will-to-Good which is animating the entire evolutionary process—a process in which humanity (again for the first time) is intelligently participating and cooperating" (A. A. Bailey, *The Externalization of the Hierarchy*, p. 685).

[136] "Disciples will come deliberately into incarnation and will take office in institutions of higher learning and in the churches, and will exert such pressure that old and obsolete methods, ancient outworn theologies and selfish and competitive techniques will be ended and the sciences of cooperation, of right human relations and of correct adjustment to life through meditation and right vision will supersede the present methods of learning; this will lead to no damage to the acquisition of academic knowledge or the right apprehension of spiritual truth" *(ibid.*, p. 577, 578).

[137] *Ibid.*, p. 698.

[138] Cf. Norman R. Gulley, "The New Age Attack on Jesus Christ," *Adventist Perspectives* 3, No. 2 (1989).

[139] It is true that Christ is spoken of as a "son of God" together with other "sons of God" *(ibid.*, p. 590).

[140] *Ibid.*, p. 644.

[141] Alice A. Bailey, *The Reappearance of Christ*, p. 10.

[142] *Ibid.*, p. 9.

[143] *Ibid.*, p. 36.

[144] *Ibid.*, p. 591.

[145] *Ibid.*, p. 140.

[146] *Ibid.*, p. 33.

[147] *Ibid.*, p. 159.

[148] *Ibid.*, p. 63.

[149] *Ibid.*, p. 9.

[150] *Ibid.*, p. 10.

[151] *Ibid.*, p. 58.

[152] *Ibid.*, p. 64.

[153] *Ibid.*, pp. 115-117.

[154] Cf. what Bailey says about Christ in Gethsemane. "Something new, yet planned for from the very depth of time, happened then in that quiet garden; Christ, representing mankind, anchored or established the Father's will on earth and made it possible for intelligent humanity to carry it out. . . . Today, because of what Christ did in His moment of crisis hundreds of years ago, humanity can add its efforts to the working out of that Plan" *(ibid.*, p. 606).

Christ Is Coming!

[155] *Ibid.,* p. 62.
[156] *Ibid.,* p. 19.
[157] *Ibid.,* pp. 71, 72.
[158] *Ibid.,* p. 40.
[159] Alice A. Bailey, *The Externalization of the Hierarchy,* p. 509.
[160] Alice A. Bailey, *The Reappearance of the Christ,* p. 21.
[161] *Ibid.,* p. 76.
[162] *Ibid.,* pp. 82, 83.
[163] *Ibid.,* pp. 76, 77.
[164] *Ibid.,* p. 122.
[165] Russell Chandler, *Understanding the New Age* (Dallas: Word, 1988), p. 50.
[166] Walter Martin, *The New Age Cult* (Minneapolis: Bethany House, 1989), p. 7.
[167] E.G. White, *The Great Controversy,* pp. 557, 558.
[168] Marilyn Ferguson, *The Aquarian Conspiracy: Personal and Social Transformation in the 1980s,* p. 51.
[169] Walter Martin, *The New Age Cult,* p. 13.
[170] E.G. White, *The Great Controversy,* p. 560.

Chapter 13

The New Age Movement and End-time Events

Matthew Huffman was 6 years old. His dad and mom were missionaries in Salvadore, Brazil. One morning he complained of fever. His temperature shot up, and he began losing his eyesight. His dad grabbed the car keys, and all three raced off for the hospital.

"As they were driving and he was lying on his mother's lap, he did something his parents will never forget. He extended his hand in the air. His mother took it and he pulled it away. He extended it again. She again took it, and he again pulled it back and reached into the air. Confused, the mother asked her son, 'What are you reaching for, Matthew?'

" 'I'm reaching for Jesus' hand,' he answered. And with those words he closed his eyes and slid into a coma from which he never would awaken. He died two days later, a victim of bacterial meningitis."[1]

If only humanity, at the end of human history, could reach up to grasp the hand of Christ! It would make all the difference! As we saw in the chapter on Theosophy, Satan is busy presenting a false picture of Christ. This continues in the contemporary New Age movement. The tragedy is that human beings feel their emptiness and know something is wrong. The intensity of life, their mistrust of people, and their dysfunctional lives drive them to cry out for a Saviour. But the New Age movement comes along and promises them that they can become God. It schools them to trust in themselves and keeps their hands from reaching up to the only hand that can help them today—and in the end-time.

When Does It Begin?

When does the New Age begin? Its adherents offer several options. The New Age is the eleventh of 12 astrological ages.[2] The several starting dates for the New Age depend upon the different calculations for the beginning of the first age.[2] So the New Age begins, for Jane Roberts, in 2075.[3] Dan Rudhyar selected either 1989-1991 or 2060,[4] though significantly for Seventh-day Adventists, he also mentions 1844.[5] In fact, he claims that the New Age was announced in 1844![6] David Spangler dubs new religious movements that sprang up in anticipation of the Second Advent to be the false labors of the real birth of the New Age.[7] Alice Bailey believed the preparation stage for the New Age took place from 1875 to 1890, the intermediate stage from 1919 to 1949, and revelation of the New Age occurred after 1975.[8] David Spangler claims it is here now,[9] having begun in 1967.[10]

Most New Agers speak of the New Age as imminent or future. To them, the New Age culminates the evolutionary process in which Christ is the essence[11] and God the driving force.[12] They picture God and Christ as both within and a part of evolution—as the mind of the universe.[13] A mingling of pantheistic and process views of God lies at the heart of New Age thinking. Thus both Christ and the truths He proclaimed 2,000 years ago are not the same today, for both have evolved and are still in process, the same viewpoint as we saw in Theosophy.

The advent of Christ two millenniums back introduced the present Piscean age. The coming of the new Christ, with a new world religion, will inaugurate the New Age of Aquarius, the central focus of "New Age eschatology."[14] The "cosmic Christ," the one present in everything, the one who is pre-Christian and not the sole possession of Christians, is the one to come.[15] Thus the coming Christ is more advanced than the Christ who came, and at least Spangler even separates the Second Advent from the coming of the cosmic Christ.[16]

New Paradigm Shift

In chapter two we talked about the changing worldviews in science. Just for quick review, we noted that paradigms, or worldviews, have radically changed since the first advent of Christ. For example, Ptolemaic cosmology, accepted for 1,400 years, posited the earth as the center of a revolving universe. In the sixteenth century Copernicus and Galileo overthrew this earth-centered cosmology with a heliocentric worldview. It thought the universe revolved around the sun. During the twentieth century Einstein, whose relativity theory views all parts of the universe, including the earth and its sun, as in motion together, challenged the heliocentric theory. Thomas Kuhn, in *The Structures of Scientific Revolution,* rightly notes that scientific worldviews are not set in concrete, for many have been overthrown.[17]

New Agers talk about a right-brain worldview. Let's see what they mean. We begin with ancient opinion. Worldviews, or paradigms, depend upon the mind's perception. Plato (428-348 B.C.) compared the two hemispheres of the brain to two horses with separate functions *(Phaedrus* 266). Neuroscience later confirmed some of Plato's philosophical ideas. A paper from Marc Dax at a medical conference in 1836 documented speech loss in more than 40 of his patients who had sustained left hemisphere brain damage.[18] Subsequently, within an evolutionary context, some considered the left side of the brain as more developed than the right hemisphere. Roger Sperry and his colleagues at the California Institute of

Technology challenged this view during the 1960s and made neurological history. Their work with epileptic patients whose corpus callosum was severed (commissurotomy—which means that the major connection between the right and left side of the brain was cut) demonstrated that "the right hemisphere is as impressive in its sphere of cognitivity as the left hemisphere."[19]

Jerry Levy, biopsychologist of Chicago University, believes that designating different functions to the two brain hemispheres is only a half truth. For "to the extent that regions are differentiated in the brain, they must integrate their activities. . . . There is no activity in which only one hemisphere is involved or to which only one hemisphere makes a contribution."[20] However, Nobel laureate John Eccles (1963) stressed the superior role of the left over the right brain.[21] By contrast, New Agers believe the right brain is more important.[22] Ongoing brain research has discovered that a bracketing out of one hemisphere of consciousness physiologically produces a condition known as "the neglect syndrome."[23] Usually "neglect syndrome" results from damage to the right brain hemisphere, and the patient is unable to see objects in the left visual range.

Laurence Wood concludes that "this medical condition of neglect syndrome is a parabolic illustration of much of the history of Western thought. We have permitted the verbal, temporal, analytical, and logical sphere of cognitive processing to restrict our vision of reality. Especially since the rise of modern philosophy and modern science, we have been largely inattentive to the realities of the unseen, the intuitive, the affective, and the feeling depths of reality. Consequently the intuitive mode of consciousness has been denigrated and subordinated to the rational mode of consciousness."[24]

David Wells agrees, noting that the scientific enterprise arose in the West and not in the East.[25] It follows that paradigm shifts have occurred in the West and not in the East. Now, many people in the West are in the midst of a new paradigm change, for New Agers are focusing on the right hemisphere of the brain, just as in the East. Although the New Agers claim a holistic view of health and say their openness to the right brain functions is a move toward completion (where the West reaches out to meet the East, and the use of the left brain hemisphere reaches out to the use of the right brain hemisphere), in actual fact, theirs is not a holistic use of the brain at all, even though they promote "whole-brain education."[26] In doing so they actually renounce the use of the logical powers of the left in favor of only employing the intuitive functions of the right, even though Marilyn Ferguson calls intuition "whole-brain knowing."[27]

Now that's the crunch. If Satan can bypass the use of the left brain, where logic resides, and if he can manipulate the right brain intuitions, he can then take over the human mind. That's his plan. And New Agers by the millions are succumbing.

Harvard professors Timothy Leary and Richard Alpert represent examples of those who exchanged the objectivity of science (left brain) for the subjectivity of mysticism (right brain).[28] Marilyn Ferguson's book *The Brain Revolution* documents the occult penetration of science through altered states of consciousness, unorthodox healing, and parapsychology.[29] In 1969 the American Academy for the Advancement of Science granted parapsychology an affiliate status, and ten years later Jeffrey Mishlove received the first Ph.D. in parapsychology from the University of California at Berkeley.[30] Such scholars have abandoned the objectivity of classical science.

The approach has been spreading into more than just the psychological sciences. For example, physicist Fritjof Capra views the mechanistic world of Cartesian-Newtonian science as outdated.[31] Reality, for him, lies beyond the seen, in the mystical realm. He sees a need to balance the rational dimension of reality with the intuitive dimension, or as the Chinese express it—the yang is to be balanced by the yin. The yang is male or rational, whereas the yin is female or intuitive. Capra notes: "We can see that our culture has consistently promoted and rewarded the yang, the masculine or self-assertive elements of human nature, and has disregarded its yin, the feminine or intuitive aspects. Today, however, we are witnessing the beginning of a tremendous evolutionary movement. The turning point we are about to reach marks, among many other things, a reversal in the fluctuation between yin and yang. As the Chinese text says, 'The yang, having reached its climax, retreats in favor of the yin.' "[32]

Capra believes that physics has gone through a number of "conceptual revolutions" during the twentieth century. Many no longer perceive the universe as a machine, with reducible parts governed by precise mathematical laws, but view it as a harmonious, indivisible whole that is alive. Einstein's relativity theory and Planck's quantum theory shattered the Cartesian-Newtonian mechanistic worldview. This "new physics," or "systems theory" (first formulated in the 1930s by Ludwig von Bertalanffy),[33] sees the unpredictable microsphere quite the opposite to the predictable macrosphere. In fact, the microsphere seems to be in flux,[34] and some have joined this view to Eastern mysticism.[35] They regard the whole world as one living system made up of interdependent parts, with no linear relation of cause and effect.[36]

Niels Bohr's "Principle of Complementarity" documents that subatomical entities behave sometimes like waves and at other times like particles. Although physics has considered such states as mutually exclusive, nevertheless the same entities exhibit them. Werner Heisenberg discovered a third behavior of subatomic entities, i.e., they react like solid bits of matter. So subatomic entities behave as either wave/particle or solid matter. This fact Heisenberg called the "Uncertainty Principle." Dean Halverson put it: "As benign as Heisenberg's Uncertainty Principle seems, it changed the nature of physics. In a science based on predictability, the Uncertainty Principle said that fundamental reality was unpredictable. Not only was the concept of predictability eroded, but so was objectivity, another foundation of classical physics."[37]

What's going on at the subatomical

level? Why is it seemingly so different from other levels of physics? *Newsweek* reported that "a new school of theoretical physicists, many of them based at the University of California's Lawrence Berkeley Laboratory, is using mystical modes of thought in an effort to create a unified philosophy of how the universe works."[38]

Not only does it view the world as one living whole, but it regards humanity as united through one unified consciousness.[39] Behind this lies a Universal Mind accessible through hypnosis or channeling, allowing one to obtain records of previous lives or other data, much as one goes to a library to check out books.[40] As former New Ager Elliot Miller warns: "As long as scientists assume that there are *no limits* to scientific inquiry and explanation, they lay themselves open to the beguiling influences of supernatural darkness."[41]

The same applies to New Agers, for in their flight from the left brain hemisphere to the right, they abandon their analytical, critical faculties and thereby lay themselves open to whatever comes through the intuitive right hemisphere. It makes them vulnerable to forces that scheme to take over by means of bypassing the conscious mind and leaves them without protection against Satan's final plan for world domination.

The New Age worldview represents an enormous paradigm shift. Researchers conclude that "today we are in the midst of a cultural/spiritual upheaval of almost inconceivable proportions. This cultural shift, like the Renaissance, is a shift in the general worldview, among other things."[42] New Agers are out to change the old, which includes old ideals, old truths, and old hopes. A new worldview fires them. As Walter Martin put it: "Every major cultural transformation rests on a shift in world views."[43] So what transformation can we expect in the New Age? New Agers work for global consciousness. Uniformity lies at the very heart of all their efforts to bypass the conscious mind.

Humanity Taking Charge of Evolution?

Perhaps the greatest paradigm shift is the belief in a quantum leap in human evolution, i.e., in the evolution of human consciousness, in which, as Alice Bailey put it, human beings for the first time participate in the evolutionary process.[44] As David Spangler said, now human beings act on their own evolution,[45] for the human mind may have reached a new stage in its development.[46] Each human being is now a "co-builder of Aquarius,"[47] also making each of us a "co-Creator."[48] We can now invoke the New Age.[49] Doesn't it remind you of readers being coauthors with the biblical texts, according to reader-response theory—the latest idea about biblical interpretation? The end-time thrusts human beings center stage. Yet it is only Satan taking over the human mind. By contrast Christians depend upon Christ and rejoice in His freedom with the whole brain.

Taking charge of evolution involves the "paradigm of self-organization."[50] Humans are supposed to be gods. When a sufficient number of them think alike, so that the evolution of the mind is both qualitative and quantitative, then the uniting of humanity will reach a "critical mass,"[51] a "Planetary Pentecost,"[52] and will bring in the Second Advent.[53] In fact, humans seem to hold the key, for they can hasten the advent.[54] But how can that be when the Second Advent inaugurates the New Age,[55] and the planets determine the New Age? Who launches this New Age—people or planets? Is it determined by consciousness or cosmic rotation? Whoever said error had to be consistent?

The new paradigm shift involves a realization that God is also imminent:[56] that the phase of personal salvation is concluding, and the phase of collective evolution beginning.[57] Some consider Lucifer the angel of human evolution. While God is in the macroworld, Lucifer is the spirit of light in the microworld and comes to give human beings the final gift of wholeness[58] called the "Luciferic initiation." Lucifer seems to take the place of Christ, for Alice Bailey speaks of Christ evolving like the rest of humanity and hence points to a new initiation, new sacrifices, and to a new salvation to come.[59] Apparently Lucifer finishes the work that Christ began.[60]

Yet the New Age, with its new paradigm, involves a third Avatar. Buddha and Christ were the Avatars of East and West, of wisdom and love respectively. The third Avatar will be the Spirit.[61] In typical dispensational fashion, Ursula Burton and Janice Dolley view the Old Testament as the Age of God the Father, the New Testament as the Age of God the Son, and "we may now be moving into the Age of God the Holy Spirit."[62]

The paradigm transformation now underway, as humanity moves from the Piscean to the Aquarian age, is a shift from authority to direct knowledge,[63] from beliefs to experience.[64] It's a time when the Masters who allegedly guide the planet teach human beings to expand their consciousness.[65] Authority has moved from an objective, external source (such as the Bible) to a subjective, internal source (human consciousness).

As mentioned previously, Teilhard de Chardin saw a parallel between our time and that of Galileo in the sixteenth century.[66] The new paradigm shift includes "collective consciousness,"[67] or "one single consciousness."[68] This unity—or better, uniformity—is a necessary prerequisite for the Second Advent. "Parousia will be realized in a creation that has been taken to the climax of its capacity for union."[69]

In this context of universal uniformity, or "mindlessness," we ponder Fritjof Capra's view that the universe is a great thought rather than a great machine (Newton), Robert Muller's statement of an "emerging planetary brain,"[70] and Erich Jantsch's perception that God is the mind of the universe.[71] David Spangler refers to "evolving a group Christ."[72] In the process of viewing all reality as "god" or mind, New Agers find themselves giving up their own minds. New Agers allege that meditation and chanting can bring the two hemispheres of the brain together in a type of transcendence.[73]

Thus New Agers claim that chanting and meditation produce holistic brain use.[74] Yet meditation opens one to spirit-guides, who take over the mind. Chanting shuts off the thinking faculties and unlocks the mind to whatever may come. The films *Angel of Light* and *Gods of the New Age* document how supernatural forces take the mind over through New Age meditation and chanting. Some practitioners have become demon possessed and insane. Fallen angels gain possession of the human mind, people lose their freedom (cf. Eph. 6:12), and Satan takes control of the planet for his finale.

Global Consciousness

As a priest in the New Age movement for 12 years, Will Baron considered himself a disciple of D.K., the alleged Ascended Master who channeled 25 books filled with New Age ideas through Alice Bailey. Baron came under the domination of the spirit-guide, who gave the young man no relief until he slavishly obeyed. For example, the spirit-guide forced Baron to give $6,000 to a New Age project during a two-week period, even though he did not have the money.[75] He forced him to buy a new car against his will,[76] and made him preach on the boardwalk against his choice.[77]

Here we encounter a paradox. Humans are alleged to be gods, yet accounts of New Age believers repeatedly describe them as in abject bondage to spirit-guides. Although humans are supposed to be taking charge to bring in the New Age, such accounts describe spirit-guides taking charge of them. Instead of being at the zenith of their evolution, the evolution of the mind, they find they are mindless. It doesn't make sense. Under the guise of whole-brain use, multitudes discover they have no use of their brain at all!

The great struggle is for possession of the human mind. Only God's Word protects from such an attack. No wonder that "Satan employs every possible device to prevent men from obtaining a knowledge of the Bible," for he knows that it is "their safeguard against . . . the delusive power of spirits of darkness."[78] Within this context, consider the following New Age view on the Bible.[79] In the old age God and humanity were separated, necessitating communication through words in the Bible. But in the New Age, communion replaces communication, energy replaces words. God and humanity are one. Such communion does not need verbal or objective communication.[80] Humanity becomes revelation itself. Thus "we are the Word of Revelation made flesh. We are the message. Now and always."[81]

Global Union and the Antichrist

A number of Christian writers, such as Constance Cumbey, Texe Marrs, Elissa McClain, and David Hunt oppose the New Age movement, viewing it as a conspiracy or as preparing for the coming antichrist—a charismatic leader who will take over the world with a global government.[82] Others claim such commentators go overboard, reading into the New Age movement their particular version of biblical prophecy.[83]

But no one I know of has viewed the New Age movement within the biblical context of Revelation 16. We must see the New Age movement within its proper context, because it is only a part of the final counterfeit. Many writers on the New Age movement regard it as alone fulfilling biblical eschatology.

They seem to overlook other important movements. While it's crucial to understand the New Age movement's role in eschatology, it must not be done in exclusion of other equally vital factors.

Remember that Revelation 16:13, 14 speaks of three avenues through which spirits of devils work.[84] The New Age movement is modern paganism. In our eagerness to see what is happening in the New Age movement, we must not overlook what takes place on other religious fronts. In other words, while focusing on the Eastern (pagan) invasion into the West to form the New Age movement, we must not ignore the fact that the uniting of churches and a church-state union is the final result of pagan infiltration of Christianity. Ellen White says, "When the early church became corrupted by departing from the simplicity of the gospel and accepting heathen rites and customs, she lost the Spirit and power of God; and in order to control the consciences of the people, she sought the support of the secular power. The result was the papacy, a church that controlled the power of the state and employed it to further her own ends, especially for the punishment of 'heresy.' "[85]

Conclusion

We need to understand the New Age movement in its biblical as well as its social context. In its social context we see it as a force that has invaded society at many levels—health, business, education, ecology, science, and even to some extent politics and the Christian church. However, on balance, it has not yet had near the impact on the Christian church as the charismatic movement, which has infiltrated practically every denomination.

However, many Christian writers focus on the New Age movement, seeing it as the avenue to bring the coming antichrist. Yet the Bible refers to a power already at work in Paul's day (2 Thess. 2:7), a power that changed divinely ordained law (Dan. 7, 8; cf. 7:25) and not to someone in the future. Just as futurism (one school of prophetic interpretation) with its projection of antichrist into the future, hid the antichrist in Catholicism, so the New Age movement serves the same function for these interpreters of eschatology.

We must place the New Age movement within its biblical context, the triumvirate of Revelation 16. At best it is but a part—albeit significant part—of just one of the three forces—paganism. It has its role, but is not the only agency Satan employs. An analogy might be helpful. The great controversy has two sides but many players—just as in a game of chess. Revelation 16 names three major agencies that Satan employs in his end-time strategy, and it will be the third one, not the New Age movement, that causes all the world to wonder (Rev. 13:3).

Yet behind each player on the chessboard stands the same mastermind. Satan's spirits work through each agency (Rev. 16:12). That is why spiritualism gets signaled out as fundamental to the final deception. Yet Sunday sacredness is the other key component to take over the world.[86] The final delusion involves counterfeit revelations, a counterfeit Sabbath, and a counterfeit appearance of Christ.

The New Age Movement and End-time Events

False revelations lead to the false Sabbath and Saviour. That is why we observe so many identical features to the different players on the cosmic chessboard. But there is only one game, and one power moves each player toward one goal. Satan is using all three of his triumvirate, just as God is using all three of the angels with the end-time message (Rev. 14). It's no more logical to focus alone on the New Age movement in final events than it would be to focus on only one, or a part of one, of the three angels' messages.

"As the spirits will profess faith in the Bible, and manifest respect for the institutions of the church, their work will be accepted as a manifestation of divine power. The line of distinction between professed Christians and the ungodly is now hardly distinguishable. Church members love what the world loves and are ready to join with them, and Satan determines to unite them in one body and thus strengthen his cause by sweeping all into the ranks of spiritualism."[87]

A fundamental difference exists between the two sides on this chessboard. Satan's triumvirate share common ground in an appeal to the senses, to manifestations and feeling, to spirit-guides, to channeled books, to subjective experience. God's three angels rest alone on the objective Word of God.

As *The Great Controversy* puts it: "The last great delusion is soon to open before us. Antichrist is to perform his marvelous works in our sight. So closely will the counterfeit resemble the true that it will be impossible to distinguish between them except by the Holy Scriptures. By their testimony every statement and every miracle must be tested. . . . None but those who have fortified the mind with the truths of the Bible will stand through the last great conflict."[88]

All those who fortify their minds with the truths of the Bible will stand through the last great delusion. There are just two sides—those who believe, study, and love God's Word and those who do not. From the Word of God we gain our perception to unmask the enemy and our protection to withstand him. "'To the law and to the testimony; if they speak not according to this word, it is because there is no light in them' (Isa. 8:20). The people of God are directed to the Scriptures as their safeguard against the influence of false teachers and the delusive power of spirits of darkness."[89]

Today a whole generation is being groomed to accept counsel from spirit-guides instead of God's Word, to read channeled books instead of the Bible, and to look for Christ to appear on the earth contrary to biblical warnings. Satan is preparing the world for the final deception. Channeled messages orient the masses for that day. Spirits of devils work through churches, the charismatic movement, spiritualism, Theosophy, and the New Age movement (to name some), each for the same purpose—to prepare the world for Satan's appearance as Christ to take over the planet.

---

[1] Max Lucado, *And the Angels Were Silent* (Sisters, Oreg.: Multnomah, 1992), pp. 22, 23.

[2] The 12 carry the names of the 12 signs of the Zodiac. They are Sagittarius, Scorpio, Libra, Virgo, Leo, Cancer, Gemini, Taurus, Aries, Pisces, Aquarius, and Capricornus.

[3] Jane Roberts, *Seth Speaks,* p. 171.

[4] Dan Rudhyar, *Occult Preparations for a New Age* (Wheaton, Ill.: Theosophical), p. 256.

[5] Dan Rudhyar, *The Astrology of America's Destiny,* pp. 8, 55, 56.

[6] Rudhyar, *Occult Preparations for a New Age,* pp. 131, 132 (cf. pp.10, 240).

[7] "Easily two hundred years before the actual beginning of a New Age, the energies that will characterize it begin to be felt. The patterns of the old cycle are agitated in anticipation as, deep within them, the unexpressed potentials that will become realized in the succeeding age begin to move to the surface. Often this produces 'false labors'" . . . False labors appeared from the womb of man's consciousness. New religious movements sprang up around the world in anticipation of the Second Coming or of new revelation" (David Spangler, *Revelation: The Birth of a New Age* [Lorian], p. 134).

[8] Alice Bailey, *Ponder on This* (New York: Lucis), p. 295.

[9] David Spangler, *Reflections on the Christ,* pp. 78, 87. "For Spangler the second coming is presently occurring on a massive level all over the earth" (Ronald C. Rhodes, "The New Age Christology of David Spangler," *Bibliotheca Sacra* 144 [October-December 1987]: 410).

[10] Spangler, pp. 44, 87.

[11] *Ibid.,* p.117.

[12] Marilyn Ferguson, *The Aquarian Conspiracy,* p. 49.

[13] Erich Jantsch, *The Self-Organizing Universe,* p. 308.

[14] From one perspective, it is a misnomer to speak of "New Age eschatology," for it has no unified belief on what is to come. New Age groups are a loose network of different programs, some of which do not say much more than how to cope with the present. As we saw in the previous chapter, Teilhard de Chardin, Helena Blavatsky, and Alice Bailey are three major sources for insights into the future as perceived by many New Agers. See *Adventist Perspectives* 4, No. 2 (1990).

[15] Matthew Fox, *The Coming of the Cosmic Christ,* pp. 7, 77, 128, 241.

[16] New Agers consider the coming of the Cosmic Christ as a greater outpouring of energies than that received in the Second Coming, with still greater "advances in consciousness to come." So the New Age is not the ultimate, but a phase along the evolutionary process as we see indicated by the fact that one more cosmological age is supposed to succeed that of Aquarius (Spangler, pp. 142, 143).

[17] Thomas Kuhn, *The Structures of Scientific Revolution* (Chicago: University Press, 1970).

[18] Cited by Laurence W. Wood, "Recent Brain Research and the Mind-Body Dilemma," *Asbury Theological Journal, the Best in Theology* (Chicago: Carol Stream, n.p.d.), vol. 2, p. 205.

[19] *Ibid.*

[20] Quoted in Russell Chandler, *Understanding the New Age* (Dallas: Word, 1988), p. 37.

[21] Wood, *Asbury Theological Journal, the Best in Theology*, pp. 211-213.

[22] It should be kept in mind that 7 percent of people are right-brained. William H. Calvin, neurophysiologist at the University of Washington, cautions against exaggerated dichotomizing of "left-brain" versus "right-brain" functions (see Chandler, p. 37).

[23] Wood, p. 214.

[24] *Ibid.,* p. 215.

[25] David W. Wells, in his introduction to the Systematic Theology section of *The Best in Theology,* vol. 2, p. 199.

[26] For example, in comparing the old and new paradigm for learning, Marilyn Ferguson in *The Aquarian Conspiracy* (Los Angeles: J. P. Tarcher, 1980), p. 290, writes of the new paradigm that it "strives for whole-brain education, augments left-brain rationality with holistic, nonlinear, and intuitive strategies. Confluence and fusions of the two processes emphasized." New Age "altered states of consciousness" techniques transcend the critical left-brain faculties by opening the recipient up to the mystical, by the right-brain faculties. Elliot Miller notes how New Agers push right-brain methods under the rubric of "whole-brained" education. "The discovery that the right hemisphere of the brain governs intuitive, creative, nonverbal activities has been seized by New Agers and used as a justification for bringing 'right-brain learning techniques' into the classroom. These include meditation, yoga, guided imagery, chanting, mandals (visual symbols used as aids to education), and fantasy-role-playing games. Children are being led into mystical and psychic experiences (including encounters with spirit guides called 'Wise Ones') on the premise that this will develop their intuitive abilities and thus provide a more balanced, holistic, or 'whole-brained' education" (p. 95).

THE NEW AGE MOVEMENT AND END-TIME EVENTS

[27] Ferguson, p. 107.

[28] Both psychologists sought to experience an altered state of consciousness, with a significant loss of objectivity. Elliot Miller comments: "To Leary and Alpert's colleagues, however, the once-respected researchers' participation in the experiments was transforming them from scientists into mystics (an allegation which the years that followed certainly substantiated)" (Elliot Miller, *A Crash Course on the New Age Movement* [Grand Rapids: Baker, 1989], p. 41).

[29] Marilyn Ferguson, *The Brain Revolution.*

[30] Miller, p. 50.

[31] Fritjof Capra, *The Turning Point* (New York: Bantam, 1982), pp. 15-18.

[32] *Ibid.,* p. 45.

[33] "This view which Capra elucidates so well was first formulated in the 1930's by Austrian-born biologist Ludwig von Bertalanffy (d. 1972). By the 1950s his General Systems Theory (GST) had generated an interdisciplinary movement. Although von Bertalanffy was not the first to advocate a holistic perspective (for example, see South African statesman-philosopher Jan Christian Smuts' 1925 treatise *Holism and Evolution),* he was the first to seek an all-encompassing scientific basis for it" (Miller, p. 60).

[34] K. C. Cole said, "You cannot hit an electron with a known force and say at precisely what speed and direction it will fly off. You cannot follow its movements and say precisely where or how it will wind up. You can only say where it will probably be moving. Atomic particles do not obey the classic Newtonian laws of cause and effect; they are governed by the dictates of chance" (quoted in Chandler, p. 185).

[35] "The new concepts in physics have brought about a profound change in our world view; from the mechanistic conception of Descartes and Newton to a holistic and ecological view, a view which I have found to be similar to the views of mystics of all ages and traditions" (Capra, p. 15). "If the New Age interpretations noted above were to become widely accepted in physics, we would witness the marriage of a 'hard' science to Eastern/occult mysticism. This could signal the end of classical objective science" (Miller, p. 43).

[36] Fritjof Capra, *The Turning Point,* chap. 3, "The New Physics," pp. 75-97; and chap. 9, "The Systems View of Life," pp. 265-304.

[37] Dean C. Halverson in *The New Age Rage*, Karen Hoyt, ed., p. 77.

[38] Kenneth L. Woodward with Gerald C. Lubenow, "Physics and Mysticism," *Newsweek,* July 23, 1979, p. 85.

[39] Teilhard de Chardin, *The Future of Man* (Collins, Fontana, 1969), p. 321.

[40] Woodward with Lubenow, "Physics and Mysticism."

[41] Miller, p. 49.

[42] The Spiritual Counterfeits Project researchers in Karen Hoyt's *The New Age Rage* (New Jersey: Fleming H. Revell, 1987), p. 198.

[43] Walter Martin, *The New Age Cult,* p. 70.

[44] Alice A. Bailey, *The Externalization of the Hierarchy,* p. 685.

[45] David Spangler, *Reflection of the Christ,* p. 11.

[46] Marilyn Ferguson, *The Aquarian Conspiracy,* p. 67.

[47] Barbara M. Hubbard, *Happy Birthday Planet Earth,* p. 17.

[48] Spangler, p. 87.

[49] Benjamin Creme, *The Reappearance of Christ and the Masters of Wisdom,* p. 200. For the New Age prayer of invocation, see Alice A. Bailey, *The Externalization of the Hierarchy,* pp. 40, 45.

[50] Erich Jantsch, *The Self-Organizing Universe,* p. xiii.

[51] De Chardin, p. 280.

[52] Barbara M. Hubbard, *Happy Birthday Planet Earth,* pp. 9, 10.

[53] Alice Bailey, *The Externalization of the Hierarchy,* p. 650.

[54] *Ibid.,* p. 562. Bailey says that when the world follows the eightfold path of Buddha, then Christ will come *(The Reappearance of Christ,* pp. 20, 21).

[55] Alice A. Bailey, *The Externalization of the Hierarchy,* p. 666.

[56] Alice A. Bailey, *The Reappearance of the Christ,* p. 36.

[57] Hubbard, p. 21.

[58] Spangler, pp. 37-45.

[59] Alice A. Bailey, *The Externalization of the Hierarchy,* p. 663.
[60] The work of Christ was unfinished according to Alice A. Bailey *(The Externalization of the Hierarchy,* p. 595).
[61] Alice A. Bailey, *The Reappearance of the Christ,* pp. 10, 11.
[62] Ursula Burton and Janice Dolley, *Christian Evolution Towards a Global Spirituality* (Northamptonshire: Turnstone, 1984), 101. Theosophical theory presupposes seven ages of humanity in cyclic succession (Viva Emmans, *The Roots of Peace, a Study of Human Potential in Relation to Peace* [Wheaton, Ill.: Theosophical, 1969], p. 108).
[63] Alice A. Bailey, *The Externalization of the Hierarchy,* p. 3.
[64] Elliot Miller, *A Crash Course in the New Age Movement,* p. 16.
[65] Alice A. Bailey, *The Externalization of the Hierarchy,* p. 509.
[66] De Chardin, pp. 269-271.
[67] *Ibid.,* p. 16.
[68] *Ibid.,* p. 321.
[69] *Ibid.,* p. 322.
[70] Miller, p. 70.
[71] Erich Jantsch, *The Self-organizing Universe,* p. 308.
[72] Spangler, *Reflection on the Christ,* p. 10.
[73] "Meditation, chanting, and similar techniques increase the coherence and harmony in the brain-wave patterns; they bring about greater synchrony between the hemispheres, which suggests that higher order is achieved" (Ferguson, p. 79).
[74] *Ibid.*
[75] Will Baron, *Deceived by the New Age* (Boise, Idaho: Pacific Press, 1990), pp. 91-97.
[76] *Ibid.,* p. 54.
[77] *Ibid.,* pp. 132-136. It forced him to witness (p. 137).
[78] E. G. White, *The Great Controversy,* p. 593.
[79] David Spangler, *Revelation,* pp. 204, 232.
[80] *Ibid.,* p. 233.
[81] *Ibid.,* p. 235.
[82] Constance Cumbey, *Hidden Dangers of the Rainbow* (Shreveport, La.: Huntington, 1983); Texe Marrs, *Dark Secrets of the New Age: Satan's Plan for a One World Religion* (Westchester, Ill.: Crossway, 1987); Elissa L. McClain, *Rest From the Quest* (Shreveport, La.: Huntington, 1984); Dave Hunt and T. A. McMahon, *The Seduction of Christianity* (Eugene, Oreg.: Harvest House, 1985).
[83] "The New Age movement could certainly play a part in the great deception of the tribulation described in various biblical prophecies, and we should definitely keep it under observation. But it would be counterproductive for the body of Christ to respond to this movement with hysteria over a public declaration that the New Age movement is involved in conscious conspiratorial activities that cannot be factually substantiated" (Walter Martin, p. 20). "We must think in global terms, say New Age political activists. National boundaries are obsolete. Yet to most New Agers the notions of top-down bureaucratic government or a one-world global ruler are repugnant because these models shift power from grass-roots individuals. A minority of New Agers, however—particularly those influenced by the writings of Theosophy disciple Alice Bailey—buy into the concept of an elite, ruling hierarchy such as her 'New Group of World Servers'" (Russell Chandler, *Understanding the New Age,* pp. 197, 198; cf. chap. 24, "Conspiracy Theories," pp. 227-234). "Some Christians have viewed them as demonized Luciferians, consciously conspiring to usher in the Antichrist, and have thus regarded them with mixed fear and loathing. Though there may be a limited basis in fact for some of these views, as general descriptions they are grossly misleading" (Miller, pp. 20, 21). "In dealing with the subject many authors have had such an eschatological bias (seeking always to show how it fulfills prophecy) that they have handled the facts selectively, and consequently left many Christians with a distorted picture of the movement. Also, because many believers see the movement in exclusively eschatological terms, several moral and social issues that it raises for the church are never even considered" (Miller, p. 129).
[84] *The Seventh-day Adventist Bible Commentary,* vol. 7, p. 844; cf. E. G. White, *The Great Controversy,* pp. 588, 589.

[85] White, *The Great Controversy,* p. 443.

[86] "Through the two great errors, the immortality of the soul and Sunday sacredness, Satan will bring the people under his deceptions. While the former lays the foundation of spiritualism, the latter creates a bond of sympathy with Rome" *(ibid.,* p. 588).

[87] *Ibid.*

[88] *Ibid.,* pp. 593, 594.

[89] *Ibid.,* p. 593.

Chapter 14

The New Age Attack on Jesus Christ

Maximilian Kolbe was incarcerated in Auschwitz in February 1941. Four months later someone escaped from prison. The German military guarding the Jews had a punishment for escapes. The crack SS would shoot 10 prisoners for each person who managed to escape.

Prisoners gathered in the courtyard that July day.

The camp commandant had the roll book. "Goldstein!" he barked, "Frankenstein, Liechtenstein." He went back and forth in the list, choosing randomly as if it were a lottery. He had selected nine names. The prisoners held their breath. Would they be the tenth?

"Gojowniczek," snarled the commandant.

A young man broke down and began to sob. "My wife and my children," he wept.

"The officers turn as they hear movement among the prisoners," says Max Lucado. "The guards raise their rifles. The dogs tense, anticipating a command to attack. A prisoner has left his row and is pushing his way to the front."

"It is Kolbe. No fear on his face. No hesitancy in his step. The capo shouts at him to stop or be shot. 'I want to talk to the commander,' he says calmly. For some reason the officer doesn't club or kill him. Kolbe stops a few paces from the commandant, removes his hat, and looks the German officer in the eye.

"'Herr Kommandant, I wish to make a request, please.'"

That no one shot him is a miracle.

"'I want to die in the place of this prisoner.' He points at the sobbing Gojowniczek. The audacious request is presented without stammer.

"'I have no wife and children. Besides, I am old and not good for anything. He's in better condition.' Kolbe knew well the Nazi mentality.

"'Who are you?' the officer asks.

"'A Catholic priest.'

"The block is stunned. The commandant, uncharacteristically speechless. After a moment, he barks, 'Request granted.'"[1]

Someone who didn't even know Gojowniczek was willing to die for him! Christ died for you. The best news anyone can get, it means that He will get us through final events. His longing for our homecoming gives us assurance. Heaven is ours because of His death and not because of our life. True we love Him and keep His commandments (John 14:15), but there's no way we can ever be worthy of His gift.

That's the good news that Satan's studied strategy strives to keep from those seeking and searching for security. He desperately tries to hide it from those who feel condemned. Many sense they will die without hope. The world has countless Gojowniczeks. Knowing his time is short, Satan does everything he can to keep the good news from those who need it so desperately. "Your enemy the devil prowls around like a roaring lion looking for someone to devour" (1 Peter 5:8).

In the End-time

Satan pushes for world domination. Fallen angels channel their ideas as solace to human beings at the breaking point, as light to those in darkness, as hope to those believing themselves doomed by a nuclear holocaust or other global disaster.

"Channelmania" captivates large sections of the public. More than 1,000 people in Los Angeles alone claim to channel. A New Age/occult bookstore in Berkeley has seven shelves full of channeled material. Four of the shelves—recent publications—outsell all the rest of the books in the entire store. As *Christianity Today* put it: "That's not a mere publishing trend; it's a stampede."[2]

Earth's inhabitants clutch at straws as does a drowning victim. Aching for security, vulnerable for any seeming sure word, they pay $275 per person to hear a channeler for a weekend, or $60 for a videotape. For just one seminar, the Channeler Lazarus channeled $190,000 to the bank.[3]

False Gospel Promoted

Satan and his fiends push their version of the gospel.[4] They fill in the lost years of Jesus (ages 12-30), give alleged lost teachings, and provide further insights to well-known stories, sometimes changing the meaning of passages or introducing new doctrines. Such unfolding of "truth" has devastating results for the biblically illiterate.

Satan's struggle focuses primarily against God's Son. He hates Him, because Michael and His angels fought against Satan and his host and threw them out of heaven (Rev. 12). Although Satan flung all his fury and artifice against the vulnerable Jesus in Palestine, he failed. No wonder that now, in the end-time, he musters all his cunning for the final onslaught with a clever attack on Christ, one garbed as illumination from heaven.

We will limit our attention to three of the major channeled "bibles" that currently influence the New Age movement.[5] We could include others,[6] but these three give insight into the nature and extent of Satan's end-time attack.[7]

***The Aquarian Gospel of Jesus the Christ,* 1907**

Levi H. Dowling was born May 18, 1844, in Ohio. "Early in life, when but a mere lad, he had a vision in which he was told that he was to 'build a white city.' This vision was repeated three times with years intervening. The building of the 'white city' was *The Aquarian Gospel of Jesus the Christ.* This book was transcribed between the early morning hours of two and six—the absolutely 'quiet hours.' "[8]

The book claims that Christ and Jesus are two different entities,[9] even though joined together temporarily during earth-life. For Christ is God's love[10] that came to live on earth 11 times[11] before dwelling in Jesus.[12] For example, He lived in Enoch and Melchizedek. Also, the persons whom "the Christ" came to inhabit had apparently been prepared for this by many past lives. At least this was so for the man Jesus.[13] Therefore, both "the Christ" entity and Jesus had lived many times on earth before they joined together nearly 2,000 years ago.[14] Such "reincarnation," in different ways, is basic to New Age Christology.[15]

To understand the function of "the Christ" and Jesus in *The Aquarian Gospel,* we will consider (1) monism, (2) mission, and (3) moral influence.

1. Monism

"Before the worlds were formed all things were One; just spirit, Universal Breath."[16] Jesus taught that "Man is the Breath made flesh,"[17] "that God and man are one."[18] Although humanity did not have a beginning,[19] creation and salvation are somewhat synonymous, for "when all the essences of carnal things have been transmuted into soul, and all the essences of soul have been returned to Holy Breath, and man is made a perfect God, the drama of Creation will conclude,"[20] since "man is saved when he has reached deific life; when he and God are one."[21] If everything is one, then there's no distinction between God and humanity. The New Age bibles consistently push the concept. As we'll see later, it's precisely this distinction between God and humanity that is crucial for a safe passage through last-day events.

The fallen angels try to palm off the spiritual as more important than matter, very much as the soul is supposedly more important than the body. As *The Aquarian Gospel* puts it, everything was originally "spirit." Matter is merely spirit moving at a lower vibration.[22] The Fall was simply a slowing of the vibrational level—when the ethers became more dense.[23] Hence "the lower self is an illusion, and will pass away" while "the higher self is God in man, and will not pass away."[24] "Study self," for "the only devil from which men must be redeemed is self, the lower self," and "if man would find his savior, he must look within."[25] No surprise then that angels never fell[26] and that the devil and hellfire are both human inventions,[27] or that Jesus taught that heaven is not a place but a state of mind.[28]

You get the thrust. The Fall exists only in the mind. You're your own savior. Such a theory needs only revelation to change thoughts, not redemption to change destiny. So here comes the revelation—in multiple channeled bibles and other books!

Fallen angels claim Jesus taught that the house of God is within the soul, so "look deep within the temple of your brain" for there "you are in the Holiest of All, where rests the Ark of God, whose covering is the Mercy Seat." "Fear not to lift the sacred board; the

Tables of the Law are in the Ark concealed. Take them and read them well; for they contain all precepts and commands that men will ever need. And in the Ark, the magic wand of prophecy lies waiting for your hand; it is the key to all the hidden meanings of the present, future, past. And then, behold the manna there, the hidden bread of life; and he who eats shall never die."[29] No wonder prayer is only an inner meditation,[30] that human beings worship God in the temple of the heart,[31] and that healing is "not a special gift of God" but merely issues from faith.[32]

Thinking, or meditation, is a key concept in New Age thought. For "God made the universe by thought."[33] If the Fall was a lowering of the vibrational level to the physical, then the opposite raising of the vibration level comes through thought (light).[34] Jesus said: "By the power of holy thought, my body will be changed from carnal flesh to spirit form; and so will yours."[35]

2. Mission

It follows that Jesus came merely to change thinking—to enlighten, not to redeem, for "when men have needed added light a master soul has come to earth to give that light."[36] No wonder Jesus went to India,[37] Tibet,[38] Persia,[39] Assyria,[40] Greece,[41] and Egypt[42] to study the writings of the Masters—to obtain knowledge or enlightenment—during the "lost" or "silent years" between the ages of 12 and 30.[43]

The Aquarian Gospel presents Jesus as the "pattern" for other humans.[44] In Egypt, the last country in which He learned from the Masters, Jesus takes the seven degrees of brotherhood. The hierophant addresses Jesus, saying: "Brother, man, most excellent of men, in all the temple tests you have won out. Six times before the bar of right you have been judged; six times you have received the highest honors man can give; and now you stand prepared to take the last degree. Upon your brow I place this diadem, and in the Great Lodge of the heavens and earth you are THE CHRIST. This is your great Passover rite. You are a neophyte no more, but now a master mind. Now man can do no more; but God himself will speak, and will confirm your title and degree."[45]

As a human being, Jesus had to work Himself up until He became good enough to be "christed" by God.[46] First, He had all the carnal passions of a human being.[47] He was therefore "subjected to the hardest test of human life, and he has conquered all the appetites and passions of the carnal man, and by the highest court of heaven, has been declared a man of such superior purity and holiness that he can demonstrate the presence of Christ on earth. Lo, love divine, which is the Christ, abides in him, and he is pattern for the race. And every man can see in him what every man will be when he has conquered all the passions of the selfish self."[48]

So Jesus merely shows the way for everyone to be "christed," or infilled with "the Christ," which is to realize the divine already within. He is not a unique incarnation, but an example of what all can achieve or realize. That is why a Master says not to worship Jesus,[49] and Jesus refused worship in India, declaring, "I am your brother man just come to show the way to God;

you shall not worship man; praise God, the Holy One."[50] In fact, Jesus said: "I lived to show the possibilities of man. What I have done all men can do, and what I am all men shall be."[51]

Christian religious legalists can think the same kind of thing as we move into the great time of trouble. They also focus too much on what they have to do for salvation and heaven. Satan's strategy is always to direct human beings to what they can do, irrespective of whether they can really do it or not. By contrast, Christ invites people to come to Him (Matt. 11:28) and abide in Him, for apart from that relationship we can do nothing concerning salvation and heaven (John 15:5).

3. Moral Influence

From such New Age reasoning, it follows that Calvary is unnecessary. Throughout *The Aquarian Gospel of Jesus the Christ* we observe a hatred of any substitutionary sacrifice for human sin. For example, John the Baptist "could not understand how sin could be forgiven by killing animals." Matheno, priest of Egypt, tells him, "the God of heaven and earth does not require sacrifice. This custom with its cruel rites was borrowed from the idol worshipers of other lands. . . . The Vedas say that none can right the wrong but he who does the wrong."[52]

At the age of 10 Jesus went to the Jerusalem Temple and "watched the butchers kill the lambs and birds and burn them on the altar in the name of God. His tender heart was shocked at this display of cruelty; he asked the serving priests, What is the purpose of this slaughter of the beasts and birds? Why do you burn their flesh before the Lord?

The priest replied, "This is our sacrifice for sin." To which Jesus replied, "A God that takes delight in sacrifice, in blood and burning flesh, is not my Father-God. I want to find a God of love."[53] Then at the age of 12 Jesus said, "The sacrifices and the offerings of Israel are but abomination unto God. The only sacrifice that God requires is self."[54]

We need to think long about this when some Christians downgrade Calvary from a sacrifice to only a revelation of God's love. What revelation does it make anyway if it does not involve redemption?

On the other hand, the passages do contain some elements of truth. God does not delight in the sacrifice of animals (1 Sam. 15:22; Isa. 1:11; Ps. 51:16) any more than in the sacrifice of His Son, but sin required God's self-sacrifice (John 3:16, 17; 14:6). This substitutionary sacrifice is what *The Aquarian Gospel of Jesus the Christ* apposes,[55] declaring, "You are, each one, a priest, just for yourself; and sacrifice of blood God does not want. Just give your life in sacrificial service to the all of life, and God is pleased."[56] Salvation is not through God's incarnation and crucifixion, but through each human being's life and reincarnations. Jesus taught reincarnation. "Affliction is a prison cell in which a man must stay until he pays his debts unless a master sets him free that he may have a better chance to pay his debts. . . . Behold this man! Once in another life he was a cruel man."[57]

If going through many lives enables human beings to pay back their debts (karma), then what function does Calvary have? *The Aquarian Gospel of Jesus the Christ*'s rendering of John 3:16 is insightful: "For God so loved the world that he sent forth his only son to be raised up that men may see the love of God."[58] Calvary, at best, gets reduced to a mere moral influence.

The cross also led to resurrection. Yet this New Age bible questions whether the man Jesus really died,[59] even though conquering death is crucial. According to *The Aquarian Gospel,* Jesus passed through the Calvary-resurrection experience to show that death does not exist at all. Before dying He said: "And I am now about to demonstrate the power of man to conquer death; for every man is God made flesh."[60] After His resurrection Jesus assured, "What I can do all men can do. Go preach the gospel of the omnipotence of man."[61]

The Urantia Book, 1955

Another New Age bible declares that when Jesus was 5, a "Thought Adjuster" came to abide in Him. "Jesus was no more aware of the coming of the divine Monitor than are the millions upon millions of other children who, before and since that day, have likewise received these Thought Adjusters to indwell their minds and work for the ultimate spiritualization of these minds and the eternal survival of their evolving immortal souls."[62] Here's a new twist on Satan's desire to take over human minds. He is the ultimate thought adjuster!

The fourteenth and fifteenth years of Jesus were "the real temptation" for Him. "These two years, after he began to be self-conscious of divinity and destiny, and before he achieved a large measure of communication with his indwelling Adjuster, were the most trying of his eventful life on Urantia."[63]

In His twenty-seventh year "Jesus made great advances in the ascendant mastery of his human mind and attained new and high levels of conscious contact with his indwelling Thought Adjuster."[64] During His twenty-ninth year "Jesus made great advances in his human task of mastering the material and mortal mind, and his indwelling Adjuster made great progress in the ascension and spiritual conquest of this same human intellect. By the end of this tour Jesus virtually knew—with all human certainty—that he was a Son of God, a Creator Son of the Universal Father. The Adjuster more and more was able to bring up in the mind of the Son of Man shadowy memories of his Paradise experience in association with his divine Father."[65]

The great temptations of Jesus took place before, not after, His baptism. The indwelling Thought Adjuster led Him to go up Mount Hermon.[66] There "He went into the great test with only his indwelling Adjuster to guide and sustain him."[67]

The above references reveal that *The Urantia Book* considers human thought processes as important as does *The Aquarian Gospel of Jesus the Christ.*[68] The inward focus is crucial too. Jesus did not seek divine power from above or depend upon God beyond Him, but looked solely within for both guidance and power. The term "Thought Adjuster" is significant too, for the life of Jesus was one of learning from others, and of also being changed in thought from within.

In direct contrast to *The Aquarian Gospel of Jesus the Christ,*[69] *The Urantia Book* has Jesus studying from synagogue teachers within Palestine[70] (Nazareth,[71] Capernaum,[72] and Jerusalem[73]) rather than in different foreign countries, up until the last two years (His twenty-eighth and twenty-ninth). (Cayce's channeled material differs from both.)[74] During those two years, before His public ministry, Jesus traveled around the Mediterranean world. By contrast with *The Aquarian Gospel of Jesus the Christ, The Urantia Book* seems to portray Jesus as teaching people of other nations more than learning from them.[75]

We will consider two aspects of the Urantia gospel: (1) the humanity of Jesus and (2) the crucifixion.

1. Humanity of Jesus

Jesus knew the "urges and impulses" of other human beings.[76] How did He meet temptation? "He went into the great test with only his indwelling Adjuster to guide and sustain him . . . and did not hesitate to assert the ascendancy of his divine nature over his human nature"[77] In fact, in His twentieth year, "he began anew the task of further weaving his mortal and divine natures into a simple and effective *human individuality.*"[78] By the following year, He "had already effectively combined these natures into one—Jesus of Nazareth."[79]

2. Crucifixion

The boy Jesus' visit to the Jerusalem Temple devastated Him. He witnessed the sacrifice of lambs. "The terrible sight sickened this boy of Nazareth; he clutched his father's arm and begged to be taken away."[80] "Even at this early date, though he said nothing about such matters to his parents, Jesus had begun to turn over in his mind the propriety of celebrating the Passover without the slaughtered lamb. He felt assured in his own mind that the Father in heaven was not pleased with this spectacle of sacrificial offerings, and as the years passed he became increasingly determined someday to establish the celebration of a bloodless Passover." That night Jesus slept little. "His rest was greatly disturbed by revolting dreams of slaughter and suffering. His mind was distraught and his heart torn by the inconsistencies and absurdities of the theology of the whole Jewish ceremonial system."[81]

The third day in the Temple the boy Jesus asked many questions, one of which was "If God is a father who loves his children, why all this slaughter of animals to gain divine favor—has the teaching of Moses been misunderstood?"[82]

During His twentieth year Jesus desired to celebrate the Passover in the house of Lazarus. But Lazarus had no paschal lamb. Then "Jesus entered upon a prolonged and convincing dissertation to the effect that the Father in heaven was not truly concerned with such childlike and meaningless rituals. After solemn and fervent prayer they rose, and Jesus said: 'Let the childlike and darkened minds of my people serve their God as Moses directed; it is better that they do, but let us who have seen the light of life no longer approach our Father by the darkness of death. Let us be free in the knowledge of the truth of our Father's eternal love.' "[83]

In His thirtieth year Jesus observed the Day of Atonement services in Jerusalem, where He "remained a thoughtful and silent spectator. To the Son of Man this performance was pitiful and pathetic. He viewed it all as misrepresentative of the character and attributes of his Father in heaven. He looked upon the doings of this day as a travesty upon the facts of divine justice and the truths of infinite mercy. He burned to give vent to the declaration of the real truth about his Father's loving character and merciful conduct in the universe, but his faithful Monitor admonished him that his hour had not yet come."[57]

When that hour arrived, Jesus did not just reject the misunderstanding of those sacrifices, but the very sacrifice itself. In fact, months before His baptism, He completed His task.[85] Thus *The Urantia Book* jettisoned His entire public ministry, viewing it as merely subsequent to the completion of His mission. What was that mission? Merely to live an incarnational life, to ascend up to the seventh bestowal,[86] to show what all other humans can do. Thus, "at the time of the Master's baptism he had already completed the technique of the required experience on earth and in the flesh which was necessary for the completion of his seventh and last universe bestowal. At this very time Jesus' duty on earth was done. All the life he lived thereafter, and even the manner of his death, was a purely personal ministry on his part for the welfare and uplifting of his mortal creatures on this world and on other worlds." The crucial reason follows—*"The gospel of the good news that moral man may, by faith, become spirit-conscious that he is a son of God, is not dependent on the death of Jesus.* True, indeed, all this gospel of the kingdom has been tremendously illuminated by the Master's death, but even more so by his life."[87]

So the Urantia gospel claims "no direct relation between the death of Jesus and the Jewish Passover," stating that "it was man and not God who planned and executed the death of Jesus on the cross."[88] Instead, the Father in heaven desired His Son to have a natural death, not the Crucifixion.[89]

Therefore, Calvary was unnecessary for salvation. Atonement was not made through the death of Jesus, because "the salvation of God for mortals of Urantia would have been just as effective and unerringly certain if Jesus had not been put to death by the cruel hands of ignorant mortals. If the Master had been favorably received by the mortals of earth and had departed from Urantia by the voluntary relinquishment of his life in the flesh, the fact of the love of God and the mercy of the Son—the fact of sonship with God—would have in no wise been affected. You mortals are the sons of God, and only one thing is required to make such a truth factual in your personal experience, and that is your spirit-born faith."[90] Hence the one thing required for salvation is not crucifixion but spirit-born faith.

The Urantia gospel calls for people to "utterly abandon all those primitive motions about God" that include a substitutionary sacrifice on Calvary. "The whole idea of ransom and atonement is incompatible with the concept of God as it is taught and exemplified by Jesus of Nazareth. The infinite love of God is not secondary to anything in the divine nature."[91] "We know that the death on the cross was not to effect man's reconciliation to God but to stimulate man's *realization* of the Father's eternal love."[92]

Not only is Calvary unnecessary for salvation, but *The Urantia Book* presents it as the evidence for human immortality. It argues that the death of Jesus "did much to make forever plain the certainty of mortal survival after death in the flesh."[93] The body of Jesus decomposed, but the process was greatly accelerated.[94] His body was not a part of Jesus' resurrection,[95] and His spirit-resurrection apparently underscored the immortality of the soul, which has no beginning or end, comes from and goes to God, and hence needs only to *realize* this rather than be *redeemed.*

A Course in Miracles, 1976

Helen Schuman and William Thetford, professors of medical psychology at Columbia University College of Physicians and Surgeons in New York City, received and recorded the channeled material found in the *A Course in Miracles* text, student workbook, and manual for teachers.[96] Helen Thetford received the "voice," or "inner dictation," and William Thetford typed as Helen dictated. The process took seven years. They believed that Jesus dictated the channeled materials.[97]

A Course in Miracles, unlike *The Aquarian Gospel of Jesus the Christ* and *The Urantia Book,* does not pre– sent another life and teachings of Jesus, but like them radically calls into question the biblical gospel. Reminiscent of Greek dualism, it divides the unreal world of perception from the real world of knowledge, or the inner voice of the Holy Spirit. Thus the visible world is not the real world—consciousness is.[98] Within this context, the worldview is monistic, so that "God and His Creation share one will,"[99] and each person is a part of God's Mind.[100]

"Since love is all there is, sin in the sight of the Holy Spirit is a mistake to be corrected, rather than an evil to be punished."[101] Thus sin is an illusion.[102] Salvation is simple, it says. "What was never true is not true now, and never will be."[103] Thus humanity needs *revelation* or *realization* rather than *redemption. A Course in Miracles*, with its workbook, teaches the student to seek within and depend upon the internal Teacher. Because God and humanity are one, "this is a course in how to know yourself."[104] Humanity is really God, and needs merely to discover this fact.

Atonement

Atonement, the "essence" or "core" of *A Course in Miracles,*[105] aims at a "complete reversal of thought,"[106] a "correction of perception."[107] No wonder, then, that "the crucifixion had no part in the Atonement,"[108] and should be considered "the last useless journey the Sonship need take, and that it represents release from fear to anyone who understands it."[109]

A Course in Miracles teaches that "Easter is the sign of peace, not pain. A slain Christ has no meaning. But a risen Christ becomes the symbol of the Son of God's forgiveness on himself; the sign he looks upon himself as healed and whole. . . . This week we celebrate life, not death. And we honor the perfect purity of the Son of God, and not his sins."[110] The Course continues, "You stand beside your brother, thorns in one hand and lilies in the other, uncertain which to give. Join now with me and throw away the thorns, offering the lilies to replace them."[111]

The soul has no beginning—and no end.[112] In fact, "there is no need for help to enter Heaven for you have never left."[113] So why did "the Christ" come to the man Jesus and thus to earth? "In his complete identification with Christ—the perfect Son of God, His one creation and His happiness, forever like Himself and one with Him—Jesus became what all of you must be. He led the way for you to follow Him. He leads you back to God because He saw the road before Him, and He followed it. He made a clear distinction, still obscure to you, between the false and true. He offered you *a final demonstration that it is impossible to kill God's Son.*"[114]

Is One Greater Than Christ to Come?

The Urantia Book points to a greater one who has already arrived. Pentecost is the climax of that gospel story. The apostles made "more individual spiritual progress" in less than a month than during nearly four years with Christ.[115] Pentecost was brighter and more joyous than resurrection, for on that day the Spirit of Truth became "the personal gift from the Master to every soul."[116] "At last true religion is delivered from the custody of priests and all sacred classes and finds its real manifestation in the individual souls of men."[117] Now we witness "the great effort of the spirit to liberate the religion of Jesus from its inherited Jewish fetters."[118] A religion of the spirit, beyond Jewish roots, beyond Christ in Jesus, brings humanity to greater heights of illumination and perfection.

In *The Aquarian Gospel of Jesus the Christ* Christ's so-called incarnations took place at the beginning of every New Age. He came to Jesus at the start of the Piscean Age.[119] Now humanity approaches the Aquarian Age, which is "pre-eminently a spiritual age."[120] Will Christ come again in yet another incarnation? *The Aquarian Gospel of Jesus the Christ* says a greater one will come, but does not specify who. For "in the ages yet to come, man will attain to greater heights, and lights still more intense will come. And then, at last, a mighty master soul will come to earth to light the way up to the throne of perfect man."[121]

Conclusion

"Jesus the Christ," in New Age philosophy, is merely an example to humanity in that He showed all human beings what they can become. Thus the Jesus of *The Aquarian Gospel of Jesus the Christ* could say: "I lived to show the possibilities of man. What I have done all men can do, and what I am all men shall be."[122] His message was "the Fatherhood of God" and the "brotherhood of men." It meant that all are equally sons and daughters of God. There's not just one son of God (Jesus), for "the Christ" entity can indwell all humanity just as He did the man Jesus. This radically questions the uniqueness of the Incarnation.

It also repudiates the purpose of incarnation—to become humanity's sin substitute and intercessor. Humanity is merely infilled with "the Christ" entity, the Spirit of Truth, in an evolutionary process that ignores incarnation and crucifixion. The hatred toward viewing the atonement as a sacrifice,[123] the focus on Calvary as only a revelation of the Father's love, and the view of the Father as too loving to necessitate the present intercession of Christ[124] are essential ingredients of New Age Christology.

If New Age philosophy, applied to human need, bypasses the conscious mind, then New Age anthropology (view of man) bypasses incarnation, crucifixion, and intercession. Any understanding of the atonement that does not give full place to them is in company with New Age thinking, whether the proponent realizes it or not.

Channeled "gospels" call into question the only gospel revelation—they tamper with God's authoritative Word. But that is precisely what liberal scholarship has also done in its historical-critical work on the Bible. For example, the three quests for the historical Jesus do not accept the Gospels as an inspired revelation about Jesus Christ. They consider them to be a product of the faith of the believers. Just as George Washington and Abraham Lincoln have risen in stature since their death, such scholars see the same thing happening in the minds of those who wrote about Jesus—for the synoptic Gospels were scribed some 30 and John was written 60 years after Calvary. Thus we must accordingly discount the Gospels' ideas about His divinity and the accounts of His miracles. The scholarly quest has been to get back beyond the inflated Christ of faith (memory) to the real Jesus of history.

And what do they have left? Thomas Sheenan put it this way: "Christianity begins not with Jesus but with Simon Peter, and it maintains itself throughout history by staying in continuity with that first believer. Christianity essentially *is* its sense of history, its unique claim of historical continuity—but the continuum is with Peter and the first disciples rather than directly with Jesus. That is the meaning of the Catholic dictum *Ubi Petrus, ibi ecclesia*: Christianity is present wherever someone traces his or her faith back to that of Simon and the first believers. Those who choose to preserve continuity, in one way or another, with Simon Peter's evaluation of the prophet from Galilee can rightly lay claim to the title 'Christian.' Ultimately, Jesus' understanding of himself is not essential to Christianity. But Peter's is."[125]

In other words, people place culture and tradition above God's Word, because they put the assumed faith of the biblical writers above the revelation of God to man. Humanity becomes the judge of divine revelation rather than the other way round. Thus the Christ of faith (the first believers, including the biblical writers) overshadows the historical authenticity of God's revelation in Jesus Christ.

But any questioning of the authority of God's Written Word results in a reduced view of His Living Word (Jesus Christ, John 1:1, 14). After shredding Scripture through historical-critical methods, all one has left is a vulnerability to channeled gospels and the like. God's authoritative Word is the only objective basis to expose any counterfeit. Those who throw away this standard, replacing it with human wisdom, are like sailors lost at sea after jettisoning their only compass.

God warned that false Christs and false prophets would come in the end-time (Matt. 24:4, 11, 23-26). That "evil spirits" would deceive the entire world (Rev. 16:13, 14). We have seen the results of their onslaught upon Christianity. Christians have given up "the Reformed faith for the Age of Aquarius precisely because they could not tell the difference."[126] Alice Bailey, successor of Helena Blavatsky—"grandmother of the New Age" movement[127]—was once an orthodox Christian.[128] Other Christians read channeled gospels. "Indeed, some in mainline churches appear to believe the *Course* is Christian. I am aware of at least three churches in California's San Francisco Bay Area where the *Course* is being preached from the pulpit or studied in Sunday School. A pastor of one of these churches said, 'I believe in the *Course* and I teach it in our church.' In another church, one young man described the *Course* to his pastor as a new revelation that superseded scripture."[129]

It's important to note that "*A Course in Miracles* is one of the more popular channeled writings on the market. . . . It is firmly established in New Age circles and has been for some time, which is not surprising. But it has also found a ready and expanding audience within the Christian Church, which is not surprising either. Biblical illiteracy is rampant and commitment to orthodoxy often less than vigorous and sometimes consciously absent."[130]

We live in a time of ultimate paradox as channeled books sell out while the Bible gathers dust. It's high time to "put on the full armor of God so that you can take your stand against the devil's schemes. For our struggle is not against flesh and blood, but against the rulers, against the authorities, against the powers of this dark world and against the spiritual forces of evil in the heavenly realms" (Eph. 6:11, 12).

For "none but those who have fortified the mind with the truths of the Bible will stand through the last great conflict."[131] And concerning the study of the gospel, "it would be well for us to spend a thoughtful hour each day in contemplation of the life of Christ. We should take it point by point, and let the imagination grasp each scene, especially the closing ones. As we thus dwell upon His great sacrifice for us, our confidence in Him will be more constant, our love will be quickened, and we shall be more deeply imbued with His spirit. If we would be saved at last, we must learn the lesson of penitence and humiliation at the foot of the cross."[132]

No wonder Satan and fallen angels distort the true story of Jesus and His crucifixion. They are bent on destroying the human race. But, as God's Word abides in us, we will abide in Him (cf. John 15:1-5; James 1:21). Then "neither angels nor demons, neither the present nor the future, nor any powers . . . will be able to separate us from the love of God that is in Christ Jesus our Lord" (Rom. 8:38, 39).

Even some Seventh-day Adventists have dabbled in the New Age movement, including swinging pendulums and other occult practices. In his *Coming of the Cosmic Christ,* Matthew Fox observed: "At a recent workshop on creation spirituality in North Carolina there were not only Roman Catholics and Quakers, Anglicans and Methodists, but Southern Baptists and Seventh-day Adventists."[134]

In the end-time we approach the greatest crisis ever brought upon our church. Soon "the church may appear as about to fall."[135] "When the law of God is made void, the church will be sifted by fiery trials, and *a larger proportion than we now anticipate, will give heed to seducing spirits and doctrines of devils.* Instead of being strengthened when brought into straight places, many prove that they are not living branches of the True Vine, they bore no fruit, and the husbandman taketh them away."[136]

---

[1] Max Lucado, *Six Hours One Friday* (Multnomah, 1989), pp. 66, 67.

[2] Brooks Alexander, "Theology from the Twilight Zone. Spirit channeling is the latest fad in upscale New Age spiritism," *Christianity Today,* Sept. 18, 1987, p. 26.

[3] *Ibid.,* p. 22.

[4] We will focus on the false gospel of channeling, as it relates specifically to Jesus Christ, but other false ideas appear throughout the channeled material, such as there is no sin, no death, and humanity is God.

[5] Although New Agers do not necessarily consider them as Bibles, they are believed to be revelations. New Age thinking does regard other books as fundamental in the sense of Bibles. For example, William Irwin Thompson calls *Revelation: The Birth of a New Age* by David Spangler "the 'Bible' of the movement" in his introduction to Spangler's book (San Francisco, Rainbow Bridge, 1976, 11, 12). Also Norman L. Geisler views *Isis Unveiled* (1877) and *The Secret Doctrines* (1988) by Helena Petrova Blavatsky as "mystical 'Bibles' of New Age thought" in "The New Age Movement," *Bibliotheca Sacra*, vol. 144 (January-March, 1987): 85, 86 (reprinted in *Evangelical Review of Theology* [October 1987]: 302-320).

[6] For example, Edgar Cayce, perhaps America's most famous clairvoyant, began giving medical diagnoses in 1902 and continued for 43 years, channeling more than 14,000 recorded statements for more than 6,000 people. These documents, referred to as "readings," are housed in the Association for Research and Enlightenment, in Virginia Beach, Virginia. The documents contain messages given to people who allegedly lived in past lives at the time of Jesus. The readings contain information about Jesus and His times. See Anne Read (ed. by Hugh Lynn Cayce) *Edgar Cayce on Jesus and His Church* (New York: Warner, 1970).

Mark L. Prophet and Elizabeth Clare Prophet, between 1965 and 1973, wrote down alleged dictations from Jesus, producing a series of volumes entitled *The Lost Teachings of Jesus.* Published in 1986 by Summit University Press, volume 1 was subtitled *Missing Texts/Karma and Reincarnation.* The four volumes reveal an Eastern religious worldview permeated with doctrinal ideas from Hindu-Buddhist religion. They claim that from the ages of 12 to 29 Jesus was in India, Nepal, Lakakh, and Tibet.

Janet Bock, in her *The Jesus Mystery: Of Lost Years and Unknown Travels* (Los Angeles: Aura, 1980), ponders whether an 1890 Notovitch manuscript was the source for the 1911 *The Aquarian Gospel*, or if they merely corroborate each other (see p. 4). The Notovitch manuscript has only 14 chapters (20-30 pages) compared to the 182 chapters of *The Aquarian Gospel* (246 pages). The Notovitch manuscript is entitled "The Life of Saint Issa, Best of the Sons of Men" (Issa being the Buddhist equivalent of Jesus). See Janet Bock, pp. 207-227, or Elizabeth Prophet, *The Lost Years,* pp. 191-221.

[7] The very fact of various lives and teachings of Jesus (see footnote 6) indicates that the attack is not new in the end-time, but is part of the consistent effort by Satan to distort the truth about God and His Son.

[8] Levi, *The Aquarian Gospel* (Marina Del Rey, Calif.: DeVorss, 1987), p. 1.

[9] The following are all channeled sources, and reflect a spectrum of claims of who, or what, Christ is, as well as noting that Christ and Jesus are two different entities. They radically oppose the biblical view.

Edgar Cayce explained that "Jesus is the man . . . He grew faint, he grew weak, and yet gained that strength that he has promised in becoming the Christ by fulfilling and overcoming the world. We are made strong in body, in mind, in soul and purpose by that power in Christ. The power, then, is in the Christ. The pattern in Jesus." Or put in another reading—"Jesus was the man; Christ the messenger. Christ in all ages—Jesus in one, Joshua in another, Melchizedek in another . . ." (Anne Read, *Edgar Cayce on Jesus and His Church*, pp. 107, 108).

David Spangler has greatly influenced the New Age movement. Ronald C. Rhodes in "The New Age Christology of David Spangler" (*Bibliotheca Sacra* 144 [October-December, 1987]: pp. 402-418) documents this influence and shows that Jesus and Christ are "two distinct beings" in Spangler's thinking. That is, Christ as a "spirit being" or "force," "utilized the body of Jesus in order to become a potent evolutionary influence in man's development on earth" (p. 404). Christ was once human, then evolved. He is now a universal spirit that has manifested Himself in all the religions of the world, "for no one religion can contain Him" (p. 405). Therefore, "Christ is not so much a religious figure, 'but rather a cosmic principle, a spiritual presence whose quality infuses and appears in various ways in all the religions and philosophies that uplift humanity and seek unity with spirit.' Clearly Spangler's Christ is a highly impersonal being or force" (p. 406). "Christ is an expression of divinity whose goal is to draw out man's inner divinity. . . . Christ's goal is to keep humanity dynamically moving and evolving and manifesting greater and greater degrees of divinity. This is a central facet of New Age thought" (p. 407). Spangler believes in a "mass incarnation" so that "the Word will eventually be made *all flesh*" (p. 409).

Benjamin Creme states that "the Christ" "is not the name of an individual but of an office in the Hierarchy" of occult masters (quoted by Norman L. Geisler, "The New Age Movement," in *Bibliotheca Sacra* 144 [January-March 1987]: 92). Creme says further, "Christians hope for the Christ's return, the Buddhists look for the coming of another Buddha, the Lord Maitreya, while the Muslims await the coming of the Imman Mahdi, the Hindus, the Bodhisattva or Krishna, and the Jews the Messiah . . . Esotericists know them all as one Being, the World Teacher, the supreme Head of the Spiritual Hierarchy of Masters, and look for His imminent return now as we enter the Aquarian age" (*The Reappearance of the Christ and the Masters of Wisdom,* p. 28).

Seth, who channeled messages through Jane Roberts, presented Christ as a multiple entity. "During break I went over a few questions about the relationships between the three members of the Christ entity—John the Baptist, Jesus Christ, and Paul" (Jane Roberts, *Seth Speaks* [Toronto: Bantam, 1983], p. 383). Cf.: "The three Christ personalities were born upon your planet, and indeed became flesh among you. None of these was crucified" (*ibid.,* p. 232).

H. P. Blavatsky's *Isis Unveiled,* which was mostly channeled through her (see book 1, pp. 4, 11, 17, 22, 23, 33, 37) wrote: "In the ideas of the Christians, Christ is but another name for Jesus. The philosophy of the Gnostics, the initiates and hierophants, understood it otherwise . . . Thus Christos, as a unity, is but an abstraction: a general idea representing the collective aggregation of the numberless spirit-entities, which are the direct emanations of the infinite, invisible, incomprehensible *first cause*—the individual spirits of men, erroneously called the souls. They are the divine sons of God, of which some only overshadow mortal men—but these the majority; some remain forever planetary spirits, and some—the smaller and rare minority—unite themselves during life with some men. Such Godlike beings as Gautama Buddha, Jesus, Lao-Tse, Krishna, and a few others had united themselves with their spirits permanently—hence, they became gods on earth. Others, such as Moses, Pythagoras, Apollonius, Confucius, Plato, Iamblichus, and some Christian saints, having at intervals been so united, have taken rank in history as demigods and leaders of mankind. When unburdened of their terrestrial tabernacles, their freed souls, henceforth united forever with their spirits, rejoin the whole shining host, which is bound together in one spiritual solidarity of thought and deed, and called 'the anointed'" (H. P. Blavatsky, *Isis Unveiled* [Wheaton, Ill.: Theosophical, 1972], vol. 2, pp. 158, 159). Cf. Blavatsky's comment on Paul: "For Paul, Christ is not a person, but an embodied idea" (*ibid.,* vol. 2, p. 574).

[10] David Spangler's channel information relegates Christ to a lower level of being—one able to incarnate. "There are Beings of Light and power who cannot take on human form, for they are far too extended in the range of their consciousness to be placed in any single kingdom. Their energies, their beings, can express only through a vehicle composed of the united effort and blending of several kingdoms and people" (David Spangler, *Revelation: The Birth of a New Age* [Madison, Wis.: Lorian, 1976], p. 58).

[11] Compare this with the classic list of ten Avatars of the great Indian epic, the Mahabharata (Geoffrey Parrinder, *Avatar and Incarnation: A Comparison of Indian and Christian Beliefs* [New York: Oxford University, 1982], pp. 19-31).

For Benjamin Creme, "the Christ is not God. When I say, 'the coming of Christ,' I don't mean the coming of God, I mean the coming of a divine man, a man who has manifested His divinity by the same process that we are going through—the incarnational process, gradually perfecting Himself" *(The Reappearance of the Christ and the Masters of Wisdom* [North Hollywood, Calif.: Tara, 1980], p. 115).

Compare with the fact that the Buddha incarnates five times (Helena Blavatsky, p. 275).

[12] Cf. with the channeled information received by David Spangler. He was told there have been 12 fully Christed Beings, and 12 more to come (David Spangler, *Revelation: Birth of a New Age,* p. 58).

[13] Edgar Cayce records the previous lives of Jesus as Adam, Enoch, Melchizedek, Joseph, Joshua, and Jeshua. Through each incarnation he brought the "physical body, with its inherent desires, more into harmony with the spiritual" (Anne Read, *On Jesus and His Church,* pp. 32, 33).

[14] The Incarnation of Christ and the coming of the Avatars are distinct, for the former is a "once-for-all" entrance of God into human history to become the God-man forever, whereas Avatars are theophanies—manifestations of alleged divinity (person) in history in both a Docetic (nonontological, or nonenfleshment) and repetitive process (Geoffrey Parrider, *Avatar and Incarnation,* pp. 7, 223-279). The manifestations of God in New Age thinking are within a monistic worldview in which "God is all and all is God" (pantheism), so that "a coming of God" is, on the one hand, nonpersonal, and on the other hand, it has to do with enlightenment.

[15] Properly understood, there can only be one incarnation—Christ becoming the God-man. This is irreversible and unrepeatable. Nevertheless, New Agers use the term as Christ's numerous "incarnations" to the world through history. This view is essentially the same as the one incarnation of adoptionism, in which Christ allegedly assumed the use of the body of Jesus from either birth to death, or from baptism to death. Such a putting off of humanity for a temporary time is no more an ontological incarnation than putting on a coat for a time. Reincarnation, when applied to the man Jesus (or to any other), is also a misnomer, because it also is a temporary inhabiting of bodies with no lasting commitment.

[16] *The Aquarian Gospel* 9:15, 24.

[17] *Ibid.* 22:13, 40.

[18] *Ibid.* 22:31, 41.

[19] *Ibid.* 32:18, 52.

[20] *Ibid.* 59:16, 88.

[21] *Ibid.* 22:31, 41.

[22] *Ibid.* 10.

[23] *Ibid.* 32:30-31, 53.

[24] *Ibid.* 8:8, 22.

[25] *Ibid.* 8:14, 21, 22, 23.

[26] *Ibid.* 32:32, 53.

[27] *Ibid.* 39:18, 62.

[28] *Ibid.* 33:8, 54.

[29] *Ibid.* 40:16-24, 63, 64. Cf. "And Issa made answer to them that God had not in view temples erected by the hands of man, but he meant that the human heart was the true temple of God. 'Enter into your temple, into your heart. Illumine it with good thoughts and the patience and immovable confidence which you should have in your Father. And your sacred vessels, they are your hands and your eyes. See and do that which is agreeable to God, for in doing good to your neighbor you accomplish a rite which embellishes the temple wherein dwells he who gave you life'" (chapter 9, verses 11-13, Elizabeth Prophet, *The Lost Years,* p. 208).

[30] "It is not prayer to tell the Holy One how great he is, how good he is, how strong and how compassionate . . . The fount of prayer is in the heart; by thought, not words, the heart is carried up to God, where it is blest, Then let us pray. They prayed, but not a word was said; but in that holy Silence every heart was blest" *(The Aquarian Gospel* 12:7, 11, 12, 27). Cf. the thought prayer of the sick woman healed by Jesus *(ibid.* 84:14-20, 115).

[31] *Ibid.* 81:26, 112.

[32] *Ibid.* 41:8, 9; 64.

[33] *Ibid.* 84:23, 115.

[34] *Ibid.* 56:9, 23; 84; 85.

[35] *Ibid.* 84:25, 115.

[36] *Ibid.* 14:15-22, 30, 31.

[37] *Ibid.* 21-35; 39-57.

[38] *Ibid.* 36:37; 58-60.

[39] *Ibid.* 38:41; 61-65.

[40] *Ibid.* 42:43; 66-68.

[41] *Ibid.* 44-46; 69-72.

[42] *Ibid.* 47-60; 73-89.

[43] "And Jesus said, In every way of earth-life I would walk; in every hall of learning I would sit; the heights that any man has gained, these I would gain" *(ibid.* 47:12, 73).

[44] *Ibid.* 64:7, 94; 79:12, 110; 174:18, 249.

[45] *Ibid.* 55:4-8, 82.

[46] *Ibid.* 69:13, 99. This sounds like adoptionism, which suggests that Jesus, in nature as a man, was adopted by God, and used for a time, usually considered as between baptism and crucifixion. The earliest expression of Adoptionism is that of the Shepherd of Hermas, written about A.D. 150. However, the panentheistic worldview of *The Aquarian Gospel* suggests that all humans are pervaded (from birth) by the life-force that is God, so that the moment of adoption (for the Adoptionists) is really the moment of realization (for the Panentheists).

[47] In response to a beautiful maiden, he sat entranced for days, "a love-flame had been kindled in his soul, and he was brought to face the sorest trial of his life. He could not sleep nor eat. Thoughts of the maiden came; they would not go. His carnal nature called aloud for her companionship" *(ibid.* 53:16, 17, 80). Concerning the wilderness temptations, "for forty days did Jesus wrestle with his carnal self" *(ibid.* 65:16, 95).

[48] *Ibid.* 79:10-13; 109; 110.

[49] *Ibid.* 4:10-12, 18.

[50] *Ibid.* 26:24, 46.

[51] *Ibid.* 178:46, 255.

[52] *Ibid.* 13:13-20, 29, 30.

[53] *Ibid.* 18:2-4, 12, 13; 35.

[54] *Ibid.* 19:25, 37.

[55] Pantheism, or belief in God's pervading everything as a life-force, is tantamount to God's being involved in animal sacrifices.

[56] *Ibid.* 28:24, 25; 48.

[57] *Ibid.* 138:10-12, 188.

[58] *Ibid.* 75:23, 106.

[59] Jesus predicted: "And in the tomb I will remain three days in sweet communion with the Christ, and with my Father-God and Mother-God. And then, symbolic of the ascent of the soul to higher life, my flesh within the tomb will disappear; Will be transmuted into higher form, and, in the presence of you all, I will ascend to God" *(ibid.* 127:28-30, 173). If Jesus communed with the Christ in the grave, then both aspects of His God-man reality were conscious, and hence not dead.

[60] *Ibid.* 163:37, 230.

[61] *Ibid.* 178:13, 14; 254.

[62] *The Urantia Book,* p. 1357.

[63] *Ibid.,* p. 1386. Urantia is the name given to Planet Earth.

[64] *Ibid.,* p. 1421.

[65] *Ibid.,* p. 1424.

[66] *Ibid.,* p. 1492.

[67] *Ibid.,* p. 1493.

[68] Cf. The Life of Saint Issa, chapter 1, verse 3: "Which was incarnate in a simple mortal in order to do good to men and to exterminate their evil thoughts" (Elizabeth Prophet, *The Lost Years of Jesus,* p. 191).

[69] Cf. Issa studied the laws of the great Buddhas (4:13), and the sacred writings of the Sutras (6:3) (Claire Prophet, *The Lost Years,* pp. 197, 200).

[70] Jesus, claimed Father Rebold, had been educated "among the Essenian priests of (Egypt or) Judea" (quoted by Helena Blavatsky, *Isis Unveiled,* p. 305, 306).

[71] *The Urantia Book,* p. 1362.

[72] *Ibid.,* p. 1420.

[73] *Ibid.,* pp. 1420-1422.

Christ Is Coming!

[74] According to Cayce, Jesus studied in the Essene Brotherhood at Mount Carmel from His twelfth to fifteenth or sixteenth year, after which He went abroad to study in Egypt for a short time, in India for three years, then a year in travel and in Persia. He returned to Judea when Joseph died, and then went back to Egypt to complete his studies (Anne Read, *Edgar Cayce on Jesus and His Church,* p. 70).

[75] *The Urantia Book,* p. 1427-1482.

[76] *Ibid.,* p. 1425. Cf., The Creator Son was made flesh and dwelt among us. "He labored, grew weary, rested, and slept. He hungered and satisfied such cravings with food; he thirsted and quenched his thirst with water. He experienced the full gamut of human feelings and emotions; he was 'in all things tested, even as you are,' and he suffered and died" *(ibid.,* p. 1407).

[77] *Ibid.,* p. 1493.

[78] *Ibid.,* p. 405.

[79] *Ibid,* p. 1407.

[80] *Ibid.,* p. 1378.

[81] *Ibid.,* p. 1379.

[82] *Ibid.,* p. 1382.

[83] *Ibid.,* p. 1404.

[84] *Ibid,* p. 1494.

[85] *Ibid.,* p. 1494.

[86] Cf.: "The great Pyramid was built, Cayce says, 'to be the Hall of the Initiates of that sometimes referred to as the White Brotherhood. In that same pyramid did the Great Initiate, the Master, take those last of the Brotherhood degrees with John, the forerunner of him at that place'" (Anne Read, *Edgar Cayce on Jesus and His Church*, p. 33).

[87] *The Urantia Book,* p. 2002.

[88] *Ibid.,* p. 2002.

[89] *Ibid,* p. 1972.

[90] *Ibid,* p. 2003.

[91] *Ibid,* p. 2017.

[92] *Ibid,* p. 2019.

[93] *Ibid.,* p. 2017.

[94] *Ibid.,* p. 2024.

[95] *Ibid.,* p. 2021.

[96] Helen Schuman and William Thetford, *A Course in Miracles,* three vols. in one combined volume (Tiburon: Foundation for Inner Peace, 1985), preface. The *text* (vol. 1: 622 pages), followed by the *Workbook for Students* (vol. 2: 478 pages) and the *Manual for Teachers* (vol. 3: 88 pages).

[97] *Ibid.,* vol. 3, p. 56, and *SCP Journal* 7, No. 1 (1987): 9. Benjamin Creme disagrees. He stated: *"A Course in Miracles* is inspired by the Master Jesus—it is His concept, His idea, it embodies His teaching, but it was not given by Him; it was given by one of His disciples on a higher astral plane through a medium. The Master Jesus Himself would not use a medium in that way" (Benjamin Creme, *Transmission: A Meditation From the New Age* [California: Tara, 1984], p. 74).

[98] *A Course in Miracles,* preface.

[99] *Ibid.*

[100] *Ibid.,* vol. 1, p. 180.

[101] *Ibid.,*,preface.

[102] *Ibid.,* vol. 1, p. 490. Cf.: "True perception is the means by which the world is saved from sin, for sin does not exist" ("Terms Defined," vol. 3, p. 81). This section follows the *Manual for Teachers.*

[103] *Ibid.,* vol. 1, p. 600.

[104] *Ibid.,* vol. 1, p. 312.

[105] *Ibid.,* vol. 3, p. 67.

[106] *Ibid.,* vol. 3, 57.

[107] Terms defined, a separate section following the *Manual for Teachers*, vol. 3, p. 73.

[108] *Ibid.,* vol. 1, p. 264.

[109] *Ibid.,* vol. 3, p. 85.

[110] *Ibid.*, vol. 1, p. 396.
[111] *Ibid.*
[112] *Ibid.*, vol. 3, p. 75.
[113] *Ibid.*, vol. 3, p. 83.
[114] *Ibid.*
[115] *The Urantia Book.*
[116] *Ibid.*, p. 2063.
[117] *Ibid.*
[118] *Ibid.*, p. 2064.
[119] *Ibid.*, pp. 3, 7.
[120] *Ibid.*, p. 5.
[121] *Ibid.*, p. 31.
[122] *Ibid.*, p. 255.

[123] "How strangely illogical is this doctrine of the Atonement. . . . It has proved one of the most pernicious and demoralizing of doctrines. . . . How the faintest glimmering sense of Justice revolts against this Vicarious Atonement . . . by believing that the spilling of one blood washed out the other blood spilt—this is preposterous!" (H. P. Blavatsky, *Isis Unveiled,* vol. 2, p. 542).

"The vicarious at-one-ment has been substituted for the reliance which Christ Himself enjoined us to place upon our own divinity . . ." (Alice A. Bailey, *The Reappearance of the Christ,* p. 63).

" It is interesting to remember that when the Buddha came, approximately five hundred years before Christ (for the exact date of Christ's birth remains debatable), the first dim influences of the Piscean Age could be felt, impinging upon the powerful quality of the age of Aries, the Scapegoat or the Ram. It was the influence of this age—persisting throughout the Jewish dispensation—which led eventually to the distortion of the simple teaching of the Christ when He came. He was erroneously presented to the world as the living Scapegoat, bearing away the sins of the people, and thus originating the doctrine of the vicarious at-one-ment. It was St. Paul who was responsible for this emphasis. A paralleling instance of a similar distortion was also of Jewish origin and appeared in the early stages of the cycle of Aries, the Ram. We are told that the Children of Israel fell down and worshiped the golden calf, the symbol of Taurus, the Bull; this was the preceding astronomical cycle" *(ibid.,* p. 106).

Concerning the mission of Christ, "The Christian Church has so distorted that mission and ruthlessly perverted the intention for which He originally manifested that a consideration of that mission is deeply needed and should be revolutionary in its effects. Starting with St. Paul, the theologians interpreted His words in such a manner that they served to bridge the gap between the spiritual future of the world and the Jewish dispensation which should have been passing out. So effective had been their work that the teachings of the loving, simple Son of God have been largely ignored; the failure of Christianity can be traced to its Jewish background (emphasized by St. Paul), which made it full of propaganda instead of loving action, which taught the blood sacrifice instead of loving service, and which emphasized the existence of a wrathful God, needing to be placated by death, and which embodied the threats of the Old Testament Jehovah in the Christian teaching of hell fire" (Alice A. Bailey, *The Externalization of the Hierarchy,* pp. 542, 543).

Benjamin Creme said: "People have been led to leave the Churches in large numbers because the Churches have presented a picture of the Christ impossible for the majority of thinking people today to accept—as the One and Only Son of God, sacrificed by His loving Father to save humanity from the results of its sins; as a Blood Sacrifice straight out of the old and outworn Jewish Dispensation . . . The majority of thinking people today have rejected this view" *(The Reappearance of Maitreya the Christ and the Masters of the Wisdom,* p. 1).

[124] Monism knows no real intercession of a God-man between God and man. This is why "New Agers believe in 'prayer' not as intercession but as meditation" (Norman L. Geisler, "The New Age Movement," *Bibliotheca Sacra* 144 [January-March 1987]: 94).

[125] Thomas Sheehan, *The First Coming: How the Kingdom of God Became Christianity* (New York: Vintage Books, Random House, 1988), p. 6.

[126] John W. Cooper, "Testing the Spirit of the Age of Aquarius: The New Age Movement" *Calvin Theological Journal* 22 (November 1987): 304.

[127] Norman L. Geisler, "The New Age Movement," in *Bibliotheca Sacra* 144, (January-March 1987): 85.

[128] *The Unfinished Autobiography of Alice A. Bailey* (New York: Lucis, 1951), p. 1.

[129] *SCP Journal* 7, No. 1 (1987): 23. The examples may appear as isolated, but in view of Revelation 16:12-16—Satan's final push to take over the world through the spirits of devils—it is perhaps more correctly representative of what is going on in many places. Channeled gospels and doctrines are just as much an attack upon the only authentic gospel and Scripture as the charismatic focus on tongues in place of biblical truths.

[130] *Ibid.,* p. 9.

[131] E. G. White, *The Great Controversy,* pp. 593, 594.

[132] E. G. White, *The Desire of Ages,* p. 83.

[133] "The New Age Movement and Seventh-day Adventists," a 27-page document prepared by the Biblical Research Committee, July 1987. "A nurse places her hands in certain positions on her own abdomen for 20-minute periods several times a day. Although formerly a sufferer from chronic constipation, she now has relief by correcting the disordered electrical currents of her body. A concerned mother swings a pendulum over her cancer-afflicted son to discover what herbs are needed to cure his diseased condition. A lady suspends a lead crystal pendant over a handful of vitamin C pills to determine her daily dosage. The number varies from day to day. . . . A young man in ill health is tied to a tree with his back to its 'window' or 'door.' The aperture has been located by means of a pendulum. It is believed that electrical energy will flow into the patient to bring renewed vigor. . . . Housewives, shopping for groceries, hold their pendulum over lettuce and other products to determine freshness or wholeness" (pp. 1, 2). These are just five examples of the eleven given in the BRI paper. The paper states: "These experiences could be multiplied. They all involve Seventh-day Adventist church members; in certain instances, personnel in denominational churches and schools. Professional and college-educated persons are engaged in these practices as well as individuals with lesser educational backgrounds. Actually, the above experiences have a common denominator: We believe they reflect an intrusion here and there of some aspects of the so-called New Age movement into the ranks of Seventh-day Adventists" (p. 2).

[134] M. Fox, *Coming of the Cosmic Christ* (San Francisco: Harper and Row, 1988), p. 239. It is not known what motivated the Adventists to attend, whether as observers or willing participants, nor is the number of attendees known.

[135] E. G. White, *Selected Messages,* book 2, 380. "The church may appear as about to fall, but it does not fall. It remains, while the sinners in Zion will be sifted out—the chaff separated from the precious wheat. This is a terrible ordeal, but nevertheless it must take place."

[136] E. G. White in *General Conference Bulletin,* 1891, p. 257.

Chapter 15

The Christian Coalition and the Endgame

In America, a bastion of religious liberty, forces are at work to tear down the wall of separation between church and state. A relentless attack wages against the First Amendment of the Constitution, and leading the fight is the Christian Coalition. Prophecy tells us that America will exercise "all the authority of the first beast" and will make "the earth and its inhabitants worship the first beast" (Rev. 13:12). In fact, America will set up an image that involves the union of church and state (verses 13, 14). When church and state unite in America, then the church will use the government to enforce its agenda. The issue in Revelation 13 involves worship (verses 4, 8, 12, 15). Whoever refuses to participate in the mandated false worship will face the threat of death (verses 15-17).

Are we quickly losing religious liberty? In this chapter we need to look at the following topics: (1) the purpose of the Constitution, and its First Amendment; (2) attacks on the First Amendment; (3) Christian Coalition attacks on the First Amendment; (4) the game plan of the Christian Coalition; (5) the 1995 Coalition "Road to Victory" convention; (6) secular or spiritual power? and (7) the impending conflict.

1. The Purpose of the Constitution and Its First Amendment

In their book *The Godless Constitution: The Case Against Religious Correctness,*[1] Isaak Kramnick and R. Laurence Moore document that the Constitution is a secular document, even though Christians took part in producing it. The framers of the Constitution believed religion to be a personal matter between Christians and God, and so considered church matters as not something for government to involve itself in. Church and state were to be two separate powers, one to serve the spiritual and the other the secular needs of citizens. The First Amendment is a two-way street, in which the government must not meddle in religion, and religion must not interfere in governing. A wall of separation kept them apart. History had proven the wisdom of such a separation of powers (see chapter 17). The framers of the Constitution knew the necessary limits of both church and state to keep the new nation safe from the loss of religious liberty so often experienced in countries where they merged.

In their *Liberty* article "Our Godless Constitution," Kramnick and Moore note that the constitutional framers, building on good English political theory derived from John Locke, limited government "to protect people's rights to life, liberty, and property, not to tell them how and when to pray." Nowhere does the Constitution mention Christianity or even God. The Constitutional Convention offered no prayers for guidance. Although the founders generally believed in God, "they did not want a godless America, just a godless Constitution."[2] However, the framers of the Constitution did not have "a radical secular agenda for the nation."[3] Obviously they were interested only in separating church and state, a perspective anathema to the Christian Coalition.

2. Attacks on the First Amendment

The First Amendment reads "Congress shall make no law respecting an establishment of religion, or prohibiting the free exercise thereof." Here are two important principles—the establishment clause and the free exercise clause. The government must stay out of the sphere of religion, which also means that religion should not force government to legislate in matters of religion. The Christian Coalition supports candidates for government who will promote their own religious agenda. They have all but taken over the Republican Party, and are out to get a Republican president elected. No wonder they hate the separation of church and state![4]

The Berlin Wall came crashing down in Germany. Forces are now seeking to tear down the wall of separation between church and state in America. As Rob Boston observes, Christian Coalition critics "insist that destruction of the wall of separation between church and state remains a key goal of Robertson and the Coalition." In October 1981 "Robertson's *700 Club* aired what amounted to a week long attack on the separation of church and state." Robertson spent much of a *700 Club* broadcast lambasting church-state separation.[5] He wants his Christian Coalition to rule. He once said, "We have enough votes to run the country. . . . And when people say, 'We've had enough,' we're going to take over."[6] Pat Robertson sees no problem with the church ruling the state, governing the people. It's as if the First Amendment had never existed or as if he had amnesia about other church-state regimes that inflicted religious bigotry and intolerance on dissenting minorities (see chapter 17).

"In 1992 the American Center for Law and Justice, a legal group founded by Robertson, printed an article titled 'TEAR DOWN THIS WALL!' in its *Law & Justice* newsletter. The article, written by ACLJ director Keith Fournier, compared the wall of separation between church and state to the Berlin Wall and demanded that it be demolished. Fournier insisted that religious liberty in the United States 'has been hampered by this fictitious wall that was never intended by the founding fathers and one which militates against the First Amendment.' In the same newsletter, Robertson raged against the 'so-called "wall of separation"' between church and state."[7]

The New Christian Right is out to Christianize America. Randall Terry, founder of Operation Rescue, has stated, "Our goal is a Christian nation. We have a biblical duty, we are called by God, to conquer this country."[8] The Bible does not call for any Christianizing of America. But it does warn about the result of uniting church with state (Rev. 13:11-17). In commenting on the Coalition's "Contract With the American Family," Sandy Alexander stated that the Christian Coalition aims to "abolish the long-held Constitutional doctrine of separating church and state."[9] In speaking about the "many religious conservatives" who "would like to junk" church-state separation, *American Business Review* republished a Chicago *Tribune* editorial stating that "church and state stand best apart."[10]

"Not true!" thunders the Coalition. Church and state were never supposed to be apart. "Indeed," they say, "America was a Christian nation," a fact that James Madison denied, and he was one of the principal designers of the Constitution.[11] Furthermore, *The Federalist,* a series of 85 letters written by James Madison, Alexander Hamilton, and John Jay right after the Constitutional Convention, are the most authoritative commentary on the Constitution. The letters appeared under the pseudonym "Publius" in several New York newspapers, and as Clifford Goldstein concludes, "are almost as secular as the Constitution itself. They never once use the name 'Jesus Christ' or 'Christian.' The word 'Christianity' appears once, in *Federalist* No. 19, in this context: 'In the early ages of Christianity, Germany was occupied by seven distinct nations.' A handful of references to 'Providence' (No. 2), 'heaven' (No. 20), and 'the Almighty' (No. 37) show that the authors believed in God, not that they were establishing a Christian republic." The most significant refutation of the Christian nation idea was in *Federalist* No. 69. "Hamilton contrasted the [president of the United States with the king of England]. 'The one has no particle of spiritual jurisdiction; the other is the supreme head and governor of the national church!'"[12]

The difference couldn't be greater. The British monarch is head of the secular state and the national church of England, thus imaging the papacy to the extent that the pope presides over both the Vatican state and the Catholic Church. It is precisely this image to the beast, this union of church and state and its resultant legislation, that Scripture warns about in Revelation 13, and that the Christian Coalition seems to be on a fast track to fulfill.

Not persuaded by the facts about the Constitution, its First Amendment, and *The Federalist,* the Christian Coalition maintains that the "wall of separation" is simply a bad metaphor that appeared in a quick letter from President Thomas Jefferson to the 26 churches that formed the Danbury Baptist Association of Connecticut, a religious minority that longed for religious liberty in a state in which Congregationalism was the established religion. A Coalition representative further declares that "the wall of separation between church and state was erected by secular humanists and other enemies of religious freedom. It has to come down."[13]

Thomas Jefferson's January 1, 1802, letter to the Danbury Baptist Association said, "Believing with you that religion is a matter which lies solely between man and his God, that he owes account to none other for his faith or his worship, that the legislative powers of government reach actions only, and not opinions, I contemplate with sovereign reverence that act of the whole American people which declared that their legislature should 'make no law respecting an establishment of religion, or prohibiting the free exercise thereof, thus building a wall of separation between church and state.'"[14] Jefferson's words spoke to the lack of liberty suffered by the Danbury Baptist Association because of an established religion, and also represent the real intent of the First Amendment.

How can the Coalition escape the clear intent of the First Amendment and Jefferson's letter? "Christian Coalition materials state that Jefferson's letter asserted the United States government should be based on Christian principles, and the wall of separation meant only that the government should not interfere with churches, not the other way around." But that is revisionist history. A church discriminated against the Danbury Baptist Association, not the state. The nation's founders intended the separating wall to work both ways. The Christian Coalition sees the state as interfering with religion when Christian prayer is not a part of the public school experience, or Bible reading is not in the public school curriculum, or secular government property excludes Christian religious symbols. What they utterly fail to realize is that any place given to one religion above others in the secular sphere would be an establishment violation as surely as Jefferson and the Danbury Baptist Association discerned in Connecticut.

David Barton's book *The Myth of Separation: What Is the Correct Relationship Between Church and State?* also puts a revisionist spin on things. He says, "There is no 'wall of separation' in the Constitution, unless it is a wall intended by the Founding Fathers to keep the government out of the church."[15] The Christian Coalition is not alone in its antipathy to Jefferson's wall metaphor. Chief Justice of the United States Supreme Court William H. Rehnquist concludes, "The 'wall of separation between church and state' is a metaphor based on bad history, a metaphor which has proved useless as a guide to judging. It should be frankly and explicitly abandoned."[16] I agree with Robert Alley that Rehnquist's conclusion rests on "a remarkably weak historical argument," which one can follow in his article "Mr. Rehnquist's Misplaced Metaphor."[17] I also agree with Haig Bosmajian that the Supreme Court justices are revisionists when they base their argument on Justice Holmes' aphorism that "a page of history is worth a volume of logic."[18]

For, when arguing about the free exercise clause of the First Amendment, Justice Sandra Day O'Connor and Justice Antonin Scalia arrive at opposite conclusions.

3. Christian Coalition Attacks on the First Amendment

It is important to understand the worldview of the Christian Coalition. Pat Robertson, founding president of the Coalition and now chairman of the board, in his book *The New World Order* sees two forces at work on the planet: the "Babylonian humanistic and occultic traditions to unify against the people of the Abrahamic, monotheistic tradition." Hence "the world government of the new world order will one day become an instrument of oppression against the Christians and Jews around the world." In light of this worldview he describes the mission of the Christian Coalition. "We must rebuild the foundation of a free, sovereign America from the grass roots, precinct by precinct, city by city, state by state."[19] What he fails to see in his scenario is the parallel between the two forces, with the Babylonian forces ruling the world and the Christian Coalition ruling America.

A part of the Christian Coalition worldview is the misguided sense that Christians are being persecuted in America today. Sam Munger, in *The Nation,* wrote of "martyrs before Congress." Brittney Settle Gossett stands before a giant American flag in a Capitol Hill hearing room. "She leans toward the microphone and declares, in a voice heavy with indignation, that religious persecution exists in the United States. In fact, because of such bigotry she received a failing grade on a high school writing assignment. The crowds nodded sympathetically." She claimed that she failed because her subject was Jesus Christ. But the teacher advised her to choose another topic because she already knew that topic. The U.S. Court of Appeals for the Sixth Circuit concluded, "The student has no constitutional right to do something other than that assignment and receive credit for it."

Audrey Pearson, confined to a wheelchair, had her school principal ask her not to read her Bible on the school bus (1989). When he realized his mistake, he reversed his decision. "'Within days Audrey was back reading her Bible on the bus,' reported the Washington *Times.* Eight years later the coalition is still outraged." In 1990 Kelly DeNooyer was selected VIP of the Week and asked to make a presentation. She chose to bring a videotape of her singing a religious song. The Christian Coalition is incensed that her choice was turned down. But it wasn't based on the Christian song, but on the assignment. The purpose was "to make students feel comfortable giving speeches." Ralph Reed, former executive director of the Christian Coalition, reported the three stories, stating, "And thousands of other stories just like them underscore the fundamental need for the Religious Freedom Amendment."[20] (We will look at this below.) For more Religious Right public school horror stories that don't stand up under scrutiny, see *Church and State,* May 1997. Compare them with the 160,000 Christians martyred worldwide every year, reported by Jeff Taylor, managing editor of *Compass Direct,* which monitors real Christian persecution.[21] Clifford Goldstein rightly says that "the rhetoric sounds as if the authors were Christians in Nero's Rome, not evangelicals living in a nation that allows them the freedom they would use to destroy freedom for others."[22]

Here are the facts about religious persecution. For Christian Coalitionists it's persecution of Christians when government cannot legislate school prayers and Bible reading, and the Ten Commandments cannot hang in secular government places—ignoring the fact that this discriminates against the Veda for Buddhists and other such religious prayers, readings, and documents for other religions. It's as if the Christian Coalition believes that God owns America, and so Christians have a right to make all other religions toe the line according to the Christian agenda. What kind of persecution will this lead to? It's sad that on March 5, 1997, by a 295-125 vote, the U.S. House of Representatives adopted a nonbinding resolution that endorses the display of the Ten Commandments in government buildings and courtrooms.[23]

At the fiftieth anniversary celebration of the Americans United for the Separation of Church and State, on November 1-3, 1997, in the Hotel Washington in Washington, D.C., a debate occurred between Americans United president Barry Lynn and Oliver North. During questions from the audience, a Rochester, New York, woman who said she was pagan asked North about Judge Moore's display of the Ten Commandments in his courtroom in Alabama. She asked if "he would support the right to post the Wiccan Rede [a religious code for witches] on her courtroom wall if she were a judge. 'No,' replied North curtly. When the crowd jeered, North added, 'I believe that this country's whole premise going back to the seminal documents of this country were based on Judeo-Christian principles, and you don't have to like it but they were.'

"Lynn said the Religious Right wants to interfere in the personal decisions of family and individuals. 'I don't want people meddling in my moral choices.'" Pointing out that since the Supreme Court's landmark 1947 *Everson v. Board of Education* decision emphasizing church-state separation "religious beliefs and practices have not suffered," Lynn "derided North's claim that religion is being squelched in America. Citing Princeton Research Center polls, Lynn noted, 'In 1947 when this organization [Americans United] was founded, a whopping 90 percent of Americans said they prayed regularly. Fifty years later in 1997. a mere 90 percent say the same thing. Fifty years ago 41 percent of Americans went to church frequently and today that percentage has plummeted to 41 percent. In 1947, 95 percent of all Americans believed in God. After 50 years of cultural warfare against heaven itself, 96 percent believe in God . . . It looks like religion in America is doing just fine.'"[24]

But Christian Coalition advocates don't think so. They look at the moral degradation in the country and rush to legislate morality. "Make this a Christian nation," they cry as their sledgehammers pound the wall of separation.

In its intent to break down the wall of separation, the Christian Coalition is using "stealth" candidates. They get them elected to Congress on "balance the budget" and other neutral issues, and then when they are there, they are ready to work on the religious (nonneutral) agenda of the Coalition. This same "stealth" method appears in the "Samaritan Project" unveiled January 30, 1997, in Washington, D.C. Here the Coalition took up a neutral project—to help the poor. Reed said, "We believe that government and the church can be partners in undertaking this great endeavor." The trouble is that the second item in a list of eight[25] speaks of "Opportunity Scholarships," really another name for religious school vouchers, or a way to get government to spend tax dollars to fund sectarian education.[26]

We should remember that former secretary of education, William Bennett opposes the wall of separation. *Church and State* reports that "according to Bennett, there really is no wall, only 'a pile of stones here and a pile of stones there.'" He dodged the July 1, 1985, U.S. Supreme Court decision in *Aguilar v. Felton* (which disallowed federal funds for remedial education) by launching a van program to take federal remedial education close to private schools so that parochial students could receive government education. For example, in New York "126 vans are leased at an annual cost of more than $106,000 apiece, which includes salaries for security personnel and drivers. The end result is that New York's Catholic schools are being bombarded with federal dollars."[27] The Christian Coalition wants to increase the flow of government aid to churches through the "Samaritan Project." But in this case, no bus drives to a neutral place—rather, the poor will come to churches and receive government aid through religious leaders, with all of the religious impact that could make. Government funding to parochial schools, or to the poor through the church, violates the wall of separation.

The next example of the Christian Coalition's attack on the First Amendment involves their backing of Judge Roy Moore, of Etowah County, Alabama, and Alabama governor Fob James. The American Civil Liberties Union sued Judge Moore for sponsoring religion in the courtroom by opening each session with prayer and by hanging the Ten Commandments in the courtroom. Montgomery County circuit judge Charles Price ruled against Judge Moore in November 1997. Judge Moore defied the order. Governor Fob James backed Judge Moore. In a speech he thundered, "I say to my fellow Alabamians at this moment, the only way those Ten Commandments and that prayer will be stripped from that court is with the force of arms. Make no mistake about that statement." He had been inspired by a speech from Richard Land, director of the Southern Baptist Christian Life Commission, who "encouraged people to work through government to legislate morality."[28]

Legislate morality—that's precisely the plan of the Christian Coalition. Doesn't that sound like Revelation 13? Pat Buchanan "hailed

Governor James' threat of force and suggested it may be the start of a national showdown similar to the American Revolution." Buchanan asked, "Are the Ten Commandments a religious document?" Then he answered, "Of course they are. . . . They were a foundation of American law. From Sunday blue laws to anti-blasphemy laws, to laws against adultery, false witness, and murder, they served as the basis upon which we built much of our civil code and public life. Who is to tell us they cannot so serve again?" And they will, with a national Sunday law that transcends Sunday blue laws! The Mobile, Alabama, *Register* said that the governor pledged his "maximum effort" to keep the Ten Commandments in the courtroom and indicated that he might defy both the state and the federal courts if necessary. "The governor suggested that his ultimate goal is to overturn the Supreme Court's decisions on church and state, complaining that citizens didn't do enough to fight the court's 1962 and 1963 decisions against public school-sponsored prayer and Bible reading." And that's why the Christian Coalition has thrown its full support behind the governor and Judge Moore.[29]

Governor James "threatened to call out the National Guard and state troopers if necessary to keep the government-sponsored Christian religious expressions in place." Ralph Reed, then executive director of the Christian Coalition, said, "As long as there is breath in our bodies the Ten Commandments will never come down from this courthouse." Americans United director Barry W. Lynn said, "The organizers of this rally are courting anarchy and promoting theocracy. Many Christians have been fooled into thinking this rally is about support for the Ten Commandments. In fact, it's about the rule of law and church-state separation. When public officials threaten to defy lawful court orders and vow to enforce their personal religious agenda, the American form of government is placed in jeopardy."[30]

4. The Game Plan of the Christian Coalition

On September 13, 1997, Christian Coalition state leaders in Atlanta held a closed-door breakfast. Pat Robertson "offered a detailed 'game plan' for delivering the White House to a hand-picked Christian Coalition GOP candidate in the year 2000." "According to Robertson, the nation faces the threat of annihilation by God due to legal abortion. The only way to save the country from God's wrath, he added, is for the Christian Coalition to elect a president who will implement the organization's agenda." Someone taped Robertson's speech, and it went public. He called for his Coalition to get behind one Republican candidate for president, and so revealed the partisan nature of the scheme.[31]

For the Coalition to seek religious tax-exempt status when engaged in partisan politics shows how blind they are to the moral issue involved. No organization with any partisan agenda can legally claim religious tax-exempt status. But it comes as no surprise to find the Coalition seeking such a status when they reject the separation of church and state.

Church and State journal reports that "Robertson insisted that the time has come for the Coalition to demand that Congress implement its agenda. . . . 'We just tell these guys, "Look, we put you in power in 1994, and we want you to deliver. . . . Don't give us all this stuff about you've got a different agenda. This is your agenda. *This is* what you're going to do this year. And we're going to hold your feet to the fire while you do it." . . . We're going to say, "Gentlemen, it's time." You know, our time has come.' "[32] This is the kind of church control of the state that caused pilgrims to flee from Europe to the American continent. And it is the kind of church control of Congress that we can expect to fulfill Revelation 13. Right now it seems that the Christian Coalition is on a fast track to fulfill that chapter.

Even those who know nothing about Revelation 13 and the endgame in America are alarmed at the Christian Coalition. Robert Boston's book *The Most Dangerous Man in America? Pat Robertson and the Rise of the Christian Coalition* gives important insights. Presbyterian minister Robert H. Meneilly dubbed the New Right as "a present danger greater than 'the old threat of Communism.' "[33] What makes the Coalition so dangerous is their deep conviction that God is using them to redeem America, to restore it as a Christian nation, to enforce a Christian agenda on the nation in spite of what non-Christians think. William Martin's book *With God on Our Side* expresses their sentiments well. The Religious Right believes it has a God-given mandate to break down the wall of separation, to force its moral agenda, and to wash away moral degradation. Instead the wall will come crashing down with the onrush of religious intolerance.

An enigma in the Coalition's takeover of the Republican Party is that the party itself opposes big government and has traditionally concerned itself with individual freedom. Yet the Coalition ignores individual free choice about prayer and Bible study in the public square by mandating it for all. The New York *Times* editorial for May 17, 1995, said, "It ought to terrify Republicans who believe in their party's traditional concern for individual liberty and constitutional integrity. That tradition is about to be hijacked by religious activists who value the party not as a political institution but as a vehicle for promoting their churches' social agendas."[34]

5. The 1995 Coalition "Road to Victory" Convention

I attended the Christian Coalition Road to Victory 1995 convention in Washington, D.C., September 8, 9, 1995. The Washington Hilton ballroom was packed. I thought about the first meeting, just five years before, when 250 delegates attended. In 1995, 4,260 came. Of the 143 speakers on the program, seven of the nine Republican presidential candidates spoke. Others included William Bennett, Newt Gingrich, Dick Armey, Pat Robertson, Phyllis Schlafly, Robert Bork, Peter Marshall, Ralph Reed, Keith Fournier, Jay Sekulow, E. V. Hill, and Oliver North. Clearly the elections of November 1994 that catapulted the Republican Party into control of both the Senate and Congress stirred the delegates to further conquests as they geared up for 1996.

Some of the speakers really got the delegates riled up. "Let's get rid of Kennedy of Massachusetts!" Thunderous applause ripped through the crowd. "Take the nation back for God!" "Out with the liberals!" "Away with their agenda!"

"Crucify them!" I heard that refrain break into my mind from other religionists bent on getting the state to do their bidding. "We have no king but Caesar!" You can't join state and religion any closer than that. For properly understood, any church joining the state is an illegitimate marriage—Caesar replaces Christ.

As I listened, I wondered. The Christian Coalition wallows in spiritual adultery, and knows it not. The very movement opposed to moral degradation is up to its neck in it. Another love has captured its heart. Caesar beckons. "Get power! Control the future! Be in charge!" The One who said, "My kingdom is not of this world" (John 18:36) lays trampled on the "road to victory." His words "Go ye into all the world, and preach the gospel" (Matt. 16:15, KJV) got drowned out. "Get those God-hating dummies out!" "That's the way to go. Christ needs to be relevant. This is the eve of the third millennium. Everyone knows that power means everything. The way to take the gospel to the world is to take over the world and legislate your agenda. Sure beats going from door to door, and having it slammed in your face!"

I attended Keith Fournier's afternoon session. Fournier is one of the leaders in the Christian Coalition. He's Catholic. An all-Catholic panel led out. I sensed they felt at home. "About 250,000 of Christian Coalition's 1.7 million members nationwide [in 1995] are Catholics, according to Mike Russell, the Christian Coalition communications director."[35] Think of it. Protestants and Catholics have slung heresy charges at each other for centuries! They've died for doctrine. Not now. Here they sit cozily snug in a common cause. They sense victory in the air, and it's not Calvary but Caesar.

"Catholics are 15 years behind Protestant evangelicals," Catholic Deal Hunson reported in that afternoon session. Two months later, in November 1995, Catholics organized at the grass roots. They formed the Catholic Alliance, a spin-off of the Christian Coalition.

"'We can no longer afford to be divided. It is a luxury that is no longer ours,' said Ralph Reed to a gathering in Boston, Massachusetts, 'The left wants you and I to be divided,' he said. 'Nothing frightens them more than Christians shattering the barriers of denomination.'"[36]

In his book *Politically Incorrect* Ralph Reed says, "The future of American politics lies in the growing strength of evangelicals and their Roman Catholic allies. If these two core constituencies—evangelicals comprising the swing vote in the South, Catholics holding sway in the North—can cooperate on issues and support like-minded candidates, they can determine the outcome of almost any election in the nation. . . . No longer burdened by the past, Roman Catholics, evangelicals, Greek Orthodox, and many religious conservatives from the mainline denominations are forging a new alliance that promises to be among the most powerful and important in the modern political era."[37]

6. Secular or Spiritual Power?

The fact that America is morally awash pushes the churches together. If only they can have a united front, they'll make a difference. Isn't this the way to be salt in the world, its light? Even the Promise Keepers men's movement, founded by Bill McCartney, with its desire to make men keep their promises to wives and family, focuses on the uniting of denominations. As L. Dean Allen II stated, "Promise Keepers' 1996 conference theme, 'Break Down the Walls,' was intended to refer to removing the racial, denominational and other barriers between Christian men."[38] A commitment to truth is far more important than any other commitment. Breaking down the wall of separation between church and state or between churches is not a goal of the "Spirit of truth" (John 15:26). Any union not based on truth is suspect, because all the world will unite in false worship in the end-time (Rev. 13:3, 9, 12-17).

The book *Power Religion: The Selling Out of the Evangelical Church?* offers a powerful critique of evangelicals who have taken up political issues while forgetting issues of the gospel. In it Charles W. Colson says, "Today's misspent enthusiasm for political solutions to the moral problems of our culture arises from a distorted view of both politics and Christianity—too low a view of the power of a sovereign God and too high a view of the ability of man."[39] The Christian Coalition rushes to become sovereign, with little thought about the One who truly is.

Does the end justify the means? Has it ever? Consider the evangelical reaction to the 1988 MCA/Universal film *The Last Temptation of Christ.* "There are many ironies in *The Last Temptation* affair," observes Kenneth A. Myers in *Power Religion,* "that make it a microcosmic example of the great temptation facing American evangelicals. Stated simply, that temptation is to become so preoccupied with power *in the service* of holiness and truth that holiness and truth become eclipsed. As more and more Christians succumb to that temptation, a further problem is increasingly evident: Theology, the biblically rooted study of God, His Word, and His will, is gradually replaced by ideology, a system of assertions, theories, and goals that constitute a sociopolitical program."[40]

"Although one might respect the intentions of people who promote them," says Myers, "the use of boycotts in the name of Christ is always liable to distract attention from the prophetic, authoritative proclamation of truth and repudiation of error that is the first duty of the church of Jesus Christ. . . . If the tactics of the parachurch dominate Christian activity as it confronts a post-Christian culture, protest and politicking will loom larger *in the public mind* than the proclamation of the church. . . . The E. T. boycott attempted to render judgment on MCA/Universal by a jury of angry consumers. That is a fine way to distract New York and Hollywood executives from contemplating a judgment that will render all profit and loss statements meaningless."[41]

We see a new twist in church relations today. No more battle for the truth. Only war against those who don't have the truth. "Doctrinal distinctives are simply treated with indifference," comments Myers, for "one is most trusted in evangelical leadership if he adheres to social, cultural, and political conservatism, regardless of whether or not he can define 'justification,' which, according to Martin Luther, was 'the article by which the church stands or falls.' "[42]

Let's face it. The Christian Coalition justifiably is appalled at the moral disarray in the country, but winks at the doctrinal disarray in the church. They shout out against moral degradation, but don't even whimper about doctrines on the trash heap. Such uniting for a moral cause is a moral disaster. One of the leading thinkers of our day, David F. Wells, writes about the danger of imposing laws in a time when morality has ebbed. He states the principle: "When moral principle breaks down, of course, we are left with no other recourse than that of law." Then he comments, "Today we stand at the turbulent meeting place of these two swirling, swollen currents. From one side, the loss of moral vision threatens to undo culture along its entire front; from the other side comes the escalating recourse to law in order to contain a society that is splitting its own seams. This contest between license and law is one that, in the absence of recovered moral fiber, can only become more shrill, more frustrating, more culturally destabilizing, more damaging, and more dangerous, and it is one that poses both temptations and opportunities to Christian faith."[43]

Ervin S. Duggan warns that "the evangelical church must hold to its historic priorities of worship, teaching, pastoral care, and evangelism—and not imagine that political shortcuts can further the work of the kingdom. To renounce such shortcuts can further the work of the kingdom. To renounce such shortcuts will not diminish the power of the church to do good in the world; it will enhance it."[44]

Edward G. Dobson, senior editor of *Christianity Today* and pastor of the Calvary Church, Grand Rapids, Michigan, wrote a powerful article entitled "Taking Politics Out of the Sanctuary." Nearly every week he receives letters or phone calls soliciting his church's involvement in a political issue for the community. "If I decline their request (which I do), they are often upset with me, and in subtle ways they call into question my Christian convictions. Nearly every pastor I know faces this same pressure on a regular basis." He makes sound judgments that the Christian Coalition needs to heed: 1. "We should keep the church out of partisan politics and political action." It's one thing for individuals to be involved politically; it's quite another thing for the institutional church. 2. "We are against abortion, but what alternatives are we providing? What kind of love and concern do we demonstrate for the mothers who walk into abortion clinics and the people who work in them?" 3. "Ultimately, the Great Society and the Contract With

America will fail. The only solution is the gospel of Christ, which changes people from the inside out. Some Christians have lost this perspective."[45]

Today we find a uniting of church and a uniting of churches with the state that tries to cover the lack of the churches uniting with Christ. Secular power has never been a substitute for spiritual power. To the degree that Christians seek the former is the degree to which they may not seek the latter.

7. The Impending Conflict

The Great Controversy comments, "Let the restraint imposed by the divine law be wholly cast aside, and human laws would soon be disregarded."[46] A necessary relationship exists between the divine and the secular when it comes to morality. For example: "Had the Sabbath been universally kept, man's thoughts and affections would have been led to the Creator as the object of reverence and worship, and there would never have been an idolater, an atheist, or an infidel."[47] Separation of church and state doesn't mean separation of the influence of the moral from the secular. All moral laws of society reflect moral values. This is not the issue. Rather it is the danger of moralists attempting to legislate their moral values on minorities. It is the danger of the Christian Coalition agenda, and that of Dominion theology (see next chapter). In chapter 17 we look at how other Christians, even Protestants, have legislated their view of morality on the rest, and how religious bigotry and persecution followed. But this has happened even in pagan religious persecution, as seen in Plato's *Republic* and *Laws*.

As Clifford Goldstein points out: "In fact, Plato even urged the death penalty for those whose worship deviated from the state religion, because, he wrote in *Laws*, those who do deviate 'increase infinitely their own iniquity, whereby they make themselves and those better men who allow them guilty in the eyes of the gods, so that the whole state reaps the consequences of their impiety to some degree—and deserves to reap them.' "[48]

During the 1990s unprecedented natural disasters, including earthquakes, floods, tornadoes, and hurricanes, have struck the world. Each year 6,000 major earthquakes occur, and 1993 witnessed a record 1,297 tornadoes. The Christian Coalition and the New Right consider such natural disasters as God's judgment acts for human moral degradation. And this fires them up in their push to place secular leaders in power to push their religious agenda. But *The Great Controversy* gives the real purpose of the disasters. Satan "will bring disease and disaster, until populous cities are reduced to ruin and desolation. Even now he is at work. In accidents and calamities by sea and by land, in great conflagrations, in fierce tornadoes and terrific hailstorms, in tempests, floods, cyclones, tidal waves, and earthquakes, in every place and in a thousand forms, Satan is exercising his power. He sweeps away the ripening harvest, and famine and distress follow. He imparts to the air a deadly taint, and thousands perish by the pestilence. These visitations are to become more and more frequent and disastrous."[49]

Christ Is Coming!

As we watch the Christian Coalition out to force through its social revolution, we remember that "Protestant churches shall seek the aid of the civil power for the enforcement of their dogmas."[50] Then, as a part of their moral agenda, Christians will paradoxically cause the moral law to be repudiated (fourth commandment, Ex. 20:8-11) by enforcing a Sunday law human substitute (Rev. 13:12-15). But such a law is a moral outrage—a defiance of God's moral law! What right have any humans to tamper with God's moral law in their quest to legislate "Christian" morality? So the church will use the state to impose morality and tear down the very Sabbath law that, if it had been kept from the beginning, could have safeguarded the world from immorality. What a paradox! So even "in free America, rulers and legislators, in order to secure public favor, will yield to the popular demand for a law enforcing Sunday observance. Liberty of conscience, which has cost so great a sacrifice, will no longer be respected."[51] That's where the union of church and state is heading.

"This very class put forth the claim that the fast-spreading corruption is largely attributable to the desecration of the so-called 'Christian sabbath,' and that the enforcement of Sunday observance would greatly improve the *morals* of society."[52] At that time, "those who honor the Bible Sabbath will be denounced as enemies of law and order, as breaking down the *moral* restraints of society, causing anarchy and corruption, and calling down the judgments of God upon the earth."[53] That's the endgame.

---

[1] Isaac Kramnick and R. Laurence Moore, *The Godless Constitution: The Case Against Religious Correctness* (New York: W. W. Norton, 1996).

[2] Isaac Kramnick and R. Laurence Moore, "Our Godless Constitution," *Liberty,* May/June 1996, pp. 13, 14.

[3] Isaac Kramnick and R. Laurence Moore, "Yes! A Godless Constitution," *Liberty,* November/December, 1996, p. 12. This article was in answer to "A Godless Constitution?" by Daniel L. Dreisbach in the same issue of *Liberty,* pp. 10-13.

[4] Robert Boston, *The Most Dangerous Man in America? Pat Robertson and the Rise of the Christian Coalition in America* (Amherst, N.Y.: Prometheus Books, 1996), p. 69.

[5] Rob Boston, "Ralph Reed's War on Poverty: Hope or Hype?" *Church and State,* March 1997, p. 6.

[7] Pat Robertson, quoted by Clifford Goldstein, " 'Him Whose Name Is Above All Names," *Liberty,* May/June 1996, p. 30.

[7] Rob Boston, *The Most Dangerous Man in America?* p. 76.

[8] Randall Terry, quoted in Clifford Goldstein, *One Nation Under God? Bible Prophecy—When the American Experiment Fails* (Boise, Idaho: Pacific Press, 1996), p. 37.

[9] Sandy Alexander, "The Re-Packaged Bigotry of the Christian Coalition," *NOW,* August 1995.

[10] Editorial from the Chicago *Tribune,* "Church and State Stand Best Apart," in *American Business Review,* May 21, 1997.

[11] Robert H. Meneilly, "New Right Wrongs," *Liberty,* March/April 1994, p. 16.

[12] Clifford Goldstein, *One Nation Under God,* p. 69.

[13] *Liberty,* November/December 1992, p. 5.

[14] Derek H. Davis, "What Jefferson's Metaphor Really Means," *Liberty,* January/February 1997, p. 17.

[15] David Barton, *The Myth of Separation: What Is The Correct Relationship Between Church and State?* (Aledo, Tex.: Wallbuilder Press, 1992), p. 45.

[16] William H. Rehnquist in *Wallace v. Jaffree,* p. 2517, quoted in Davis.

The Christian Coalition and the Endgame

[17] Robert Alley, "Mr. Rehnquist's Misplaced Metaphor," *Liberty,* January/February 1997, pp. 19, 20.

[18] Haig Bosmajian, "Aphoristic History: Is a Page of History Worth a Volume of Logic?" *Liberty,* November/December 1997, pp. 20-24.

[19] Pat Robertson. *The New World Order* (Dallas: Word, 1991), pp. 258, 261.

[20] Sam Munger, "Martyrs Before Congress," *The Nation,* June 23, 1997, p. 5.

[21] Jeff Taylor, "Hollow Cries," *Liberty,* January/February 1998, pp. 27-29.

[22] Clifford Goldstein, *One Nation Under God?* p. 37.

[23] *Church and State* published a list of each member of the House and how they voted, April 1997, p. 7.

[24] Joseph L. Conn, "50 Years of Freedom," *Church and State,* December 1997, pp. 12, 13.

[25] Faye Bowers, "Christian Coalition Tempers Its Wish List for Congress in '97," *The Christian Science Monitor,* Jan. 31, 1997, p. 4.

[26] Rob Boston, "Ralph Reed's War on Poverty: Hope or Hype?" *Church and State,* March 1997, p. 4.

[27] Rob Boston, "Religious Schools, Tax Dollars, and the Supreme Court," *Church and State,* April 1997, pp. 10-12.

[28] Joseph L. Conn, "Armed and Dangerous?" *Church and State,* March 1997, p. 9.

[29] *Ibid.*

[30] Joseph L. Conn, "Tear Down the Wall," *Church and State,* May 1997, pp. 9-12.

[31] Rob Boston and Joseph Coon, "Boss Pat," *Church and State,* October 1997, pp. 4-9.

[32] *Ibid.*

[33] Robert H. Meneilly, "New Right Wrongs," *Liberty,* March-April 1994, p. 14.

[34] "Prayer, by Government Order," New York *Times,* May 17, 1995, p. A18.

[35] Martin Finucane, "Coalition Seeking Catholic Support," Bowling Green, Kentucky, *Daily News,* Dec 10, 1995.

[36] *Ibid.*

[37] Ralph Reed, *Mainstream Values Are No Longer Politically Incorrect: The Emerging Faith Factor in American Politics* (Dallas: Word, 1994), p. 16.

[38] L. Dean Allen II, "Breaking Down the Wall?" *Church and State,* January 1997, p. 13.

[39] Michael Scott Horton, ed., *Power Religion: The Selling Out of the Evangelical Church?* (Chicago: Moody, 1992), p. 32.

[40] *Ibid.,* p. 39.

[41] *Ibid.,* pp. 46, 47.

[42] *Ibid.,* pp. 48, 49.

[43] David F. Wells, "Our Dying Culture," in James Montgomery Boice and Benjamin E. Sase, eds., *Here We Stand: A Call From Confessing Evangelicals* (Grand Rapids: Baker, 1996), p. 40.

[44] Ervin S. Duggan, "The Living Church," in *Here We Stand,* p. 55.

[45] Edward G. Dobson, "Taking Politics Out of the Sanctuary," *Christianity Today,* May 20, 1996.

[46] E. G. White, *The Great Controversy*, p. 585.

[47] *Ibid.,* p. 438.

[48] Clifford Goldstein, "Shipwrecked?" *Liberty,* September/October 1997, p. 14.

[49] E. G. White, *The Great Controversy,* pp. 589, 590.

[50] E. G. White, *Last Day Events* (Boise: Pacific Press, 1992), p. 228.

[51] E. G. White, *The Great Controversy,* p. 592.

[52] *Ibid.,* p. 587. (Italics supplied.)

[53] *Ibid.,* p. 592. (Italics supplied.)

Chapter 16

Dominion Eschatology

After looking at the Christian Coalition, we next consider a movement similar in many ways with some of the same goals. Together they form a major factor for the fulfilling of end-time prophecy. Here are Christians mobilizing to Christianize America (Christian Coalition) and to Christianize the world (Dominionists).

Dominionists are also called Reconstructionists, since they seek to reconstruct society according to Christian norms. Another name they have received is that of Theonomists, because they focus on the place of biblical law (theonomy) to guide society. Through reconstructing society on biblical law, the movement works for dominion, to make society come under God's rule. It is a kingdom-of-God-on-earth view that is typical of postmillennialists. That is to say, God's kingdom rule is to be global before the Second Advent.

In his book *Paradise Restored: A Biblical Theology of Dominion,* Dominionist David Chilton gives insight into the eschatological beliefs of those who espouse dominion theology. "God wants us to apply Christian standards everywhere, in every area," he writes. "Spirituality does not mean retreat and withdrawal from life; it means *dominion.*"[1] He claims that "the Bible gives us *an eschatology of dominion,* and eschatology of victory."[2] By this he believes that Christians will take over the world for Christ, that this world is not getting worse and will become ripe for destruction, but rather, that it will become converted to Christ as a result of the original dominion given to humanity at Creation and in the Great Commission given to the Christian church by Christ. In short, "Christians are destined for dominion."[3]

Chilton speaks of two opposite eschatologies: the eschatology of defeat and the eschatology of dominion.[4] He assures the reader that salvation "restores the original calling and purpose, and guarantees that man's original mandate—to exercise dominion under God over the whole earth."[5] It follows that dominion eschatology radically differs from dispensational eschatology. The latter believes that God will rapture the church out of the world before the time of tribulation. Chilton rejects the concept,[6] and also seeks to show that Christ's reign on David's throne is not some future event but has been ongoing since His ascension.[7] In those two respects, dominion eschatology is right.

However, dominion eschatology includes a preterist reading of the book of Revelation. That is, it focuses on a past fulfillment rather than on a future one. For example, the great tribulation ended in A.D. 70[8] and the biblical "last days," "last times," or "last hour" *"is the period between Christ's birth and the destruction of Jerusalem,"*[9] that is, the first 70 years of the Christian Era. Chilton claims that John wrote the book of Revelation before the destruction of Jerusalem in A.D. 70,[10] and that the book of Revelation is not about the Second Advent,[11] nor does it make any other predictions.[12] So Revelation does not give an insight into eschatology. It has nothing to say about final events leading to the world's destruction. Rather, it speaks only of events culminating in the destruction of Jerusalem.

It follows from his reasoning that eschatological events in the book of Revelation confine themselves to past or present events without any future eschatological significance. Thus the millennium (Rev. 20) began in the First Advent and is in process now;[13] the New Jerusalem is the present-day church.[14] Chilton presents God's kingdom in a three-dimensional way. It "was established *definitively* in the finished work of Christ, it is established *progressively* throughout history (until it is established *finally* on the Last Day)."[15]

Goal: World Dominion

Within the context given above, we now consider the way dominion theology looks at the Great Commission (Matt. 28:19, 20) of Christ. Chilton says, "The Great Commission to the Church does not end with simply witnessing to the nations. Christ's command is that we disciple the nations—all the nations. The kingdoms of the world are to become the kingdoms of Christ. They are to be discipled, made obedient to the faith. This means that every aspect of life throughout the world is to be brought under the lordship of Jesus Christ: families, individuals, business, science, agriculture, the arts, law, education, economics, psychology, philosophy, and every other sphere of human activity. Nothing may be left out. Christ 'must reign, until he has put all enemies under his feet' (1 Cor. 15:25). We have been given the responsibility of converting the entire world."[16]

He refers to 2 Corinthians 10:3-6 as Paul's *"strategy for worldwide dominion."* "Paul tells us that the goal of our warfare is total victory, complete dominion for the Kingdom of Christ. We will not settle for anything less than the entire world. 'We are ready to punish all disobedience, once your obedience is complete,' Paul says. The Moffatt translation renders it this way: *I am prepared to court-martial anyone who remains insubordinate, once your submission is complete.* Paul's goal is universal obedience to our Lord."[17]

The church has a central role to

play in the goal for global dominion. As Chilton puts it: "*The center of Christian reconstruction is the Church.* The River of Life does not flow out from the doors of the chambers of Congresses and Parliaments. It flows from the restored Temple of the Holy Spirit, the Church of Jesus Christ. Our goal is world dominion under Christ's lordship, a 'world takeover' if you will; but our strategy begins with the reformation and reconstruction of the Church. From that will flow social and political reconstruction, indeed a flowering of Christian civilization (Haggai 1:1-15, 18-23)."[18]

Chilton looks to the imprecatory Psalms as a blueprint for the way the church should relate to oppressors. These Psalms, with their curses against the wicked, include Psalms 35, 55, 69, 79, 83, 109 and 140. "Church officers must pronounce sentence against oppressors, and Christians must follow this up by faithful prayers that the oppressors will either repent or be destroyed."[19]

Reconstructionists look for a Christianized world, with Christianity as a universal religion. They foresee the time when Christian culture will dominate all culture. Therefore, in the meantime they call their people to behave as conquerors, not as if they are in the minority—as is actually true today. Chilton exhorts: "We must stop acting as if we are forever destined to be a subculture. We are destined for dominion; we should straighten up and start acting like it. Our life and worship should reflect our expectation of dominion and our increasing capacity for responsibility. We should not see ourselves as lonely outposts surrounded by an increasingly hostile world; that is to bear false witness against God. The truth is just the opposite of that. It is the devil who is on the run, it is paganism which is doomed to extinction. Christianity is ultimately the dominant culture, predestined to be the final and universal religion. The Church will fill the earth."[20]

Dominion theologians believe in a worldwide theocracy in which God rules the nations. They consider that Christ has given, through the Great Commission, "the theocratic mandate." "Our goal is a Christian world, made up of explicitly Christian nations. How could a Christian desire anything else? Our Lord Himself taught us to pray: 'Thy kingdom come, *Thy will be done, on earth as it is in heaven'* (Matt. 6:10). We pray that God's orders will be obeyed on earth, just as they are immediately obeyed by the angels and saints in heaven. The Lord's Prayer is a prayer for the worldwide dominion of God's Kingdom—not a centralized world government, but a world of decentralized theocratic republics."[21]

Clearly, Dominion theology looks for a kingdom of God established on earth. We have noted that, for Dominionists, the millennium began with the first advent of Christ. Their goal is a Christianization of the entire world, a setting up of God's kingdom through the discipling of peoples. So the Great Commission of Christ and His Lord's Prayer, to Dominionists, both point to a coming global theocracy in which each republic is a Christian nation. Evidently the Second Advent is the climax of a restored world. How long will this process take?

To answer the question, Chilton refers to Deuteronomy 7:9, where it states that the faithful God keeps His covenant to the thousandth generation of those who love Him and keep His commandments. He says that God made the promise about 3,400 years ago. A generation is 40 years, so a thousand of those would be 40,000. Take away 3,400 years, and we have still 36,600 years to go. Chilton concludes that "this world has tens of thousands, perhaps hundreds of thousands of years of increasing godliness ahead of it, before the Second Coming of Christ."[22] In some ways this reminds one of evolutionary theory. Given sufficient time in the past, even the impossible microbe to human development seems possible (at least to evolutionists). And given sufficient time in the future, even the impossible Christianization of the world, the setting up of God's kingdom, the return to paradise, appears possible (at least to Dominionists).

In 1987 David Chilton wrote a commentary on the book of Revelation titled *The Days of Vengeance*. The publisher's preface claims that Dominion theology "was the reigning faith of the Puritans in that first generation (1630-1660) when they began to subdue the wilderness of New England. It was also the shared faith in the era of the American Revolution." It goes on to claim that "the Christian Reconstruction movement has recruited some of the best and brightest young writers in the United States. Simultaneously, a major shift in eschatological perspective is sweeping through the charismatic movement. This combination of rigorous, disciplined, lively, dominion-oriented scholarship and the enthusiasm and sheer numbers of victory-oriented charismatics has created a major challenge to the familiar, tradition-bound, aging, and, most of all, present-oriented conservative Protestantism. It constitutes what could become the most important theological shift in American history, not simply in this century, but in the history of the nation."[23]

Rousas John Rushdoony's book *The Institutes of Biblical Law* (1973) is a massive 1,600-page study that presents biblical law as the necessary law for society. It applies the Ten Commandments to American society. In his *Westminster Theological Journal* article, John M. Frame speaks of Rushdoony as "one of the most important Christian social critics alive today."[24] Rushdoony declares in his *Institutes:* "As the new chosen people of God, the Christians are commanded to do that which Adam in Eden, and Israel in Canaan, failed to do. One and the same covenant, under differing administrations, still prevails. Man is summoned to create the society God requires. The determination of man and of history is from God, but the reference of God's law is to this world."[25]

Rushdoony explains that "the state was created in order to keep man's sin in check and invoke penalties up to death in judgment on sin. The state is thus God's hangman, an institution which exists between the fall and the second coming to keep man in order." "The *first* and basic duty of the state is to further the Kingdom of God by recognizing the sovereignty of God and His word and conforming itself to the law-word of God. The state thus has a duty to be Christian. It must be Christian even as man, the family, the church, the school, and all things else must be Christian. To hold otherwise is to assert the death of God in the sphere of the state."[27]

Rushdoony looks at Dominion in the light of Christ's exhortation to meekness. He says: "The blessed meek are those who submit to God's dominion, have therefore dominion over themselves, and are capable of exercising dominion over the earth. They therefore inherit the earth. This point is of very great importance. Apart from it, the gospel is perverted. Man has a God-given urge to dominion, to power. The purpose of regeneration is to reestablish man in his creation mandate, to exercise dominion and to subdue the earth. The purpose of the law is to give man the God-appointed way to dominion. The purpose of the call to obedience is to exercise dominion."[28]

In Rushdoony's words we see a clear case for taking charge, of making the world Christian, as a result of salvation. It is a call for Christians to use the law to gain dominion of a world lost through the Fall. But it ignores the fact that God actually gave humanity dominion over the natural world, not over society (Gen. 1:26).

One day government will force a Sunday law upon humanity, with a death decree to enforce it. It will be done in the cause of Christianizing the world. Already we can see the groundwork laid out in the writings of Dominionists.

G. Bahnsen's book *Theonomy in Christian Ethics* (1979) says: "The Christian is obligated to keep the whole law of God as a pattern of sanctification and . . . this law is to be enforced by the civil magistrate where and how the stipulations of God so designate."[29] Commenting on this statement and others, Douglas E. Chismar and David A. Rausch in the *Journal of the Evangelical Theological Society* express their concern.[30] I do too. It seems to me that the state enforcing God's law describes exactly what is coming in the imposition of a counterfeit Sabbath, Sunday, by the state (Rev. 13:12-15).

Gary North, another Dominion leader, calls "for international theocracy, . . . for this international theocracy is exactly what the Bible requires. . . . Every nation is as much under God's sovereign rule as every individual is. The goal of the gospel is to subdue every soul, every institution, and every nation under God."[31]

Those wishing to delve more fully into Dominion theology can gain insights from a critique of it by H. Wayne House and Thomas Ice in *Dominion Theology: Blessing or Curse?*[32] with a reply to the book by Greg L. Bahnsen and Kenneth L. Gentry, Jr., in *House Divided: The Breakup of Dispensational Theology*.[33] House and Ice sum up the goal of Christian Reconstructionists: "The promised land belonged to Israel, but first Joshua and company had to claim it by annihilating its occupants. A similar situation exists in America today. Those forces mitigating against God's kingdom must be challenged and destroyed by a church militant and confidant of triumph."[34]

Dominionists often cite Holland as an example of Christianizing a nation. Theologian Abraham Kuyper (1837-1920) led a movement from 1870 to

1920 that took over the largest newspaper in the country, founded the Free University in Amsterdam, established a national Christian day school movement, launched a new Christian denomination, organized a new political party that controlled the government for more than 10 years, and elected Abraham Kuyper as prime minister for four years.[35]

The Netherlands Reformed Church was becoming liberal. To counteract the trend, a coalition of Protestant churches organized and called itself "The Reformed Churches in the Netherlands." The conservative churches united to defeat a common liberal foe. Historian Kenneth Scott Latourette writes, "The movement was a protest against the liberalism of the Netherlands Reformed Church. It crystallized a discontent which had long been simmering, a discontent which had given rise to private schools in which the historical confessions of the Reformed Churches were made the basis of religious instruction and to the founding, by Kuyper, of the Free University of Amsterdam. Beginning with 1887 the dissenting congregations began the development of a national ecclesiastical structure. Kuyper was a vigorous leader, carried his principles into politics, and from 1901 to 1905 as premier was the real executive head of the state."[36]

As he established a moral Christian society, Kuyper made it clear that Sunday had replaced the Sabbath. In his magnum opus, *The Work of the Holy Spirit,* which John W. Montgomery in *Christianity Today* called "an unsurpassed classic," Kuyper wrote, "The Decalogue alone is occasionally cause of contention, especially the Fourth Commandment. There are still Christians who allow no difference between that which has a passing, ceremonial character and that which is perpetually ethical, and who seek to substitute the last day of the week for the Day of the Lord."[37]

Dominionists regard Holland as a success story that can be accomplished anywhere. They hope for theocracies in every country, so that the final global church is really a Christian Coalition of church-state theocracies around the world, operating in a way similar to that of Holland under theologian-prime minister Abraham Kuyper. Brian Tierney, specialist in the history of medieval Europe and Professor of Medieval History at Cornell University, documented in his book *The Crisis of Church and State 1050-1300* the attempts at theocracy during the 250 years of medieval history.[38] Tierney reminds his readers that "the pharaohs of Egypt, the Incas of Peru, the emperors of Japan were all revered as divine beings; the Roman Caesars bore the title *Pontifex Maximus.* In modern totalitarian despotism, where the party structure provides a travesty of a church, the simultaneous control of party and state is the very essence of a dictator's authority." During the medieval period "there were rulers who aspired to supreme spiritual and temporal power." For centuries neither church nor state was able to dominate the other. Such a duality "was eventually rationalized in works of political theory and ultimately built into the structure of European society. This situation profoundly influenced the development of Western constitutionalism. The very existence of two power structures competing for men's allegiance instead of only one compelling obedience greatly enhanced the possibilities for human freedom."[39]

During the centuries preceding the medieval period, the Christian church reigned supreme. But this was already being called in question during the 250 years from 1050 to 1300, or nearly 200 years before the Protestant Reformation. The proper separation of church and state provided religious freedom. The problem is Dominionists, like the Christian Coalition adherents, ignore such historical realities, and failing to learn from history, they are plunging back to the premedieval model of a church-state theocracy, thus providing the framework in which all the world will wonder after and worship the restored and globally dominant religious power in the end-time (Rev. 13:1-17).

Joseph L. Conn in his article "Tear Down the Wall!" speaks of Dominionists (or Reconstructionists) as "the most extreme component of the Religious Right. Leaders of Reconstructionism want to scrap democracy and replace American secular government with a theocratic regime that enforces the harsh legal code of the Old Testament." This includes R. J. Rushdoony's call for the death penalty for 18 offenses, including adultery, homosexuality, and worship of false gods. George Grant, a Tennessee historian and director of the King's Meadow Study Center, wrote a book titled *Legislating Immorality* (1993) pushing the death penalty for homosexuals. Conn points out that anti-abortionist Randall Terry, founder of Operation Rescue, insists that "we must have a Christian nation built on God's law, on the Ten Commandments. No apologies." Conn comments that "Terry's 1995 book, *The Sword,* gives the 'biblical foundation' for overthrowing the government. In one section, Terry argues that 'lower magistrates' (state local officials) may 'raise a revolution' against a 'wicked, unrepentant' central government that refuses to enforce 'God's law.'" "Terry appears to have adopted a sweeping agenda that reflects Reconstructionist influence."[40]

Bishop Earl Paulk is probably the best known exponent of "Dominion Theology" according to H. Wayne House and Thomas Ice. They cite his thoughts on the kingdom of God. Seeing disunity among the churches as preventing the coming of the kingdom, he calls for unity—but only at the price of forgetting doctrines. "What would a meeting be like which brought together liberal evangelicals, such as we are, conservative theologians, represented by Holiness groups and Southern Baptists, and Catholics, Seventh-day Adventists, and members of the Church of Jesus Christ of Latter-Day Saints? Many of these groups have become so different that we almost regard them as enemies, rather than as brothers and sisters in the faith. How can we step over these walls that have been built so high? It is my honest opinion that bridging these walls is what Paul is talking about when he says that the Kingdom of God cannot come to pass until 'we all come in the unity of the faith.' He specifically does not say anything about doctrine, because he is not concerned about doctrinal points."[41]

Besides breaking down the constitutional wall separating church and state, here is a call to remove the doctrinal walls separating churches. By so doing Bishop Paulk ignores the very reason why walls exist between churches—because their doctrines are different. In rushing to establish the kingdom on earth, to force the world to become theocracies, Dominionists throw away doctrinal truth that is the only basis of unity and of the kingdom. By pushing to establish a Christianized world, Dominionists bypass the very truths of Christianity. And through working to establish a moral kingdom Dominionists overlook moral truths. They ignore the truth of Christ's clear statement, "My kingdom is not of this world" (John 18:36).

Although differences exist between the Christian Coalition adherents and Dominionists, they share some common concerns about the end-time. Both believe Christians will rule over America (Christian Coalition) and the world (Dominionists). They both call for Christianizing government. Neither do justice to biblical eschatology that ends in Armageddon, with most of the world fighting against a Christian remnant.

Their designs to rule and enforce their views of Christianity on the rest fits in with the prophetic scenes of Revelation 13 of a mandated morality enforced by a death decree. Also their rhetoric suggests that Satan is preparing the world for the fulfillment of the scenes of Revelation 13.

---

[1] David Chilton, Paradise Restored: A Biblical Theology of Dominion (Ft. Worth, Tex.: Dominion Press, 1987), p. 4.

[2] *Ibid.*, p. 5.

[3] *Ibid.*, p. 7.

[4] *Ibid.*, p. 15.

[5] *Ibid.*, p. 25.

[6] *Ibid.*, p. 54.

[7] *Ibid.*, p. 71.

[8] *Ibid.*, p. 88.

[9] *Ibid.*, p. 115.

[10] *Ibid.*, p. 159.

[11] *Ibid.*, p. 166.

[12] *Ibid.*, p. 175.

[13] *Ibid.*, p. 172.

[14] *Ibid.*, p. 205.

[15] *Ibid.*, p. 73.

[16] *Ibid.*, p. 213.

[17] *Ibid.*, pp. 213, 214.

[18] *Ibid.*, p. 214.

[19] *Ibid.*, p. 216.

[20] *Ibid.*, p. 218.

[21] *Ibid.*, p. 219.

[22] *Ibid.*, p. 221, 222.

[23] David Chilton, *The Days of Vengeance: An Exposition of the Book of Revelation* (Ft. Worth, Tex.: Dominion Press, 1987), p. xxi.

[24] John M. Frame, "The Institutes of Biblical Law," *Westminster Theological Journal* 38 (Winter 1976): 195. It is an excellent article for evaluating the Institutes. Frame points out that almost all Old Testament civil law is literally normative for society today, but he says it is not clear what laws are binding today and in what sense they are binding.

[25] Rousas John Rushdoony, *The Institutes of Biblical Law* (Phillipsburg, N.J.: Presbyterian and Reformed, 1973), p. 4.

[26] *Ibid.,* p. 238.

[27] *Ibid.,* p. 240.

[28] *Ibid.,* p. 450.

[29] Greg Bahnsen, *Theonomy in Christian Ethics* (Nutley, N.J.: Craig, 1979), p. 45.

[30] Douglas E. Chismar and David A. Rausch, "Regarding Theonomy: An Essay of Concern," *Journal of the Evangelical Theological Society* 27 (September 1984): 315.

[31] Gary North, *Healer of the Nations: Biblical Principles for International Relations* (Fort Worth, Tex.: Dominion, 1987), pp. 56, 57.

[32] H. Wayne House and Thomas Ice, *Dominion Theology: Blessing or Curse?* (Portland, Oreg.: Multnomah, 1988).

[33] Greg L. Bahnsen and Kenneth L. Gentry, Jr., *House Divided: The Breakup of Dispensational Theology* (Tyler, Tex.: Institute of Christian Economics, 1989).

[34] House and Ice, p. 23.

[35] *Ibid.,* pp. 336, 337.

[36] Kenneth Scott Latourette, *A History of Christianity: Reformation to the Present,* rev. ed. (Peabody, Mass.: Prince Press, 1997), vol. 2, p. 1151.

[37] Abraham Kuyper, *The Work of the Holy Spirit* (Grand Rapids: Eerdmans, 1979), p. 53.

[38] Brian Tierney, *The Crisis of Church and State 1050-1300* (Englewood Cliffs, N.J.: Prentice-Hall, 1964).

[39] *Ibid.,* pp. 1-2.

[40] Joseph L. Conn, "Tear Down the Wall!" *Church and State,* May 1997, pp. 10, 11.

[41] House and Ice, pp. 379, 380.

Chapter 17

Precursors of End-time Eschatology

We have looked into the Christian Coalition and Reconstruction, or Dominion, movements and noted their interest in merging church and state as a likely prelude to the final union of church and state prophesied in Revelation 13. In so doing we have examined movements at work in America, an incredible situation when we realize that America has been the bastion of religious freedom. Surely religious persecution could never happen here. But it already has, and in other places too.

The fact is religious persecution has occurred many times before. Often church and state have combined to enforce morality. What is coming is not something novel, but rather the final outworking of a scheme that Satan has successfully employed countless times in different countries throughout history. It is a global finale of what Satan has conducted in local situations so many times before. His schemes involve human attempts to set up God's kingdom on earth, various forms of postmillennialism, and the merging of church and state in a form of theocracy. What has happened often on a local level gives insight into what awaits us on a global scale.

Although the topic deserves a book in and of itself, our purpose here is much more modest. We will look at (1) Savonarola in Florence, (2) John Calvin in Geneva, (3) Oliver Cromwell in England, (4) the Puritans in England and New England, (5) the Fifth Monarchists in Puritan England, and (6) how religion and state have united in other countries.

Savonarola in Florence

Savonarola was born September 21, 1452, and died May 23, 1498. In 1481 he joined St. Mark's convent in Florence. "At the time of Savonarola's arrival, the city was at the height of its fame as a seat of culture and also as the place of light-hearted dissipation under the brilliant patronage of Lorenzo the Magnificent."[1]

In his *Liberty* article on Savonarola, Dennis Pettibone speaks of the conditions of the time. "The preacher turned away in disgust from the lurid woman. This was the second time today that a prostitute had propositioned him. Had decency fled this Christian nation? Immorality was glaringly, daringly rampant. Almost as if sinners were deliberately defying Jehovah, daring Him to retaliate, daring Him with gambling, avarice, fraud, sexual impurity, and that most disgusting of sins—homosexuality. Even the nation's leader was said to be a practitioner of this vile vice. If heaven delayed its vengeance much longer, would not Sodom itself cry out 'Why us?'" Savonarola saw a twofold solution: "to proclaim Jesus Christ the nation's king and to enact moral legislation."[2]

Savonarola was "the most imposing preacher of the Middle Ages and one of the most noteworthy preachers of righteousness since St. Paul."[3] However, he thundered from the pulpit rather than presenting divine compassion. Basing his sermons on the book of Revelation, he applied them to present conditions. The people flocked out to hear him. "In the time of his greatest popularity, the throngs waited hours at the doors of the cathedral for the preacher's arrival and it has been estimated by Villari that audiences of 10,000 or 12,000 hung on his discourses."[4]

Claiming to be a prophet, Savonarola wrote the *Manual of Revelations* in 1495 and a *Dialogue Concerning Truth and Prophecy* in 1497. His prophesies and intense presentations gripped the people. In one sermon he describes his visit to Paradise in March 1495. "With the help of angels, the visitor [Savonarola] mounted a ladder to the throne of the Virgin who gave him a crown and a precious stone and then, with Jesus in her arms, supplicated the Trinity for Savonarola and the Florentines."[5]

Savonarola saw the expulsion of the Medici as the chance to establish an ideal government in Florence, "a theocracy with Christ as its head." The "reorganization of the state and the new constitution, largely a matter of Savonarola's creation, involved him inextricably in civic policies and the war of civic factions." It thrust him into the political scene. "Remonstrating with God for imposing this duty upon him, he declared, 'I will preach, if so I must, but why need I meddle with the government of Florence.' And the Lord said, 'If thou wouldst make Florence a holy city, thou must establish her on firm foundations and give her a government which cherishes righteousness.' Thus the preacher was committed."[6]

Consider how Savonarola approached his mission. "'If you desire a good government,' he declared, 'you must restore it to God.' Only a good Christian could be a good citizen, he said." "He also demanded the death penalty for incest and gambling. Blasphemers, he said, should have their tongues nailed to a block of wood." "He called for Sunday legislation. 'Whoever keeps his business open on Sunday,' he said, 'desecrates the Lord's day. He should be hauled before the magistrates and forfeit the earnings of an entire week.'"[7]

What was the result of Savonarola's theocracy in Florence? "To many Florentines . . . the tragedy of Savonarola's three and a half years of dominance was not that he failed to eradicate sin, but that he succeeded too well. They felt that their personal freedom was being sacrificed to someone else's conscience. Regulations suffocated their accustomed lifestyle." As Pierre Van Passen concludes, "To the great majority of the people of Florence the yoke of Savonarola's asceticism became unbearable in the long run. His attempts to have his proposals and suggestions of reform placed on the statute books . . . with binding force on all were more and more resented as interference in state affairs, as a form of ecclesiastical authoritarianism."[8]

His experience serves as a warning to other well-meaning contemporary church leaders who wish to legislate their form of morality through government legislation.

John Calvin's Geneva

John Calvin (1509-1564) believed that "Christianity was intended to reform all of society." His first stay in Geneva was 1533 to 1534. During that time the government enacted strict laws relative to Sunday sermons, ordering that "'neither butchers, nor tripe sellers, nor others, nor second-hand dealers shall stay open beyond the last stroke of the great bell; that those who have idols at home break them up forthwith; that there is to be no singing of idle songs and no playing of games of chance; nor are the pastry cooks to cry their wares during the time of sermon.'"[9]

Calvin's second stay in Geneva occurred during 1541 to 1564.[10] His ruling body, the Consistory, or Presbytery, consisted of a mixture of ministers and laypersons. "It represented the union of Church and State," and met every Thursday. Many have called Calvin "the Pope of Geneva" because of the strict rules he enforced in the city. For example, his legislators regulated the number of dishes at a meal and fined citizens three *sols* if they did not attend compulsory public worship. "Watchmen were appointed to see that people went to church. The members of the Consistory visited every house once a year to examine into the faith and morals of the family."[11]

The theocracy of Geneva meted out such punishments as banishing a man for three months for saying a baying ass "prays a beautiful psalm" and imprisoning three men three days for laughing in a sermon. It had a girl beheaded for hitting her parents and executed a banker for repeated adultery. Men and women perished at the stake for witchcraft as well as the Catholic theologian and physician Michael Servetus for heresy and blasphemy, and Servetus was only traveling through Geneva when apprehended! "From 1542 to 1546 fifty-eight judgments of death and seventy-six decrees of banishments were passed. During the years 1558 and 1559 the cases of various punishments for all sorts of offenses amounted to four hundred and fourteen—a very large proportion for a population of 20,000."[12]

Oliver Cromwell in England

Oliver Cromwell (1599-1658) was a Calvinistic Puritan. King Charles I had become overbearing in taxation, and his support of bishops irked the Puritans. "Cromwell, in fact, distrusted the whole hierarchy of the Church of

England, though he was never opposed to a state church." When those wanting reform revolted against the monarchy, Oliver Cromwell fought in the two ensuing English civil wars and never lost a battle. His military men, called Ironsides, he trained vigorously. "If they swore, they were fined; if drunk, put in the stocks; if they called each other Roundheads—thus endorsing the contemptuous epithet the Royalists applied to them because of their close-cropped hair—they were cashiered; and if they deserted, they were whipped."[13]

Cromwell finally signed, with others, the execution order for King Charles I. On April 20, 1653, he expelled all the members from Parliament. "He asserted that they were 'corrupt and unjust men and scandalous to the profession of the Gospel.'" By July 4 he set up a new assembly and told them "that they must be just, and, 'ruling in the fear of God,' resolve the affairs of the nation. Cromwell seems to have regarded this 'Little Parliament' as a constituent body capable of establishing a Puritan republic." But he considered this "Assembly of Saints" was "too hasty and too radical."[14]

Finally, believing that providence had chosen him to rule, from 1653 to 1658 he served as Lord Protector of the republican Commonwealth of England, Scotland, and Ireland. "Although Cromwell was a determined opponent of absolutism, he governed almost as absolutely as had Charles I. The troubled conditions of the times forced him to adopt stern measures."[15]

Although we could say many good things about both John Calvin and Oliver Cromwell, what we have recorded here shows what the establishment of a religious state or republic through governmental force and the union of church and state can lead to.

Puritans in England and New England

1. Old England

King Henry VIII separated the Church of England from the Catholic Church in 1534. Protestantism advanced during the reign of Edward VI (1547-1553), but suffered many martyrs under the reign of Catholic Queen Mary (1553-1558). Many fled to John Calvin's Geneva. Protestants welcomed Queen Elizabeth's accession to the throne in 1558.[16] Although she adhered to Protestantism because her throne depended on it,[17] she still disappointed those wishing reform. Believers desirous of a complete break from Catholicism, and thus a purifying of the church, received the name Puritans in the 1560s. Puritans believed they were "called upon to create a commonwealth in accordance with God's will."[18]

In his book on Elizabethan Puritanism, editor and historian Leonard J. Trinterud records the thinking of Puritan William Fulke. "Of this honorable subjection to God and his church, Isaiah prophesieth, chapter 49:23: 'Kings shall be thy nursing fathers and queens shall be thy nurses. They shall worship thee with their faces towards the earth and lick the dust of thy feet, and thou shalt know that I am the Lord.' The prophet meaneth that kings and queens shall be so careful for the preservation of the church that they shall think no service too base for them, so they may profit the church of Christ withal. Unto this honorable subjection the Holy Ghost exhorteth princes in the second Psalm, after that they have tried that they prevail nothing in striving against the kingdom of Christ: 'Be now therefore wise (O ye kings); be learned that judge the earth. Serve the Lord with fear, and rejoice unto him with trembling' (Ps. 2:10, 11), declaring that it is a joyful service to be obedient to Christ, yea to serve God is indeed to reign."[19]

As John Wilson notes: "The Puritans were English patriots who construed their nation's historical destiny in terms of the biblical drama. England had been the seat of the pure church and the great locus of resistance to Antichrist through Christian history. In turn they believed it would be the fountainhead of a purified Europe delivered from the Roman incarnation of Antichristian power. Englishmen generally cherished their native land and held it to be unique. This Reformed Protestant movement elaborated these strong sentiments in theological images which led to a vision of England as instrumental in the regeneration of the Christian world."[20]

The Puritans "sought parliamentary support for an effort to institute a presbyterian form of polity for the Church of England." "When civil war broke out between Parliament and Charles in the 1640s, Puritans seized the opportunity to urge Parliament and the nation to renew its covenant with God."[21] From 1640 until 1649 Puritans preached to the Long Parliament (1640-1653) in London in an attempt to get the government to promote their religious values.[22] They believed that the millennium was imminent. In 1643-1644 Puritan minister Stephen Marshall preached about the ultimate king above King Charles I, declaring, "This is, the Lord Jesus Christ, whom we are endeavouring to set upon his throne, that he might be Lord and King in his Israel, over his Church, amongst us."[23] Many Puritans called for a uniting of Christ with the state, a theocracy. As M. M. Knappen, historian from the University of Chicago, put it: "Puritans felt that a state-supported church required a Christian magistrate to wield the temporal sword."[24] Both in old and New England a Christian society ruled by Christians left no room for those who were not Christians. In the future those who do not adhere to the prevalent type of Christianity will face the enforced worship of Revelation 13.

2. New England

As *The New Encyclopedia Britannica* states, "the Puritan ideal of realizing the Holy Commonwealth by establishing of a covenanted community was carried to the American colony of Virginia by Thomas Dale."[25]

Puritans in Massachusetts Bay, such as the Pilgrims, came to the New World to escape "religious restraints." Whereas the Pilgrims separated from the church, the Puritans wanted to reform the church from within. The problem came when some persons wanted to abandon the majority belief and practice. "When these tendencies or any other hinting of deviation from orthodox Puritan doctrine developed, those holding them were either quickly corrected or expelled from the colony."

The leadership intended Massachusetts Bay Colony to "be a 'Zion in the wilderness,' a model of purity and orthodoxy, with all backsliders subject to immediate correction."[26] Now, the Puritans persecuted others in the New World just as they had endured persecution in England. Religious leaders used the state to enforce their dogmas. As a result many New Englanders fled to regions that later became the states of Connecticut and Rhode Island. Roger Williams, who founded Rhode Island, had been banished from Massachusetts.[27] Seventh Day Baptists in America first kept the seventh-day Sabbath in Rhode Island.[28] The Sabbath could enter the New World there because the colony espoused religious liberty, a freedom not found in most of the other colonies.

In some respects Puritan eschatology is a precursor to earth's final events. We will look at various aspects of it. The first has to do with a strong postmillennialism, or a belief that humanity must establish the millennium on earth before Christ returns in the Second Advent.

3. Puritan Postmillennialism

Thomas Brightman made the first English revision of the concept of the millennium as held by Augustine, Bishop of Hippo. Augustine identified the millennium with the history of the church. Brightman, born in 1562, became a Fellow of Queen's College, Cambridge University, in 1584 and thought in terms of two millennia: 300-1300, and 1300-2300. He held an optimistic view of history, believing that things will get better before the final tribulation and coming of Christ.[29]

The future of the Jews became a part of Puritan eschatology long before the emergence of dispensationalism. Many looked for a Jewish return to Palestine and conversion to Christ. John Owen and the Savoy Declaration of Faith and Order (1658) offer one example. The declaration speaks of a better future that includes the Jews. "So according to his [Christ's] promise we expect that in the latter day Antichrist being destroyed, the Jews called, and the adversaries of his dear Son broken, the churches of Christ being enlarged and edified through a free and plentiful communication of light and grace, shall enjoy in this world a more quiet, peaceable and glorious condition than they have enjoyed."[30]

Peter Toon called the concept "the Latter-day glory." John Owen believed that it would come as a result of the outpouring of the Holy Spirit and that all nations would be "subservient to the interests of the kingdom of Christ." The "influence of Satan both in politics and religion would be more than checked."[31] John Durham (1622-1658) was "perhaps the most persuasive advocate of this pristine Scottish postmillennialism."[32]

"In both Old and New England as well as in Scotland the eschatological doctrine now usually called postmillennialism has continued to the present day to have many supporters. Some of its more famous advocates include Jonathan Edwards in his *History of Redemption,* Daniel Whitby in his *Paraphrase and Commentary on the New Testament,* Charles Hodge and Augustus Strong in their works on *Systematic Theology* and Patrick Fairburn in his *The Interpretation of Prophecy.*"[33]

4. Christ and the Millennium

Contemporary belief in the millennium often includes the presence of Christ. As we will study in chapter 36 the millennium takes place in heaven and not upon earth. Interestingly, the Puritans were divided as to whether Christ will be here on earth during the millennium. Joseph Meade, for example, gives a glorious view of the millennium during which Christ has victory over His enemies and binds Satan so that he can no longer deceive the nations. During this period, the Church would enjoy a happy peace and security from the persecution and sufferings of former times. Meade described the presence of Christ in this kingdom as glorious and evident, yet he did not believe that He would be visible upon earth. He reminded his readers that "the kingdom of Christ has always been one in which Christ's throne and kingly residence are in heaven." Further, Meade suggested that "Christ may come to earth for a brief moment to set up the kingdom and to gather the Jews to Himself."[34]

5. The Fifth Monarchists in Puritan England

Not content to allow God to establish His own millennium, the Fifth Monarchists were an extremist group bent on establishing it by force. In this respect they remind us of the Christian Coalition and Dominion movements of our time. The Fifth Monarchists were strong in England during the mid-1660s but ceased to exist in the 1680s. Fired by the book of Revelation, they interpreted its symbols, such as the little horn, to represent contemporary institutions in English political life, and they had much to say about the "political, social and economic structure of the millennium."[35]

The Monarchists discussed as to whether Christ would be present or not during the millennium on earth. Some thought that the saints in heaven could not do without Christ for 1,000 years. "If Christ did come, the government would naturally be monarchial. Otherwise it was to be according to an Old Testament pattern."[36] They perceived a hierarchic society during the millennium equivalent to that then in existence in England. "The saints would tyrannize (with divine approval) over their former oppressors and over the unregenerate masses. For though most of the Fifth Monarchists came from the lower classes, they did not conclude that all the lower classes were saints. They warned that the ungodly beggar would suffer as much as the ungodly king. The chief function of the government in the millennium, besides supervising the new social order, would be the establishment of the laws of God."[37]

Note two things running through their beliefs: that the millennium was apparently an opportunity to get equal, to punish oppressors, and also that it would be a time to establish God's laws and enforce them on others. Reminiscent of contemporary Theonomists, Fifth Monarchists promoted all Old Testament laws, both in England as well as projecting them into the millennium. B. S. Capp, lecturer in history at Warwick University, said of the Fifth Monarchists, "Having adopted the governmental forms of the Old Testament Israel as their ideal, the saints adopted also the Old Testament laws. They called for the abolition of all existing laws and Courts, and the introduction of the Mosaic Code. By this they meant not merely the Ten Commandments or moral law (Ex. 20), but all the judicial laws and penalties derived from them and scattered throughout the five books of Moses." It included the death penalty for some offenses.[38]

A Fifth Monarchist sermon could last seven hours and "usually contained political as well as spiritual teaching." B. S. Capp notes that the saints "disputed whether infant or adult baptism was correct, whether the laying on of hands was an additional ordinance, and whether Saturday or Sunday was the true Lord's Day. But when the millennium arrived, all ordinances would be abolished."[39]

In January 1661 a small group of Fifth Monarchists became violent. A man named Venner "led about fifty followers through the streets of London in an attempt to set up God's kingdom by force, with the daunting cry 'King Jesus and the heads upon the gates.' The rebels were not suppressed until the fourth day, having held at bay far greater forces sent against them. Twenty-six of the saints were killed and twenty captured; Venner was wounded nineteen times before he was taken. Venner and a dozen others were executed, and it was their own heads, not their enemies', that were set up on London Bridge. Venner's plot was largely a London affair, but there were echoes in Exeter which he had visited a few weeks before, and a hundred suspects were seized. There were other minor outbreaks of violence in London, including a riot by Fifth Monarchist prisoners in Newgate, and the discovery of a party of the saints tearing down and burning the decorations put up for the coronation."[40]

Religion and State United in Other Countries

Ancient and modern examples of the merger of religion and state abound. Often they combined in the person of the leader. Sometimes the people considered their leader a god. Ancient countries that persecuted God's people in biblical times often reflected this pattern. Muslim countries, such as Iraq and Iran, offer modern examples in which religion dominates the state, its citizens, and both internal and foreign policy. All such countries reject religious liberty and give us insight into the future when such things will happen in all nations during the final global union of church and state (Rev. 13:12-15).

Confusion of God's Kingdom With the World's Kingdoms

Philip Yancey in his book *The Jesus I Never Knew*[41] expresses his concern with Christians confusing the kingdom of God with the kingdoms of this world. "How easy it is to join the politics of polarization, to find myself shouting across the picket lines at the 'enemy' on the other side. How hard it is to remember that the kingdom of God calls me to love the woman who has just emerged from the abortion clinic (and, yes, even her doctor), the promiscuous person who is dying with AIDS, the wealthy landowner who is exploiting God's creation. If I cannot show love to such people, then I must question whether I have truly understood Jesus' gospel."[42]

Yancey refers to times in history when Christians have become like the wrong kingdom. "The Crusaders who pillaged the Near East, the conquistadors who converted the New World at the point of a sword, the Christian explorers in Africa who cooperated with the slave trade—we are still feeling aftershocks from their mistakes. History shows that when the church uses the tools of the world's kingdom, it becomes as ineffectual, or as tyrannical, as any other power structure. And whenever the church has intermingled with the state (the Holy Roman Empire, Cromwell's England, Calvin's Geneva), the appeal of the faith suffers as well. Ironically, our respect in the world declines in proportion to how vigorously we attempt to force others to adopt our point of view."

I agree with Yancey that Christ's parables about the kingdom all express a kind of "secret force" that works from within. They contain such metaphors as yeast in bread dough, tiny seeds in a garden, sheep amidst wolves, and salt in food. "He said nothing of a triumphant church sharing power with the authorities. . . . For this reason," Yancey continues, "I must say in an aside, I worry about the recent surge of power among U.S. Christians, who seem to be focusing more and more on political means. Once Christians were ignored or scorned; now they are courted by every savvy politician. Evangelicals especially are identified with a certain political stance, so much so that the news media use the terms 'evangelical' and 'religious right' interchangeably. When I ask a stranger, 'What is an evangelical Christian?' I get an answer something like this: 'Someone who supports family values and opposes homosexual rights and abortion.'" "If a century from now all that historians can say about evangelicals of the 1990s is that they stood for family values, then we will have failed the mission Jesus gave us to accomplish: to communicate God's reconciling love to sinners."[43]

Philip Schaff, in his *History of the Christian Church,* speaks of the sudden change that came when church and state united under Constantine in the fourth century. "The Christianizing of the state amounted therefore in great measure to a paganizing and secularizing of the church. The world overcame the church, as much as the church overcame the world, and the temporal gain of Christianity was in many respects cancelled by spiritual loss."[44] Church leaders considered such a union of church and state as "a restoration of the Mosaic and Davidic theocracy on Christian soil."[45]

"Ever since Constantine, the church has faced the temptation of becoming the 'morals police' of society. The Catholic Church in the Middle Ages, Calvin's Geneva, Cromwell's England, Winthrop's New England, the Russian Orthodox Church—each of these has attempted to legislate a form of Christian morality, and each has in its own way found it hard to communicate grace. . . . Listening to sermons and reading the writings of the contemporary church in the U.S., I sometimes detect more of Constantine than of Jesus."[46]

The Kingdom in Premodern Times

We will give only a brief overview, making no attempt to provide a complete picture here, but only sufficient examples to be representative.

The kingdom did not interest the early Church Fathers. Irenaeus equated the "times of the kingdom" with "the seventh day," which is the coming "true Sabbath of the righteous."[47] He regarded the kingdom as the future millennium. Tertullian states: "A kingdom is promised to us upon the earth, although before heaven, only in another state of existence; inasmuch as it will be after the resurrection for a thousand years in the divinely-built city of Jerusalem."[48] As James Leo Garrett says: "The kingdom of God was not a prominent theme for the Church Fathers."[49]

The early Church Fathers lived during a period that established some major church doctrines, such as the Trinity and the person of Jesus Christ. It was a time for apologetics—a defense of the faith against critics, as in Justin Martyr's *Dialogue With Trypho the Jew* and against heretics, as in Irenaeus' answers to Gnostics. But no one did any major work on the kingdom until Augustine of Hippo.[50]

The Constantinian Catholic Church union of church and state led church historian Eusebius to believe that the millennial kingdom had arrived. With some influence from Augustine, he identified the kingdom with the church. The millennium was the history of the church in human history, a concept that remained the position of the medieval church and Reformers such as Martin Luther and John Calvin. The way Luther related to the Turks and Calvin administered Geneva showed a continuation of the older position.

The Kingdom in Modern Times

Again we will not give a complete presentation of the topic, but selective examples.

1. Friedrich Schleiermacher

In 1924, when Karl Barth was working on his theological system (finally launched eight years later), he recorded in two letters to his friend Thurneysen the breadth of the theological background he was working against. "Where actually is the divine Providence at work in the history of theology as we now have to see it? Three centuries of rubbish? That in itself is really a problem! And to what extent was the Reformation in some measure jointly responsible for this rubbish?"[51] "O this swamp of many hundreds of years in which we are stuck! It is so fearfully hard just to keep thinking the opposite always, to say nothing of speaking it, or of formulating it and setting it in its context."[52]

Barth has questioned the lack of eschatology in Reformation theology and its effect on succeeding centuries. Nor was he alone in his concern. The post-Reformation centuries were the time during which, as J. P. Martin says, Protestant theology gradually became de-eschatologised, particularly during the latter half of the seventeenth century and the first part of the eighteenth century.[53] Emil Brunner noted that the eschatological question remained almost completely outside of the theological debate, referring specifically to the eighteenth and nineteenth centuries.[54] The Reformers did not work with eschatology as they did soteriology and ecclesiology, perhaps contributing to a weak focus in later centuries.

a. Nineteenth Century

Barth noted two lines of theological thought in the nineteenth century, stressing respectively, reason and feeling.[55] K. Heim saw three main lines of development: the moral autonomy or the individual, speculative theology, and religious feeling.[56] From whichever standpoint we view the nineteenth century, it still appears as the century of anthropocentrism. Theologically speaking, Barth considered lines from everywhere, both positive and negative, to lead to Schleiermacher, for it was "his century." He was right in his assessment, for Schleiermacher dominated the century and still has influence today (e.g., on Rudolph Bultmann and existentialism).

b. Schleiermacher's *The Christian Faith*

As we saw earlier, Schleiermacher dominated the theology of the century. His *Christian Faith* was amazingly coherent and consistent.

To Schleiermacher, as we explored in a previous chapter, piety was a state made up of feeling, knowing, and doing.[58] For him, then, the starting point in theology is the self-consciousness of the individual,[59] the God-consciousness of the redeemed person.[60] Only in the contemplation of Christian self-consciousness can the believer discover doctrines.[61] Theology articulates the inner life of Christian piety,[62] because doctrines are but religious affection set forth in speech.[63] Thus Schleiermacher begins with the human being in his attempt to get to the divine. But he ends up with an anthropology rather than a theology.

It follows that to Schleiermacher the kingdom is an inner reality. He can even say that Christ, as our new corporate life, was in actuality the kingdom of God.[64] Thus in the narrower sense he confined the kingdom to Christ alone.[65] Schleiermacher dismissed a future kingdom and saw the kingdom as a kingdom of grace, because it alone can emerge in moral devotions.[66]

2. Albrecht Ritschl

As we have noted previously, many consider Albrecht Ritschl's book *Justification and Reconciliation*[67] the greatest theological treatise since Schleiermacher's *The Christian Faith.*[68] Being more pragmatic than Schleiermacher, Ritschl revolted against all mysticism, pietism, and romanticism, turning from the sole emphasis upon "feeling" to include also "knowledge" and "will." He considered all three psychological areas as being concerned with religious functions, for they mutually condition one another.[69]

a. The Kingdom

For Ritschl the kingdom is no realm within the Christian (versus mysticism),[70] nor is it identical with the church (versus Augustinianism).[71] It is therefore not a devotional or a spiritual kingdom, but as with Kant, a moral kingdom.[72] As a moral society of nations,[73] a universal moral fellowship,[74] a moral commonwealth[75] or moral unification of the race,[76] it seeks to develop one whole supernatural humanity through receiving believers into the religious community of Christianity that will enable them to reach the highest morality.[77]

Although Christ founded the kingdom through His moral task,[78] it cannot reach its full realization without the moral works of Christians.[79] Does that mean that the kingdom has some special future existence? Can he perceive any true eschatology? Ritschl says: "Hitherto we have been accustomed to regard the early Christian expectation of the nearness of the world's end as belonging to the shell and not to the kernel. And there the matter will rest, for that anticipation has not acted prejudicially on any of the positive social duties which follow from Christianity."[80] As we have stated before, such disposable, time-related words or ideas as those within the category of the "shell" were the very materials Bultmann later demythologized in his radical gospel-reductionism. I agree with H. R. Mackintosh that in Ritschl, "the Kingdom of God, stripped of the eschatological transcendence that belongs to it in the Gospels, is not hardly more than (as with Kant) a realm of moral ends, 'a purely present mundane commonwealth.'"[81]

Neither the immanental kingdom of Schleiermacher nor the moral kingdom of Ritschl were eschatological due to their preoccupation with the human and the anthropocentric pole of revelation. Rather than a kingdom *in* humanity or *by* humanity, we need an emphasis on a kingdom *to* humanity. That is the biblical emphasis, and it radically calls into question human kingdom building.

Biblical Views of the Kingdom

1. Old Testament

The words "kingdom of God" do not appear in the Old Testament, although it mentions the concept of kingdom in numerous contexts. Israel's kingdom was a type of Christ's kingdom, just as the sacrifices, priests, prophets, and kings were types of Christ. Christ was born of the line of David (Matt. 1:6-17). In this respect the rule of David and his kingdom became particular types of Christ's rule and kingdom.

Consider David's comments. "Yours, O Lord, is the kingdom; you are exalted as head over all. . . . You are the ruler of all things" (1 Chron. 29:11, 12). "For dominion belongs to the Lord and he rules over the nations" (Ps. 22:28). "The Lord has established his throne in heaven, and his kingdom rules over all" (Ps. 103:19). "Your kingdom is an everlasting kingdom, and your dominion endures through all generations" (Ps. 145:13). Here David speaks of the kingdom as present and future, and of rulership that encompasses heaven and all the nations of earth. It is a cosmic rule.

The book of Daniel speaks of God's kingdom, indicating how God rules over human affairs. "He sets up kings and deposes them" (Dan. 2:21). Establishing Nebuchadnezzar on his throne (verse 37), God spoke to him, saying, "The Most High is sovereign over the kingdoms of men and gives them to anyone he wishes" (Dan. 4:32).

Eventually Nebuchadnezzar found himself able to proclaim, "His dominion is an eternal dominion; his kingdom endures from generation to generation" (verse 34). King Darius admitted the same (Dan. 6:26). God's rescue of the three from the fiery furnace (Dan. 3:16, 17, 25-27) and of Daniel from the lions' den (Dan. 6:22) illustrate His rule among His followers.

Daniel also mentions the future kingdom. Speaking of the last days, he said, "In the time of those kings, the God of heaven will set up a kingdom that will never be destroyed" (Dan. 2:44). Christ, as the Son of man, comes to the Father to receive the results of the cosmic judgment verdict. "He was given authority, glory and sovereign power; all peoples, nations and men of every language worshiped him. His dominion is an everlasting dominion that will not pass away, and his kingdom is one that will never be destroyed" (Dan. 7:14). Furthermore, the judgment verdict will affect Christ's followers—"'The saints of the Most High will receive the kingdom and will possess it forever—yes, for ever and ever'" (verse 18; cf. verse 22). "Then the sovereignty, power and greatness of the kingdoms under the whole heaven will be handed over to the saints, the people of the Most High. His kingdom will be an everlasting kingdom, and all rulers will worship and obey him" (verse 27).

2. Intertestamental Period

The people at Qumran, an eschatological community, "pinned their hopes on the belief that God would intervene on their behalf and overthrow their enemies. The War Scroll suggests that they had in mind an earthly kingdom in which the Sons of Light would be victorious over the Sons of Darkness (those outside the Qumran community). They did not believe they had to bring in the kingdom by their own words, but rather they withdrew from society. By contrast, the zealots believed political action was necessary to bring in the kingdom, and they used their swords to this end."[82]

The Qumran community and the zealots represent two ways of looking at the kingdom. Is it a kingdom that comes solely by God's initiative, as believed by the Qumran community? Or does the kingdom result through human political or other activities? Is it a gift, or is it earned? Does it come from God, or does it originate through human efforts? Such questions have continually confronted believers, and the preoccupation with the human participation has often led to wresting the kingdom building out of the hands of a Sovereign God who alone can build His kingdom. That is to say, often believers have looked more to the state for help than to God.

3. The New Testament

a. Israel and the Kingdom

John the Baptist appears in the desert of Judea, proclaiming, "Repent, for the kingdom of heaven is near" (Matt. 3:2) and "The kingdom of God is near" (Mark 1:15). Matthew is the only one to mention the kingdom of heaven, the latter word probably used as a synonym for God in respect to the holiness of the divine name. The announcement did not surprise people, for they expected the coming of the

Messiah to bring present history to an end. But they had no comprehension that the kingdom must first draw near, be inaugurated, and wait for its final coming in a Second Advent. Nor did they envisage a church age.

The Jews, looking for deliverance from the hated Romans, believed the Messianic kingdom would bring them freedom and establish them once again as an independent people. Thus the kingdom was a national dominion to be established on earth exclusively for Jews. Then John the Baptist announced the kingdom. He said it was near (Gr. *engiken),* or "has come, or drawn near." The verb suggests a movement of the kingdom toward the human realm. It does not suggest arrival, but a coming or approaching close.

John the Baptist declared, "Look, the Lamb of God, who takes away the sin of the world!" (John 1:29). The prophet clearly linked Jesus with His mission to die for humanity. Jesus continued this focus when He said, "For God so loved the world that he gave his one and only Son, that whosoever believes in him shall not perish but have eternal life" (John 3:16). No confined nationalism here. The Jews had not understood the suffering-servant passages in Isaiah that marked out what the Messiah would have to endure before He would establish His eternal kingdom. They had no idea of the cosmic controversy and the necessity of crucifixion to precede the kingdom.

Then Jesus, the King of kings incarnate, came. The King had entered human history. Christ speaks of "his kingdom" (Matt. 13:41; 16:28). Coming to His own people, the Jewish nation, He sends out the 12 disciples, saying, "Do not go among the Gentiles or enter any town of the Samaritans. Go rather to the lost sheep of Israel. As you go, preach this message: 'The kingdom of heaven is near. Heal the sick, raise the dead, cleanse those who have leprosy, drive out demons. Freely you have received, freely give" (Matt. 10:5-8). Clearly the Jewish nation received first opportunity to accept the kingdom. It was a kingdom in which God performed mighty miracles through His followers.

Throughout the mission of Christ and His disciples the Jewish leaders refused to accept His works. Rejecting the evidences of the kingdom in their midst, they put themselves on a fast track that would lead inexorably to crucifixion and those chilling words, "We have no king but Caesar" (John 19:15). In view of such stubborn and blind refusal, Christ sadly told them, "Therefore I tell you that the kingdom will be taken away from you and given to a people who will produce its fruit" (Matt. 21:43). Christ scathingly rebuked the Jewish religious leaders. "Woe to you, teachers of the law and Pharisees, you hypocrites! You shut the kingdom of heaven in men's faces. You yourselves do not enter, nor will you let those enter who are trying to" (Matt. 23:13). This was not a racist statement, since Jesus was also a Jew. But with a breaking and aching heart He announced the result of their free choice. Still He welcomes Jews into the Christian church as equally loved as people of any nation.

The Father conferred the kingdom on Christ (Luke 22:29), and Christ in turn will confer it on all who follow Him. Notice that Christ said they will "sit on thrones, judging the twelve tribes of Israel" (verse 30). Clearly this suggests that the physical nation of Israel will never fulfill its kingdom promises. It had the opportunity, turned it down, and Christ established the Christian church as the new "Israel of God" (Gal. 6:16), "a holy nation" (1 Peter 2:9), "the twelve tribes" (James 1:1). Christ purchased its members "from every tribe and language and people and nation" and "made them to be a kingdom" (Rev. 5:9, 10).

b. Kingdom as Rule or Realm

Is the kingdom God's rule or His realm? Or both? When Jesus exorcised a demon-possessed man, "all the people were astonished and said, 'Could this be the Son of David?'" (Matt. 12:23). That is, could Jesus be the Messiah? The Pharisees hurriedly accused Christ of casting out the spirits by the power of Beelzebub, prince of demons. "If Satan drives out Satan," Jesus responded, "he is divided against himself. How then can his kingdom stand?" (Matt. 12:26). Note that Satan has a kingdom. The gospel writer now introduces us to the cosmic battle that pits Satan's kingdom against Christ's kingdom. "But if I drive out demons by the Spirit of God," Christ concluded, "then the kingdom of God has come upon you (Gr. *eph humas)"* (verse 28; Luke 11:18). As Donald Guthrie rightly observes: "There is here a strong contrast implied between the kingdom of God and the kingdom of Satan. This is in line with the spiritual conflict which is seen throughout the ministry of Jesus and reached its climax in the passion."[83]

So with Jesus the kingdom has arrived. God acts in the midst of human history as the power of Christ meets Satan's power head-on. The rule of Christ overcomes the rule of Satan to inaugurate Christ's kingdom on earth. Although it is not yet the fullness of the kingdom, God's rule is breaking through to humanity. As G. E. Ladd put it, "the kingdom is not an abstract principle; the kingdom *comes*. It is God's rule actively invading the kingdom of Satan."[84]

c. Kingdom Is Not Political

While the kingdom is God's rule in the human realm, is it a political kingdom that Christians today should help to establish? What does Matthew 11:12 mean when it says, "From the days of John the Baptist until now, the kingdom of heaven has been forcefully advancing"? Above all, we must remember that the passage speaks of Christ's time. Nowhere does Scripture record that He joined with a political group to advance His kingdom. Even in face of death, "Jesus said, 'My kingdom is not of this world. If it were, my servants would fight to prevent my arrest by the Jews. But now my kingdom is from another place'" (John 18:36). The verb *biazetai* can be in the middle tense ("has been forcefully advancing") or the passive ("suffereth violence," KJV). R. T. France gives the latter interpretation,[85] D. A. Carson the former.[86] We should note that the political force view does not harmonize with the rest of the emphasis in the Gospels. In Christ's day "the kingdom was not being established by physical or political force." Nor should it in our day.

The kingdom came with Christ as its king. He is the one who establishes His kingdom, though it is true that the kingdom's extension in history and throughout the world does include human participation. Christ said, "This gospel of the kingdom will be preached in the whole world as a testimony to all nations, and then the end will come" (Matt. 24:14). Preaching—not politics—extends the kingdom.

d. Kingdom on Earth

The Jews in Christ's day expected a kingdom of God on earth, when the Messiah would liberate them from the hated Roman rule. They failed to recognize Christ as the true Messiah and did not understand when He pointed forward to the time that He would set up the kingdom. It does not take place at the Second Advent, because the saints then ascend to meet Christ in the air (1 Thess. 4:16-18) and He conducts them to the mansions He has prepared for them in heaven (John 14:1-3). It is only after the millennium (Revelation 20) that He returns again. This time He brings the New Jerusalem and all the saints, makes the earth new, and establishes His eternal kingdom on this world (Rev. 21, 22).

All attempts to establish the kingdom on earth in human history are premature. As a visible realm the kingdom is yet future. Then the whole world will be the kingdom with all its inhabitants its citizens. In the meantime the kingdom is invisible, as the reign or rule of God in human hearts, a kingdom of grace that moves toward a future day when the kingdom of grace will become the kingdom of glory. All efforts to establish the kingdom in human history are only attempts to make the kingdom of grace the kingdom of glory before its proper time. Furthermore, the kingdom of glory is solely God's work and not a human task. No human being can make a new heavens and a new earth. No human has built the New Jerusalem. The kingdom of glory is just as much the work of God as is the kingdom of grace. Human beings can no more establish the kingdom than they can save themselves.

It is therefore incredible that the Reformers, who taught the doctrine of salvation by Christ alone, did not follow through with a doctrine of the kingdom by Christ alone. We could say the same thing of contemporary evangelical thinking. A great danger, I fear, lurks in all human efforts to change society. They can easily deteriorate into human attempts to build God's kingdom. Instruction is appropriate. Being salt and light is vital. But getting into the political arena to influence the state to mandate even Christian moral and family values runs the danger of forgetting that the kingdom, like salvation, rests in the hands of a sovereign God. For after all, there is no essential difference between saving a nation/world and saving the individual.

---

[1] Philip Schaff, *History of the Christian Church* (Grand Rapids: Eerdmans, 1960), Vol. V, pp. 685, 686.

[2] Dennis Pettibone, "The Preacher Who Politicked What He Preached," *Liberty,* May/June 1988, p. 2.

[3] Schaff, Vol. V, p. 685.

[4] *Ibid.,* p. 687.

[5] *Ibid.*, pp. 690, 691.
[6] *Ibid.*, p. 696.
[7] Dennis Pettibone, *Liberty,* May/June 1988, p. 3.
[8] *Ibid.*, Pierre Van Passen, quoted from *A Crown of Fire: The Life and Times of Girolamo Savonarola* (New York: Charles Scribner's, 1960), pp. 235, 236.
[9] T.H.L. Parker, *John Calvin* (Batavia, Ill.: Lion, 1975), p. 77.
[10] *World Book Encyclopedia* (Chicago: Field Enterprises Educational Corporation, 1973), vol. 3, p. 59.
[11] Schaff, Vol. VII, pp. 481-491.
[12] *Ibid.*, pp. 489-493.
[13] *New Encyclopaedia Britannica* (Chicago: University of Chicago, 1993), 15th edition, vol. 16, p. 823.
[14] *Ibid.*, p. 824.
[15] *World Book Encyclopedia,* vol. 4, p. 918.
[16] *New Encyclopedia Britannica,* vol. 9, p.809.
[17] Emily Easton, *Roger Williams, Prophet and Pioneer* (New York: Houghton Mifflin, 1930), p. 6.
[18] Paul S. Seaver, *The Puritan Lectureships: The Politics of Religious Dissent, 1560-1662* (Stanford, Calif.: University Press, 1970), p. 290.
[19] Leonard J. Trinterud, *Elizabethan Puritanism* (New York: Oxford University Press, 1971), p. 299.
[20] John F. Wilson, *Pulpit in Parliament: Puritanism During the English Civil Wars, 1640-1648* (Princeton, N.J.: University Press, 1969).
[21] *New Encyclopedia Britannica,* vol. 9, p. 809.
[22] Wilson, p. 18.
[23] Quoted in Wilson, p. 233.
[24] M. M. Knappen, *Tudor Puritanism: A Chapter in the History of Idealism* (Chicago: University Press, 1939), p. 401.
[25] *New Encyclopedia Britannica,* vol. 9, p. 810.
[26] *Ibid.*, vol. 29, p. 204.
[27] *Ibid.*
[28] William G. McLoughlin, *Rhode Island: A Bicentennial History* (New York: Norton, 1978), p. 13.
[29] Peter Toon, ed., *Puritans, the Millennium and the Future of Israel: Puritan Eschatology 1600-1660* (Cambridge: James Clarke, 1970), p. 31.
[30] *Ibid.*, p. 37.
[31] *Ibid.*, p. 39.
[32] *Ibid.*, p. 40.
[33] *Ibid.*, p. 41.
[34] R. G. Clouse, "The Rebirth of Millenarianism," in *Puritans*, pp. 60, 61.
[35] B. S. Capp, "Extreme Millenarianism," in *Puritans*, pp. 68, 87.
[36] *Ibid.*, p. 72.
[37] *Ibid.*, p. 73.
[38] *Ibid.*, p. 74.
[39] *Ibid.*, p. 76.
[40] *Ibid.*, p. 88.
[41] Philip Yancey, *The Jesus I Never Knew* (Grand Rapids: Zondervan, 1995).
[42] *Ibid.*, p. 245.
[43] *Ibid.*, pp. 246, 247.
[44] Schaff, Vol. III, p. 93.
[45] *Ibid.*, p. 136.
[46] Yancey, pp. 260, 261.
[47] Irenaeus, *Against Heresies, the Ante-Nicene Fathers* (Grand Rapids: Eerdmans, 1989), vol. 1, p. 562.
[48] Tertullian, *Against Marcion, ibid.*, vol. 3, p. 342.
[49] James Leo Garrett, *Systematic Theology: Biblical, Historical and Evangelical,* (Grand Rapids: Eerdmans, 1995), vol. 2, p. 733.

[50] Alister E. McGrath, *Christian Theology: An Introduction* (Oxford: Blackwell, 1994), p. 13.
[51] J. D. Smart, *Revolutionary Theology*, p. 68.
[52] *Ibid.*, p. 183.
[53] J. P. Martin, *The Last Judgment in Protestant Theology From Orthodoxy to Ritschl* (Edinburgh, Scotland: Oliver and Boyd, 1963), p. 30.
[54] Emil Brunner, *Eternal Hope* (London: Lutterworth, 1954), p. 213.
[55] Karl Barth, *From Rousseau to Ritschl* (London: SCM, 1959), p. 190.
[56] K. Heim, *Expository Times* (October 1936-September 1937).
[57] Karl Barth, *Die Protestantische Theologie im 19 Jahrhundert* (Zurich: EVZ, 1947), pp. 377, 381. "Aber es ist auf dem Feide der Theologie doch sein Jahrhundert gewesen."
[58] Friedrich Schleiermacher, *The Christian Faith* (Edinburgh, Scotland: T & T Clark, 1928), pp. 8, 9, 11.
[59] *Ibid.*, p. 501.
[60] *Ibid.*, pp. 541, 542.
[61] *Ibid.*, pp. 84, 85.
[62] *Ibid.*, pp. 428, 485.
[63] *Ibid.*, pp. 66, 67, 76, 91, 92, 127, 132, 141, 142.
[64] *Ibid.*, p. 360; cf. p. 444.
[65] *Ibid.*, p. 568.
[66] *Ibid.*, pp. 468, 470.
[67] Albrecht Ritschl, *The Christian Doctrine of Justification and Reconciliation,* H. R. Mackintosh and A. B. Macaulay, eds. (Edinburgh, Eng.: T & T Clark, 1900).
[68] *Ibid.*, preface.
[69] *Ibid.*, p. 652.
[70] *Ibid.*, pp. 112, 113.
[71] *Ibid.*, p. 289.
[72] *Ibid.*, pp. 284, 285.
[73] *Ibid.*, p. 10.
[74] *Ibid.*, p. 252.
[75] *Ibid.*, p. 92.
[76] *Ibid.*, p. 280.
[77] *Ibid.*, p. 138.
[78] *Ibid.*, p. 589.
[79] *Ibid.*, p. 511.
[80] *Ibid.*, p. 613.
[81] H. R. Mackintosh, *Types of Modern Theology,* p. 149.
[82] Donald Guthrie, *New Testament Theology* (Downers Grove, Ill.: InterVarsity, 1981), p. 411.
[83] *Ibid.*, p. 413.
[84] George E. Ladd, "Kingdom of Christ, God, Heaven," *Evangelical Dictionary of Theology,* Walter A. Elwell, ed. (Grand Rapids: Baker, 1987), p. 608.
[85] R. T. France, *Tyndale New Testament Commentaries, Matthew* (Grand Rapids: Eerdmans, 1985), vol. 1, pp. 195, 196.
[86] D. A. Carson, *The Expositor's Bible Commentary,* Frank E. Gaebelein, ed. (Grand Rapids: Zondervan, 1984), vol. 8, pp. 265-268.

Chapter 18

You Will Not Surely Die

Allicin Titus, a popular student at Southern Adventist University, wrote for *Southern Accent,* the student paper, served as a Student Association officer, and was in her third year as a journalism major. On Sabbath afternoon, January 27, 1996, she hiked with some other students in a state park. Then suddenly something terrible happened. She slipped off a ledge and plunged head-first 30 feet to her death.

The university family mourned her loss and prayed for the great day when they would meet her again. They had the blessed hope that she rests in the grave until resurrection morning. But that's not the way many other Christians would view it. They think their souls live on after death. For after all, famous people have described their alleged after-death experiences (for example, Dwight Moody, Carl Jung, Thomas Edison, Benjamin Franklin, Elizabeth Browning, and Eddie Rickenbacker).[1]

The first shot in the cosmic controversy on earth came with the words "You will not surely die" (Gen. 3:4). Lethal as any bullet, it sank into Eve's mind, causing her to doubt God's word. After all, the serpent munched the forbidden fruit as he spake. He was very much alive and could even speak human language too. "For God knows," said the crafty serpent, "that when you eat of it your eyes will be opened, and you will be like God" (Gen. 3:5). "Think of it, Eve, if I a mere serpent can speak your language through eating the fruit, why, you will become as God!" "When the woman saw that the fruit of the tree was good for food and pleasing to the eye, and also desirable for gaining wisdom, she took some and ate it" (verse 6).

"Seeing is believing." That's how it all began that day long ago in the garden. Satan stashed that trump card in his back pocket and pulls it out when needed. He has it ready for the end-time game. Since it worked so well to get the controversy launched, it'll work again in its climax. "Through the two great errors," Ellen G. White warns, "the immortality of the soul and Sunday sacredness, Satan will bring the people under his deceptions."[2]

The Trump Card in the End-time

We always think of Sunday laws in the end-time, but what about the false doctrine about human survival beyond death? It will become increasingly dangerous in the end-time. "Many will be confronted by the spirits of devils personating beloved relatives or friends and declaring the most dangerous heresies. These visitants will appeal to our tenderest sympathies and will work miracles to sustain their pretensions. We must be prepared to withstand them with the Bible truth that the dead know not anything and that they who thus appear are the spirits of devils."[3]

Fallen angels will appear as loved ones. Satan "has power to bring before men the appearance of their departed friends. The counterfeit is perfect; the familiar look, the words, the tone, are reproduced with marvelous distinctness."[4] Just as Sunday counterfeits the Sabbath, so such manifestations appear to duplicate the real people. Satan specializes in deception. Through deception he took the world captive in the beginning, and through deception he captures it during the end-time.

In fact, "it is Satan's most successful and fascinating delusion—one calculated to take hold of the sympathies of those who have laid their loved ones in the grave. Evil angels come in the form of those loved ones and relate incidents connected with their lives, and perform acts which they performed while living. In this way they lead persons to believe that their dead friends are angels, hovering over them and communicating with them. These evil angels, who assume to be the deceased friends, are regarded with a certain idolatry, and with many their word has greater weight than the Word of God."[5]

There you have it. Full circle from Eden.

Have you met a fallen angel in human disguise? "Evil angels in the form of believers," Ellen G. White tells us, "will work in our ranks to bring in a strong spirit of unbelief. . . . These powers of evil will assemble in our meetings, not to receive a blessing, but to counterwork the influences of the Spirit of God."[6] Imagine evil angels going to church, sitting in your Sabbath school class, and attending board meetings! But don't try to pick them out. That will only lead to paranoia. Mrs. Smith may really be Mrs. Smith. Let God take care of things; we don't have to do His work.

Debate About Death

The idea of not dying is found in spiritualism, Theosophy, and the New Age movement. It's espoused by most Christians too, who unlike these other views do not reject Christ and Calvary. But if you really don't die, why do you need Christ and Calvary? Because it's all a part of Satan's attack, we really have to know our Bible on this one. That's why we'll study this carefully. We need to expose this conspiracy before it takes over in the end-time.

1. Biblical Terms

Scripture has several ways of looking at death. It speaks of *physical death* (2 Sam. 14:14; Rom. 6:23; Heb. 9:27); *spiritual death,* an alienation from God due to sin (Gen. 2:17; Matt. 8:22; John 5:24; 8:21, 24; Rom. 6:23; Eph. 2:1; James 5:20; Jude 12; Rev. 3:1); *second death,* a permanent separation of the unrighteous from God (Matt. 10:28; Rev. 2:11; 20:6, 14, 15; 21:8); and *death to sin* (Rom. 6:4, 6, 11).[7] So death and eternal life are not merely eschatological events (individual or corporate) but apply to human beings in their present life.[8]

a. Old Testament

A number of Hebrew words in the Old Testament derive from the common Semitic root *mwt.* For example, the verb *mut,* "die" (Gen. 2:17) and the noun *mawet,* "death" (Ps. 6:5). Other terms include *'abad,* "perish" (Job 4:7, 9, 11, 20); *harag,* "murder" (Gen. 12:12; 2 Sam. 3:30; cf. *hala,* Ps. 88:5) and *naka* (Gen. 4:15; Ps. 135:10) and *tam,* "consume, destroy" (Deut. 2:14, 15, 16).[9] The Old Testament uses the verb *mut* and the noun *mawet* more than 900 times.[10]

Sheol (Heb. *s'ol)* is the place mentioned in the Old Testament where one goes at death. Three major synonyms of Sheol appear in the Old Testament: *bor,* "cistern" or "pit" (Ps. 28:1; 30:3; 88:6; Lam. 3:53, 55; Eze. 32:30); *sahat,* "destruction" or "pit" (Job 33:18, 22, 24, 28, 30; Ps. 16:10; 30:9; 103:4) and *'badon,* "destruction" (Job 26:6; 28:22; 31:12; Ps. 88:11).[11] Both the wicked and the righteous go to Sheol. Scripture offers no hint that the righteous can escape Sheol. It is the other side of death for all humanity.

b. New Testament

The Greek words for death in the New Testament are the nouns *thanatos* and *teleutē* (death), adjective *nekros* (dead), and the verbs *apothnesko, apokteino, anaiareo, apollymi,* and *thanatō* (die). "The verb *apothneskein,* 'to die,' is used 75 times in the New Testament, and the verb *teleutoun,* 'to end life,' seven times. The noun *thanatos,* 'death,' appears 115 times in the New Testament."[12] We are to understand all of the terms in the context of death as an enemy (Rom. 5:12-21) that has been dealt a fatal blow by the death of Christ (2 Tim. 1:10; Heb. 2:9, 14), but which is still the last enemy (1 Cor. 15:26) until the eschatological eradication of all death (Rev. 20:14).

2. Patristic Teaching

Socrates (469?-399 B.C.), Plato (427?-347? B.C.), Aristotle (384-322 B.C.), and Philo (c. 20 B.C.-42 A.D.), to name some ancients, believed human souls are immortal, so that death is a mere passage into another more glorious existence, because, in this life, the body confines, imprisons, and binds the immortal soul. Death is therefore a liberating event. Platonic anthropology taught the preexistence of souls and that souls are divine and migrate to the realm of pure forms, to ready themselves to reincarnate into other bodies. So, according to them, your soul has been around for a very long time. It has just come recently in your body to spend time on the planet, but can hardly wait to escape the body at death.

Early church fathers, such as Irenaeus and Tertullian, considered that souls are naturally immortal by virtue of an inherent quality. That is, immortality is just as much a natural endowment as reason. Both immortality and the ability to reason separate humans from the animal kingdom.

Later Christian scholars considered that God gave this inherent immortality as a gift of grace to human beings at their creation or birth. To them, the image of God (Gen. 1:26, 27) *(imago Dei)* means that humans are invested with immortal souls.

Clement of Alexandria, born about A.D. 150 and later head of the school of Alexandria, taught the eternity of matter,[13] a view contrary to philosophical ideas elevating the spiritual above the material. Now where would that place the body in comparison to the soul? Clement's successor at the Alexandrian school, Origen, allowed Platonic ideas to mold his theology, as seen in the belief that souls have a preexistence.[14] Another world preceded the present visible world. "The preexistent human souls are spirits who fell away from God in the preceding world and are therefore now enclosed in material bodies,"[15] imprisoned in the body for a previously committed sin.[16]

Origen believed in the immortality of the soul but could also cite two ways in which the soul is mortal (death to sin, Rom. 6:2; and death to God, Eze. 18:4).[17] Pierius (d. c. 309), a later head of the School of Alexandria, called Origen's preexistence of the soul an "absurd idea."[18] Methodius (d. A.D. 311), "one of the most distinguished adversaries of Origen," also refuted his view of the soul's preexistence.[19] Methodius believed that "in the beginning man was immortal in soul and body. Death and the separation of body from soul were caused by the envy of the devil only. The purpose of the redemption is to unite that which has been unnaturally divided."[20]

Some ancients believed that once the soul left the body it began a long and arduous journey from one heaven to another.[21] The Greek-speaking church father Irenaeus held that "body and soul await reunion in different places or conditions without imputing an active existence to the soul."[22] By contrast the Latin fathers spoke "more freely of the soul's activity during the interim after death."[23] Influenced by Greek philosophy and the church fathers, the Catholic Church, like so many early church theologians, has taught the immortality of the soul.

3. Immortality of the Soul

Most Protestant churches also hold to the immortality of the soul. Here are three Reformers who advocated it.

a. Martin Luther

For a time Luther believed in soul-sleep. "We are to sleep until he comes and knocks on the grave and says, 'Dr. Martin, get up.' Then I will arise in a moment and I will be eternally happy with him."[24] He wrote about it, in part to counteract the Catholic doctrine of purgatory, the destination of those dying with venial sins, sins that Catholics believe can still be atoned for. Purgatory alleges that the dead are very much awake after death as they work to make atonement. Later, Luther came to deny soul-sleep. Speaking of Abraham, he said, "It is divine truth that Abraham (after death) lives with God, serves Him, and also rules with Him. But what sort of life that is, whether he be asleep or awake, that is another question. How the soul rests, we are not to know; it is certain, however, that it lives."[25]

b. John Calvin

Calvin was careful to vindicate God's justice in the human Fall. For, "God having not only deigned to animate a vessel of clay, but to make it the habitation of an immortal spirit, Adam might well glory in the great liberality of his Maker."[26] He calls the soul "his nobler part" and shows his dependence upon Plato in referring to the death of Stephen as an example of how the "soul is freed from the prison-house of the body."[27] He opposed the view that the soul is the breath of God. Rather he saw a number of proofs in human ability as evidence of an immortal soul. For example, conscience "is an undoubted sign of an immortal soul," "the mere knowledge of a God sufficiently proves that souls which rise higher than the world must be immortal."[28]

Further he affirms, "Were not the soul some kind of essence separated from the body, Scripture would not teach that we dwell in houses of clay, and at death remove from a tabernacle of flesh; that we put off that which is corruptible, in order that, at the last day, we may finally receive according to the deeds done in the body. These, and similar passages which everywhere occur, not only clearly distinguish the soul from the body, but by giving it the name of man, intimate that it is his principal part. Again, when Paul exhorts believers to cleanse themselves from all filthiness of the flesh and the spirit, he shows that there are two parts in which the taint of sin resides. Peter, also, in calling Christ the Shepherd and Bishop of souls, would have spoken absurdly if there were no souls towards which he might discharge such an office,"[29]

Calvin considered that "though the whole man is called mortal, the soul is not therefore liable to death." The idea came from his understanding of the image of God, where "the proper seat of the image is in the soul,"[30] even though "there was no part even of the body in which some rays of glory did not shine." Nevertheless, "the primary seat of the divine image was in the mind and heart, or in the soul and its powers."[31]

c. Francis Turretin

The Bible that says God alone is immortal (1 Tim. 6:16). But those who defended the concept of the immortal soul attempted to work around the passage. For example, Francis Turretin makes a distinction between the "essential and absolute immortality" that God alone possesses (1 Tim. 6:16) from "comparative and participative immortality" that he believed belongs to humans. So human beings are not immortal by nature (as is God) but through their living. "It does not concern the immortality of the soul in the genus of being and as to the state of nature (belonging to it in any state), but concerns the immortality of man in the genus of morals and as to happiness."[32]

But Scripture not only says God alone has immortality but also that humans will be given immortality at the Second Advent (1 Cor. 15:53). How can you receive something that you already have? So any idea that souls are inherently immortal owes much to Platonic dualism and more to Satan's first lie, "You will not surely die." ❧

CHRIST IS COMING!

---

[1] Maurice Rawlings, *Beyond Death's Door* (New York: Bantam, 1979), pp. 53, 54.

[2] E. G. White, *The Great Controversy,* p. 588.

[3] *Ibid.,* p. 560.

[4] *Ibid.,* p. 552.

[5] E. G. White, *Last Day Events,* p. 161.

[6] *Ibid.*

[7] M. J. Harris, article on "Death" in the *New Dictionary of Theology,* Sinclair B. Ferguson, David F. Wright, and J. I. Packer, eds. (Downers Grove, Ill.: InterVarsity, 1988), p. 188.

[8] Cf. *Baker Encyclopedia of the Bible,* Walter A. Elwell, ed. (Grand Rapids: Baker, 1988), vol. 1, p. 604.

[9] Kent Harold Richards, "Death: Old Testament," in *The Anchor Bible Dictionary* (New York: Doubleday, 1992), vol. 2, p. 110.

[10] James Leo Garrett, *Systematic Theology: Biblical, Historical, and Evangelical* (Grand Rapids: Eerdmans, 1995), vol. 2, p. 661.

[11] *Ibid.,* p. 662.

[12] *Ibid.,* p. 664.

[13] Johannes Quasten, *Patrology* (Westminster, Md.: Christian Classics, 1990), vol. 2, p. 17.

[14] *Ibid.,* p. 42.

[15] *Ibid.,* p. 91.

[16] *Ibid.,* p. 115.

[17] *Ibid.,* p. 64.

[18] *Ibid.,* p. 112.

[19] *Ibid.,* p. 129.

[20] *Ibid.,* p. 135.

[21] *Ibid.,* vol. 3, p. 154.

[22] Milton McC. Gatch, *Death,* p. 131.

[23] *Ibid.,* p. 132.

[24] Martin Luther, *Martin Luther Werke,* 37:151.

[25] Quoted by Francis Pieper, *Christian Dogmatics* (Saint Louis: Concordia, 1953), vol. 3, p. 512, n. 21.

[26] John Calvin, *Institutes of the Christian Religion,* Henry Beveridge, trans. (London: James Clarke, 1962), vol. 1, p. 160.

[27] *Ibid.*

[28] *Institutes*, vol. 1, p. 161.

[29] *Ibid.,* pp. 161, 162.

[30] *Ibid.,* p. 162.

[31] *Ibid.,* p. 164.

[32] Francis Turretin, *Institutes of Elenctic Theology,* vol. 1, pp. 473, 474.

Chapter 19

The Intermediate State

Most Christians expect to live on at death. They say their souls enter another sphere of existence. But there's a problem with that. Their gaze has slipped away from Christ's return to their own death. Personal survival has replaced the blessed hope.

"But wait a minute," someone might protest. "Didn't Paul 'desire to depart and be with Christ' (Phil. 1:23)?"

Yes, Christians cite this as proof that the soul goes straight to Christ at death. But does it? "If Paul intended to teach the reality of an intermediate state," suggests Stephen H. Travis, "might we not reasonably expect him to say so more clearly?"[1]

Paul didn't say when he would go to be with Christ, whether at death or at Christ's return. For after all, what difference would it make to him? The moment he died the next awareness to him would be the Second Advent. "There is no indication that this 'being in Christ' is only an interim state before the resurrection," comments Travis. "And how is a bodiless 'being with Christ' to be envisaged?"[2] If Christ fashioned human bodies in the first place, why does He now want bodiless souls floating around?

"The idea of being in Christ as only half a person," Russell Aldwinckle observes, "does not make sense."[3] Terence Penelhum considers that the idea of a disembodied person as unintelligible.[4] By contrast, Paul Helm argues for a "minimal person" in the intermediate state.[5] Ever seen a minimal person? How much is required to maintain such a state?

So the intermediate state has its premise in the concept that souls live on without the body, but that in the Second Advent God will reunite them with the body. Many regard the experiences of those who have been resuscitated as evidence for human immortality. It's as if the new Bible for modern humanity is human experience rather than God's Word. The problem with human experience is that it leads to conflicting theories. Satan has removed the gaze away from God's Word to the natural and human realm, just as he did in Eden when he questioned God's Word and appealed to Eve's observation (Gen. 3:4).

He Saw Her Last Night

He had eked out a lonely existence since his wife passed away. The house was empty. His heart ached. A void lay heavy on him day and night.

One night he sensed light shining into his bedroom. Awakening, he sat up in bed and glanced toward the window. There a being walked toward him. Suddenly he saw her. It seemed to be his wife.

"Darling," she said, "I've come to be with you. I'm lonely too." She called him by an endearing name that only the two of them knew. Speaking with his wife's voice, walking as she did, and using her hands as she talked as she did, the apparition looked like her with her long flowing hair.

"Begone," he shouted. "In the name of Jesus begone. I know you're not my wife." It took all the energy within him to blurt out the words. Immediately the fallen angel vanished. The man sank back in bed and wept at the cruelty of such an impersonation. What such angel manifestations ignore is the "not yet" of the biblical story—the "not yet" that will give way to the "now" at the Second Advent, when all will meet their dead loved ones with whom they then will go to heaven (1 Thess. 4:16-18).

The "Already" and "Not Yet" Eschatological Tension

"At death Christians do not immediately pass into the full presence of Christ," says Thomas N. Finger. Thus "to be 'at home with the Lord' is not to go where he presently is but to experience his full presence in time to come."[6] However, Finger concludes that "the dead in Christ are in some passive state. Perhaps it is not wholly unconscious. It may well approximate pleasant dreaming. It is a 'rest from their labors.' Their sufferings are over. Nevertheless, they still exist within the tension of the 'already/not yet.' Until Christ's cosmic victory is consummated, they too will not experience the fullness of his presence and the fulfillment of their individual destinies."[7] Some long dream that would be for Adam and Eve!

Scripture presents an "already" of eternal life in Christ (John 6:40, 47) in the present, and a "not yet" of eternal life with Him after the Second Advent (1 Thess. 4:16-18). The life of the Christian in the present must always take into account the life of the Christian at the Second Advent. The "not yet" remains throughout the interim, so that no postulation of an intermediate state can legitimately call the "not yet" of Scripture into question. To the extent that intermediate views eradicate the "already"/"not yet" tension, they contradict this eschatological tension in the New Testament. As mentioned in my *Anchor Bible Dictionary* article, "The tension between the 'already' and the 'not yet' maintains an 'eschatological reserve,' for 'the last enemy to be destroyed is death' (1 Cor. 15:26)."[8]

Intermediate State

Many Christians believe their souls live on after death in an intermediate state.

The Intermediate State

1. Conscious or Unconscious in Death

What happens to people at death? Do they live on in another place? Are they conscious or unconscious there? Or is their experience somewhere between the two options, just as some consider purgatory as a place between heaven and hell? At least some have chosen this third option. As Loraine Boettner points out in his book *Immortality,* "The doctrine commonly held by the Jews and by the early medieval Church was that believers after death were in a dreamy, semiconscious state, neither happy nor miserable, awaiting the resurrection of the body."[9] This is not a major view today.

M. J. Harris suggests that Paul's nine uses (1 Thess. 4:13-15; 1 Cor. 7:39; 11:30; 15:6, 18, 20, 51) of the verb "to sleep" (Gr. *koimasthai)* suggests an intermediate state "of depressed consciousness and reduced vitality perhaps spent in Sheol as a 'paralyzed personality.' On this view, the intermediate state would be an interval of reduced consciousness—not of unconsciousness, suspended consciousness, or latent existence—which is but a shadowy counterpart of either earthly or heavenly existence."[10] Can you picture yourself as a "paralyzed personality"? And this is supposed to be better than "imprisonment" in the body?

Most Christians believe in an intermediate state during which the soul remains conscious. Death serves merely as a transition from this life to the next life. Actually, the person really does not cease to exist. Death is therefore not death.

But here we have a fundamental problem. If the immortal soul survives the body at death and continues on for thousands of years before the resurrection of that body, then the soul has had its own existence far longer than it lived joined with the body. Thus at the resurrection of the body, the body and soul are essentially two different beings. "Placing the soul in any state of conscious existence beyond death," says Stanley J. Grenz, "means that the disembodied soul participates in new experiences apart from the body (such as disembodied cognition of events happening on earth, disembodied relationships with other souls, or disembodied experiences of bliss or torment). But because the soul brings with it these additional postmortem experiences, the resurrected person who meets God at the judgment is not identical with the earthly person."[11]

2. Embodied or Disembodied

Some believe that the intermediate state is a disembodied experience for the soul,[12] and others suggest that the soul receives a spiritual body at death.[13] If the soul sheds the body, and lives on by itself, it necessarily must be less than the whole person it was before. "In a certain sense," Peter Toon observes, "the interim period between death and the Parousia represents an 'inferior' or 'diminished' mode of existence when compared with the final state after the Parousia and general resurrection of the dead."[14]

Those believing that a period of "nakedness" intervenes between death and the Parousia, between the natural and spiritual bodies, include Ronald Berry.[15] By contrast E. Earle Ellis states that "it is not at death but at the Parousia that those without the wedding garment (Matt. 22:11), the spiritual body (1 Cor. 15:44, 53f.), the heavenly house (2 Cor. 5:1f.) to be put on will be discovered stripped and naked (verse 3f.)."[16]

3. Second-chance Theory

Does death introduce a person to a second chance? Is it really extra time to get ready for heaven? Christians traditionally believe that the present is the only life one has in which to accept Christ. "Now is the day of salvation" (2 Cor. 6:2; cf. Phil. 2:12). "For those who are self-seeking and who reject the truth and follow evil, there will be wrath and anger" (Rom. 2:8). "For we must all appear before the judgment seat of Christ, that each one may receive what is due him for the things done while in the body, whether good or bad" (2 Cor. 5:10). "He will punish those who do not know God and do not obey the gospel of our Lord Jesus" (2 Thess. 1:8). "How shall we escape if we ignore such a great salvation?" (Heb. 2:3). God did not spare even fallen angels (2 Peter 2:4). All this is not the language of a second chance beyond death. Wayne Grudem says, "Jesus' story about the rich man and Lazarus gives no hope that people can cross from hell to heaven after they have died."[17] We have no second chance, no extra time. For as Charles Hodge put it, "the destiny of the soul is decided at death."[18]

On the other hand, what about those who lived in lands where no Christian messenger ever came, and so never had a first chance to accept Christ? Will they be confronted with Christ in the intermediate state and receive a first chance, extra time to accept Him, as taught by Dale Moody?[19] Gordon R. Lewis and Bruce A. Demarest in their *Integrative Theology* discuss this question. Scholars offer various opinions relative to a second or first chance. Some say God extends it to those who have never heard of Christ; others, to those who never understood the terms of salvation; and still others, to those who did not choose to accept Christ in this life. A number of people believe such individuals get extra time after death.[20]

4. Preaching to Spirits in Prison

The primary biblical passage used to allegedly support a second-chance theory is 1 Peter 3:18-20, in which it appears that Christ between His death and resurrection goes to some dead spirits and offers them salvation. Christ's death "illustrates the separation of body and soul which takes place when death occurs," claims Robert A. Morey. "Thus, when He died, His body remained intact in the tomb while in His spirit or soul He went to Hades according to Peter in Acts 2:27 and in 1 Peter 3:18-20." If Morey is right, then Christ's experience would support Platonic dualism between soul and body. "This is a more wonderful text (1 Peter 3:18-20) and a darker saying than almost any in the New Testament," admits Martin Luther, "so that I do not rightly know what St. Peter means."[22]

Philip E. Hughes has called the passage "one of the most difficult and most widely controverted passages in the New Testament."[23] John Calvin observes that "the obscurity of this passage has produced, as usual, various explanations."[24] Paradoxically, his interpretation is a prime example of obscuring the passage. He apparently overlooked that the text (1 Peter 3:18-20) says Christ spoke to unbelievers (Gr. *apeithesasi),* for "the manifestation of Christ's grace was made to godly spirits, and that they were thus endued with the vital power of the Spirit." He continues, "I allow that the Greek construction is at variance with this meaning, for Peter, if he meant this, ought to have used the genitive case absolute. But as it was not unusual with the Apostles to put one case instead of another, and as we see that Peter here heaps together many things, and no other suitable meaning can be elicited, I have no hesitation in giving this explanation of this intricate passage; so that readers may understand that those called unbelieving are different from those to whom he said the gospel was preached."[25]

When we look at the history of the interpretation of the passage, the idea of Christ's "descent into hell," or Hades, did not appear in the first Christian centuries. The earliest example occurs in the Fourth Formula of Sirmium, A.D. 359. The Nicene Creed does not include the phrase, and only the Apostolic and Athanasian Creeds have it. Hans Küng notes that the phrase "descent into hell" did not enter the Creed until the middle of the fourth century,[26] and Martin H. Scharlemann says it "was not in general use until the sixth century."[27] Now these facts should tell us that those nearest the apostles didn't believe it.

Catholic Karl Rahner regards Christ's descent into hell a redemptive activity after His death and considers "such a descent into hell . . . as an essential element in human death."[28] Does the passage teach a soul/body separation in death or is it too difficult to interpret? Or is there a third alternative between these two choices?

Wayne Grudem finds five different interpretations of this passage. (1) In Noah's day Christ "in spirit" preached to that generation through Noah to unbelievers whose spirits were in hell when Christ died. (2) In His death Christ went to people in hell to give them a second chance. (3) After His death Christ preached to those in hell, telling them that their condemnation was final because of His triumph over them. (4) After His death Christ came to release those in purgatory who had repented just before they died in the Flood. (5) After His resurrection, and before His ascension,[29] Christ went to hell to proclaim His triumph over fallen angels who had sinned by marrying human women before the Flood.[30]

Edwin A. Blum's interpretation provides a sixth view. He says Christ made a "victorious proclamation to the fallen angels during his ascension."[31] C.E.B. Cranfield's interpretation gives a seventh view—that if the people of Noah's day get another chance, it is a hint that all who have not accepted Christ "will not perish eternally without being given in some way that is beyond our knowledge an opportunity to hear the gospel and accept Him as their Savior."[32] Anthony Hanson believes the passage teaches "the universality of God's redemption in Christ."[33] The Lutheran

Formula of Concord states an eighth view. "We simply believe that the entire person, God and man, after the burial descended into hell, conquered the devil, destroyed the power of hell, and took from the devil all his might."[34]

Let us analyze the various options. As noted above, Scripture does not substantiate a second-chance theory (numbers 2, 7). The present life is the one during which we determine our eternal destiny. The other options (numbers 3-5) are all creative ideas, most involving a body/soul dichotomy and hence opposed to biblical holism. The idea of Christ's proclaiming His victory after His ascension (number 6) has no biblical backing. The last one (number 8), though true to biblical anthropology, otherwise lacks biblical evidence. The view that avoids these problems (number 1) is the one, in my opinion, that takes seriously the context of the passage. Peter has just said that Christ was "made alive by the Spirit" (1 Peter 3:18). The apostle is addressing the function of the Spirit here. It was through the same Spirit that Jesus preached to unbelievers before the Flood (verse 19). Augustine was the first to suggest that the passage refers to Christ's preaching at the time of Noah, and others since, such as S.D.F. Salmon,[35] W. D. Morris,[36] and Donald Guthrie[37] have in turn accepted it. The *Tyndale New Testament Commentary* also persuasively argued it.[38]

Christ preached through Noah to the "disobedient" rather than to "disembodied" spirits. This agrees with the biblical texts considered in the previous section that state sinful beings have no second chance. Furthermore, if Christ preached to the spirits only from Noah's day, what about the rest of the unbelievers from other generations? Is He a respecter of persons after all? The principle that "God does not show favoritism" (Acts 10:34) opposes this approach.[39] Christ did not preach while in the grave. Unlike fellow Catholic Karl Rahner, Catholic Hans Küng is right in stating that "the New Testament *has nothing to say about a passion or an action of Jesus between death and resurrection.*"[40]

5. Baptism for the Dead

Mormons and Catholics have a different view than the above examples of a second probation, although they share common ground with the second-chance theories. We will take up the Mormon baptism for the dead now, and in the next chapter consider Catholic purgatory.

Mormons have compiled the largest genealogical files in the world as they try to gather the name of everyone who has ever lived on the planet since the Flood. This Mormon doctrine derives from one verse in Scripture, 1 Corinthians 15:29: "Now if there is no resurrection, what will those do who are baptized for the dead? If the dead are not raised at all, why are people baptized for them?"

F. W. Grosheide considers this to be "one of the most difficult passages in the New Testament."[41] The scholarly literature presents as many as 36 interpretations,[42] which leads Conzelmann to say, "The ingenuity of the exegetes has run riot."[43] Rather than present the various views, it will suffice to attempt to grasp the meaning of the Greek phrase *huper ton nekron* ("for the dead"). The literal meaning of the Greek preposition *huper* means "on behalf of." Clearly it speaks of "proxy," or as Leon Morris calls it, "vicarious baptism."[44] This rules out the idea that believers were baptized above the graves of relatives who died as Christians, for as W. Harold Mare rightly notes, "such a locative meaning as 'above' or 'over' for the preposition *hyper* with the genitive is not found elsewhere in the NT."[45]

John Calvin notes that the common exposition of this text by Chrysostom, Ambrose, Grotius, and Tertullian was that "the Corinthians were accustomed, when any one had been deprived of baptism by sudden death, to substitute some living person in the place of the deceased—to be baptized at his grave." Such persons claimed that the Corinthians, "while they denied that there was resurrection, they in the mean time declared in this way that they believed in it." Calvin's reply to the ancients was, "For my part, however, I cannot by any means be persuaded to believe this." He contrasts the silence of Paul on this practice with his speaking against various other faults of the Corinthians. How could "the Apostle, after reproving almost all their faults, . . . have been silent as to this one?"[46]

However, Calvin apparently overlooks the fact that Paul does not disapprove of all their faults. What about "eating in an idol's temple" (1 Cor. 8:10)? Leon Morris is right to suggest that "Paul is quite capable of reasoning from a practice of which he disapproves . . . shown by the way he refers to sitting at a meal in an idol's temple without saying anything about this being wrong (1 Cor. 8:10), though in a later passage he connects idol feasts with demons (1 Cor. 10:21-23). It is perhaps significant that, while Paul does not stop to condemn the practice of which he speaks here, he dissociates himself from it ('what will *those* do . . . ?'; contrast 'why do we endanger ourselves?' [verse 30]). He simply mentions the practice as taking place, and asks what meaning it can possibly have if the dead do not rise."[47] In short, if you don't believe in their resurrection, why get baptized for someone?

"This much is clear," says F. W. Grosheide, "that Paul refers to a custom that clearly presupposed the resurrection of the dead. He does not state explicitly whether he approved of that custom. Probably he did not disapprove of it."[48] However, Grosheide's conclusion fails to distinguish between what Paul taught from what he did not teach.

Biblical interpretation first begins with the local context (passage, book), but then goes to the sum of Scripture, in which one allows Scripture to interpret Scripture. It is in this broadest context that we find the clue to interpreting 1 Corinthians 15:29. Meaningful baptism requires certain conditions. Peter says, "Repent and be baptized, every one of you, in the name of Jesus Christ for the forgiveness of your sins" (Acts 2:38). Forgiveness does not rest upon baptism but upon personal repentance. John writes, "For God so loved the world that he gave his one and only Son, that whoever believes in him shall not perish but have eternal life" (John 3:16). Even Christ's baptism in death (cf.

Rom. 6:3-8) by itself is not sufficient to bring salvation. It requires personal belief in Christ to receive eternal life.

You can't be a proxy for someone, not even if you are the most worthy of saints such as Noah, Daniel, or Job. "Even if these three men—Noah, Daniel and Job—were in it, they could save only themselves by their righteousness, declares the Sovereign Lord" (Eze. 14:14). Character is not transferable. Scripture has only one vicarious sacrifice, and that is Christ's. If any other could offer an atoning vicarious substitution in baptism for another, it would deny the uniqueness and sole right of Christ's atoning sacrifice. "No man can redeem the life of another," said the psalmist, "or give to God a ransom for him" (Ps. 49:7). Humans have only one probationary lifetime. "Man is destined to die once, and after that to face judgment" (Heb. 9:27). Dunking for someone else doesn't count before death, let alone after.

---

[1] Stephen H. Travis, *Christian Hope and the Future* (Downers Grove, Ill.: InterVarsity, 1980), p. 110.

[2] *Ibid.*

[3] Russell Aldwinckle, *Death in the Secular City* (London: Allen & Unwin, 1972), p. 144.

[4] Terence Penelhum, *Survival and Disembodied Existence* (London: Routledge and Kegan Paul, 1970), p. 103.

[5] Paul Helm, "A Theory of Disembodied Survival and Re-Embodied Existence," *Religious Studies* 14, No. 1 (March 1978) pp. 15-26.

[6] Thomas N. Finger, *Christian Theology*, vol. 1, p. 140.

[7] *Ibid.*, p. 141.

[8] Norman R. Gulley, "Death: NT," in *The Anchor Bible Dictionary,* vol. 2, p. 111.

[9] Loraine Boettner, *Immortality* (Philadelphia: Presbyterian and Reformed, 1971), p. 91.

[10] M. J. Harris, "2 Corinthians 5:1-10: Watershed in Paul's Eschatology," *Tyndale Bulletin,* vol. 22 (1971), pp. 49, 50.

[11] Stanley J. Grenz, *Theology for the Community of God* (Nashville: Broadman & Holman, 1994), p. 770.

[12] This is probably the preponderant view of those who reject the "soul sleep" view of the intermediate state and look for the bodily resurrection at the Parousia, as mentioned in the various creeds. Ronald Berry rejected the view of a spiritual body at death as proposed by R. F. Hettlinger *(Scottish Journal of Theology* 10: 174-194) in "Death and Life in Christ: The Meaning of 2 Corinthians 5:1-10," *Scottish Journal of Theology* 14 (1961): 60-76; Oscar Cullmann, *Christ and Time,* pp. 238-242.

[13] For example, Murray Harris, *Raised Immortal* (London: Marshall Morgan & Scott, 1983), pp. 159-161, and "2 Corinthians 5:1-10: Watershed in Paul's Eschatology," *Tyndale Bulletin* 22 (1971): 39-42; F. F. Bruce, "Paul on Immortality," *Scottish Journal of Theology* 24 (1971): 457-471, and *1 and 2 Corinthians* (London: 1971), p. 204; C. L. Mitton, "Paul's Certainties," *Expository Times* 69 (1958): 261; R. H. Charles, *Eschatology* (London: A. & C. Black, 1899), pp. 394, 395; R. F. Hetteinger, "2 Corinthians 5:1-10," *Scottish Journal of Theology* 10 (1957): 174-194; Aldwinckle, p. 144.

[14] Peter Toon, *Heaven and Hell: A Biblical and Theological Overview* (Nashville: Nelson, 1986), p. 112.

[15] Ronald Berry, "Death and Life in Christ: The Meaning of 2 Corinthians 5:1-10," *Scottish Journal of Theology* 14 (1961): 60-76.

[16] E. Earle Ellis, "2 Corinthians 1-10 in Pauline Eschatology," *New Testament Studies* 6 (1959-1960): 221.

[17] Wayne Grudem, *Systematic Theology: An Introduction to Biblical Doctrine* (Grand Rapids: Zondervan, 1994), pp. 822, 823.

[18] Charles Hodge, *Systematic Theology,* vol. 3, p.725.

[19] Dale Moody, *The Hope of Glory* (Grand Rapids: Eerdmans, 1964), p. 61.

[20] "Advocates of a second chance include the nineteenth-century authorities F. D. Maurice, I. A. Dorner, F. Delitzsch, and F. Godet; the twentieth-century scholars P. T. Forsyth, L. H. DeWolf, F. W. Farrar, R. Aldwinckle, D. L. Edwards, B. Hebblethwaite; and the American evangelicals D. Moody, D. Bloesch, and

C. Pinnock. Louis Berkhof adds for the nineteenth-century Mueller in Germany, Gretillat in Switzerland, Maurice and Plumptre in England, and Newman Smythe, Munger, Cox, Jukes, and several Andover theologians in America" (Louis Berkhof, *Systematic Theology,* p. 692).

[21] Robert A. Morey, *Death and the Afterlife*, p. 102.

[22] Quoted by Anthony Hanson in "Salvation Proclaimed: 1 Peter 3:18-22," *Expository Times* 93 (1982): 100.

[23] Philip E. Hughes, *The True Image,* p. 398.

[24] John Calvin, *Calvin's Commentaries, 1 Peter,* vol. 22, p. 112.

[25] *Ibid.,* p. 115.

[26] Hans Küng, *Eternal Life*, p. 128.

[27] Martin H. Scharlemann, "'He Descended Into Hell': An Interpretation of 1 Peter 3:18-20," *Concordia Theological Monthly* 27, No. 2, (1956): 81.

[28] Karl Rahner, *On the Theology of Death,* p. 57.

[29] William J. Dalton believed it was either during His death or perhaps after His resurrection ("The Interpretation of 1 Peter 3:19 and 4:6; Light From 2 Peter," *Biblica* 60, No. 4 [1979]: 548).

[30] Wayne Grudem, *Tyndale NT Commentaries, 1 Peter,* p. 204.

[31] Edwin A. Blum, *The Expositor's Bible Commentary, 1 Peter*, 241.

[32] C.E.B. Cranfield, "The Interpretation of 1 Peter 3:19 and 4:6," *Expository Times* 69, (1957-1958): 369-372.

[33] Anthony Hanson, "Salvation Proclaimed: 1 Peter 3:18-22," *Expository Times* 93 (1982): 103.

[34] Martin H. Scharlemann, "He Descended Into Hell," p. 84.

[35] S.D.F. Salmon, *The Christian Doctrine of Immortality* (Edinburgh, Scotland: T & T Clark, 1897), 471, 472.

[36] W. D. Morris, "1 Peter 3:19," *The Expository Times*, vol. 38, (1926-1927): p. 470.

[37] Donald Guthrie, *New Testament Theology* (Downers Grove, Ill.: InterVarsity, 1981), p. 842.

[38] Wayne Grudem, *Tyndale NT Commentary, 1 Peter,* pp. 205-239.

[39] William J. Dalton believes that Christ spoke "to all those in the world of the dead," and not just to those of Noah's day (*Biblica* 60, No. 4 [1979]: 548). C.E.B. Cranfield believes the people of Noah's day received mention only because they were the most notorious, and were not the sole recipients of Christ's preaching *(Expository Times* 69 [1957-1958]: 372).

[40] Hans Küng, *Eternal Life? Life After Death as a Medical, Philosophical, and Theological Problem* (Garden City, N.Y.: Doubleday, 1984), p. 127.

[41] F. W. Grosheide, *The New International Commentary on the New Testament, 1 Corinthians* (Grand Rapids: Eerdmans, 1983), p. 371.

[42] *The Seventh-day Adventist Bible Commentary,* vol. 6, p. 807.

[43] Conzelmann, as quoted by Leon Morris, *Tyndale New Testament Commentaries, 1 Corinthians* (Grand Rapids: Eerdmans, 1988), vol. 7, p. 215.

[44] Leon Morris, *1 Corinthians,* vol. 7, pp. 214, 215.

[45] W. Harold Mare, *The Expositor's Bible Commentary, 1 Corinthians*, Frank E. Gaebelein, ed. (Grand Rapids: Zondervan, 1976), vol. 10, p. 287.

[46] John Calvin, *Calvin's Commentaries, 1 Corinthians,* John Pringle, trans. (Grand Rapids: Baker, 1989), vol. 22, pp. 34, 35.

[47] Leon Morris, *1 Corinthians,* p. 214.

[48] F. W. Grosheide, *1 Corinthians,* pp. 373, 374.

Chapter 20

Purgatory

The final exam was three hours of essay questions. It still seems like yesterday. I was at Newbold College, in England. Five questions. I took them in the order given and wrote furiously. My hand ached as I sped across the paper, as if taking a "how many words a minute" typing test. Pressure, stress, speed, all wrapped into one. Then, just in time, I put the pen down. All five questions answered.

Suddenly I glanced at the instructions. They glared as a neon light blinking in the dark night: "Choose any three."

Was I seeing straight? Yes, that's what it said. My heart sank. The questions I knew best were the last two. Oh, if I'd only done those first! If I'd only read the instructions!

I got up and limped down the aisle to the professor and weakly blurted out, "I did all five. May I have more time to work on the last two?" I implored.

"No!" she said firmly. "Get your sleep next time." I must have looked like someone dragged through the wringer. At least I felt like it—especially then.

"I'll grade just the first three. The others don't count." That's all there was to it.

She was right. How stupid of me to stay up all night and cram. I learned a lesson that I'll never forget. But oh how I wished I had had more time to put all I knew on that paper.

More Time

Dr. Wiltse of Skiddy, Kansas, went four hours in 1889 without a recorded pulse and 30 minutes without any detectable respiration. He lay on a couch in a coma produced by fulminating typhoid fever. The *St. Louis Medical and Surgical Journal* recorded his case.

Later he described his experience. "I saw a number of persons sitting and standing about the body and particularly noticed two women apparently kneeling by my left side, and I knew they were weeping. I have since learned that they were my wife and sister. . . . I now attempted to gain the attention of the people with the object of comforting them as well as assuring them of their own immortality."

He then goes on to portray a journey through space. Three huge rocks appeared before him. They separated the present world from the one beyond. A being told him, "'This is the road to the eternal world. Yonder rocks are the boundary between the two worlds and the two lives. Once you pass them, you can no more return into the body. If your work is complete on earth, you may pass beyond the rocks. If, however, upon consideration you conclude that . . . it is not done, you can return into the body.'"[1] Apparently Dr. Wiltse assumed that he received a second chance—an option for extra time.

Even Christians live on the fast lane and make mistakes. It goes with the territory, they say. Have to keep up with modern demands. Hard to get time to pray and read the Bible when you have to make a living. There's never enough time. Catholics, however, do believe that they have extra time. Time after the exams are due. But it is not a coming back to life after seeing three rocks. It is going on with life in the next alleged stage. One that allows time to get ready for heaven. A person continues on after death to enter purgatory. There one has more opportunity to get ready for heaven. Still other ideas exist about a possible intermediate state. I want you to hear about some of them, see the biblical data they use, and then be able to know how to answer them.

You've just driven your new car off the lot. How it sparkles! Ten minutes down the pike a thunderstorm leaves a muddy highway and splatters and splashes the sheen. "Horrible storm," you mutter, "Why did this have to happen?" Roaring trucks spray more muddy water on windshield and body. You're sick. Ten miles farther you drive out of the storm and into sunshine. But the damage is done. You head for the nearest drive-in car wash, go through the sprays and brushes, the polish and drying—and it is clean at last.

That's like purgatory. Catholics believe that most die a muddy mess. They still have sins to clean away. In death the soul pulls off the highway of life and heads into an automatic car wash. The building is an extremely long one, perhaps a mile. The soul goes slowly through until it sparkles at the other end. Then it's on to heaven.

Where Did the Idea Come From?

The roots of purgatory go back to the early Church Fathers. I "do now beseech Thee for the sins of my mother,"[2] prayed Augustine of Hippo after her death. "At Thy altar remember Monica, Thy handmaid, together with Patricius, her sometime husband."[3] Yet the word *purgatorium* did not appear until Pope Innocent IV used it in 1254. Pope Gregory the Great considered the Eucharist as a repetition of Christ's sacrifice, rather than just a remembrance. He declared that it was efficacious for releasing souls from purgatory.[4] The Jubilee Indulgences (1300) "which made provision for the promotion from purgatory to heaven of certain classes of the faithful"[5] furthered the teaching, which the second Council of Lyons (1274), the Council of Florence (1439), the Council of Trent (1563), and the Roman catechism of 1566 subsequently set forth as doctrine. Dante Alighieri's *Purgatorio* popularized the doctrine, as did the classic expositions by Robert Bellarmine (d. 1621) and Francisco de Suarez (d. 1617).[6]

"The Roman Pope, as the successor of the keys of Peter and the representative of Christ on earth," declared Pope Leo X in 1815, "can through the power of the keys . . . grant to those who are faithful Christians . . . in this life and in purgatory remission through the exceeding merits of Christ and the saints."[7]

Thomas Aquinas gives a scholastic presentation of purgatory in his *Summa Theologica.* The suffering of purgatory results from "the delay of the divine vision, and the pain of sense, namely punishment by corporeal fire." This "surpasses all the pains of this life."[8] Those confined to purgatory often pray for release. They are "cleansed after this life by Divine justice alone."[9] In fact, "those who deny Purgatory speak against the justice of God."[10] Aquinas makes a difference between mortal and venial sins.[11] "Some are tormented in Purgatory longer than others, for as much as their affections were steeped in venial sins," yet "one may be delayed longer who is tormented less, and *vice versa."*[12]

How does purgatory compare with hell? Aquinas asserts that "purgatory is situated below and in proximity to hell." "The fire of Purgatory is eternal in its substance, but temporary in its cleansing affect."[13] Does it mean that the fire of purgatory will continue to burn after the last cleansed soul leaves? It's anyone's guess.

Christians without mortal sins (that exclude a person from heaven) but with venial sins (atoneable sins) at the time of death can work off the debt due from the latter sins. It's like taking your final exam again after failing first time. Most of the faithful land in purgatory.[14] Purgatory is a halfway place between earth and heaven. How long you spend there depends on how much purification you need.

"Purgatory is not a probation," Catholics say. "It's just a final clean-up before meeting God."

"Not so," replies the Greek Orthodox Church. "Catholicism links purgatory with the notion of satisfaction for sins, whereas Eastern Orthodoxy views the purifying fire mystically as a means of spiritual growth."[15]

Both Mormons and Catholics consider that a further work for human salvation is possible beyond death; hence the intermediate state serves as an opportunity to complete what was done during life.

"It is possible that one must remain in purgatory until the time of the last judgment," Louis Berkhof states. "The Pope is supposed to have jurisdiction over purgatory. It is his peculiar prerogative to grant indulgences, lightening the purgatorial sufferings or even terminating them."[16]

The concept of purgatory does not appear in Scripture, and hence evangelical Christians reject it. The Roman Catholic Church bases the concept upon some of the apocryphal writings. For example, 2 Maccabees 12:42-45 tells how Judas Maccabeus "took up a collection, man by man, to the amount of two thousand drachmas of silver, and sent it to Jerusalem to provide for a sin offering. In doing this he acted very well and honorably, taking account of the resurrection. For if he were not expecting that those who had fallen would rise again, it would have been superfluous and foolish to pay for the dead. But if he was looking to the splendid reward that is laid up for those who fall asleep in godliness, it was a holy and pious thought. Therefore he made atonement for the dead, that they might be delivered from their sin."

The 1994 *Catechism of the Catholic Church* refers to the Maccabees passage. But 2 Maccabees 12:42-46 is only one of the sources upon which the church bases its doctrine. Article 1031 of the catechism says: "The Church formulated her doctrine of faith on Purgatory especially at the Councils of Florence and Trent. The tradition of the Church, by reference to certain texts of Scripture, speaks of a cleansing fire."[17]

The catechism then quotes St. Gregory the Great with alleged further biblical support: "As for certain lesser faults, we must believe that, before the Final Judgment, there is a purifying fire. He who is truth says that whoever utters blasphemy against the Holy Spirit will be pardoned neither in this age nor in the age to come [Matt. 12:31]. From this sentence we understand that certain offenses can be forgiven in this age, but certain others in the age to come."[18]

Article 1032 of the catechism notes that "this teaching is also based on the practice of prayer for the dead, already mentioned in Sacred Scripture: 'Therefore . . . [Judas Maccabeus] made atonement for the dead, that they might be delivered from their sin' (2 Macc. 12:46). From the beginning the Church has honored the memory of the dead and offered prayers in suffrage for them, above all the Eucharistic sacrifice, so that, thus purified, they may attain the beatific vision of God [note the Mass, not Calvary, helps those in purgatory]. The Church also commends almsgiving, indulgences, and works of penance undertaken on behalf of the dead." The catechism then cites John Chrysostom: "Let us help and commemorate them. If Job's sons were purified by their father's sacrifice, why would we doubt that our offerings for the dead bring them some consolation? Let us not hesitate to help those who have died and to offer our prayers for them."[19]

Besides the texts already cited, Gordon R. Lewis and Bruce A. Demarest add Malachi 3:2, 3, Luke 12:59, and Jude 23 as further passages used as alleged evidence for purgatory. Louis Berkhof adds Isaiah 4:4.[20] So besides the passage from the Apocrypha (2 Macc. 12:42-46), eight biblical passages (Job 1:5; Isa. 4:4; Mal. 3:2, 3; Matt. 12:32; Luke 12:59; 1 Cor. 3:15; 1 Peter 1:7; and Jude 23) supposedly support the idea of purgatory. Let's take a look at them.

1. Job 1:5

Job offered sacrifices for his children while living, not after their death. Christ also intercedes for the living. His high priestly ministry in the heavenly sanctuary is the theme of the book of Hebrews. "He is able to save completely those who come to God through him, because he always lives to intercede for them" (Heb. 7:25). Nowhere in Hebrews, nor in the rest of Scripture, do we find even one text that says Christ intercedes for the dead. Nor do we encounter the suggestion that human beings should intercede for the dead.

2. Isaiah 4:4

"The Lord will wash away the filth of the women of Zion; he will cleanse the bloodstains from Jerusalem by a spirit of judgment and a spirit of fire" (Isa. 4:4). But the passage has no hint that such cleansing takes place after death for each person individually. Rather, it harmonizes with all the Old Testament prophecies about judgment, and applies to events that will take place in history. The following two verses (5, 6) give the result: "Then the Lord will create over all of Mount Zion and over those who assemble there a cloud of smoke by day and a glow of flaming fire by night; over all the glory will be a canopy. It will be a shelter and shade from the heat of the day, and a refuge and hiding place from the storm and rain."

The flaming fire echoes the pillar of cloud and fire found in Exodus 13:21; 14:19; 16:10; 33:9; 40:36; Numbers 9:17; 10:11; 12:5; 16:42; Deuteronomy 1:33; 31:15; Nehemiah 9:12; Psalm 78:14; 105:39; and Isaiah 4:5. The cloud by day and the fire by night represented the presence of God in the midst of His people. God desires to purify His people so that they may safely dwell in His midst.

The passage has a historical focus, and it has nothing to do with cleansing fires in purgatory. "The pictures of cloud and fire over Jerusalem," John D. W. Watts says, "are reminiscent of the priestly narrative of the presence accompanying the desert pilgrimage toward the promised land (Ex. 13:21)."[21] The fire in this context is historical and corporate, not beyond history and individualistic, and so applies before death rather than afterward.

3. Malachi 3:2, 3

"But who can endure the day of his coming? Who can stand when he appears? For he will be like a refiner's fire or a launderer's soap. He will sit as a refiner and purifier of silver; he will purify the Levites and refine them like gold and silver. Then the Lord will have men who will bring offerings in righteousness" (Mal. 3:2, 3). Here we have not purgatory after death, but glorification at the Second Advent. "Behold, I shew you a mystery; We shall not all sleep, but we shall be changed, In a moment, in the twinkling of an eye, at the last trump: for the trumpet shall sound, and the dead shall be raised incorruptible, and we shall be changed. For this corruptible must put on incorruption, and this mortal must put on immortality. So when this corruptible shall have put on incorruption, and this mortal shall have put on immortality, then shall be brought to pass the saying that is written, Death is swallowed up in victory" (1 Cor. 15:51-54, KJV).

God transforms both the living saints and the righteous resurrected at the same time. This text refers to the coming of God and not purgatory after individual death. Change occurs at His coming, when dead and living saints meet their Saviour for the first time (1 Thess. 4:16-18). It is important to note that the final gift of change takes place at the time when mortals become immortal for the first time. Humans gain both gifts from Christ at the Second Advent. No biblical text says that we receive the gift of purification or the gift of immortality at death or during an interim state.

4. Matthew 12:32

"Anyone who speaks a word against the Son of Man will be forgiven, but anyone who speaks against the Holy Spirit will not be forgiven, either in this age or in the age to come" (Matt. 12:32). Is this verse suggesting any age to come in which we can seek forgiveness? Or is it declaring that if we don't accept such forgiveness in the present time, it will not be available in the age to come? Forgiveness—not purification—is the focus. It would seem that purgatory is for forgiven sinners, who still need to atone for forgiven venial sins. But the passage here deals with pardon and not purgatory. Scripture does talk about an age to come (e.g., 1 Thess. 4:16-18; Rev. 21:1-22:6), but instead of a purgatory experience in an intermediate state, it's a new heavens and a new earth.

5. Luke 12:59

"I tell you, you will not get out until you have paid the last penny" (Luke 12:59). Christ here speaks not about death, but He rebukes His hearers for knowing how to predict weather without knowing "how to interpret this present time" (Luke 12:56). "Judge . . . what is right," He appeals (verse 57). "Be reconciled with a magistrate so that he will not put you into prison. For once in that place, there will be no release until the last penny is paid" (Matt. 5:25, 26). All this happens during the present life. It focuses on how to live and not how to get purified after death.

Many commentators see Christ's parable as portraying the importance of getting right with God now before the final judgment.[22] The concept of the urgency of immediate action is far removed from any idea of being able to pay for the debt after death. Scripture clearly indicates that "multitudes who sleep in the dust of the earth will awake: some to everlasting life, others to shame and everlasting contempt" (Dan. 12:2). But it tells of no interim place called purgatory where added work can be accomplished after death. Death seals human destiny.

6. 1 Corinthians 3:15

"If it is burned up, he will suffer loss; he himself will be saved, but only as one escaping through the flames" (1 Cor. 3:15). Thomas Aquinas refers to verse 12 (wood, hay, stubble) as denoting different kinds of venial sins, taking different lengths of punishment in purgatory.[23] But the passage has nothing to do with a purgation experience subsequent to death. Rather it speaks of the Christian's good works in the light of the Second Advent. "The Day that Paul refers to is the Day when Christ will come again," says William Barclay. "Then will come the final test. The wrong and the inadequate will be swept away. But, in the mercy of God, even the inadequate builder will be saved, because at least he tried to do something for Christ. At best all our versions of Christianity are inadequate."[24] "The imagery is that of one who has to dash through the flames to escape to safety," suggests Leon Morris.

"The fire is, of course, a fire of testing, not one of purifying, and the passage lends no support to the doctrine of purgatory as some claim."[25]

The expression "escaping through the flames" (1 Cor. 3:15) reminds one of the "burning stick snatched from the fire" mentioned in Amos 4:11 and Zechariah 3:2. "The doctrine of purgatory is not taught here," concludes F. W. Grosheide, "since the apostle has in view works rather than persons."[26] W. Harold Mare adds: "Those whose works are consumed by the fire will themselves escape the flames (as if they were to jump out of the burning wooden structure they had built) and will be saved alone, without any works of praise to present to Christ."[27]

7. 1 Peter 1:7

"These have come so that your faith—of greater worth than gold, which perishes even though refined by fire—may be proved genuine and may result in praise, glory and honor when Jesus Christ is revealed" (1 Peter 1:7). Again the passage speaks of the Christian life before, not after, death. Notice the verse preceding verse 7. "In this you greatly rejoice, though *now* (Gr. *arti,* "yet," in the present) for a little while you may have had to suffer grief in all kinds of trials" (verse 6). "Peter comes to the actual situation in life in which his readers found themselves," comments William Barclay. "Their Christianity had always made them unpopular, but now they were facing almost certain persecution."[28]

8. Jude 23

The last text used to support purgatory is Jude 23. We will add verse 22 to get the context. "Be merciful to those who doubt; snatch others from the fire and save them; to others show mercy, mixed with fear—hating even the clothing stained by corrupt flesh." The context is Jude's appeal to Christians to "keep yourselves in God's love as you wait for the mercy of our Lord Jesus Christ to bring you to eternal life" (Jude 21); for these are "the last times" (Jude 18). A part of the preparation to be ready for Christ's Second Advent is to confront those who live without any thought of His coming. We need to snatch them from the fire, as it were. "They need a direct frontal approach," Michael Green comments. "They are on the wrong path and need to be told as much, and then rescued."[29]

Edwin A. Blum concurs. This "group needs to be dealt with directly and vigorously. Salvation is God's work, and here Christians are portrayed as God's instruments for snatching brands out of the fire."[30] Clearly this is a task that we do for people while they are still alive and not something done for them after they are dead.

In recent times Catholic writers appeal more to the Church Fathers than to Scripture when presenting purgatory. R. J. Bastian in the *New Catholic Encyclopedia* recognizes that "in the final analysis, the Catholic doctrine on purgatory is based on tradition not Scripture."[31]

Protestants Take Note

"All views positing a conscious existence of the soul beyond death potentially share the theological problem Protestants find reprehensible in the Roman Catholic doctrine of purgatory," challenges theologian Stanley J. Grenz. "In various ways all these views play down the finality of earthly life. Lying behind the postulate of a postmortem abode for the soul is dichotomist anthropology dividing the human person into two substantial entities, soul and body, and elevating the soul as the true bearer of personhood. This anthropology risks placing our confidence for surviving death in the innate immortality of the soul."[32]

[1] Maurice Rawlings, *Beyond Death's Door,* pp. 49-52.

[2] Augustine, The Confessions of Augustine, in *The Nicene and Post-Nicene Fathers,* First Series, Philip Schaff, ed. (Grand Rapids: Eerdmans, 1988), vol. 1, p. 140.

[3] *Ibid.,* p. 141.

[4] Hans Schwarz, *On the Way to the Future,* p. 168.

[5] Peter Toon, *Heaven and Hell,* pp. 118, 119.

[6] *Ibid.,* pp. 114, 115; Schwarz, p. 169.

[7] Schwarz, p. 168.

[8] Thomas Aquinas, *Summa Theologica* (Westminster, Md.: Christian Classics, 1948), vol. 5, p. 3006.

[9] *Ibid.,* p. 3000.

[10] *Ibid.,* p. 3007.

[11] *Ibid.,* p. 3010.

[12] *Ibid.,* p. 3009.

[13] *Ibid.,* p. 3011.

[14] Louis Berkhof, *Systematic Theology,* p. 686.

[15] Gordon R. Lewis and Bruce A. Demarest, *Integrative Theology,* vol. 3, p. 447.

[16] Berkhof, p. 686.

[17] *Catechism of the Catholic Church,* pp. 268, 269.

[18] *Ibid.,* p. 269. Matthew 12:31 in the catechism should be Matthew 12:32.

[19] *Ibid.,* p. 269.

[20] Louis Berkhof, *Systematic Theology,* p. 687.

[21] John D. W. Watts, *Word Biblical Commentary, Isaiah 1-33* (Waco, Tex.: Word, 1985), vol. 24, p. 51.

[22] A few examples are: John Nolland, *Word Biblical Commentary, Luke 9:21-18:34* (Waco, Tex.: Word, 1993), vol. 35B, p. 715; Norval Geldenhuys, *The New International Commentary on the NT, Luke* (Grand Rapids: Eerdmans, 1983), pp. 368, 369; Leon Morris, *Tyndale NT Commentary, Luke* (Grand Rapids: Eerdmans, 1988), pp. 241, 242; and Walter L. Liefeld, *The Expositor's Bible Commentary, Luke* (Grand Rapids: Zondervan, 1984), p. 969.

[23] Thomas Aquinas, *Summa Theologica,* vol. 5, p. 3007 (Appendix Q.2, Art.4); 3009 (Appendix Q.2, Art.6).

[24] William Barclay, *The Letters to the Corinthians* (Philadelphia: Westminster, 1956), pp. 32, 33.

[25] Leon Morris, *Tyndale NT Commentaries, 1 Corinthians,* p. 66.

[26] F. W. Grosheide, *The New International Commentary on the NT, 1 Corinthians* (Grand Rapids: Eerdmans, 1983), p. 88.

[27] W. Harold Mare, *The Expositor's Bible Commentary, 1 Corinthians,* Frank E. Gaebelein, ed. (Grand Rapids: Zondervan, 1976), vol. 10, p. 208.

[28] William Barclay, *The Letters of James and Peter* (Philadelphia: Westminster, 1960), p. 176. It is significant that Peter uses the Greek word *peirasmoi* (trials) rather than *diogmoi* (persecutions) or *thlipseis* (tribulations). See Edwin A. Blum, *The Expositor's Bible Commentary, 1 & 2 Peter* (Grand Rapids: Zondervan, 1981), p. 221.

[29] Michael Green, *Tyndale NT Commentaries, 2 Peter and Jude* (Grand Rapids: Eerdmans, 1988), p. 203.

[30] Edwin A. Blum, *The Expositor's Bible Commentary, Jude* (Grand Rapids: Zondervan, 1981), p. 395.

[31] R. J. Bastian, *New Catholic Encyclopedia,* article "Purgatory." "In the final analysis, the Catholic doctrine on purgatory is based on tradition not scripture" (New York: McGraw-Hill, 1967), vol. 11, p. 1034.

[32] Stanley Grenz, *Theology for the Community of God,* p. 770.

Chapter 21

Holistic View of Human Nature

The two brothers had a well-deserved reputation as being the worst people in town. "They've fleeced us," people would shout after dealing with them. "Rotten cheats," others would yell.

Then one day news passed rapidly through the town that one of the brothers had died. The surviving brother came to a local pastor. "Will you have the funeral? I'll give you a large sum of money if you say my brother was a saint." He told him the amount.

The pastor thought for a while. "OK. I will," he replied softly.

Time came for the funeral. The surviving brother sat on the front row near the casket. He had defrauded people just as much as his dead brother. Both had been shrewd and unfair. The pastor preached about the bad financial problems suffered by the people of the community. Everyone knew what he meant. The brother wondered if he would follow through on the promise. When would he say his brother was a saint? He didn't have to wait much longer. Pausing and pointing to the casket, the minister said, "Compared to his brother, this man was a saint!"

Now that's not the way it usually goes. Right? It seems that pastors can preach anyone into heaven, but have you ever heard someone acknowledge at a funeral that anyone might go to hell? That wouldn't be polite, would it? The famous evangelist Dwight Moody said in August 1899, "Someday you will read in the papers that Moody is dead. Don't you believe a word of it. At that moment I shall be more alive than I am now. . . . I was born of the flesh in 1837. I was born of the Spirit in 1855. That which is born of the flesh may die. That which is born of the Spirit shall live forever.' "[1] He certainly had no holistic view of human nature.

The immortality-of-the-soul idea "is one of the greatest misunderstandings of Christianity,"[2] said New Testament scholar Oscar Cullmann. Most Christians believe they go straight to heaven when they die. But new studies about human nature shatter that idea.

Holistic View of Human Nature

Contemporary Holistic Anthropology

1. Two Starting Places

Assumptions determine our view of death. Beginning with the premise that human anthropology allows the soul to separate from the body at death, then one approaches the biblical texts that speak of the intermediate state in a way that will emphasize such a division. But those who approach the biblical data from the perspective that the Bible presents human beings holistically, that the soul is bound inextricably with body, will view the biblical texts that speak of the intermediate state in a way consistent with such holism. The basic presupposition determines the way one comes to interpret the biblical data. It is therefore crucial that we examine such passages with an appropriate premise deduced from Scripture itself.

2. Sensitive Doctrine

Realizing that the state of the dead is a sensitive topic, I am extremely sympathetic with those who have lost loved ones and who believe they are in heaven now. As has everybody else, I have lost parents, other family members, and friends to death. Death is a terrible tragedy in human history. Human beings need all the solace they can get from the Bible, and our purpose in this section and the next one is to lay out the good news of Scripture on this complex topic.

3. The Biblical View of Human Nature

Scripture long ago anticipated the findings of modern anthropology on holism, which contradict the Platonic and Cartesian dualism that have had such a major influence on philosophy and theology for so many centuries. The soul of Scripture *(nefesi* in Hebrew and *psuchē* in Greek) has a far wider meaning than the narrow focus given to it in Greek philosophy. Rather than limited to some immaterial essence within a human body, the biblical usage applies to the total person: what we refer to as body, soul, and spirit.

Scholars usually translate the Greek word *psuchē* as soul. Yet, as Thomas N. Finger reminds us, "like *sarx* and *soma, psuchē* can simply mean the whole person."[3] When Jesus said, "For whoever wants to save his life will lose it, but whoever loses his life for me and for the gospel will save it" (Mark 8:35), the word He used for "life" was *psuchē* (soul). "The term *'nefesi'* (just as *'psyche')* often means nothing more than 'life,'" G. C. Berkouwer reminds us, "and is thus used not to distinguish one part of man from other parts, but rather to refer to man himself, who can be described in so many varying ways."[4]

Together with this broader meaning of the "soul" as the total person, we need to put the word "body." For example, we say, "Somebody told me." It does not mean a body spoke, but a person communicated. "The Bible, we are told, tends to think of a human individual as precisely what 'individual' implies," remarks C.F.D. Moule, "—one and indivisible: He is not a soul inside a body; he is a person with a body, or a body that is a person; one might almost say that the most biblical word we could find in English for an individual would, indeed, be 'somebody'—

'some-*body.*' "[5] Modern parlance also speaks of "that poor soul," or "he baptized so many souls," both meaning the total person. Can you imagine baptizing a soul without the body?

4. Body and Soul Fell in Eden

The Platonic view of an inherent immortality separated the soul from the physical body, destroying their proper unity. "To contend that only the human soul is innately immortal is to maintain a position which is nowhere approved in the teaching of Scripture," Philip Edgcumbe Hughes declared, "for in the biblical purview human nature is always seen as integrally compounded of both the spiritual and the bodily. If this were not so, the whole doctrine of the incarnation and of the death and resurrection of the Son would be despoiled of meaning and reality. Man is essentially a corporeal-spiritual entity. God's warning at the beginning, regarding the forbidden tree, 'In the day that you eat of it you shall die,' was addressed to man as a corporeal-spiritual creature—should he eat of it, it was as such that he would die. There is no suggestion that a part of him was undying and therefore that his dying would be in part only."[6]

5. Inflated Souls

Classical philosophy and Christian theology have raised the soul to a level above the body. Both studies have given the soul inherent immortality, whereas the body is the soul's imprisonment (philosophy) or clothing (theology) only for the life span on earth, with a spiritual body awaiting it later. Philosophy and theology both regard the soul as able to exist without the body. The Bible's view of the soul is far lower, for at least 11 places in the Old Testament declare that animals are or possess a "soul." Here the soul "is clearly equated with the concept of life (e.g., Lev. 24:17, 18; 1 Kings 3:11). In Genesis 6:17 (cf. Gen. 7:15) breath *(ruach)* is given to both humans and animals."[7]

6. Interdependence of Soul and Body

Modern anthropological studies document the interdependence of body and mind. What affects the one affects the other. Out of such studies has come the view that we must consider humans holistically. The many body systems are inseparably linked to the mind. It is not intelligible to think of a separate soul and body, for the two function only—if they exist at all—when joined. It's like taking an engine out of a car, and believing that the engine and car can function effectively without each other. "In the past few decades a good many able philosophers have become convinced that there are new and decisive objections to the notion of disembodied survival," Richard L. Purtill reports, "objections which show the concept of disembodied survival to be unintelligible."[8]

"Many earlier cultures gave the self-conscious human soul a greater measure of independence vis-à-vis the body than our modern knowledge of the close mutual interrelations of physical and psychological occurrence will permit," theologian Wolfhart Pannenberg comments. "In the history of modern thought, advances in nuanced knowledge of these interrelations have robbed of their credibility the traditional ideas of the soul as a substance that is distinct from the body and that is detached from it in death."[9]

"In the light of *modern anthropology* the Platonic-Augustinian-Cartesian body-soul dualism has largely ceased to count," declares Hans Küng. "The designation 'soul'—understood as the nearer (substrate) of psychological events and phenomena or as the Aristotelian 'form' (entelechy) of the body—is scarcely used any longer as a scientific term; the designation 'psyche' more generally used does not mean a substantial principle of life, distinct from the body, but simply the totality of conscious and unconscious emotional events and spiritual (intellectual) functions."[10]

Modern psychology and medicine recognize our psychosomatic unity. Hans Küng suggests that "it is obvious then that biblical and modern anthropological thinking converge in their conception of man as a body-soul unity, a fact that is of crucial importance also for the question of life after death. When the New Testament speaks of resurrection, it does not refer to the natural continuance of a spirit-soul independent of our bodily functions. What it means—following the tradition of Jewish theology—is the *new creation, the transformation of the whole person by God's life-creating Spirit.*"[11] Otto Kaiser and Eduard Lohse agree. "The resurrection of the dead is a resurrection of the whole man, and therefore a bodily resurrection. . . . The apostle is thinking of man as a unity that may not be divided into a higher part that is preserved in an immortal soul and a lower part that passes away with the deceased body. Instead, man is, with his body, soul, and spirit, God's creation."[12] They reflect the views of some of the leading theological thinkers of our time.

7. Survival of the Soul

So many scholars look to a survival of the soul in death that enables it to continue the identity of the person in the bodily resurrection. But we must ask ourselves, Is the assurance of this continuity of the person best found in a surviving soul or in the Creator God? In other words, is God dependent upon a surviving soul in order to maintain a proper continuity, or is the God who created everything *"out of nothing"* able to recreate the identical individual who holistically died in death? "The emphasis here is not on some quality of mine that outlasts death," declares Helmut Thielicke, "but on the quality of my Lord not to desert me."[13]

What About Soul Sleep?

Sleep is a common biblical synonym for death. It appears 66 times in 17 biblical books, and Jesus used it in Matthew 9:24, Mark 5:39, Luke 8:52, and John 11:11.[14] The Greek writer Didorus Siculus (15, 25.2) represents death as a sleep.[15]

1. Soul Sleep as Inadequate

First we turn to a basic presupposition. If we accept the findings of modern anthropology, which I believe confirm the biblical view of human wholeness, then the term "soul sleep" is inadequate to describe death. For it implies that the soul alone is asleep while the body decays. It continues the dichotomous view of human nature, with its Cartesian dualism.

2. Body Sleep No Better

Here's a surprising idea. "Everyone acknowledges, of course, that the body does sleep until the resurrection, that is, it becomes unconscious, insensible," declares Loraine Boettner. "The sleep spoken of is that of the body, not of the soul. Those who teach soul sleep have simply confused the sleep of the body with that of the soul."[16] Although body-sleep is his alternative for soul-sleep, it still favors a dualistic anthropology. Both perspectives are wrong.

3. Proponents of Soul-Sleep

The doctrine of soul-sleep has not been widely held throughout the history of dogma. Eusebius mentions that some in Arabia believed in soul-sleep.[17] Anabaptists and Psychopannychians during the Protestant Reformation taught soul-sleep. John Calvin wrote his *Psychopannychia* to combat the belief. Although Martin Luther taught soul-sleep as a reaction to Catholic purgatory[18] and also spoke of his own death in terms of soul-sleep, later he jettisoned the idea.

4. Popes Disagree

Pope John XXII considered that the soul does not go to be with God (beatific vision) until the eschatological judgment and that it merely sleeps after death. But his successor, Benedict XII, issued an edict in 1336 stating that souls do go immediately at death to experience the beatific vision.[19] During the nineteenth century Irvingites in England subscribed to soul-sleep, as Russellites, or Millennial Dawnists, did later in America.[20] Today evangelical Christians are divided between support for soul-sleep and support for an immediate journey of the soul to be with Christ. However, the latter view is the preponderant one.

5. Asleep or With Christ?

Asleep or not asleep? That is the question. Here are two ways of looking at it.

Gordon R. Lewis and Bruce A. Demarest note that proponents of soul-sleep do so typically on the basis of the following three reasons. 1. Persons are unitary beings with no separate existence apart from the body (monism); 2. Scripture often depicts death as an unconscious state of sleep (Jer. 51:39, 57; Acts 7:60; 13:36; 1 Cor. 15:6, 18, 20, 51). If human beings received their reward immediately at death, what is the need for Christ's second coming, the general resurrection, and the final judgment? Often scholars link these concerns with conditional immortality, in which they do not see human beings as inherently immortal, but will at the Second Coming receive this gift.[21] The three biblical reasons radically call into question the idea that souls go immediately to heaven, hell, or purgatory at death.

Then there's the other side. Souls supposedly go to be with Christ. It hardly seems fair that they get there before their bodies. Thus G. C. Berkouwer's view of "continuous communion" with Christ in death, or a "dying in the Lord" rejects soul-sleep. "Accordingly," he adds, "the doctrine of soul-sleep has become an anthropological argument in direct opposition to the confession of the victory of the Lord over death. It should be dismissed by the church as a distortion of the secret of God."[22]

Louis Berkhof, rejecting the proposition that entrance into rewards at death undermines the final judgment, comes up with a creative solution. "The day of judgment is not necessary to reach a decision respecting the reward or punishment of each man, but only for the solemn announcement of the sentence, and for the revelation of the justice of God in the presence of men and angels." It's as if God were saying, "Listen up, all you souls in heaven. You are here because you passed the judgment." Wouldn't that be obvious already? "The surprise of which some of the passages give evidence," says Berkhof, "pertains to the ground on which the judgment rests rather than to the judgment itself."[23] But it's the other way round. Some will be surprised at the judgment verdict (e.g., Matt. 7:21-23; Luke 13:25-28) but not about its ground.

How will it be a surprise that only those who do the will of the Father (Matt. 7:21), love others (Matt. 25:40), and know Christ (Luke 13:25-27) gain entrance to heaven? The three criteria (doing God's will, loving fellow humans, and knowing Christ) are expected as the basis for the judgment since Jesus clearly declared that all the law hangs on love to God (i.e., obedience, John 14:15) and love to human beings (Matt. 22:37-40), and "This is eternal life: that they may know you, the only true God, and Jesus Christ" (John 17:3).

Wayne Grudem denies the idea of soul-sleep on the basis of texts he believes indicate that souls go straight to heaven to be with Christ (2 Cor. 5:18; Phil. 1:23; Luke 23:43; and Heb. 12:23). In his promise to the thief on the cross, Grudem notes, "Jesus did not say, 'Today you will no longer have consciousness of anything that is going on,' but, 'Today *you will be with me in paradise'* (Luke 23:43). Certainly the conception of Paradise understood at that time was not one of unconscious existence but one of great blessing and joy in the presence of God. Paul did not say, 'My desire is to depart and be unconscious for a long period of time,' but rather, 'My desire is to depart *and be with Christ'* (Phil. 1:23)." His is a persuasive argument. We will examine the answer in the next chapter.

---

[1] Maurice Rawlings, *Beyond Death's Door,* p. 53.

[2] Oscar Cullmann, *Immortality of the Soul or Resurrection of the Dead? The Witness of the NT* (London: Epworth, 1964), p. 15.

[3] Thomas N. Finger, *Christian Theology,* vol. 2, p. 123.

[4] G. C. Berkouwer, *Man: The Image of God,* pp. 200, 201.

[5] C.F.D. Moule, "The Meaning of 'Life' in the Gospels and Epistles of St. Paul," *Theology* 78 (1975): 115.

[6] Philip E. Hughes, *The True Image: The Origin and Destiny of Man in Christ* (Grand Rapids: Eerdmans, 1989), p. 400.

[7] Stanley Grenz, *Theology for the Community of God,* p. 209.

[8] Richard L. Purtill, "The Intelligibility of Disembodied Survival," p. 3.

[9] Wolfhart Pannenberg, *Systematic Theology* (Grand Rapids: 1994), vol. 2, p. 182.

[10] Hans Küng, *Eternal Life? Life After Death as a Medical, Philosophical, and Theological Problem,* p. 110.

[11] *Ibid.,* p. 111.

[12] Otto Kaiser and Eduard Lohse, *Death and Life,* John E. Steely, trans. (Nashville: Abingdon, 1981), p. 139.

[13] Helmut Thielicke, *Death and Life,* Edward H. Schroeder, trans. (Philadelphia: Fortress, 1970), p. 186.

[14] LeRoy Edwin Froom, *The Conditionalist Faith of Our Fathers* (Washington, D.C.: Review and Herald, 1966), vol. 1, p. 81. See list of texts on pages 81, 82.

[15] Norman R. Gulley, "Death: New Testament," *Anchor Bible Dictionary,* vol. 2, p. 110.

[16] Loraine Boettner, *Immortality,* p. 112.

[17] Louis Berkhof, *Systematic Theology,* p. 688.

[18] Gordon R. Lewis and Bruce A. Demarest, *Integrative Theology,* vol. 3, p. 451.

[19] Grenz, p. 767.

[20] Berkhof, p. 688.

[21] Lewis and Demarest, vol. 3, p. 451.

[22] G. C. Berkouwer, *The Return of Christ,* pp. 60, 61.

[23] Berkhof, p. 689.

Chapter 22

The Christian View of Death

Victor Solow bolted upright on the emergency-room table after being clinically dead 23 minutes. It was 11:15 a.m. at the United Hospital in Port Chester, New York. Solow, 56-year-old head of the Solow Productions, Inc., a film-making company, had died at 10:52 a.m. of a heart attack after jogging. What happened during those 23 minutes?

As two internists, two surgeons, two cardiac technicians, two respiratory therapists, and four nurses busily worked to resuscitate his body, Solow felt himself rise from his body.

"I was moving at high speed toward a net of great luminosity," he later said. "The strands and knots where the luminous lines intersected were vibrating with a tremendous cold energy. The grid appeared as a barrier that would prevent further travel. . . . Then I was in the grid. The instant I made contact with it, the vibrant luminosity increased to a blinding immensity which drained, absorbed and transformed me at the same time."[1]

Many who have had such near-death experiences believe that their soul rose up a corridor of light on its way to heaven. Dr. Elizabeth Kübler-Ross,[2] Dr. Raymond Moody,[3] and Drs. Karlis Osis and Erlendur Haraldsson[4] have interviewed resuscitated patients and found a similar pattern. The problem is, how come people of all kinds of character were going to the same place? Is heaven a place for Hitler as well as Mother Teresa?

Dr. Maurice Rawlings also conducted interviews with such patients. Here's his comment: "A dying person simply faints or painlessly loses consciousness as death occurs, and yet he is still able to hear himself pronounced dead by his doctor. He then discovers that he is out of his own body, but still in the same room, looking on as a bystander and observing the procedures. He watches himself being resuscitated, and frequently is compelled to walk around other people who might be obstructing his view. Or he may look down upon the scene from a floating position near the ceiling in which he sometimes finds himself. Often he is standing or floating behind the doctor or the nurse, looking down on the back of their heads as they work to revive his body. He notices who is in the room and knows what they are saying. He has difficulty believing that he is dead, that the lifeless body used to be his. He feels fine! The body has been vacated as if it were a strange object."[5]

Rawlings' interviews showed some people believed they were headed for hell. In the article "Life After Death—What About the New Evidence?" in *These Times* (April 1982, pp. 3-7) I documented the fact that this century has been one of intense research on the study of death. Interestingly, non-Christian views on death differ from the traditional concept of an immediate passage to heaven or hell. The Tibetan Book of the Dead *(Bardon Thodol)* states that it takes the spirit three or four days to leave the body. Citizens of Borneo consider that death releases seven souls that pass through the big toe in the shape of a butterfly, and then remain near relatives and friends, rather than flying away to some other realm. In Manila, Philippines, I saw the sumptuous mansions built by Chinese businessmen for their departed loved ones. It's a veritable ghost town. According to the Chinese only departed spirits live in the mansions. Visiting Japan, I watched people put rice and fish at the graves of their departed loved ones, presumably for the spirits who live there. The squirrels were the real beneficiaries.

The point is that wherever you go, you will find belief in life after death, making the whole world vulnerable to fallen angels impersonating departed loved ones. The only safety is in knowing what the Bible says about death. And that's the problem. Most who revere the Bible come away with the wrong view about what happens after death. The near-death experience stories seem to confirm their wrong view. So it's important that we really look at the evidence.

So what is death? Satan said that human beings would not really ever cease to exist. God said that they would. So the lines were drawn from the beginning (Gen. 3:1-4). Who's right? The Old Testament gives us insights, and so does Christ.

Old Testament Insights

1. No Independent Soul in Creation Record

Ecclesiastes 12:7 says about death: "The dust returns to the ground it came from, and the spirit returns to God who gave it." Speaking of human creation, the Bible declares: "And the Lord God formed man of the dust of the ground, and breathed into his nostrils the breath of life; and man became a living soul" (Gen. 2:7, KJV). The RSV and NIV versions translate soul *(nephes),* "living being." Do these passages speak of humans as composed of body and soul, the body from dust and the soul from God? Or does God breathe into the whole person His life-giving power, so the potential whole person becomes a living person?

Derek Kidner rightly notes "that man neither 'has' a soul nor 'has' a body, although for convenience he may be analysed into two or more constituents (e.g., 1 Thess. 5:23). The basic truth is here: he is a unity. *Nephes,* translated *being* (RSV) or *soul* (AV, RV), is often the equivalent of 'life,' and often of 'person' or 'self,' according as one emphasizes the aliveness of the creature or the creature who is alive."[6] Even for C. F. Keil and F. Delitzsch, who support the idea of a soul, *nephesh haya* "does not refer to the soul merely, but to the whole man as an animated being."[7]

Gordon J. Wenham recognizes that the term *nephesh haya* "breath of life" is a near synonym to *ruah* "wind, spirit." When Genesis 2:7 says "God blew into man's nostrils the breath of life, it is affirming that God made him alive by making him breathe." The term *nephes* "is one of the most common words in the OT (754 occurrences), and it has a wide range of meaning—'appetite, throat, person, soul, self, corpse,' among others." "It is not man's possession of 'the breath of life' or his status as a 'living creature' that differentiates him from the animals," for Scripture uses *nephes* of both animals and humans. It is the image of God that distinguishes humans and animals.[8] So *nephes* as soul is not the intent in this passage. Put another way, a human being does not *possess* a soul; he or she *is* one. A man or a woman is a living being without any part metaphysically distinguished from the rest. No immortal substance lurks within the mortal. Each individual came alive as a holistic person.

Death is merely the reverse of creation. In creation God joined the dust of the ground with His life-giving breath, and the first human being became a living person. But in death the life-giving principle departs from the human being, and the body goes back to dust. The process involves no soul. The equation is dust + God's inbreathing = living person. Or the reverse: Person – living principle = death of total person.

2. No Inherent Immortality

Inherent immortality would mean that human beings could never die. If we attribute such an immortality to the soul, and if the soul can exist disembodied after death, then human souls do not need the death of Christ to save them. Their own intrinsic immortality saves them. But the Christian view of death takes the purpose of Christ's death seriously. Scripture is clear that God "alone is immortal" (1 Tim. 6:16). Nowhere does Scripture ascribe the word "immortal" (Gr. *athanasia)* to humans before the *second coming of Christ.*

3. Origin of Death

Just as God did not institute natural immortality for human beings, so He did not intend that death would be a natural part of existence. Whereas the concept of an immortal soul gave to humans something greater than they actually possessed, so the concept of humans having only a finite time for existence is less than what their Creator created them for. We call the biblical view between these two extremes conditional immortality. It believes that God created humans with the possibility of becoming immortal, as in fact they will become at the eschatological resurrection when they receive immortality as a gift (1 Cor. 15:53, 54). God had to withdraw potential immortality at the Fall, and death took its place. Yet, through Christ, those who believe in Him receive everlasting life (John 3:16).

It is important to study what happened in humanity's Fall. Genesis 3 records how Eve told the tempter that God said, "You must not eat fruit from the tree that is in the middle of the garden, and you must not touch it, or you will die" (verse 3). Satan replied, "You will not surely die" (verse 4). The Creator speaks of death as being annihilation, and Satan redefines it as being continued existence. God did not say to Adam and Eve, "Your bodies will die, but your souls will live on as if you had never sinned." That would question the fact that they would actually die. But that is in fact what Satan proposed. It should cause us to hesitate when faced with any proposed concept about an intermediate state between death and the resurrection. We must ask ourselves whether such a view of the intermediate state reflects God's prediction about the first sin (verse 3), or actually echoes Satan's rebuttal, "You will not surely die" (verse 4).

Paul compares the origin of death with the origin of immortal life for humanity. Adam inflicted death on the human race by his disobedience in Eden, and Christ introduced eternal life through His death at Calvary (Rom. 5:15-19).

4. Sin Brings Death

It follows that death entered the world as a result of sin (Rom. 5:12, 15-19). Throughout the Old Testament God's people remembered this truth through the sacrificial services. A sinner could atone for a sin only through offering a substitutionary sacrifice. The lamb died in the place of the sinner. Its death was only due to the sin. Of course the sacrifices at the same time also pointed to the coming of the Lamb of God, who would pay the price for all human sin in His death at Calvary. Although that was the good news, it was never presented apart from the bad news that human sin brings death. Paul presents both sides of the issue when he declares that "the wages of sin is death, but the gift of God is eternal life in Christ Jesus our Lord" (Rom. 6:23). Here again the fact of human mortality is clear. Eternal life is a gift, not something inherent in us.

Another important fact that we need to understand is that sin does not pay its wages just to the body, but to the total person. Some believe that the essence of the person is the soul. It's the soul that sins. On that basis we must acknowledge that the soul must die, the opposite to the popular belief.

But the Bible never confines sin to one part of a human being. The total person sins and receives the wages of sin, just as it is not a part of the person that receives the gift of eternal life, but the whole individual.

5. The Soul That Sins Dies

"The soul who sins is the one who will die" (Eze. 18:20). Here the word "soul" (Heb. *nephesh)* is the same used for the soul of a person in other passages. In the light of those passages one may conclude that since the soul can die, then it is not inherently immortal. However, it is equally clear that Ezekiel 18:20 employs soul for the total person.

6. Banned From the Tree of Life

After the Fall of Adam and Eve,

God said, "The man has now become like one of us, knowing good and evil. He must not be allowed to reach out his hand and take also from the tree of life and eat, and live forever. So the Lord God banished him from the Garden of Eden" (Gen. 3:22, 23). Evidently the tree of life was necessary for continued human existence before the Fall, again indicating that human beings had no inherent immortality. They depended upon the tree of life.

Because of the Fall God removed any chance of their eating from that tree, so that death indeed would eventually overtake them. When we consider the function of the tree of life, we realize that its life-giving fruit affected the whole person; and likewise, no longer having access to its life-sustaining fruit also had an impact on the whole person. Again, nowhere in the passage do we find any suggestion that only the soul received the life-sustaining fruit before the Fall or that only the soul no longer received it after the Fall. Even if it did single out the soul, the passage would teach the soul's nonimmortality while eating the fruit, and therefore its certain death after it lost access to the fruit.

New Testament Insights

When Christ came to earth and Satan had Him put to death, it was the only time that Satan fully intended death to mean death. He wanted Christ to be gone forever. Let us look at how the New Testament regards death. As we do so we will consider some arguments used to support death as just a transition to further life for the soul. Because Christians employ such arguments, and at first glance they appear to be biblical, we need to examine them so Christians can awaken to the danger of believing in an immortal soul. For in the end-time, demons will use the belief to cause great damage.

1. God of the Living, Not of the Dead

Christ says "even Moses showed that the dead rise, for he calls the Lord 'the God of Abraham, and the God of Isaac, and the God of Jacob.' He is not the God of the dead, but of the living, for to him all are alive" (Luke 20:37, 38). Leon Morris suggests that this "can be true only if they are alive beyond the grave. . . . To us they are dead, but not to God. Death cannot break their relationship to him."[9] But such an interpretation overlooks the context of the resurrection. Christ is not speaking of the state in which the patriarchs presently exist (or nonexist) but rather of their existence at the eschatological resurrection.

Walter L. Liefeld grasped this fact. "God's children are also 'children of' (i.e., are characterized by) the Resurrection. Note the repetition of the word 'resurrection' and the absence of any reference to the Greek concept of 'immortality.' It is not persistence of life but that 'the dead rise' (v. 37) that Jesus is teaching."[10]

Many scholars, such as Norval Geldenhuys, link the "God of the living" with the interim state rather than with the resurrection, what the context actually calls for. Geldenhuys maintains that if the patriarchs are not immortal, then it would be unworthy of God, for He has established an everlasting covenant with them. However, if God brings them to life in the eschatological resurrection and gives them all the benefits of the everlasting covenant, would He not then be fulfilling His covenantal promises? Nowhere in the covenant did God promise the patriarchs, "You will never die, but live beyond death till the eschatological resurrection."[11]

2. Enoch, Elijah, and Moses

The Old Testament saints died, because they did not have access to the tree of life and received the wages of sin. Hebrews 11 records the great faith they had, though. Abraham "was looking forward to the city with foundations, whose architect and builder is God" (Heb. 11:10). His descendants "were still living by faith when they died. They did not receive the things promised" but were "longing for a better country—a heavenly one" (verses 13-16). Chapter 11 concludes: "These were all commended for their faith, yet none of them received what had been promised. God had planned something better for us so that only together with us would they be made perfect" (verses 39, 40). This points to the corporate *eschaton,* when the resurrected and living will receive the promises together (1 Thess. 4:16-18; cf. John 14:1-4). The passage does not suggest that they received the promise in death but that they wait until God gives them in the new heaven and new earth (Rev. 21, 22). Not even Moses has obtained the promises yet, even though he is the only one in the list who lives today.

Clearly the promises were not talking just about the land of Canaan but the heavenly city and country. It is this greater blessing, of which the earthly land of promise was but a type, that all of them still lacked when they died. Donald Guthrie notes the corporate nature of "made perfect" (Gr. *teleiothosin).* "No part of the true Christian community can be complete without the rest."[12] Leon Morris states that "the plan provides that the heroes of the faith throughout the ages should not 'be made perfect' apart from Christians. Salvation is social. It concerns the whole people of God."[13] William L. Lane adds that "God in his providence deferred the bestowal of the final reward until the advent of Christ and the enactment of the new covenant. . . ." In this context he suggests that *teleioun* "should be interpreted in terms of entrance into the promised eternal inheritance."[14]

Elijah and Moses visited Jesus on the Mount of Transfiguration (see Matt. 17:1-3). So they must have been alive centuries after their life on earth. Do they offer concrete evidence of a transition through death to continued living? It should be noted that Scripture mentions only Samuel, Moses, and Elijah as appearing to individuals in history subsequent to the end of their earth-life. We will consider Samuel immediately below. But for now, we must understand what took place at the transfiguration visitation of Moses and Elijah. The earthly life of both individuals was unique. Moses forfeited entrance into the land of Canaan because he disobeyed God by striking the rock, rather that speaking to it (see Num. 20:1-13; Deut. 1:37). Deuteronomy 34 records his death. After showing Moses the land of promise from the top of Mount Nebo, God evidently then caused Moses to die, despite the fact that "his eyes were not weak nor his strength gone" (verse 7). The New Testament picks up the story. There Christ ("archangel Michael," see Daniel 10:13; 12:1; 1 Thess. 4:16; John 5:26-28) disputes with the devil over Moses' body. One can imagine that Satan intended to keep him in the grave, but Christ wanted to resurrect him. Christ then raised Moses to be a type of those whom He will resurrect at His return.

By contrast Elijah, like Enoch before him (Gen. 5:24), received translation to heaven without seeing death (2 Kings 2:1-11). It is significant that Enoch, Elijah, and Moses are the only three people in Scripture who had an unusual departure, and Moses and Elijah are the only ones who appear in human history long after their earth-life.[15] Christ, in Matthew 16:28, said that some standing before Him would not see death until they witnessed the Son of Man coming in His kingdom. The very next verse introduces the reader to the Transfiguration, which took place only six days later. There Peter, James, and John saw Christ glorified and talking with Elijah and Moses. They beheld a proleptic view of the eschatological kingdom, for Christ was glorified with Moses, who represented the resurrected in the kingdom, and Elijah, those to be translated. The glorified King stands with a resurrected and translated first-fruits of His coming kingdom.

Paul teaches the same idea in 1 Thessalonians 4:16-18: "For the Lord himself will come down from heaven, with a loud command, with the voice of the archangel and with the trumpet call of God, and the dead in Christ will rise first. After that, we who are still alive and are left will be caught up together with them in the clouds to meet the Lord in the air. And so we will be with the Lord forever. Therefore encourage each other with these words." Here Paul summarizes what we have been considering in this section. Two groups will enter the eschatological rewards of the everlasting covenant at the same time and meet the Lord together. They are the resurrected saints and the translated saints. It's important to realize that both groups encounter the Lord in the air at the same time, emphasizing the corporate nature of eschatological fulfillment. Here corporate eschatology defines the limits of private eschatology. The dead saints wait for the resurrection. The only thing that the resurrected saints have experienced different from the translated ones is death.

3. Who Comes With Christ in the Second Advent?

Because Paul speaks of the two groups that await the return of Christ, the resurrected and translated, who both meet Him in the air (1 Thess. 4:16-18), then what does he mean when he says, "Our Lord Jesus comes with all his holy ones" (1 Thess. 3:13)? Does the verse suggest that human beings accompany Christ in the Second Coming? First, we should note that Paul makes his statement just a few verses prior to the passage that clearly designates the two groups of humans as either resurrected and translated. Is this a picture of disembodied spirits coming to join their resurrected bodies? The Scriptures never articulate such a position. Rather, those who in all sincerity believe that death is only a transition for the soul that waits for the reembodiment with the body at the eschatological resurrection are the ones who assume that the Bible teaches it.

Also, nowhere in Scripture does it state that the "holy ones" accompanying Christ in the Second Advent are humans, even though it is a popular belief.[16] But Paul elsewhere specifically states who they are: "when the Lord Jesus is revealed from heaven in blazing fire with his powerful angels" (2 Thess. 1:7). It is logical that angels will attend Christ. Always a vital part of the plan of salvation, God sent them to give messages to His saints or to battle with the enemy in their behalf. The Old Testament mentions angels at least 99 times, and the New Testament, 172 times. They have fulfilled an essential role and will do so in the Second Advent.

Revelation 14:14-20 describes events at the Second Coming, when angels assist Christ in the harvest of the wicked. It is the final act of the judgment that they have been involved in during the pre-Advent plagues (Rev. 16:1-21). The same Second Advent scene appears in Revelation 19:11-21, in which an angel cries in a loud voice (verse 17) and which describes Christ as a "rider on the horse" who comes with "his army" (verse 19) to bring the "fury of the wrath of God" (verse 15) upon the wicked. So Scripture is clear that angels return with Christ in the Second Advent, yet it never says that humans will accompany Him.

4. What Does It Mean to "Seek Immortality"?

God has promised that He "'will reward each person according to what he has done'" (Ps. 62:12; see also Prov. 24:12). "To those who by persistence in doing good seek glory, honor and immortality, he will give eternal life" (Rom. 2:7). Clearly the saints do not now possess immortality, but they seek it and will receive it at some future time. But when? Paul answers this question in 1 Corinthians 15. The saints, both resurrected and translated, will obtain it at the Second Advent, when "this mortal must put on immortality" (verse 53, KJV).

5. What Does It Mean to Have Eternal Life Now?

The biblical view of experiencing eternal life now differs from the philosophical view of inherent immortality. In Scripture, immortality belongs inherently to Christ, and He only imparts it as a gift to Christians. Berkouwer was right to say that "theologians spoke about the natural immortality of the soul as a 'truth' which was known more from reason than from revelation."[17]

Romans 6:7 mentions the future gift of immortality as the reception of eternal life. But do not Christians already have eternal life in the present? Jesus said, "Whoever eats my flesh and drinks my blood [i.e., has fellowship with me] has eternal life" (John 6:54). "God has given us eternal life, and this life is in his Son. He who has the Son has life. . . . I write these things to you who believe in the name of the Son of God so that you may know that you have eternal life" (1 John 5:11-13). Clearly, whoever is in fellowship with Christ has eternal life now. Thus Romans 6:7 has in mind the gift of eternal life yet to come at the Second

Advent, when the mortal will put on immortality, the corruptible will put on incorruption, and the redeemed will enter the fullness of eternal life, including face-to-face communion with Christ.

The passages under consideration mention two dimensions of eternal life. Eternal life has a present aspect of eternal life that is the "real thing" (with Christ), yet we can experience it only in our limitations (corruptible, mortal bodies without sight) compared to the future gift of eternal life when all the limitations will vanish forever. It is important to realize that no Scripture says we presently have immortal life. As far as human beings are concerned, immortality has only a future dimension, since in the present only God has immortality (1 Tim. 6:16). Eternal life in the present is the "already" of the eschatological tension that separates it from the "not yet" of eternal life to be gifted to Christians when they become immortal at the second coming of Christ. The fact that Christ "has destroyed death and has brought life and immortality to light through the gospel" (2 Tim. 1:10) does not contradict this eschatological truth but speaks of the gospel that proclaims it.[18]

Death and Spiritualism

As we have seen previously, in the end-time "many will be confronted by the spirits of devils personating beloved relatives or friends and declaring the most dangerous heresies."[19] Death makes Spiritualism possible.

Paul Althaus rejects the concept of eschatology through death as spiritualistic and acosmic. If a person privately arrives at the goal through death, there exists no need of a cosmic eschatological goal. It substitutes individual salvation in place of the community.[20] Jesus did not say to His disciples just before His departure, "Cheer up, you will be with Me soon when you die." Rather, He said, "In my Father's house are many rooms; if it were not so, I would have told you. I am going there to prepare a place for you. And if I go and prepare a place for you, I will come back and take you to be with me that you also may be where I am" (John 14:2-4).

It agrees with Paul, who said the dead in Christ will rise at the Second Coming and go to be with Christ (1 Thess. 4:16-18). Jesus said that "a time is coming when all who are in the graves will hear his voice and come out—those who have done good will rise to live, and those who have done evil will rise to be condemned" (John 5:28, 29). The New Testament does speak of Paul's longing to depart to be with Christ, but he does not contradict Christ's promise as to when his desire will be realized. We must always understand Pauline texts within the biblical worldview expressed by Christ. Then we will see that the New Testament consistently points to the second advent of Christ, and not individual death, as the goal for all humans.

As Stanley Grenz rightly says, "the goal of our hope is the resurrection, not an intermediate state."[21] And G. C. Berkouwer reminds us that there has "been sharp criticism from various quarters of the doctrine of the intermediate state, and often in unmistakable relation to criticism of the soul's immortality."[22] Philip Edgcumbe Hughes states, "As sleeping is followed by waking so the

Christian believer has the certain knowledge that, though overtaken by death, he will awaken at the resurrection to fullness of life in the presence and likeness of his Redeemer."[23] Holistic anthropology is biblical. The soul has no fast track to the goal ahead of the body. Christ died for the total person, and the total person awaits the Second Coming resurrection, or translation.

Scripture speaks of death as "rest" or "sleep" (Heb. *shakab:* Deut. 31:16; 2 Sam. 7:12; 1 Kings 2:10; Gr. *koimao:* John 11:11-14; Acts 13:36; 1 Cor. 15:51; 1 Thess. 4:13, 14). The image of sleeping, or resting, appears throughout both Testaments. Just as we saw the focus on the second coming of Christ rather than personal death as the moment for reaching the eschatological goal in the New Testament, so we see the same in the Old Testament. For example, "multitudes who sleep in the dust of the earth will awake: some to everlasting life, others to shame and everlasting contempt" (Dan. 12:2).

The Old Testament comments on the interim state in ways that reinforce the sleeping or resting description. For example, "the dead know nothing" (Eccl. 9:5); "in that very day [of death] his thoughts [Heb. *heshtonah,* not "plans," as in NIV] perish" (Ps. 146:4, KJV). The dead have no love, hatred, or jealousy (Eccl. 9:6). The wise man exhorts his readers to do all in this life, "for in the grave, where you are going, there is neither working nor planning nor knowledge nor wisdom" (Eccl. 9:10). "It is not the dead who praise the Lord," says the psalmist, who describes them as "those who go down to silence" (Ps. 115:17). The two Testaments have a consistent approach to death.

By contrast with this biblical view, Spiritualism assumes that it is possible for the living to communicate with the dead. What do we do with 1 Samuel 28, in which the deceased Samuel apparently speaks to King Saul? Ralph W. Klein believes it was a real interview with Samuel.[24] C. F. Keil and F. Delitzsch saw such a position as the "unanimous" opinion of "modern orthodox commentators."[25]

But what does Scripture say? "Do not turn to mediums or seek out spiritists, for you will be defiled by them. I am the Lord your God" (Lev. 19:31). In fact, any person in Israel who was a medium or spiritist "must be put to death" (Lev. 20:27). Even if someone consulted a medium or spiritist, God said, "I will cut him off from his people" (Lev. 20:6). In obedience to God, "Saul had expelled the mediums and spiritists from the land" (1 Sam. 28:3). Then why would he want to consult the medium at Endor? He inquired of God, but the Lord did not answer him (verse 6). So in desperation Saul sought a source that God had condemned. It seems logical that if God did not answer in the usual manner, then He hardly would reply through a means He had condemned. It would be inconsistent for Him to employ a method that He rejects elsewhere in Scripture.

Yet Keil and Delitzsch claim that "God brought up" Samuel "from Hades through an act of His omnipotence." They further suggest that "the reality of the appearance of Samuel from the kingdom of the dead cannot therefore be called in question, especially as it has an analogon in the appearance of Moses and Elijah at the transfiguration of Christ."[26] We have noted previously that Elijah and Moses are exceptions in their transfiguration and resurrection. The appearance of Samuel as a result of God's omnipotence would be comparable to a resurrection from the dead such as experienced by Moses. Yet why would God go to that incredible extent when He could have answered Saul directly? Saul had forgotten God's omnipotence for the coming battle and chose rather to rely upon his own efforts, consulting a medium who belonged to those God had already rejected. God had now also abandoned him, and so He remained silent when Saul inquired of Him. To attribute Samuel's appearance to the omnipotence of God overlooks these facts and denies the biblical picture of death noted above, particularly the fact that "never again will they [the dead] have a part in anything that happens under the sun" (Eccl. 9:6).

Death as the Last Enemy

"The last enemy to be destroyed is death" (1 Cor. 15:26), an event that takes place in the eschatological future. In the meantime, death remains an enemy as it robs Christians of their life with Christ in the present, even though it cannot separate them from Christ (see Rom. 8:38, 39). So I cannot follow Anthony A. Hoekema when he says that our last enemy "has through the work of Christ become our friend."[27] His conclusion seems prefaced on the fact that death is a mere transition that brings us to be with Christ, rather than an interruption of fellowship with Christ that lasts until the eschatological resurrection.

However, it is true that the death of Christ has radically altered death's finality. His death has made possible the future destruction of death itself. The blessed hope of an eschatological resurrection rests on the death and resurrection of Christ. Nowhere in Scripture is that final deliverance called into question by a deliverance from death at death. One can say that "with Christ's resurrection, the resurrection of the dead has already begun."[28] And as Otto Kaiser and Eduard Lohse rightly comment, "the resurrection of the dead is a resurrection of the whole man, and therefore a bodily resurrection. . . . The apostle is thinking of man as a unity that may not be divided into a higher part that is preserved in an immortal soul and a lower part that passes away with the deceased body."[29]

Christ's Return and the Resurrected Saints

Repeatedly Scripture compares death to sleep. But it is not a soul-sleep, that is, of the soul alone but the sleep of the total person. Paul longed to depart and be with Christ. From the perspective of Paul in death, that is precisely what happens. Even though centuries of human history have passed since the apostle died, the moment he closed his eyes in death was to him the moment he will rise to be with Christ in the resurrection at His second coming. As Stephen H. Travis rightly discerns, "from the viewpoint of the person who dies, resurrection is instantaneous."[30]

In the New Testament the blessed hope never focuses on individual death, but always on the return of Christ and the resurrection and translation of the saints to meet Him together, at the same time. It is in this future, and not what happens at death, that saints can find comfort (1 Thess. 4:16-18). "There has been a sharp reaction against the post-Enlightenment idealistic belief in immortality," says G. C. Berkouwer, "based on an optimistic view of natural immortality, as demonstrable by reason. There can then be no idea that death affects merely the body, as a part of man; the soul is also affected by death, so that after man dies there remains only one eschatological perspective; awakening from death. That is a perspective which has nothing to do with the 'natural' immortality or indestructibility of the soul, but comes exclusively from God's future creative act in Jesus Christ."[31]

Christ's Teaching

Christ presented the parable of the rich man and Lazarus (Luke 16:19-31), which some believe indicates that individuals go to heaven and hell at death. He also said to the thief on the cross, "Today you will be with me in paradise" (Luke 23:43). Do these two incidents from Christ's life contradict all that we have said thus far? And what does Christ's raising of Lazarus tell us (John 11:1-44)? We will consider these three incidents and then ask how Christ's death informs us about the state of the dead. But first, note the startling fact that Jesus said the believer does not die.

1. The Christian Will Never Die

In the Gospel of John Christ spells out in great detail what it means for a Christian to die. He says, "whoever hears my word and believes him who sent me has eternal life and will not be condemned: he has crossed over from death to life," yet He adds that "the dead will hear the voice of the Son of God, and those who hear will live" (John 5:24, 25). Further, He declares that whoever "looks to the Son and believes in him shall have eternal life, and I will raise him up at the last day" (John 6:40). "Whoever eats my flesh and drinks my blood [i.e., has fellowship with me] has eternal life, and I will raise him up at the last day" (John 6:54). Christ says, "I tell you the truth, if anyone keeps my word, he will never see death" (John 8:51). "I give them eternal life, and they shall never perish" (John 10:28). For "whoever lives and believes in me will never die" (John 11:26). Does it sound like Satan's promise in Eden, "You will not surely die" (Gen. 3:4)?

In a breathtaking and startling manner, Christ describes fellowship with Him as not only having eternal life; He says the experience means a Christian has already crossed over from death to life, and therefore does not die. Yet (and this is the point) He holds the concept in careful tension with the promise that the resurrection is eschatological and does not occur at death. We find no hint here that Christ speaks of the survival of the soul (that does not die) in death, contrasted with the future resurrection of the body. He has the whole person in mind. It's the total person that does not die. Why? A Christian is one who has partaken of the divine nature (2 Peter 1:4); who has Christ, and therefore eternal life (1 John 5:11, 12); who cannot be separated from Christ in death (Rom. 8:38, 39), and therefore has "crossed over from death to life" (John 5:24) and cannot die (John 11:26), or perish (John 10:28). Christ will resurrect the total person (John 5:26-28; 1 Thess. 4:16-18).

2. Parable of the Rich Man and Lazarus

In Christ's parable the rich man goes to hell, and Lazarus enters heaven. The rich man sees Abraham with Lazarus by his side and requests that Lazarus bring water on the tip of his finger to place on the rich man's tongue, because he is in agony in the fire. Abraham refuses the request. The rich man then begs Lazarus to warn his five brothers still living on earth, for they will surely believe if someone comes from the dead with such a message.

Those believing that souls survive death and go directly to their rewards consider this parable vital. For example, Ronald Cassidy sees it as evidence for a "continuity of consciousness."[32] Edward G. Kettner even considers the parable "a proof text for the existence of the intermediate state."[33]

It seems to me what Jesus teaches here is that we receive rewards based on things done, or not done, in the present life. Such an interpretation harmonizes with the rest of the scriptural teaching we have examined. So Philip Edgcumbe Hughes is right to question if the parable has anything to do with an intermediate state.[34] John Calvin says the parable "represents the condition of the life to come."[35]

If there are immediate rewards, as the parable seems to suggest, it repudiates the concept that we receive our rewards at the final judgment. I agree with Stanley Grenz that "the narrative cannot be historical because it contradicts the biblical teaching concerning the judgment."[36] Not only this, but it would require us to jettison the rest of the biblical insights about life after death. And I concur with Donald Guthrie that "it would be precarious to regard the parable as a sufficient basis for deducing the nature of the afterlife as understood by Jesus, for the intention of the parable was clearly not doctrinal, but moral."[37]

3. Promise to the Thief on the Cross

"Today you will be with me in paradise" (Luke 23:43) Jesus said to the crucified thief. Did Christ, who comforted His disciples to look to His second advent as their time of meeting Him again (John 14:1-4), give the thief on the cross, not long afterward, an earlier schedule than He gave them? Would He meet the thief on Crucifixion Friday while His beloved disciples had to wait until His return centuries later? Most commentators believe that Christ and the thief went to Paradise that day.

Some have devised rather creative ways of looking at the passage. If Jesus is to be consistent with the rest of the biblical worldview, where the "already" of death takes seriously the "not yet" of resurrection in a holistic view of humans, then we need to consider some alternative understandings. The fact that a comma after "today" would alter the meaning is granted. Then Jesus would be saying, "I say to you today, you will be with me in paradise" (at the eschatological resurrection).

Hughes, however, finds the suggestion unacceptable, because a few hours earlier Jesus used the same formula in speaking to Peter in Mark 14:30.[38] "'I tell you the truth,' Jesus answered, 'today—yes, tonight—before the rooster crows twice you yourself will disown me three times.'" For Stanley Grenz, Christ was "promising the thief that he would enjoy the Lord's presence even in death ('today'). The focal point of Jesus' reply was not the location of the two beyond death ('paradise'), but the promise of his personal presence ('Today you will be with me')."[39]

Rather than looking to these replies, it seems best to consult words Jesus uttered after His resurrection on Sunday, the third day after His death. When Mary discovered who He was, she clung to Him in understandable emotion. Jesus kindly said to her, "Do not hold on to me, for I have not yet returned to the Father" (John 20:17). He was asking her to release Him so that He could go to heaven. Evidently He had not ascended to heaven on Crucifixion Friday with the thief. If Jesus did not visit heaven until the third day, why should anyone else ascend at his or her death? It seems clear to me that Jesus' promise to the thief was the same as the one that He made to the disciples—that when He returns in His kingdom, they would all be with Him. Therefore, the promise was made "today" about that future tomorrow.

4. The Death of Lazarus

Christ refers to Lazarus as "fallen asleep" when he died (John 11:11, 14), a description in keeping with the texts we examined above about death as a sleep. This is the time of repose between death and eschatological resurrection, not an intermediate state. Should we understand sleep as figurative and death as real? Or are both terms speaking about reality? Berkouwer is right to conclude that "we would reach a wholly wrong conclusion if we viewed Christ's first words as figurative, and His later words as 'real.'"[40]

The resurrection of Lazarus is the greatest miracle Christ performed, culminating His work for humanity prior to His death and resurrection. It was an amazing miracle, because Lazarus had been dead for four days (John 11:17). A believer, Lazarus experienced the eternal life that Christ gives to those in whom He indwells. If such persons go immediately to heaven at death, then the soul (at least) of Lazarus had already been in heaven four days when Jesus resurrected the total person Lazarus. And if it was a recall from heaven, it is the only example found in Scripture and it would mean that Christ brought Lazarus back from heaven to live on earth again.

Why would He ever do such a thing? Why wrest him away from the joys of heaven to return to the struggles of earthly life? And what happened to his body? Did he get a spiritual body in death and then have to exchange that for his old body in the resurrection? C.B.D. Moule exclaimed that the entire story is "positively confusing."[41]

But it is not confusing when seen in the light of the biblical worldview on the one hand and the light of its purpose on the other hand. When Lazarus died, the whole person lay in the grave. He did not go anywhere, although the life principle from God was no longer present. Christ did not bring him back from heaven—He brought him back from the grave, back into existence. The purpose of the exercise, so it appears, was to emphasize His mission as "the resurrection and the life" (John 11:25). At the beginning of His ministry Christ raised Jairus' daughter (Mark 5:22-43) and the widow's son at Nain (Luke 7:11-17).

Now near the end of His ministry He performs a far greater resurrection, for it followed four days of decomposition. This parallels the fact that Christ cleansed the Temple at the beginning of His ministry (John 2:12-22) as He did again near its close (Matt. 21:12-16; Mark 11:15-19, 27-33; 12:1-12; Luke 19:45-48; 20:1-19). Such events seem to draw attention to the purpose of His mission among humanity. R.V.G. Tasker is right that "through the miracle of his restoration Jesus desires to manifest Himself as *the resurrection, and the life.*"[42]

The important fact to note is that He performed the miracle of resurrection to point to His own coming resurrection, on which the resurrection of all human beings depend. The focus is ultimately on the eschatological resurrection. That of Lazarus was a proleptic type. It did not include glorification any more than receiving eternal life in the present includes immortality. So it has much more to do with the eschatological resurrection than any emphasis on the intermediate state.

Christ's Death

If Christ was a real man, then did He have a soul that went to heaven as soon as He died? No. Buried on Good Friday (John 19:42), He rose on Easter Sunday (Mark 16:9). He did not go to preach to souls in prison, as shown in chapter 16, but lay in the grave holistically until resurrection morning. In doing such, He gave us insight into the death of His followers. They rest holistically in the grave until He calls them from the graves in His second advent (1 Thess. 4:16-18). Christ's death, and not the alleged "after-death experiences" of Christians, must guide our understanding of death itself.

---

[1] Victor Solow, "I Died at 10:52 a.m.," *Reader's Digest,* October 1974, p. 181.

[2] Elizabeth Kübler-Ross, *On Death and Dying* (New York: MacMillan, 1969).

[3] Raymond Moody, *Life After Life* (Covington, Ga.: Mockingbird, 1975).

[4] Karlis Osis and Erlendur Haraldsson, *At the Hour of Death* (New York: Avon, 1977).

[5] Maurice Rawlings, *Beyond Death's Door* (New York: Bantam, 1978), p. 44.

[6] Derek Kidner, *Tyndale OT Commentaries, Genesis* (Downers Grove, Ill.: InterVarsity, 1967), p. 61.

[7] C. F. Keil and F. Delitzsch, *Commentary of the OT,* James Martin, trans. (Grand Rapids: Eerdmans, 1986), vol. 1, p. 79.

[8] Gordon J. Wenham, *Word Biblical Commentary, Genesis 1-15,* David Hubbard and Glenn W. Barker, eds. (Waco, Tex.: Word, 1987), vol. 1, pp. 60, 61.

[9] Leon Morris, *Tyndale NT Commentaries: Luke* (Grand Rapids: Eerdmans, 1988), vol. 3, pp. 292, 293.

[10] Walter L. Liefeld, *The Expositor's Bible Commentary,* Frank E. Gaebelein, ed. (Grand Rapids: Zondervan, 1984), vol. 8, p. 1017.

[11] Norval Geldenhuys, *The New International Critical Commentary on the NT, Luke* (Grand Rapids: Eerdmans, 1983), pp. 511, 512.

[12] Donald Guthrie, *Tyndale NT Commentaries, Hebrews,* vol. 15, p. 247.

[13] Leon Morris, *The Expositor's Bible Commentary, Hebrews,* vol. 12, pp. 132, 133.

[14] William L. Lane, *Word Biblical Commentary: Hebrews 9-13* (Waco, Tex.: Word, 1991), vol. 47b, p. 393.

[15] I consider the appearance of Samuel to King Saul as an apparition, and not the real person Samuel.

[16] For example, Edward G. Kettner, "Time, Eternity, and the Intermediate State," p. 98; Otto Kaiser and Eduard Lohse, *Death and Life,* p. 127.

[17] G. C. Berkouwer, *Man: The Image of God,* p. 242.

[18] Ralph Earle, *The Expositor's Bible Commentary, 2 Timothy,* vol. 11, pp. 396, 397.

[19] E. G. White, *The Great Controversy,* p. 560.

[20] Paul Althaus, *Die Letzten Dinge,* pp. 149-152.

[21] Stanley J. Grenz, *Theology for the Community of God,* p. 775.

[22] G. C. Berkouwer, *Man: The Image of God,* p. 249.

[23] Philip E. Hughes, *The True Image,* p. 393.

[24] Ralph W. Klein, *World Biblical Commentary* (Waco, Tex.: Word, 1983), vol. 10, pp. 270-273.

[25] C. F. Keil and F. Delitzsch, *Commentary of the OT,* vol. 2, p. 266.

[26] *Ibid.,* p. 268.

[27] Anthony A. Hoekema, *The Bible and the Future,* p. 85.

[28] Otto Kaiser and Eduard Lohse, *Death and Life,* p. 134.

[29] *Ibid.,* p. 139.

[30] Stephen H. Travis, *Christian Hope and the Future,* p. 116.

[31] G. C. Berkouwer, *Man: The Image of God,* pp. 250, 251.

[32] Ronald Cassidy, "Paul's Attitude to Death in 2 Corinthians 5:1-10," *The Evangelical Quarterly* 43, (October-December 1971): 216.

[33] Edward G. Kettner, "Time, Eternity, and the Intermediate State," p. 98; cf. Anthony A. Hoekema, *The Bible and the Future,* p. 101.

[34] Philip Edgcumbe Hughes, *The True Image,* p. 394.

[35] John Calvin, *Commentary on a Harmony of the Evangelists: Matthew, Mark, Luke,* William Pringle, trans. (Grand Rapids: Baker, 1989), vol. 2, p. 188. We will not discuss at this juncture the future focus that Calvin has or his immortality-of-the-soul teaching.

[36] Grenz, p. 772.

[37] Donald Guthrie, *New Testament Theology,* p. 820.

[38] Hughes, p. 395.

[39] Grenz, p. 773.

[40] Berkouwer, p. 246.

[41] C.F.D. Moule, "The Meaning of 'Life' in the Gospels and Epistles of St. John," *Theology* 78 (1975): 115.

[42] R.V.G. Tasker, *Tyndale NT Commentaries, John* (Grand Rapids: Eerdmans, 1988), vol. 4, p. 138.

Chapter 23

The Debate on Hell Heats Up

Thomas Welch in his booklet *Oregon's Amazing Miracle* describes his visit to hell. He worked as an engineer's helper at the Bridal Veil Lumber Company, 30 miles east of Portland, Oregon. Part of his job was to walk over a trestle 55 feet above a dam. One day, as he headed out across the trestle, he fell headfirst onto a beam 30 feet down, and then tumbled from one beam to another until he hit the water and disappeared. Immediately the mill shut down and a rescue search began. Finally, after 45 minutes to an hour, M.J.H. Gunderson found him.

Welch describes his experience. "I was dead as far as this world is concerned. But I was alive to another world. There was no lost time. I learned more in that hour out of the body than I could ever learn while in this body. All I could remember is falling over the edge of the trestle. The locomotive engineer watched me go all the way down into the water. The next thing I knew I was standing near a shoreline of a great ocean of fire. It happened to be what the Bible says it is in Revelation 21:8 'the lake which burneth with fire and brimstone.' This is the most awesome sight one could ever see this side of the final judgment."[1] He believed that he had arrived at the edge of hell.

Pondering why nearly all cases in the literature speak of the resuscitated as returning from a good experience, Maurice Rawlings says, "It then occurred to me that some of the 'good' experiences could have been false impressions, perhaps created by Satan appearing as an 'angel of light' (see 2 Cor. 11:14)."[2] But he apparently never concluded that Satan could give false impressions of hell too.

Hell holds an important place in the final events of most Christians. We cannot ignore it if we wish to help those who believe in this myth.

The Hell-Death Connection

The way one views death affects the way one regards the concept of hell. Those who believe in the innate immortality of the soul find it necessary to have an eternal hell, for both good and evil souls live forever. Those who deny the inherent immortality of the soul do not have to accept an eternal hell. Proponents of both sides come to the same biblical texts with their different assumptions. Finding the texts speaking of eternal punishment, they conclude that such punishment is either eternal in process (unending) or in its effects (total and final destruction). Each side claims that its view is biblical and that the opposite view is not. Both hold that their interpretation better represents God's justice. And both sides claim that their perspective provides the best motivation for evangelization. Here are two diametrically opposed claims. The simple fact is that both cannot be right.

It is important to step back from the debate and look at it in context. Proponents on both sides are sincere Christians who really believe that they are upholding Scripture and are attempting to be true to God's nature. Yet we all know that it is possible to be sincerely wrong. When we encounter two mutually opposed views, both claiming to have Christ and Scripture on their side, it is good to look over both views from the vantage point of the biblical worldview. Before doing that, we will pause and consider the history of the doctrine of hell.

Those Opposing Hell

The debate on hell is heating up these days. We will look at seven leading antagonists.

1. Nels Ferre

Nels Ferre, in his book *The Christian Understanding of God* (1951), said, "Eternal hell is naturally out of the question, both as subjustice and as sublove. The very conception of eternal hell is monstrous and an insult to the conception of last things in other religions, not to mention the Christian doctrine of God's sovereign love. Such a doctrine would make God a tyrant, where any human Hitler would be a third-degree saint, and the concentration camps of human torture the king's picnic grounds. That such a doctrine could be conceived, not to mention believed, shows how far from any understanding of the love of God many people once were and, alas, still are!"[3]

2. G. C. Berkouwer

G. C. Berkouwer, in his *The Return of Christ* (1972), observes, "Perhaps no single New Testament word has stimulated the imagination more or drawn so many conflicting reactions as the term 'Gehenna.'" Hell is a translation of Gehenna. In time it became "divorced from the relationships in which it is invariably found in Scripture, and came to be treated by many as a ruthless threat, an expression of extreme harshness, in which all feelings of compassion had perished. When this happened, the critical relationship in the New Testament between 'Gehenna' and the invitation, love, and covenant of God was lost."[4] So he rejects any presentation of hell that overlooks its proper context in the gospel.

3. William Barclay

William Barclay, in his *A Spiritual Autobiography* (1975), goes beyond the concept of God as a judge or a king to the fact that He is also a father. In fact, he concludes that "he is indeed Father more than anything else." Therefore he asserts, "no Father could be happy while there were members of his family forever in agony." But he also believes that no father could be happy "to obliterate" his family members either. Barclay believes in universalism, which we will need to address later, but for our purposes now, he cannot see how God as Father would be happy if His children suffered eternally in hell.[5]

4. Edward W. Fudge

Edward William Fudge, in his *The Fire That Consumes* (1982), takes the position that "the Passion of Jesus Christ revealed in a unique way God's judgment against sin, and that in a genuine way it revealed also what awaits at the end of the world for those who reject Christ now." As Christ was "utterly forsaken by God," so will be the ultimate punishment of the wicked.[6]

Two years later Fudge pointed out that most Christians misunderstand the New Testament phrase "unquenchable fire," being unaware that it has its roots in the Old Testament, where the word "quench" means "destruction that cannot be resisted." Psalm 118:12 (KJV) says about the writer's enemy, "They compassed me about like bees; they are quenched as the fire of thorns: for in the name of the Lord I will destroy them." Here "quench" and "destroy" are synonymous. Fudge goes to Isaiah 66:24 for the roots of the phrase "their worm does not die" (Mark 9:48). He notes that the language is figurative, using the undying worm and unquenchable fire in reference to carcasses of the wicked. "[The righteous] view their destruction, not their misery. . . . The final picture is one of shame, not pain."[7]

Fudge notes that the phrase "gnashing of teeth" also has Old Testament roots in Job 16:9; Psalm 35:16; 37:12; and Lamentations 2:16, indicating anger, as we also see in Acts 7:54 demonstrated by Stephen's enemies. Psalm 112:10 (KJV) reads: "The wicked shall see it, and be grieved; he shall gnash his teeth, and melt away: the desire of the wicked shall perish." Here Scripture links gnashing with perishing, not an eternal response. The phrase "the smoke of their torment rises for ever and ever" (Rev. 14:11) finds a root in Isaiah 34:10, where Edom's fire "will not be quenched night and day; its smoke will rise forever." Fudge rightly says, "The verses following describe a land empty of people, the haunt of desert creatures. Conscious pain has ended there, but 'its smoke will rise forever'—the extinction is perpetual."[8]

Next Fudge examines the punishment of the wicked in Revelation 14. They "will be tormented with burning sulfur in the presence of the holy angels and of the Lamb. And the smoke of their torment rises for ever and ever. There is no rest day or night" (verses 10, 11). He notes that burning sulfur destroyed Sodom and Gomorrah (Gen. 19:23-28). The biblical usage of "fire and brimstone" (burning sulfur) is that of "total destruction," not only at Sodom and Gomorrah, but thereafter (Deut. 29:23; Job 18:15-17; Isa. 30:27-33; 34:9-11; Eze. 38:22-24). "The cup of God's wrath" in Revelation 14:9-11 "is a common figure of God's punishment in both OT and NT (see Job 21:20; Ps. 60:3; 75:8; Isa. 51:17, 22; Jer. 25:27, 28; Obadiah 16; Matt. 26:39)."[9]

The devil will be "thrown into the lake of burning sulfer, where the beast and the false prophet had been thrown. They will be tormented day and night for ever and ever" (Rev. 20:10). Fudge considers the verse "is the single most problematic text in the whole Bible for the extinction of all evil," but reminds readers of the hermeneutical principle of interpreting the more obscure in the light of the clearer.[10]

The fate of Satan in Ezekiel 28:18, however, offers a better solution. After speaking of the "guardian cherub" (verse 14) expelled from heaven (verse 16) to earth (verse 17) and who was in Eden (verse 13), the passage points to the future punishment of Satan in the past tense, indicating its certainty. "So I made a fire come out from you, and it consumed you, and I reduced you to ashes on the ground in the sight of all who were watching." Here "ashes" qualifies the "tormented day and night for ever and ever" (Rev. 20:10). It is a process of torment that ends in ashes, in which the result, rather than the process, is eternal.

Paul's focus is also total extinction. "The wicked, he warns, will die (Rom. 6:21, 23), perish (2:12), be destroyed (Gal. 6:8; 1 Cor. 3:17; 2 Thess. 1:9; Phil. 1:28; 3:19; see also Jude 10)." Nor will they ever come back, for this destruction is to be "everlasting" (2 Thess. 1:9). Fudge reminds us that the word "eternal" used of salvation is the result. For "we do not look for an eternal act of 'saving.'"[11] So it is when Scripture employs "eternal" to explain God's punishment.

5. Hans Küng

Hans Küng, in his *Eternal Life: Life After Death as a Medical, Philosophical, and Theological Problem* (1984), responds to the common view that God casts people into hell as revenge for their rebellion against Him and then keeps them there forever, because His anger is never assuaged. "What would we think of a human being who satisfied his thirst for revenge so implacably and insatiably?"[12]

6. John Stott

In *Evangelical Essentials* (1988) David L. Edwards and John Stott dialogue together on numerous topics, including hell. John Stott says: "I want to repudiate with all the vehemence of which I am capable the glibness, what almost appears to be the glee, the *Schadenfreude*, with which some Evangelicals speak about hell. It is a horrible sickness of mind or spirit." Noting the fact that Jesus and His apostles used the phrases "the lake of fire, the outer darkness, the second death," he says we cannot interpret them literally, "since fire and darkness exclude each other."[13]

Stott considers Scripture to teach annihilation, so eternal torment is merely a tradition. He suggests that Scripture documents this through language, imagery, justice, and universalism. Relative to language, he cites the Greek verb *apolumi* (to destroy) and the noun *apoleia* (destruction). Matthew 10:28 declares: "'Be afraid of the One [God] who can destroy both soul and body in hell.'" He then comments, "If to kill is to deprive the body of life, hell would seem to be the deprivation of both physical and spiritual life, that is, an extinction of being."[14]

Concerning the biblical imagery, Stott observes that "the main function of fire is not to cause pain, but to secure destruction. . . . The fire itself is termed 'eternal' and 'unquenchable,' but it would be very odd if what is thrown into it proves indestructible." In Matthew 25:46 the comparison between "eternal life" and "eternal punishment" is *"contrasting* the two destinies: the more unlike they are, the better."[15] Stott questions whether it is just to give eternal punishment for sins committed in time, "unless perhaps (as has been argued) the impenitence of the lost also continues throughout eternity." He opposes universalism, but cannot see a part of God's creation as being punished or still in rebellion, when Scripture speaks of "Christ drawing all men to himself (John 12:32), and of God uniting all things under Christ's headship (Eph. 1:10), reconciling all things to himself through Christ (Col. 1:20), and bringing every knee to bow to Christ and every tongue to confess his lordship (Phil. 2:10, 11), so that in the end God will be 'all in all' or 'everything to everybody' (1 Cor. 15:28)."[16]

7. Clark H. Pinnock

In the *Criswell Theological Review* (1990) Clark H. Pinnock wrote an article, "The Destruction of the Finally Impenitent." As the title conveys, its emphasis is on destruction, and therefore against eternal punishment. "I consider the concept of hell as endless torment in body and mind an outrageous doctrine, a theological and moral enormity, a bad doctrine of the tradition which needs to be changed." To him such a doctrine "is one nearly like Satan than like God." He asks a crucial question. "Does the one who told us to love our enemies intend to wreak vengeance on his own enemies for all eternity?"[17]

Pinnock reminds us that "the Bible repeatedly uses the language of death, destruction, ruin, and perishing when speaking of the fate of the wicked. It uses the imagery of fire consuming (not torturing) what is thrown into it." Then he puts his finger on a key assumption behind eternal hell, the immortality of the soul.[18] He believes hell "makes God into a bloodthirsty monster who maintains an everlasting Auschwitz for victims whom he does not even allow to die," and wonders "what atrocities have been committed by those who have believed in a God who tortures his enemies." For, after all, "what purpose of God would be served by the unending torture of the wicked except sheer vengeance and vindictiveness?"[19]

Then in his book *A Wideness in God's Mercy* (1992) Clark Pinnock quotes Elton Trueblood approvingly. "What kind of God is it who consigns men and women and children to eternal torment, in spite of the fact that they have not had even a remote chance of knowing the saving truth? What sort of God would create men and women in love, only to irrationally punish the vast majority of them? A God who would thus play favorites with his children, condemning some to eternal separation from himself while admitting others, and distinguishing between them wholly or chiefly on the basis of the accidents of history or geography, over which they had no control, would be more devil than God. In any case he would not even resemble Jesus Christ, and thus there is a contradiction at the heart of the system."[20]

From the discussion above, it is clear that many leading theologians are questioning the doctrine of hell just as they are doubting the immortality of the soul. We continue to examine the discussion in the next chapter.

---

[1] Thomas Welch, *Oregon's Amazing Miracle* (Dallas: Christ for the Nations, Inc.), p. 8, quoted by Maurice Rawlings, *Beyond Death's Door,* pp. 86, 87.

[2] Rawlings, pp. 46, 47.

[3] Nels Ferre, *The Christian Understanding of God* (New York: Harper, 1951), p. 228.

[4] G. C. Berkouwer, *The Return of Christ* (Grand Rapids: Eerdmans, 1972), pp. 415, 416.

[5] William Barclay, *A Spiritual Autobiography* (Grand Rapids: Eerdmans, 1975), pp. 60, 61.

[6] Edward William Fudge, *The Fire That Consumes* (Falbrook, Calif.: Verdict, 1982), p. 221.

[7] *Ibid.,* pp. 111, 112.

[8] *Ibid.,* p. 330.

[9] *Ibid.,* pp. 295, 331.

[10] *Ibid.,* p. 332.

[11] *Ibid.,* p. 333.

[12] Hans Küng, *Eternal Life, Life After Death: as a Medical, Philosophical, and Theological Problem* (New York: Doubleday, 1984), p. 136.

[13] David L. Edwards and John Stott, *Evangelical Essentials: A Liberal-Evangelical Dialogue* (Downers Grove, Ill.: InterVarsity, 1988), pp. 312-314.

[14] *Ibid.,* p. 315.

[15] *Ibid.,* pp. 316, 317.

[16] *Ibid.,* pp. 318, 319.

[17] Clark H. Pinnock, "The Destruction of the Finally Impenitent," *Criswell Theological Review* 4 (1990): 246, 247.

[18] *Ibid.,* pp. 250-252.

[19] *Ibid.,* pp. 253, 254.

[20] Clark H. Pinnock, *A Wideness in God's Mercy: The Finality of Jesus Christ in a World of Religions* (Grand Rapids: Zondervan, 1992), p. 150.

Chapter 24

The Cases for and Against Hell

Let's look at the debate over the reality of hell. Some facts seem to make a case for hell, and others oppose it. First we'll examine the case for hell.

Taught in Scripture

A number of scholars state that they believe Scripture clearly teaches hell.[1] That's why Clark Pinnock rightly says, "The majority of conservative theologians" support the doctrine.[2] Wayne Grudem believes hell "tends to be one of the first doctrines given up by people who are moving away from a commitment to the Bible as absolutely truthful in all that it affirms."[3] In the book *Four Views on Hell,* which examines the literal, metaphorical, purgatorial, and conditional views, John Walvoord suggests that "those who deny scriptural innerrancy naturally have no problem in supporting the idea that eternal punishment does not exist."[4] He claims that "doubting the matter of eternal punishment requires either doubting the Word of God or denying its literal, normal interpretation."[5] Clearly many claim Scripture itself as the reason for their belief in an eternally burning hell.

Taught by Christ

If we can substantiate that Scripture and also Christ teach the concept of hell, then the case for hell would be irrefutable. Scholars believe not only that Scripture presents hell but that Christ was the doctrine's chief exponent. For example, Augustine asked, Who is not terrified by hell as "uttered so vehemently by the lips of the Lord Himself?"[6] Charles Hodge noted that Christ Himself stated "the most solemn and explicit declarations of the everlasting misery of the wicked recorded in the Scriptures."[7] William G. T. Shedd claims that "the strongest support of the doctrine of Endless Punishment is the teaching of Christ, the Redeemer of man."[8] In fact, Shedd says, "Jesus Christ is the Person who is responsible for the doctrine of Eternal Perdition. He is the Being with whom all opponents of this theological tenet are in conflict. Neither the Christian church, nor the Christian ministry are the authors of it."[9]

Gordon R. Lewis and Bruce A. Demarest quote Harry Buis approvingly: "The knowledge of hell comes almost exclusively from the teachings of Christ, who spoke emphatically on the subject on a number of occasions."[10] Harry Buis maintains that Christ "has more to say about hell than any other individual in the Bible."[11] John Walvoord concurs, declaring, "One of the most significant aspects of the doctrine of everlasting punishment is the fact that Jesus himself defined this more specifically and in more instances than any New Testament prophet. All the references to gehenna, except James 3:6, are from the lips of Christ."[12] Donald Guthrie adds: "There is no way of avoiding the conclusion that Jesus firmly accepted that there was a counterpart to heaven for those who were condemned before God."[13]

The issue before us is vital: If Christ taught hell more than any other person in Scripture, then it should become an important part of Christian final events. But if it proves to be false, then the doctrine of hell, like Spiritualism, the Charismatic movement, and the New Age movement come between the Christian and Christ to hide Christ from view.

Examples Seeming to Confirm Hell

Many scholars note that Scripture speaks of eternal life and eternal hell. If the word "eternal" (Gr. *aionios)* means forever for one destiny, then they believe the other destiny is forever also. "Then they will go away to eternal punishment, but the righteous to eternal life" (Matt. 25:46). The words "everlasting" and "eternal" appear repeatedly in connection with hell. For example, Christ says to the wicked, "Depart from me, you who are cursed, into the eternal fire prepared for the devil and his angels" (verse 41). The book of Revelation states that the wicked "will drink of the wine of God's fury, which has been poured full strength into the cup of his wrath. He will be tormented with burning sulfur in the presence of the holy angels and of the Lamb. And the smoke of their torment rises for ever and ever. There is no rest day or night for those who worship the beast and his image, or for anyone who receives the mark of his name" (Rev. 14:10, 11). The passage clearly mentions the duration of time for the punishment.

Scholars refer to the lake of fire mentioned at both ends of the millennium. The beast and the false prophet are "thrown alive into the fiery lake of burning sulfur" (Rev. 19:20) before the millennium, and then after the millennium "the devil, who deceived them, was thrown into the lake of burning sulfur, where the beast and the false prophet had been thrown. They will be tormented day and night for ever and ever" (Rev. 20:10). Thus they believe the fiery lake will blaze for a millennium, after which the devil joins the others, and they all burn forever.

The Case Against Hell

Much of the debate about whether hell is eternal or not depends upon a basic presupposition brought to the biblical texts. We have seen above that one can clearly read eternal hell into the texts given. But that is not the only way Scripture describes the future of the wicked. Many passages speak of their destruction, focusing on the eternity of the result of punishment rather than on the eternity of the process.

1. Annihilation and Justice

A myth holds that the wicked are annihilated at death. Perhaps Wayne Grudem had this in mind when he said that if there is no eternal hell, then "Hitler and Stalin would have nothing coming to them, and there would be no ultimate justice in the universe. Then people would have great incentive to be as wicked as possible in this life."[14] It is an important point, for truly if death is the only end for the wicked, then how would justice be served? Below, we will examine the doctrine of hell from the broader standpoint of God's justice. Here we ask the narrower question, "Can a temporary hell punish Hitler and Stalin more than others?"

Justice demands that punishment be proportionate to the crimes committed. Thus one would expect Satan and fallen angels, who caused all the unredeemed to be lost, would suffer greater punishment than humans. The fact that Satan and his angels get thrown into the fiery lake a thousand years after the beast and the false prophet (mentioned above, see Rev. 19:20, 21; 20:10), and after many more millennia if the wicked go straight to hell at death (as some believe), then it raises drastic questions about God's justice. Why should humans suffer so much longer than Satan, who caused them to sin in the first place (assuming that the intensity of heat is the same for all)?

If Scripture teaches the annihilation of the wicked, then we need to interpret the language of eternity accordingly. For the wicked cannot be both burning and burnt up. Nor can they be both suffering eternal torment and annihilated. The two are mutually exclusive. And if Scripture presents both unending torment and annihilation, then it needs to qualify the word "unending" within the context of the process, as unending until annihilation takes place. That is, the punishment is continuous until complete. In this context God can mete out appropriate punishment on an individual basis, fulfilling the demands of justice.

2. Is Universalism a Viable Option?

Origen (c. 185-254) is the father of universalism, even saying that Satan and his angels will eventually be redeemed. Only a few, such as Gregory of Nyssa (c. 385-394), John Scotus of Erigena (c. 810-877), and John Denck (1500?-1527), espoused it before the seventeenth century. Since then numerous individuals, including Friedrich Schleiermacher, the leading theologian of the nineteenth century, and Karl Barth, the leading theologian of the twentieth century until the 1960s,[15] have advocated it.

Its proponents give various reasons for universalism. The most important is the outworking in history of what Christ completed on the cross. He died for everyone, so eventually God's irresistible grace will convert all. A classic example of this view is Karl Barth's system. His christology is so universalistically focused that the momentum of his system inevitably ends in universalism, his belated protestations not withstanding. Barth's system resembles a train that has gone a long journey (8,000 pages) and comes too quickly into the station and cannot stop, even though the engineer applies the brakes just before impact.

Universalism has also developed as a reaction to the doctrine of endless torture in hell. Whereas the love of God gets lost in an eternal hell, the doctrine of universal salvation seems to capture it. Although they are opposite emphases, they share a common problem. Both are thought through within a confined biblical worldview. When one looks at both from the vantage of the cosmic controversy worldview, then it would not be just for God to save those who do not desire salvation. He would be forcing people into a destiny not of their choosing, and this is no different from decreeing that some should be lost in hell simply as God's choice.

But when we view things within the framework of a cosmic struggle between good and evil, we recognize that the two sides of the conflict will exist right up to the end. The fact that the world is full of people who hate God and have nothing to do with Him is evidence that their destiny is not the same as those who love and serve Him. God will be seen as just by the fact that He will honor the choice of both groups, and hence universalism is no better an option than eternal hell as far as the issue in the universe about God's justice is concerned.

3. Is Annihilation a Viable Option?

If Scripture presents annihilation as well as eternal hell, then it's not correct to view them as mutually exclusive, as systems of theology almost universally do. Rather than an "either or" approach, one must be open to both views, allowing both to inform each other of their biblical meaning. If Scripture teaches both, then both are equally biblical and are a part of the inerrant Word of God. When both sides of the debate claim that Scripture and Christ are on their side, we need to penetrate to the fact that both are right. Instead of the two options sparring, biblical hermeneutics must accept both views and work out their interrelationship.

Supposing that both eternal hell and annihilation appear in Scripture, then it must present both in the context of God's judgment on the wicked. Both concepts form a part of His punishment of the lost. Eternal hell explains the process of punishment, whereas annihilation completes it. If there is a process, then it cannot be an instantaneous annihilation, and so the biblical perspective seriously takes the question about the justice in punishing Hitler or Stalin. There are degrees of punishment. I believe most theologians do not think of annihilation in this context. For example, James Leo Garrett affirms that "annihilation undermines the biblical teaching on degrees of punishment."[16] Annihilation is not instantaneous, however, but comes after the process of punishment, with persons such as Hitler and Stalin receiving longer or greater punishment. Because God is just, He metes out a just punishment for each. Given the cosmic controversy over divine justice, it is necessary that both the process and completion of punishment reflect His justice. We'll address this in the next section. For now, we'll consider if annihilation is a viable biblical option.

In Scripture the phrase "the day of the Lord" often refers to a time of destruction. It has in mind both the Second Advent and the final judgment at the end of the millennium. Sometimes the Old Testament links a present day of the Lord with the eschatological day of the Lord. "Wail, for the day of the Lord is near; it will come like destruction from the Almighty" (Isa. 13:6). "What a dreadful day! For the day of the Lord is near; it will come like destruction from the Almighty" (Joel 1:15). The Old Testament witnesses to a past day of the Lord that destroyed the world in a deluge, in which the inhabitants all perished (Gen. 7; 8).

Paul says of those who live as enemies of the cross of Christ, "Their destiny is destruction" (Phil. 3:19). At the second advent of Christ, "while people are saying, 'Peace and safety,' destruction will come on them suddenly" (1 Thess. 5:3). For God will appear "destroying those who destroy the earth" (Rev. 11:18). The apostle emphasizes the justice of God in His punishment of the wicked. "God is just: He will pay back trouble to those who trouble you and give relief to you who are troubled, and to us as well. This will happen when the Lord Jesus is revealed from heaven in blazing fire with his powerful angels. He will punish those who do not know God and do not obey the gospel of our Lord Jesus. They will be punished with everlasting destruction and shut out from the presence of the Lord and the majesty of his power on the day he comes" (2 Thess. 1:6-10).

Scripture repeatedly associates the Second Advent with destroying fire. "See, the Lord is coming with fire, and his chariots are like a whirlwind; he will bring down his anger with fury, and his rebuke with flames of fire. For with fire and with his sword the Lord will execute judgment upon all men, and many will be those slain by the Lord" (Isa. 66:15, 16). Note that the fire and sword slay humans rather than place them in eternal torment. Zephaniah emphasizes the same thing. "The great day of the Lord is near. . . . That day will be a day of wrath. . . . In the fire of his jealousy the whole world will be consumed, for he will make a sudden end of all who live in the earth" (Zeph. 1:14-18).

Peter says that just as a flood destroyed the world, so "the present heavens and earth are reserved for fire, being kept for the day of judgment and destruction of ungodly men. . . . The heavens will disappear with a roar; the elements will be destroyed by fire, and the earth and everything in it will be laid bare. . . . That day will bring about the destruction of the heavens by fire, and the elements will melt in the heat. But in keeping with his promise we are looking forward to a new heaven and a new earth, the home of righteousness" (2 Peter 3:7-13). The burning of the old earth and heavens will purify them, eradicating sin and sinners. Hell is not purgatorial, but penal and purificatory. "'Surely the day is coming; it will burn like a furnace. All the arrogant and every evildoer will be stubble, and that day that is coming will set them on fire,' says the Lord Almighty. 'Not a root or a branch will be left to them'" (Malachi 4:1).

Here in Malachi God makes very clear that the fire consumes, destroying the wicked and preparing the way for new heavens (surrounding our planet) and a new earth. Such a hell will be intense and will be eternal in endurance until it has completed its work. It's significant that Christ speaks of hell in 11 places, using the word *Gehenna*. It was the name for a rubbish dump south of Jerusalem, where the flames burned constantly. That fire was eternal, in that it remained alight until it had burned up everything possible, a perfect representation of the Gehenna eschatological hellfire. The fire in Jerusalem's *Gehenna* went out nearly 2,000 years ago. So the future *Gehenna* hellfire will cease when it has consumed everything, and all is purified, ready for Christ to recreate the heavens and the earth.

The Bible clearly connects destruction with Christ's return. The fire consumes rather than remaining forever, thus qualifying the "fiery lake" (Rev. 19:20), the "eternal fire" (Matt. 25:41), and "no rest day or night" (Rev. 14:11). The "eternal fire" leads to "everlasting destruction" (2 Thess. 1:9). It is the means to the end of everlasting destruction. As for the two sides of the presentation about hell in Scripture, we need to hold them together. They are the two parts of God's one judgment on the wicked. Hell is a process of being consumed rather than of eternal life. Only the saints receive the gift of eternal life, never the wicked.

If we maintain this balance between the process and its penal and purification consummation, then we will more clearly understand God's true justice. This leads us to think about the debate between eternal hell or annihilation from the vantage point of the biblical worldview. Hellfire does have an end. God is not a cosmic cook, miraculously keeping human bodies alive so they can roast forever. Fire will do what fire always does, just as the floodwaters did what they always do in Noah's day. "'Then you will trample down the wicked; they will be ashes under the soles of your feet on the day when I do these things,' says the Lord Almighty" (Mal. 4:3). This divine commentary must interpret the words of Christ when He said of hell, "the fire never goes out" (Mark 9:43). Members of the Godhead spoke both passages describing the same hell judgment. God does not lie (Num. 23:19). We must do equal justice to both divine statements. They tell us that the fire never goes out until it has accomplished its purpose, including the annihilation of the wicked.

Scripture mentions the process and completion of hell in connection with Satan. He is "thrown into the lake of burning sulfur" to "be tormented day and night for ever and ever" (Rev. 20:10) and will be "consumed" and reduced "to ashes" (Eze. 28:18). Now, if that is true of the arch rebel in the cosmic controversy, then it's also true of all others, both angels and humans, who joined him in rebellion.

The book of Revelation gives the destiny of the nations of the world. The biblical writer presents it in the past tense to indicate its certainty, and it takes place at the close of the millennium at the destruction of Satan.

"They marched across the breadth of the earth and surrounded the camp of God's people, the city he loves. But fire came down from heaven and devoured them" (Rev. 20:9). All the wicked perish, so that this second death (verse 6) is really death in its finality. Here is the final realization that when God said in Eden that sin brings death, He was right. The universe truly sees that Satan's denial that sin brings death is false. There is no eternal hell as a process, but there is an eternal result to hell as penalty.

[1] For example, Millard J. Erickson, *Christian Theology* (Grand Rapids: Baker, 1986), p. 1235; Harry Buis, *The Doctrine of Eternal Punishment* (Grand Rapids: Baker, 1957), p. ix.

[2] Clark Pinnock, "The Destruction of the Finally Impenitent," *Criswell Theological Review* 4 (1990): 248.

[3] Wayne Grudem, *Systematic Theology* (Grand Rapids: Zondervan, 1994), p. 1151.

[4] John Walvoord in *Four Views of Hell* (Grand Rapids: Zondervan, 1992), p. 12.

[5] *Ibid.,* pp. 26, 27.

[6] Augustine, "The City of God," *The Nicene and Post-Nicene Fathers,* First Series (Edinburgh, Scotland: T & T Clark, 1988), vol. 2, p. 461.

[7] Charles Hodge, *Systematic Theology* (Grand Rapids: Eerdmans, n.p.d.), vol. 3, p. 880.

[8] William G. T. Shedd, *Dogmatic Theology* (Grand Rapids: Zondervan, n.p.d.), vol. 2, p. 675.

[9] *Ibid.,* p. 680.

[10] Gordon R. Lewis and Bruce A. Demarest, *Integrative Theology* (Grand Rapids: Zondervan, 1994), vol. 3, p. 478.

[11] Harry Buis, *The Doctrine of Eternal Punishment* (Grand Rapids: Baker, 1957), p. 33.

[12] Walvoord, *Four Views of Hell,* pp. 19, 20.

[13] Donald Guthrie, *New Testament Theology,* p. 888.

[14] Wayne Grudem, *Systematic Theology* (Grand Rapids: Zondervan, 1994), p. 1151.

[15] See James Leo Garrett, *Systematic Theology,* vol. 2, pp. 795, 796, for names of those who taught universalism.

[16] *Ibid.,* p. 806.

Chapter 25

The Biblical Worldview and Hell

Hell, no!" the bystander blurted. "I wouldn't be seen dead with him for anything!" "We had a hell of a time." The frightened mother clasped her child close. "The police caught the kidnapper three hours after the abduction."

"Go to hell!" the teenager shouted at a gang member.

The trouble is that people use the word "hell" today more than the word "heaven." That's because life is a stress-filled, hectic-paced existence. It's more like the one than the other. What a tragedy that so many misunderstand hell! God has received a bad reputation over the doctrine. Countless millions of people have rejected Him because of it. "If He does that to His children, forget it! His love is just a farce!" So we need to penetrate to who is behind this bad press about God. Satan has pushed the concept of hell to obscure Calvary. They are mutually exclusive. How can God love to the depths if He punishes without mercy? It's the same old game we've noticed throughout the book. He hates the cross because he lost there, and he will do anything to make the Crucifixion appear unimportant. Hell suits his purpose well.

We have seen that we need to harmonize both the data about eternal hell and annihilation, because both appear in Scripture. But we must view the topic from a further vantage point as we take a more careful look at the debate, thus enabling us to find a definitive answer.

The biblical worldview is greater than just the issue of human salvation or damnation. It transcends human destiny to the cosmic controversy between God and Satan. In chapter 2 we saw that Satan envies God and wants to take His place. The fact that he influenced a third of the holy angels to join him in rebellion against God indicates that he must have distorted the truth about God. What would lead holy angels to war against the One who created them? Only if Satan portrayed God to them as unjust, arbitrary, severe, and as keeping something back from them would even angels join the rebellion. Satan wanted to become like God, sit on His throne, and rule. What better way to stir the angels to rebel than to promote the view that God had been unjust to him (Satan) and his angels.

After his expulsion from heaven, Satan in Eden tempted Eve to disbelieve God's word about death. "You will not surely die" (Gen. 3:4), he assured her. It was as if he had said, "God is keeping something back from you. Eat the fruit, and you will become as God." The devil's temptation to Eve gives insight into the same approach Satan probably used in heaven. His studied strategy sought to cause angels and humans to doubt God, His word, and hence His justice.

If Satan is right that humans do not die, then they live on at death and will do so for eternity; hence there must be an eternal hell. Immortal souls simply cannot be annihilated. By contrast, the Creator Christ warned that eating the fruit would bring death (Gen. 2:17), and that final disobedience will bring the second death (Rev. 20:6). The debate over hell brings us squarely back to the two opposing predictions of God and Satan about human death in Eden.

The Question of Justice

We have seen that a temporary hell with the process ending in annihilation seems to fit the biblical data better if we follow the Protestant principle of *sola Scriptura,* in which Scripture interprets Scripture. Thus we interpret the eternity of hell by the destruction caused by hell. It becomes an even more important conclusion when we face the fact that theologians use the eternity of hell as evidence for divine justice. But to burn them forever because they messed up for 70 years? What kind of justice is that?

1. Hell as a Demonstration of God's Justice

Catholic theologian Karl Rahner suggests that hell is "a manifestation of the justice of God," that "the just God is 'active' in the punishment of hell only insofar as he does not release man from the reality of the definitive state which man himself has achieved on his own behalf, contradictory though this state be to the world as God's creation."[1] It reminds us of Thomas Aquinas, who said, "Fire continues in that place for all eternity by the ordering of Divine justice,"[2] for "it seems just that for a mortal sin a man should be punished for ever."[3] Aquinus even declares that the wicked "are punished less than they deserve."[4]

He further suggests that everlasting punishment has two purposes. "First, because thereby the Divine justice is safeguarded which is acceptable to God for its own sake." For, quoting Gregory, "He is for ever unappeased by the punishment of the wicked." "Secondly, they are useful, because the elect rejoice therein, when they see God's justice in them, and realize that they have escaped them."[5] Gregory says that "it belongs to the great justice of the judge that those should never cease to be punished, who in this life never ceased to desire sin."[6] Did these men ever put themselves in the place of the lost? It seems that they glibly speak such things, smug in the thought that they won't have to experience them.

Wayne Grudem quotes two texts in Revelation: "'The smoke from her

[Babylon] goes for ever and ever' (Rev. 19:3)" and "'they will be tormented day and night for ever and ever' (Rev. 20:10)." He then comments that "these verses should make us realize the immensity of the evil that is found in sin and rebellion against God, and the magnitude of the holiness and the justice of God that calls forth this kind of punishment."[7] In other words, the eternity of hell reveals the enormity of sin and God's holiness and justice. It is the last word that is of interest to us as Grudem identifies God's justice with the unending punishment of hell. "It may help us to realize," he says, "that if God were not to execute eternal punishment, then, apparently, his justice would not be satisfied."[8]

William G. T. Shedd believed that punishment satisfies justice.[9] In hell, "justice is the very first thing, and constitutes the essence of it."[10] If we deny that God is just, that human beings have free will and sin is voluntary, then "there can be no defense of endless punishment."[11] Clearly, in his view, God's justice is linked with the everlastingness of hell. Harry Buis points out "that God would have been perfectly just with men if he had let all go their way to their own condemnation. Men ought not to criticize God for sending some to hell, but rather praise God for lifting some above that fate which they absolutely deserved, and giving them the gift of eternal life."[12]

Charles Hodge concludes his three-volume *Systematic Theology* by answering objections about hell, attempting to refute those who believe hell is not "consistent with the justice of God."[13] First, he suggests that "we are incompetent judges of the penalty which sin deserves." By contrast, "God only knows; and, therefore, the penalty which He imposes on sin is the only just measure of its ill desert." Second, "if it be inconsistent with the justice of God that men should perish for their sins, then redemption is not a matter of grace, or undeserved mercy."[14] Third, sin is infinite because human beings commit it "against a person of infinite dignity." Fourth, because while in hell "the lost continue to sin forever they may justly be punished forever."[15]

Hodge then gives three points relative to God's goodness in his attempt to respond to the charge that hell is incompatible with divine goodness. First, he says if the goodness of God allowed sin and misery to be the lot of the human race since the Fall, why could not this same goodness allow "some of them to remain miserable forever"? Two, the number of lost compared "with the whole number of the saved will be very inconsiderable." And third, "it should constrain us to humility, and to silence on this subject, that the most solemn and explicit declarations of the everlasting misery of the wicked recorded in the Scriptures, fell from the lips of Him, who, though equal with God, was found in fashion as a man, and humbled Himself unto death, even the death of the cross, for us men and for our salvation."[16] With these words Charles Hodge ends his systematic theology.

Whereas Charles Hodge believed that only a few humans will go to hell, Augustine concluded the majority would. After thinking through several alternatives in examining God's justice, he said, "If all had remained under the punishment of just condemnation, there would have been seen in no one the mercy of redeeming grace. And, on the other hand, if all had been transferred from darkness to light, the severity of retribution would have been manifested in none. But many more are left under punishment than are delivered from it, in order that it may thus be shown what was due to all. And had it been inflicted on all, no one could justly have found fault with the justice of Him who taketh vengeance; whereas, in the deliverance of so many from that just award, there is cause to render the most cordial thanks to the gratuitous bounty of Him who delivers."[17]

In his 1995 book *Whatever Happened to Hell?* John Blanchard concurs with Paul Helm in stating that "hell is a place of justice, where punishment is dispensed not in accordance with the warped and partial and ignorant procedures of human society, but immaculately, in accord with the standards of him who is supremely just."[18] In another place Blanchard approvingly quotes Helm, saying that hell "is not a demonic colony which has gained unilateral independence from God. Because there is full recognition of God's justice, God's character is vindicated."[19] Blanchard believes that God's eternal hatred of the wicked is a manifestation of His justice.[20] "Nothing will more vividly demonstrate God's awesome power and justice than the fact that unrepentant sinners will be unable to escape the consequences of their impenitence or to bring either ease or end to the punishment that their wickedness properly deserves. God glorifies Himself in their eternal damnation."[21]

He further contends that annihilation of the wicked would be unjust and immoral. If hell is for the punishment of sins, and that payment has been made in full, Blanchard asks, "surely a God of justice would then welcome them into heaven, rather than consign them to non-existence."[22] Of course he does not believe such infinite evil can ever be paid for. Rejection of God is an infinite evil, he holds, and it demands infinite punishment, so that "the infinite sufferings of hell exactly fit the crime of which the wicked are guilty and are ultimate example of God's perfect justice."[23]

Blanchard recognizes that "the character of God is at stake here. God's punishment of sinners is not something done in a fit of temper which might blow over after a while. Instead, it is the outcome of His perfect justice and unchanging hatred of evil. That being the case, there will never be a time when God will 'cool off' and take a more lenient view of the sinner's stubborn rebellion."[24] As a result, he dismisses the need for human beings to understand the justice of hell. "If we are honest," he says, "must we not say that there are times when even the Bible's record of God's dealings with His people 'makes no sense'? Does this mean that we must find some explanation that will fit in with our own earth-bound ideas of love, or justice, or fairness? To do that would be tantamount to making God in our own image."[25]

2. Evaluation of God's Justice

God's justice is the central issue in the cosmic controversy. A part of the larger biblical worldview overlooked by most Christians, it also constitutes a vital aspect of final events, as we'll see later. Thus it is crucial that we examine any defense of hell in the light of this broader biblical worldview. As we have seen, the cosmic controversy involves an attack of creaturely beings against their Creator. Satan and his angels rebelled against God, believing that He was unjust and that their existence would be better if they severed their connection from Him.

We should not forget that many scholars see the greatest defense for eternal hell as coming from the teaching of Christ Himself.[26] Yet the same Christ taught human beings to love their enemies (Luke 6:27) and those who persecute them (Matt. 5:44). On the cross He prayed for forgiveness to those who crucified Him (Luke 23:34). We know that He practices what He teaches and will not treat His enemies in the future any different than the way He did in His human life. To say that hell is eternally punishing those who rejected Him, that God does so because He hates them, and that He is eternally revengeful against them is to accept the picture of God that Satan all along has foisted onto the universe. The life and death of Jesus resoundingly refuted such a portrayal. And God is no different from Christ. Jesus assured His disciples that in seeing Him they had witnessed the true revelation of God the Father (see John 14:9).

Furthermore, when Jesus became humanity's substitute and bore the sins of all (see 2 Cor. 5:21), dying for a lost world (John 3:16), He did not suffer eternally in a place called hell. The sins He assumed quickly crushed out His life as He died the death of a sinner. His death was separation from His Father that wrung from Him the mournful words, "My God, my God, why have you forsaken me?" (Mark 15:34). If Christ had been only human, His separation from God would have been eternal. If He had really been a sinner, He would have died what Scripture calls the second death (see Rev. 20:6), the final death as judgment for sins.

As noted in the previous chapter, death is a cessation of life. Any view of death that presupposes it as an entrance into a different kind of existence is no different from the pagan views of inherent immortality. God warned in Eden that eating the fruit from the forbidden tree would result in death. Since then death has been humanity's lot. If Christ had not come to die in our place, then death would have been an eternal separation from God. Because Christ died, a resurrection now awaits us, at which time those choosing eternal life will be with Christ forever.

The difference between the saved and the lost concerns this matter of separation from God. The saved will remain with God because they have accepted Christ's death in their place. But the lost will be sundered from God because they have rejected it. In this way the justice of God is upheld. He does not force either group in their decisions and hence does not predetermine their destiny. God issues no eternal decree to predestine some for salvation and the rest to be lost. This would not be just, because it would ignore the response of human freedom to God's love for all humanity. Life is probationary time to give human beings opportunity to respond to Him out of their God-given freedom. He respects creaturely freedom, and as such is just.

Life's decisions form character, character makes us who we are, and who we are determines whether we would enjoy being with God for eternity or not. The reason why God does not save the lost is because they could not stand being in His presence. In mercy God will allow them to be separated from Him forever, because to go to heaven would be a hell-like experience for them. They would be eternally miserable in the presence of infinite purity. By contrast, the saved will revel in His presence forever. A God of justice and love has no delight in making people miserable. To suggest that He will forever delight in the writhings of His children in hell is the most grotesque perversion of God's character possible, and makes Him out to be like Satan, His archrival, whose fiendish cunning would delight in such horrendous injustice.

Satan's studied strategy seeks to present a false picture of God. When God said sin would bring death, the devil responded, "You will not surely die." From his premise has issued a false view of survival of the soul beyond death and an accompanying view of eternal punishment. If the alleged essence of humans is beyond death, then there has to be an unending punishment for the lost to deal with that fact. I believe that the idea of an eternal burning hell is one of the most powerful weapons Satan has used in the cosmic controversy to get human beings to reject God. Such a view destroys the revelation of God's love made at Calvary. How can anyone associate such a demonstration of utter love with such a picture of endless punishment? The effects, and not the process, of Calvary are eternal. Likewise, the effects of hell, and not the process, are final. The eternal result of Calvary and the eternal process of hell are mutually exclusive. The Christ of Calvary is not the God of eternal hell.

3. Second Death and God's Justice

Yet those espousing eternal hell do so from the perspective of what they offer as God's justice. They believe that it is just for God to eternally burn humans who have sinned against Him, an infinite Being. Some even suggest that one sin against an infinite Being merits infinite punishment. Wayne Grudem says in humility, "We have to admit that the ultimate resolution of the depths of this question lies far beyond our ability to understand, and remains hidden in the counsels of God."[27] I can appreciate his point, as it comes from within the confined salvation-damnation worldview. But from the broader cosmic controversy biblical worldview, in which it matters very much that humans understand whether God is just or not, we cannot have anything hidden somewhere in divine counsels. If that were the case, the cosmic-controversy issue would forever remain unresolved. In fact, it is the view of hell espoused by Wayne Grudem and others that calls divine justice into question. Many theologians from the Calvinistic-Reformed wing of the Reformation approach this question in relation to a hidden decree by a *Deus absconditus,* or hidden God, behind Christ, a position that Karl Barth rejected vigorously.

Our reply to this logic is to point out that God does want to solve the question of His justice before the universe from the perspective of creaturely beings. Created beings act as the jury. The revelation of God's dealings with created beings has to be seen as just from their perspective, and not merely from the divine perspective. To say God is just and then expect intelligent created beings to submissively accept that claim is not good enough. God desires to be seen as just in all that He has done for created beings, including their future destiny in heaven or hell.

If God permits the cosmic controversy so that created beings can see the evidence and vote accordingly, then no amount of pleading that hell is just from God's perspective will be helpful. In fact, if God's justice is locked into His perspective and not that of created beings, then God could have destroyed Satan and the fallen angels at the inception of their rebellion and expected all other creaturely beings to accept such an act as perfectly just. Though their rebellion deserved such an end, God knew that if He had destroyed the rebels immediately, created beings would then have served Him out of fear and not from love. The very fact of a continuing rebellion suggests that God desires created beings to see that He is just, so that after the controversy reaches its conclusion, rebellion will never arise again. Here is what is really at stake rather than a mere divine definition of justice. God has the good of the universe in mind. Its inhabitants need to *see* that He is just and not just hear from Him that it is the case. They must arrive at this decision on the basis of concrete evidence.

But what about the second death? Why does God resurrect the lost only to destroy them? Is this fair? Revelation 20 mentions two resurrections. Martyrs of the end-time, who refused to worship the beast and his image, rise to reign with Christ for 1,000 years (verse 4; cf. Rev. 13:11-15), and finally the rest of the dead who do "not come to life until the thousand years were ended" (Rev. 20:5). So two separate resurrections bracket the millennium. Those raised at the beginning of the millennium also include all the righteous, for at the second advent of Christ "the dead in Christ will rise" (1 Thess. 4:16). "Given authority to judge" (Rev. 20:4), they are "blessed and holy," for they "have part in the first resurrection. The second death has no power over them" and they "reign with him [Christ] for a thousand years" (verse 6).

By contrast, the second resurrection brings to life those subject to the second death—the lost of all generations. If the first resurrection returns to life those who will participate in the process of judgment, what does the second resurrection say about those raised in it? They too will have opportunity to judge. First each will individually receive a judgment. "The dead were judged according to what they had done as recorded in the books" (verse 12). Those who judged during the 1,000 years looked into those same records to see if God was just to confine them to the second death. The redeemed are satisfied that God has judged justly. They see that such people are unfitted for fellowship with a holy God and that in mercy God allows the unrepentant wicked to have their choice to be separate from Him. The lost multitudes rise from the grave to receive their just punishment. A Hitler or a Stalin faces no simple death. Justice demands just retribution. That is why God will return to life all the wicked who have ever lived. But before they receive their punishment, they have the chance to see where their life has brought them, and each one will realize that lurking behind all they have done is their own deliberate rejection of Christ's gift of salvation.

The important fact is that each person will see and admit that God is truly and undeniably just. The millennial and postmillennial judgments have everything to do with God's justice. The fact that God will take some fallen humans to heaven and not others makes these judgments necessary. God does not require them Himself because He is omniscient (Ps. 33:13-15; 56:8; 104:24; Isa. 44:28; 46:9, 10; Mal. 3:16; Rom. 11:33; Eph. 3:10), and hence He recognizes who will be saved and who will be lost. But because the cosmic controversy has raised that question of God's justice, His omniscience is not sufficient basis for ignoring investigative judgments. God wants His created beings to see for themselves that He is just, and so He allows the righteous to examine the records of the lost during the 1,000 years so that they completely satisfy themselves with His justice. Then He provides time for the resurrected wicked to consider if it is fair that they have forfeited heaven and life. We need to realize that unfallen and fallen angels, as well as the saved and lost humans, all participate in this examination of God's justice. If the universe had no question about God's justice, then He could unilaterally decide who will be lost and who saved without any reference to creaturely questioning, just as He could have destroyed Satan and his rebels in the beginning.

Revelation 5 provides insight into the fact that the question of God's justice involves all creaturely beings. Christ as the slain Lamb (verse 6) takes the scroll from the Father on the throne (verse 7). It causes redeemed humans (the 24 elders) to sing, "You are worthy to take the scroll and to open its seals, because you were slain, and with your blood you purchased men for God from every tribe and language and people and nation. You have made them to be a kingdom and priests to serve our God, and they will reign on the earth" (verses 9, 10).

John introduces a second group. "Then I looked," the apostle said, "and heard the voice of many angels, numbering thousands upon thousands, and ten thousand times ten thousand. They encircled the throne and the living creatures and the elders. In a loud voice they sang: 'Worthy is the Lamb, who was slain, to receive power and wealth and wisdom and strength and honor and glory and praise!'" (verses 11, 12).

Still another group joins the redeemed humans and unfallen angels. "Then I heard every creature in heaven and on earth and under the earth and on the sea and all that is in them, singing: 'To him who sits on the throne and to the

Lamb be praise and honor and glory and power for ever and ever' " (verse 13).

I believe they represent all the other created beings throughout the cosmos, whether fallen or unfallen, thus including fallen angels and humans as well as the unfallen created beings from any inhabited planets throughout the universe. Thus fallen human beings will also sing praise to God and to Christ as a result of their own self-judgment. In that final moment they clearly see the issues of the cosmic controversy. They recognize that Christ has given the ultimate revelation of what God is like in His death at Calvary. The lost acknowledge that God has done everything to assure their salvation. Only by their own rejection of that gift have they made themselves unfit for heaven, and although forced from unwilling lips, they cannot help but proclaim the justice of God in view of the overwhelming evidence. Only then will God allow them their choice to be forever separate from Him. This is the second death.

4. Second Death as Death

The second death is both like and unlike the first death. Like the first death, it really means a cessation of existence. Death in Scripture is never non-death. Unlike the first death, no resurrection will ever follow it. It is the final death, the death that comes to all the wicked, the same death that would have happened to Satan and his angels and to each human who has ever died if there had been no cosmic controversy about God's justice before the universe. It's only after all the universe has acknowledged God's justice—and this includes all the fallen angels and humans—that God can safely destroy the wicked. When every created being who ever lived votes about divine justice—and votes unanimously in support of His justice—they can accept their destiny as the inevitable result of their own choice. Thus God is seen to be just. No hidden divine decree has made the difference. Nor are people in heaven through fear of hell. The cross alone drew people to Christ. But its rejection unfits people for heaven. All see that salvation rests not with creaturely merit but solely with divine grace.

When the vast multitude of the saved and lost coexist together momentarily at the end of the millennium, all view their lives in the light of Christ's death for them. They see that judgment day has already taken place. It occurred at Calvary (Rev. 12:9-11). There Christ was judged a sinner in their place. There He took the punishment due them. There He died the second death that all humans deserve. And there He conquered hell for them.

5. Earth Made New

If one works out his or her theology within the confines of a salvation-damnation worldview, then the eternity of both may seem to be no problem. And this is essentially how most have reasoned about hell during most of the history of Christian thought. But when we break beyond the confines of salvation-damnation to the cosmic controversy before the universe, then the conflict necessitates a resolution. Is God just or not? As noted above, all created beings will vote on the issue; then there will be a New Jerusalem on a new earth (Rev. 21:1, 2). God "will wipe every tear from their eyes. There will be no more death or mourning or crying or pain, for the old order of things has passed away. He who was seated on the throne said, 'I am making everything new!' Then he said, 'Write this down, for these words are trustworthy and true'" (verses 4, 5). The universe returns to the pristine harmony present before the cosmic controversy began.

It is important that we unpack the two verses just quoted. God emphasized that they are true. Satan questioned His first words about death in Genesis 3:1-4, and now at the end of Scripture God speaks about death again and underlines that what He says is accurate. There will be no more death. So far the concept of eternal hell could go along with such a view, for none will die in hell. But the verses go further than that. There will be no more tears or pain. God makes no exception such as "except those who suffer in hell." In fact, Scripture says "the old order of things has passed away." This is the key. The old earth with sinners and sin is no more. The new earth and New Jerusalem and the redeemed have replaced it.

The passage goes on to show why it is a new order, for the wicked are thrown into "the fiery lake of burning sulfur. This is the second death" (Rev. 21:8). Here the book of Revelation defines the fiery lake (viewed as hell by most) as the second death, and not as an eternal existence.

A number of those espousing an eternal hell think of God as eternally hating the wicked, and, as Thomas Aquinas believes, the wicked will eternally hate God.[28] But this does not resolve the cosmic controversy. It is not good enough for William G. T. Shedd to suggest that "the Bible teaches that there will always be some sin, and some death, in the universe. Some angels and men will forever be the enemies of God."[29] The fact of the matter is "the wages of sin is death" (Rom. 6:23), and "the last enemy to be destroyed is death" itself (1 Cor. 15:26).

The fuzzy idea of what constitutes death lies behind William Shedd's statement and the various views of eternal hell. Precisely this question of death is what launched the cosmic controversy on our planet (Gen. 3:1-4). God has always taken death seriously, as we best see in the death of Christ. Satan has attempted to remove the seriousness of death by rejecting death as the price of sin in the garden of Eden and then getting Christians to accept both the continued existence of the soul beyond death and of the wicked forever in hell.

Satan foists his view of death upon the whole world in a variety of ways. Pagan religions, such as Hinduism and Buddhism, believe in the transmigration of souls, just as the New Age movement postulates multiple lives for souls joining different bodies. The devil's view of death has also permeated philosophy. The concept of the immortality of the soul fills the Greek philosophical writings of Socrates and Plato. But Satan has not stopped at getting the pagan religions and philosophies to accept his position on death. He has penetrated into biblical and theological study throughout much of Christian thought. They echo pagan sources in that they share the same basic assumption that death is not really the end of existence, but some passage to further existence in an intermediate state until Christ's return, and that the second death is not death but a further eternal existence in hell.

The non-Christian views of multiple lives in different bodies have obvious differences when you compare them to the multiple experiences (embodied and disembodied) that most Christians espouse. Living many lives in order to become fitted for heaven in non-Christian thinking is not totally the same as living one life on earth (evangelical) or one extended beyond in purgatory (Catholic) in Christian thought. Although such differences are not inconsequential in themselves, they are inconsequential, though, when compared to the basic assumption that gives them status. That basic premise, shared across the board by both pagan and Christian thinking, holds that death is not death, is not a cessation of all existence. Once you accept that assumption, then an eternal existence in hell logically follows.

We see the reason Satan is so interested in the question of death demonstrated several ways in Eden. He wanted Eve to doubt God's word ("You will surely die"), and he sought to get her to question God's justice (God held back something from humans by forbidding them to eat the fruit). Also he aimed to get her to misunderstand the enormity of sin (sin will not bring death). If sin does not bring death, then it cannot be that bad. Having deceived Eve, and subsequently the human race, he shifted tactics. What we hear now from scholars is that only one finite sin against an infinite God is sufficient to condemn the sinner to eternal torture at the hands of a just God. The enormity of sin was less than it should have been in Satan's lie in Eden and is now far greater than it should have been in the doctrine of hell today.

I believe that the doctrine of hell has done more than any other to drive people away from God. The picture of an arbitrary, severe, heartless, and angry God who delights in the eternal torture of His children has repulsed countless numbers of individuals. Especially when Christians argue that hell includes those that God did not elect to save, and then confined them to endless agony, merely because it is His will. The heartless idea that saints will rejoice to see the wicked writhing in hell because they will realize how gracious God is to save them; that they will rejoice as they see their own mother cast into hell; that God will be eternally angry at the wicked—all ideas show to what extent Satan's cunning has worked even among Christians, as he foists his picture of an unjust God upon all humanity.

The terrible paradox is that people consider such an unjust portrayal of God as actually evidence of His justice. As we saw earlier, some claim that God is just in condemning the wicked to eternal torture. It seems to me that the existence of an eternal hell would forever have the potential of causing created beings to raise the same question about God's justice as Satan did in the beginning. An eternal hell means that the universe has an eternal dualism. Good and evil will coexist, as if God were not greater than evil. But the fact that sin cannot exist in the presence of a holy God, who is a consuming fire, must always guide our understanding of the destruction of the wicked. The second death is not eternal hell. It's the last enemy—permanent death. A cleansing fire, it eradicates all evil from the universe, so that sin and sinners are no more, restoring harmony to all existence.

Furthermore, if God makes a new earth, then where will hell be? Jonathan Edwards said that "the world will probably be converted into a great lake or liquid globe of fire, in which the wicked shall be overwhelmed, which shall always be in tempest."[30] Such a view of hell contradicts the biblical promise of a new earth (Rev. 21:1).

6. No Immortality for the Lost

The second and third (Gen. 2:9 and 3:22) and final chapter (Rev. 22:2) of Scripture mention the tree of life. Only Genesis 2:9 and 3:2-6 refer to the forbidden tree. Nothing in the new earth will remind one of the sorry history of sin. "No longer will there be any curse. The throne of God and the Lamb will be in the city, and his servants will serve him. They will see his face, and his name will be on their foreheads. There will be no more night" (Rev. 22:3, 4).

After Adam and Eve sinned in eating the forbidden fruit in Eden, God said, "He [generic for Adam and Eve, see Gen. 1:26, 27] must not be allowed to reach out his hand and take also from the tree of life and eat, and live forever" (Gen. 3:22). Clearly, fallen humans are not immortal, a gift that even the righteous do not receive until the Second Advent (1 Cor. 15:53). God banished Adam and Eve from the garden so they would not live forever. Only eating of the tree of life, a symbol of partaking of eternal life through Christ, gifts human beings with immortality in the final eschatological events. This denies the ability of humans to live in hell at death or to live in hell eternally. For in death there is no impartation of immortality, and the impossibility of a future eternal hell is linked to the fact that immortality is imparted only to the righteous and never to the wicked.

[1] Karl Rahner, "Hell," *Sacramentum Mundi,* vol. 2, pp. 8, 9.

[2] Thomas Aquinas, *Summa Theologica,* vol. 5, p. 2989.

[3] *Ibid.,* p. 2996.

[4] *Ibid.,* p. 2999.

[5] *Ibid.,* p. 2997.

[6] Gregory, quoted in Thomas Aquinas, *Summa Theologica,* vol. 5, p. 2997.

[7] Wayne Grudem, *Systematic Theology: An Introduction to Biblical Doctrine,* p. 1149.

[8] *Ibid.,* p. 1152.

[9] William G. T. Shedd, *Dogmatic Theology* (New York: Scribner's, 1891), p. 716.

[10] *Ibid.,* p. 717.

[11] *Ibid.,* p. 715.

[12] Harry Buis, *The Doctrine of Eternal Punishment* (Grand Rapids: Baker, 1957), p. 133.

[13] Charles Hodge, *Systematic Theology* (Grand Rapids: Eerdmans, n.p.d.), vol. 3, p. 878.

[14] Harry Buis concurs with this argument in *The Doctrine of Eternal Punishment,* p. 120.

[15] Hodge, vol. 3, pp. 878, 879.

[16] *Ibid.,* pp. 879, 880.

[17] Augustine, "The City of God," *The Nicene and Post-Nicene Fathers,* First Series (Edinburgh, Scotland: T & T Clark, 1988), vol. 2, p. 463.

[18] John Blanchard, *Whatever Happened to Hell?* (Wheaton, Ill.: Crossway, 1995), pp. 173, 174.

[19] *Ibid.,* p. 221.

[20] *Ibid.,* p. 163.

[21] *Ibid.*

[22] *Ibid.,* p. 223.

[23] *Ibid.,* p. 224.

[24] *Ibid.*

[25] *Ibid.,* p. 218.

[26] Augustine, *The Nicene and Post-Nicene Fathers,* vol. 2, p. 461; Hodge, vol. 3, p. 880; Shedd, vol. 2, pp. 75, 680; Gordon R. Lewis and Bruce A. Demarest, *Integrative Theology,* vol. 3, p. 478; Guis, p. 33; John Walvoord, *Four Views of Hell,* pp. 19, 20; Donald Guthrie, *New Testament Theology,* p. 888.

[27] Grudem, p. 1151.

[28] Aquinas, vol. 5, pp. 2993.

[29] Shedd, vol. 2, p. 746.

[30] Jonathan Edwards, quoted in Vernon C. Grounds, "The Final State of the Wicked," *Journal of the Evangelical Theological Society* 24, No. 3 (September 1981): 217.

Chapter 26

The Battle Against the Sabbath

"Give us change," yells a voter to a candidate.

"We're fed up with gridlock and the government," another retorts.

"Change" is a catchword of those fed up with government. "If only change could come, life would be better," the masses say.

Satan wants to change God's government. He claims to be capable of doing a better job at governing. His miserable demonstration on earth will be a part of the end-time scenario, because he will have his chance after the close of probation.

"Change" also describes Satan's schemes in the meantime. He altered true Christianity by blending into it paganism, and transformed Calvary into a mass and tradition and New Age-channeled bibles into God's Word. Through him death became soul survival and the annihilation of sinners an eternal burning hell.

In the next few chapters we will consider what Satan has done to God's law. By attacking the law he undermines the basis of God's government. It's a part of his takeover bid as he questions the constitution of heaven in his bid to unseat its King. As in the case of death and hell, most Christians have accepted Sunday in place of the seventh-day Sabbath. Because the Sunday issue will be center stage in final events, we need to understand it in the context of the cosmic controversy.

God and the principles of His law are eternal. The law is an outward manifestation of His essence. The two are inseparable and unchangeable. "His law is without variableness, unalterable, eternal," Ellen G. White wrote, "because it is the transcript of his character."[1] "'God is love' (1 John 4:16). His nature, His law, is love. It ever has been; it ever will be. 'The high and lofty One that inhabiteth eternity,' whose 'ways are everlasting,' changeth not. With Him 'is no variableness, neither shadow of turning.' (Isa. 57:15; Hab. 3:6; James 1:17)."[2]

The unchangeable God (Mal. 3:6) gives expression of Himself in His unchanging law (Matt. 5:18; Luke 16:17).

We can no more alter His law than we can alter God Himself. Both God and His law transcend created beings in such a way that they function, in different ways, to transform human beings rather than to be changed by them. That transformation comes from the law exposing human need (Rom. 7:7). The law shows people what they are really like (Rom. 3:20). It reveals their desperate need of God.[3] God's law corrects their distorted self-esteem. He enables them to see their true self-worth—in Him (Eph. 1:3, 4; 2 Cor. 3:18).

Satan's Guise in Attacking Christ and His Law

Sin originated in a being bent on changing the law and disputing Christ's supremacy (cf. Isa. 14:12-15; Eze. 28:13-15). "In heavenly council the angels pleaded with Lucifer. The Son of God presented before him the greatness, the goodness, and the justice of the Creator, and the sacred, unchanging nature of His law."[4] What was his response? "While claiming for himself perfect loyalty to God, he urged that changes in the order and laws of heaven were necessary for the stability of the divine government. Thus while working to excite opposition to the law of God and to instill his own discontent into the minds of the angels under him, he was ostensibly seeking to remove dissatisfaction and to reconcile disaffected angels to the order of heaven. While secretly fomenting discord and rebellion, he with consummate craft caused it to appear as his sole purpose to promote loyalty and to preserve harmony and peace."[5]

Behind his pretense, jealousy of Christ consumed Lucifer, despite the fact that all he was and had came from Christ. Holding the place of highest honor among created beings, he stood as the covering cherub at the throne (Eze. 28:14). Above all, he owed his very existence to Christ, because Christ created everyone and everything (Col. 1:15, 16; Heb. 1:1, 2). Yet Lucifer plunged down a path that led inexorably to Calvary.

He would kill the One who gave him life. Then, during the Christian age, he would overthrow the Sabbath that reminds human beings of their Creator (Ex. 20:11). Satan's whole rebellion is aimed at Christ. Calvary and Sunday expose his hatred of Christ. Sunday is Satan's creation, not a day in honor of Christ's resurrection. Whether realized or not, Sunday honors Satan's work (change of a commandment) rather than Christ's work (resurrection). Sunday is Satan's fourth commandment in place of the Sabbath command of the preincarnate Christ (Deut. 5:22).

In his counterfeit role as promoter of loyalty to God, Satan reacted against those angels who were really loyal. "Rejecting with disdain the arguments and entreaties of the loyal angels, he denounced them as deluded slaves. The preference shown to Christ he declared an act of injustice both to himself and to all the heavenly host, and announced that he would no longer submit to this invasion of his rights and theirs. He would never again acknowledge the supremacy of Christ. He had determined to claim the honor which should have been given him, and take command of all who would become his followers; and he promised those who would enter his ranks a new and better government, under which all would enjoy freedom. Great numbers of the angels signified their purpose to accept him as their leader."[6]

Since that time Satan's purpose has been "to secure the abolition of law"[7] and he has "exerted all his power and cunning to destroy Jesus."[8] He despises God's law because he hates Christ. His long campaign of deception has been to oust Christ and His law, and take their place. In the end-time on earth it will appear that he has succeeded. With consummate cunning Satan comes pretending to be Christ and promotes Sunday. "Satan's policy in this final conflict with God's people is the same that he employed in the opening of the great controversy in heaven. He professed to be seeking to promote the stability of the divine government, while secretly bending every effort to secure its overthrow. And the very work which he was thus endeavoring to accomplish he charged upon the loyal angels. The same policy of deception has marked the history of the Roman Church. It has professed to act as the vicegerent of Heaven, while seeking to exalt itself above God and to change His law."[9]

God's name appears in only one commandment, in the "sabbath of the Lord thy God" (Ex. 20:9). An attack against the Sabbath is a thrust against God. It also wars against all that the Sabbath represents. The Sabbath is a memorial of Christ's creation (verse 11), His liberation (Deut. 5:15), and His relationship with His followers (Eze. 20:12). To set up a substitute Sabbath (Sunday) is the work of a substitute Christ (Satan). The bottom line is that Satan hates Christ, wants to overthrow Him and wrench from Him His rule, and does so, in part, by promoting Sunday as the Christian Sabbath. Satan's coming advent as Christ to push Sunday sacredness is the ultimate attack against Christ and His day.

In these chapters on Sabbath/Sunday we will see that throughout church history Satan promoted Sunday by falsely linking it with Christ. Satan hides the fact that he transferred Christian worship to another day by giving credit to Christ for the shift. With cunning deception he promoted his work against Christ as the doing of Christ Himself. In the name of Christ, countless Christians have fought, and will fight for, what they believe to be the Sabbath of Christ, not knowing that it is the sabbath of Satan. Let's look at history.

A Look at History

1. Early Church Fathers

Early Church Fathers who speak about the Sabbath include Justin Martyr, Barnabas, Ignatius, Tertullian, and Victorinus.[10] Our reference to them will necessarily be brief. They discussed a number of matters. One had to do with when God instituted the Sabbath. Was it at Creation or much later at the time of Israel? Justin Martyr believed that God's followers before Moses and Abraham "observed no sabbaths,"[11] and so it is not a Creation ordinance, whereas Tertullian held that Adam, Abel, Enoch, Noah, Abraham, and Melchizedek observed it.[12] Barnabas concurred that "the Sabbath is mentioned at the beginning of the creation."[13] So the Church Fathers could not agree when the Sabbath began. The difference of opinion developed into two views. One saw the Sabbath as relevant to all human beings, because God gave it at the creation of the human race. The other group saw the Sabbath as applying only to the Jews, because God instituted it for that nation alone.

Besides the two beginning dates, Tertullian thought Scripture had two different Sabbaths—the "temporal Sabbath," considered human, and the "eternal Sabbath," regarded as divine. The temporal Sabbath was merely "temporary" and foreshadowed the eternal Sabbath.[14] Here is a type/antitype paradigm that would become a persuasive evidence for the temporal nature of the Old Testament Sabbath, because many would conclude that it merely pointed to Christ who came to fulfill/replace/transcend it.

Another question concerned what Christ thought of the Sabbath. Tertullian suggested that Christ broke the Sabbath when He excused His hungry disciples after they plucked some ears of grain to rub them in their hands to get food. The Church Father qualified this statement by saying, "Christ did not at all rescind the Sabbath; He kept the law thereof, and both in the former case did a work which was beneficial to the life of His disciples, for He indulged them with the relief of food when they were hungry, and in the present instance cured the withered hand."[15]

Barnabas was one of the early Church Fathers who projected the six days of Creation onto history, with each Creation day representing 1,000 years of historical time. He said: " 'He finished in six days.' This implieth that the Lord will finish all things in 6,000 years, for a day is with Him a thousand years. . . . Therefore, my children, in six days, that is, in 6,000 years, all things will be finished. 'And He rested on the seventh day.' This meaneth: when His Son, coming [again], shall destroy the time of the wicked man, and judge the ungodly, and change the sun, and the moon, and the stars, then shall He truly rest on the seventh day."[16]

An eighth day will follow that future seventh day. Putting words into the Lord's mouth, Barnabas wrote: "I shall make a beginning of the eighth day, that is, a beginning of another world. Wherefore, also, we keep the eighth day with joyfulness, the day also on which Jesus rose again from the dead."[17] Here is an early reference to Sunday observance. It ignores the obvious parallel of Creation Friday and Crucifixion Friday being followed by a seventh-day Sabbath celebration, with Sunday as merely the first day of the next week. Rather, it invents an eighth-day, never found in Scripture, and attempts to identify the first day of the week with some supposedly eighth-day new-world time. It operates under the assumption that human history is to be 6,000 years and the millennium is the seventh day, followed by the new earth time as the eighth day.

Interestingly the time grids of Barnabas and Tertullian do not synchronize. For how can the eternal Sabbath of Tertullian function from the Second Advent onward, when Barnabas awaits the new world for the eighth-day Sabbath to begin? It leaves the millennium hanging. Even though Barnabas refers to the Psalms as the source for his eighth-day idea (Ps. 6; 12), we find no such reference. Scripture mentions the "eighth day" only 20 times in Scripture, and not one of them refers to the imaginary views of Barnabas and other early Church Fathers.

2. Augustine of Hippo (354-430)

Augustine of Hippo was not only the greatest theologian of his time, but one of the greatest of all time. His voluminous writings became the basis of Catholic theology for centuries. He is also the most quoted theologian by the Reformers in their attempt to attack the Catholic Church, which speaks of the selectivity at work by both sides as they looked to him as authority. Behind this is the fact that Augustine presented contradictory ideas in his writings.

By the time we come to Augustine, we have moved away from the early Church Fathers' thinking about the Sabbath. Even though some of Augustine's ideas find their roots in theirs, he is much clearer in his antipathy to the Sabbath. Augustine said that the Sabbath "ought not to be kept by a Christian."[18] He reasoned that the Sabbath merely "prophesied" Christ's first advent. After Christ arrived on earth, the Sabbath had no more usefulness than any other prophecy about His birth. As Augustine put it, "The Lord did break the Sabbath; but was not therefore guilty. What is that that I have said, 'He broke the Sabbath'? He, the Light had come, He was removing the shadows."[19] Thus Augustine dismisses all of Christ's Sabbath miracles and instruction about the Sabbath as a process of removing the shadows (the Sabbath) now that He, the Light, had arrived. Just as the sacraments of wine and bread show forth the Lord's death till He comes the second time, so Augustine's Sabbath was a sacrament fulfilled by Christ's first advent.[20]

Hence, according to Augustine, Christ replaced the Sabbath when He came. But when did He come? Augustine answers his question by looking at Creation days as types of historical periods. "For these days were not without reason ordained in such order, but for that ages also were to run in a like course, before we rest in God. . . . As therefore God made man in His own image on the sixth day: thus we find that our Lord Jesus Christ came into the sixth age, that man might be formed anew after the image of God. . . . The sixth day beginneth from the preaching of John, and lasteth unto the end: and after the end of the sixth day, we reach our rest."[21]

Apparently humanity is still in the sixth day, with the Sabbath in the post-advent future, for the Creation Sabbath being open-ended it can be fully realized only in the open-endedness of eternity. Thus Augustine's time periods do not agree with those of Barnabas. Augustine's sixth historical day began a millennium before the sixth historical day of Barnabas.

To Augustine the Creation account in Genesis is mystical, for God merely spoke things into existence by His omnipotent power during six days. Because His Creation work was easy for Him, how could He possibly need the seventh-day Sabbath rest that followed? Augustine asked, "How could

He require rest after the world was made, as if to enjoy leisure after toil, He who in commanding never toiled?"

Obviously Augustine makes too much of the anthropomorphism of rest, not allowing the word "rest" to mean anything other than physical recovery from toil. He apparently has no room for *"rest" meaning a change from creation-work to its celebration, without reference to any toil.* And he certainly ignores the concept of the Sabbath being a celebration of Christ's finished work either of Creation or of redemption. Not only that, Augustine goes on to conjure up a meaning not found in the text. "Consequently these sayings are mystical, and are laid down in this wise that we may be looking for rest after this life, provided we have done good works."[22] Just as Christ's work issued in rest after its completion, so will Christians rest in the eternal day after their life of works. Again he restricts the Sabbath to the eternal future.

Although he believes that Christians should not keep the sacramental/typical Sabbath signifying Christ any more than they should sacrifice lambs, Augustine paradoxically (in view of what has been said thus far) urges Christians to be even more diligent in their observation of the Sabbath than the Jews. " 'Observe the Sabbath-day' is enjoined on us more than on them, because it is commanded to be spiritually observed. . . . The Christian observes the Sabbath spiritually, abstaining from servile work. For what is it to abstain from servile work? From sin."[23] "For this is the spiritual Sabbath, to have no sin. In fact, brethren, it is of this that God admonishes us, when He commends the Sabbath to our notice: 'Thou shalt do no servile work."[24] For Augustine, the Sabbath seems to be a seven-day experience of sinlessness.

He sees the 50 days from Passover to the day Moses received the Ten Commandments at Sinai as typical of the 50 days between the death of Christ and Pentecost. He recognizes that Scripture calls the Holy Spirit "the finger of God" (Luke 11:20). Just as God wrote the Decalogue with His finger on external tables, so the Holy Spirit, as the finger of God, writes "the new law" on the tables of the heart.[25] The new law within does not include the Sabbath as a day, but as an experience.

One must keep in mind that contemporary Jewish Sabbath observance often lurked in the background of his Sabbath comments. Like Barnabas,[26] Augustine speaks of Sunday observance contrasted with Jewish Sabbath-keeping. His revulsion for the Jewish observance of Sabbath caused him to overreact to the Sabbath itself. His mystical bent shows up in the way he compares the Sabbath for Christians with the Sabbath for the Jews. "Lo, this day is the Sabbath, which the Jews at this period observe by a kind of bodily rest, languid and luxurious. They abstain from labors, and give themselves up to trifles; and though God ordained the Sabbath, they spend it in actions which God forbids. Our rest is from evil works, theirs from good; for it is better to plough than to dance. They abstain from good, but not from trifling, works. God proclaims to us a Sabbath. What sort of Sabbath? First consider, where it is. It is in the heart, within us; for many are idle with their limbs, while they are disturbed in conscience. . . . That very joy in the tranquility of our hope, is our Sabbath. This is the subject of praise and of song in this Psalm, how a Christian man is in the Sabbath of his own heart, that is, in the quiet, tranquility, and serenity of his conscience, undisturbed; hence he tells us here, whence men are wont to be disturbed, and he teaches thee to keep Sabbath in thine own heart."[27]

This existential, rather than weekly, Sabbath ignores the uniqueness of the scriptural Sabbath. Augustine projects the Sabbath into the future and within, to the eternal and internal, to the eschatological and to the existential. But he does so at the expense of the present historical claims of the Sabbath. He ignores them, reminding us of later Preterist and Futurist schools of prophetic interpretation that pay no attention to the historical. Furthermore, Augustine can even merge these two horizons (eschatological/existential). For example, in the last paragraphs of *The City of God,* he speaks of the perpetual Sabbath, saying, "There shall be the great Sabbath which has no evening, which God celebrated among His first works, as it is written, 'And God rested on the seventh day from all His works which He had made. And God blessed the seventh day, and sanctified it; because that in it He had rested from all His work which God began to make.' For we shall ourselves be the seventh day, when we shall be filled and replenished with God's blessing and sanctification."[28]

3. Thomas Aquinas (1225-1274)

Satan camouflages his attack against Christ with a Christian guise. Tragically, many Christians through the centuries have jettisoned the Sabbath in what they thought was showing support for Christ. Think of the terrible irony: They rallied to be true to Christ, only to help His enemy. Here we find Satan's deceptive front, clothing Sunday with Christ's garb to deceive as verily as he will clothe himself as Christ in the endtime. Fooled by the Christian garb, the vast majority of Christians fall into the enemy's camp without knowing it. Early church fathers and Augustine stumbled into the trap. What about Aquinas and Calvin?

Thomas Aquinas, the second most influential theologian in Catholic theology, contrasted the old and new laws. "The New Law is compared to the Old as the perfect to the imperfect. . . . The New Law gives what the Old Law promised."[29] To Aquinas the Old Law merely pointed to the New Law, as shadow to substance. "The reality is found in Christ. Wherefore the New Law is called the law of reality; whereas the Old Law is called the law of shadow or of figure."[30]

Here Aquinas treats the Old Law, including the Sabbath, as merely a shadow that its reality in Jesus Christ overtook. To observe the seventh-day Sabbath would be no better than slaying lambs in the Christian age.

However, unlike so many since his day, Aquinas understood why Jesus seemed to break the Sabbath command. Whereas many scholars believe Christ ignored Sabbath restrictions to show that He transcended the divine law, Aquinas saw it differently. "But He did seem to break the Sabbath according to the superstitious interpretation of the Pharisees, who thought that man ought to abstain from doing even works of kindness on the Sabbath; which was contrary to the intention of the Law."

Aquinas speaks of God's resting on the seventh day as a cessation "from creating new creatures."[31] Because God had no need of the creatures He made, Aquinas can say, "When all things were made He is not said to have rested *in* His works, as though needing them for His own happiness, but to have rested *from* them, as in fact resting in Himself, as He suffices for Himself and fulfills His own desire."[32] He also believed that "God rested in giving rest to us."[33] But the most important fact for our purpose is Aquinas' focus on Christ taking the place of the Old Law, including the Sabbath. For Aquinas, Christ, and not the seventh-day Sabbath, is meant for Christians.

4. John Calvin (1509-1564)

Calvin believed that God enforced no commandment more strictly than the Sabbath one. He concurs with those who hold that the Old Testament Sabbath was typical of Christ, and like all other types met its fulfillment in Christ. Christ "is the truth, at whose presence all the emblems banish; the body, at the sight of which the shadows disappear. He, I say, is the true completion of the Sabbath."[34] But he says this is only half of the Sabbath's meaning. "First, under the rest of the seventh day, the divine Lawgiver meant to furnish the people of Israel with a type of the spiritual rest by which believers were to cease from their own works, and allow God to work in them. Secondly, he meant that there should be a stated day on which they should assemble to hear the Law, and perform religious rites, or which, at least, they should specially employ in meditating on his works, and be thereby trained to piety. Thirdly, he meant that servants, and those who lived under the authority of others, should be indulged with a day of rest, and thus have some intermission from labor."[35]

Like others before him, Calvin distinguished between the meaning of the Sabbath as "the mystery of perpetual resting from our works," from the ceremonial part of the Sabbath. He affirms that "on the advent of our Lord Jesus Christ, the ceremonial part of the commandment was abolished." But the existential part of the Sabbath continues every day of our lives. It is a daily experience. "Christians, therefore, should have nothing to do with a superstitious observance of days."[36] In this way Calvin jettisons the weekly Sabbath. So what is the purpose of the Sabbath commandment? Calvin sees its intent in providing a day for public worship and a day for the laborer's vacation.[37]

Calvin rejected any continuance of the seventh day as a holy day given to humanity to observe. He identified the seventh day with Jewish superstitions. Therefore Christians chose another day to distance themselves from the Jews. But why Sunday? "It was not, however, without a reason," Calvin said, "that the early Christians substituted what we call the Lord's day for the Sabbath. The resurrection of our Lord being the end and accomplishment of that true rest which the ancient Sabbath typified, this day, by which types were abolished, serves to warn Christians against adhering to a shadowy ceremony."[38]

He went on to say, "I do not cling so to the number seven as to bring the Church under bondage to it, nor do I condemn churches for holding their meetings on other solemn days, provided they guard against superstition."[39] So Calvin advised Christians to choose any day they wished as long as it was free from superstition. The distinction between the seventh day from the rest of the week was only typical.[40]

5. Overview

In our brief overview of the early Church Fathers, Augustine, Aquinas, and Calvin, we noticed some differences among them but also a theme running throughout them. That theme is that Christ is the antitype of the seventh-day Sabbath just as He was the antitype of all christological types in the Old Testament. Even though they saw the Sabbath as vested with more than typical value, it is the typical that designates it as temporary and fulfilled/transcended by Christ. We have observed that Satan's cunning deception has been to pretend to promote Christ, while behind that guise he actually attacks Christ and His Sabbath. It is a forceful argument that recurs again in later times, as we will notice in the next chapter.

---

[1] Ellen G. White, *Signs of the Times,* Mar. 12, 1896, p. 6.

[2] E. G. White, *Patriarchs and Prophets,* p. 33.

[3] Ellen G. White put it this way: "The law makes sin appear exceedingly sinful. It condemns the transgressor, but it has no power to save and restore him. Its province is not to pardon. Pardon comes through Christ, who lived the law in humanity. Man's only hope is in the substitute provided by God, who gave His Son, that He might reconcile the world to Himself" *(Review and Herald,* July 25, 1899, p. 1).

[4] E. G. White, *Patriarchs and Prophets,* p. 36.

[5] *Ibid.,* p. 38.

[6] *Ibid.,* p. 40.

[7] E. G. White, *The Great Controversy,* p. 499.

[8] *Ibid.,* p. 501.

[9] *Ibid.,* p. 591.

[10] For further insights see Samuel Bacchiocchi, *From Sabbath to Sunday* (Rome: Pontifical Gregorian University, 1977), pp. 27-29.

[11] Justin Martyr, *The Ante-Nicene Fathers* (afterward as *ANF),* vol. 1, p. 208.

[12] Tertullian, *ANF,* vol. 3, p. 155.

[13] Barnabas, *ANF,* vol. 1, p. 146.

[14] Tertullian, *ANF,* vol. 3, p. 155.

[15] *Ibid.,* vol. 3, p. 363.

[16] Barnabas, *ANF,* vol. 1, p. 146.

[17] *Ibid.,* vol. 1, p. 147.

[18] Augustine, *Nicene and Post-Nicene Fathers of the Christian Church* (afterward as *NPNF),* Philip Schaff, ed. (Edinburgh, Scotland: T & T Clark, 1987), vol. 5, p. 93.

[19] *Ibid.,* vol. 6, pp. 515, 516.

[20] *Ibid.,* vol. 7, pp. 115, 132.

[21] *Ibid.,* vol. 8, pp. 456, 457.

[22] *Ibid.,* vol. 7, p. 132.

[23] *Ibid.,* p. 24.

[24] *Ibid.,* p. 247.

[25] *Ibid.,* vol. 5, pp. 95, 96.

[26] Ignatius wrote: "'He will come and save us.' Let us therefore no longer keep the Sabbath after the Jewish manner, and rejoice in days of idleness; for 'he that does not work, let him not eat.' For say the [holy] oracles, 'In the sweat of thy face shalt thou eat thy bread.' But let every one of you keep the Sabbath after a spiritual manner, rejoicing in meditation on the law, not in relaxation of the body, admiring the workmanship of God and not eating things prepared the day before, not using lukewarm drinks, and walking within a prescribed space, nor finding delight in dancing and plaudits which have no sense in them. And after the observance of the Sabbath, let every friend of Christ keep the Lord's Day as a festival, the resurrection-day, the queen and chief of all the days [of the week]" *(ANF*, vol. 1, pp. 62, 63).

[27] Augustine, *NPNF*, vol. 8, p. 453.

[28] *Ibid.,* vol. 2, p. 511.

[29] Thomas Aquinas, *Summa Theologica,* vol. 2, p. 1110.

[30] *Ibid.*

[31] *Ibid.,* vol. 1, p. 354.

[32] *Ibid.*

[33] *Ibid.*

[34] John Calvin, *Institutes of the Christian Religion,* vol. 1, p. 340.

[35] *Ibid.,* p. 339.

[36] *Ibid.,* vol. 2, p. 341.

[37] *Ibid.,* vol. 1, p. 342.

[38] *Ibid.,* p. 343.

[39] *Ibid.*

[40] *Ibid.,* p. 344.

Chapter 27

The Sabbath in Crisis?

The beginning of the 1990s saw the publication of a book entitled *Sabbath in Crisis,*[1] in which the author rejected the seventh-day Sabbath as a day for Christians to keep holy. The tragedy is that the author, Dale Ratzlaff, is a former Seventh-day Adventist minister.[2]

D. A. Carson supplied the foreword. Carson also edited the book *From Sabbath to Lord's Day* (1982).[3] Written by a group of scholars at Cambridge University, the latter volume was essentially a response to Adventist Samuel Bacchiocchi's book *From Sabbath to Sunday* (1977).[4] Ratzlaff's book is a popularized version of the basic thesis found in the more scholarly one edited by Carson.[5]

Three Views on the Sabbath

Three views about the Sabbath have the greatest circulation among Christians today.[6]

1. Sunday sabbatarianism, which considers Sunday as the Christian Sabbath (transfer/modification). This view alleges that the New Testament transferred the Sabbath of the Old Testament to Sunday and modified the Sabbathkeeping regulations.

2. Saturday sabbatarianism, which considers Saturday as the continued Sabbath (reformation/continuation). Held most prominently by Seventh-day Adventists, this view believes that Jesus observed the Sabbath of the Old Testament. He reformed Sabbath-keeping by overthrowing the human rules that bound it. This reformed Sabbath of the Old Testament continues to be the Sabbath of the New Testament.

3. Nonsabbatarianism, which considers the Sabbath to have culminated in Christ (fulfillment/transformation). This view claims that Jesus fulfilled the Sabbath of the Old Testament and that the symbolism of the Sinaitic Sabbath has been transformed into other symbols in the new covenant. The Ratzlaff/Carson books subscribe to this nonsabbatarian view. Their view, though different in some details, is in essential agreement with the early Church Fathers, Augustine, Aquinas, and Calvin. All replace the Sabbath with Christ.

The nonsabbatarian thesis holds that the fourth-commandment Sabbath existed only for Israel,[7] is essentially different than the Creation Sabbath,[8] and is merely a type of the salvation-rest that Christ brought.[9] Hence, like the priesthood, sacrifices, and Messianic prophecies, the Sinaitic Sabbath met both its reality[10] and fulfillment in Christ.[11] So the Sabbath has undergone transformation from physical rest to salvation instead of transference from Saturday to Sunday.[12]

Old and New Covenant Dichotomy

Behind their thesis, the Carson and Ratzlaff books posit a radical difference between the old covenant and its Sabbath and the new covenant and Christ.[13] But does not such a distinction between the two covenants question the unity of the Old and New Testaments and the unity of the plan of salvation? Does God change? Is He different in the New Testament and its covenant from what He was in the Old Testament and its covenant? The Bible is clear that God changes not (Mal. 3:6). He "is the same yesterday and today and forever" (Heb. 13:8).

In fact, the new covenant is the same as the everlasting covenant (Gen. 17:13; Heb. 13:20), with the old covenant a temporary teaching device God used to meet people fresh out of slavery, with a view to preparing them to enter into the everlasting covenant, which by contrast to this old covenant, Scripture refers to as the new covenant. The "historical period" view of the covenants regards the new as really older than the old, even though the old covenant is a historical period that precedes the new covenant as a historical period.

Still another way to look at the two covenants is the "existential," or "experience" view. Here the old covenant is a works, or legalistic, response to God, whereas the new covenant is a faith or relationship response to Him. In this view David, who delighted in God's law (Ps. 119:70), had the new-covenant experience though living in the old-covenant historical period; whereas some legalistic believers in Galatia (Gal. 1:6-9) experienced the old covenant while living in the new-covenant period.

Therefore, if the new covenant is the same as the everlasting covenant, then both are the same as the one plan of salvation. Sabbath, salvation, and everlasting covenant each reveal God's desire to be with humanity. All three are equally a part of the everlasting gospel. As such, the Sabbath is a Creation ordinance and not tied to the temporary and passing old covenant. The Carson/Ratzlaff books fail to relate the new covenant to the everlasting covenant and the Sabbath to Creation. In linking the Sabbath only to a temporary covenant, they make an unbiblical dichotomy between law in the Old Testament and gospel in the New Testament.

Sabbath Not Rejected in the New Covenant

We must note that besides the fact that no New Testament writer doubts the importance of the new covenant, none of them speak against the seventh-day Sabbath, or suggest its replacement through Christ's salvation. Given the sacredness of the seventh-day (Ex. 20:8-11), the death penalty for failure to keep it in the past (Ex. 31:14), the Babylonian captivity caused in part through Sabbath-breaking (Jer. 17:19-27), and the prophets' support of the Sabbath (Eze. 20:12-24; 22:8, 26; 23:38; Isa. 56:2-6; 58:13, 14; Neh. 10:31; 13:15-22), one would expect a clear announcement of any Sabbath change if it constituted a part of the gospel good news. No command to forsake the seventh-day Sabbath or to observe any other day exists in the New Testament. Equally significant, Christ never suggested a change of His Sabbath, which He Himself kept (Mark 1:21; 3:1, 2; Luke 4:16-27; 13:10). Yet He instituted the Lord's Supper to replace the Passover (Matt. 26:17-30), even designating the cup as "the new covenant in my blood" (Luke 22:20; cf. verses 7-19).

In spite of these facts, the Carson/Ratzlaff books seek to replace the old-covenant law by the new covenant Holy Spirit.[14] The Lord's Supper takes the place of the Sabbath.[15] They do not consider the moral/ceremonial distinctions of law the self-evident biblical basis for any continuity/discontinuity.[16] In other words, the Sabbath as moral law does not remain for Christians on the basis of being in the moral law (Decalogue).[17] Carson's book shoves the Sabbath within the ceremonial category.[18] Whereas historically many theologians have dichotomized the fourth commandment as moral (time for God) and ceremonial (time of week), with the moral "rest" remaining, while the ceremonial "seventh" does not,[19] these books view the salvation-history mission of Jesus as fulfilling/transforming/transcending/replacing the old-covenant Sabbath.[20]

"In short the physical rest of the Old Testament Sabbath has become the salvation rest of the true Sabbath. . . . The Sabbath keeping now demanded is the cessation from reliance on one's own works (Heb. 4:9, 10)." The Old Sabbaths have been "superseded," "transformed."[21] Christ's mission "brought the true Sabbath rest of the end time into the course of history,"[22] throwing the law into eclipse,[23] making it obsolete,[24] so that He taught a new Sabbath law,[25] and His resurrection "fulfills the rest signified by the Old Testament Sabbath."[26]

At best the Ratzlaff/Carson books do attempt to understand the Sabbath in the light of Christ, even though their quest is a dismal failure. But at least they tried. That's more than many of the Jews did in the time of Christ with all their 600 *halakah,* or human-made laws, to keep the Sabbath. Such Jews, bent on trying to earn their own salvation through the Sabbath, did not see through the Sabbath to the Saviour. At least the Ratzlaff/Carson books make the attempt. But, as we will see later, their authors missed the most important aspect of the relationship between the Sabbath and the Saviour.

Sabbath Not a Creation Ordinance?

Carson and Ratzlaff deny that the Sabbath is a Creation ordinance,[27] stating that it began only with Israel. They claim that the Creation Sabbath was different in quality (different rest) and time (permanent, not one day) from the Sinaitic Sabbaths.[28] It reminds one of Tertullian's "eternal Sabbath" and "temporal Sabbath." They note that Genesis does not mention the evening and morning in connection with the seventh day (Gen. 2:2) as it had for the other six days of Creation (Gen. 1:5, 8, 13, 19, 23, 31). Thus they believe that the seventh day of Creation was open-ended, that the Sabbath rest continued until the Fall. Christ's salvific mission was a new creation through His death and resurrection. Just as Creation week concluded in an open-ended Sabbath,[29] so Christ's re-creation brings "the divine rest of Genesis 2:2, 3."[30] Ratzlaff claims that "the New Testament testing truth is faith in Jesus. It is *not* the seventh day of the Sinaitic Covenant."[31] He dismisses Christ's Sabbath observance as not a valid example for Christians,[32] even though He was rejecting the *halakah* rather than God's commandment.[33] Both claim that the Jerusalem Council (Acts 15) did not require Gentiles to keep the Sabbath.[34]

Sabbath as Temporary

To summarize the major thrust of Ratzlaff's book, for example, it views Creation Sabbath as a permanent rest (not a seventh day). When sin interrupted the permanent Sabbath, it was acted out by the Sinaitic Sabbath and restored with Christ's rest. Now Christ's rest has arrived, replacing the seventh-day Sabbath. Ratzlaff interprets biblical passages within this framework.[35]

Ratzlaff compares the Sabbath to a map. I believe such an analogy gives insight into Satan's consistent attempt to garb falsehood with truth, to present Christ as the reason for replacing the Sabbath, when all the time the devil himself is the cause for the change. Here is the analogy. "The map and trail guide served important functions. But upon arrival at the destination it is time to put the map down and look up. So it is with the Sabbath. Rather than seek to keep a *day* holy let us put the day down and step into the arms of our holy *Creator*. Let us enter 'today' into fellowship, into a 'rest' which *remains* for those who have believed."[36]

But the only way to step into the arms of our Creator is to come with the Sabbath, the memorial of His creation. There is no either-or here. It's not Christ *or* the Sabbath. Nowhere does Scripture set the two up as mutually exclusive. We come to Him for rest (Matt. 11:28), the only way to experience the Sabbath rest. We go to Him so that we can honor all His law, including the Sabbath command. Disobedience, including Sabbath disobedience, robs one of rest (Heb. 4:3-11). When we step into the arms of our holy Creator, we find ourselves embraced by the arms of the "Lord of the Sabbath" (Matt. 12:8). "What God has joined together, let man [or devil] not separate" (Matt. 19:6) is good theological as well as marital advice.

Sabbath as a Creation Ordinance

Although Carson and Ratzlaff deny the Sabbath as a Creation ordinance,[37] scholars of the past supported the concept. For example, Philo described the Sabbath as "'the birthday of the world' and 'the festival not of a single city or country but of the universe.'" We have seen that Tertullian and Barnabas believed that God instituted the Sabbath at Creation. Others supporting Sabbath as a Creation ordinance include Martin Luther,[38] John

Calvin,[39] Alfred Edersheim,[40] C. F. Keil and F. Delitzsch,[41] Gordon J. Wenham,[42] Robert L. Dabney,[43] Roger T. Beckwith and Wilfrid Stott,[44] John Skinner,[45] John P. Lange[46] and James G. Murphy,[47] to name a few, together with *The Bible Commentary,*[48] and *A Commentary, Critical, Experimental and Practical on the Old and New Testaments.*[49]

Also some contemporary scholars recognize the Sabbath as a Creation ordinance. For example, R. Alan Cole says: "It is highly likely that the origins of Sabbath (like the origins of tithing and circumcision) go back well beyond the law, even though there is no direct biblical evidence for its observance."[50] Walter Elwell declares, "The Sabbath's setting in the biblical account of creation implies that it is one of those OT standards which are meant for all men, and not just for Israel."[51] Some other scholars include D. A. Rausch,[52] J. C. McCann, Jr.,[53] and J. H. Sailhamer.[54] Gordon J. Wenham states, "The Sabbath idea is as old as creation itself."[55]

The fact of manna not falling on Sabbath before the proclamation of the Ten Commandments at Sinai (Ex. 16), and the very term "remember" referring to the Sabbath in the fourth commandment (Ex. 20:8), both presuppose a Sabbath commandment in existence before Sinai.[56] Thus evidence supports the Sabbath as a Creation ordinance. It is not good enough to say that the biblical record has no evidence that the patriarchs kept the Sabbath. It is equally true that we have no biblical evidence that they didn't observe it. Arguments from silence are not sufficient to make a case, as we can also present them as evidence for the opposite conclusions. At best, such arguments cancel out one another. Far more important is the fact that the biblical record refers to Sabbath observance before Sinai. The logical conclusion is to ask where such Sabbath observance came from. It involved a miracle from God, that is, manna not falling on the seventh day. In this way God's action in supplying a double quantity of manna on Friday so that the seventh day could be a day of rest shows the sanctity of the Sabbath before Sinai. It would appear that such a practice has its roots in God's blessing of the Sabbath at the end of Creation week (Gen. 2:3).

The fact that the seventh day does not have the usual "evening and morning" designation (verse 2), as do the other six days of Creation (Gen. 1:5, 8, 13, 19, 23, 31), in no way suggests that it was an eternal Sabbath interrupted merely by sin, to be restored after the consummation, as some suggest. Though the Creation record does not use the word "Sabbath," nor mention a Sabbath command, God's act of blessing the seventh day (Gen. 2:2) must be understood in the context of His other two blessings of animals (Gen. 1:22) and humanity (Gen. 1:28). As J. G. Murphy discerned, "the solemn act of blessing and hallowing is the institution of a perpetual order of seventh-day rest: in the same manner as the blessing of the animals denoted a perpetuity of self-multiplication, and the blessing of man indicated further a perpetuity of dominion over the earth and its products."[57] Subsequent Sabbath commandments identify the seventh day of Creation as the day that God blessed and set apart as His holy Sabbath (e.g., Ex. 20:11; 31:15).

In the Carson tome, A. T. Lincoln admits that "if the hypothesis of the Sabbath as a creation ordinance could be established, then, whatever the temporary nature of the Sabbath as part of the Mosaic covenant, the appeal could still be made to the permanence of the mandate for one day of rest as inherent to humanity made in the image of God."[58] The Bible supports the seventh-day Sabbath as a Creation ordinance, divinely given to humanity as a perpetual memorial to celebrate Christ's finished works.

The Creator/Redeemer Dichotomy

In my opinion, the most serious failure of the Carson and Ratzlaff books is their unbiblical dichotomy between the work of Christ as Creator and His role as Redeemer, with the resulting discontinuity between the Sabbath of the Old and New Testaments. Scripture is clear that the Christ who came as humanity's Saviour in the New Testament is the same One who created the human race as recorded in the Old Testament (Heb. 1:1-3; Col. 1:15-17). Both were acts of Christ as gifts to all humanity. Both were creative gifts, creation out-of-nothing *(ex nihilo)* before sin and creation without human contribution after sin. Humanity made no contribution to either divine act of Christ. Both were His doing, performed by His power, voluntarily and decisively as gifts to all the human race.

The same Christ who created the Sabbath blessed it and set it apart from the other six days as a type of the difference between human working days and our need to rest in Christ's work. The Sabbath, when compared to the six days of Creation, was a powerful type signifying that human work has a limit. Humans can do many awesome things, but no human can make himself or herself, and no human being can save himself or herself. The Sabbath followed both gifts, for Christ created humans on Creation Friday and redeemed them on Crucifixion Friday. The first full day to follow both creations by Christ was a Sabbath to celebrate His finished work and to rest in that work.

What is missing in the Ratzlaff/Carson books, as well as in the theology of the early Fathers, Augustine, Aquinas, and Calvin, is the deeper christological significance of Christ's acts in both Creation and salvation with respect to the Sabbath celebration of His accomplished work. The wedge they try to drive between the Old and New Testaments fails to do justice to the everlasting gospel revealed throughout Scripture. And the severance of Christ from the Sabbath fails to see the salvific meaning of the Sabbath throughout Scripture (see chapter 29). In other words, while these authors thought they exalted Christ by rejecting the seventh-day Sabbath, they really spurned the significance of Christ as Creator-Redeemer.

Those who believe another day replaced the Jewish Sabbath in honor of the resurrection of Christ have traditionally recognized Sunday. That has been by far the prevailing view of Christians from earliest times till the present. Linking Sunday with a great salvific event of Christ offers a further example of how Satan clothes his attacks against the seventh-day Sabbath in a Christian garb. Most Christians have bought the identity without stopping to think through the christological insights that such a view jettisons.

But not all have viewed Sunday in this way. It is of interest that scholars writing in Carson's book conclude that "it is all but impossible to believe that Sunday was established as the Lord's Day, as a holy convocation, and as a Christian response to a creation ordinance in Palestine shortly after the Resurrection. The arguments against this position are virtually conclusive"[59] (M. Turner). Later the same work states: "It cannot be argued that the New Testament itself provides warrant for the belief that since the Resurrection God appointed the first day to be observed as the Sabbath."[60] Concerning the Sabbath, the book admits that "there is no biblical or compelling theological reason why it has to be Sunday"[61] (A. T. Lincoln).

---

[1] Dale Ratzlaff, *Sabbath in Crisis* (Applegate, Calif.: Life Assurance Ministries, 1989, 1990).

[2] *Ibid.*, p. 310.

[3] D. A. Carson, ed., *From Sabbath to Lord's Day: A Biblical, Historical and Theological Investigation* (Grand Rapids: Zondervan, 1982). That same year the Seventh-day Adventist Church published its own contribution: Kenneth A. Strand, ed., *The Sabbath in Scripture and History* (Washington, D.C.: Review and Herald, 1982). The two books do not mention each other, but some of the arguments found in *From Sabbath to Lord's Day* are answered in *The Sabbath in Scripture and History*.

[4] Samuel Bacchiocchi, *From Sabbath to Sunday: A Historical Investigation of the Rise of Sunday Observance in Early Christianity* (Rome: Pontifical Gregorian University, 1977).

[5] In the *Journal of the Adventist Theological Society* 2, No. 1 (1991): 153, 154, I made reference to the books, noting the need for a separate article (footnote 6). The present chapter is, in part, to meet this need.

[6] Ratzlaff, pp. 274-277.

[7] *Ibid.*, p. 41. The Sabbath originated in Israel (Carson, pp. 23, 24), was not a Creation ordinance (p. 34, cf. pp. 349, 350), and is transcended by Christ (p. 364).

[8] Ratzlaff, pp. 245, 263. Genesis 1, 2 does not institute a weekly Sabbath (Carson, p. 198).

[9] The new covenant interprets, modifies, and transforms the old-covenant laws (including the Sabbath) with reference to Christ as center of the new covenant (Ratzlaff, p. 81).

[10] Ratzlaff compares the Sabbath to a map that serves merely to get one to a destination. Upon arrival it has no further function (p. 267). With obvious reference to Hebrews 4:9, Ratzlaff claims, "The *'sabbatismos'* (Gr.) rest of the new covenant is better than the *'sabbaton'* (Gr.) rest of the old covenant for it deals with the *reality* to which the old covenant only *prefigured*. It moves from *observance* to *experience" (ibid.*, p. 268).

"Jesus views the law as essentially prophetic of Himself and His ministry" (Carson, p. 84). "Christ's life, death, resurrection, and teaching threw the law into eclipse" *(ibid.*, p. 126). The OT law was transitory, imperfect and inferior to Christ (Ratzlaff, pp. 376, 377). "Christ brings the spiritual reality; His work fulfills the intent of the Sabbath, and with Christ comes that for which the Sabbath existed. The reality of salvation rest supersedes the sign" (Carson, p. 215).

[11] Ratzlaff, pp. 223-236, 293; Carson, pp. 113, 369, 373, 374.

[12] Ratzlaff, p. 265; Carson, pp. 134, 135, 214, 216, 374. Cf. p. 282. Those denying any connection between Sunday and the fourth commandment include Tyndale, Peter Helyn, J. A. Hessey, and Willy Rordorf. Among those accepting Sunday as connected to the fourth commandment are Roger Beckwith and Wilfrid Stott. See Roger T. Beckwith and Wilfrid Stott, *The Christian Sunday: A Biblical and Historical Study* (Grand Rapids: Baker, 1980), pp. vii-x.

[13] Cf. "One cannot go both directions; he is a disciple of Jesus or a disciple of Moses" (Ratzlaff, p. 128; cf. pp. 135, 138).

[14] Ratzlaff, pp. 187, 188; cf. The Resurrection fulfills/replaces the Sabbath (Carson, p. 205).

[15] Ratzlaff, p. 265. "It is no longer 'remember the Sabbath day to keep it holy,' but *DO THIS IN REMEM-*

BRANCE OF ME" (p. 274). Cf. "It is just possible, in the Fourth Gospel, Jesus Himself replaces the Sabbath" (Carson, p. 84).

[16] Carson, p. 68; cf. pp. 79, 80.

[17] However, Ratzlaff claims, "The *moral principles* upon which the Sinaitic Covenant laws were based are included in the *moral principles* of the new covenant" (p. 264).

[18] Carson, p. 69. The Sabbath law is not moral law (p. 85). Cf. Second-century writers believed the Sabbath commandment, though in the Decalogue, was classified with the ceremonial ordinances that passed when Christ fulfilled them (pp. 267, 268). "The writers of this period take one attitude towards the Decalogue but a different one towards the Sabbath" (p. 378). "The majority of second-century writers seem to have been sound in their instinct to treat the Sabbath as a temporary Mosaic institution" (p. 381).

[19] For example, Thomas Aquinas (Carson, pp. 305-307). The moral/ceremonial distinctions of the fourth commandment originated with Thomas Aquinas. For historical insights see Samuel Bacchiocchi, *Divine Rest for Human Restlessness* (Rome: Tesar, 1980), pp. 45-57.

[20] Ratzlaff, p. 293; Carson, pp. 113, 205, 373, 374; cf. p. 84.

[21] Carson, p. 215.

[22] *Ibid.,* p. 346.

[23] *Ibid.,* p. 126.

[24] *Ibid.,* p. 378.

[25] *Ibid.,* p. 202.

[26] *Ibid.,* p. 205.

[27] Ratzlaff, p. 21; Carson, pp. 28, 34, 198; cf. p. 65.

[28] Ratzlaff, pp. 22, 23, 245, 246, 263; Carson, pp. 349-351.

[29] Ratzlaff, p. 20; Carson, p. 348.

[30] Carson, p. 215; cf. Ratzlaff, pp. 245, 246.

[31] Ratzlaff, p. 333.

[32] *Ibid.,* p. 88.

[33] *Ibid.,* p. 115; Carson, pp. 73, 76, 345, 361, 362; cf. an exception, p. 364.

[34] Carson, pp. 117, 118, 366, 375; cf. Ratzlaff, p. 218.

[35] For example, Ratzlaff uses the Pharisees' words ("You are this fellow's disciple! We are disciples of Moses!" [John 9:28]) to say "One *cannot* go both directions; either he is a *disciple of Jesus* or a *disciple of Moses"* (p. 135). "This is a key verse in this chapter and a very important one in our study of the Sabbath" (p. 135). Here his presupposition does not stop him from borrowing language from those in error to support his claim.

[36] Ratzlaff, p. 267.

[37] "The Sabbath is not viewed as a universal ordinance for all mankind but as a specific institution for Israel. As a sign of the covenant it was to last as long as that covenant" (Harold H. P. Dressler, in Carson, p. 34). Keil-Delitzsch denies a pre-Sinaitic Sabbath commandment *(Commentary on the Old Testament,* James Martin, trans. [Grand Rapids: Eerdmans, 1986], vol. 2, p. 119). "The evidence thus leads us to the conclusion that while the notion of God's rest in Genesis 2 was treated eschatologically by the biblical writers, it was not held by them to be a 'creation ordinance'" (A. T. Lincoln, in Carson, p. 351).

Lincoln argues that the Sabbath is no more binding than marriage, for "marriage can be considered a creation ordinance (Gen. 1:28; 2:24) but it is not binding on all men and women for all time, for . . . celibacy is . . . at least an equal option for obeying God (Matt. 19:10-12) and Paul considers it preferable (1 Cor. 7)" (p. 347). In so doing Lincoln fails to distinguish between obedience and free choice. Scripture never gives the Sabbath in Scripture as optional, while marriage is. Calvin rightly said of the Sabbath command, "Indeed there is no commandment the observance of which the Almighty more strictly enforces" (John Calvin, *Institutes,* vol. 1, p. 339). Wilfrid Stott concurs: "No other commandment is so strongly emphasized as this, showing what great importance it held in Israel's history and carrying the death penalty for its infringement (Ex. 31:14; cf. Ex. 35:3; Num. 15:32-36)." (Colin Brown, gen. ed., *The New International Dictionary of New Testament Theology* [Grand Rapids: Zondervan, 1986], vol. 3, p. 405).

[38] Martin Luther, *Luther's Works,* J. Pelikan, ed. (St. Louis: Concordia, 1958), vol. 1, pp. 79-82.

[39] John Calvin, *Genesis* (Grand Rapids: Baker, 1989), vol. 1, p. 106.

[40] Alfred Edersheim, *Old Testament Bible History* (Grand Rapids: Eerdmans, 1982), p. 113.

[41] C. F. Keil and F. Delitzsch, *Commentary on the Old Testament,* vol. 1, pp. 69, 70.

[42] John Skinner, *Word Biblical Commentary* (Waco, Tex.: Word, 1987), pp. 34-36.

[43] John P. Lange, *Lectures in Systematic Theology* (Grand Rapids: Zondervan, 1980), p. 376.

[44] James G. Murphy, *This Is the Day: The Biblical Doctrine of the Christian Sunday* (Greenwood, S.C.: Attic, 1978), p. 2.

[45] S. R. Driver, A. Plummer, C. A. Briggs, eds., *Genesis, International Critical Commentary* (Edinburgh, Scotland: T & T Clark, 1963), vol. 1, p. 35.

[46] P. Schaff, trans., *Genesis, Commentary on the Holy Scriptures, Critical, Doctrinal and Homiletical* (Grand Rapids: Zondervan, n.p.d.), vol. 1, pp. 196, 197.

[47] *Barnes Notes: A Commentary on the Book of Genesis* (Grand Rapids: Baker, 1983), vol. 1, p. 71.

[48] *The Biblical Commentary,* F. C. Cook, ed. (Grand Rapids: Baker, 1981), vol. 1, p. 37.

[49] Robert Jamieson, A. R. Fausset, D. Brown, *A Commentary, Critical, Experimental and Practical in the Old and New Testaments* (Grand Rapids: Eerdmans, 1982), vol. 1, pp. 28, 29.

[50] R. Alan Cole, *Exodus, Tyndale OT Commentary,* D. J. Wiseman, gen. ed. (Leicester, Eng.: InterVarsity, 1972), p. 158.

[51] *Baker Encyclopedia of the Bible,* Walter A. Elwell, gen. ed. (Grand Rapids: Baker, 1988), p. 1874.

[52] D. A. Rausch, *Evangelical Dictionary of Theology,* Walter A. Elwell, ed. (Grand Rapids: Baker, 1987), p. 964.

[53] J. C. McCabb, Jr., *The International Standard Bible Encyclopedia* (Grand Rapids: Eerdmans, 1988), p. 249.

[54] J. H. Sailhamer, *The Expositor's Biblical Commentary,* Frank E. Gaebelein, gen. ed., *Genesis* (Grand Rapids: Zondervan, 1990), vol. 2, pp. 38, 39.

[55] Gordon J. Wenham, *Word Biblical Commentary,* D. A. Hubbard, G. W. Barker, eds. (Waco, Tex.: Word, 1987), vol. 1, p. 36.

[56] One commentary claims that the Genesis Sabbath account is a command, as follows: "And God rested on the seventh day from all His work, which He made; and God commanded (man) to bless and worship on the seventh day, and ordered (him) to sanctify it" (Jamieson, Fausset, Brown, pp. 28, 29).

[57] J. G. Murphy, *Barnes Notes: A Commentary on the Book of Genesis* (Grand Rapids: Baker, 1983), vol. 1, p. 71.

[58] Carson, p. 346.

[59] M. Max B. Turner in Carson, pp. 133, 134.

[60] A. T. Lincoln in Carson, p. 386.

[61] *Ibid.,* p. 404.

Chapter 28

Satan's Sunday Sabbath

"I didn't know there was such a church as Seventh-day Adventists." He spoke thoughtfully. He was a student who had promised God to read the Bible through because He had answered a prayer.

"I followed through. It took me a year to read the Bible. I was amazed that many times through the 66 books I found references to the seventh-day Sabbath."

"What effect did they have on you?" I asked.

"I became convicted that Christians were keeping the wrong day. I didn't have any idea why or where they got the idea. All I know was the Bible doesn't say anything about Sunday as the Sabbath. But it repeatedly says that the seventh day is the Sabbath. I decided to keep the Sabbath on Saturday, even if I was the only person in the world doing it. In fact, I thought I was."

This teenager read himself into the Sabbath from the Bible, without any other books. It was a joy to have him in classes at Southern Adventist University.

Is Sunday the Christian Sabbath? Most Christians say yes. They base that on their understanding of certain biblical passages. For example: Christ rose from the dead "on the first day of the week" (Mark 16:2). He "appeared to his disciples on a Sunday (John 20:1-18; Luke 24:15, 34; John 20:26; 21:3-17; Acts 1:10) and sent them the Spirit on a Sunday (Acts 2:1-3). Sunday is thus the weekly Easter, the 'celebration of the paschal mystery on the eighth day, which is therefore rightly called the day of the Lord or the Lord's Day,' "[1] states the Catholic *Sacramentum Mundi.* The 1994 *Catechism of the Catholic Church* adds, "The Sunday celebration of the Lord's Day and his Eucharist is at the heart of the Church's life."[2]

The Catholic Church puts mass and Sunday together each week. But both are human inventions and take the place of a work of Christ. The mass replaces Calvary, and Sunday substitutes for the Sabbath He gave to humanity in Eden (Gen. 2:2, 3; Ex. 20:8-11; John 1:1-4, 14; Col. 1:16; Heb. 1:1-3). That's not all. Tradition has cloaked the mass in Christian garb, as is also the case with Sunday. Linking Sunday with the Resurrection gives it credibility to many Christians, but not to Christ and His followers.

Sunday in the New Testament

Christians of all denominations believe that the New Testament changed Sabbath to Sunday. Look at Christ's resurrection on the first day of the week, they point out, or at Pentecost and the various first-day meetings. But all these are descriptive passages, not prescriptive. In other words, the fact that some events and meetings took place on the first day of the week doesn't prove that Sunday succeeded the seventh-day Sabbath. When it comes to His Ten Commandments, the constitution of heaven, surely God Himself would announce such a radical change. The fact He didn't should cause those who observe Sunday to ask why. Let's analyze the first-day texts.

1. John 20:19-23

On the day of His resurrection Jesus appeared to His disciples who had locked themselves in a room out of fear of the Jews. The incident took place after Christ's encounter with two disciples on the Emmaus road (Luke 24:36-40), who had urged Him, "Stay with us, for it is nearly evening; the day is almost over" (verse 29). As Leon Morris explains, the phrase "toward evening" "meant that it was time to stop normal traveling. After dark the going would be difficult on unlit paths and there might be dangers from robbers and wild beasts. It was better to call a halt."[3] The Greek literally means "the day has declined into evening."[4] It is likely that Jesus appeared to the disciples after dark, since the Jews reckoned days from sunset to sunset (Gen. 1:5, 8, 13, 19, 23, 31), so He actually appeared to them on Monday.

2. Acts 20:6, 7

"On the first day of the week we came together to break bread. Paul spoke to the people." Is this evidence that early Christians met regularly on Sunday to worship and partake of the Lord's Supper? F. F. Bruce says this passage "is the earliest unambiguous evidence we have for the Christian practice of gathering together for worship on that day."[5] But does the text really substantiate this? First, "Paul spoke . . . until midnight" and was to leave the next day (verse 7). It appears to be a farewell meeting to say goodbye to Paul, as well as an evening meeting, and hence the reference "first day of the week" would be Saturday evening (Jewish reckoning) or Sunday evening (Roman reckoning). Whichever it is, we have no hint it was a normal event or that Sunday had replaced the Sabbath. The passage just doesn't offer any "unambiguous evidence" for Sunday worship.

3. 1 Corinthians 16:1, 2

Paul asked that each member in Corinth set aside money for the poor in Jerusalem "on the first day of the week" that he would then collect when he came to Corinth. Does it suggest a change of Sabbath to Sunday? W. Harold Mare sees it as urging that "Christians were to bring their offerings to church on Sunday."[6] F. W. Grosheide believes that

Paul "does not ask them to hand in their collection on a weekly basis," yet also suggests that the singling out of the first day of the week shows that "Sunday was destined for the special service of the Lord."[7] But the passage contains no hint that it was a public meeting for worship, or that the collection request was destined to make Sunday the new Sabbath. It's simply a request from Paul for each member to save money at home, on a regular basis, so that when he came they would have a good collection to give to him.

4. Revelation 1:10

"On the Lord's Day I was in the Spirit," John reports. Most Christians link this with Sunday, which they call the Lord's day. The Lord's day in the Greek is *kyriake hemera,* the only time the term appears in the New Testament. As Alan F. Johnson rightly points out, commentators have made several interpretations, such as the future day of judgment (unlikely because the eschatological day of the Lord is *hemera kyriou* in Greek), Easter Sunday, or Sunday (favored by most commentators).[8] Leon Morris supports the interpretation as Sunday, stating "this is the first use of the term for a day of worship, a weekly commemoration of the resurrection."[9]

However, this takes the term "Lord's day" as used in later Christian writings and reads it back into the text. It is important to examine the passage within its biblical context. Scripture is clear that the Lord's day is the seventh-day Sabbath (Ex. 20:11; Isa. 58:13), for "the Son of Man is Lord even of the Sabbath" (Mark 2:28).

Sunday Worship in the New Testament Questioned

From the passages we have examined in the previous section, it is clear that they do not prescribe any change of the Sabbath from Saturday to Sunday. One must remember that the Gospels, for example, were written around A.D. 60 (Matthew, Mark, Luke) and A.D. 90 (John), and thus 30 and 60 years (in round numbers) since the Resurrection. Yet nowhere does the New Testament say Sunday is to be the Sabbath in honor of the Resurrection. In fact, Jesus was crucified on the preparation day, rested in the grave on the Sabbath, and arose on Sunday morning (Matt. 28:1-3; Mark 15:42-16:6; Luke 23:50-24:6; John 19:38-20:2). Even though John calls Friday the "Jewish day of preparation" (John 19:42), he says nothing about the Sabbath shifting to Sunday for Christians.

The consistent problem with the passages reviewed above is that to support Sunday as the new Sabbath is that each one has a later practice projected back into the texts. But the biblical passages do not support such a later inclusion. The arguments that Sunday was the Christian Sabbath in the New Testament are simply not persuasive.

Interestingly, as we saw in the previous chapter, the scholars writing in D. A. Carson's book *From Sabbath to Lord's Day* conclude that "it is all but impossible to believe that Sunday was established as the Lord's Day, as a holy convocation, and as a Christian response to a creation ordinance in Palestine shortly after the Resurrection. The arguments against this position are virtually conclusive."[10] Later the same work states: "It cannot be argued that the New Testament itself provides warrant for the belief that since the Resurrection God appointed the first day to be observed as the Sabbath."[11] As for the Sabbath, they admit that "there is no biblical or compelling theological reason why it has to be Sunday."[12]

So it seems clear that the New Testament doesn't support the transfer of Sabbath from Saturday to Sunday. Nor does the New Testament associate the so-called Sunday meetings with a worship day. In addition, the New Testament is completely silent as to any such shift. If the change was God-ordained, as a new interpretation of the sacred law of God, Scripture should have stated it as clearly as the fourth commandment in the Old Testament. We cannot just guess at any alteration of divine law. It's like changing the constitution of a country. In order for Christians to know of any modification of the day of the Sabbath, God would have clearly announced it; this is particularly true in light of the fact that Christ promised to send the Holy Spirit to "guide you into all truth" (John 16:13). Because God does not change, and hence the law, as a transcript of His character, does not alter, when did the transfer from Saturday to Sunday take place? Do we have any evidence from nonbiblical sources that tell us?

Origin of Sunday Observance

God's law is as unchangeable as He is. This means that the Sabbath is, in principle, as everlasting as God. Anyone attempting to shift the Sabbath to another day is in essence trying to change God. The Bible predicts that a power would attempt to make such a change. Daniel 7:25 refers to a little-horn power (Dan. 7:21) that "will speak against the Most High and oppress his saints and try to change set times and the laws." History shows this power opposes God and His law, and seeks to change the law. The *Catechism of the Council of Trent for Parish Priests* records what the early church did: "The Church of God has thought it well to transfer the celebration and observance of the Sabbath to Sunday."[13] So the human church inaugurated Sunday, whereas the Sabbath is Christ's creation.

Stephen Keenan, in *A Doctrinal Catechism,* raises the question "Have you any other way of proving that the Church has the power to institute festivals of precept?" The answer he gives is "Had she not such power, she could not have done that in which all modern religionists agree with her—she could not have substituted the observance of Sunday the first day of the week, for the observance of Saturday the seventh day, a change for which there is no Scriptural authority."[14]

In the *Catholic Mirror* (Sept. 23, 1893) we read: "The Catholic Church for over one thousand years before the existence of a Protestant, by virtue of her Divine mission, changed the day from Saturday to Sunday. We say by virtue of her Divine mission because He [who] has so called Himself 'the Lord of the Sabbath' . . . commanded all, without exception, 'to hear His Church,' under penalty of being classed by Him as 'the heathen and the publican. . . .' But the Protestant says: How can I receive the teachings of an apostate Church? How, we ask, have you managed to receive her teaching all your life, *in direct opposition* to your recognized teacher, the Bible, on the Sabbath question?"[15]

Gaspare de Fosso, archbishop of Reggio, in his address to the seventeenth session of the Council of Trent, January 18, 1562, cites the change of Sabbath from Saturday to Sunday as an evidence of the Church's authority. "The authority of the church, then, is illustrated most clearly by the Scriptures; for while on the one hand she recommends them, declares them to be divine, offers them to us to be read, in doubtful matters explains them faithfully, and condemns whatever is contrary to them; on the other hand, the legal precepts in the Scriptures taught by the Lord have ceased by virtue of the same authority. The Sabbath, the most glorious day in the law, has been changed into the Lord's day."[16] "The Archbishop of Reggio . . . openly declared that tradition stood above Scripture. The authority of the church could therefore not be bound to the authority of the Scriptures, because the church had changed circumcision into baptism, Sabbath into Sunday, not by the command of Christ, but by its own authority."[17]

Johann Eck, Luther's opponent at Leipzig, argued for the Church's superiority over Scripture. "The Scripture teaches 'Remember that you sanctify the day of the Sabbath; six days shall you labor and do all your work, but the seventh day is the Sabbath of the Lord your God,' etc. But the Church has changed the Sabbath into the Lord's [day] by its own authority, concerning which you have no Scripture. Christ said to his disciples in the mount, 'I have not come to dissolve the law but to fulfill it'; and yet the church of the Apostles in the first council has boldly spoken out concerning the cessation of legal things. . . . The Scripture decrees in the [apostolic] council . . . that you abstain from . . . blood and from a strangled thing; a matter so clearly defined and expressed the Church has changed by her own authority, for she used both blood and things strangled. See the power of the church over Scripture.

"The Sabbath is commanded many times by God; neither in the Gospels nor in Paul is it declared that the Sabbath has ceased; nevertheless the Church has instituted the Lord's day through the tradition of the Apostles without Scripture."[18]

We see no attempts to prove Sunday from the New Testament here. Rather the change to Sunday demonstrates the authority of the Catholic Church above Scripture. That should tell us something about the church and Sunday. The day does not have divine credentials.

Sabbath as a Type

The Catholic *Sacramentum Mundi* states: "The old Sabbath ended with the Passover of the Lord, but as a type (like the temple, etc.) it had its fulfillment in Christ (2 Cor. 1:20)."[19] Thus the Sabbath is "a prefiguration of Sunday in the history of salvation."[20] So the seventh-day Sabbath gets yanked out of the Ten Commandments and put down with the ceremonial laws such as lamb sacrifices and circumcision.

The recent *Catechism of the Catholic Church* declares that "Sunday is expressly distinguished from the Sabbath which it follows chronologically every week; for Christians its ceremonial observance replaces that of the sabbath. In Christ's, Passover Sunday fulfills the spiritual truth of the Jewish Sabbath and announces man's eternal rest in God."[21] In fact, "the Sabbath, which represented the completion of the first creation, has been replaced by Sunday which recalls the new creation inaugurated by the Resurrection of Christ."[22]

Sunday as a Moral Commandment?

God's moral law is as eternal and unchanging as God. Yet the Catholic Church wrenched the law from its proper place and changed Sabbath from seventh to first day. Look what it says about Sunday: "The celebration of Sunday observes the moral commandment inscribed by nature in the human heart to render to God as outward, visible, public, and regular worship 'as a sign of his universal beneficence to all.' Sunday worship fulfills the moral command of the Old Covenant, taking up its rhythm and spirit in the weekly celebration of the Creator and Redeemer of his people."[23]

But if the church wants to celebrate the Creator and Redeemer, that is, praising Him for His gifts of life and salvation, why do they not praise Him for His Sabbath gift, which celebrates both? The choice of their own day in place of the one Christ gave humanity is tantamount to rejecting Christ as Creator and Redeemer. So the use of words such as "Creator" and "Redeemer" are hollow. They are a Christian garb that cloaks a human replacement for what Christ has given. The human has so replaced the divine that it rejects Christ's gifts.

Sunday and Religious Liberty

How can Sunday and religious liberty be thought of together? After all, the coming Sunday law will rob saints of their societal liberty, but not liberty in Christ (Rom. 8:38, 39). Yet the *Catechism of the Catholic Church* declares that "in respecting religious liberty and the common good of all, Christians should seek recognition of Sundays and the Church's holy days as legal holidays."[24]

Sunday will become a legal holiday according to human regulations, but not according to God's law. "But in vain they do worship me," Christ said, "teaching for doctrines the commandments of men" (Matt. 15:9, KJV). No good to claim Sunday as the Lord's day since Christ is Lord of the Sabbath (Mark 2:28), not Sunday. Christ still invites Christians, "If you love me, you will obey what I command" (John 14:15).

CHRIST IS COMING!

---

[1] *Sacramentum Mundi* (New York, NY: Hermann-Herder, n.p.d.), vol. 5, p. 189.

[2] *Catechism of the Catholic Church,* p. 525.

[3] Leon Morris, *Tyndale New Testament Commentaries, Luke,* rev. ed. (Leicester, Eng.: InterVarsity, 1988), vol. 3, pp. 339, 340.

[4] John Nolland, *World Biblical Commentary,* David A. Hubbard, gen. ed. (Dallas: Word, 1993), vol. 35c, p. 1205.

[5] F. F. Bruce, *The New International Commentary on the New Testament* (Grand Rapids: Eerdmans, 1984), pp. 407, 408.

[6] W. Harold Mare, *The Expositor's Bible Commentary,* Frank E. Gaebelein, gen. ed. (Grand Rapids: Zondervan, 1976), vol. 10, p. 293.

[7] F. W. Grosheide, *The New International Commentary on the New Testament, 1 Corinthians* (Grand Rapids: Eerdmans, 1983), p. 398.

[8] Alan F. Johnson, *The Expositor's Bible Commentary, Revelation,* vol. 12, pp. 424, 425.

[9] Leon Morris, *Tyndale New Testament Commentaries, Revelation,* rev. ed. (Leicester, Eng.: InterVarsity, 1988), vol. 20, p. 52.

[10] M. Max B. Turner in *From Sabbath to Lord's Day,* pp. 133, 134.

[11] A. T. Lincoln in *From Sabbath to Lord's Day,* p. 386.

[12] *Ibid.,* p. 404.

[13] *Catechism of the Council of Trent for Parish Priests,* trans. by McHugh and Call, 2nd rev. ed. (1937), p. 402, quoted in T. H. Jemison, *Christian Beliefs: Fundamental Biblical Teachings for Seventh-day Adventist College Classes* (Boise, Idaho: Pacific Press, 1959), p. 289.

[14] Stephen Keenan, *A Doctrinal Catechism,* 3rd American ed., rev. (New York: T. W. Strong, Late Edward Dunigan & Bro., 1876), p. 174, quoted in the *Seventh-day Adventist Bible Students' Source Book* (Washington, D.C.: Review and Herald Pub. Assn., 1962), p. 886.

[15] *The Christian Sabbath,* 2nd ed. (Baltimore: *The Catholic Mirror,* 1893), pp. 29-33, quoted in the *SDA Bible Students' Source Book,* p. 885.

[16] Gaspare (Ricciulli) de Fosso in J. D. Mansi, ed., *Sacrorum Conciliorum . . . Collectio,* cited in *SDA Bible Students' Source Book,* p. 887.

[17] Heinrich Julius Holtzmann, *Kanon und Tradition* (Ludwigsburg: Druck und Verlag von Ferd. Riehm, 1859), p. 263, cited in *SDA Bible Students' Source Book,* p. 888.

[18] Johann Eck, *Enchiridion Locorum Communinium . . . Adversus Lutheranos* (Venice: Ioan. Antonius & Fratres de Sabio, 1533), fold. 4v, 5r, 42v. Latin. Trans. by Frank H. Yost, cited in *SDA Bible Students' Source Book,* p. 888.

[19] *Sacramentum Mundi* (Basle, Montreal: Hermann-Herder, n.p.d.), vol. 5, p. 189.

[20] *Ibid.,* p. 190.

[21] *Catechism of the Catholic Church,* pp. 524, 525.

[22] *Ibid.,* p. 529.

[23] *Ibid.,* p. 525.

[24] *Ibid.,* p. 528.

Chapter 29

The Christian Sabbath

"Wake up, son!" Father gently shook me. Slowly I awoke. Then I heard them. German bombers droned in the night sky as air-raid sirens wailed. I jumped onto the floor. Dad led the way as Mother, my brother Bernard, and I followed down the stairs, through the living room, kitchen, and den, with only a small dull light to guide us.

Outside, searchlights crisscrossed the sky. In the distant city, enemy bombs whistled in their descent. Antiaircraft guns blazed up at the planes. You never knew if it would be your last night. We lived near Watford, not too far from the outskirts of London. Hitler sent many planes to destroy England's capital.

Dad opened the back door. We followed gingerly down the small path past the pear tree, walking across the small lawn, by the apple tree, and through the vegetable garden to a camouflaged shelter. It lay half submerged in the ground. The door opened, we climbed down the steps, got up on the bunks, and closed the door—safe at last.

Down on the south coast of England, in Weymouth, Grandad and Grandma came out of their back door.

"Come and join us," Granddad called to his neighbors.

"Thanks. We're going inside to get a cup of tea. Then we'll stay under the stairs."

"You're more than welcome to join us," Grandma urged as they quickly made for the shelter. No sooner had they gotten inside and the door closed than they heard a terrible shrill noise coming closer, followed by a tremendous explosion. Debris rattled outside. Their hearts sank. What about their neighbors? They waited until all became quiet before opening the door. Outside they saw houses leveled and neighbors dead.

I thank God for those shelters. They remind me of the Sabbath. Just as those air-raid shelters offered an escape from the perils of war, so the Sabbath provides a refuge from the pressures of the week. The Sabbath brings protection amidst the cosmic controversy.

Christ began His ministry on a

Sabbath (Luke 4:16), proclaiming His mission to set the oppressed and prisoners free and to announce "the year of the Lord's favor" (verses 18, 19). As Samuel Bacchiocchi notes, most commentators refer this year to the Jubilee or sabbatical year.[1] Christ cited Isaiah 61:1, 2, claiming that "today this scripture is fulfilled in your hearing" (verse 21). Bacchiocchi asks a crucial question about this fulfillment. Did Christ view the Sabbath as a type that met its fulfillment in Him, or did He identify His mission with the Sabbath?[2]

I believe the Sabbath was a type of the Incarnation. Every week it comes to bring relief from the burdens of work. It sets workers free for a day. Thus the weekly Sabbath gives insight into Christ's mission to release those burdened with sin.

Sabbath as Essence of the Gospel

Yet the Sabbath was not a type in the sense that it met its fulfillment in the antitype and afterward had no function. In His announcement Christ identified His mission with the essence of the Sabbath. He had come to bring rest to sin-sick and weary people. Jesus had come to liberate them in Himself and would demonstrate through miracles the total freedom He had to offer. In fact, He often chose a Sabbath to perform that healing (Matt. 12:9-21; Luke 4:31-40; 13:10-17; John 5:1-18; 9:1-41) so that the physical release could give some insight into the spiritual salvation He came to provide. Christ offered both the Sabbath and salvation to humanity and illustrated the salvation gift through the Sabbath miracles.

The Sabbath gift of freedom had for many deteriorated into a day of work in Christ's day. Some 600 *halakah,* or man-made requirements, smothered the day with legalistic burdens. The Sabbath was no longer an invitation to set the burdened free. It had become itself an instrument to shackle. In stark contrast Christ came to liberate the prisoners, and He illustrated His deliverance through the Sabbath. He came to demonstrate the forgotten essence of the Sabbath (cf. Matt. 5:17-19). Like His mission, the Sabbath had liberation as its goal.

Christ, well aware of the ceremonial law, knew that it was a type of Himself. The function of the earthly sanctuary/Temple came to an end at Calvary. The sacrifices ceased in His sacrifice, circumcision gave way to adult baptism. The Jerusalem Council (Acts 15:1-29) met to consider the claim that Gentiles must be circumcised according to the law of Moses (verse 5). Peter reported to the council that Gentiles had received the Holy Spirit without being circumcised (verses 5-11). Paul and Barnabas told of the miraculous signs and wonders God did among the Gentiles (verse 12). But nowhere do we read that Christian believers replaced the Sabbath with Sunday.

Types Met Fulfillment in Christ

Types met their fulfillment in Christ, to whom they pointed and in whom they found their meaning. And these included ceremonial Sabbaths, Sabbaths connected with festivals such as unleavened bread (Lev. 23:6-8), the Feast of Weeks (verses 15, 16, 21), the Feast of Trumpets (verses 24, 25), the Day of Atonement (verses 26-28), and the Feast of Tabernacles (verses 33-36). These ceremonial Sabbaths lost their predictive meaning along with the ceremonial feasts of which they formed a part.

The cessation of these ceremonial Sabbaths forms the content of Paul's statement in Colossians 2:16, 17: "Therefore do not let anyone judge you by what you eat or drink, or with regard to a religious festival, a New Moon celebration or a Sabbath day. These are a shadow of the things that were to come; the reality, however, is found in Christ." Clearly Paul was not speaking about the moral law of the Ten Commandments. The separation of the Sabbath day "one-day-in-seven" rest from the specified seventh day, calling the Sabbath by itself moral and its connection with the seventh-day ceremonial, has no logical or biblical foundation.

Sabbath More Than a Type

The seventh-day Sabbath must be more than a type. The fact that Christ saw the Sabbath in a far greater context appeared when He said, "The Son of Man is Lord of the Sabbath" (Matt. 12:7; see also Mark 2:28; Luke 6:5). Christ also said: "The Sabbath was made for man, not man for the Sabbath" (Mark 2:27). Christ did not state that God established the Sabbath for the Jewish race, but for humanity. Clearly Christ is rejecting the national confines placed on the Sabbath by human thinkers and placing it squarely into its global context. It is tantamount to declaring the Sabbath a Creation ordinance. The Sabbath, as understood by Christ, breaks beyond national and typical confines and is placed solidly in its broadest context as transcultural and transgenerational.

As Gerhard Hasel expressed it: "The Son of Man as Lord determines the true meaning of the Sabbath. The Sabbath activities of Jesus are neither hurtful provocations nor mere protests against rabbinic legal restrictions, but are the kingdom of God in which man is taught the original meaning of the Sabbath as the recurring weekly proleptic 'day of the Lord' in which God manifests His healing and saving rulership over man."[3]

Sabbath Remains for Christians

The New Testament corroborates Hasel's conclusion. The secondary meaning of Hebrews 4 states that there still remains a seventh-day Sabbath rest *(katapausis)* for the people of God (Heb. 4:9, 10), and Hebrews was most likely written in A.D. 70, nearly 40 years after Christ's crucifixion (which many scholars consider as discontinuing the Sabbath because it was merely a type) and resurrection (to which still other scholars look to as changing the Sabbath to the first day). Hebrews 4 denies the possibility of either reason for the Sabbath's demise or its change. The chapter agrees with Christ's linkage of the Sabbath with the entire human race without exception relative to the Old and New Testament periods.

The Christian Sabbath is the day Christ made holy at the creation of the world. Christ created our planet and Adam and Eve. He rested on the seventh day, setting it apart as holy. Jesus observed it while He lived on earth as the God-man. He did not keep the Sabbath because He was a Jew, even though we can say that about His circumcision and Passover observance.

Rather He honored the Sabbath as He did all Ten Commandments, setting an example for all humans and not just for the Jews. It is the same Sabbath Christ kept that the redeemed will observe forever in the new earth (Isa. 66:22, 23). The Jerusalem Conference (Acts 15:1-29) said nothing about transferring the Sabbath from Saturday to Sunday.

The End-time Sabbath Test

In his book *Sabbath in Crisis* (studied in chapter 27), Dale Ratzlaff rejected the Sabbath as the seal of God and as an end-time testing truth. "Nowhere in the New Testament is this type of evangelism *taught* or *practiced,"* he says. "Rather, New Testament evangelism is *always* a proclamation of the *good news of the gospel of Jesus Christ!"* Furthermore, he adds, "The SDA 'traditional evangelistic method,' as mentioned above, undermines the gospel. It takes the gospel out of the center and makes Sabbath observance 'the testing truth.' "[4]

I believe that Ratzlaff is the one who removes the Sabbath from its gospel context and excises the good news about coming events. Furthermore, no careful reading of Revelation 13-20 can escape the fact that the beast and its image are a significant factor in an end-time test over the gospel of Christ. We shall consider this omitted dimension of the gospel in this section and see that the Sabbath is actually the very essence of the gospel in the last days. There is no gospel without the Sabbath, and no Sabbath without the gospel. Scripture inextricably combines the two, especially in end-time events. An attack against one is an attack against both, a serious problem of Ratzlaff's book that he totally overlooks. While attempting to champion the gospel he rejects Christ's Sabbath that magnifies it. The sad fact in the end-time is that separation from Christ's Sabbath leads inexorably to alienation from Him, and rejection of Christ leads to denial of His Sabbath.

Satan has ever claimed to offer a more exalted existence to those who would free themselves from Christ. He did it in heaven, Eden, and will again try it during the end-time. "To the very close of the controversy in heaven the great usurper continued to justify himself. When it was announced that with all his sympathizers he must be expelled from the abodes of bliss, then the rebel leader boldly avowed his contempt for the Creator's law. He reiterated his claim that angels needed no control, but should be left to follow their own will, which would ever guide them right. He denounced the divine statutes as a restriction of their liberty and declared that it was his purpose to secure the abolition of law; that, freed from this restraint, the hosts of heaven might enter upon a more exalted, more glorious state of existence. With one accord, Satan and his host threw the blame of their rebellion wholly upon Christ."[5]

In Eden Satan said Eve would become as God if she ate the fruit (Gen. 3:5). "As she ate, she seemed to feel a vivifying power, and imagined herself entering upon a higher state of existence."[6] And during the end-time "through spiritualism, Satan appears as a benefactor of the race, healing the diseases of the people, and professing to present a new and more exalted system of religious faith; but at the same time he works as a destroyer."[7]

Throughout his struggle with Christ he has equated this more exalted experience with freedom from God's law. As noted above, in heaven Satan "boldly avowed his contempt for the Creator's law. . . . He denounced the divine statutes as a restriction of their liberty."[8] Yet, in the end-time, Satan will come to enforce his Sunday law with a death decree (Rev. 13:11-15). "The last great conflict between truth and error is but the final struggle of the long-standing controversy concerning the law of God. Upon this battle we are now entering—a battle between the laws of men and the precepts of Jehovah, between the religion of the Bible and the religion of fable and tradition."[9]

In the great time of trouble Satan will manifest himself as Christ and reign on earth. He has always wanted to take Christ's position and receive the worship due Him alone. Although he will rule over billions of humans as their savior, really he has robbed them of eternal life. "While appearing to the children of men as a great physician who can heal all their maladies, he will bring disease and disaster, until populous cities are reduced to ruin and desolation."[10] Satan will send tornadoes, hailstorms, floods, earthquakes "in every place and in a thousand forms" and declare "that men are offending God by the violation of the Sunday-sabbath; that this sin has brought calamities which will not cease until Sunday observance shall be strictly enforced; and that those who present the claims of the fourth commandment, thus destroying reverence for Sunday, are troublers of the people, preventing their restoration to divine favor and temporal prosperity."[11]

When the angels release the winds of strife in the end-time (Rev. 7:1-3), unprecedented troubles will deluge the planet. "Those who honor the Bible Sabbath will be denounced as enemies of law and order, as breaking down the moral restraints of society, causing anarchy and corruption, and calling down the judgments of God upon the earth."[12] "Communications from the spirits will declare that God has sent them to convince the rejecters of Sunday of their error, affirming that the laws of the land should be obeyed as the law of God. They will lament the great wickedness in the world and second the testimony of religious teachers that the degraded state of morals is caused by the desecration of Sunday. Great will be the indignation excited against all who refuse to accept their testimony."[13]

After probation's close Satan will cause havoc. "The same destructive power exercised by holy angels when God commands, will be exercised by evil angels when He permits. There are forces now ready, and only waiting the divine permission, to spread desolation everywhere."[14]

"The Sabbath question is to be the issue in the great final conflict in which all the world will act a part."[15] The Sabbath issue "will agitate the whole world,"[16] as all the world wonders after the beast (Rev. 13:3). "The substitution of the laws of men for the law of God, the exaltation, by merely human authority, of Sunday in place of the Bible Sabbath, is the last act in the drama. When this substitution becomes universal, God will reveal Himself. He will arise in His majesty to shake terribly the earth."[17]

In the coming conflict, "the whole world is to be stirred with enmity against Seventh-day Adventists because they will not yield homage to the papacy by honoring Sunday, the institution of this antichristian power."[18] "As the Sabbath has become the special point of controversy throughout Christendom, and religious and secular authorities have combined to enforce the observance of the Sunday, the persistent refusal of a small minority to yield to the popular demand will make them objects of universal execration."[19] "There will come a time when, because of our advocacy of Bible truth, we shall be treated as traitors."[20]

"Wealth, genius, education, will combine to cover them with contempt. Persecuting rulers, ministers, and church members will conspire against them. With voice and pen, by boasts, threats, and ridicule, they will seek to overthrow their faith."[21] "Satan has a thousand masked batteries which will be opened upon the loyal, commandment-keeping people of God to compel them to violate conscience."[22] "All who in that evil day would fearlessly serve God according to the dictates of conscience, will need courage, firmness, and a knowledge of God and His word; for those who are true to God will be persecuted, their motives will be impugned, their best efforts misinterpreted, and their names cast out as evil."[23]

How to Prepare for the Coming Crisis

1. To Survive the Sabbath Test We Need to Experience the Sabbath Rest.

The Sabbath test involves far more than a question of mathematics. Transcending which day is the seventh, it goes to the essence of the Sabbath itself. The Sabbath teaches "the distinction between the Creator and His creatures."[24] It is precisely what Satan has refused to acknowledge since he began his rebellion. In the end-time Satan seeks to replace his Creator when he comes impersonating Christ and promoting Sunday. The end-time saints will not worry about the worldwide opposition against them, because Sabbathkeeping is more than a day—it is an experience. Through observing Christ's Sabbath they can rest in Him. They experience the Sabbath by resting in a Creator who alone can take them through the crisis. All of them recognize that they didn't do anything to enter this world and they cannot do anything to earn the right to get into the next one. Christ has done for them that which they could never do for themselves—He created them and redeemed them. The Sabbathkeeping is resting in His double finished work.

2. The Sabbath Rest in Christ Our Refuge

This is why a Sabbath follows Creation Friday (Gen. 2:2) and Crucifixion Friday (Luke 23:54-24:1). Properly understood, both Sabbaths were time to celebrate Christ's finished work, His completed task, both of Creation and of redemption. Resting in these works of Christ is the very essence of the Sabbath rest. We rest in Him as our Creator-Redeemer.

Psalm 91 speaks of this rest. "He who dwells in the shelter of the Most High will rest in the shadow of the Almighty. I will say of the Lord, 'He is my refuge and my fortress, my God, in whom I trust.' Surely he will save you from the fowler's snare and from the deadly pestilence. He will cover you with his feathers, and under his wings you will find refuge; his faithfulness will be your shield and rampart. You will not fear the terror of night, nor the arrow that flies by day, nor the pestilence that stalks in the darkness, nor the plague that destroys at midday. A thousand will fall at your side, ten thousand at your right hand, but it will not come near you. You will only observe with your eyes and see the punishment of the wicked. If you make the Most High your dwelling—even the Lord, who is my refuge—then no harm will befall you, no disaster will come near your tent" (Ps. 91:1-10).

---

[1] Samuel Bacchiocchi, *From Sabbath to Sunday,* p. 20.

[2] *Ibid.,* p. 21.

[3] Gerhard F. Hasel, "Sabbath," *The Anchor Bible Dictionary,* David Noel Freedman, ed. (New York: Doubleday, 1992), vol. 5, p. 855.

[4] Dale Ratzlaff, *The Sabbath Crisis,* p. 304.

[5] E. G. White, *The Great Controversy,* p. 499.

[6] E. G. White, *Patriarchs and Prophets,* p. 56.

[7] E. G. White, *The Great Controversy,* p. 589.

[8] *Ibid.,* p. 499.

[9] *Ibid.,* p. 582.

[10] *Ibid.,* p. 589.

[11] *Ibid.,* p. 590.

[12] *Ibid.,* p. 592.

[13] *Ibid.,* p. 591.

[14] *Ibid.,* p. 614.

[15] E. G. White, *Testimonies for the Church,* vol. 6, p. 352.

[16] E. G. White, *Evangelism* (Washington, D.C.: Review and Herald, 1946), p. 236.

[17] E. G. White, *Testimonies,* vol. 7, p. 141.

[18] E. G. White, *Testimonies to Ministers* (Mountain View, Calif.: Pacific Press, 1944), p. 37.

[19] E. G. White, *The Great Controversy,* p. 615.

[20] E. G. White, *Testimonies,* vol. 6, p. 394.

[21] *Ibid.,* p. 450.

[22] E. G. White, *Last Day Events,* p. 147.

[23] E. G. White, *The Acts of the Apostles* (Mountain View, Calif.: Pacific Press, 1911), pp. 431, 432.

[24] E. G. White, *The Great Controversy,* pp. 437, 438.

Chapter 30

The Real Issue in the Coming Sunday Law

I'd rather be a Sundaykeeper who loves the Lord than a Sabbathkeeper who doesn't!"

"What do you mean?" a friend asked.

"Salvation is premised on knowing Christ. Look at John 17:3," the other replied.

"So what's that got to do with the coming Sunday law?" came the retort.

"Everything! Many Sundaykeepers really know Jesus. They'll get a chance to learn of the seventh-day Sabbath in the end-time final invitation of Revelation 18:1-4. Accepting the news, they'll be God's end-time saints, having already experienced the meaning of the Sabbath in their Sunday observance!"

"OK. But what about Sabbathkeepers in the end-time?" the other pressed.

"Remember the Jews of Christ's day observed the Sabbath but crucified Jesus. The test then wasn't over a day but over a Person. All admitted that the seventh day is God's Sabbath. They knew the Sabbath of the Lord, but not the Lord of the Sabbath. Seventh-day Sabbathkeepers were those who yelled, 'Crucify!'"

"But, wait a minute," the other interrupted. "The Sabbath is the issue in the end-time."

"Yes and no. The end-time test is more than mathematics. More than which is the seventh day, it has far more to do with who is the Lord of the Sabbath—do I have a relationship with Him, is He giving to me the Sabbath experience that will protect me in the end-time?"

"So it's a package deal—the Saviour and the Sabbath?"

"Right! The primary test is whether we are in a deep saving relationship with Jesus. The seventh-day Sabbath will become the ultimate outward manifestation of this relationship. The Sunday-law test is more than a day—it's a test of a relationship."

We'll take a look at this real issue in this chapter.

What's the deeper meaning of the Sabbath in light of Satan's final attack against God's Decalogue in the approaching international Sunday-law crisis? We will consider (1) the purpose of the Sabbath, (2) Sabbath as a Creation ordinance, (3) its meaning unfolded in salvation history, and (4) the real issue in the coming Sunday law.

The Purpose of the Sabbath

The entrance of sin is one of the two greatest mysteries in the universe (cf. 2 Thess. 2:7). The other is the plan of salvation from sin (Eph. 1:9, 10; 6:19; Col. 1:26). The fact that sin could enter a perfect universe is inexplicable.[1] Lucifer claimed "equality with Christ."[2] He wanted to be "equal with God Himself"[3] (cf. Eze. 28:1-19). The Father made all the worlds and their inhabitants through Christ (Col. 1:16; Heb. 1:2); that would include Lucifer. So he owed everything to Christ, yet in utter insensitive ingratitude came to desire equality with Him.

Sin is a leap into the dark—because it leads away from the One who is the light. Separation from God, sin at its deepest level, is the ignoring of the distinction between the Creator and creatures. Here we find the root problem behind transgression of the law. Satan's broken relationship with Christ led inevitably to law-breaking.[4] Law-keeping issues out of a dependent relationship upon the Lawgiver—"If you love me, you will obey what I command" (John 14:15). In the Decalogue the Sabbath command is the only one that has no immediate rational basis except that God gave it. To not kill, steal, or commit adultery makes sense in our everyday human life, but not so with a seventh day as holy, set apart from the six—except that God decreed it.[5] Like the "tree test" in Eden, the only difference between that tree and other trees was the fact that God had set it apart. That is why the looming Sunday-law test will find humanity facing the same issue as in Eden. Both constitute a loyalty test.[6] If sin is alienation from God, then of all commandments kept, Sabbath-keeping manifests a deep loyal relationship with God—obedience based solely upon His wishes.

At the very moment sin began, a new reality burst into the universe—the great controversy. Now for the first time a created being ignored his necessary dependence upon his Creator and set out on a flight of independence. How would God respond? His first tangible response was to institute the Sabbath.[7] The Sabbath would remind created beings that they are dependent creatures, for, as Kierkegaard observed, an infinite qualitative distinction exists between God and humanity.[8]

Thus before human beings took their leap into the dark—into sorry "independence" from their Maker—Christ gave them the Sabbath. It constituted as vital a gift as life itself, and within this context of the great controversy and Creation, we come to discover the deeper meaning of the Sabbath. As Ellen White put it: "'The importance of the Sabbath as a memorial of creation is that it keeps ever present the true reason why worship is due to God'—because He is the Creator, and we are His creatures. The Sabbath therefore lies at the very foundation of divine worship, for it teaches this great truth in the most impressive manner, and no other institution does this. The true ground of divine worship . . . is found in the distinction between the

Creator and His creatures."[9]

When friends look at Seventh-day Adventists and believe they keep a Jewish Sabbath according to the old law and that such a thing is legalism, they overlook the fact that the Sabbath reveals the very heart of the gospel—dependence upon Christ (the creature depending upon his Creator for everything).

If the purpose of the Sabbath is to remind human beings of their total need of the Creator for everything and that Christ is the One who created all things, then the Sabbath is distinctly Christian.

Sabbath as Creation Ordinance

Every nation has needed the Sabbath to remind it of the distinction between God and humanity. Humanity's quest (1) for godhood, found in eastern religions, Mormonism, and the New Age movement; his search (2) for other gods or (3) for no God—all evidence this need. Ellen White observed that "had the Sabbath been universally kept, man's thoughts and affections would have been led to the Creator as the object of reverence and worship, and there would never have been an idolater, an atheist, or an infidel."[10]

These categories, found around the world and throughout human history, indicate humanity's serious need to recognize the distinction between God and itself. This is particularly important in end-time events. All the saints will feel their absolute dependence upon Christ, and not upon themselves. They will have given up on themselves.

While some relatively recent publications endorse the Sabbath as a Creation ordinance,[11] the book *From Sabbath to Lord's Day,* as we saw in a previous chapter, rejects it.[12] On the other hand, a leading theologian of the twentieth century, Karl Barth, recognized it.[13] As we shall see later, the Sabbath as a Creation ordinance, with relevance for all humanity, will be crucial in the final crisis on earth.[14]

Sabbath Unfolded in Salvation History

As in the unfolding of progressive revelation, it took time to disclose the full meaning of the Sabbath. We see creaturely dependence upon the Creator illustrated throughout salvation-history, so that the meaning of the Sabbath unfolds as we move through the Bible. We will consider some of the key moments in that process.

The Sabbath is a revelation of Christ. Just as He comes to be with humanity on the seventh day,[15] so He entered the world as Immanuel, "God with us" (Matt. 1:23). In Old Testament times, to the enlightened, each Sabbath was a microcosm of the Incarnation. Each Sabbath renewed the promise of a coming Messiah. In Creation He had made space and time—He filled space with created things and entered time as the Creator.[16] He was not satisfied with created space and its lower inhabitants, even though they were "very good" (Gen. 1:31). As Heschel suggests, He made humans in order to be with them in time.[17]

Prior to the Creation week of Genesis we have no evidence of marriage, the weekly cycle, or the Sabbath.[18] Each is important to Creation's purpose. Creation week has "companionship" as a theme running through it (Gen. 1; 2). 1. Creatures provided for human enjoyment were His companions at the lowest level. 2. Moving through the week to Friday, God created man and woman for each other to be companions at a much higher level. But Creation week does not climax in human creation, although human beings are the crowning work of physical creation. 3. Creation week culminates in the Sabbath, in which we see humans made for God—companionship at the highest possible level.

Being omnipotent (Job 42:2; Ps. 115:3; Isa. 43:13; Jer. 32:17; Luke 1:37), God could have brought everything into existence instantaneously. But He did not. He chose to take a week in order that, subsequently, humans might be able to focus on the ultimate purpose for their creation. God did not create human beings just for the animals nor just for fellowship with each other. He made them for Himself. Can we grasp what this means? Can we enter into the depths of Christ's desire to be with us? Not as much in creation as in re-creation—at the cross. There we see Christ willing to die for humanity in order to have us live with Him forever. Properly understood, each Sabbath has this commitment of Christ as its very essence—Christ gives everything so that we can be with Him. If Christ goes to that extent, then the Sabbath, far from being legalistic, opens up the very heart of the gospel.

Humanity's first full day was a Sabbath.[19] Adam and Eve spent it in Sabbath fellowship with Christ. What a vantage point from which to go down into the work-a-day week that followed.[20] Here's an insight into the Christian life: work issues out of time spent with Christ, never the other way round.[21]

Just as Creation week has a theme that unfolds to its climax in the Sabbath, so the Sabbath itself has an unfolding of its meaning throughout Scripture. As we move through the canon we find that later texts add to the depth already found in earlier ones. As they occur, the events of Creation week make the purpose of human creation more understandable; similarly, the key events in salvation history throughout Scripture unfold the fuller significance of the Sabbath.

Old Testament Examples

With respect to the meaning of the Sabbath, we will briefly consider three major texts: Exodus 20:8-11; Deuteronomy 5:12-15; and Ezekiel 20:12. The first insight into the Sabbath occurs in the setting of Creation. Exodus 20 calls us to remember the Sabbath, to keep it holy, in memory of Creation (Ex. 20:8-11). The Sabbath reminds us that we are not God,[22] or emanations from God,[23] but merely creatures. An infinite qualitative distinction separates the Creator and human beings. Our creaturely dependence is fundamental to our very existence. We are totally and forever indebted to Christ's power, outside of and beyond ourselves, to give us life. Each Sabbath summons us to remember that fact because it is easy for us to think that we are independent and can make it on our own. The Sabbath reminds the human race that there really is no "self-made" human being.

Deuteronomy 5 asks us to consider something other than Creation in the Sabbath command. "Remember that you were slaves in Egypt and that the Lord your God brought you out of there with a mighty hand and an outstretched arm. Therefore the Lord your God has commanded you to observe the Sabbath day" (verse 15). Here the fourth commandment asks that Israel honor the Sabbath and keep it holy in memory of the Exodus.

The two renditions of the fourth commandment, in Exodus and Deuteronomy, offer complementary presentations. The Sabbath is both a memorial of Creation and of the Exodus. Although God gave both to Israel, we cannot apply the first to humanity as a whole and limit the second to the "called-out" nation.

Until the Exodus, Sabbaths represented only a memorial of Creation. But following the Exodus, the newly "called-out" people had another divine act to remember. The same preincarnate Christ, who created the whole human race, had now liberated Hebrew slaves from Egypt, and through the Exodus formed a new people, a new nation, the covenant movement through whom He wished to prepare the whole world for His incarnation. The Sabbath now took on added meaning as it celebrated two completed works of Christ—Creation and Exodus.

Ezekiel 20 focuses on that Exodus, unfolding an additional significance of the Sabbath. It was an unrepresentative people that Christ rescued from Egypt. Because they were enslaved to false idols as well as to the Egyptians, Christ longed to free them from this greater slavery. The Exodus itself acted as a self-revelation of Christ to them. "I had revealed myself to the Israelites by bringing them out of Egypt. Therefore I led them out of Egypt and brought them into the desert. I gave them my decrees and made known to them my laws, for the man who obeys them will live by them. Also I gave them my Sabbaths as a sign between us, so they would know that I the Lord made them holy" (Eze. 20:9-12).

The word "holy," in the Hebrew *(qodesh)* and the Greek *(hagion),* means to "set apart." In the Exodus Christ set His people apart from the Egyptians, with a view to taking them into Canaan to become a separate nation. The Exodus therefore typified historically what Christ longed for His people experientially—separation from the world to be one with Him. Just as He removed them geographically from slavery in Egypt to bring them into their own Promised Land, so He longed to free them from the deeper slavery within—to bring them to the Promised One—Himself.

In this context He gave them Sabbaths as the sign of their freedom. They were not set apart merely to be different, but precisely to be with Christ. And only in that relationship with Him could they come to be really set apart. Just as the Sabbath is time "set apart" from the other six days, and Israel was a nation "set apart" from the other nations, so each freed slave was "set apart" to Christ—to be sanctified, changed or re-created, and thus to experience what "being set apart" really means. The Sabbath is "sacred relationship-time" when both Christ and the Christian enjoy togetherness, sharing deeply with each other.[24]

Primarily the Sabbath is a state of "being," rather than "doing," but the "being together" moves the Christian to worship Christ. The exuberance of Psalm 92 shows the freedom of such a "set-apart" person. To such an individual the Sabbath rest is not merely a cessation from work but an entering into works of adoration, praise, and worship of his or her Creator-Redeemer, in utter joyful celebration.[25] Unless Sabbath-keeping opens up the deepest expressions of praise, we have not experienced the first angel's message, even though we may be Seventh-day Adventists.[26] The coming Sunday law is, in part, a test of worship,[27] which has everything to do with our inner relationship with Christ.

Ezekiel speaks of the re-creative work within each one of us that only the Creator can accomplish. Just as Christ brought human beings into existence in the first place, so only He can re-create humanity. This is what sanctification is—a work of God, not humanity. The Sabbath is a sign of sanctification because it focuses on the distinction between the Creator who alone sanctifies and the creature who receives this sanctification. The Sabbath symbolizes sanctification because in it human beings unite with His sanctification, for Christ is humanity's "sanctification" (1 Cor. 1:30, NASB). The Sabbath rest reveals where our sanctification is—in Him alone. Resting in Him is sanctification.

New Testament Examples

Again we will focus on just three texts: John 5:1-15; Luke 23:54-24:1; and Hebrews 4:4-10. When He announced His mission, Christ said He came to set prisoners free (Luke 4:18, 19; cf. Isa. 61:1, 2). Israel groaned before Him in worse slavery than it had had under Egyptian taskmasters. Bound by their own traditional chains, they attempted to work their way to heaven. Two tractates of the Mishna focus exclusively on Sabbath rules and regulations—with one tractate containing 39 sections defining laborious "do's" and "don'ts" of Sabbathkeeping.[28] Rabbi Johanan states that post-exilic Judaism had "1,521 derivative laws."[29] The laws were not only numerous but involved wearisome minutia.[30]

Christ strode among such spiritual prisoners, calling them to a new Exodus as real as the first. To do this He exposed their slavery by revealing the truth about the Sabbath. He came to show that "the Sabbath was made for man, not man for the Sabbath" (Mark 2:27). To dramatize this, He often healed on the Sabbath to reveal His desire to set human beings free. Those languishing in "Sabbath-keeping bondage" desperately needed to hear and see this good news. So, to the woman crippled for 18 years, He proclaimed, "Woman, you are set free from your infirmity" (Luke 13:12). Christ used the Greek verb *luein,* "to free," or "to loose."[31] Physical freedom promised spiritual deliverance. Here was good news to those tired of Sabbath slavery. Christ longed to liberate the prisoners. So He demonstrated the Sabbath truth through Sabbath healings.[32] He realized that knowing the truth makes one free (John 8:32).

Some scholars disagree that Christ was healing on the Sabbath to reveal its real meaning. They see His Sabbath miracles as either simply helping the needy,[33] or purposely violating the Sabbath laws because He intended thereby to overthrow the Sabbath.[34] The truth is that He healed not to nullify the Sabbath but to abolish the false understanding of it.[35] He repudiated the Jewish misunderstanding of the Sabbath by revealing its true meaning through good works. Some Jews would save life on the Sabbath, but not do good works such as healing.[36] Christ's placing of human need above human tradition riled legalists and presented a recurring problem.[37] "The strongest clashes between Jesus and His religious contemporaries were occasioned by disputes over the Sabbath."[38] They became one of the factors behind the Jerusalem leaders' hostility toward Christ,[39] although it did not appear in the charge they brought against Him at His trial.[40]

Consider one Sabbath miracle of healing. The man at Bethesda's pool had lain there for 38 years (John 5:5)—a span of time beginning some five to six years before Christ's incarnation. Could Jesus not have waited one more day—till Sunday—to heal him? (The fact that He would not wait till Sunday then, and yet waited till Sunday in His grave—gives us additional insights into His teaching about the Sabbath).[41] No! He gazed on the emaciated remains of a man ravaged by disease and decided He would re-create him. His miracle of healing was a work of creation. Christ knew that the man would always link his miraculous "re-creation" with the Sabbath. Forever he would associate the Sabbath with the restorative presence of Christ. The Sabbath—to be what God intended it to be—must open up to humanity the presence of Christ to make a radical difference in their lives. Anything less is not the "Sabbath-experience," even if it takes place on the seventh day.

The second Sabbath passage raises the question "Why did Christ die on Friday?" The answer derives from a comparison of Creation Friday and Crucifixion Friday, both marking an end for the human race—the end of Creation and the "it is finished" sacrifice for sin (re-creation sacrifice). But those two Fridays also define two beginnings for the human race. Humanity began its mortal existence that first Friday, and then began eternal life that second Friday.[42] For on those two Fridays the planet had an Adam.[43]

This new beginning for the race necessarily took place on a Friday. Just as humanity's beginning was on Creation Friday to enable the original couple's first full day of life to be a Sabbath celebration of Christ's finished creative work, so Christ completed His substitutionary life/death for us on Crucifixion Friday in order that the first full day following could be a Sabbath celebration of His finished work of redemption. The Sabbath always celebrates a finished work of Christ.

Therefore, with Crucifixion weekend, the Sabbath took on additional meaning. Subsequently the Sabbath would be a memorial not only of Creation and the Exodus—as finished works of Christ—but of the cross—as Christ's greatest possible finished work, His "once-for-all" *(hapax,* Heb. 9:26, 27) blood-sacrifice *(aimatekchusias,* Heb. 9:22) for humanity. His crucifixion constituted the greatest Exodus ever, the ultimate re-creation for the world by divine provision for its deliverance from sin. No mere moral influence here, but a work, a very costly work—infinitely more expensive than Creation and Exodus. If no one else could create or liberate as He did, then a thousand times more true it is that no other one could die that human beings may live.

Hence, at Calvary the Sabbath reaches its fullest unfolding. For here we see that human works are not only impossible but unnecessary! We speak here of human works in which humanity seeks to save itself. The "it is finished" of Calvary calls into question any other human work and invites humanity to rest in Christ's work alone—to rest in it as completed.[44] All along the unfolding process the Sabbath celebrates the incomparable and finished work of Christ.

No wonder Hebrews 4 speaks of a seventh-day Sabbath-rest *(sabbatismos)* that still remains. Although not primarily concerned with the weekly Sabbath (but rather the resting in Christ[45] that Israel failed to participate in when they entered Canaan), it does secondarily apply to weekly Sabbaths (Heb. 4:4; cf. Isa. 66:22, 23). Just prior to A.D. 70, the approximate date when the Epistle to the Hebrews appeared,[46] a Sabbath rest remained for Christ's followers, because the Sabbath celebration followed His death on the cross as it had His work of creation in the beginning. (That is why He could warn people not to flee on the Sabbath in the coming destruction of Jerusalem—40 years after Calvary [Matt. 24:20]). Those who consider Sunday as replacing the Sabbath do not give the powerful parallel between Creation and Crucifixion Sabbaths its proper place.[47]

The Real Issue in the Sunday Law

While it is important to observe the right day, it is even more important to have the right experience. Better to have the right experience with Christ and keep the wrong day than to observe the right day and have the wrong experience. Some of the Jews honored the right Sabbath day but crucified the "Lord of the Sabbath" (Matt. 12:8). When the final "loud cry" invitation goes to the world (Rev. 18:1-4), "notwithstanding the agencies combined against the truth, a large number take their stand upon the Lord's side."[48] Many consist of Sundaykeepers who already have a right relationship with Christ. All they need to do is to change a day, and they have time to do that.

By contrast, some observe the correct day but do not have a right relationship with Christ. Because "the final movements will be rapid ones,"[49] there may not be time enough to transform an experience—to get to know Christ. To change a day takes a moment—to alter a relationship requires much longer. Sabbathkeeping does not necessarily mean one will remain committed to Christ when the Sunday laws come. In fact, in that imminent crisis "a larger proportion than we now anticipate will give heed to seducing spirits and doctrines of devils"[50] and depart from the church. How many will that be? So many will leave that "the church may appear as about to fall, but it does not fall. It remains, while the sinners in Zion will be sifted out—the chaff separated from the precious wheat. This is a terrible ordeal, but nevertheless it must take place."[51]

When Sabbathkeepers face starvation through not being able to buy or sell (Rev. 13:16, 17), and death through a universal decree threatens them (Rev. 13:15),[52] what will cause them to stand true to the Sabbath? What will commit them to die rather than give up the Sabbath? Far more than just knowing which day of the week it is. Not until they consider that abandoning the Sabbath is rejecting Christ will anyone be willing to die for the Sabbath. For Sabbathkeeping is not so much keeping a day as it is being kept by Christ in that day. At its deepest level, Sabbath observance is not something humans can do—but something Christ does. The very essence of the Sabbath—the distinction between the Creator and creature—radically affects the way we honor the Sabbath.

Translated into human experience, this means that a radical difference exists between God's department and that of human beings. He brought humans into the world—humans did not create themselves. Similarly it is His responsibility—not humanity's—to get them into the next world. The only difference between the two entrances is that human beings had nothing to do with the first one, but they can accept or turn down the second. It is therefore useless to worry about any "how questions," such as how will one withstand the pressures of a world against them (cf. Rev. 13:3). Rather one must be preoccupied with the "who question"—with Jesus, whom to know is life eternal (John 17:3). It is whom we know that makes the decisive difference—and the Sabbath is precisely time given for humans to get to know Christ ever more intimately.

To get to know Him is humanity's responsibility, while to get the human race to heaven is His—just as it was the Hebrews' assignment to stand loyal on Dura's plain, and God's assignment to keep them alive in the fiery furnace (Dan. 3:1-30; cf. 2 Tim. 4:16-18; Heb. 11:33, 34). It is vital that we recognize the distinction between the Creator and His creatures. And it is imperative that we realize that only resting in Him will carry the remnant through the final crisis. We must rest in Christ's finished work at Calvary—realizing that His death irreversibly assures us that this world is His, that human history is ultimately under His control, and that eternal life is certain for those who abide in Him (cf. John 15:1-11). Calvary ushered in the great Sabbath rest—a resting in the Creator's finished task that guarantees that nothing in the present or future, demons or world powers, can separate His people from Him (Rom. 8:38, 39). For it is the Conqueror of Calvary "who is able to keep" them "from falling and to present" them "before his glorious presence without fault and with great joy" (Jude 24).

The Final Exodus

Many Old Testament texts function as types of the last battle between truth and error. It is good to read them again and again to fix them in our memory to give us courage as we face the time when the Sabbath "will be the great point at issue."[53] Such passages include Joshua 10:7-14 and Job 38:22, 23.

They indicate that God uses hail as a weapon against the enemies of His people. Revelation 16:17-21 shows that He will employ it again in the seventh plague. A number of texts speak of God causing the enemy to kill each other, e.g., Judges 7:19-23; 1 Samuel 14:19, 20; 2 Chronicles 20:22-24; Isaiah 19:2; 31:21-23; Ezekiel 38:14-23; and Haggai 2:22. Other battles that typify Armageddon appear in Judges 4, 5; 1 Kings 18:16-40; Isaiah 34:8-10; Jeremiah 25:12-15, 29-38; and Zechariah 14:13. Finally, Isaiah 63:1-6 is typical of the description of Armageddon in Revelation 19:14-21. All of these texts share one common fact: Without Christ the victory is impossible. In past battles God's people were completely outnumbered. They felt helpless, but they rested in their only Helper. Here is the essence of the Sabbath rest in the coming battle.

The exodus out of Egypt is a type of the exodus through final events. It was important for the children of Israel to recognize their utter need of God in their escape. God and they both had a part. Their part was infinitesimally small but essential. God said to their leader, "Step into the water, and I will do the rest." The Israelites entered the Red Sea and crossed over as God opened up the waters for a safe crossing. As they traversed the passage through the sea, with the world's then greatest army pursuing, they could only look to God for survival. Whether they knew it or not, they experienced the essence of the Sabbath—experienced the distinction between the Creator and themselves as creatures.

In the final exodus God's saints will have every earthly support taken from them. They can neither buy nor sell (Rev. 13:17), the world is against them (verses 3, 12), and a death decree hangs over their heads (verse 15). All they can do is rest in God, realizing that it is His department to get them through. Their role is merely to trust in Him implicitly. They will cry out as Israel did in the time of Jehoshaphat, "O our God, will you not judge them? For we have no power to face this vast army that is attacking us. We do not know what to do, but our eyes are upon you" (2 Chron. 20:12). God answered, "Do not be afraid or discouraged because of this vast army. For the battle is not yours, but God's. . . . You will not have to fight in this battle. Take up your positions; stand firm and see the deliverance the Lord will give you" (verses 15-17).

So it was in the Exodus. "Moses answered the people, 'Do not be afraid. Stand firm and you will see the deliverance the Lord will bring you today. The Egyptians you see today you will never see again. The Lord will fight for you; you need only to be still'" (Ex. 14:13, 14). All Israel had to do was to follow God's instruction to cross over. He did the rest as He protected His people (verse 19). "The Israelites went through the sea on dry ground, with a wall of water on their right and on their left. That day the Lord saved Israel from the hands of the Egyptians" (verse 29), and threw the Egyptians into confusion. "He made the wheels of their chariots come off so that they had difficulty driving. And the Egyptians said, 'Let's get away from the Israelites! The Lord is fighting for them against Egypt'" (verse 25), and "not one of them survived" (verse 28). He wrought mightily for Israel in a deliverance that was swift, complete, and final.

No wonder liberated Israel sang the song of Moses: "I will sing to the Lord, for he is highly exalted. The horse and its rider he has hurled into the sea. The Lord is my strength and my song; he has become my salvation. He is my God, and I will praise him. . . . Your right hand, O Lord, was majestic in power. Your right hand, O Lord, shattered the enemy. In the greatness of your majesty you threw down those who opposed you. You unleashed your burning anger; it consumed them like stubble. By the blast of your nostrils the waters piled up. The surging waters stood firm like a wall; the deep waters congealed in the heart of the sea. . . . In your unfailing love you will lead the people you have redeemed. In your strength you will guide them to your holy dwelling" (Ex. 15:1-13).

After the Exodus Christ added a new reason for Sabbathkeeping beyond honoring Him as Creator. "Remember that you were slaves in Egypt and that the Lord your God brought you out of there with a mighty hand and an outstretched arm. Therefore the Lord your God has commanded you to observe the Sabbath day" (Deut. 5:15). Properly understood, our utter dependence upon Christ in the exodus is the essence of the Sabbath rest in Him.

The way to prepare for the coming crisis is to remember that Christ is our Creator and Deliverer. We need to enter the shelter of God's presence, abide in Him, and allow Him to deepen our relationship with Him through Bible study and communion, and through the infilling of the "Spirit of Christ" (Rom. 8:9). Not until we realize the distinction between ourselves and our Creator, not until we find nothing in ourselves to commend us to Him and to fit us for heaven, will we really rest in Him. Resting in Him is the heart of the gospel. It is the good news that in Him alone is our title and fitness for heaven.[54] Having done all good things, we are still unprofitable servants (Luke 17:10). Gone is confidence in works, in position and title. We have become as little children (Matt. 18:3)—trusting in Christ alone. Sabbathkeeping is more than observing a day—it is being kept by Christ in that day. It is a day that reminds us that He means everything to us, a day in which we find in Him alone our self-worth. The Sabbath tells us that He made us and redeemed us. We matter to God.

Modern Israel will come to the banks of the Red Sea when the Sunday law and death decree move in against them and the whole world surrounds them as their enemy. Now the exodus type is to meet its cosmic antitype. A planetwide escalation, including the worst time of trouble ever (Dan. 12:1), closes in on God's remnant. Every earthly support has vanished. God's people have only One to whom they can cling. Like Jacob, they hold on to Christ (Gen. 32:22-26). Christ promised the saints, "Never will I leave you; never will I forsake you" (Heb. 13:5) for "I am with you always, to the very end of the age" (Matt. 28:20). Standing with us in the final fiery furnace (Dan. 3:25), "he will not let you be tempted beyond what you can bear. But when you are tempted, he will also provide a way out so that you can stand up under it" (1 Cor. 10:13). He promised, "I will also keep you from the hour of trial that is going to come upon the whole world to test those who live on the earth" (Rev. 3:10). Dark will be the night of our world's end, but brighter and more glorious the deliverance. Christ will stand there with us in the trenches and open up a way through final events.

The saints will cross over on dry ground as Christ holds back the devastating waters threatening to destroy the remnant. Deliverance will come, and the saints will sing "a new song before the throne and before the four living creatures and the elders. No one could learn the song except the 144,000 who had been redeemed from the earth" (Rev. 14:3). It is "the song of their experience—an experience such as no other company have ever had. . . . 'These are they which came out of great tribulation;' they have passed through the time of trouble such as never was since there was a nation; they have endured the anguish of the time of Jacob's trouble; they have stood without an intercessor through the final outpouring of God's judgments."[55]

What is this song they sing? They sing the song of Moses and the Lamb. "Great and marvelous are your deeds, Lord God Almighty. Just and true are your ways, King of the ages. Who will not fear you, O Lord, and bring glory to your name? For you alone are holy. All nations will come and worship before you, for your righteous acts have been revealed" (Rev. 15:3, 4). Like ancient Israel after the Exodus, they do not sing about themselves. Their song is only about Christ. They worship and praise Him alone, revealing how opposite they are to Satan. Whereas they know the distinction between the Creator and creatures, Satan denies this fact. The lost are those who try to take God's place and lose their own. The saved acknowledge Christ's place and remain content in theirs. They do not try to be God but rest in their Creator-Redeemer. Thus they keep the Sabbath of Christ because He keeps them.

The crucial difference between the saved and the lost is this understanding and acceptance of Christ's distinction from them. The saved will experience this distinction as they rest in Him. It will get them through the final exodus of end-events and is the essence of the Sabbath. They rest in Christ alone, and throughout eternity will sing about Him and their experience in the end-time (Rev. 14:3). We need to consider final events from this perspective, for they will experience Sabbath resting in Him that will cause them to sing the song of deliverance in the life to come.

Central to the deliverance through the Red Sea and final events is the deliverance of Calvary. There Christ did not go through the waters but succumbed to the death we deserve. He became the enemy in our place. It was as if He turned into the Egyptian army and the Babylonian beast. He who knew no sin became sin for us (2 Cor. 5:21), took our place, and died our death (Rom. 4:25) so that we could cross over on dry ground. No wonder we will forever sing the song of Moses and the Lamb, the song of deliverance. Resting in His salvation is the heart of the gospel and the very meaning of the

Sabbath. All attempts to change the Sabbath, even through a Christian guise, are a rebellious attempt to save oneself, to cross over in one's own might, and to deny to the Saviour the proper distinction between Him as Creator-Redeemer and human beings as His dependent creatures.

---

[1] Scholars have attempted to explain the inexplicable for centuries. Such theodicies seek to answer why sin entered God's universe, whether He is responsible or not. If God is all-loving and all-powerful, then how could sin enter? The all-loving attribute gave us creaturely freedom. Our misuse of it led to sin. See *Evangelical Dictionary of Theology,* Walter A. Elwell, ed. (Grand Rapids: Baker, 1987), pp. 1083-1086.

[2] E. G. White, *Patriarchs and Prophets,* p. 38.

[3] *Ibid.,* p. 40.

[4] When Keil-Delitzsch noted that "doubt, unbelief, and pride were the roots of the sin of our first parents, as they have been of all the sins of their posterity" *(Commentary on the Old Testament in Ten Volumes,* James Martin, trans. [Grand Rapids: Eerdmans, 1986], vol. 1, p. 96), they focused on the fact that doubt leads to disobedience, separation to outward sin. So it was with Lucifer. "Little by little Lucifer came to indulge the desire for self-exaltation" (E. G. White, *Patriarchs and Prophets,* p. 35). Pride separated him from a dependent relationship upon his Creator, and led eventually to outward rebellion.

[5] This is why the Sabbath is perhaps the best indicator of our spiritual experience. If Sabbathkeeping is a joy to us, it gives insight into our relationship with God, and the reverse is also true. Cf. "As the Christian takes heed of the Sabbath day and keeps it holy, he does so purely in answer to God's command, and simply because God is his Creator. Thus, the Sabbath command comes nearer being a true measure of spirituality than any other of the commandments, and, as in the days of Israel of old, it is often more of a test of loyalty to God than is any of the others" (Raoul Dederen, "Reflection on a Theology of the Sabbath," *The Sabbath in Scripture and History,* Kenneth Strand, ed. [Washington, D.C.: Review and Herald, 1982], p. 302).

[6] The tree "in the middle of the garden" (Gen. 3:2) of Eden was part of the creation that God pronounced "very good" (Gen. 1:31). In itself it was good for food just as much as the seventh-day Sabbath is as good for work as the six. But God set both the tree and the Sabbath apart for different reasons; yet they share a common purpose in being chosen as a visible test of loyalty to Christ, shown by staying away from the tree and by entering into deep fellowship. Both were not optional, and both determine destiny—not in and of themselves, but because they manifest the commitment, or lack of it, between the creature and his or her Creator.

[7] After the fall of Satan and his expulsion from heaven (Rev. 12:7-9), Christ created Planet Earth with Adam and Eve (Gen. 1; 2) and then instituted the Sabbath (E. G. White, *Patriarchs and Prophets,* p. 336; *Prophets and Kings* (Mountain View, Calif.: Pacific Press, 1917), p. 183; *The Desire of Ages,* pp. 281, 288; and *Testimonies for the Church,* vol. 2, p. 582). Literally, "the Sabbath was made for man" (Mark 2:27). So both the entrance of sin and the Sabbath's institution were new realities in the universe. I believe the Sabbath was God's response to the sin problem because it focused on the very problem that caused sin, i.e., failure to recognize the distinction between the Creator and creatures. One may be tempted to ask why God had not inaugurated the Sabbath before. Would this have kept sin back? Obviously, coming into the very presence of God's majesty did more than anything could to remind created beings that they were not comparable to the unsurpassed majesty, omnipotence, omniscience, omnipresence, and eternity of God.

[8] Soren Kierkegaard, *Philosophical Fragments* (Princeton, N.J.: University Press, 1962).

[9] E. G. White, *The Great Controversy,* pp. 437, 438.

[10] *Ibid.,* p. 438.

[11] "Generally speaking, Jewish writers who lived outside Palestine (so-called Hellenists) stressed the creation aspect of this Sabbath teaching, while those who lived and wrote in the Holy Land itself (the Palestinians) placed far more emphasis on the special relationship between the Lord and Israel that the Sabbath signified. Some Palestinian Pharisees, for example, denied that the Sabbath had any relevance for gentiles at all; while the Hellenist writer Philo described the Sabbath day as 'the birthday of the world' and 'the festival not of a single city or country but of the universe'" *(Baker Encyclopedia of the Bible,* Walter A. Elwell, ed. [Grand Rapids: Baker, 1988], p. 1877).

"It was not because the 'rest' of God was not yet available that the wilderness generation of Israelites failed to enter into it; it had been available ever since creation's work was ended. When we read that God 'rested on the seventh day from all his work which he had made' (Gen. 2:2), we are to understand that He *began* to rest then; the fact that He is never said to have completed His rest and resumed His work of creation implies that His rest continues still, and may be shared by those who respond to His overtures with faith and obedience. This interpretation which views the divine Sabbath as beginning from the moment when creation's work came to an end and going on to the present time is paralleled in Philo" (F. F. Bruce, *The New International Commentary on the New Testament, Hebrews* [Grand Rapids: Eerdmans, 1984], p. 74).

[12] See chapter 27, footnote 37.

[13] Barth views Creation as the presupposition for the incarnation of Christ, as "the external basis of the covenant *(Church Dogmatics* [Edinburgh, Scotland: T & T Clark, 1960], vol. 3, part 1, pp. 94-228); cf. the covenant as the internal basis of Creation *(ibid.,* pp. 228-329). Cf. "We have already said that not man but the divine rest on the seventh day is the crown of creation" *(ibid.,* p. 223); "the seventh day as the coronation of creation" *(ibid.,* p. 225).

[14] See the final section of this chapter and footnote 55.

[15] It is true that Christ is with us every day (Matt. 28:20; Heb. 13:5), having all the time needed for humanity. However, because of human preoccupation with living, we need a day set aside to have significant time for God. In this qualified sense, Christ comes to us each Sabbath in a way and to a depth that we do not enter into during the other six days of work. Entering into Christ's rest on the Sabbath does, however, necessitate an entering into His rest each day (cf. Heb. 4:1-11).

[16] This opposes the pantheistic view that sees no distinction between the Creator and His creation. God is present to His creation in time rather than identified with it in space.

[17] Abraham Heschel, *The Sabbath, Its Meaning for Modern Man* (New York: 1951). Compared to objects in space, the Sabbath is incorruptible and universal; see Samuel Bacchiocchi, *Divine Rest for Human Restlessness* (Rome: Pontifical Gregorian University, 1980), p. 118.

[18] Years are determined by the sun's rotation, months by the moon's rotation, but the weekly cycle depends upon the Sabbath, the day instituted in Eden.

[19] Because the Sabbath was the first full day of Adam and Eve's existence, Karl Barth applies this to the first day of the week and Sundaykeeping. "Basically, then, it was no innovation when the early Christians (1 Cor. 16:2; Acts 20:7) adopted the first day of the week as a holiday instead of the seventh and called it the *kuriake hemera* (Rev. 1:10). On the contrary, it was a discovery and application of the chronology implicit in Genesis 1-2. For they began the week with a holiday instead of ending it with one" *(Church Dogmatics,* vol. 3, part 2, p. 458). He overlooks the basic, unchangeable, fact that God chose the seventh day for His Sabbath, and the fact that it was humanity's first day cannot alter His choice any more than our "birthday" day becomes the Sabbath day for us.

[20] Barth makes an insightful comment on rest preceding work. "Ought not 'rest' to be earned by preceding work? Should not what we say about it be in terms of what has already been said about work? The question may seem obvious, but it must actually be reversed. Can we understand the working day, the day of labor in relationship to our fellowmen, or any of its commands, before we have understood the holy day? Can we hear the law before we have heard the Gospel? Can man view and tackle his own work under the command of God without first, as the same command of God enjoins, pausing, resting and keeping holy-day in the sight of God, rejoicing in freedom? Can he value and do justice to his work except in the light of its boundary, its solemn interruption? Is not this interruption the true time from which alone he can have other time?" (Karl Barth, *Church Dogmatics,* vol. 3, part 4, p. 51).

[21] The fact that Adam and Eve spent their first full day with Christ and then went into their first week of work illustrates the Christian life. Christians work because they love Christ (John 14:15). Non-Christians work for godhood, enlightenment, or Nirvana. They work to *be* "saved." Christians work because they *are* saved. The basic difference results from Christian awareness of the distinction between the Creator and creatures. The Creator's department is giving salvation. Human beings can no more earn salvation than to give it. As a gift salvation cannot be earned, even though it is received and can be lost. It is not possible for a created being to earn that which can only be given. The deeper meaning of the Sabbath makes this clear. For that which makes the Sabbath the joy it is, beyond other days, is not the day itself, but God's blessing of the day (Gen. 2:3; Ex. 20:11) and therefore His gift. It is true that He comes to be with us every day, but on the Sabbath we also have more time to come to Him.

Christ Is Coming!

Christ gave us the gift of Sabbath time so that we could receive the gift of Himself.

[22] All non-Christian religions fail to understand the distinction between the Creator and His creatures. Pantheism and panentheism ignore this distinction. Satan's first temptation to Eve involved a supposed progression to become like God through transgression (Gen. 3:1-5). Keil-Delitzsch notes that "the illusive hope of being like God excited a longing for forbidden fruit" *(Commentary on the Old Testament in Ten Volumes, Pentateuch* [Grand Rapids: Eerdmans, 1986], vol. 1, p. 95). Obviously transgression of God's Word was not the pathway to becoming godlike, but supposedly to become God. Evidently even a perfect human could be tempted quickly to wish to become as God. Note: "The fatal steps are described in a series of eleven *waw*-consecutive clauses that suggest rapidity of the action—'she saw,' 'she took,' 'she gave'" (Gordon J. Wenham, *World Biblical Commentary,* Genesis 1-15, David A. Hubbard and Glenn W. Barker, eds. [Waco, Tex.: Word, 1987], vol. 1, p. 75).

[23] For example, Gnostic and Neoplatonic views. "In the Middle Ages the Neoplatonic ideas of Plotinus and others were mixed with Christian perspectives and gave birth to the mysticism of thinkers like John Scotus Erigena. The universal is real and a causal process gives birth to the particular. Thus, the created order is really God unfolded into particularities" *(Evangelical Dictionary of Theology,* p. 351).

[24] "We must rest entirely, in order that God may work in us" (John Calvin, *Institutes of the Christian Religion,* vol. 1, p. 340).

[25] "Nowhere does the OT express its sheer joy in Sabbath worship more exuberantly than in Psalm 92, which has the title *A Song for the Sabbath" (Baker Encyclopedia of the Bible,* p. 1876).

[26] The first angel's message, experientially, is worshiping Christ as Creator, and can issue only out of a heart/mind that keeps the distinction between Creator and creatures uppermost. Worship wells up in the heart/mind of one who knows the "worth" of the one he or she worships. "Fear God and give him glory, because the hour of his judgment has come. Worship him who made the heavens, the earth, the sea and the springs of water" (Rev. 14:7).

[27] The three angels' messages describe the two groups of humanity in the end-time as those who worship Christ (Rev. 14:7) and those who worship the beast (Rev. 14:9). The historical examples in Daniel, that give insight into the eschatological confrontation, indicate that worship was a key factor. For example, (1) worshiping the golden image (Dan. 3), and (2) worshiping King Darius (Dan. 6). The three Hebrew worthies in the fiery furnace and Daniel in the lions' den represent those who will stand true in their worship to Christ in the coming Sunday-law test. Genuine Sabbathkeeping will see them through, as we will note in the final section of this chapter.

[28] *Baker Encyclopedia of the Bible,* p. 1877.

[29] "The multitude of meticulous and causistic regulations (according to Rabbi Johanan there were 1,521 derivative laws) produced to guard the Sabbath turned the observance of the day into a *legalistic ritual"* (S. Bacchiocchi, *From Sabbath to Sunday,* p. 33).

[30] "Some of the detailed regulations are passing wonderful. For example, (On the Sabbath) a man may borrow of his fellow jars of wine or jars of oil, provided that he does not say to him, 'Lend me them' (Shab. 23:1). This would imply a transaction, and a transaction might involve writing, and writing was forbidden. Or again, 'If a man put out the lamp (on the night of the Sabbath) from fear of the gentiles or of thieves or of an evil spirit, or to suffer one that was sick to sleep, he is not culpable; (but if he did it with a mind) to spare the lamp or to spare the oil or to spare the wick, he is culpable' (Shab. 2:5). The attitude to healing on the Sabbath is illustrated by a curious provision that a man may not put vinegar on his teeth to alleviate toothache. But he may take vinegar with his food in the ordinary course of affairs, and the Rabbis philosophically concluded, 'if he is healed he is healed' (Shab. 14:4)!" (Leon Morris, *The New International Commentary: NT, John,* p. 305, fn. 25).

[31] If it is permissible to loose an ox on the Sabbath (for mercenary, not merciful considerations) then why not loose a woman (Luke 13:15, 16)? "With a stress on the word *luein* the conclusion is thus drawn: How much more should this daughter of Abraham be loosed from her bond on the Sabbath (verse 16!)" *(Theological Dictionary of the New Testament,* Gerhard Kittel, Gerhard Friedrich, eds., G. W. Bromiley, trans. [Grand Rapids: Eerdmans, 1983], Eduard Lohse, vol. 7, p. 25. See "The Sabbath Conflicts of Jesus," pp. 21-28).

[32] Leon Morris is right in observing His purposeful choice of Sabbath healings. "Jesus' act of compassion had not been inhibited because there were scribal regulations forbidding works of healing on that day. Perhaps He even chose the day for His deed in order that the issues might be made clear" *(The New International Commentary: NT, John,* p. 305).

[33] "He heals on a Sabbath because the opportunity presents itself and not because it is a Sabbath" (A. T. Lincoln in *From Sabbath to Lord's Day,* p. 360).

[34] J. Danilelou, *Bible and Liturgy* (South Bend, Ind.: University of Notre Dame Press, 1956), p. 226. W. Rordorf, *Sunday: The History of the Day of Rest and Worship in the Earliest Centuries of the Christian Church* (Philadelphia: Westminster), p. 70.

[35] "His point of collision with the Pharisees was the point at which their tradition departed from biblical teaching. . . . Rabbinic tradition had exalted the institution above the people it was meant to serve. . . . Jesus fearlessly exposed the callousness and absurd inconsistencies to which this attitude led. How, he asked, could it be right to circumcise a baby or lead an animal to water on the Sabbath day (which tradition allowed), but wrong to heal a chronically handicapped woman and a crippled man—even if their lives were not in immediate danger (Luke 13:10-17; John 7:21-24)? The Sabbath, he taught, was a particularly appropriate day for acts of mercy (Mark 3:4, 5). If tradition said otherwise, it was high time to get back to the Bible (Matt. 12:7)" *(Baker Encyclopedia of the Bible,* vol. 2, p. 1877).

[36] "Clearly, their principle implied, that it was lawful on the Sabbath to do that which would save life or prevent death. To have taught otherwise, would virtually have involved murder" (Alfred Edersheim, *The Life and Times of Jesus the Messiah* [Grand Rapids: Eerdmans, 1986], vol. 3, p. 60).

[37] "One Sabbath healing becomes an example of the recurring controversy of the Jews with Jesus about the Sabbath" (George R. Beaseley-Murray, *World Biblical Commentary, John,* D. A. Hubbard, G. W. Barker, eds. [Waco, Tex.: Word, 1987], vol. 36, p. 72).

[38] Donald Guthrie, *New Testament Theology,* p. 942.

[39] Merrill C. Tenney, *The Expositor's Bible Commentary, John,* Frank E. Gaebelein, ed. (Grand Rapids: Zondervan, 1981), vol. 9, p. 62.

[40] Such a religious charge, involving Jewish legal tradition, was of no interest to Roman law. But the charge against destroying the Temple, something the Romans had helped to build, carried clout. Cf. "It is strange that the accusation of Sabbath breaking was not pressed at his trial. Possibly it was because the Pharisees disagreed so much among themselves that they could not have made such a charge stick" *(Baker Encyclopedia of the Bible,* vol. 2, p. 1877).

[41] He healed persons to show that the Sabbath exists for humanity—for human benefit (Mark 2:27). He rested in the grave to honor the Sabbath-rest command (Luke 23:56), indicating that we should keep it after His death.

[42] Eternal life begins in the present. The finished work of Christ brought the inbreaking of the future into the present, as seen in the inbreaking of Pentecost.

[43] Adam stood full-grown Creation Friday, which was not true of the Second Adam, Christ (Rom. 5) when born in Bethlehem. But on Crucifixion Friday this Second Adam was now fully grown—He had completed His mission with the words "It is finished." What was finished, for us, was a perfect human life, character, wedding garment, or robe, or righteousness, which is as necessary for salvation as was His death for our sins.

[44] The payment, or sacrifice for sin, is completed. In that sense the atonement has been made. But the application of atonement continues subsequently, so that Christ still ministers in heaven, and the "Spirit of Christ" still ministers on earth till the ultimate consummation of the completed atonement.

[45] Some believe the Sabbath rest comes after death, according to Scripture (Rev. 14:13). But Hebrews 4:9 does not use *katapusis* but *Sabbatismos.* F. F. Bruce sees an eschatological fulfillment to entering into Christ's rest. "This rest which is reserved for the people of God is called a 'Sabbath rest'—a *sabbatismos* or 'Sabbath keeping'—because it is their participation in God's own rest. When God completed His work of creation, He 'rested;' so His people, having completed their service on earth, will enter into His rest" *(The New International Critical Commentary: NT, Hebrews,* p. 77; cf. p. 78).

Leon Morris notes: "Bruce thinks it is 'an experience which they do not enjoy in their present immortal life, although it belongs to them as a heritage, and by faith they may live in the good of it here and now' (in loc.). I should reverse his order and say that they live in it here and now by faith, but what they know here is not the full story. That will be revealed in the hereafter. There is a sense in which to enter Christian salvation means to cease from one's works and rest securely on what Christ has done" *(The Expositor's Bible Commentary,* vol. 12, p. 43. Cf. "The writer pictures salvation as God's rest which man is to share and God will have perfect satisfaction when man is in harmony with him (Dods)" (A. T. Robertson, *Word Pictures in the New Testament* [Grand Rapids: Baker, 1960], vol. 5, p. 362).

John Calvin affirmed: "We here begin our blessed rest in him, and daily make new progress in it; but because we must still wage an incessant warfare with the flesh, it shall not be consummated until the fulfillment of the prophecy of Isaiah: 'From one new moon to another, and from one sabbath to another, shall all flesh come to worship before me, saith the Lord' (Isa. 66:23, KJV); in other words, when God shall be 'all in all' (1 Cor. 10:28)" *(Institutes,* p. 340).

[46] See F. F. Bruce, *The New International Critical Commentary: NT, Hebrews,* pp. xlii-xliv.

[47] The following comparison misses the real parallel: "Saturday was seen as a memorial of the first creation and Christ's part in it, while Sunday commemorated the inauguration of the second creation through Christ" (A. T. Lincoln, in *From Sabbath to Lord's Day,* p. 382).

[48] E. G. White, *The Great Controversy,* p. 612.

[49] E. G. White, *Testimonies for the Church,* vol. 9, p. 11.

[50] E. G. White, *Selected Messages,* book 2, p. 368.

[51] *Ibid.,* p. 380.

[52] The test will be as worldwide as the Sabbath command itself. Now will be seen that the Sabbath is a "Creation ordinance," as a "loyalty test" for the race as was the "tree" in Eden. Both the Sabbath and that tree have universal implications, far beyond a national significance as some confine the Sabbath to Israel.

[53] E. G. White, *Last Day Events,* p. 124.

[54] E. G. White, *The Desire of Ages,* p. 300.

[55] E. G. White, *The Great Controversy,* p. 649.

Chapter 31

Evolution: A Theory in Crisis

So far we've discussed several movements and ideas that push Christ out of sight. Spiritualism, Theosophy, New Age and charismatic movements, Catholic tradition, channeled Bibles, false concepts about death, the doctrine of hell, and Sunday, all are ways to hide Christ from view.

As history entered the end-time, Satan added a powerful new weapon—evolution. Through it he distances humanity from the Creator by making their origin the result of chance and natural selection in nature. If a product of an evolutionary development, human beings have lost their creation by Christ, and hence the Sabbath to celebrate it and even the need for human salvation. Instead of a Fall, humanity is involved in a process of upward development.

In the beginning Satan told Eve "You will not surely die" (Gen. 3:4). But in the end-time he declares, "You have not surely fallen." So the fact of Christ as Creator and Redeemer gets thrown on the trash heap.

The Mission of Seventh-day Adventists

Seventh-day Adventists are an end-time people, raised up by God to be His church. Through them God restores Christ and truths about Him to their proper place. Adventists have brought Calvary, the heavenly intercession, the function of Scripture, the importance of the Sabbath, the great controversy, the truth about death and hell, and the fact that Jesus Christ is the Creator of the universe all more clearly to the world's attention.

In fact, the three angels' messages call human beings to "worship him who made the heavens, the earth, the sea and the springs of water" (Rev. 14:7). Christ was the Creator. "Through him all things were made; without him nothing was made that has been made" (John 1:3). "For by him all things were created: things in heaven and on earth, visible and invisible" (Col. 1:16). For the Father "has spoken to us by his Son, whom he appointed heir of all things, and through whom he made the universe" (Heb. 1:2).

The mission of Seventh-day Adventists, in part, is to summon the human race to worship their Creator. For, in the end-time "men worshiped the dragon [Satan, Rev. 12:9] because he had given authority to the beast [apostate religion], and they also worshiped the beast" (Rev. 13:4). All humanity will worship something in the end-time. Will it be the Creator, Christ, or Satan, the author of evolutionary theory? Because of this important end-time scenario we now look at the theory of evolution. But it has begun to face a crisis itself. We need to know this in our sharing of truth to an end-time generation that uncritically accepts evolution as fundamental. Human beings need to see Christ as the true Creator He is.

Massive Influence of Evolution

Evolution is possibly the most influential worldview ever to affect the human race. It has become all-pervasive in nearly every modern discipline. Darwin believed that "his theories would necessitate a complete redrafting of the problems and scope of several sciences, including psychology, paleontology, and comparative anatomy."[1] The theory has radically altered biology and later shaped most other scientific disciplines.

The Origin of Species, published in 1859, "has had a massive influence not only on the sciences, which increasingly are built on evolutionary assumptions, but on the humanities, theology, and government."[2] As Ernst Mayr noted, Darwin's book "brought about a fundamental reorientation in the study of behavior."[3] Darwin's influence was so great that with him came a new paradigm change. Ernst Mayr, professor of zoology at Harvard University, says of Darwin's theory: "It was one of the most novel and most daring new conceptualizations in the history of ideas."[4] No wonder scholars widely consider him the Newton of biology.

Alfred R. Wallace[5] and Charles Darwin independently thought of natural selection as the mechanism for evolution. Both took theology before going on to make contributions to evolutionary studies, and Darwin drifted into agnosticism and atheism through his study into evolutionary theory. He lost his faith during the years 1836-1839, some 20 years before publishing *The Origin of Species*.[6] His loss of faith was one major factor in Darwin's adoption of natural selection as the mechanism for his theory.[7] In turn, his evolutionary theory has caused many others to lose their faith. Martin Lings contends that "more cases of loss of religious faith are to be traced to the theory of evolution . . . than to anything else."[8]

Evolution has also shaped social theory. Some applied the concept of "survival of the fittest" to the extermination of six million Jews in the holocaust under Hitler's Third Reich. And it continues to influence society. In the August 15, 1994, issue of *Time* Robert Wright wrote a major article entitled "Our Cheating Hearts." He promotes male promiscuity as a product of evolution. "According to evolutionary psychology, it is 'natural' for both men and women—at some times, under some circumstances—to commit adultery." Wright claims that "nearly 1,000 of the 1,154 past or present human societies studied . . . have permitted a man to have more than one wife." Furthermore, the article contends that "it is to a man's evolutionary advantage to sow his seeds far and wide." Wright concludes that "lifelong monogamous devotion just isn't natural, and the modern environment makes it harder than ever."[9] With the belief that humans are mere animals, no wonder we witness so much moral disarray in a world that considers life as well as marriage disposable.

As Henry Morris rightly observes: "Untold damage has been wrought, especially during the past century, by this dismal doctrine that man is merely an evolved animal. Racism, economic imperialism, Communism, Nazism, sexual promiscuity and perversions, aggressive militarism, infanticide, genocide, and all sorts of evils have been vigorously promoted by one group or another on the grounds that, since they were based on evolution, they were 'scientific' and, therefore, bound to prove beneficial in the long run. Even cannibalism, of all things, is beginning to receive favorable attention by certain evolutionists."[10] Blind to these possibilities, Darwin even said that the evolutionary theory ennobles![11]

Influence on Christians

Evolution has even made remarkable inroads into Christian theology by calling into question the historicity of the Genesis account of Creation. Paul K. Jewett notes that "few who confess the Christian doctrine of creation would suppose that the world was fashioned in a week of time some six thousand to ten thousand years ago. Drafts of time of a vastly different magnitude are indicated by the findings of the natural sciences."[12] The scientific worldview has led to an accommodation with science in interpreting the Genesis record.[13] Some evangelical theologians believe that death existed in the human race prior to the Fall,[14] which undercuts the biblical concept of death as sin's wages and ultimately, the need for atonement.

If we consider death as an inherent part of the natural order of things, death cannot be a result of human sin. Karl Barth, one of the most influential theologians, claims that death is a part of being finite. Because God has no beginning or end, by contrast humans have a beginning and an end. Thus death is an aspect of being human.[15]

Theistic evolution is an attempt to give validity to evolutionary theory while holding onto the fact that God as Creator launched the process. Several advocates even suggest that He then superintended it. Some contemporary theologians "deny any original act of creation, and equate creation with that universal, continuing activity which traditional theology called 'preservation' or 'providence.'"[16] Calling it "continuing creation," process theologians influenced by Alfred Whitehead have espoused it,[17] and it appears in the theology of John Macquarrie.[18] Theistic evolutionists look at the Genesis account of Creation as either a myth, saga, or poetry, in which the only factual information is that God created through natural processes. Many hold that the other Creation stories in eastern Mesopotamia, such as the Enumah Elish account, influenced the Genesis description of Creation. All this questions the authority of the biblical record of Creation and shoves it aside to make room for evolutionary theory to explain the alleged mechanism of creation by random genetic mutation and natural selection.

The root problem of theistic evolution (God using evolution as His way to create) is that it overlooks the worldview of evolution. Darwin did not believe in miracles, or in the intervention of God either at the beginning or anywhere else along the evolutionary process. His worldview was a closed system that removed God from the natural laws of cause and effect. His theory focuses on the concept that nature, left to itself without God, has achieved the evolutionary development.

Clearly, anyone accepting biblical creationism believes in the supernatural act of God in creating. Theistic evolution is logically a misnomer. It's as if saying God began the process and yet had no part in it. Behind the term "theistic evolution" lie two opposing philosophical views, and hence opposing paradigms: supernaturalism and naturalism. A marrying of the two doesn't explain anything, for one cancels the other. On the basis of logic alone, theistic evolution cannot explain the origin of human beings. Merging opposites doesn't produce harmony. The Jesuit paleontologist Pierre Teilhard de Chardin espoused theistic evolution.[19] Augustine of Hippo[20] and Thomas Aquinas[21] believed in progressive creation.[22]

What about Catholic theology? The Second Vatican Council addressed the relation between Scripture and science, and spoke of "the rightful independence of science"[23] and of "the legitimate autonomy of human culture and especially of the sciences."[24] This is in keeping with the Catholic division between Scripture and tradition. The Document on Revelation places "sacred tradition" before "sacred revelation."[25] In the same way it is expected that science takes precedence over Scripture in the area of evolution. The recently released *Catechism of the Catholic Church* comments: "The question about the origins of the world and of man has been the object of many scientific studies which have splendidly enriched our knowledge of the age and dimensions of the cosmos, the development of life-forms and the appearance of man." The catechism then gives thanks "for the understanding and wisdom he gives to scholars and researchers."[26] So Catholic theology mixes two worldviews.

Evolution of Evolution

Darwin became an evolutionist in March 1837, or certainly by July 1837.[27] Although Darwinian evolution began with his *The Origin of Species*, various forms of evolution reach back through Hume to the classical philosophers such as Democritus, Epicurus, Aristotle, and the Ionian nature philosophers such as Empedocles.[28] As Isaac Asimov points out in his *New Guide to Science*, "From Aristotle on, many men speculated on the possibility that organisms had evolved from one another."[29] Evolution as the transmutation of species, though, goes back only to the eighteenth-century Enlightenment,[30] as indicated by Peter J. Bowler,[31] Loren Eiseley,[32] and John C. Green.[33]

We should keep in mind that evolutionary theory has had its own evolution. It has developed from classical Darwinism (1858-1890s) to the modern synthesis,[34] also called neo-Darwinism (1915-1930s),[35] to post-Darwinianism,[36] questioned by DNA and molecular biology (1950s), to the current Punctuated Equilibria views and Cladistic taxonomy (1980-onward).[37] The classical period focused on natural selection as the sole mechanism for evolution until Mendelian genetics forced a synthesis with natural selection to form neo-Darwinism, labeled also the modern synthesis. In the 1950s the discovery of DNA by Watson and Crick in molecular biology caused a new analysis of evolutionary theory.[38]

Throughout these first two periods most scientists considered gradualism, or a series of micro-evolutionary changes over sufficient time, as the way evolution occurred. Not so today. Punctuated equilibrium (Stephen Jay Gould, Niles Eldredge) suggests that new species appeared abruptly, as we observe in the fossil records. Historians and philosophers of science have rightly called this new focus a major paradigm change in evolutionary theory[39] because, in part, it rejects natural selection as the sole mechanism for change and gradualism as the time-frame for change. The modern form of taxonomy, called cladistics (Simpson, Cox, Halstead, Hennig, Greenwood, Forey, Gardiner, Patterson, Nelson),[40] finds a distinct gap between major taxonomic groups, with no ancestral linkage. Those whose research supports the post-Darwinian view include paleontologists, geneticists, immunologists, embryologists, and taxonomists.

Although evolution has had its own evolution, it is still evolution. Therefore, in the scientific literature, when later evolutionary views criticize former views, it does not mean to say that the various exponents have given up evolutionary theory. It simply indicates that scientists who belong to the post-Darwinian evolution camp now question both Darwinian evolution as well as neo-Darwinian evolution. In this chapter we will consider some evidence that challenges the theory of evolution in its various stages. We should keep in mind that the various experts we cite still support evolution. As Peter J. Bowler, historian of science at Queen's University, Belfast, states, "biologists have begun a more active campaign to defend the theory (Eldredge, 1982; Godfrey, 1983; Halstead, 1983; Kitcher, 1982; Montagu, 1982; Newell, 1982; Ruse, 1982; Futuyma, 1982)."[41]

Recent Publications Calling Evolutionary Theory Into Question

We will mention a few of the recent major publications that challenge evolutionary theory. They include Scott Huse's *The Collapse of Evolution;*[42] Michael Denton's *Evolution: A Theory in Crisis;*[43] Phillip Johnson's *Darwin on Trial;*[44] *The Creation Hypothesis: Scientific Evidence for an Intelligent Designer,* edited by J. P. Moreland;[45] *Of Pandas and People: The Central Question of Biological Origins,* by Percival Davis and Dean H. Kenyon;[46] Brian Leith, *The Descent of Darwin: A Handbook of Doubts About Darwinism;*[47] Alvin Platinga's seminal article, "When Faith and Reason Clash: Evolution and the Bible," in *Christian Scholar's Review;*

from an earlier time, Michael Polanyi's insightful article "Life's Irreducible Structure" in *Science;*[48] and a book by W. R. Bird, *The Origin of Species Revisited: The Theories of Evolution and of Abrupt Appearance.*[49] Such publications together make a formidable attack on evolutionary theory.

The Parameters of Science

Evolution claims to be a science and therefore to be able to demonstrate its theory through empirical evidence. By contrast, evolutionists argue that creationism is nonempirical and hence nonscientific. Such a comparison has problems, however. It is true that we can demonstrate change in nature, but the evidence is confined to microevolution and does not offer proof of macroevolution, or change from one major kind of life form to an entirely different life form. The empirical evidence is simply insufficient to prove the claims made. The idea of reading from microevolutionary change and extrapolating macroevolutionary change is merely an unproved and untestable theory. The basis of the evidence itself throws it into question. One can accept macroevolution only on faith. And that is no different from accepting by faith that God created the world and all within it. While science does offer a few examples of what appear to be major changes, such exceptions still seem to prove the rule of no macroevolutionary change.[50]

Faith in either macroevolution or in Creation by God is still only faith. It's not empirical evidence. Because it is faith and not empirical evidence, and because it is a given and not something that we can demonstrate in the lab today, humanity's origin, whether either by evolution or God's creation, lies beyond the proper domain of science. Science has to limit itself to what we can test or demonstrate through natural and repeatable processes. That which stands beyond the currently demonstrable falls into the realm of philosophy or metaphysics. Colin Patterson, senior paleontologist at the British Natural History Museum, characterized evolution and creationism "as scientifically vacuous concepts which are held primarily on the basis of faith."[51]

Is evolution a science? Most people automatically consider it as one. But true empirical science is testable, being either verified or falsified through experimentation. Can evolutionary theory qualify as science on those terms? Different scholars have offered different answers. At one time, Karl Popper, a leading exponent of the philosophy of science, questioned whether evolution is scientific because it is not falsifiable. In 1974 he wrote: "I have come to the conclusion that Darwinism is not a testable scientific theory, but a metaphysical research programme."[52] Later he conceded that parts of evolution are testable, and to that extent it is scientific.[53] But much of evolutionary theory still remains beyond the objectivity of science, such as the origin of life in the beginning, the assumed process of gradualism in which extremely small transitional stages during billions of years produced the ascendancy of species from living molecule to human being. The claim that random genetic mutation and natural selection, without any evidence of transitionals in the fossil record, produces complexity has thrown into question the scientific nature of the theory. To these matters we will return.

What about biblical creationism—is it scientific? Gunther S. Stent considers that "the very term 'Scientific Creationism' is an oxymoron,"[54] and Judge William Overton, commenting on the Arkansas law that mandated the teaching of creationism, ruled that creation science does not constitute a genuine science.[55] J. P. Moreland rightly shows that the statements "By its very nature, Natural Science must adopt Methodological Naturalism" (in support of evolution) and "Theistic science is religion and not science" (in opposition to biblical creationism) are not first-order claims of science about some scientific phenomenon. "Rather, they are second-order philosophical claims *about* science. They are meta-claims that take a vantage point outside science and have science itself as their subject of reference. Thus the field of philosophy, especially philosophy of science—not science—will be the proper domain from which to assess these claims. Scientists are not experts in these second-order questions, and when they comment on them, they do so qua philosophers, not qua scientists."[56] A leading philosopher of science, Alvin Platinga, says, "we need Theistic Science."[57]

Theistic science takes the position that we need not restrict scientific methodology to methodological naturalism, as in evolutionary theory. Philosopher and historian of science Michael Ruse confines the scope of science to "unbroken, natural regularity."[58]

Why should science limit itself to the natural realm? Although empirical evidence lies at the core of scientific enquiry, Paul K. Feyerabend speaks about the various problems in empiricism. Different thinkers have "proceeded in different ways and thereby given rise to different kinds of scientific knowledge." As a result, he warns, "the unity of doctrine insinuated by the scientist's appeal to experimentation and by his hostility toward 'hypotheses' must therefore be viewed with extreme caution."[59]

So there are different kinds of scientific knowledge. Why cannot the action of God, or the supernatural, be seen as one kind of scientific thinking, in which God is the cause of Creation in theistic science? After all, as Charles B. Thaxton notes, "Science includes many elements; it includes asking what causes things."[60]

Causation as a Part of Science

Darwin's central thesis was evolution through natural selection. Such methodological naturalism cannot, however, be cut loose from causation. Darwin's *Origin of Species* never explains anything about the origin of life from some prebiotic soup. The term *"Origin"* is a misnomer, in that Darwin never tells how that first beginning was possible. Nevertheless, the fact that he mentions origin means that he assumes causation. It is not good enough to speak about natural laws as if they somehow transcend causation. J. P. Moreland said it well: "It is simply false to assert that scientists explain things merely by using natural laws, say by invoking a covering law model of scientific explanation. Scientists also explain certain aspects of the universe not only by using natural laws but also by citing the big bang as a single causal event."[61]

If evolutionary theory can speak of causation, why cannot theistic science? Henry M. Morris was right when he said that science is assumed to be "rational and causal and unified" and yet "banning by definition even the possibility of a supernatural First Cause of the rationality, causality, and unity of the universe with which science deals." Then that "assumption is purely arbitrary."[62]

Dr. Abraham Wolf, one of the greatest philosophers of science and former professor and head of the Department of the History of Method of Science at London University, said every event has a cause. "This assumption is commonly known as the Postulate or Principle of Universal Causation." He pointed out that "the principle of conservation of matter or energy would lose all significance without the idea of causal continuity, according to which certain successive events not only *follow* but *follow from* one another. In fact, mere laws of sequence are intelligible only in the last resort, when they can be shown to result from direct or indirect causal connections."[63]

Sir Julian Huxley said of Darwin that "he had a passion for natural history, which showed itself from early childhood."[64] The evolutionary view is historical, for it believes that every living animal is related by common ancestry. I contend that Darwin, even though focusing on natural selection in evolution, was still enamored with history (ancestral line) when he wrote his *Origin of Species*. Steven C. Meyer points out correctly that Darwin's *Origin of Species* "does not explain by natural law. Common descent explains by postulating a hypothetical pattern of historical events which, if actual, would account for a variety of presently observed data. . . . In Darwin's historical argument for descent, as with historical explanations generally, postulated past causal events (or patterns thereof) do the primary explanatory work. Laws do not."[65] For example, "the law 'Oxygen is necessary to combustion' does not explain why a particular building burned at a particular place and time."[66] Many different factors, such as an arsonist, lack of security, faulty wiring, a malfunctioning kerosene stove, a smoldering cigarette, or lack of a sprinkler system could be possible causes.

So evolutionary theory premises itself on causality through the ancestral line. Is it not hypocritical of evolutionary theorists to reject supernatural causation when they believe in natural causation? To restrict causation to the natural realm alone limits the search for possible evidence.

Is such confining really true to a scientific objectivity that seeks to keep itself open to all evidence? Does not the precluding of the supernatural interpose a subjective assumption before anyone even considers the facts? Natural theory presupposes descent. Supernatural theory presupposes design. How can a scientist determine whether homology (the correspondence of structures between different organisms) among animals results from descent rather than design? How objective can the scientist be when he or she has prescribed the area of search through biased presuppositions? What would happen if the scientist could really be objective and consider all the options, both supernatural and natural? Does the empirical evidence support descent or design? To this question we now turn.

The Origin of Life

The origin of life is unknown to empirical science, though evolutionists have suggested various ideas. A popular thesis assumes that life arose out of a prebiotic soup when molecular complexity crossed the divide from organic chemistry to biology, from nonliving to living. While at the University of Chicago in 1953, graduate student Stanley Miller, in Harold Urey's lab, experimented with amino acids in a mixture of water, methane, ammonia, and hydrogen, substances assumed to be present in the atmosphere and oceans of the primitive earth. He exposed the chemicals to an electrical spark.[67] "Because amino acids are used in building proteins, they are sometimes called the 'building blocks of life.' Subsequent experiments based on the Miller-Urey model produced a variety of amino acids and other complex compounds employed in the genetic process, with the result that the more optimistic researchers concluded that the chemicals needed to construct life could have been present in sufficient abundance on the early earth."[68]

During the 1980s a major skepticism of the Miller-Urey experiments began to arise. Atmospheric physicists now doubt that the early earth's atmosphere contained significant amounts of ammonia, methane, or hydrogen to allow the kind of reactions that the experiments produced to have actually occurred. Molecular biologists discovered that RNA—a bridge from the chemicals to DNA—is "exceedingly difficult to synthesize under the conditions that likely prevailed when life originated." Moreover, they no longer believe that RNA can replicate itself as easily as once believed.[69] "Perhaps the most discouraging criticism has come from chemists, who have spoiled the prebiotic soup by showing that organic compounds produced on the early earth would be subject to chemical reactions making them unsuitable for constructing life. In all probability, the prebiotic soup could never have existed, and without it there is no reason to believe that the production of small amounts of some amino acids by electrical charge in a reducing atmosphere had anything to do with the origin of life."[70]

Thus we have no empirical evidence for how life began. Science has not been able to deny the biblical record of Creation by God. Cambridge University astrophysicist Sir Frederick Hoyle in his book *Evolution From Space* (1981) quoted a statement that said: "'The likelihood of the spontaneous formation of life from inanimate matter is one to a number of 40,000 naughts after it!'" He concludes, "It is big enough to bury Darwin and the whole theory of evolution."[71]

It is incredible that some scholars believe life began many times in the universe (Dawkins, Asimov, Billingham).[72] They teach it, even though they have found no evidence of life anywhere in the universe outside of the earth. Yet the winner of the Nobel Prize for physiology and medicine in 1962 for his work on DNA, Francis Crick, postulates that life began on some other planet some 9 billion years ago.[73] In his view of "Directed Panspermia," Crick believes that alien beings packed bacteria, such as *Escherichia coli*, about one micron wide and two microns long, and put them aboard a space ship and sent them to other planets, including earth. The advantage of such bacteria is they can be frozen alive and most of them will survive. "At a very low temperature, such as that of space, many of them might well survive for well over ten thousand years. They would be almost immune to impact shock and other similar hazards."[74]

Human imagination is amazing! What such scholars fail to do is to explain how life itself began on those hypothetical other planets. We cannot solve science's failure to explain how life started on our own planet (prebiotic soup) by transporting bacteria on a space ship from outer space. The question simply gets removed to that planet—how did life originate there? Furthermore, we have no empirical evidence that bacteria can evolve into a complex organism, as the first stage of the evolutionary climb to ever greater complexity. In addition, as far as our planet is concerned, we have no evidence of a prebiotic soup in the earliest rocks.[75] And even if there was evidence, Klaus Dose from the Institute of Biochemistry, Johannes Gutenberg University, Germany, concludes: "It is extremely unlikely that the first forms of life could have evolved spontaneously in a primordial soup."[76]

---

[1] Michael Bartholomew, Bernard Norton, and Robert M. Young, *Block VI, Problems in the Biological and Human Sciences* (London: The Open University, 1981), p. 17.

[2] W. R. Bird, *The Origin of Species Revisited: The Theories of Evolution of Abrupt Appearance* (New York: Philosophical Library), vol. 1, p. 1.

[3] Ernst Mayr, "Behavior Programs and Evolutionary Strategies," *American Scientist* 62 (November-December 1974): 650.

[4] Ernst Mayr, "Darwin and Natural Selection: How Darwin May Have Discovered His Highly Unconventional Theory," *American Scientist* 65 (May/June 1977): 321.

[5] Naturalist Alfred R. Wallace wrote a paper on natural selection and sent it to Charles Darwin in 1858. It shocked Darwin, who had been working on his theory for 20 years, and he feared that his own work on natural selection was now at risk as an original idea, even though both men had done their work independently. Charles Lyell, a friend of Darwin, arranged with the Linnean Society in London that Darwin and Wallace could both present their papers in 1858.

From 1869 onward, Wallace had an important difference with Darwin. He concluded that natural selection was not responsible for the emergence of humans. In 1910, at the age of 87, Wallace made a second major step away from Darwin. He wrote: "After 40 years of further reflection, I now uphold the doctrine that not only man but the whole world of life leads us to the same conclusion—that to afford any rational explanation or its phenomena, we require to postulate the continuous action and guidance of a higher intelligence." He thereby broke beyond the naturalistic paradigm of Darwin to allow for the supernatural (Paul Kildare, "Monkey Business," *Christian Order,* December 1982, p. 592). See also Bartholomew, Norton, and Young, pp. 19, 20.

[6] Henry M. Morris, *The Biblical Basis for Modern Science* (Grand Rapids: Baker, 1990), p. 111.

[7] Ernst Mayr, "Darwin and Natural Selection," p. 327.

[8] Martin Lings, quoted by Huston Smith, "Evolution and Evolutionism," *Christian Century,* July 7-14, 1982, p. 755.

Evolution: A Theory in Crisis

[9] Robert Wright, "Our Cheating Hearts," *Time,* Aug. 15, 1994, pp. 44-52.

[10] Morris, p. 403.

[11] Charles Darwin, *The Origin of Species* (New York: Carlton), p. 373.

[12] Paul K. Jewett, *God, Creation and Revelation* (Grand Rapids: Eerdmans, 1991), pp. 479, 480.

[13] Here are a few of the scholars who, in varying degrees, place evolutionary theory as the context in which to interpret the Genesis account of Creation: Augustus Strong, *Systematic Theology* (Philadelphia: Judson, 1907), pp. 465, 466; Bernard Ramm, *The Christian View of Science and Scripture* (Grand Rapids: Eerdmans, 1954), pp. 76-79; Langdon Gilkey, *Maker of Heaven and Earth* (Garden City, N.Y.: Doubleday, 1965); Millard J. Erickson, *Christian Theology* (Grand Rapids: Baker, 1986), pp. 381, 382; Paul K. Jewett, *God, Creation and Revelation* (Grand Rapids: Eerdmans, 1991), pp. 478-484.

[14] Marco T. Terreros, "Death Before the Sin of Adam: A Fundamental Concept in Theistic Evolution and Its Implications for Evangelical Theology" (Ph.D. dissertation, Andrews University Theological Seminary, 1994). See *Andrews University Seminary Studies* 32, Nos. 1, 2 (Spring-Summer 1994): 114.

[15] Karl Barth, *Church Dogmatics,* vol. 3, part 2, pp. 511-640. Cf. Barth (1966), vol. 2, part 1, pp. 608-677.

[16] Thomas N. Finger, *Christian Theology: An Eschatological Approach* (Scottdale, Pa.: Herald, 1989), vol. 2, p. 413.

[17] Alfred Whitehead, *Process and Reality* (New York: Free, 1929), pp. 25, 26.

[18] John Macquarrie, *Principles of Christian Theology* (New York: Scribner, 1966).

[19] Pierre Teilhard de Chardin, *The Phenomenon of Man,* Bernard Wall, trans. (New York: Harper, 1959).

[20] Augustine seems to posit the idea that God implanted seeds in the natural order for an ongoing creation *(On the Holy Trinity* (3.8), *The Nicene and Post-Nicene Fathers,* First Series [Edinburgh, Scotland: T & T Clark, 1988], vol. 3, pp. 60, 61).

[21] In his *Summa Theologica,* Thomas Aquinas, after considering the procession in the Trinity (Q 27-43), takes up the procession of creatures from God (Q 44-49). He views these two processions in a type/antitype correspondence (45.6). Thus "every being in any way existing is from God" (44.1), a concept that seems to echo progressive creation *(Summa Theologica,* vol. 1, pp. 229-256).

[22] Theistic evolution is a divine working immanental in nature, whereas progressive creation focuses on the transcendental activity of God. See Bernard Ramm, *The Christian View of Science and Scripture* (Grand Rapids: Eerdmans, 1971), p. 147.

[23] "The Church Today," *The Documents of Vatican II,* p. 234.

[24] *Ibid.,* p. 265.

[25] *Ibid.,* p. 117.

[26] *Catechism of the Catholic Church,* p. 74.

[27] Ernst Mayr, "Darwin and Natural Selection: How Darwin May Have Discovered His Highly Unconventional Theory," *American Scientist* 65 (May/June 1997): 321.

[28] Michael Denton, *Evolution: A Theory in Crisis* (Bethesda, Md.: Adler and Adler, 1986), p. 37.

[29] Isaac Asimov, *Asimov's New Guide to Science* (New York: Basic Books, 1972), p. 772.

[30] Marvin L. Lubenow, "Augustine: Evolutionist or Creationist" (an unpublished paper presented to the Evangelical Theological Society, Nov. 17-19, 1994, Chicago).

[31] Bowler argues that Aristotle was not the real discoverer of evolution. Rather, Darwin's natural selection was a "genuine scientific revolution" (Peter J. Bowler, *Evolution: The History of an Idea* [Berkeley, Calif.: University of California, 1989], pp. 20, 21.

[32] Eiseley argues that eighteenth-century biologists contributed to a new understanding of evolution, such as Buffon's premonition of the Law of Succession, that animals developed in the area in which they are now found, rather than coming from Noah's ark (p. 44). Other ideas include the belief of Darwin's grandfather, Erasmus Darwin, "in the inheritance of acquired characteristics" (p. 48). Jean Baptiste Lamarck held a similar view (p. 49). "Both he and Erasmus Darwin placed . . . an emphasis upon volition, the 'striving' of the organism for survival and adjustment" (p. 51). "Lamarck appears to have been the first to grasp the importance of the concept of use and disuse in their effect upon individual organs. Later on this was to be appropriated by Charles Darwin" (p. 55) (Loren Eiseley, *Darwin's Century* [Garden City, N.Y.: Doubleday, 1958], pp. 44-55).

[33] Green argues that "Buffon was very close to the idea of natural selection" (p. 152). "The mutability of

species, a conception toward which Buffon had slowly groped his way, became Lamarck's starting point" (p. 159). Lamarck's "developmental hypothesis" was fundamental to his view of evolution (p. 161). "Lamarck provided the first systematic elaboration of the evolutionary idea," although it goes back to Darwin's grandfather, Erasmus Darwin (p. 166) (John C. Greene, *The Death of Adam: Evolution and Its Impact on Western Thought* [Ames, Iowa: Iowa State University, 1959], pp. 145-169).

[34] In 1942 Julian Huxley coined the term *modern synthesis* (Roger Lewin, "Evolutionary Theory Under Fire: An Historical Conference in Chicago Challenges the Four-Decade Long Dominance of the Modern Synthesis," *Science* 210 [Nov. 21, 1980]: 883).

[35] Sir Julian Huxley mentions the 1915 date and Ernst Mayr cites the 1930s date. Perhaps this is the time during which the synthesis of Darwin's natural selection with Mendel's genetic heredity took place. See Sir Julian Huxley in *The Evolution of Life: Its Origin, History and Future,* Sol Tax, ed. (Chicago: University, 1960), p. 10; Ernst Mayr, *Populations, Species, and Evolution* (Cambridge, Mass.: Harvard, 1970), p. 1. Theodosius Dobzhansky was one of the architects of the Neo-Darwinian Modern Synthesis. Brian Leith, *The Descent of Darwin: A Handbook of Doubts About Darwinism* (London: Collins, 1982), p. 19.

[36] *Post-Darwinianism* is a term I coined to represent the demise of the strictly Darwinian model. Although the Modern Synthesis added random genetic mutation to Darwin's sole principle of natural selection, the marriage proved to be an assumed strengthening of Darwin's basic thesis. The advent of molecular biology and the study of DNA brought a persuasive challenge to the central thesis of Darwinian evolutionary theory. This continued in the work of Niles Eldredge and Stephen Jay Gould in their view of "punctuated equilibrium." The sudden appearance of species in the fossil record radically called into question Darwinian gradualism.

[37] In 1980 Stephen Jay Gould and Niles Eldridge proposed a new theory of abrupt, rather than gradual, changes in evolutionary development. See Phillip E. Johnson, *Darwin on Trial* (Downers Grove, Ill.: InterVarsity, 1991), pp. 11, 39, 50.

[38] Brian Leith, *The Descent of Darwin: A Handbook of Doubts About Darwinism* (London: Collins, 1982), pp. 13, 14.

[39] Phillip Johnson, *Darwin on Trial* (Downers Grove, Ill.: InterVarsity, 1991), p. 118.

[40] L. Beverly Halstead, "Halstead's Defense Against Irrelevancy," *Nature* 292 (July 30, 1981): 404.

[41] Bowler, p. 356.

[42] Scott M. Huse, *The Collapse of Evolution* (Grand Rapids: Baker, 1983).

[43] Michael Denton, *Evolution: A Theory in Crisis* (Bethesda, Md.: Adler & Adler, 1986).

[44] Johnson.

[45] J. P. Moreland, ed., *The Creation Hypothesis: Scientific Evidence for an Intelligent Designer* (Downers Grove, Ill.: InterVarsity, 1994).

[46] Percival Davis and Dean H. Kenyon, *Of Pandas and People: The Central Question of Biological Origins* (Dallas: Haughton, 1989).

[47] Leith.

[48] Michael Polanyi, "Life's Irreducible Structure," *Science* 160 (June 1968): 1308-1312.

[49] W. R. Bird, *The Origin of Species Revisited: The Theories of Evolution and of Abrupt Appearance* (New York: Philosophical Library, 1954), vol. 1.

[50] In fairness it may be claimed that science has discovered a few transitional organisms, such as the *Archaeopteryx,* but they seem to prove the rule as exceptions. The *Archaeopteryx* looks like the small dinosaur called *Compsognathus*, is mostly birdlike with wings and feathers, but has claws on its wings and teeth in its mouth. See Phillip E. Johnson, *Darwin on Trial*, p. 78.

[51] Johnson, p. 9.

[52] Karl Popper, quoted in Leith, p. 26.

[53] *Ibid.,* p. 28.

[54] Gunther S. Stent, in *Science and Creationism,* Ashley Montagu, ed. (Oxford: University Press, 1984), p. 137.

[55] Michael Ruse, ed., *But Is It Science?* (Buffalo, N.Y.: Prometheus, 1988), p. 6.

[56] J. P. Moreland, *The Creation Hypothesis: Scientific Evidence for an Intelligent Designer,* J. P. Moreland, ed. (Downers Grove, Ill.: InterVarsity, 1994), p. 43.

[57] Alvin Platinga, "When Faith and Reason Clash: Evolution and the Bible," *Christian Scholar's Review* 21, No. 1 (1991): 30.

[58] Michael Ruse, "Creation Science Is Not Science," *Science, Technology, and Human Values* 7, No. 40 (Summer 1982): 74.

[59] Paul K. Feyerabend in *Beyond the Edge of Certainty: Essays in Contemporary Science and Philosophy,* Robert G. Colodny, ed. (Englewood Cliffs, N.J.: Prentice-Hall, 1965), p. 146.

[60] Charles B. Thaxton, ed., *Of Pandas and People: The Central Question of Biological Origins* (Dallas: Haughton, 1989), p. viii.

[61] Moreland, p. 55.

[62] Henry M. Morris, *The Biblical Basis for Modern Science* (Grand Rapids: Baker, 1990), p. 31.

[63] Abraham Wolf, quoted in *ibid.,* p. 35.

[64] Sir Julian Huxley in *Evolution After Darwin,* vol. 1, p. 2.

[65] Stephen C. Meyer in *The Creation Hypothesis,* p. 81.

[66] *Ibid.,* p. 79.

[67] Julius Rebek, Jr., "Synthetic Self-Replicating Molecules," *Scientific American,* July 1994, p. 48.

[68] Johnson, p. 102.

[69] Walter L. Bradley and Charles B. Thaxton in *The Creation Hypothesis,* p. 175.

[70] Johnson, p. 103.

[71] Sir Frederick Hoyle, quoted by Paul Kildare, "Monkey Business," *Christian Order* 23 (December 1982): 589.

[72] Richard Dawkins in *But Is It Science?* p. 202.

[73] Francis Crick, *Life Itself: Its Origin and Nature* (New York: Simon and Schuster, 1981), p. 116.

[74] *Ibid.,* p. 128.

[75] Michael Denton, *Evolution: A Theory in Crisis,* p. 263.

[76] Klaus Dose, "The Origin of Life: More Questions Than Answers," *Interdisciplinary Science Reviews* 13, No. 4 (1988): 352.

Chapter 32

Evidences Against Evolution

Many forms of evidence question the Darwinian theory of evolution. We'll note a number of them as we proceed through the next two chapters.

Descent or Design

Some biologists have used demarcation arguments to separate the so-called scientific approach to origins (descent) from what they consider the nonscientific (design). Such demarcation arguments derive from a philosophy of science called logical positivism.[1] Logical positivism has its roots in a seminar by Moritz Schlick at the University of Vienna in 1923. Others joining the movement were A. J. Ayer, Rudolf Carnap, Herbert Feigel, and the early Ludwig Wittgenstein. They set up what they considered as standards for meaningfulness. As Millard Erickson notes: "According to the view, there are only two types of meaningful language: (1) mathematico-logical truths, in which the predicate is contained within the subject, such as 'the sum of the angles of a triangle is 180 degrees,' and (2) empirical truths such as 'the book is on the table.' Empirical truths are propositions which are verified by sense data. These are the only meaningful types of language. All other propositions, that is, propositions which are neither mathematical-type nor empirical or scientific-type statements verified by sense data, are literally 'nonsense' or meaningless."[2]

As Erickson rightly concludes, logical positivism consigned the language of metaphysics, ethics, theology, and other disciplines to meaninglessness. The problem with that conclusion is that we cannot verify it by using the confined criteria of logical positivism itself. So logical positivism fails because it cannot meet its own criteria.

With the collapse of logical positivism, analytical philosophy came to study language in the context of its use, an approach known as functional analysis. This means that we must evaluate language employed in biology and theology from within the different contexts of the two fields. Thus the criteria for evaluating the authenticity of the one cannot evaluate the authenticity of the other.

Ludwig Wittgenstein, in his later thinking, compared the different contexts to different games. No one would apply the rules of baseball to football. Each game is played according to its own rules. Likewise, the language of theology in discussing Creation and design must be true to its own context and is as valid within that context as any other use of language in other contexts, including biological views on descent.

Stephen Meyer has written on the methodological equivalence of intelligent design and naturalistic descent. "Design and descent prove equally scientific or equally unscientific depending upon the criteria used to adjudicate their scientific status and provided metaphysically neutral criteria are selected to make such assessments."[3] The fact is that the word "design" has come back into scientific vocabulary, on account of the work of physicists. They have "unveiled a universe apparently fine-tuned for the possibility of human life."[4]

"Despite this renewal of interest in the (intelligent) design hypothesis among physicists and cosmologists, biologists have remained reluctant to consider such notions. As historian of science Timothy Lenior has observed, 'Teleological thinking has been steadfastly resisted by modern biology. And yet, in nearly every area of research biologists are hard pressed to find language that does not impute purposeness to living forms.'"[5] Yet, as Mae-Wan Ho and Peter T. Saunders have stated, "the all-powerful force of natural selection has come more and more to resemble explanation in terms of the conscious design of the omnipotent Creator."[6]

The Function of DNA

In 1953 Francis Crick and James Watson discovered the architecture of the double helix DNA molecule.[7] DNA has added enormously to our understanding of how living things develop. Research on it has shown that the idea of natural selection and random genetic mutation, with their emphasis on descent, has been too narrow a view, because DNA is a unique method of storing information that speaks far more of design by an intelligent Creator.

Michael Denton, in his seminal book *Evolution: A Theory in Crisis,* speaks of the amazing ability of DNA to contain biological data. "The capacity of DNA to store information vastly exceeds that of any other known system; it is so efficient that all the information needed to specify an organism as complex as man weighs less than a few thousand millionths of a gram. The information necessary to specify the design of all the species of organisms which have ever existed on the planet, a number according to G. G. Simpson of approximately one thousand million, could be held in a teaspoon and there would still be room left for all the information in every book ever written."[8]

John W. Oller, Jr., and John L. Omdahl compared human language capacity with the capacity of DNA. They noted that "the origin of the human language capacity is not unlike the problem of the origin of life itself."[9] They conclude that "the intricate and articulate structures of language are mirrored in the delicate arrangements of biological representations in correspondence to information coded in DNA. We have shown logically that the language capacity cannot have originated in a purely materialistic manner. The logical gulf that separates mind from matter really is an uncrossable barrier to any materialistic origin. If the definitions of Peirce and Einstein are accepted, the gulf they describe cannot be crossed without the intervention of a truly transcendent Intelligence—a conclusion both of them accepted."[10]

It is not good enough to say, with Oxford University zoologist Richard Dawkins, that God cannot be the origin of DNA. "To explain the origin of the DNA/protein machine by invoking a supernatural Designer is to explain precisely nothing, for it leaves unexplained the origin of the Designer. You have to say something like 'God was always there,' and if you allow yourself that kind of lazy way out, you might as well just say 'DNA was always there,' or 'Life was always there,' and be done with it."

What Dawkins completely overlooked was the two-leveled reality at work in the living organism, that is, the DNA at the higher level suggesting design and the physical-chemical development at the lower level, which some claim to illustrate descent. What Dawkins needs to do is to take seriously the seminal work done by another Oxford University professor, Michael Polanyi.

In an influential article entitled "Life's Irreducible Structure," Polanyi, former Fellow of Merton College, Oxford University, compared machines to evolutionary theory. Human beings make machines, even though the former operate according to laws of inanimate nature. "So the machine as a whole works under the control of two distinct principles. The higher one is the principle of the machine's design, and this harnesses the lower one, which consists in the physical-chemical processes on which the machine relies."[11]

Polanyi considers live mechanisms and information in DNA as boundary conditions, with a sequence of boundaries above them. He reasons that "a boundary condition is always extraneous to the process which it delimits." For example, when Galileo conducted his experiment of balls running down a slope, the choice of the slope had nothing to do with the laws of mechanics. Furthermore, the shape and manufacture of test tubes have nothing to do with the laws of chemistry. Nor can we define the structure of machines by the laws they harness. "Thus the morphology of living things transcends the laws of physics and chemistry," he concludes.[12]

Relative to DNA, Polanyi questions evolutionary theory. "In the light of the current theory of evolution, the codelike structure of DNA must be assumed to have come about by a sequence of chance variations established by natural selection. But this evolutionary aspect is irrelevant here; whatever may be the origin of a DNA configuration, it can function as a code only if its order is not due to the forces of potential energy. It must be as physically indeterminate as the sequence of words is on a printed page. As the arrangement of a printed page is extraneous to the chemistry of the printed page, so is the base sequence in a DNA molecule extraneous to the chemical forces at work in the DNA molecule."[13]

"Can the control of morphogenesis

by DNA be likened to the designing and shaping of a machine by an engineer?" Polanyi asks.[14] He answers in the positive. The codelike structure of DNA, with all its information that affects the growth of the organism, acts on the organism as an engineer does on a machine. The fact that the organism harnesses the physical-chemical substances within it in no way fully defines the organism which is under dual control—from DNA and the physical-chemical substances, with DNA being the primary level of influence. It would seem to me that this model places design (not descent) from the DNA as the primary influence in the development of living things.

Scott M. Huse, commenting on DNA, observes that "computer scientists have demonstrated conclusively that information does not and cannot arise spontaneously. Information results only from the expenditure of energy (to arrange the letter and words) and under the all-important direction of intelligence. Therefore, since DNA is information, the only logical and reasonable conclusion that can be drawn is that DNA was formed by intelligence."[15]

On the basis of the work done on DNA, it seems more reasonable to say that it demonstrates an intelligent Creator and thus speaks eloquently on behalf of design rather than on descent.

Complexity

Evolutionary theory is a paradigm, a concept not yet proved but accepted as a basic presupposition. Within this assumed paradigm science studies nature in a search to find evidence to support the paradigm itself. Thus the paradigm itself biases or shapes the search. When we come to consider complexities in nature, we find them on every level. One has to ask the serious question: How can such complexity develop just from random genetic mutation and natural selection? Michael Denton puts well the enormity of the problem when he speaks about DNA. "To the skeptic, the proposition that the genetic programmes of higher organisms, consisting of something close to a thousand million bits of information, equivalent to the sequence of letters in a small library of one thousand volumes, containing in encoded form countless thousands of intricate algorithms controlling, specifying and ordering the growth and development of billions and billions of cells into the form of a complex organism, were composed by a purely random process is simply an affront to reason. But to the Darwinist the idea is accepted without a ripple of doubt—the paradigm takes precedence."[16]

With such complexity at the infinitesimal level in DNA, what observed process do we know to be responsible for its development? The fact of the matter is that evolutionary theory has not come up with any clue as to how such complexity can exist at the very basic level of living organisms. Brian Leith, in his insightful book *The Descent of Darwin,* comments: "I don't think there is an evolutionist alive who is particularly happy with existing ideas about how complex features arise."[17]

Richard Dawkins, in the *New Scientist* journal, notes that only two alternatives to Darwinism exist to explain "the organized and apparently purposeful complexity of life. These are God and Lamarkism." It is incredible to what lengths the evolutionary paradigm pushes Dawkins as he rejects the idea of God as a reasonable origin for complexity in nature. "I am afraid I shall give God rather short shrift. He may have many virtues: no doubt he is invaluable as a pricker of the conscience and a comfort to the dying and the bereaved, but as an explanation of organized complexity, he simply will not do. It is organized complexity we are trying to explain, so it is footling to invoke in explanation a being sufficiently organized and complex to create it."[18]

Dawkins at least admits the existence of God who "pricks" and "comforts" human beings. He accepts, to that degree, the supernatural. Why does he then limit causation to the natural? Does not his paradigm prejudice confine him so that he refuses to take in all of the possibilities, as we would expect from normal scientific methodology to do? Stephen C. Meyer was right when he observed, "If competing hypotheses are eliminated before they are evaluated, remaining theories may acquire an undeserved dominance."[19] This has happened in the self-confined naturalistic paradigm of evolutionary theory. What science needs to do is to allow supernatural causation as a more reasonable cause for complexity than random genetic mutation and natural selection. From the megauniverse to the microuniverse, we find complexity everywhere, and it staggers the mind if such complexity is the result only of random and purposeless evolution.

Kurt P. Wise speaks of complexity as evidence that evolution has to leave unexplained. "Anyone who has taken college biochemistry has been impressed with the extraordinary complexity of replication, transcription, the Krebs cycle, and other features of living things. For those who did not take such a course, these are a few of the many chemical processes that occur within any one of your trillions of body cells at any given moment. Photosynthesis, as an example on a subcellular process, is thought to involve as many as five hundred chemical steps—of which we 'fully' understand only a few. Yet a number of these kinds of processes occur spontaneously within individual cells."[20] He traces complexity up through different levels, from the chemical processes in the cell to human organs and their interrelationships, to communities of organisms and their network of complex interactions, and finally to the earth and the complex arrangement of astronomical bodies that allow life to exist on our planet. "Macroevolutionary theory has never successfully explained the acquisition of any level of this complexity, let alone the total complexity."[21] As Michael Denton has said, "In practically every field of fundamental biological research ever-increasing levels of design and complexity are being revealed at an ever-accelerating rate."[22] This effectively calls into question the theory of evolution.

Beyond complexity itself lies the question of integration. "As if the basic complexity of things were not enough, the integration of that complexity is truly astounding. Not only do subcellular chemical processes involve a large number of complex molecules and chemical steps, but those items and events are connected in a well-balanced and well-timed series of items and steps to produce a well-integrated process. Similarly, the workings of subcellular organelles, cells in tissues, tissues in organs, organs in systems, systems in bodies, organisms with other organisms, organisms in communities in the biosphere, all show staggering integration. As with the complexity of these items and events on any given level, such a level of integration has never been observed to arise from nonintelligent natural law and process. Integration seems to argue for intelligent cause."[23]

"The integration that is so striking *within* levels is even more striking *between* levels. Not only do subcellular organelle systems and chemical processes show integration, but the chemical and organelle systems are themselves linked together, and must be for the cell to survive. Even more impressive, a similar integration exists between all levels. Once again, this level of integration is unexplained by evolutionary theory but is addressable by intelligent-cause theory."[24]

The Human Eye

In 1861, two years after the publication of his *Origin of Species,* Darwin wrote a letter to biologist Asa Gray saying that "'The eye to this day gives me a cold shudder.'"[25] "To suppose that the eye," he wrote, "with all its inimitable contrivances for adjusting the focus to different distances, for admitting different amounts of light, and for the correction of spherical and chromatic aberration, could have been formed by natural selection, seems, I freely confess, absurd in the highest possible degree. . . . The belief that an organ as perfect as the eye could have formed by natural selection is more than enough to stagger anyone."[26]

If the eye made Darwin shudder, imagine what today's additional knowledge of the eye would do to him! "Electrophysiological studies have recently revealed very intricate connections among the nerve cells of the retina, which enable the eye to carry out many types of preliminary data processing of visual information before transmitting it in binary form to the brain. The cleverness of these mechanisms has again been underlined by their close analogy to the sorts of image intensification and clarification processes carried out today by computers, such as those used by NASA, on images transmitted from space. Today it would be more accurate to think of a television camera if we are looking for an analogy to the eye."[27]

Darwin had every reason to shudder at an examination of the human eye, for how could natural selection produce such ordered and precise design and complexity? Furthermore, how could natural selection, an incredibly slow process, have a workable eye at every stage of its development? Richard Dawkins admits that the human eye "could not possibly come into existence through single-step selection."[28] He believes the human eye could have taken several hundred million years to evolve.[29] Yet Dawkins can say elsewhere, "The eye is, par excellence, a case where a fraction of an organ is better than no organ at all; an eye without a lens or even a pupil, for instance, could still detect the looming shadow of a predator."[30]

But how can a fraction of an eye really be an eye? How can the allegedly slow process to produce the eye really be possible when the eye is only a part of a wider complex network of interdependent parts comprising the visual network? As Alvin Platinga said, "Here is the problem: how does the lens, for example, get developed by the proposed means—random genetic variation and natural selection—when at the same time there has to be development of the optic nerve, the relevant muscles, the retina, the rods and cones, and many other delicate and complicated structures, all of which have to be adjusted to each other in such a way that they can work together? Indeed, what is involved isn't, of course, just the eye; it is the whole visual system, including the relevant parts of the brain. Many different organs and suborgans have to be developed together, and it is hard to envisage a series of mutations which is such that each member of the series has adaptive value, is also a step on the way to the eye, and is such that the last member is an animal with such an eye."[31]

The eye is too complex in itself and in its visual network to be a product of random development. This is why Dawkins' idea that an eye functions as an eye even during its early stages of development does not make sense. Harvard scholar Stephen Jay Gould asked what good is 5 percent of an eye? Realizing that it could not see, he thought it might have some other function than sight. Dawkins disagreed with Gould and said that the 5-percent eye was used "for 5 percent vision." But how can 5 percent of an eye have 5 percent of vision, when vision does not function until the eye is 100 percent an eye, with all the parts in place and fully functioning as noted above by Plantinga? Lawyer Phillip E. Johnson saw the illogic of Dawkins' conclusion, stating, "The fallacy in that argument is that '5 percent of an eye' is not the same thing as '5 percent of normal vision.' "[32]

Dan-E. Nilsson and Susanne Pelger of Lund University considered that the human eye could have developed in "a few hundred thousand generations" in "1829 steps,"[33] yet they start with a flat, light-sensitive patch of cells. They say nothing about how those light-sensitive cells came into being. The two researchers assume their presence rather than realizing that how the cells formed is itself a fundamental part of what they should be proving, rather than assuming, if they wish to demonstrate how the eye evolved. True science begins the process at the beginning, not way down the line.

What we have said about the eye applies to many other organs, or body parts, such as the avian lung[34] and bird wings, to name but two. Each has a complex network involved, so that no one part can evolve without all parts developing at the same time. The problem is, how can an emerging lung be a lung, or a wing be a wing? How can an avian lung, through which air passes only one way, develop from the two-way passage found in all other vertebrates?

Beyond all this is the complexity of the human brain. Cal Tech neurobiologist Roger Sperry, winner of the 1981

Nobel Prize for study on the two hemispheres of the human brain, argues "that the brain system as a whole somehow controls its parts in ways that supersede the mechanistic physical states of the brain's 10 billion neurons."[35] Although he dismisses the supernatural, Sperry at least apparently realizes that the brain involves more than "mechanistic physical" dimensions. The intricacies of the human brain are equivalent to the most complex computer network known to humanity and speak eloquently for a Creator rather than random chance for its existence.

Michael Denton observes, "If complex computer programs cannot be changed by random mechanisms, then surely the same must apply to the genetic programmes of living organisms."[36] It is not correct to compare the "evolution" of planes from Bleriot's monoplane to Boeing's 747, for their development did not depend upon chance.[37] We cannot explain the sheer perfection throughout the universe at every level on the basis of chance and random natural processes.[38]

Random chance introduces the theory of probability into evolutionary theory. Enormous amounts of time have been a safe haven for the evolutionary hypothesis, because its theorists believe that, given sufficient time, any evolutionary development is possible. With sufficient time, as on a roulette wheel, the number 26, for example, could come up exactly when needed along the evolutionary line. But this loophole is no longer available today, since science better understands the complexities of evolution. "We now see that significant organic changes require that innumerable component developments occur *simultaneously* and *independently* in bones, nerves, muscles, arteries and the like," Huston Smith reports. "These requirements escalate the demand on probability theory astronomically. It would be like having 26 come up simultaneously on 10 or 15 tables in the same casino, followed by all the tables reporting 27, 28 and 29 in lockstep progression; more time than the earth has existed would be needed to account for the sequences that have occurred."[39]

The Cell

Darwinian evolution believes that gradual microevolutionary steps explain the development of life from the prebiotic soup all the way to human beings (some even posit that human beings will progress beyond their present stage[40]). Most people understand evolution as change from the simple to the complex. We have already noted how complex the human species is, and we could say much about the complexity of the animal kingdom too. Our point here is that complexity is not the end result of some evolutionary process but appears even in the smallest building block of life, as in DNA and the single cell itself.

Molecular biology has opened up a whole new world of complexity that staggers the imagination and exposes how incredulous is the theory of evolution. W. R. Bird, in his book *The Origin of Species Revisited,* speaks of the enormous complexity of a single cell. Quoting Sagan, he concludes that the simple cell has "information . . . comparable to about a hundred million pages of the *Encyclopaedia Britannica.*"[41] Richard Dawkins compares it to 30 volumes of the encyclopedia.[42] Whichever analogy one takes, it's a staggering storage in one tiny cell! *Of Pandas and People* goes so far to say that "if the amount of information contained in one cell of your body were written out on a typewriter, it would fill as many books as are contained in a large library."[43] Tiny bacterial cells are incredibly small, and "each is in effect a veritable microminiaturized factory containing thousands of exquisitely designed pieces of intricate molecular machinery, made up together of one hundred thousand million atoms, far more complicated than any machine built by man and absolutely without parallel in the non-living world."[44]

Who can explain how the simplest, tiniest cell became complex? No known evolutionary process can account for even these so-called primitive cells. In fact, as Jacques Monad rightly states, "the simplest cells available to us for study have nothing 'primitive' about them."[45]

---

[1] Stephen C. Meyer in *The Creation Hypothesis,* p. 72.

[2] Millard J. Erickson, *Christian Theology* (Grand Rapids: Baker, 1986), p. 49.

[3] Meyer, p. 71.

[4] *Ibid.,* p. 67.

[5] *Ibid.,* p. 68.

[6] Mae-Wan Ho and Pewter T. Saunders, eds., *Beyond Neo-Darwinism: An Introduction to the New Evolutionary Paradigm* (London: Academic, 1984), p. x.

[7] Percival Davis and Dean H. Kenyon, *Of Pandas and People,* p. 61.

[8] Michael Denton, *Evolution: A Theory in Crisis,* p. 334.

[9] John W. Oller, Jr., and John L. Omdahl in *The Creation Hypothesis,* p. 238.

[10] *Ibid.,* p. 265.

[11] Michael Polanyi, "Life's Irreducible Structure," p. 1308.

[12] *Ibid.,* p. 1309.

[13] *Ibid.*

[14] *Ibid.*

[15] Scott M. Huse, *The Collapse of Evolution* (Grand Rapids: Baker, 1983), p. 95.

[16] Denton, p. 351.

[17] Brian Leith, *The Descent of Darwin: A Handbook of Doubts About Darwinism,* p. 36.

[18] Richard Dawkins, "The Necessity of Darwinism," *New Scientist,* Apr. 15, 1982, p. 130.

[19] Meyer, p. 100.

[20] Kurt P. Wise, in *The Creation Hypothesis,* p. 228.

[21] *Ibid.,* p. 230.

[22] Denton, p. 342.

[23] Kurt P. Wise in *The Creation Hypothesis,* p. 230.

[24] *Ibid.*

[25] Charles Darwin, quoted in Denton, p. 326.

[26] Charles Darwin, quoted in Scott M. Huse, *The Collapse of Evolution* (Grand Rapids: Baker, 1992), p. 73.

[27] Denton, p. 333.

[28] Richard Dawkins, *The Blind Watchmaker,* p. 140.

[29] *Ibid.,* p. 40.

[30] Richard Dawkins in *But Is It Science? The Philosophical Question in the Creation/Evolution Controversy,* Michael Ruse, ed. (Buffalo, N.Y.: Prometheus, 1988), p. 210. Cf. *The Blind Watchmaker,* p. 41.

[31] Alvin Platinga, "When Faith and Reason Clash: Evolution and the Bible," p. 25.

EVIDENCES AGAINST EVOLUTION

[32] Phillip E. Johnson, *Darwin on Trial,* p. 34.

[33] Dan-E. Nilsson and Susanne Pelger, "A Pessimistic Estimate of the Time Required for an Eye to Evolve," *Nature,* Apr. 21, 1994.

[34] The avian lung has a one-way flow of air through the parabronchi, whereas inhalation and exhalation is a two-way passage of air in all other vertebrates. It speaks eloquently for discontinuity rather than continuity between reptiles and birds. See Michael Denton, *Evolution: A Theory in Crisis,* pp. 209-213.

[35] John Gliedman's comment in "Scientists in Search of the Soul," *Science Digest* 90 (July 1982): 78. Roger Sperry dismisses the supernatural and the existence of extra-physical phenomena.

[36] Denton, p. 315.

[37] *Ibid.,* pp. 316, 317.

[38] *Ibid.,* p. 342.

[39] Huston Smith, "Evolution and Evolutionism," *Christian Century,* July 7-14, 1982, p. 756. See also Scott M. Huse, *The Collapse of Evolution,* p. 92, in which he argues that "the handiwork of time is disassociation and disintegration, not synthesis."

[40] Richard Dawkins suggests that "human vanity cherishes the absurd notion that our species is the final goal of evolution" *(The Blind Watchmaker* [London: Norton, 1987], p. 50).

[41] W. R. Bird, *The Origin of Species Revisited,* p. 300.

[42] Dawkins, p. 18.

[43] Charles B. Thaxton, ed., *Of Pandas and People,* p. 7.

[44] Denton, p. 250.

[45] Jacques Monod, *Chance and Necessity: An Essay on the Natural Philosophy of Modern Biology,* trans. from French by Austryn Wainhouse (London: 1972), p. 134.

Chapter 33

Evolution Under Fire and an End-time Challenge

Even the central mechanism that Darwin believed to cause evolutionary development has come under question today. It seems that even he knew he was on shaky grounds. In *The Origin of Species* Darwin spells out the difficulties to his theory in chapter 6. "Can we believe that natural selection could produce," he questions, "on the one hand, an organ of trifling importance, such as the tail of a giraffe, which serves as a fly-flapper, and, on the other hand, an organ so wonderful as the eye?"[1]

Natural Selection

During the nineteenth century, scientists, while accepting evolution as a fact, increasingly came to question the supposed mechanism of evolution through natural selection.[2] Today, some have even said that natural selection has been "relegated to a back seat in terms of its shaping power in the origin of species."[3]

In the *Origin of Species* Darwin speaks of domestic breeding and comments, "There is no reason why the principles which have acted so efficiently under domestication should not have acted under nature."[4] Although he did not have any examples of natural selection when he wrote his *Origin of Species,* he did have extensive knowledge of the way animal breeders selected and bred domesticated animals to improve the stock. Much evidence shows that selective breeding does improve both animals and plants. But such a comparison is valid only if the human owners of animals will do the same as the animals would do if left to themselves.

Paradoxically, Darwin excludes an intelligent God from the process of natural selection, but he finds in intelligent humans an empirical evidence for natural selection. This represents a basic logical inconsistency in his claim. He is not comparing apples with apples, even though a partial analogy is involved. As Phillip Johnson rightly comments, "The analogy to artificial selection is misleading. Plant and animal breeders employ intelligence and specialized knowledge to select breeding stock and to protect their charges from natural dangers. The point of Darwin's theory, however, was to establish that purpose-lessness natural processes can substitute for intelligent design."[5]

What Darwin should have learned from domestic breeding is that changes have definite boundaries that they do not want to go beyond. "Mutations are almost always (99.995) harmful, if not lethal, to the unfortunate organism in which they occur. In other words, mutations produce organisms that are weaker and at a marked disadvantage; they are less able to compete for survival. This fact directly contradicts the assumptions of the modern evolutionary theory."[6] Mutations need to be understood for what they are. It is not a case that they are always beneficial or plentiful. In fact, "mutations are quite rare. This is fortunate, for the vast majority are harmful, although some may be neutral. Recall that DNA is a molecular message. A mutation is a random change in the message akin to a typing error. Typing errors rarely improve the quality of a written message; if too many occur, they may even destroy the information contained in it. Likewise, mutations rarely improve the quality of the DNA message, and too many may even be lethal to the organism."[7]

Even if mutations are good, how likely is it that they can occur to form even one new structure? Suppose an insect wing requires only five genes, a very low estimate, and suppose that the new wing information could come from a single mutation per gene, then it is estimated that a single mutation will occur in only one individual out of 1,000. The probability of two mutations within the same individual is one in 1,000,000. "The odds of five mutations occurring are one in one thousand million million." Such an occurrence during the life cycle of one organism is not realistic. And this is only one mutation. "Yet, an organism is made of many structures that must appear at the same time and work together in an integrated whole, if they are not to work to its disadvantage."[8]

Few deny the reality of microevolution. The question is whether one can extrapolate it to macroevolution. Alvin Platinga points out that "there is some experiential reason to think not; there seems to be a sort of envelope of limited variability surrounding a species and its near relatives. Artificial selection can produce several different kinds of fruit flies and several different kinds of dogs, but, starting with fruit flies, what it produces is only more fruit flies. As plants or animals are bred in a certain direction, a sort of barrier is encountered; further selective breeding brings about sterility or a reversion to earlier forms."[9]

Whereas Darwin looked to natural selection as the central driving force for his theory of evolution, today "a growing number of scientists accept natural selection as a reasonable explanation for the modification of traits but not for the origins of new structures." And even if natural selection did operate on genetic variability to produce new species, "then the Darwinist is faced with several difficult problems. First of all, if organisms can be modified easily by natural forces to produce all of the variety we see among species today, why does any line exist at all that is stable enough and distinct enough to be called a species? Why is the world not filled with intermediate forms of every conceivable kind? In fact, the world corresponds much more closely to what can be expected from the intelligent design point of view: it is filled with distinct and stable species that retain their identity over long periods of time, and intermediate forms expected by Darwinists are missing."[10] Constancy, rather than change, seems to be the basic pattern found in nature.

We need to take a closer look at natural selection. First, we must recognize that it doesn't explain the arrival of the fittest,[11] the origin of species,[12] the altruism we find in nature,[13] or entropy.[14] If we credit natural selection with producing all the species extant today, why do we still find so much stasis—that is, organisms that don't change?[15] Actually we have no evidence that natural selection has creative power.[16] Natural selection predates Darwin, and Edward Blyth considered it as maintaining the fixity of species, an idea "postulated by virtually all proponents of intelligent design, including the father of taxonomy, Carolus Linnaeus."[17] How do evolutionists validate their premise that natural selection produces species under the descent model when others also see it as maintaining the fixity of species under the design model, particularly when it is unknown if natural selection can produce a new species?[18] We must remember that Darwin's loss of faith acted as a major contribution to his substituting natural selection in place of the work of God in Creation. Rejecting God behind nature, he had to come up with something else. So he grasped at natural selection.

Furthermore, for Darwin natural selection explained everything. But if it explains everything, does it really explain anything? As Brian Leith observed, "If the presence of adaptations is evidence for selection, but the absence of adaptations is not evidence *against* selection, then is it possible to deny the existence of selection at all? In other words, if selection can explain everything then it really explains nothing. Good scientific theories should be testable and even falsifiable."[19]

The Fossil Record Doesn't Support Darwin

Concerning fossils, A. Hallam of the Department of Geological Sciences, University of Birmingham, Great Britain, observes that "they are the only direct evidence we have of the history of life on our planet, and in particular of the course of evolution."[20] If that is so, then scientists have an extremely flimsy basis for believing evolutionary theory, as we will see in this section. In fact, a tautological relationship exists between evolution and fossils. "The only justification for assigning fossils to specific time periods in that chronology is the assumed evolutionary progression of life. In turn, the only basis for biological evolution is the fossil record so constructed. In other words, the assumption of evolution is used to arrange the sequence of the fossils, then the resultant sequence is advanced as proof of evolution."[21]

Paleontologists have found nearly 100,000 fossil species, and yet "where sequence does exist it is exceptional or relatively trivial."[22] Moreover, 99 percent of the biology of any organism resides in the soft anatomy which isn't preserved, and so the fossil record represents only 1 percent of the organism.[23] At best, it is estimated that 87.8 percent of the 329 living families of terrestrial vertebrates were fossilized. Birds have had poor fossilization.[24]

Evolution necessitates a change from one species to another up the increasingly complex progression from the first cell to the human. If that, in fact, happened, we would expect to find evidence of transitional forms between the various categories. But we can search the fossil record at every level and find no such evidence. In the first edition of *The Origin of Species,* Darwin admits that the fossil record is "the most obvious and gravest objection which can be urged against my theory."[25]

Instead of giving up his theory, however, he seemed to blame the fossil record for the absence of the transitional forms. "I do not pretend that I should ever have suspected how poor a record of the mutations of life, the best preserved geological section presented, had not the difficulty of our not discovering innumerable transitional links between the species which appeared at the commencement and close of each formation, pressed so hardly on my theory."[26]

Darwin clearly faults the adequacy of the fossil record in a chapter in his *Origin of Species* on the "Imperfection of the Geological Record." Elsewhere he says that the reason why we do not find innumerable transitions is due to "the record being incomparably less perfect than is generally supposed. The crust of the earth is a vast museum; but the natural collections have been imperfectly made, and only at long intervals of time."[27] He decided that "the geological record is far more imperfect than most geologists believe."[28] Darwin concluded that "the noble science of Geology loses glory from the extreme imperfection of the record," because fossils are "a poor collection made at hazard and at rare intervals."[29]

Apparently Darwin came to the fossil record with his own preconceived assumption about evolution and forced that belief upon the fossil record, rather than allowing the absence of transitional forms to call his theory into question. And he did it in the name of science. Such a procedure runs counter to scientific methodology, which allows the objective data or experimentation to verify or falsify a theory.

Martin J. S. Rudwick, lecturer in history and philosophy of science, Cambridge University, in his book *The Meaning of Fossils,* notes the subjectivity of fossil study. "The 'meaning' of fossils has been seen in many different ways in different periods. Indeed, the same fossil specimens (for example sharks' teeth) have been reinterpreted several times within different frames of reference—they have, as it were, been seen with different eyes."[30] Moreover, study has shown that "there was no fossil evidence of one species changing gradually into another when traced through successive strata; and—much more seriously—there was no fossil evidence that any of the major groups, with their distinct types of anatomical organization, had any common ancestors."[31] L. Beverly Halstead, in *Nature,* agrees, stating "no fossil species can be considered the direct ancestor of any other."[32]

Evolutionary paleontologists attempt to find evidence for evolution in the fossils. "The Darwinist approach has consistently been to find some supporting evidence, claim it as proof for 'evolution,' and then ignore all the difficulties."[33] On the other hand, perhaps what is surprising to many people is the fact that the fossil experts, rather than clergymen, have been "Darwin's most formidable opponents."[34]

Punctuated Equilibrium

In spite of more than 130 years of study of the fossil record, the lack of evidence for transitional forms is the same today as in Darwin's time.[35] That is why, during the 1970s, Harvard professor Stephen Jay Gould and paleontologist Niles Eldredge proposed a theory we have already alluded to called "punctuated equilibrium." They advanced the theory of punctuated equilibrium to deal with the absence of transitional forms in the fossil record. It was clear that the fossil record gives evidence of stasis (no directional change) as opposed to evolutionary gradualism. Also, species appear suddenly in the fossil record, without any sign of transitional forms. Stasis always follows such sudden appearance. This fact radically throws evolutionary theory into question. As Phillip Johnson says, "the fossil problem for Darwinism is getting worse all the time."[36]

Gould and Eldredge were not the first to question gradualism by suggesting an "abrupt evolution." Hugo de Vries "led the Continental 'mutationists' with ideas of large-scale, abrupt evolution."[37] Scientists have modified "Darwin's basic tenet of gradual change to the concept of stasis (no change) alternating with episodes of rapid change," because the "pattern of fossil organism is not, by and large, a graded series, but clusters separated by gaps."[38]

Going beyond the idea of "abrupt evolution," "explosive evolution,"[39] "'instant' speciation,"[40] or "punctuated equilibrium," and yet inextricably linked to them, is the discovery that new species appearing suddenly in the fossil record have no trace of ancestral linkage. "The new data from biochemistry where organismal differences can be measured somewhat more quantitatively, generally confirm this pattern of clustering. By studying sequences of amino acids in proteins, it has been found that organisms cannot be lined up in a series, A-B-C, where A is an ancestor of B and B an ancestor of C, but are instead, approximately equidistant from most other organisms in a different taxon. This feature remains reasonably consistent over a wide range of species."[41] In agreement, Alvin Platinga notes that "nearly all species appear for the first time in the fossil record fully formed, without the vast chains of intermediary forms evolution would suggest."[42]

Cambrian Explosion

As geologists study the stratified layers in the geological column they operate on the assumption that the oldest strata contain primitive fossils, and the later strata enclose more complex fossils. Thus they consider the geological column to support the evolutionary development from primitive to more complex as we move through the time layers. However, it is well known that the early strata, known as the Cambrian, has evidence of a plethora of organisms.

"There is a virtual 'explosion' of life forms recorded in the rocks at the beginning of the Cambrian. Any theory of the origin and development of life must explain how such a dramatic range of body plans made the early, abrupt appearance they did."[43]

The abrupt arrival of complex animals in the Cambrian strata raises serious questions about the idea of ancestral linkage. Whereas Darwin's evolutionary tree has all species linked through one ancestral line, Stephen Jay Gould, with his punctuated equilibria, questions the one ancestral line. Bernhard Rensch, professor of zoology, University of Münster, speaks of "parallel evolution" rather than one ancestral line.[44] Phillip Johnson considers that "one of the most powerful examples" against a single ancestral line "is the Cambrian Explosion, in which the complex animal groups appear suddenly, without any evidence of step-by-step descent from single-celled predecessors."[45]

In fact, the geological column displays some more complex animals in lower strata, and some less complex animals in higher ones. The assumption behind the geological column, that it was laid down during a period of more than 4 billion years, turns upside down if one accepts the biblical story of a worldwide Flood (Gen. 7; 8). The Flood would lay the geological column as it is. Geologists should be studying the geological column as evidence of the demise of the pre-Flood world rather than its evolution.

Cladistics

Whereas Darwin believed in an infinite number of intermediary links,[46] typologists (those who study the bodies or forms of living organisms) did not believe in a common ancestor theory.[47] Typologists and taxonomists had carefully classified the species before Darwin wrote his book in 1859. Actually, classification goes all the way back to Aristotle, and Linnaeus gave it new strength in his *Systema Naturae* during the eighteenth century.[48] The most influential of the new schools of taxonomy is known as Cladistics, founded during the early 1960s by German systematist Willi Hennig.[49] Cladistics emphasizes the distinctness of biological classes, with no ancestral linkage, thus raising serious questions about the evolutionary theory.

The British Museum of Natural History decided to exhibit "Man's Place in Evolution" in 1980. The museum's book *A New Look at Dinosaurs* included, as Halstead reports, "that no fossil species can be considered the direct ancestor of any other."[50] The comment caused a great stir as we see exhibited in the pages of the journal *Nature*. Cladistics and evolutionary theory were at loggerheads. Keith Thompson of Yale University commented on the battle: "No one needs reminding that we are well into a revolutionary phase in the study of evolution, systematics, and the interrelationships of organisms. . . . To the thesis of Darwinian evolution . . . has been added a *new cladistic antithesis* which says that the search for ancestors is a *fool's errand,* that all we can do is determine sister group relationships based on the analysis of derived characters. . . . It is a change in approach that is not easy to accept for, in a sense, it runs counter to what we have all been taught."[51]

Molecular Biology

Molecular biology has taken the debate between evolutionists and those who question the theory to a more profound level. We have already noted how the complexity of one cell creates fundamental questions about the idea of development from the simple to the complex, for nature even at its micro level is already incredibly complex. Furthermore, a study of molecules has provided further evidence for stasis. "As more protein sequences began to accumulate during the 1960s, it became increasingly apparent that the molecules were not going to provide any evidence of sequential arrangements in nature, but were rather going to reaffirm the traditional view that the system of nature conforms fundamentally to a highly ordered hierarchic scheme. . . . Moreover, the divisions turned out to be more mathematically perfect than even most die-hard typologists would have predicted."[52]

The Darwinian thesis that life arose through a naturalistic process now faces serious challenges. "Darwin thought this claim very chancy; discoveries since Darwin and in particular recent discoveries in molecular biology make it much less likely than it was in Darwin's day," Alvin Platinga has said.[53] According to the evolutionary paradigm, how did human beings come to talk, to reason, to ask questions, to have a conscience? Microbiologist Michael Denton and Dimitri Kouznetsov find a profound similarity between human language capacity and "the unfolding series of biological language systems including the genetic code. For this reason, it is nearly impossible to address the question of how the human language capacity came to be without coming eventually to consider the closely related mystery of how life itself came to be. Conversely, biologists today are increasingly aware that insights from linguistics are apt to aid our understanding of molecular biology and biophysics (and vice versa)."[54]

Molecular study has shown molecular distance instead of ancestral linkage between fundamental groups of living things.[55] Also "at the molecular level, the effect of natural selection is therefore mainly to prevent change."[56]

Evolutionary Logic Questioned

Phillip E. Johnson, in his book *Darwin on Trial,* brings his legally-trained mind to evaluate the claims of Darwinian evolution. After admitting that he is not a defender of creation science, he gives as his stated purpose "to examine the scientific evidence on its own terms." He assumes that "creation-scientists are biased by their precommitment to Biblical fundamentalism," and investigates "whether Darwinism is based upon a fair assessment of the scientific evidence, or whether it is another kind of fundamentalism."[57] Throughout the book Johnson separates scientific empirical evidence from metaphysical or philosophical presuppositions. Repeatedly he concludes that evolution derives from theory lacking empirical evidence. We will consider only one example of the kind of faulty logic that he critiques.

Stephen Jay Gould's article, "Evolution as Fact and Theory," included the following comparison: "Facts are the world's data. Theories are structures of ideas that explain and interpret facts. Facts do not go away while scientists debate rival theories for explaining them. Einstein's theory of gravitation replaced Newton's, but apples did not suspend themselves in mid-air pending the outcome. And human beings evolved from apelike ancestors whether they did so by Darwin's proposed mechanism or by some other, yet to be identified."[58] Here Gould compares the fall of apples with evolutionary ascent. The problem with this kind of illustration is that we can demonstrate the fall of apples, whereas we cannot evolutionary ascent.

As Johnson rightly says: "The analogy is spurious. We observe that apples fall when dropped, but we do not observe a common ancestor for modern apes and humans. What we do observe is that apes and humans are physically and biochemically more like each other than they are like rabbits, snakes, or trees. The apelike common ancestor is a hypothesis in a theory, which purports to explain how these greater and lesser similarities came about. The theory is plausible, especially to a philosophical materialist, but it may nonetheless be false. The true explanation for natural relationships may be something much more mysterious."[59]

One of the major weaknesses of evolutionary theory, from every aspect, is its tendency to accept evolutionary theory as a fact, then interpret empirical data from that perspective. The quest is biased with more basic presuppositions than we would expect in a traditional objective scientific study. The lack of empirical evidence for the theory, and the faith required to believe in it, makes evolution more of a philosophy than a science. But even more than a philosophy, it is also a religion.

Evolution as a Religion

When we remove God, or the supernatural, from the realm of causality, something has to fill the vacuum. Not only has naturalism substituted for God, but evolution has become a religion in place of the biblical religion that worships the Creator. Physicist H. S. Lipson observed that "evolution became in a sense a scientific religion: almost all scientists have accepted it, and many are prepared to 'bend' their observations to fit in with it."[60] Alvin Platinga noted that "evolution has deep religious connections; deep connections with how we understand ourselves at the most fundamental level,"[61] and that it "is by no means religiously or theologically neutral."[62]

Scripture and science conflict when it comes to the doctrine of Creation. We should remember that it is not just the historicity of Genesis that scientists question, for the doctrine of Creation occurs in 60 places throughout the New Testament.[63] The doctrine of God, and not nature, as Creator is fundamental to the biblical worldview. So scientists rejecting the Genesis account of Creation are really abandoning the biblical worldview. Thomas Kuhn has persuasively shown that current teachings of science may not be correct, and that scientific paradigms have changed through the years. Although Kuhn never mentioned the naturalistic evolutionary worldview, his thesis applies to it.

Platinga opposed the surrender of science to Scripture or Scripture to science, for how do we know if the position to which either side subscribes to is the right one? "The belief that when there is a conflict, the problem must inevitably lie with our interpretation of Scripture, so that the correct course is always to modify that understanding in such a way as to accommodate current science—is every bit as deplorable as the opposite error. No doubt science can correct our grasp of Scripture; but Scripture can also correct current science."[64]

Platinga believes that a battle rages between perennial naturalism, enlightenment humanism, and Christian theism, all "three basically religious ways of viewing ourselves and the world." He observes that "according to a popular contemporary myth, science is a cool, reasoned, wholly dispassionate attempt to figure out the truth about ourselves and our world, entirely independent of religion, or ideology, or moral convictions, or theological commitments. I believe this is deeply mistaken. Following Augustine (and Abraham Kuyper, Herman Dooyeweerd, Harry Jellema, Henry Stob, and other Reformed thinkers), I believe that there is conflict, a battle between the *Civitas Dei*, the City of God, and the City of the World."[65]

The Changing Evolutionary Worldview and the Challenge to Seventh-day Adventist Mission

Seventh-day Adventists believe that Satan lies behind the various forms of evolutionary theory locked into the naturalistic worldview. Peter predicted uniformitarianism, so important to evolution, when he said that "in the last days scoffers will come, scoffing and following their own evil desires. They will say, 'Where is this "coming" he promised? Ever since our fathers died, everything goes on as it has since the beginning of creation'" (2 Peter 3:3, 4). That everything goes on as it has since Creation means there was no Flood, and history will continue as it always has continued. Such uniformitarianism is a basic premise for evolutionary theory, because most scientists consider the geological columns not as evidence for the demise of the world by a global deluge, but the evolving of the world ever since its beginning. During the nineteenth century catastrophism, or belief in a global flood, collapsed under the new doctrine of uniformitarianism predicted in Scripture.

Sir Julian Huxley speaks about Darwin's reluctance to write out his theory. In 1842 he first put his ideas down on paper. Then, "two years later, in 1844, he enlarged this into an 'Essay.' As a matter of fact, this so-called essay was a sizeable book of 230 pages, covering almost the same ground as the *Origin*, and more than adequate as an exposition of the whole subject."[66] So Darwin wrote out his theory in full in 1844, or 15 years before its publication as *The Origin of Species* in 1859. To Seventh-day Adventists 1844 is a significant date. It also saw the launching of the first angel's message to "every nation, tribe, language and people" (Rev. 14:6), calling them to "worship him who made the heavens, the earth, the sea and the springs of water" (verse 7).

The Seventh-day Adventist Church movement began the precise hour that

Darwin wrote out his frontal attack on the Creator. God called us out to lead humanity to worship Christ as Creator. The first angel's message arose on time to meet the enormous challenge of the counterfeit creation theory of evolution.

As we move toward the time of Christ's return, we find major new developments in evolutionary thinking. The inclusion of causation in science, the utter marvels of DNA, the sheer complexity of nature, the impossibility of the various parts of the visual network developing at the same time to produce an eye, as well as such other examples as the enormous complexity of a single cell, the total absence of support for Darwinian evolution in the fossil record on the one hand and plentiful evidence of abrupt appearance of new species with no intermediaries (punctuated equilibrium) on the other hand, the work of Cladistics providing empirical evidence for definite gaps between the species, the revolutionary research in molecular biology that finds complexity at the microsphere without any trace of prior development—all these point to the same conclusion, to design by the Creator instead of descent through natural selection and random genetic mutation. The many interconnected levels of nature offer overwhelming evidence of purpose rather than purposelessness. In place of the assumptions of evolutionary theory, which lack empirical support, we find much empirical evidence for an intelligent Designer/ Creator behind the complexities of His interdependent universe.

Two worldviews are locked in deadly battle today—naturalism, with its evolutionary theory, and supernaturalism, with its belief in Jesus Christ as Creator. This is a major aspect of the struggle in the end-time controversy between Satan and Christ. Evolutionary theory is one of the devil's many schemes to take attention away from Christ. Belief in evolution distances Christ from any involvement in human origin, removing the Fall of man and denying any need for the atonement. Some have claimed that we do not need to be saved by Christ. We have evolved through natural means. In fact, humans are still evolving. New Age philosophy, the writing of Catholic paleontologist Teilhard de Chardin, and Mormon theology, as well as the reincarnational beliefs of eastern religions, to name a few, all speak of human beings as advancing to godhood. This is the same lie that Satan gave to Eve in Eden. "'You will not surely die,' the serpent said to the woman. 'For God knows that when you eat of it your eyes will be opened, and you will be like God'" (Gen. 3:4, 5).

In the light of this ancient battle in its modern form, it is inconsistent for Christians to subscribe to theistic evolution. With so many questions being raised today against the various phases of evolution, Seventh-day Adventists have a window of opportunity[67] to proclaim the first angel's message intelligently to a world that needs to know that Christ created human beings (Heb. 1:2), made them in His image (Gen. 1:27), creates a new person within them now (Ps. 51:10; 2 Cor. 3:18) and will create them again when He makes the living saints immortal (1 Cor. 15:54), resurrects the dead saints (1 Thess. 4:16), establishes a new heaven and a new earth, and comes to dwell with humanity forever (Rev. 21:1-4).

Because Christ is in the business of creating along the historical continuum, from Eden to beyond the millennium, humanity has hope. To hide that hope and thrust humanity back into a jungle of survival of the fittest with its degrading social results, Satan has promoted evolutionary theory. It is a counterfeit religion that takes the place of Christ. The challenge to Seventh-day Adventists is to lift up Christ as central in all their beliefs, showing how all their fundamental doctrines find their inner coherence in the message of Christ as Creator/Redeemer.

Evolution is a theory in crisis. Christians put too much stock in it and far less in Scripture. It is time to return to the biblical account of Christ as Creator. Its narrative of Creation in Genesis 1, 2, along with 60 other references in Scripture, is His Word about the origin of life. In Genesis 3:4 Satan caused Eve to doubt Christ's word about death. He also used evolution to cast doubt on Christ's word about Creation. Sunday sacredness and evolutionary theory counterfeit the Sabbath of the Lord (Ex. 20:10; Matt. 12:8) and creation by Christ (John 1:1-3; Col. 1:16; Heb. 1:1, 2). Now it is time for Christians to give up theistic evolution and to accept Christ's word about Creation. And as they do it is also time to honor His memorial for Creation in the seventh-day Sabbath. That Sabbath is central in final events; hence the importance that we examine Satan's counterfeit theory of origins.

---

[1] Charles Darwin, *The Origin of Species* (New York: Carlton, 1859), p. 124.

[2] Michael Bartholomew, Bernard Norton, and Robert M. Young, *Block VI: Problems in the Biological and Human Sciences,* p. 34. Ronald L. Numbers claims that perhaps most professional naturalists remained skeptical of the primacy of natural selection from the mid-1870s *(The Creationists* [New York: Knoff, 1992], p. 5).

[3] Brian Leith, *The Descent of Darwin,* p. 60.

[4] Darwin, pp. 358, 359.

[5] Phillip E. Johnson, *Darwin on Trial,* p. 17.

[6] Scott M. Huse, *The Collapse of Evolution,* p. 90.

[7] Charles B. Thaxton, ed., *Of Pandas and People,* p. 12.

[8] *Ibid.,* pp. 13, 14.

[9] Alvin Platinga, "When Faith and Reason Clash: Evolution and the Bible," pp. 23, 24.

[10] Thaxton, p. 88.

[11] Huse, p. 89.

[12] Leith, p. 78.

[13] Leith, p. 56. Richard Dawkins' selfish gene cannot be reconciled with altruism in nature. See Richard Dawkins, *The Selfish Gene* (London: Oxford University, 1976).

[14] Henry M. Morris, *The Biblical Basis for Modern Science,* p. 205. Morris claims that "a law of science (entropy) should take precedence over a scientific belief (evolution)."

[15] Thaxton, p. 88.

[16] Johnson, p. 96.

[17] Thaxton, p. 67.

[18] Leith, p. 59.

[19] *Ibid.,* p. 21.

[20] A. Hallam, ed., *Patterns of Evolution as Illustrated by the Fossil Record* (New York: Elsevier Scientific, 1977), preface.

[21] Huse, p. 14.

Evolution Under Fire and an End-time Challenge

[22] Michael Denton, *Evolution: A Theory in Crisis,* p. 185.
[23] *Ibid.,* p. 177.
[24] *Ibid.,* p. 189.
[25] Darwin, *The Origin of Species.*
[26] *Ibid.*
[27] *Ibid.,* p. 125.
[28] *Ibid.,* p. 356.
[29] *Ibid.,* p. 372.
[30] Martin J. S. Rudwick, *The Meaning of Fossils: Episodes in the History of Paleontology* (London: Macdonald, 1972), p. 266.
[31] *Ibid.,* p. 229.
[32] L. Beverly Halstead, "Halstead's Defence Against Irrelevancy," *Nature* 292 (July 30, 1981): 403.
[33] Johnson, p. 84.
[34] *Ibid.,* p. 45.
[35] The archaeopteryx, a claimed intermediate between reptiles and birds, because it has certain skeletal features similar to both, is only an assumed intermediary in a fossil record that fails to give any certain examples.
[36] Johnson, p. 57.
[37] Leith, p. 65.
[38] Thaxton, 39.
[39] Ernst Mayr *(Populations, Species, and Evolution,* p. 6), uses the expression "explosive evolution."
[40] Roger Lewin, "Evolutionary Theory Under Fire: An Historic Conference in Chicago Challenges the Four-Decade-Long Dominance of the Modern Synthesis," *Science* 210 (Nov. 21, 1980): 884.
[41] Thaxton, p. 40.
[42] Platinga, p. 24.
[43] Thaxton, p. 22.
[44] Bernhard Rensch, *Evolution Above the Species Line* (New York: Columbia University, 1960), p. 191.
[45] Johnson, "Response to Hasker," *Christian Scholar's Review,* pp. 299, 300.
[46] Denton, p. 69.
[47] *Ibid.,* p. 132.
[48] *Ibid.,* pp. 122, 123.
[49] Leith, pp. 102, 103.
[50] Halstead.
[51] Keith Thompson, quoted in Denton, p. 139.
[52] Denton, pp. 277, 278.
[53] Platinga, p. 20.
[54] John W. Oller, Jr., and John L. Omdahl, in *The Creation Hypothesis,* p. 242.
[55] Johnson, *Darwin on Trial,* pp. 90-93.
[56] *Ibid.,* p. 96.
[57] *Ibid.,* p. 14.
[58] Quoted in Phillip Johnson, *Darwin on Trial,* pp. 66, 67.
[59] *Ibid.,* p. 67.
[60] H. S. Lipson, "A Physicist Looks at Evolution," *Physics Bulletin* 31, No. 138 (1980).
[61] Platinga, p. 17.
[62] *Ibid.,* p. 15.
[63] Henry M. Morris, *The Biblical Basis for Modern Science,* p. 392.
[64] Platinga, p. 14.
[65] *Ibid.,* p. 16.
[66] It was reprinted with Darwin's sketch of 1842, in C. Darwin and A. R. Wallace, *Evolution by Natural Selection,* G. R. de Beer, ed. (Cambridge: University Press, 1958). Sol Tax, ed., *The Evolution of Life: Its Origin, History and Future,* p. 5.
[67] I concur with John T. Baldwin's conclusion in his article "Inspiration, the Natural Sciences, and a Window of Opportunity," *Journal of the Adventist Theological Society* 5, No. 1 (Spring 1994): 131-154.

Chapter 34

The Pre-Advent Judgment

She is a college student in her early 20s. Her conscientious mother finds it hard to let go and constantly pushes Serita (a pseudonym) to achieve. The student showed me a letter she had written to her mother and gave me permission to use it in this book. In part, it says, "I may never be a household name or greatly travel the world, but I will be a blessing to people no matter where I am. Because, most importantly, I have dedicated myself and my career to God. Isn't that what every mother wants? Why isn't that enough? It's everything to God! Yes, I am going to be on my own and you need to let go, but don't push me away."

That went straight to my heart as I read it. I put the letter down and looked at Serita. She was a kind and committed Christian. "You said it from the heart," I responded. "How hard it is to be pushed away, just because you cannot be made in your mother's image. You long for acceptance for who you are, and not just for what you do. Right?"

"Yes." She nodded.

Jesus Understands

Some accepted Jesus for what He did, but few just for who He was. Thus He understands young people who struggle with Serita's problem. I felt I could never satisfy my mother either. She was a wonderful mom, but even after she was dead I struggled with the feeling that I could never come up to her expectations. At such times I found it a great solace to experience the acceptance of Christ. He accepts us just as we are, even though He longs to make us what we can become!

No one ever lived who had such a tender heart. He loved people, not because they were good but because He is good. Jesus treated them not as they deserved, but He met their need. Yet they treated Him terribly. They lunged into Him with clenched fists, yanked hair out of His beard, threw curses His way, and spat at Him. Mobs tried to pull Him limb from limb. The Roman soldiers lacerated His back with spiked thongs.

Now He hung bleeding, bruised, broken.

He looked at His tormentors, those

who cried "Crucify Him," and meekly said, "Father, forgive them, for they do not know what they are doing" (Luke 23:34). Incredible! Unbelievable! Yet true.

That's the picture of His intercession. And that's the kind of Person He is in the pre-Advent judgment. He's your defense attorney.

Christ lost the world when Adam and Eve accepted Satan's lie about death (Gen. 3:1-4). Then He won back the world through His death on Calvary. Satan hates Christ and the cross. He is doing everything he can to make Calvary of no effect. While he cannot deny the cross, if he can rob everyone of its gift; then he will have won.

The devil pours all his fiendish energy through apostate Christianity, Spiritualism, the New Age movement, the charismatic movement, the doctrine of an immortal soul, Sunday worship, and the evolutionary theory, to wrench Christ from the hearts and minds of humanity. He is preparing for his own counterfeit second coming of Christ, which will climax his scheme to take Christ's place and rule in His stead.

But beyond the planet, in heaven's throne room, a judgment is in process. This judgment has everything to do with end-time events. Its verdict will make itself felt around the globe in plagues and a battle called Armageddon. Satan doesn't want anyone to know what is happening. For many, human priesthoods take the gaze away from Christ's priestly ministry in the pre-Advent judgment today.

Unfortunately, many Seventh-day Adventists fear the pre-Advent judgment. They know it is under way but wonder if they will make it through. Has the judgment reached their name yet? What if it came up when they were sinning? Is there any hope that they will pass the judgment? The purpose of this chapter is to see the good news in the pre-Advent judgment and to gain biblical insights that will help Seventh-day Adventists to share it with their friends. The pre-Advent judgment is wonderful news for all good Christians.

The Pre-Advent Investigation in Its Biblical Context

Only a few non-Seventh-day Adventist scholars believe in a pre-Advent judgment. Studies of the book of Daniel almost universally overlook it.[1] By contrast, Seventh-day Adventists find in Daniel 7 and 8, together with Revelation 14:6, 7, biblical evidence for a pre-Second Coming judgment. Adventists call this judgment "pre-Advent," denoting its time, and "investigative," indicating its method.

This chapter attempts to follow the Bible's self-interpretation of the pre-Advent judgment in Daniel. After defining the way we employ "pre-Advent judgment," we'll document evidence for it in Daniel, evaluate the alternative view held by most historical-critical scholars, and consider the Danielic presentation in the light of Leviticus 16, Zechariah 3, the book of Hebrews, and Revelation 13-19. Then we'll see the good news of the pre-Advent judgment in the biblical salvation-history context, with Calvary before it, Christ's intercession during it, and Armageddon after it.

Pre-Advent Judgment in Daniel

1. Who Are Judged?

The usual definition for the "pre-Advent judgment" focuses on the investigation of God's people of all ages. That is a fundamental aspect of it. But many of God's end-time saints who live during the end-time judgment look on the pre-Advent judgment as anything but good news, even though the first angel's message places the judgment in the context of the "eternal gospel" (Rev. 14:6). They apparently consider the judgment apart from its relationship to the little horn in Daniel and apart from its roots in the cross, its relationship to Christ's intercession, and its outworking in Armageddon.

The everlasting gospel is the truth about Calvary. If "the sacrifice of Christ as an atonement for sin is the great truth around which all other truths cluster" and if "in order to be rightly understood and appreciated, every truth in the Word of God, from Genesis to Revelation, must be studied in the light that streams from the cross of Calvary,"[2] then Calvary must give us insight into the pre-Advent judgment. No subsequent judgment calls into question the cross's judgment; neither is it different from, nor does it add to, but it only reveals and applies what Christ completed there.

In other words, judgment day was primarily and initially at Calvary.[3] Jesus said of the cross, "Now is the time for judgment on this world; now the prince of this world will be driven out" (John 12:31). Calvary judgment means ultimate deliverance for God's people and destruction of their enemy. God works it out in salvation history through the pre-Advent, millennial, and postmillennial series of judgments. Calvary's double verdict of "deliverance destruction" needs to guide our definition of the pre-Advent judgment verdict.

a. Professed Christians Judged

According to biblical typology, the pre-Advent judgment, which concludes human history (see next section), finds its type in the annual Day of Atonement (Lev. 16). God intended that annual judgment only for Israel, and it never included other nations (verse 16). One would expect a correspondence to it in the antitype (Dan. 7). Although Daniel 7 does not name who is being judged in the pre-Advent judgment, it designates those who will receive the judgment verdict (verses 22, 26). It is logical to assume that the judgment investigation will include the recipients of the verdict. The two groups receiving the verdict are: (1) God's people attacked by the little horn (verses 20-22, 25-27); (2) the little horn, as a professedly Christian system (verses 22, 26).

b. Catholic System Judged

But is it legitimate to include the little horn (the Catholic system)? Seventh-day Adventist scholars answer this question in various ways.[4] Ellen White says "the only cases considered are those of the professed people of God,"[5] and further defines them as "all who have believed on Jesus,"[6] yet it also significantly includes "all those who have ever taken upon themselves the name of Christ."[7] If two groups come to view here, that is, genuine believers and those taking on Christ's name, then the little horn corresponds to both. For the little horn has members within it who love God and the saints, whereas Satan uses the system in his hatred of God and the saints. It would seem reasonable that the judgment includes: (1) "All persons (of whatever communion) who profess a relationship to God," as Bill Shea concludes;[8] and (2) the little horn, as a counterfeit system, because it masquerades as Christian, taking "the name of Christ."

We need to remember that Israel also consisted of the genuine and the nominal, so type and the antitype correspond to each other. In addition, we should consider that Christ mentions a pre-Advent inspection in Matthew 22:1-14, which Ellen White refers to as "a mixed company," for "not all who profess to be Christians are true disciples."[9] Remember too that Lucifer made his original attack against Christ and His position in heaven while he still pretended to be a loyal angel. He works through this same guise in the warfare of the little horn as a professedly Christian system.

It's also instructive that the immediate background to Daniel (2 Kings 21-25; 2 Chron. 33-36),[10] as well as his contemporary prophets, Jeremiah and Ezekiel,[11] all document that God judged Judah for desecration of His sanctuary and for setting up other gods in His place—the precise thrust of the little horn against Christ and His New Testament sanctuary service. Also we should keep in mind that, in contrast with the secular nations mentioned in Daniel (all which also lose their dominion [Dan. 7:12]), the saints and the little horn both claim to be Christian and either receive or lose their dominion subsequent to the judgment.[12]

As Joyce G. Baldwin puts it, "the heavenly court decrees that *his dominion shall be taken away,* and that he whose rule has been destructive will in turn see his dominion totally destroyed."[13] *The Seventh-day Adventist Commentary* states: "The judgment will pass sentence of extinction upon the papacy. This power will continue its war against the saints to the very last. Then its dominion over them will be forever removed, and it will be consumed."[14]

Internal contextual evidence suggests that the saints and the little horn equally share in the pre-Advent judgment verdict, which includes three interrelated acts: (1) dominion is given to the Son of man (Dan. 7:14; cf. verse 13); (2) dominion is taken from the little horn (verse 26); and (3) dominion is given to the saints of the Most High (verses 18, 27). The three acts represent judgment in favor of the saints (verse 26) and judgment against their little-horn enemy (verses 21, 22). Note that the loss of the little horn's dominion is eschatological (verses 21, 22, 25-27), unlike the loss of dominion by the beast powers (verse 12). Christ comes in the Second Advent "for judgment" (Mal. 3:5), which Ellen White says is "His coming for the execution of the judgment,"[15] i.e., the implementation of the pre-Advent verdict, which destroys the little horn/beast in Armageddon, as we will note later.

Scriptural evidence for including the little horn in the judgment appears in the book of Hebrews, which describes backsliding Christians *(katapatesas,* Heb. 10:29; cf. verses 30, 31) in similar terms to the way Daniel depicts the little horn *(mirmac* [MT],

Sunpatethesetai [LXX], Dan. 8:13; cf. verse 10)—both "trample" *(pateo)* on Christ, and both have an anti-Christ thrust. It is interesting that, in speaking of backsliding Christians, to whom the book of Hebrews was written, Calvin compared them to the papacy: "Our business with the Papists is similar in the present day; for they confess with us that Christ is the Son of God, the Redeemer who had been promised to the world: but when we come to the reality, we find they rob him of more than one-half of his power."[16] Precisely this same kind of backsliding, with its rebellion against God (Jer. 6:28; Eze. 2:3; Dan. 7:12) and desecration of His Old Testament Temple (2 Kings 21, 23; Jer. 23:11; Eze. 5:11; 8:1-18) brought judgment on Judah in the time of Daniel as noted above (see footnotes 9 and 10).

We find further scriptural evidence for including the little horn in the pre-Advent judgment in 2 Thessalonians 2:2-4, in which Paul speaks of a coming apostasy *(apostasia)* that opposes God sitting in the temple of God *(naon tou Theo),* as if he were God himself. Here the apostle describes a religious power usurping Christ's place in His New Testament temple. The passage has its roots in Ezekiel 28:2, Isaiah 11:4, and Daniel 11:36, in which the latter text speaks of the little horn. Hans LaRondelle rightly concludes that "Paul did not think of the Antichrist as an atheistic power but as a staunchly religious one, who will claim to speak instead of and on behalf of Christ."[17]

Still more evidence occurs in the book of Revelation, with its reference to the true and false Christian churches—the two women of chapters 12 and 17, respectively. Also in Revelation, the three angels' messages allude to the "beast" (little horn) in the context of the pre-Advent judgment (Rev. 14:6-11). So biblical evidence suggests that the little horn is a counterfeit Christian system, and as such gets included in the pre-Advent judgment.

Daniel 7 is the first time the little horn appears in Scripture, and each of the three times he refers to the little horn, Daniel immediately mentions the judgment (verses 7 and 8, followed by verses 9 and 10; verses 11 and 12, followed by verses 13 and 14; verses 20 and 21, followed by verse 22). In the light of what we have said thus far, it seems that the repeated mention of the little horn within the context of the pre-Advent judgment is significant.

The little horn is the beast in Revelation (e.g., Rev. 13:1-10). It is united with the dragon and false prophet (Rev. 16:12-16), which together constitute the enemy of God's end-time remnant. They gather the entire world against the saints (Rev. 16:14; 13:3; cf. 12:17). So the little horn of Daniel 7 is a type of the end-time global alliance against God's saints, according to the hermeneutical principle of escalation, a principle well demonstrated by Richard M. Davidson.[18] We need to put with this fact of escalation the equally important principle that the Day of Atonement typifies not only the pre-Advent judgment but also the millennial and postmillennial judgments.[19] Thus the judgment of Daniel 7 corresponds to only part of the Day of Atonement type in Leviticus 16. The Day of Atonement includes judgment against the scapegoat (verses 20-22), the enemy of God's people that corresponds with judgment against the little-horn enemy in Daniel 7.[20]

c. Judgment's Double Verdict

The pre-Advent judgment has a double verdict: (1) deliverance for God's saints and (2) destruction for their enemy, an unfolding of the double verdict of Calvary. Internal contextual evidence in Daniel beyond chapter 7 seems also to support such a double verdict. Thus the "deliverance" *(sh zab,* Dan. 3:17, 28; 6:20; *nesal,* Dan. 3:29; 6:16; *malat,* Dan. 12:1) of Daniel and his three friends from the lions' den and from the fiery furnace gives us insight into the eschatological rescue of those who have their names written in the "book" *(sepher,* Dan. 12:1), the record used in the pre-Advent judgment (Dan. 7:10). Here local deliverances escalate to a universal rescue.[21] The historical deliverances for God's people also include destruction of their enemies in both the fiery furnace (Dan. 3:22) and the lions' den (Dan. 6:24).[22] Likewise, the eschatological rescue of the saints has its counterpart in the destruction of their enemy (little horn; Dan. 7:26, 27).[23]

Corroborating this conclusion is the fact that Babylon, as a literal enemy nation of God's people in Daniel, acts as a type of spiritual Babylon, the enemy of God's people in the end-time in Revelation. Here the escalation goes from one nation (Dan. 1:1, 2) to all the world (Rev. 13:3; 17:1-19:21). Babylon is a type of the enemy of God's people, spoken of as the little horn in Daniel 7 and as the woman, or beast, in Revelation 13-19. Daniel 7 and Revelation 13-19 clearly speak of the same power that attacks God's people. So Daniel says, "As I watched, this horn was waging war against the saints and defeating them" (Dan. 7:21). The book of Revelation records: "MYSTERY, BABYLON THE GREAT, THE MOTHER OF PROSTITUTES AND OF THE ABOMINATIONS OF THE EARTH. I saw that the woman was drunk with the blood of the saints" (Rev. 17:5, 6).

The pre-Advent judgment does not investigate ancient Babylon because it never claimed allegiance to God. But antitypical Babylon apparently enters the pre-Advent judgment precisely because it considers itself to be Christian. I doubt if there is much need to investigate the little horn as a system,[24] for its actions are blatant against God and His saints (Dan. 7:21-22, 25, 26; 8:9-11, 25, 26; 11:28-32; 12:11), but it seems clear that both the little horn and the saints receive the pre-Advent judgment verdict, which is not true of any other nation presented in Daniel.

Now to some other important details about the pre-Advent judgment.

2. Time of the Pre-Advent Judgment

Do we have any internal contextual evidence that the judgment of Daniel 7 is pre-Advent? The answer is yes. Daniel 7:21, 22 has a triple sequence of time: 1. The little horn wages war against the saints in phase one. 2. "Until," a temporal adverb, introduces the second phase in the time sequence, the phase of judgment at the end of which God pronounces a verdict in favor of the saints. 3. "At that time," another time expression, introduces the third phase. It indicates that the time of judgment ends when another time comes, and that particular time is the occasion of the saints taking possession of the kingdom at the Second Advent. Daniel 7:25-27 repeats the triple time sequence. Clearly this repeated triple sequence places the investigative phase of the judgment prior to the Second Advent.

The larger context of Daniel corroborates the pre-Advent time focus. Daniel traces the rise and fall of human kingdoms till God sets up His own kingdom. God's ongoing judgment lies behind these changes, since "he . . . sets up kings and deposes them" (Dan. 2:21). Note the parallel sequence in Daniel 2, 7, and 8, as follows:

Dan. 2:37-44: Babylon, Medo-Persia, Greece, Rome, divided kingdoms, God's kingdom

Dan. 7:4-14, 22, 27: Babylon, Medo-Persia, Greece, Rome, little horn, God's kingdom

Dan. 8:2-9, 20-26: Medo-Persia, Greece, little horn (Rome, pagan-papal)

Daniel names three of the kingdoms as Babylon (Dan. 2:24, 38), Medo-Persia (Dan. 8:20), and Greece (verse 21). The data on Medo-Persia and Greece, from chapter 8, informs us of the two nations to follow the Babylonian kingdom of chapter 2. History corroborates this sequence (Babylon, Medo-Persia, Greece),[25] and records that Rome followed Greece. According to Daniel 7:7, 8, the little horn comes after the fourth kingdom (Rome). The crucial fact is that the little horn not only succeeds Rome, but God's kingdom comes after it, according to Daniel 7:14, 22, 26, 27. So Daniel 7 reveals that a judgment convenes and concludes by (1) taking away the dominion of the little horn (verses 23-26) and in (2) establishing the dominion of God's eternal kingdom (verses 27, 28). The removal of the one opens the way to the establishing of the other. This judgment must therefore be pre-Advent in its investigation and execution.[26]

The placement of the little horn in this sequence of nations clearly puts it beyond the time (second century B.C.) of Antiochus IV Epiphanes (believed by most scholars to be the little horn), as he is not alive in this end-time when the dominion of the little horn is about to vanish because of the arrival of God's eschatological kingdom.

3. Other Reasons for Rejecting Antiochus IV Epiphanes

Scholars have noted the close relationship between Daniel 2 and Daniel 7,[27] but have overlooked the same eschatological conclusion given in both (Dan. 2:31-35, 44, 45; 7:13, 14, 17, 18, 21, 22, 27).[28] It's precisely this eschatological time-frame that disqualifies Antiochus IV Epiphanes. Maurice Casey's assertion that the destruction of Antiochus inaugurates the eternal kingdom of the Jews lacks empirical evidence.[29] Jerome answered this question in refuting Porphyry. He said that if the Jew, Judas Maccabaeus, defeats Antiochus, how does Judas come with the clouds of heaven like a Son of man to the Ancient of Days in heaven (see Dan. 7:9, 13), how was royal power bestowed upon him, and how is his kingdom eternal (see Dan. 7:14)?[30] Obviously the scene in Daniel 7 is far larger than Judas and Antiochus. By contrast, G. K. Beale rightly refers to the judgment "books" of Daniel 7 and 12 as appearing "in contexts of eschatological persecution."[31]

Nevertheless, interpreters believe almost universally that Antiochus is the "abomination of desolation" of the sanctuary mentioned in Daniel 8:11-13; 9:27; 11:31; and 12:11. But Christ referred to the "abomination of desolation" as still future in His day. "So when you see standing in the holy place 'the abomination that causes desolation,' spoken of through the prophet Daniel—let the reader understand" (Matt. 24:15). We must allow Scripture to interpret Scripture, particularly when Christ gives specific guidance and urges that we seek understanding in a matter. We could have no clearer refutation of a second century B.C. interpretation, nor a better mandate to seek for another solution (cf. 2 Thess. 2:1-12) than His command.

The pagan neoplatonist philosopher Porphyry (third cent. A.D.) is the earliest known source for supporting the Antiochus interpretation.[32] According to Jerome, "Porphyry wrote his twelfth book against the prophecy of Daniel."[33] Whereas Christ accepted Daniel's prophecy of a coming desolation (Matt. 24:15), Porphyry rejected Daniel's ability to predict the future. So he jettisoned a sixth-century B.C. date for Daniel's composition, opting for a second-century date so that the prophecies were merely events recorded after the fact. Jerome, Eusebius of Caesarea, Apollinarius of Laodicea, and Methodius rejected Porphyry's views.[34]

But historical-critical scholars have all followed Porphyry. The basic difference between Christ and such critics is their worldview. Christ believed in a God who is in control of human history, who knows the end from the beginning, who can therefore predict future events, and who evidently inspired Daniel to present authentic predictions. In fact, it is a fundamental theme in the book. Recent scholarship provides evidence for a sixth-century B.C. date for Daniel, and therefore for its authentic predictions.[35]

Scholars have four schools of interpretation for Daniel.[36] Some preterists (sixth-century date for Daniel) and all historico-critical (second-century date for Daniel) scholars believe the little horn was Antiochus. The other two views reject Antiochus, regarding the papacy (historicist) or some future antichrist (futurist) as the little horn.

4. Daniel Compatible Only With Historicist View[37]

Daniel speaks of only one little horn, not two. Samuel Nuñez documents nine different interpretations from 1700-1850 of the little horn in Daniel 8.[38] Calvin believed the little horn in Daniel 7 was Julius Caesar and the other Caesars,[39] and Antiochus in Daniel 8. Also he held that the little horn of Daniel 8 reaches up only to the first advent of Christ.[40] By contrast, Daniel presents the little horn as having a history that reaches back to Roman times and forward into the eschatological future. Paul corroborates this view, speaking of an anti-God power already at work in the first century and to be revealed before Christ's return (2 Thess. 2:1-12). This differs from preterism, historical-criticism, and futurism.

5. The 2,300 Literal Years

Daniel names the little horn three times (Dan. 7:8, 21; 8:9) and links its attack upon the daily *(tamid)* ministry of the sanctuary (Dan. 8:11) to "2,300 evenings and mornings" (Dan. 8:14). First Maccabees[41] and Josephus' *Antiquities of the Jews*[42] describes the desecration of the Jerusalem temple by Antiochus IV Epiphanes. Historical-critical scholarship interprets the 2,300 "evening-morning" period as the time when sacrifices to God ceased, because of the desecration of the Temple/altar by Antiochus. The sacrifices halted for either 2,300 literal days or 2,300 literal sacrifices. The latter would compute to 1,150 days to account for the morning and evening sacrifices.[43]

But the biblical period calls for more than six years (2,300 days), double the time length of the gap in sacrifices caused by Antiochus. On the fifteenth of the ninth month (Casleu) of the 145th year, Antiochus "set up the abomination of desolation upon the altar" (1 Macc. 1:54) and on the twenty-fifth day of the ninth month of the 148th year, Jews "offered sacrifice according to the law upon the new altar of burnt offerings, which they had made" (1 Macc. 4:52). The time period is only 10 days more than three years.

The problem is obviously worse for the shorter 1,150 days. Beyond that, the 1,150 days choice is not possible on linguistic grounds, because the words *ereb boqer* are both in the singular, representing a full day, as it is in Genesis 1 for the days of Creation (Gen. 1:5, 8, 13, 19, 23, 31). As Scripture classified the Creation days as *ereb boqer,* it is logical to equate the 2,300 days similarly. Because of this, Sigfried Schwantes believes Daniel borrowed the phrase from Genesis 1.[44] In spite of the glaring differences between the 2,300 years of Daniel 8:14 and the attempts to fit them to the strictures of Antiochus, writers gloss over the gaps with creative imagination, such as "these 2300 days cover *about* the period of time during which Antiochus Epiphanes did his wicked deeds,"[45] or the time from the Temple's desecration by Antiochus till deliverance by Judas Maccabees "was *exactly* two thousand three hundred days."[46] If Daniel was written after the events *(vaticinia ex eventu)* as critical scholarship claims, then why is the computation of the 2,300 days so far off?

Only the historicist interpretation subscribes to the 2,300 years in Daniel 8:14, basing it on the "a day for a year" principle found within Scripture.[47] Such an approach best describes the Messianic context of Daniel 9:24-27 and allows the historical time-frame of the little horn to occur between pagan Rome and God's eschatological kingdom. Is there internal contextual evidence for the "day for a year" principle? Yes there is. In Daniel 8:13 the angel asks "until when" *('ad-mathay),* not "how long" (NIV) "will be the vision, *which includes* the continual service and the transgression causing horror, to make both sanctuary and host a trampling?"[48] What is the term the text uses for "vision" here? Is it the entire vision, or only its latter part? The answer to this question determines the length of the 2,300 "evenings and mornings," and therefore its length in the answer of verse 14, "Until 2,300 evenings and mornings, then the sanctuary shall be cleansed."

Internal contextual evidence demonstrates that the vision includes the entire period and not just a final segment.[49] Here is the internal evidence. 1. The term for vision is *hazon* and not *mar'eh,* which refers to a subelement of the vision (to be considered later). 2. What is included in the *hazon,* according to what Daniel was shown? Daniel 8:1, 2 employs the term *hazon* three times, and it encompasses all that follows. Thus the *hazon* vision begins with the ram (Medo-Persia [verses 3, 4]), continues through the goat (Greece [verses 5-8]) and into the latter part of the little-horn power (verses 8-12), because the angel says, "Son of man, . . . understand that the vision *(hazon)* concerns to the time of the end" (verse 17).

Thus the *hazon* reaches from the beginning of the vision to the last days. It covers the entire period from the Medo-Persian empire to the "time of the end," thus including the entire history of Greece and the entire period of the little horn in its pagan and ecclesiastical phases all the way to the "end of time" (verse 17). It can only be 2,300 years. Therefore, the sequence of question and answer demands that we equate "evenings and mornings" with literal years. No other equivalent will reach from Medo-Persia till the "time of the end," when the sanctuary will be cleansed.

Luther identified the little horn as the papacy. H. C. Leupold said, "We also hold that in stating that the pope is the Antichrist the Lutheran Confessions were correct much as some men have derided and belittled that view. Such belittling grows out of forgetting how thoroughly the reformers understood the papacy."[50] But not Calvin. He said of the little horn in Daniel 7:8: "Some twist this to mean the Pope, and others the Turk; but neither opinion seems to me probable; they are both wrong." Calvin believed the prophecy reached up only to the First Advent.[51] He computed the 2,300 as literal days.[52]

We should keep in mind that classical prophecy generally speaks in literal terms and times, whereas apocalyptic prophecies communicate more through symbols and symbolic time. Hence the image and beasts, symbolizing kingdoms in Daniel 2, 7, 8, occur in a context in which time appears symbolically as "time, times and half a time" (Dan. 7:25; cf. Rev. 12:6, 14), "2,300 evenings and mornings" (Dan. 8:14), and "seventy weeks" (Dan. 9:24, KJV). All three are identical to or associated with the 2,300-year prophecy. It would take us beyond the confines of our topic to study the 2,300 years, reaching from 457 B.C. to A.D. 1844. Scholars have done extensive work documenting this historicist view,[53] supporting 1844 as the beginning of the pre-Advent judgment in heaven's sanctuary.

Thus, rather than forcing onto the biblical text a preconceived interpretation from the second century B.C., it is incumbent upon the biblical student to allow the Bible to interpret itself. This opens up the biblical meaning of these numbers. Having already noted the internal contextual evidence for 2,300 years, we now need to examine the term "evenings and mornings" *(ereb boqer,* Dan. 8:14) linguistically. Is it a term used of sacrifices, as supporters of the Antiochus interpretation claim? Is it Temple language? Only in part. Scripture employs it relative to tending the lamps *(me ereb 'ad boqer,* Ex. 27:20, 21), but never of the daily sacrifices. Scripture always refers to them as "morning and evening."[54] For example, "morning and evening burnt offerings" *(laboqer wela'areb,* 1 Chron. 16:40). So the term does not endorse the division of the 2,300 "evenings and mornings" into 1,150 literal sacrifices, since it stands only for a full day, never for the sacrifice sequence.

6. Contribution of the Last Half of Daniel

Daniel 8:26 refers to the term "evenings and mornings" (Dan. 8:14) as the "morning and evening vision." In both the Aramaic and Hebrew sections up to this point in Daniel, the word for "vision" has been the same in 12 occurrences (in Heb. *hazon:* Dan. 2:19; 4:5; 7:1, 2, 7, 13, 15; 8:1, 2, 13, 15, 17). Only once is it *mar eh* (Dan. 8:16). Daniel 9 and 10 employ the word *mar eh* six times (Dan. 9:23; 10:1, 7, 8, 16). The reason for this change of word seems deliberate, for every subsequent mention of *mar eh* links the explication given with the "morning and evening *mar eh"* of Daniel 8:14. Thus the new word connects these chapters to the topic of the little horn, and therefore to the pre-Advent judgment context.

Daniel 8 mentions the little horn's attack upon the *tamid* (Dan. 8:11). We will look at the term's meaning and its relationship to the little horn and the sanctuary later. Suffice it to note now that like the term *mar eh,* the word *tamid* appears in several chapters of the second half of Daniel (Dan. 8:11, 13; 11:31; 12:11), and provides further evidence that these chapters have the little horn in mind, therefore providing insight into the pre-Advent context. Thus much of the final half of Daniel has to do with the little horn and contributes to our understanding of the pre-Advent judgment.

7. An Overview of Daniel 7-9

H. H. Rowley rightly maintained that Daniel 7 has connections with both halves of Daniel.[55] It should be interpreted in the light of the historical and prophetic insights. Andre Lacocque notes that Daniel 7 is "intimately linked" with the rest of the book.[56] J. J. Collins sees Daniel 7-12 as complementing and clarifying each other.[57]

Although defending an Antiochus interpretation, which we deny, these scholars are right in estimating the importance of Daniel 7 and its relationship to subsequent chapters. W. H. Shea has demonstrated convincingly that chapters 7-9 are arranged in an "effect-cause" sequence, the inverted order to that which we follow in the West.[58] The Eastern mind goes to the result first, and then into the factors that lead up to it. In a sense, one may say that some insights in chapters 10-12 further corroborate this sequence.

We will follow this "effect-cause" sequence, beginning with Daniel 9 and working back to chapter 7. The "seventy weeks" *(shabu im shib im,* Dan. 9:24-27) are "cut off" *(nehtak)* in this *mar eh* from the 2,300 years' *mar eh* of Daniel 8:14. This 70 times 7, or 490 years, is the first part of the 2,300 years. It speaks of making atonement for sins (Dan. 9:24) and the Messiah being "cut off" *(yikkarith,* verse 26), which brings us down to Calvary.[59]

The fact of Calvary already takes us past the time of Antiochus IV Epiphanes and substantiates the principle of a literal year for a symbolic day. As Gerhard Hasel notes, "Daniel 9:24-27 is one of the most controversial in the entire OT."[60] Hasel's article conclusively demonstrates the validity of the historicist's Christological interpretation, employing the "year-for-a-day" principle.

Chapter 8 traces the little horn as it comes out from one of the four winds of the heavens (Dan. 8:8, 9)[61] after the time of Greece (Dan. 8:5-8, 21, 22). The little horn spans the pagan-papal Roman powers, and expands horizontally (verses 9, 10) and vertically against the host, causing them to be trampled (verse 10). He magnifies himself against the Prince *(sar),* thus affecting His continual *(tamid)* ministry. Three times Daniel refers to the *tamid* (verses 11, 12, 13) in the context of His sanctuary being cast down (verse 11) and truth being "thrown to the ground" (verse 12). The *tamid* has the supplied word "sacrifice" in several versions.[62] But the *tamid* is broader than sacrifice. It is the entire sanctuary service or ministry. Then the question rises, "until when" is the vision that includes the attack on the continual sanctuary service in heaven by this little horn (Dan. 8:13)? The answer comes, "until" two thousand, three hundred evenings and mornings, then the sanctuary will be vindicated/cleansed *(nisdaq,* verses 13, 14).[63] The angel interpreter is clear that the time focus is the duration of the entire vision and not just on the little horn's role.

The solution to the problem of chapters 8 and 9 appears in chapter 7 (following the effect-cause sequence). As Heaton pointed out, Daniel 7 is the apex of Daniel.[64] Arthur Ferch has convincingly shown that Daniel 7 is a literary unit.[65] The vision of Daniel 7 came to the prophet Daniel two years before that of chapter 8 (Dan. 7:1; 8:1), and it forms the content for which chapters 8 and 9 are the explication. In other words, the attack of the little horn on the heavenly sanctuary ministry, and hence its warfare against Christ, is the reason for the judgment it receives in chapter 7. Although the little horn comes out of the ten horns of pagan Rome (and hence does not cover the pagan Roman period as it does in Daniel 8 [Dan. 7:7, 8; 8:8, 9, 21]), Daniel 7 focuses upon what the little horn does in its papal period.

From the other chapters of Daniel already looked at, or referred to, the end-time is the focus of Daniel 7. God shows Daniel in vision what the little horn is doing, and at the same time what He will do to the little horn. The two scenes, earthly and heavenly, concurrently play out before the prophet. God directs him to view events in both spheres—the sphere of the little horn and the sphere of the judgment. The prophet's gaze is horizontal and vertical in continuing sequence throughout the vision. All these events do not take place on earth as some conclude.[66] Baldwin rightly says Daniel "is seeing heaven."[67]

The scene on earth traces the history of the little horn (particularly Daniel 7:1-8, 23-28), whereas the scene in heaven (besides the brief setting up of the judgment in verses 9, 10) focuses on the results of the judgment (verses 13, 14, 18, 22, 27). To this degree Daniel 7 continues to enlarge on the reasons for the judgment given in chapter 8. Three times the passage refers to the great things the little horn speaks (verses 8, 11, 20), which the vision sums up as words against the Most High (from Aramaic *'illay* [most] high, i.e., God, verse 25). This anti-God power opposes the saints of the Most High (verse 25). Together, Daniel 7 and 8 describe the little horn as opposing God, the Prince *(sar),* His sanctuary and continual *(tamid)* ministry, by speaking great words against God and persecuting His followers. But Daniel 7 shows that in spite of the great words of the little horn, God will have the last word—judgment.

So the sanctuary vindication includes a judgment that says no to the great words of the little horn. Its blasphemous words have to do with casting truth to the ground (Dan. 8:12). The little horn obscures the truth about Christ in His sanctuary ministry *(tamid)* by deflecting people's gaze to a counterfeit priesthood on earth (Dan. 8:11, 12). Its attempt to change times and laws, its persecution of the saints (Dan. 7:25), and its attack against the Prince of princes *(sar sariym,* Dan. 8:25) all present it as an anti-Christ religious power.

So the execution of the pre-Advent judgment of Daniel 7 includes God's response to the little horn's attack against the Son of Man[68] and His remnant. The watching prophet witnesses the little horn overcoming the saints until the Ancient of Days arrives and judgment goes in favor of the saints (Dan. 7:22). Then "judgment shall sit, and they shall take away his rulership, to cut off and destroy until the end" (Dan. 7:26). As Baldwin notes, "the heavenly court decrees that *his dominion shall be taken away,* and he whose rule has been destructive will in turn see his dominion totally destroyed."[69] Keil-Delitzsch suggests that verses 26 and 27 give the consequences of the judgment.[70]

Daniel 12 gives further insight into the judgment's result. It focuses on the time when Michael (or Christ, cf. Jude 9; Rev. 12:7-9) will stand up (Dan. 12:1). This is the opposite to His being seated in Daniel 7:9. Standing suggests the end of the pre-Advent judgment, as being seated suggests its beginning. For when Michael stands up, though a final great time of trouble awaits the saints—suggesting that the little horn power is still to have its final fling against them (cf. Rev. 13:3, 11-18)—it is now guaranteed that Michael will deliver His remnant, who have their names written in the book (Dan. 12:1). This book refers to the records examined in the judgment (Dan. 7:10). If our reasoning is correct, then Daniel 12:1 is a promise to the saints that in spite of an end-time final trouble, the pre-Advent judgment will result in deliverance for them and destruction for their enemies. This judgment verdict presupposes a pre-Advent judgment, for it is executed in the final moments of history and in connection with the coming of Christ's eschatological kingdom (cf. Rev. 16:12-16; 18:10-24; 19:1, 2, 11-21).

So Daniel traces the rise and fall of four major kingdoms that all come to an end within history (Babylon, Medo-Persia, Greece, and Rome) and also the little-horn power that ceases at the eschatological end-time. Just as the stone of Daniel 2 crushes the image, symbolizing the end of all political kingdoms with the arrival of God's kingdom (Dan. 2:34, 35, 44, 45), so the pre-Advent judgment issues in a verdict that takes away the counterfeit dominion of the little horn as it establishes Christ's dominion, and that of His saints, forever (Dan. 7:21-27).

---

[1] Danielic studies fall into four major schools of interpretation: (1) preterist, which considers that the scope of Daniel's prophecies reached either to the time of Antiochus Epiphanes, Christ's first advent, or Jerusalem's destruction in A.D. 70; (2) futurist (both dispensational and nondispensational), which sees Daniel's prophecies as applicable to eschatological end-time; (3) historicist, which regards the prophecies of Daniel as covering the entire historical timespan from the Babylonian empire to the Second Advent (these three schools subscribe to a sixth-century B.C. date for the book of Daniel and to authentic divine predictions); (4) the historical-critical school, which, by contrast, denies the authenticity of prophecies, for all so-called prophecies in Daniel were written in the second century B.C, as *vaticinia ex eventu.* For a thorough documentation of these schools from 1700 to 1900, see Samuel Nuñez, *The Vision of Daniel 8, the Interpretations From 1700 to 1800 (sic* 1900), Andrews University Seminary Doctoral Dissertation Series (Berrien Springs, Mich.: Andrews University, 1987).

[2] E. G. White, *Gospel Workers,* p. 315.

[3] Scholars rightly find in Calvary the antitype of the typical Day of Atonement (Lev. 16), but almost all fail to see any further correspondence in a pre-Advent judgment. Once we recognize the additional correspondence, we then need to explore the implications of the cross to comprehending the pre-Advent judgment.

[4] For example, in his systematic theology *The Reign of God* (Berrien Springs, Mich.: Andrews University, 1985), Richard Rice does not mention the little horn in reference to the investigative judgment (p. 323).

[5] E. G. White, *The Great Controversy,* p. 480.

[6] *Ibid.,* p. 483.

[7] *Ibid.,* p. 486.

[8] William H. Shea, *Selected Studies on Prophetic Interpretation* (Lincoln, Nebr.: College View Printers, 1982), vol. 1, p. 125. See pp. 123-125.

[9] E.G.White, *Christ's Object Lessons,* pp. 309, 310.

[10] During Manasseh's reign the Temple was desecrated with altars to other gods (2 Kings 21:4, 5), and in it pagan priests and mediums ministered and offered children as sacrifices (2 Kings 23:4-24). Thus Judah did more evil than the nations God had destroyed (2 Kings 21:9).

[11] Jeremiah prophesied judgments on Judah (Jer. 7:34; 15:14; 21:5, 6; 25:9-14; 32:29; 34:2, 22; 35:15; 37:3; 52:13, 14), for it had forgotten God (Jer. 2:32), become hardened rebels (Jer. 6:28), and forsaken the law (Jer. 9:13). Prophets and priests were godless, even desecrating the Temple (Jer. 23:11). Judgments came because "the Lord will take vengeance, vengeance for his temple" (Jer. 51:11). Ezekiel prophesied God's judgment because Judah had defiled God's Temple (Eze. 5:11), with its idolatry flaunted in the Temple (Eze. 8:1-18). One of his visions pictured God as coming to the Old Testament Temple to judge (Eze. 1:1, 2; 8:1).

[12] It would seem that the loss of dominion by the little horn subsequent to the judgment has more to do with the judgment than with the fact that it is also subsequent to the other nations mentioned in Daniel.

[13] Joyce G. Baldwin, *Daniel* (Leicester, England: InterVarsity, 1978), p. 146.

[14] *The Seventh-day Adventist Bible Commentary,* vol. 4, p. 834.

[15] E. G. White, *The Great Controversy,* p. 425.

[16] John Calvin, *Hebrews* (Grand Rapids: Baker, Rapids, 1989), p. xxviii.

[17] Hans LaRondelle, "The Middle Ages With the Scope of Apocalyptic Prophecy," *Journal of the Evangelical Theological Society* 32, No. 3 (1989): 351.

[18] Richard M. Davidson, *Typology in Scripture: A Study of Hermeneutical Typos Structures,* Andrews University Seminary Doctoral Dissertation Series (Berrien Springs, Mich.: Andrews University, 1981), p. 397. Kenneth A. Strand, "An Overlooked Old-Testament Background to Revelation 11:1," *Andrews University Seminary Studies* 22, No. 3: 318.

[19] Daniel and Revelation Committee Report in *Issues in the Book of Hebrews,* Frank B. Holbrook, ed. (Silver Spring, Md.: Biblical Research Institute, 1989), p. 10.

[20] The scapegoat represents the ultimate enemy, Satan, and its being led away into the wilderness to die corresponds to the millennial and postmillennial judgment upon Satan (Rev. 20:2, 3, 7-10). By contrast, the little-horn enemy operates during pre-Advent historical time. Nevertheless, the correspondence between type and antitype concerns judgment upon an enemy of God's people.

[21] Compare the deliverance from Babylonian captivity, after the 70 years, as a type of the call to come out of Babylon in Revelation 14 and 18.

[22] If looked at sequentially, the destruction came first before the deliverance in the fiery furnace incident, and the reverse in the lions' den experience. Although we should not push the typology too hard, there is correspondence in the double result of "deliverance-destruction" between these two historical events and the outcome of the pre-Advent judgment. It would appear that the historical events give some insight into the apocalyptic pre-Advent judgment, which reaches its climax in the deliverance of the saints and the destruction of their enemies in Daniel 12:1 (cf. Rev. 16-19).

[23] Hans LaRondelle rightly sees that "the historical narratives of Daniel's own experiences in Babylon and Persia carry also typological significance for the end-time ("The Middle Ages," p. 345). See Hans LaRondelle, *Chariots of Salvation* (Washington, D.C.: Review and Herald, 1987), pp. 155-157.

[24] I concur with William Shea's conclusion in *Selected Studies on Prophetic Interpretation,* page 124.

[25] H. H. Rowley gives the three interpretations of these four held through the Christian era, noting that the Babylon, Medo-Persia, Greece, and Rome "view has been by far the most popular traditional view" *(Darius the Mede and the Four World Empires in the Book of Daniel: A Historical Study of Contemporary Theories* [Cardiff, Wales: University of Wales, 1964], p. 6. Rowley is representative of critical scholars who divide the second kingdom into Media and Persia. For a full historical accounting, see Samuel Nuñez, *The Vision of Daniel 8,* particularly pages 396-408.

[26] The execution of the judgment on the little horn includes the Second Advent (see Rev. 18; 19).

[27] H. C. Leupold, *Exposition of Daniel* (Grand Rapids: Baker, 1969), pp. 276-278. Andre Lacocque, *The Book of Daniel,* David Pellaue, trans. (Atlanta: 1979), p. 122. Louise F. Hartman and Alexander A Di Lella, *The Anchor Bible. The Book of Daniel*, W. F. Albright and D. N. Freedman, eds. (Garden City, N.Y.: Doubleday, 1978), vol. 23, pp. 208, 209.

[28] An exception to scholars overlooking the eschatological implications is LaRondelle, "The Middle Ages," pp. 345-354.

[29] Maurice Casey, *Son of Man, The Interpretation and Influence of Daniel 7* (London, Eng.: SPCK, 1979), pp. 45, 46.

[30] *Jerome's Commentary of Daniel*, Gleason L. Archer, Jr., trans. (Grand Rapids: Baker, 1977), pp. 80, 81.

[31] G. K. Beale, *The Use of Daniel in Jewish Apocalyptic Literature and in the Revelation of St. John* (Lanham, Md.: University Press of America, 1984), p. 239.

[32] See *Jerome's Commentary on Daniel,* p. 80. Porphyry was not the first to question the authenticity of predictions. Celsus (A.D. 180) may well have been the first to question prophecy. See Gerhard F. Hasel in *70 Weeks, Leviticus, Nature of Prophecy,* Frank B. Holbrook, ed. (Washington, D.C.: Biblical Research Institute, 1986), p. 292.

[33] *Jerome's Commentary on Daniel,* p. 15.

[34] *Ibid.,* p. 151.

[35] See documentation for this in Gerhard F. Hasel, "The Book of Daniel and Matters of Language: Evidences Relating to Names, Words, and the Aramaic Language," in *Andrews University Seminary Studies* 19, No. 3 (1981): 211-225.

[36] See Nuñez, *The Vision of Daniel 8,* pp. 111, 409, 410, 429-432.

THE PRE-ADVENT JUDGMENT

[37] Called "continuous-historical" by Hans LaRondelle in "The Middle Ages" (p. 350) and Kenneth A. Strand, *Interpreting the Book of Revelation* (Ann Arbor, Mich.: Ann Arbor, 1976), p. 14.

[38] Nuñez, pp. 27-83.

[39] *Calvin's Commentaries,* vol. 13, p. 27.

[40] *Ibid.,* vol. 13, pp. 128f. Calvin rejects the idea that Antiochus is a type ("figure," "analogy") for the antichrist. Daniel is, to him, relevant only to the time before the first (not second) advent of Christ (pp. 128f.).

[41] First Maccabees 1:54-5:1 tells the story from the setting "up the desolation upon the altar" until a new altar was built.

[42] *The Works of Flavius Josephus,* William Whiston, trans. (Grand Rapids: Baker, 1988), vol. 3, pp. 181-183. The desecration of the Temple included sacrificing swine upon the altar.

[43] For example, Andre Lacocque, *The Book of Daniel,* p. 164, and Norman W. Porteous, *Daniel, a Commentary* (Philadelphia: Westminster, 1965), pp. 126, 127.

[44] Sigfried J. Schwantes, "Ereb Boqer of Daniel 8:14 Re-Examined," in *Symposium on Daniel,* vol. 2, p. 473.

[45] A. C. Gaebelein, *The Prophet Daniel: A Key to the Visions and Prophecies of the Book of Daniel* (Grand Rapids: Kregel, 1968), p. 99 (Italics supplied.)

[46] M. R. De Haan, *Daniel the Prophet* (Grand Rapids: Zondervan, n.p.d.), p. 230. (Italics supplied.)

[47] For an excellent exposition of the "year for a day" principle, see Shea, *Selected Studies on Prophetic Interpretation,* vol. 1, pp. 56-93.

[48] Gerhard F. Hasel, "The 'Little Horn,' the Saints, and the Sanctuary in Daniel 8," in *The Sanctuary and the Atonement,* pp. 198, 199; Gerhard F. Hasel, "The 'Little Horn,' the Heavenly Sanctuary, and the Time of the End: A Study of Daniel 8:9-14," in *Symposium on Daniel,* p. 387.

[49] I am indebted to Gerhard F. Hasel for this biblical insight on the internal evidence for the year-day principle during a dialogue with him on Daniel 8.

[50] H. C. Leupold, *Exposition of Daniel,* p. 323.

[51] John Calvin, *Commentaries on the Book of Daniel*, vol. 2, p. 26.

[52] For example, Calvin said of the 2,300 of Daniel 8:14: "Evidently we ought to understand natural days here, consisting of twenty-four hours each. Those who receive it of years and months are wretchedly mistaken, and even ridiculous in their calculations" *(Calvin's Commentaries,* vol. 13, p. 108).

[53] Gerhard Hasel's thorough study documents the first 490-year segment of the 2,300-year prophecy and conclusively rejects the Antiochus Epiphanes theory. (Gerhard F. Hasel, "Interpretations of the Chronology of the Seventy Weeks," in *Seventy Weeks, Leviticus, Nature of Prophecy,* pp. 3-63).

[54] William H. Shea, "Unity of Daniel," in *Symposium on Daniel* (Washington, D.C.: Biblical Research Institute, 1986), p. 197.

[55] H. H. Rowley, *The Unity of the Book of Daniel,* off-print from the Hebrew Union College Annual, vol. 23, part 1 (Cincinnati, 1950-1951), p. 273.

[56] Andre Lacocque, *The Book of Daniel*, p. 122.

[57] J. J. Collins, *The Apocalyptic Vision of the Book of Daniel* (Scholars Press for Harvard Semitic Museum, 1977), p. 132.

[58] William H. Shea, "Unity of Daniel," p. 168.

[59] It is a tragedy that so many critical scholars bypass the Christological content of Daniel 9:25-27 and Daniel 7:13.

[60] Gerhard F. Hasel, *Seventy Weeks, Leviticus, Nature of Prophecy,* p. 5.

[61] See Gerhard F. Hasel, "The 'Little Horn,' the Heavenly Sanctuary, and the Time of the End: A Study of Daniel 8:9-14," in *Symposium on Daniel,* pp. 387-391.

[62] "Sacrifice" in the LXX, KJV, and NIV; "offering" in Goodspeed and the Amplified OT, and "burnt offering" in the RSV. Translators have supplied all of these words and they have no support in the Hebrew word *tamid,* which includes the entire daily ministration. It seems that the interpretation of Daniel 8:13, 14 as the cessation of the sacrifice under Antiochus IV Epiphanes caused scholars to add these terms to the translation.

[63] See Niels-Erik Andreasen, "Translation of Nisdak/Katharisthesetai in Daniel 8:14," in *Symposium on Daniel,* pp. 475-496. Cf. Alberto R. Treiyer, "The Day of Atonement as Related to the Contamination and Purification of the Sanctuary," in *Seventy Weeks, Leviticus, Nature of Prophecy,* pp. 198-256.

[64] Eric W. Heaton, *The Book of Daniel,* Torch Bible Commentary (London: SCM, 1956), p. 47.

[65] Arthur J. Ferch, *The Son of Man in Daniel Seven,* pp. 108-137; cf. Arthur J. Ferch, "The Judgment Scene in Daniel 7," *The Sanctuary and the Atonement,* pp. 159-162.

[66] John E. Goldingay, *World Biblical Commentary, Daniel* (Dallas: Word, 1989), vol. 30, pp. 164-167.

[67] Joyce G. Baldwin, *Tyndale OT Commentary, Daniel* (Downers Grove, Ill.: InterVarsity, 1978), p. 141.

[68] The Son of Man is Jesus. Cf. Daniel 7:13 with Christ's own words in Matthew 26:64. The Gospels record Jesus applying this term to Himself more than 40 times.

[69] Joyce G. Baldwin, *Tyndale OT Commentary, Daniel,* p. 146.

[70] C. F. Keil and F. Delitzsch, *Commentary on the OT in Ten Volumes, Daniel,* M. G. Easton, trans. (Grand Rapids: Eerdmans, 1986), vol. 9, p. 244.

Chapter 35

The Good News of the Pre-Advent Judgment

On February 15, 1921, Dr. Evan O'Neill Kane, surgeon at Kane Summit Hospital, New York City, performed the first major surgery with local anesthetic. He had performed nearly 4,000 appendectomies in his 37-year career. Who would be willing to go through surgery with only a local anesthetic? O'Neill searched a long time for a volunteer. Many were afraid of the risk. What if they felt the pain?

Finally Dr. Kane found a candidate. The patient was prepped, wheeled into the operating room, and a local anesthetic applied. As he had done thousands of times, Dr. Kane dissected the superficial tissues and located the appendix. He skillfully excised it and concluded the surgery. During the procedure the patient complained of only minor discomfort.

Dr. Kane proved that local anesthesia works, and he made history in two ways with that operation. He did the surgery on himself since he was the volunteer. The doctor became a patient in order to convince the patients to trust the doctor.

In a similar manner Jesus became human in order to understand our human trials and win our trust.[1] "For we do not have a high priest who is unable to sympathize with our weaknesses, but we have one who has been tempted in every way, just as we are—yet was without sin. Let us then approach the throne of grace with confidence, so that we may receive mercy and find grace to help us in our time of need" (Heb. 4:15, 16). The Christ of Calvary intercedes for us during the pre-Advent judgment. That's the crucial context in which to see the good news during judgment day. Our crucified Intercessor is in charge of the pre-Advent judgment.

Day of Atonement

The annual Day of Atonement for the sanctuary and "for all the sins of the Israelites" (Lev. 16:34) came on the tenth day of the seventh month of the Jewish year. After it ended, the sanctuary and people were clean. The Feast of Tabernacles that celebrated the completed cleansing, among other things, then followed the Day of Atonement.[2] Daniel was familiar with this important annual pre-"advent-of-the-new-year" judgment. Within this context we should contemplate the words "Unto two thousand and three hundred days; then shall the sanctuary be cleansed" (Dan. 8:14, KJV); we will return to this later.

The end of the 2,300 days brought not the execution *(nisdak)* of the judgment but the beginning of the process that would produce that verdict. It was time to "fear God and give him glory, because the hour of his judgment has come. Worship him who made the heavens, the earth, the sea and the springs of waters" (Rev. 14:7). The Day of Atonement was the time to gather around the sanctuary and focus on the high priest as representative of the people ministering in the Most Holy Place before God. It was time for personal investigation.

On October 22, 1844, the antitypical day of atonement began. This pre-Advent judgment is time to focus on the second phase of Christ's ministry in heaven's sanctuary. The little horn, however, deflects human attention from Christ's sanctuary ministry by calling attention to a human priestly service.

Pre-Advent Judgment in Hebrews

Does the book of Hebrews contain a pre-Advent judgment? "In Hebrews the law/court model is not present and should not be imported nor superimposed," says William G. Johnsson. He suggests that "the court model, valuable as it is, is but one of the ways by which the human dilemma and Christ's work to solve it are set forth in the Scriptures."[3] It's true that the multiple atonement theories are evidence that Christ's work is greater than any one type can possibly contain.[4] However, Johnsson does see in Hebrews a judgment theme, "but it [Hebrews] does not pull together the concept of 9:23—the necessity of purifying the heavenly things—with this theme."[5] Johnsson sees three unambiguous references to the Day of Atonement in Hebrews 9:6, 7, 24, 25; and 10:1-4.[6] It would seem, however, that he separates the cleansing of 9:23 from the Day of Atonement in 9:24, 25 (see below for comment). He also believes "Hebrews does not take up the *time* of the cleansing of the heavenly sanctuary and the judgment (Heb. 9:23)."[7]

In contrast to Johnsson, Richard M. Davidson believes that Hebrews 9 "does provide hints of it [i.e., time] by his reference to the cleansing of the sanctuary (9:23), followed by reference to a future judgment (verse 27) and the second coming of Christ (verse 28)." Davidson further suggests that "five additional passages refer to a future judgment (2:2-4; 4:1-3; 6:7-12; 10:28-39; 12:26-29). These passages suggest an investigative (4:12; 6:10; 10:28-30), as well as executive, judgment involving the professed people of God. These hints regarding timing are consistent with the OT type."[8] George E. Rice divides Hebrews into five units, comprised of three identical elements, the third being judgment in each (Heb. 2:2-4; 4:1-13; 6:7, 8; 10:32-39; 12:25-29).[9]

The above two views (Johnsson, Davidson) demonstrate two ways of looking at the antitypical day of atonement in Hebrews. Johnsson believes the function of the day of atonement references in Hebrews is to demonstrate that even at the high point of the cultic sacrifices the old culture was inadequate. "All that the old system failed to do because of its inherent insufficiencies, all that the repeated days of atonement could not accomplish, has now been done by Calvary."[10] Hence "the leitmotif of the sacrificial argument of Hebrews (8:1-10:18) is the *better blood* rather than the Day of Atonement."[11] Then Johnsson concludes that "9:1-5 [altar of incense in Most Holy Place] should already have put us off the track of trying to reason from type to antitype in this section."[12] So efficacy of the sacrifice, and not typology, seems to be the key for Johnsson.

By contrast, Richard M. Davidson demonstrates that "typology in Hebrews is comprised of the same basic conceptual structures found in the typology of the rest of Scripture."[13] This includes both the horizontal and vertical correspondences. And as far as Hebrews 9:1-5 is concerned, the altar of incense seems to be placed in the Most Holy Place, not because of any shoddy understanding of the Old Testament sanctuary by the author, but because *echousa* (having) seems to indicate that it properly belonged to the Most Holy Place in function.[14] Furthermore, all modifications of Old Testament types in Hebrews are not further evidence of a turning away from typology, for each instance has its roots in Old Testament control passages that legitimize the modifications.[15]

What do we make of these two different views relative to the day of atonement in Hebrews? It seems to me that Hebrews, although a carefully crafted sermon, does not systematically unfold the judgment in time and does not take pains to distinguish between a pre-Advent and final judgment. Nevertheless, the writer has judgment in mind. The author uses "judgment" in *(krisis:* process, Heb. 9:27; *kriseos:* process, Heb. 10:27; *krivei:* process, Heb. 13:4; *krimatos aioniou:* result—eternal judgment, Heb. 6:2). Judgment fire is mentioned in *kausin:* Heb. 6:8; *pur katanaliskon,* Heb. 12:29). Judgment synonyms are found in no "escape" *(ekpheuzometha,* Heb. 2:3) and "giving account" *(hos logon,* Heb. 13:17). Finally, the book mentions God as "God the judge of all" *(kritei theo panton,* Heb. 12:23).

What is the significance of all this data on the judgment? That Hebrews is addressed to backsliding Christians is clear throughout the letter.[16] The writer's concern is to demonstrate that what they are giving up is the much better Christ (Heb. 1:4), "better hope" (Heb. 7:19), "better covenant" (Heb. 7:22), "better promises" (Heb. 8:6), and "better" sacrifice (Heb. 9:23) with better blood (Heb. 9:12). The key word "better" *(kreitton)* appears 13 times.[17] Although we can consider the element of judgment a passing reference, it is what they get both now and in the future in exchange for what they have given up. Both sides of the equation seem to be in the writer's mind.

Moreover, Hebrews speaks of *type (tupon,* Heb. 8:6), which necessarily corresponds to an antitype *(antitupa,* Heb. 9:24)—that is to say, the earthly sanctuary services correspond to the heavenly. Hence, returning to the question of Hebrews 9 (mentioned above), we would expect the cleansing of Hebrews 9:23 to be linked with the day of atonement of Hebrews 9:24, 25. Internal contextual evidence supports this typological correspondence. Hebrews 9:22-27 has the heavenly sanctuary to be cleansed *(katharizesthai,* verse 23), a direct reference to Daniel 8:14 *(katharizesthai* [LXX], *nizdak* [MT]). Christ entered the *antitupa* (Heb. 9:24; cf. *tupon* in Heb. 8:5) to appear in the presence of God on humanity's behalf, by offering His own sacrifice. In that "good news" context the mention of judgment then follows (verses 24-28). It would seem, consequently, that we should not separate verse 23 from verses 24 and 25. We will return to the significance of the cleansing focus in the pre-Advent judgment later.

One more text needs comment. In Hebrews 10:26-31 the writer addresses the professed Christian who has "trampled" *(katapatesas)* "the Son of God under foot, who has treated as an unholy thing the blood of the covenant that sanctified him, and who has insulted the spirit of grace" (Heb. 10:29). As Lenski insightfully says, "'To trample under foot' is illustrated by Matt. 7:6, in which the hogs trample pearls into the mire. To do this to 'the Son of God' brings to mind all that this epistle has said of his infinite exaltation from 1:2 onward. The writer does not say trample down some gift the Son of God brought as he says 'Moses law' but trample down this infinitely exalted Son who is very God himself."[18] These words applied to the backslidden Hebrew Christians remind us of the little horn magnifying itself to Christ ("leader of the host"), taking away His daily service *(tamid),* upon which it trampled *(mirmac* [MT], *Sunpatethesetai* [LXX], Dan. 8:13; cf. verse 10). The trampling (from *pateo)* in Daniel and Hebrews has the same anti-Christ thrust. This also can contribute to our understanding of the pre-Advent judgment, as we will note later.

These two passages (Heb. 9:22-28; 10:26-31) do seem to suggest some reference to the Danielic pre-Advent judgment. The first is a specific identity (cleansing the sanctuary/people) and the second alludes to a rejection of Christ that causes the negative verdict of the judgment. Although the book of Hebrews does not develop the judgment court scene as Daniel did, the writer's references to type/antitype (horizontal/vertical) suggest that it was not far from his mind.[19]

In summary, Johnsson looks from Calvary back to the whole cultic services and rightly says, "Better blood—even better than the day of atonement sacrifices." This is exceedingly important. What I believe both Johnsson and Davidson would agree on is that Hebrews also looks forward and up from Calvary and says "better priesthood." In the author of Hebrews' own summation, given in Hebrews 8:1, 2, he focuses on Christ's priesthood.

F. F. Bruce reminds us that "more than any other New Testament book it [Hebrews] deals with the ministry which our Lord is accomplishing on His people's behalf now."[20]

Johnsson is right in saying that the law-court model is only one way of expressing the work of Christ, and so were the sacrifices. Many Old Testament types found their antitype in Christ's sacrifice, yet, as Davidson reminds us, "all other aspects find their respective fulfillments in the course of Christ's priestly ministry."[21]

It is precisely in this ministry and its cleansing work that typology helps us doctrinally, for the Old Testament type was what the book of Hebrews referred to when speaking of the New Testament antitype (Heb. 9:22, 23). Hence the cleansing of Hebrews 9 finds its type in the Day of Atonement (Lev. 16), which corresponds to the pre-Advent judgment predicted in Daniel 8:14. As Calvary was better than all previous sacrifices, so the cleansing is better in heaven's sanctuary, and Christ's present intercession (also in the judgment) is better than all previous mediation. For, according to the type/antitype correspondence, it involves an escalation of that judgment.

Revelation Corroborates Daniel

Kenneth Strand has convincingly demonstrated that the book of Revelation divides into eight major prophetic sequences, with chapters 4-14 as historical-era visions and chapters 15-20 as eschatological-judgment era visions. An act, or event, of judgment culminates each of the four eschatological sections.[22] In a later chapter, I choose to make the division at chapter 13 instead of 14. The climatic focus, in both Hebrews and Revelation, is therefore on the judgment.

The books of Daniel and Revelation have some important parallels that space precludes taking up.[23] The book of Revelation designates the little horn of Daniel as the beast, as the following comparison of Revelation 13 with Daniel 7 reveals. (See chart below.)

Scripture attributes counterfeit worship both to the little horn (Dan. 8:14) and to the beast (Rev. 13:4-8, 12-15). Daniel mentions death decrees to enforce counterfeit worship (Dan. 3:4-6; 6:5-12). Just as Nebuchadnezzar raised an image on the plain of Dura, and all had to worship it or die (Dan. 3:4-6, 16-18), so Revelation says a power "ordered them to set up an image in honor of the beast," decreeing that death should come to all who refuse to worship it (Rev. 13:14, 15). Worship is the central eschatological issue. Humanity will find itself confronted with the ultimate decision—worship the beast or worship God. Beast-worship will bring God's fury/judgment (Rev. 14:9-11). Ancient Babylon set up the golden image. The beast is spiritual Babylon (Rev. 17:5). God's call is "Come out of her [Babylon], my people" (Rev. 18:2-5; cf. Rev. 14:8). "Worship him who made the heaven, the earth, the sea and the springs of water" (Rev. 14:7), "Worship God!" (Rev. 22:9). This call has its roots in the summons for Israel

Beast (Rev. 13)	Little horn (Dan. 7)
Speaks boastfully (verse 5)	Speaks boastfully (verse 8)
Wars against saints (verse 7)	Wars against saints (verses 21, 25)
In power for 42 months (verse 5)	In power for 3½ years (verse 25)

to return from Babylonian captivity under Ezra and Nehemiah. The plea to come from worshiping the beast to worship God is a crucial part of the pre-Advent judgment-hour message (Rev. 14:7).

So striking is the identity between the beast and the little horn that Gregory K. Beale believes "Revelation 13 is modeled on Daniel 7."[24] Revelation shows how God will execute the verdict against the little horn (Dan. 7:21, 22, 26, 27). It takes place in the final pre-Advent battle[25] between Christ and the beast.[26] Armageddon (Rev. 16-19) is the final pre-Advent confrontation of God against Babylon (little horn/beast and followers, Rev. 13:3), and presents God's devastating judgment on the enemies of His people.

Then "I looked, and there before me was a white cloud, and seated on the cloud was one 'like a son of man' with a crown of gold on his head and a sharp sickle in his hand" (Rev. 14:14). Here the Second Advent comes to view, with Christ riding on a cloud, which Hans LaRondelle has persuasively proved to be "His cloud chariot,"[27] for "He makes the clouds his chariot" (Ps. 104:3). Here Revelation 14:14 connects with the pre-Advent judgment scene of Daniel, in which the prophet sees "one like a son of man, coming with the clouds of heaven" (Dan. 7:13). T. Longman III believes that in Daniel 7:13 Christ is riding "the Divine War Chariot."[28] In Daniel 7 Christ goes Godward to receive the verdict of the pre-Advent judgment, whereas in Revelation 14 He comes humanward to execute that judgment. This double movement in heaven climaxes the double gathering on earth (Rev. 14:6-13; 16:12-16). The reception of the judgment verdict before its implementation offers powerful evidence for a pre-Advent judgment.

Christ, on His cloud chariot, leaves heaven's temple, and three angels also depart the temple to participate in executing the judgment (Rev. 14:14-20).[29] It is appropriate that judgment (verdict and execution) should issue from the temple, which the little horn/beast attacked (cf. Christ's second advent on a white horse, with angels on white horses, charging into battle against the little horn/beast in Rev 19:11-21).[30]

The Good News About the Pre-Advent Judgment

1. Christ Is for Us and Against Our Enemy

We are now ready to return to the book of Hebrews. No New Testament book develops so completely the post-Resurrection ministry of Christ as does Hebrews. Christ's intercession for His people is a part of the better ministry that Jesus has over Old Testament priests, even as His better sacrifice was better than the multiple cultic sacrifices. Although it is right to say that the book has no systematic development of the law court, it does have a systematic presentation of Christ's intercession, the major contribution Hebrews makes to the pre-Advent judgment doctrine. Examination of the records (Dan. 7:10) is only one side of the judgment. The other is the intercession, or advocacy, of Christ (cf. 1 Tim. 2:5; 1 John 2:1). Christ is there in the presence of God on our behalf *(huper hemon:* Heb. 9:24), where He is able to fully save *(panteles,* Heb. 7:25) and where He is ever living to intercede on behalf of His people *(pantote zon eis to entugchanein huper auton,* Heb. 7:25).

He is the advocate-intercessor portrayed in Zechariah 3, in which the cosmic/great-controversy dimensions of the pre-Advent judgment come into focus. Joshua, representative of God's people, is in dire need. Dressed in filthy garments and clearly defiled in a cultic sense, he faces accusations from Satan (Zech. 3:1-3). Zechariah's vision sees a law-court scene with an accuser and a defender of the convicted. (Joshua is unquestionably guilty. The issue is not to find out whether the priest is guilty, but what to do about it.)

The prophet refers to Joshua as "a burning stick snatched from the fire" (verse 2). Keil-Delitzsch notes that "the fire out of which Joshua had been saved like a brand was the captivity, in which both Joshua and the nation had been brought to the verge of destruction."[31] They had deserved the captivity,[32] having rebelled against God, who gave them over to their captors (Dan. 1:1, 2). God's people had nothing, save their utter need, to recommend them. This could be said also of the backslidden Christians to whom the author of the book of Hebrews addressed his Epistle. (Both the Jews of the captivity and Christian Jews reading Hebrews had rebelled like the little horn.) It is precisely for people who have sinned, but who realize their need (the little horn never does), that Christ intercedes. Isn't that good news! So Joshua stood accused by Satan, and his clothing proved the charges correct.

The high priest was desperate. Here he stood at the judgment bar, clothed in sin. Later Christ would speak of the king coming in to inspect the guests and finding "a man there who was not wearing wedding clothes" (Matt. 22:11). That man evidently thought he could make it on his own in the judgment, that he was good enough, that his garments would suffice, that his life record was sufficient. But he gets thrown out (verse 13). Unlike this man, Joshua apparently knew his need and could only look to God for help. Had not God led Israel back from Babylonian captivity just as He had out of Egypt? Could He not rescue them spiritually too? The priest had nothing to recommend him, but he simply stood there with utter faith in God alone. I must stress that Christ's intercession is not to change His Father Judge but to answer Satan's accusation. Jesus said, "I am not saying that I will ask the Father on your behalf. No, the Father himself loves you because you have loved me" (John 16:26, 27).

"Zechariah's vision of Joshua and the Angel applies with peculiar force to the experience of God's people in the closing up of the great day of atonement."[33] Zechariah 3 is therefore a type of the pre-Advent judgment. While Satan rebuked Joshua, Christ[34] said, "'Take off his filthy clothes.' Then he said to Joshua, 'See, I have taken away your sin, and I will put rich garments on you'" Zech. 3:3, 4).

No doubt Joshua exclaimed something, such as "I delight greatly in the Lord; my soul rejoices in my God. For he has clothed me with garments of salvation and arrayed me in a robe of righteousness" (Isa. 61:10). It is precisely this intercessor-advocate that comes to view in Hebrews, for Christ did not finish His intercession when the judgment began—He continues it, as demonstrated by Zechariah's vision. We should also remember that the priests also continued to offer typical daily morning and evening sacrifices on the Day of Atonement.

God's end-time remnant needs to capture the full impact of what the books of Zechariah and Hebrews have to say on the continuing intercession-advocacy of the conquering Christ during the pre-Advent judgment. His people must focus on Christ and not on themselves. During the judgment hour the saints worship Christ as their Creator (Rev. 14:7), realizing that just as He brought them into this world, so only He can get them into the next world.[35] Scripture pictures end-time saints as naked (Rev. 3:18), just as Adam and Eve were at the Fall (Gen. 3:10, 21). No fig leaves, or human works, can supply their need. Only the slain lamb can provide the covering, only the robe of Christ's righteousness (Isa. 61:10; Rev. 6:11), the wedding garment supplied by the Lord (Matt. 22:11, 12), will suffice. The prodigal son needs "the best robe" to cover his tattered rags (Luke 15:22).

The pre-Advent investigation involves the saints. God will deliver only those who have their names in the book that God will deliver (Dan. 12:1). Thus it would seem that they pass the judgment because they are different from the little horn. They do not speak great words against Christ, magnify themselves, persecute the saints, think to change God's times and laws, or put themselves in Christ's place, casting His truth to the ground.

Zechariah speaks of the pre-Advent judgment from the great-controversy perspective. The saints find themselves attacked (in the investigation process in heaven) by their ultimate enemy, while Daniel focuses on their being attacked on earth by the little-horn enemy. Christ stands up for them in the investigation (Zech. 3) and in its execution (Dan. 7; cf. Rev. 16-19).

Ellen G. White pictures the struggle. Satan "presents their sins before them to discourage them. He is constantly seeking occasion against those who are trying to obey God. Even their best and most acceptable services he seeks to make appear corrupt. By countless devices, the most subtle and the most cruel, he endeavors to secure their condemnation. Man cannot meet these charges himself. In his sin-stained garments, confessing his guilt, he stands before God. But Jesus our Advocate presents an effectual plea in behalf of all who by repentance and faith have committed the keeping of their souls to Him. He pleads their cause and vanquished their accuser by the mighty arguments of Calvary."[36]

2. Calvary Is Preeminent

We are now ready to penetrate to the heart of what is under way in the pre-Advent judgment, and for that matter, what will continue in the millennial and postmillennial judgments (Rev. 20:7-15). God does not need the judgments, because He is omniscient (Ps. 33:13-15; 56:8; 104:24; 139:2, 6; 147:4; Isa. 44:28; 46:9, 10; Mal. 3:16; Matt. 10:29, 30; Acts 15:8; Rom. 11:33; Eph. 3:10). "The

Lord knows those who are his" (2 Tim. 2:19). Rather, He conducts these judgments for the sake of created beings.[37]

In the pre-Advent judgment the universe examines the records of human works, good and bad (Dan. 7:10). But more than that, it looks to see whether individuals have accepted or rejected the saving work that Jesus did for them on the cross.[38] Their relationship to the substitutionary judgment of the covenant Saviour decides their fate (cf. John 16:26, 27; 17:3).

Precisely that, and nothing else, determines personal destiny. So the pre-Advent judgment is Christ-centered and not human-centered.[39] Not so much what individuals have or have not done per se is decisive,[40] but rather whether they have accepted or rejected what Christ has done for them when He was judged in their place at the cross (John 12:31). Also it is true that the judgment has more to do with God's vindication than humanity's, for it involves the great-controversy issue and not just human salvation.

The judgment does not repudiate Calvary. The Crucified One intercedes for us. The pre-Advent judgment is part of the unfolding in salvation history of what Christ accomplished at the cross. Calvary moves inexorably to the deliverance of God's people and the destruction of their enemies because Christ accomplished both there. Through the authority of Calvary Christ delivers His saints and destroys Satan and all their enemies. So our gaze should be backward to Calvary and upward to Christ rather than inward to character. Although we must be forgiven, forsake sin, and be fitted for heaven, that comes only through beholding Christ (2 Cor. 3:17, 18). "If they kept their eyes fixed on Jesus, who was just before them, leading them to the city, they were safe."[41] Only Jesus can say, "I am the way and the truth and the life. No one comes to the Father except through me" (John 14:6). Only Christ can clothe prodigals with the robe (Luke 15:22). And only Christ can carry the lost sheep all the way home (Luke 15:5).

We need to see through Satan's scheme. What he has done on a general level, in deflecting attention from the authentic heavenly sanctuary service to his counterfeit earthly series of priesthoods (little horn), he is doing on the personal level by misdirecting our attention away from humanity's only Substitute to ourselves. Looking to an earthly priesthood or to our own personhood equally diverts the gaze away from Christ.

The greatest need of many of us is not to be obsessed with the present judgment but to let Calvary transform us. We need to look away from our life to His, from our sins to His salvation. Long and deep was His struggle. None other will ever understand how long was the night He lived in this world that forsook Him. Even His own people rejected Him—precisely because they clung to their own works instead of accepting His works for them. They were too busy attempting to earn their right to pass a judgment, rather than accepting His judgment in their place.

The pre-Advent judgment contains wondrous news, for it does not stand by itself but is surrounded by Calvary before it, Christ's intercession in it, and

Armageddon beyond it. In all three events Christ is consistently for His people and against their enemy/enemies. (This is why judgment investigates the little horn and gives it the judgment verdict in Armageddon.) In all three events "Jesus Christ is the same yesterday and today and forever" (Heb. 13:8). What Christ accomplished on the cross is simply unfolding in all subsequent salvation history, including the pre-Advent judgment. That is why the "hour of his judgment" is part of the "eternal gospel" (Rev. 14:6, 7). In this judgment hour our crucified Saviour "is able to save completely those who come to God through him, because he always lives to intercede for them" (Heb. 7:25).

---

[1] Max Lucado, *In the Eye of the Storm* (Dallas: Word, 1991), pp. 35, 36.

[2] E. G. White, *Patriarchs and Prophets,* p. 540.

[3] William G. Johnsson, *Issues in the Book of Hebrews,* Frank B. Holbrook, ed. (Silver Spring, Md.: Biblical Research Institute, 1989), p. 90.

[4] See where I have developed this. Norman R. Gulley, "Toward Understanding the Atonement, *Journal of the Adventist Theological Society* 1, No. 1 (Spring 1990): 57-89.

[5] Johnsson, p. 96.

[6] *Ibid.,* pp. 112-114.

[7] *Ibid.,* p. 99.

[8] *Ibid.,* p. 184.

[9] George E. Rice, in *Andrews University Seminary Studies* 23, No. 1 (1985): 34, 35.

[10] Johnsson, p. 119.

[11] *Ibid.,* p. 118.

[12] *Ibid.,* p. 119.

[13] *Ibid.,* p. 154. See pp. 123-154. See also Richard M. Davidson, *Typology in Scripture.*

[14] Johnsson, pp. 178, 179.

[15] *Ibid.,* pp. 171-186.

[16] For example, in Hebrews 2:1; 3:12, 15; 4:1, 7, 11, 14; 5:6, 12; 10:26, 35-37; 12:1-6, 12-16, 25; 13:1, 2, 7-17, 22.

[17] Hebrews 6:9; 7:7, 19, 22; 8:6 (twice); 9:23; 10:34; 11:16, 35, 40; 12:24.

[18] R.C.H. Lenski, *Hebrews* (Minneapolis: Augsburg, 1966), pp. 359, 360.

[19] See Richard M. Davidson, "Typology in the Book of Hebrews," in William G. Johnsson's *Issues in the Book of Hebrews,* pp. 121-186.

[20] Bruce, p. xii.

[21] Johnsson, p. 184.

[22] Kenneth A. Strand, "The Eight Basic Visions in the Book of Revelation," *Andrews University Seminary Studies* 25, No. 1 (1987): 107-121; "The 'Victorious-Introduction' Scenes in the Visions in the Book of Revelation," *Andrews University Seminary Studies* 25, No. 3 (1987): 267-288.

[23] Like Daniel, Revelation falls into historical (1-14) and eschatological (15-21) chapters. As in Daniel, the power opposing Christ and His saints (little horn) is much larger than Antiochus of the second century B.C., so in Revelation this anti-Christian power (beast) is larger than Nero of the first century A.D. Like Daniel, the persecution spans a historical period (cf. Dan. 7:25, Rev. 12:14; see also Rev. 12:6, 13:5) and climaxes in the eschatological kingdom (Rev. 17-19); and hence is not confined to either a first-century (preterist) or last-generation (futurist) fulfillment. G. E. Ladd rightly finds that "while the churches of Asia were facing persecution, there is no known persecution in the first century A.D. which fits that portrayed in the Apocalypse. History is eschatologically interpreted" ("The New Testament Apocalypse," in *Evangelical Dictionary of Theology,* Walter A. Elwell, ed. [Grand Rapids: Baker, 1984], p. 65).

[24] Gregory K. Beale, *The Use of Daniel in Jewish Apocalyptic Literature and in the Revelation of St. John* (New York: University Press of America, 1984), p. 247.

The Good News of the Pre-Advent Judgment

[25] The pre-Advent battle is to be understood as beginning prior to the Advent and culminating with the Advent (Rev. 17-19).

[26] The unholy triumvirate of dragon, beast, and false prophet oppose the Trinity (Rev. 16:12-16; 19:11-20).

[27] Hans LaRondelle, *Chariots of Salvation,* pp. 67, 68.

[28] T. Longman III, "The Divine Warrior: The New Testament Use of an Old Testament Motif," *The Westminster Theological Journal* 44, No. 2 (1982): 290-307; see p. 297.

[29] These are the other three angels of Revelation 14. Their mission is to execute judgment on Babylon, whereas the three angels' messages (Rev. 14:6-13) are to gather people out of Babylon. The seven angels with the seven last plagues also come from the temple (Rev. 15:5-8; 16:1, 17). In Revelation 16:12 the Euphrates is dried up to prepare the way for the kings of the East. Water represents the nations (Rev. 17:15) and the kings of the East are either God the Father with Christ (Matt. 26:64; Rev. 6:16) coming from the east, or from heaven (Rev. 7:2); or Christ and His angels arriving together (Rev. 19:11-16). Mervyn Maxwell supports the "Father-Son" view in *God Cares* (Mountain View, Calif.: Pacific Press, 1985), vol. 2, p. 443; and Hans LaRondelle supports the "Christ-Angels" view in *Chariots of Salvation,* pp. 119, 120.

[30] Revelation says that "all the world wondered after the beast" (Rev. 13:3, KJV), and this includes the false prophet and dragon (Rev. 16:13; 19:20).

[31] C. F. Keil and F. Delitzsch, *Commentary on the OT,* vol. 10, p. 252.

[32] Compare Deuteronomy 28:36-64; 29:25-28.

[33] E. G. White, *Testimonies for the Church,* vol. 5, p. 472.

[34] The "angel of the Lord" (Zech. 3:1-3) is Michael of Daniel 12:1, or Jesus Christ; cf. Jude 9; Rev. 12:7-11.

[35] Compare Ellen G. White's first vision, in which she saw that only those who kept their eyes on Jesus made it up the path to heaven. Those taking their gaze away from Him fell to the world below *(Early Writings,* p. 14).

[36] E. G. White, *Testimonies for the Church*, vol. 5, pp. 470, 471.

[37] All nonhuman created beings, plus the few human representatives in heaven (of whom are Enoch, Elijah, Moses, and the 24 elders of Revelation 4 and 5), witness the pre-Advent investigation; all the redeemed observe the millennial investigation; and all the lost watch the postmillennial judgment. In this way all intelligent created beings participate in the evaluation of God's judgments, and find Him to be just (Rev. 15:3). The issue in the great controversy, calling in question the justice of God, thus receives its conclusive answer.

[38] This involves clinging not only to Calvary but to the Crucified's continuing intercession, a result of the cross.

[39] If the judgment is merely looking at what human beings have done, and the scriptural principle "by beholding we become changed" is applied (see 2 Cor. 3:18), then a millennium of poring over bad works would be dangerous. I believe that the judgments have far more to do with observing how patiently Christ has worked for each person, where each turned Him down, and so is far more Christ-centered than human-centered. Such an investigation is uplifting—it tells us more about the character of Christ than about the characters of fallen humans. To behold Christ's working will change us for the better, whereas to wallow in the morass of human sin would have the opposite effect.

[40] Throughout eternity "both the redeemed and the unfallen beings will find in the cross of Christ their science and their song" (E. G. White, *The Desire of Ages,* pp. 19, 20). We will be understanding ever greater depths of that gift and thereby receive greater revelation of God's love, in which justice and mercy met. However, the 144,000 will "follow the Lamb wherever he goes" (Rev. 14:4) to apparently relate their experience of living beyond probation's close, when they experienced spiritual and physical deliverance. So great is it they sing "the song of Moses and the Lamb—a song of deliverance. None but the hundred and forty-four thousand can learn that song; for it is the song of their experience—an experience such as no other company have ever had" (E. G. White, *The Great Controversy,* p. 649). Two pages later, *The Great Controversy* says: "The cross of Christ will be the science and the song of the redeemed through all eternity" (p. 651). The song of the Lamb (cross) has a stanza called the "song of Moses and the Lamb." The experience of the 144,000 is the final outworking of the cross in human lives during the pre-Advent judgment and before Christ returns.

[41] E. G. White, *Early Writings,* p. 14.

Chapter 36

The Millennium

Where will you spend the millennium? In heaven, on earth—or are you in it now? Christians have said yes to all three answers. Christianity has divided on the topic and has advanced more views connected with it than most other doctrines. So it is important to take a look at the various perspectives. We have noted other counterfeits Satan has promoted. The devil hates God and hides Calvary from humanity at every opportunity. He tramples the Sabbath of the Lord, throws out the pre-Advent judgment, and doesn't want anyone to understand the millennial judgment. For that judgment proves God's justice just as the pre-Advent judgment does. These doctrines repudiate Satan's challenge to God's justice. No wonder he has raised all kinds of views to hide the truth!

Revelation 20:1-7 mentions 1,000 years six times, the only chapter in Scripture that does so. Yet that period encompasses the most difficult parts of final events as far as evangelical Christians are concerned. They offer many conflicting interpretations. As J. Rodman Williams states, "the question of the Millennium has been one of the most perplexing biblical and theological issues in the history of Christendom."[1]

Christ came to earth in His first advent and lived among human beings for more than 30 years. Will Christ return the second time to earth to live with us for 1,000 years? Will He reign on earth?

The word "millennium" doesn't appear in Scripture, just as the word "trinity" is absent. But that doesn't mean that the doctrine is absent. The word is derived from two Latin words meaning a thousand years. And the thousand years is in the Bible.

Christians hold three major views about the millennium: postmillennialism, premillennialism, and amillennialism. "Post" and "pre" mean "after" or "before" Christ's second advent. These categories are "in certain respects unfortunate as the distinctions involve a great deal more than the time of Christ's return," says Robert G. Clouse. "The kingdom expected by the premillennialist is quite different from the kingdom anticipated by the postmillennialist, not only with respect to the time and manner in which it will be established but also in regard to its nature and the way Christ will exercise control over it."[2] Amillennialism means there will be no future millennium. Its advocates associate the thousand years with the Christian age itself. In terms of time, it also occurs before the Second Advent, similar to postmillennialism.

The Kingdom

Does the kingdom come suddenly, as dispensational premillennialists believe (secret rapture), or does it develop gradually (growing mustard seed) as postmillennialists and amillennialists believe? Will Christ be present during a millennial kingdom on earth with glorified saints and mortal sinners? Or is the millennial kingdom only for Christ, the Jews, and non-Christians, with the church raptured to heaven?

Is the kingdom God's rule or realm? Is it a kingdom of grace now and glory to come in the millennium, with both rule and realm present then? Where is the kingdom now—on earth or in heaven? Is the church the kingdom? Is the kingdom Christ's present reign at God's right hand? Does God reserve the kingdom until the millennium? Or is the kingdom beyond the millennium? Can it be a combination of the options above? And where does the millennium take place—on earth or in heaven? These are some of the questions that spark the millennium debate.

Tangential to them is the dispensational period between the alleged secret rapture of the church and the second advent of Christ. If there is a rapture, is it pretribulation, midtribulation, or posttribulation? That is, does it come at the beginning of the seven last earth years, in the middle, or at the end? Or are all rapture views wrong? Although we'll not take up these tangential matters, I recommend *The Blessed Hope,* by George Eldon Ladd, in which he shows that the Christian's hope is the second coming of Christ and not an alleged rapture.[3] For a further study about the kingdom, Ladd's *Jesus and the Kingdom* is an excellent source.[4]

John Bright rightly sees an organic unity between the Old and New Testaments. "It is one of beginning and completion, of hope and fulfillment. *And the bond that binds them together is the dynamic concept of the rule of God.* The Bible is *one book.* Had we to give the book a title, we might with justice call it 'The Book of the Coming Kingdom of God.'"[5]

To make it simple, Old Testament Israel was the kingdom in its original form. The Israelites longed for their Messiah-King. But they expected a king to establish the kingdom on earth and liberate them from the hated Romans. Although Jesus announced the arrival of God's kingdom, or reign (Luke 24:49), as the King in their midst, He said His kingdom was near (Luke 10:9), but "not of this world" (John 18:36). What does it mean, "For no matter how many promises God has made, they are 'Yes' in Christ" (2 Cor. 1:20)? The answer is, "What God promised our fathers he has fulfilled for us, their children, by raising up Jesus" (Acts 13:32). In other words, Christ rose and entered His reign in heaven (Heb. 1:5-13), and He will come in His kingdom at the Second Advent (Matt. 16:28). In the meantime, His kingdom can be "within you," as He rules the life (Luke 17:21). That's the fuller meaning of the kingdom promises to Israel. For that reign will continue in heaven during the millennium (Rev. 20:4) and on the new earth forever (Rev. 21:1-5; 22:1-5).

So the New Testament vastly expands the kingdom promises of the Old Testament. It's far more than any pre-Second Advent kingdom of Israel or any other earthly Christian kingdom. Put another way, the kingdom is Christ's rule in human hearts, and His reign in heaven since the ascension until after the millennium (cf. Matt. 26:28, 29). Then in the new earth His kingdom reign will be forever (Luke 1:32, 33). Thus Christ's kingdom is now a rule in the realm of human lives and a rule in the realm of heaven until the millennium's close, and then a rule with the redeemed (Rev. 22:5) in the realm of the new earth. This gives a quick overview against which you can compare the different millennial views.

Postmillennialism

The "post" in postmillennialism means "after." It places Christ's second advent after (post) the millennium. This view entered Christian thought during the fourth century. It goes back to an African named Tyconius. The great theologian Augustine of Hippo (354-430) adopted his views and made them popular in the Catholic Church. He believed the millennium began with Christ's first advent. Amillennialism also subscribes to this view. The kingdom exists in the present church age, with no future millennium. It is called postmillennialism only in reference to the Second Advent. Catholic theologians consider the kingdom to be the church, and Baptist Hezekiah Harvey, of Hamilton Theological Seminary, said, "The church is the visible, earthly form of the kingdom of Christ, and is the divine organization appointed for its advancement and triumph."[6]

Toward the end of his book *The City of God* Augustine speaks about the millennium. He describes it as the time of church history between the first and second advents of Christ. God binds Satan so he cannot seduce the church. This period ends when God frees Satan for three and a half years to gather nations for the battle of Armageddon against the church. During the 1,000 years the saints reign with Christ, the dead being in heaven and the others on earth. The church is the kingdom of Christ and the kingdom of heaven.[7] Augustine's view became church doctrine, so that in the Council of Ephesus (431), "belief in the millennium was condemned as superstitious."[8]

This view of the millennium looks to other biblical passages besides Revelation 20. It regards the gospel commission of Christ to go to all nations (Matt. 28:18-20) as evidence that the gospel will conquer the world. Parables of the gradual growth of the kingdom seem to support this. For example, the mustard seed's expansive growth (Matt. 13:31, 32) and the leaven that permeates the whole (verse 33).

Postmillenialism also uses such Old Testament passages as Psalms 47, 72, and 100; Isaiah 45:22-25; and Hosea 2:23.[9] It sees them as teaching that all nations will serve God (Ps. 72:11), worship God (Ps. 47:1), become God's people (Hosea 2:23), and bow before God (Isa. 45:23). The passages seem to picture a world won to God. But we need to remember two facts as we interpret such texts. First, Israel failed to be the medium through whom God planned to achieve this. Second, God will fulfill some things in the final judgment, when all will bow to admit that God is just (Rev. 5:13). But that is after the millennium.

Loraine Boettner teaches that the world will be Christianized, even though not all will be converted. Christ and the saints will return to a truly Christianized world. "During the millennium the saints in glorified bodies mingle freely with men who are still in the flesh." He has a heavy emphasis on the majority being saved.[10]

The idea that the world is getting better is more evolutionary than biblical. Scripture actually pictures a world becoming worse. In the end-time, Christians "will be hated by all nations because of me" (Matt. 24:9; cf. 2 Tim. 3:12, 13; 4:3, 4), society witnesses an "increase of wickedness" (Matt. 24:12), and deceivers perform miracles and signs (verses 23-27). That's a long way from a converted world! Christ also said, "When the Son of Man comes, will he find faith on the earth?" (Luke 18:8). Commenting on the Second Advent, Paul warns, "Don't let anyone deceive you in any way, for that day will not come until the rebellion occurs and the man of lawlessness is revealed" (2 Thess. 2:3). He says that "the work of Satan" will be "displayed in all kinds of counterfeit miracles, signs and wonders, and in every sort of evil that deceives those who are perishing. They perish because they refused to love the truth and so be saved" (verse 10).

Note how bad things will get in the end-time. "There will be terrible times in the last days. People will be lovers of themselves, lovers of money, boastful, proud, abusive, disobedient to their parents, ungrateful, unholy, without love, unforgiving, slanderous, without self-control, brutal, not lovers of the good, treacherous, rash, conceited, lovers of pleasure rather than lovers of God—having a form of godliness but denying its power" (2 Tim. 3:1-5).

George Ladd points out that in New Testament times the Pax Romana brought the Mediterranean world peace for 200 years, something that has never occurred since. Think of the terrible world wars in this century, besides so many others—Korea, Vietnam, Ireland, the Middle East,[11] Bosnia, and the mass slaughters in some African nations.

Dominion Theology—A Form of Postmillennialism (see chapter 16)

Christian Reconstructionism is another name for dominion theology. Launched around 1968 by Rousas J. Rushdoony, Greg Bahnsen, and Gary North, it says America must become a theocracy, just like ancient Israel. Mosaic laws are for Christians.[12] The government must enforce all judicial Mosaic laws, including capital punishment. Greg Bashan in his book, *Theonomy in Christian Ethics,* says that includes Sabbathkeeping (first day of the week), because Scripture lists it among capital crimes.[13]

CHRIST IS COMING!

Dispensationalists believe they'll be raptured anytime, but not Reconstructionists. They're here to Christianize the world to prepare it for the Second Advent. Their eschatology makes a decided difference to their ethics. Building a kingdom on earth sounds like the "Manifest Sons of God" scheme.[14] For David Chilton, re-creation of the world is already in process, with a view to recapturing the original dominion God gave to humanity in Eden.[15] The problem with his view is that God gave humanity dominion only over the natural world, not over the human race (Gen. 1:28). Reconstructionists, wanting to Christianize the world, are out to convert the human race.[16]

Whereas dispensationalists and other premillennialists expect the coming kingdom, Dominion theology says that Christ has already established the kingdom,[17] that it is now gradually being realized,[18] and it will be fully present in the last days.[19] George Grant points to a coming "world conquest. That's what Christ has commissioned us to accomplish."[20] Reconstructionists claim that the Great Commission includes more than taking the gospel to the world (Matt. 28:18-20). It has to do with dominion.

They believe that Christ bound Satan[21] and that Israel forever lost its kingdom status,[22] an idea repudiated by dispensationalists. According to reconstructionists, Christ began His reign at His ascension.[23] Christians now rule with Christ.[24] And that reign will continue for a long time. Although more excessive than other predictors, David Chilton puts Christ's return 36,000 years into the future.[25]

Both postmillennialists and reconstructionists have a lower view of the kingdom of God than they should. Postmillennialists believe that glorified saints and Christ live in the millennial kingdom with sinners, and that death is still present. How can a holy God live in such an environment? Reconstructionists believe the millennial kingdom is a time for gradual change. As God steadily lifts the curse on the world, life spans will be lengthened.[26] Again, how can things be so gradual when the Creator-King is present? Reconstructionists seem to be obsessed with the present kingdom and pay little attention to the coming kingdom. Yet Jesus taught Christians to pray "thy kingdom come" (Matt. 6:10, KJV), and said "My kingdom is not of this world" (John 18:36).

Dispensationalists have a Jewish theocracy with Temple and sacrifices reinstituted. Reconstructionists have a Christian theocracy with all Old Testament laws in operation, including capital punishment. The Bible does not prophesy any theocracy until after the millennium. After Christ's sacrifice (Heb. 9:24-28) God's people no longer need to offer additional sacrifices. The world will never be Christianized into a theocracy for it becomes ripe for destruction (2 Peter 3:1-7). Dispensationalists use Old Testament prophecies about Israel to describe the millennial kingdom of Israel. Reconstructionists apply the same Old Testament prophecies to the church when it rules the world to usher in the millennium.[27]

What about the First Amendment of the Constitution that protects religious freedom, so that American Buddhists, American Hindus, American Muslims, and American Jews can practice their religions safe from American Christians who want to Christianize the world? According to critics House and Ice, reconstructionism works to make Christianity the sole religion of the end-time. It will not tolerate other non-Christian religions as well as Catholicism and dispensationalism.[28] Its proponents seem to want a Christianized theocracy enforcing Old Testament laws.

Where does the Christian Coalition fit into the kingdom-on-earth focus of reconstructionism? In September 1980, 15,000 fundamentalists, including several thousand pastors, attended the National Affairs Briefing Conference in Dallas, Texas. The meetings urged Christians to become politically active. Reconstructionist Gary North spoke, as did Pat Robertson, then president of the Christian Coalition. Robertson "reminded the audience of the words of Genesis 1:26-28, calling Christians to exercise dominion, subdue the earth. . . . He even used the phrase, 'Christian reconstruction.'"[29]

I believe the Christian Coalition thinks more about building the kingdom on earth than looking to the kingdom of heaven. They share much with reconstructionists in their attempt to influence politics and dominate the public square with Christian values.

What both groups need to remember is the failures of the sixteenth-century Reformation. While Luther and Calvin abhorred the union of church and state in Catholicism, both stooped to do the same in their teaching and practice. In 1531 the Smalcaldic League united nine German princes and their realms to defend Protestantism against the pope's military forces. "Forsaking his earlier commitment to nonviolence and his protestations on behalf of individual liberty of conscience, Luther decided that the sword was indispensable not only for protection from the pope but for enforcement of the new truth. He was acknowledging that the Reformation which has been inspired by steadfast faith of martyrs must now look for protection to the sword wielded by earthly powers." In the same way, a few years before, Luther encouraged princes to fight in the Peasants' War (1524-1526), which slaughtered 130,000 of them.[30]

That is only seven years after he launched the Reformation cry for freedom! Just seven years since he banged 95 theses to the Wittenberg church door. In only seven short years he went from trusting God to spread His truth to a horrible massacre in the name of truth. It is a warning to reconstructionist and Christian Coalition activists!

As we saw in a previous chapter, John Calvin established a theocracy in Geneva. Its citizens labored under legislated minutia. Where had the freedom of the gospel gone? Blood flowed in the city—150 burned at the stake in just 60 years! The authorities tortured a man named Guret for three years. Finally he confessed that he had "attached a disrespectful placard to Calvin's pulpit at St. Peter's." For such a flimsy thing they executed him in 1547. Michael Servetus perished at the stake for denying the Trinity.[31]

When church and state unite in a quest to establish the kingdom of God on earth, religious freedom gets thrown to the winds. "It does not bode well that the Reconstructionists, whose influence in the church is growing rapidly, have Calvin as their faultless hero and hope to model Christianized society after his failed Geneva experiment."[32]

Another example of establishing a theocracy happened in 1534, when a splinter group of Anabaptists "forcibly installed itself as a military theocracy in Muenster in Westphalia. Grandiose plans for a New Jerusalem were set in motion and all Lutherans and Catholics were given the option of rebaptism or banishment." The leaders instituted the death penalty for a variety of trivial offenses, including complaining.[33] Those seeking to establish the kingdom on earth now need to learn from such history. Rather than Christianizing the world, they will politicize Christianity—and persecution will follow.

In spite of all such lessons from history, Gary North calls for an international theocracy. He declares that "the goal of the gospel is to subdue every soul, every institution, and every nation under God," and he goes on to say that the gospel commission is to disciple nations, "to exercise covenant control of every civil government."[34] Reconstructionists are grooming Christians to take over governments and control them by a "Christian" agenda. The political agenda of the Christian Coalition seems the same.

With this in mind, we need to realize that "the last twenty years has seen an upsurge of postmillennialism. In fact, the premillennial position is probably more on the decline at the present time [1988] than the other two views"[35] (postmillennialism and amillennialism). "This dominion eschatology seems to be especially gaining among the more politically active evangelicals and the positive confession charismatics."[36]

Charismatics have jumped on the reconstructionist bandwagon, and charismatics occur in practically every denomination. Christians are uniting to implement moral values in an attempt to Christianize the world and establish the kingdom of God on the earth. Much of this is postmillennialism, and its proponents see what they are doing as a necessary prerequisite for the second advent of Christ.

Back in 1907 Augustus H. Strong said, "Through the preaching of the gospel in all the world, the kingdom of Christ is steadily to enlarge its boundaries, until Jews and Gentiles alike become possessed of its blessings, and a millennial period is introduced in which Christianity generally prevails throughout the earth."[37] Strong concludes that the "millennial blessedness and dominion is prior to the second advent."[38]

Those attempting to establish God's kingdom forget that it is not in humanity's power to do so. Only God can establish His kingdom on earth, and biblical teaching clearly says it will happen when He re-creates a new heaven and a new earth (Rev. 21; 22), which comes after the millennium (Rev. 20).

Amillennialism

Luther and Calvin basically followed the Catholic Church in teaching amillennialism. It means they had nothing to say about a future millennium. Reformed theologian Louis Berkhof sees it as "the only view that is either expressed or implied in the great historical

Confessions of the Church," and "the prevalent view in Reformed circles."[39]

J. Rodman Williams, in his *Renewal Theology,* gives a charismatic perspective on the millennium. It spans the whole gospel era—beginning in Christ's ministry and ending in His second advent. The binding of Satan (Rev. 20:1-3) occurred during the ministry of Christ. He quotes Matthew 12:29, NASB: "How can anyone enter the strong man's house and carry off his property, unless he first binds the strong man? And then he will plunder the house." The strong man in the passage, he says, is Satan. "Christ partook of our flesh so that 'through death He might render powerless him who had the power of death, that is, the devil' (Heb. 2:14, NASB)." He equates the rendering powerless with the binding of Satan.

Satan is bound through the Christian era, fulfilling Revelation 20:3—Satan is kept from deceiving the nations for 1,000 years. Williams parallels this with the restraint of "the secret power of lawlessness" (2 Thess. 2:7). While Williams admits that Satan does still cause problems in the world, he "is incapable of preventing the gospel message from getting to the nations."[40]

The reigning with Christ takes place on earth in the victorious lives of the saints. The first resurrection of Revelation 20:4 is not at the Second Advent (see 1 Thess. 4:16-18) but in conversion. Williams quotes John 11:25, 26: "I am the resurrection and the life. . . . whoever lives and believes in me will never die." He calls it a spiritual resurrection to be followed by the second resurrection in the Second Advent. Then God will raise the body. The 1,000 years he considers as expressing "a complete but indeterminate period of time."[41]

His interpretation has many problems. Revelation 20 is a chapter full of literal events. The angel comes to bind Satan (verse 1). No longer can he deceive the nations (verse 3), a period lasting 1,000 years (verses 2, 3, 5, 6). The saints sit on thrones (verses 4, 5) and reign and judge with Christ (verse 4). A resurrection takes place at both the beginning (verse 4) and at the end of the 1,000 years (verse 5). Satan deceives the nations after the 1,000 years (verse 8), mobilizing them to fight God (verses 7, 8). When they surround the New Jerusalem, fire pours down from heaven to destroy them (verse 9). The devil is thrown into the lake of fire (verse 10), a verdict issued at the great white-throne judgment (verses 11-15).

To spiritualize this chapter is to do disservice to its message. Williams treats the first resurrection as a spiritual conversion. But the chapter speaks of martyrs who come from the grave (verse 4). The passage links their resurrection with another literal fact—that the wicked dead don't come from the graves until after the 1,000 years (verse 5). Furthermore, when it says Satan cannot deceive the nations during the 1,000 years, on what authority do we restrict it to not hindering the gospel, whereas his nefarious activity continues in everything else? The chapter says he cannot deceive. That means he cannot deceive in any way, not just in all ways except one. Williams reads into the passage a theory that's extraneous to it. The fact that saints will reign on thrones and judge cannot be reduced to victory in their lives today. Further, history is replete with examples of Satan's attempting to hinder the gospel throughout the Christian era.

Dispensational Premillennialism

Dispensational premillennialists believe that the doctrine of God's kingdom progressively unfolds throughout the Bible. It begins in Genesis where God gives humanity dominion (Gen. 1:26-28), reaches Sinai where Israel became a kingdom of priests (Ex. 19:5, 6), and continues with the promise that someone will always sit on David's throne (2 Sam. 7:12-16; 1 Chron. 28:5, 7; Isa. 9:6, 7; Dan. 2:44; 7:13, 14, 27). This kingdom is future (2 Tim. 4:1). In the last biblical book the kingdom rules on earth for 1,000 years (Rev. 20:1-7), after which it will last forever (Rev. 11:15).[42] Isn't this similar, if not the same, as the gradualism of reconstructionists?

According to some, the reign of Christ on David's throne takes place in the future millennium. Israel will be the most important nation in the world, with Christ reigning from Jerusalem. All nations will use the Temple in Jerusalem. Even though some suggest the sacrifices are a memorial of the cross, this stands in direct opposition to Hebrews 8:13, which clearly understands the sacrificial system as done away with.

During the Christian age the mediatorial kingdom remains on hold until Christ returns to earth after a seven-year period preceding it. The New Testament does not say anything about a millennial reign. Instead, dispensational premillennialists see God as fulfilling the Old Testament promises. Dispensationalists as well as postmillennialists and amillennialists employ the same passages. Whereas the latter two schools see the texts as giving insight into the present kingdom of God before the Second Advent, dispensationalists use them to illustrate the millennial kingdom after the Second Advent.

Attempting to force the fulfillment of the Old Testament texts into some present or future time is hazardous, because not just the restoration of Israel is involved. "For it involves the future restoration of all the former historical conditions of Israel's life: the great world powers of the Old Testament (Egyptians, Assyrians, and Babylonians), and the neighboring nations of Israel (Moabites, Ammonites, Edomites, and Philistines) must again appear on the scene, Isa. 11:14; Amos 9:12; Joel 3:19; Micah 4:1, 2; Zech. 14:16-22; Eze. 40-48."[43]

During the millennium dispensationalists believe that Christ's ministry "will be directed toward a progressive subjugation of all enemies to his official and personal rule." Then Christ will hand over the kingdom to the Father for the universal kingdom to begin (1 Cor. 15:24, 28).[44]

In his *Systematic Theology* Charles Hodge criticizes this type of premillennialism. He dubs it a "Jewish doctrine." "The Jews expected that when the Messiah came He would establish a glorious kingdom at Jerusalem."[45] Such premillennialism has saints reigning with Christ on earth for 1,000 years, Jews rebuilding their Temple, and Scripture superseded in the millennium. Humans continue to live forever on earth as sinners, and get to the kingdom of heaven only at their death. "What almost all Christians believe is: (1.) That all nations shall be converted unto God."[46]

Postmillennialists teach world conversion before the Second Advent. Dispensational premillennialists believe all the nations will be converted during the millennium.

Historic Premillennialism

Historic premillennialism repudiates the dispensational variety. Instead of a progressive unfolding of the kingdom throughout Scripture, we must interpret Old Testament prophecies about the kingdom by the New Testament. The New Testament becomes the expanded context in which we must understand them. We'll just mention a few examples, as we studied them in depth in chapter 6. Matthew 2:15 quotes Hosea 11:1 about Jesus' coming out of Egypt. The Hosea passage is a historical account of the Exodus. Matthew turns the historical account into a prophecy of Christ's coming out of Egypt after His flight from Herod. Thus, *"the Old Testament is reinterpreted* in the light of the Christ event."[47]

Historic premillennialists show that dispensational premillennialists put the mission of Israel on hold during the church age. They also suspend Christ's reign. But the prophecies about His reign in the Old Testament do not have to wait until the millennium. Here's the next example of the New Testament interpreting the Old. The New Testament clearly indicates that Christ ascended to heaven to begin His reign. "He sat down at the right hand of the Majesty in heaven" (Heb. 1:3). The Father announces to Christ, "Your throne, O God, will last for ever and ever, and righteousness will be the scepter of your kingdom" (verse 8). Revelation 4 and 5 documents His inauguration. Christ says to Laodicea, "To him who overcomes I will give the right to sit with me on my throne, just as I overcame and sat down with my Father on his throne" (Rev. 3:21).

"Therefore let all Israel be assured of this: God has made this Jesus, whom you crucified, both Lord and Christ" (Acts 2:36). To accept that "Jesus is Lord" is a prerequisite for salvation (Rom. 10:9). After Calvary, "God exalted him to the highest place and gave him the name that is above every name" (Phil. 2:9). The promise to David was "The Lord says to my Lord: 'Sit at my right hand until I make your enemies a footstool for your feet'" (Ps. 110:1). The New Testament takes this passage about David's rule on earth and expands it greatly. "For David did not ascend to heaven, and yet he said, 'The Lord said to my Lord: "Sit at my right hand until I make your enemies a footstool for your feet."' Therefore let all Israel be assured of this: God has made this Jesus, whom you crucified, both Lord and Christ" (Acts 2:35, 36). God said to Christ in heaven, "Sit at my right hand until I make your enemies a footstool for your feet" (Heb. 1:13). So the Old Testament prophecy about David's reign on earth becomes Christ's reign in heaven in the New Testament.

Although the millennium doesn't take place during the church age, the reign of Christ in heaven does. George Ladd believes "the millennium is part of

Christ's Messianic rule by which he puts all his enemies under his feet (1 Cor. 15:25). Another possible role of the millennium is that Christ's Messianic kingdom might be disclosed *in history.*" He says further: "The millennium will reveal to the world as we now know it the glory and power of Christ's reign." Then Ladd offers one other reason for the millennial reign of Christ: "At its close the devil will be released from his imprisonment and will find the hearts of men still responsive to his enticements, even though they have lived in a period of peace and righteousness. This will serve to commend the justice of God in the final judgment. Sin—rebellion against God—is not due to an evil society or to a bad environment. It is due to the sinfulness of the hearts of men. Thus the justice of God will be fully vindicated in the day of final judgment."[48]

Evaluation

The various schools of thought have some overlapping ideas as well as differences. The following are seven areas of comparison:

APPROACHES TO THE MILLENNIUM COMPARED

1. Gradual growth of the kingdom	Now: postmillennialists, reconstructionists, and amillennialists. In millennium: dispensationalists.
2. All nations converted	Before Second Advent: postmills., recons., and amills. In millennium: dispens.
3. Christ reigns	Now: postmills., recons., and amills. In millennium: dispens.
4. Theocracy instituted	Before Second Advent: postmills. and recons. (Christian) In millennium: dispens. (Jewish)
5. Old Testament laws valid	All before Second Coming: recons. Sacrifices: begin seven years before Second Advent: dispens.
6. Old Testament prophecies	Valid now: recons. and amills. In millennium: dispens.
7. Second Advent	First part is rapture—any moment. Not possible yet—postmills., recons., and amills.

Behind these various theories lie different hermeneutics—different ways of interpreting the Bible. Thus dispensationalists employ a literalistic interpretation that woodenly reads all Old Testament prophecies in the light of physical Israel as if the New Testament has no part in the interpretation process and as if the Christ event makes no difference. Historical premillennialists believe in a spiritual interpretation when the New Testament indicates that ethnic Israel is now spiritual Israel (Gal. 6:16), in which the church is now "a chosen people, a royal priesthood, a holy nation, a people belonging to God" (1 Peter 2:9), and "a kingdom and priests" (Rev. 1:5; 5:10). Amillennialists follow a symbolic interpretation, in which the millennium is not a literal time period to come but a symbol for the history of the church.

Behind each method of interpretation lies a set of assumptions. Dispensationalists assume that Israel and the church must forever remain apart. Historical premillennialists conclude (rightly) that Christ and the New Testament are the final words about the Old Testament. And postmillennialists, reconstructionists, and amillennialists operate from the premise that things are getting better through the spread of the gospel.

Because dispensational views of final events are so pervasive, we'll add a few words to what we presented in more depth in chapter 6. Does the present state of Israel have significance? Is what happens during the final seven years of earth's history a factual prelude to the millennium? I do not believe Israel, as a nation, has any role in final events. Consider these texts:

Abraham came to Canaan (Palestine), where God promised to make a great nation—to influence the world (Gen. 12:1-7). The promises of return to Palestine found partial fulfillment in the migration back from Babylonian captivity (Ezra-Nehemiah). In the New Testament the Promised Land has vastly expanded. Abraham and his descendants looked for "a better country" (Heb. 11:8-16), a new heaven and a new earth (Rev. 21, 22). Abraham's children are not Israel just of the Old Testament, but in the New Testament "he is the father of all who believe" (Rom. 4:11). The New Testament declares that "there is neither Jew nor Greek, slave nor free, male nor female, for you are all one in Christ Jesus. If you belong to Christ, then you are Abraham's seed, and heirs according to the promise" (Gal. 3:28).

When we examine such passages, we have to conclude that the present return of Jews to Israel is not a theologically significant event. When Pilate asked, "Shall I crucify your king?" the chief priests answered, "We have no king but Caesar" (John 19:15). And when Pilate asked, "Do you want me to release 'the king of the Jews'?" the Jewish rabble yelled back, "No, not him! Give us Barabbas" (John 18:39, 40). The Jews kept shouting, "If you let this man go, you are no friend of Caesar" (John 19:12). Christ turned to the Christian church to be the new "Israel of God" (Gal. 6:16). Today Israel has no special prophetic future, but the Israelis do have a future as Christians.

In Genesis 17:5 God said of

Abraham: "I have made of you a father of many nations." Paul in Romans expands this promise to make the patriarch "the father of all who believe" (Rom. 4:11). So the promise swelled beyond ethnicity to a belief statement for all humanity. "Therefore, the promise comes by faith, so that it may be by grace and may be guaranteed to all Abraham's offspring—not only to those who are of the law but also to those who are of the faith of Abraham. He is the father of us all" (Rom. 4:16).

All of these millennial theories share one problem. They believe the millennium takes place on earth, whether during the present or in the future.

Why the Millennium Is in Heaven, and Not on Earth

"I think it important for evangelicals to recognize that this area of study is complex," says Wayne Grudem, "and to extend a large measure of grace to others who hold different views regarding the millennium and the tribulation period."[49] Grudem then looks at where the millennium takes place. He refers to Revelation 20, in which the angel departs heaven to bind Satan (verses 1-3). "If the angel came down from heaven, then he carried out his activity on the earth, and the entire scene is set on the earth."[50]

Let's look at Revelation 20 in context and see if Scripture informs us where the millennium takes place. We begin with the previous passage, first examining the immediate context and then the rest of the New Testament.

1. Revelation 20

The angel, coming down from heaven, seizes Satan and binds him for 1,000 years, an action described as the devil being thrown into a sealed, or locked abyss "to keep him from deceiving the nations anymore until the thousand years were ended" (Rev. 20:3). This gives the impression that God seeks to prevent Satan from seducing the nations that continue on the planet during the millennium. Then it says: "When the thousand years are over, Satan will be released from his prison and will go out to deceive the nations in the four corners of the earth—Gog and Magog—to gather them for battle. In number they are like the sand on the seashore" (Rev. 20:7, 8).

A quick reading of the passage suggests that nations continue to inhabit the planet during the millennium. But such a conclusion flies in the face of the biblical passages about the Second Advent.

2. Revelation 19

Revelation 19 describes Christ's second advent. He comes as a warrior riding a white horse to execute judgment upon the living wicked (Rev. 19:11-16). An angel speaks of the decimation of the wicked (verses 17, 18). "Then I saw the beast and the kings of the earth and their armies gathered together to make war against the rider on the horse and his army. But the beast was captured and with him the false prophet who had performed the miraculous signs on his behalf [see Rev. 16:12-16]. With these signs he had deluded those who had received the mark of the beast and worshiped his image. The two of them were thrown alive into the fiery lake of burning sulphur. The rest of them were killed with the sword that came out of the mouth of the rider on the horse, and all the birds gorged themselves on their flesh" (verses 19-21).

Please note that none of the wicked survive this final battle of Armageddon. So none live on during a millennium on earth.

3. Other New Testament Descriptions of the Second Advent

Christ describes what happens at the Second Advent. Depicting humanity through the symbols of wheat and tares, He admonished: "Let both grow together until the harvest [His return]. At that time I will tell the harvesters: First collect the weeds and tie them in bundles to be burned, then gather the wheat and bring it into my barn" (Matt. 13:30). Jesus gives the interpretation when He says, "As the weeds are pulled up and burned in the fire, so it will be at the end of the age. The Son of Man will send out his angels, and they will weed out of his kingdom everything that causes sin and all who do evil. They will throw them into the fiery furnace" (verses 40-42).

Then Christ changed the metaphor. "All kinds of fish" (verse 47) represent all humanity. The fisherman pulls in the net. "Then they sat down and collected the good fish in baskets, but threw the bad away. This is how it will be at the end of the age. The angels will come and separate the wicked from the righteous and throw them into the fiery furnace" (verses 48-50). Another Second Advent scene in Revelation provides insight into this process. Seated on a white cloud, Christ carries a sickle to harvest the righteous from around the world (Rev. 14:15, 16). Then an "angel swung his sickle on the earth, gathered its grapes and threw them into the great winepress of God's wrath" (verse 19).

In these passages Christ speaks of a total annihilation of the wicked at His second advent. But what about His people? What happens to them? Do they continue to live on earth during the millennium during a time when the devil cannot tempt them?

Paul answers the question in his Second Advent scene. "For the Lord will come down from heaven, with a loud command, with the voice of the archangel and with the trumpet call of God, and the dead in Christ will rise first. After that, we who are still alive and are left will be caught up with them in the clouds to meet the Lord in the air. And so we will be with the Lord forever" (1 Thess. 4:16, 17). Not a secret rapture text as dispensationalists believe, it has to be one of the noisiest texts in Scripture. The resurrection of the righteous takes place, and the living righteous rise into the air. Both groups meet each other and Christ in the air. Notice that Christ does not land on the earth. The righteous journey away from the earth to meet Him above the surface of the planet.

Scripture corroborates this interpretation. In fact, Christ does Himself. He repeatedly warns against false Christs that we might encounter on earth (Matt. 24:23-26). "For as lightning that comes from the east is visible even in the west, so will be the coming of the Son of Man" (verse 27). In other words, don't look somewhere on earth, but look up to the heavens for the real

Christ. Remember that the disciples asked Christ, "What will be the sign of your coming and of the end of the age?" (verse 3). "At that time the sign of the Son of Man will appear in the sky, and all the nations of the earth will mourn," He answered. "They will see the Son of Man coming on the clouds of the sky, with power and great glory" (verse 30). We need to add this to what Paul tells us in 1 Thessalonians 4:16, 17—that we meet Him in the air.

A Closer Look at Revelation 20

With these insights gained from the immediate and New Testament contexts of Revelation 20, we now look further at the chapter itself. We'll enumerate points that concur with what we have seen from the two contexts. We are dealing with symbolic language. Binding Satan and locking him up in a sealed abyss has no meaning if the wicked are all dead, and the righteous dead and translated taken to heaven. So is there any other explanation? Look at verse 5. "The rest of the dead [wicked compared to the righteous resurrected mentioned in verse 4] did not come to life until the thousand years were ended." The releasing of Satan takes place when God resurrects the wicked (Rev. 20:5, 7). They are "like the sand of the seashore," because they include all the wicked who have ever lived (verse 8).

The Second Advent, we conclude from other passages, is the time when all the wicked die and the righteous leave the planet to meet Christ in the air. The planet is destitute of human beings—the first time since Creation. So Revelation 20 speaks of these dead as not coming to life until the end of the 1,000 years (verse 5).

But what about the righteous? Scripture singles out the martyrs of the end-time (verse 4). They rise in the first resurrection (verse 6), the one that takes place at the Second Advent (1 Thess. 4:16-18), and form part of those who meet Christ in the air. Revelation pictures them as seated on thrones (verse 4) and reigning with Christ as "priests of God" for 1,000 years (verses 4-6). We would expect this to be in heaven, because they ascended to meet Christ in the Second Advent.

Could they not have returned to reign here on the earth?

When Jesus sought to comfort His disciples just before His death and later departure, He said, "In my Father's house are many rooms; if it were not so, I would have told you. I am going there to prepare a place for you. And if I go and prepare a place for you, I will come back and take you to be with me that you also may be where I am. You know the way to the place where I am going. . . . I am the way and the truth and the life. No one comes to the Father except through me" (John 14:2-6).

To where did He ascend? The disciples "were looking intently up into the sky as he was going, when suddenly two men dressed in white stood beside them. 'Men of Galilee,' they said, 'why do you stand here looking into the sky? This same Jesus, who has been taken from you into heaven, will come back in the same way you have seen him go into heaven'" (Acts 1:10, 11). So the promise in John 14 declares: "I'm preparing you a place in heaven. I will come from there to take you back with me. For where I am, there you will also be."

It would seem then, that the binding and loosing of Satan has to do with the lack of people to tempt (binding) and the abundance of people to tempt (loosing). Thus the millennium is a time in which Satan and his angels have 1,000 years to contemplate their nefarious work. It is a judgment time for them that precedes their being thrown into the lake of fire some time after the end of the millennium (Rev. 20:10; cf. Matt. 25:41). So Satan and his angels are the earth's sole inhabitants during the millennium. The wicked of the end-time are dead. The righteous of all time have joined Christ in heaven.

This agrees with another insight from the book of Revelation. The book mentions a throne 38 times. God's throne is always in heaven except twice. Then it's Satan's throne on earth (Rev. 2:13) and the throne of the beast, who follows Satan (Rev. 13:2; 16:10). Never once does the book declare God's throne to be on earth. When we realize that Christ began His reign in heaven after His ascension and has reigned from heaven ever since, then it's logical to see Him take His saints to sit on thrones with Him in heaven. Revelation documents that He already did this with other human beings—the 24 elders. Surrounding the heavenly throne were 24 other thrones (Rev. 4:4).

How do we know that the 24 elders are human?[51] They wear crowns *(stepahanoi),* laurel wreaths of victory that only winners of an Olympic game wear. Here are humans who have won a victory. Redeemed, they have become victors over the devil through the power of Christ. Now in heaven, they worship God (Rev. 4:10; 5:8). When did they get there? Revelation 4 and 5 depict the inauguration of Christ after His ascension. Scripture gives us clues as to whom the 24 are. Go to the weekend of Christ's death. When Jesus cried out His last words on Calvary, the earth shook and the rocks split. The tombs broke open and the bodies of many holy people who had died were raised to life. They came out of the tombs, and after Jesus' resurrection they went into the holy city and appeared to many people (Matt. 27:51-53). Of Christ's ascension Scripture says, "When he ascended on high, he led captives in his train" (see also Eph. 4:8; Ps. 68:18).

His taking of human beings with Him to the heavenly throne is a type of what He will do again, on a much larger scale, in the Second Advent.

The Purpose of the Millennium

But what's the reason for the millennium? Why can't the Second Advent introduce the new heavens and new earth? Dispensationalists believe it offers time to fulfill all the Old Testament prophecies about Israel's greatness. But we've seen it ignores the wider interpretation the New Testament gives to those prophecies, it rejects the new definition of Israel that is far broader than ethnicity, and it overlooks the fact that spiritual Israel has replaced literal Israel. In short, it views the Old Testament as if Christ and the New Testament never existed.

We have already noticed that George Ladd believes the millennium demonstrates that rebellion can take place in a perfect environment, thus showing that God is not responsible for sin, and hence clarifying His justice.[52] Wayne Grudem also supports this view, adding, "With Satan bound for a thousand years, the fact that sin can persist will also show that the ultimate blame for sin is not demonic influence in people's lives but deep-rooted sinfulness in people's hearts."[53] Thus both authors regard theodicy, or the justice of God, as the reason for the millennium. But I don't think their concept of the rebellion of the wicked in an alleged perfect environment proves anything. It has already happened. Satan and his angels were perfect and lived in the perfect environment at heaven's throne, yet they sinned (Rev. 12:7, 8).

It is vital to keep in mind the cosmic controversy (see chapter 2). Satan has called God's justice into question. If perfect angels, including the covering cherub at the throne, can sin (Eze. 28:13-17; Rev. 12:7, 8), then who or what caused it? If God made them perfect, as we would expect on the basis of Creation of our world (cf. Gen 1:31), then their fall was their own choice. The same can be said of Adam and Eve, who also sinned in a perfect environment (Gen. 3:1-7).

As we have seen, Scripture speaks of several judgments. Daniel saw heaven in vision. "As I looked, thrones were set in place, and the Ancient of Days took his seat. . . . Thousands upon thousands attended him; ten thousand times ten thousand stood before him. The court was seated, and the books were opened" (Dan. 7:9, 10). Here is a judgment at the throne involving the cosmic controversy. And it is a pre-Second Advent judgment. The judgment verdicts indicate this. The saints will receive the kingdom forever (Dan. 7:18). "The Ancient of Days came and pronounced judgment in favor of the saints of the Most High, and the time came when they possessed the kingdom" (verse 22). The verdict in their favor follows an earlier one. "As I watched, this horn was waging war against the saints and defeating them, *until* the Ancient of Days came" (verses 22, 23).

Further, "he [little horn] will speak against the Most High and oppress his saints and try to change the set times and the laws. The saints will be handed over to him for a time, times and half a time. But the court will sit, and his power will be taken away and completely destroyed forever. Then the sovereignty, power and greatness of the kingdoms under the whole heaven will be handed over to the saints, the people of the Most High. His kingdom will be an everlasting kingdom, and all rulers will worship and obey him" (verses 25-27).

It appears that this particular judgment precedes Christ's coming when He implements both verdicts—one against the enemies of the saints and the other for the saints. The judgment process enables the onlooking universe to see why some will be saved and others lost. This is fair. It does not prove God's justice, but demonstrates it. And it is why it takes place before He comes to implement the double verdict. The human beings who ascended with Christ are human witnesses to this exhibition of His justice.

So what about the millennium? Just

as God took the 24 elders to heaven to observe the pre-Advent judgment process (Rev. 4, 5), so the saved of all time go in the Second Advent to witness the millennial judgment. "I saw thrones on which were seated those who have been given authority to judge" (Rev. 20:4). "They will be priests of God and of Christ and will reign with him for a thousand years" (verse 6). Notice the reign includes judging just as Christ's Christian-age reign also had a judgment (Dan. 7). What will they be judging? Why are so many humans not saved? Is God just in this?

They will learn that each of the lost had every opportunity for salvation. God gave His Son for the whole world (John 3:16). He sends His Spirit to enlighten everyone born on it (John 1:9). The universe observes that God did everything except force human beings to be saved. All will see that He has been just. None of the judgments would be necessary if the cosmic controversy did not question His justice. The pre-Advent judgment satisfies the onlooking universe and representative humans. The millennial judgment answers the questions of the rest of the redeemed. I believe the lost will have the same opportunity to see why they did not make it to heaven after their resurrection (Rev. 20:12, 13) and before their final destruction (verses 5-10).

The entire creation lives at the same time—all the unfallen beings, the saved and lost humans. All have seen God's justice revealed. And all realize that Satan's attacks on divine justice have no foundation. "Then I heard every creature in heaven and on earth and under the earth and on the sea, and all that is in them, singing, 'To him who sits on the throne and to the Lamb be praise and honor and glory and power, for ever and ever!'" (Rev. 5:13). Indeed, "every knee will bow" and "every tongue will confess to God" (Rom. 14:10).

The Everlasting Kingdom Reign

The everlasting reign in the kingdom begins after God implements the judgment verdicts. This means after the wicked are finally destroyed and He gives the kingdom to the saints forever (Dan. 7). It takes place after the millennium (Rev. 20:5), the implementation of the destruction of the wicked (verse 15), and the creation of "a new heaven and a new earth" (Rev. 21:1). Then the New Jerusalem comes "down out of heaven from God" (verse 2). The throne of God is in the city (Rev. 22:3) and "they will reign for ever and ever" (verse 5).

The 24 elders sing a new song of praise to Christ, "because you were slain, and with your blood you purchased men for God from every tribe and language and people and nation. You have made them to be a kingdom and priests to serve our God, and they will reign on the earth" (Rev. 5:9, 10).

---

[1] J. Rodman Williams, *Renewal Theology* (Grand Rapids: Zondervan, 1992), vol. 3, p. 421.

[2] Robert G. Clouse, ed., *The Meaning of the Millennium: Four Views* (Downers Grove, Ill.: InterVarsity, 1977), p. 7.

[3] George Ladd, *The Blessed Hope: A Biblical Study of the Second Advent and the Rapture* (Grand Rapids: Eerdmans, 1975). Ladd rightly notes that the hope of the church through the centuries has been the second coming of Christ. The idea of a secret rapture came only in the nineteenth century. For most of Christian history the rapture was not a part of the Christian hope (p. 19).

[4] George Ladd, *Jesus and the Kingdom: The Eschatology of Biblical Realism* (London: SPCK, 1966). Ladd shows that the kingdom came in the person of Christ (p. 32), but rightly adds, "The present Kingdom is not to be identified with the church. The church is the people of the Kingdom" (p. 34). For Ladd the kingdom is "the reign of God"—a reign in human hearts and human history with present and future dimensions.

[5] John Bright, *The Kingdom of God: The Biblical Concept and Its Meaning for the Church* (New York: Abingdon-Cokesbury, 1953), pp. 196, 197.

[6] Hezekiah Harvey, cited in Stanley J. Grenz, *Theology for the Community of God* (Nashville: Broadman and Holman, 1994), p. 621.

[7] Augustine, *The City of God, The Nicene and Post-Nicene Fathers,* First Series (Grand Rapids: Eerdmans, 1988), vol. 2, pp. 426-431.

[8] Robert G. Clouse, "Introduction," *The Meaning of the Millennium: Four Views,* p. 9.

[9] Millard J. Erickson, *Christian Theology* (Grand Rapids: Baker, 1986), p. 1207.

[10] Loraine Boettner, "Postmillennialism," in *The Meaning of the Millennium: Four Views,* pp. 117-141.

[11] George Ladd, "An Historic Premillennialist Response," in *The Meaning of the Millennium: Four Views,* p. 143.

[12] Greg L. Bahnsen and Kenneth L. Gentry, Jr., *House Divided: The Breakup of Dispensational Theology* (Tyler, Tex.: Institute for Christian Economics, 1989), p. 3.

[13] Greg Bashan, *Theonomy in Christian Ethics* (Nutley, N.J.: Craig, 1979), pp. 228-230, 445, 446.

[14] H. Wayne House and Thomas Ice compare them to reconstructionists in *Dominion Theology: Blessing or Curse? An Analysis of Christian Reconstruction* (Portland, Oreg.: Multnomah, 1988), pp. 384-389. One quote will suffice. " 'God's people are going to start to exercise rule, and they're going to take dominion over the power of Satan. We are rulers of this planet—it's time we take over!' " (p. 385) (not all the parallels mentioned are exact). Bahnsen and Gentry replied with a comparison of the Manifest Sons of God with dispensationalists, premillennialists, and others, in *House Divided,* pp. 320-326 (again, all the comparisons are not exact).

[15] David Chilton, *Paradise Restored: An Eschatology of Dominion* (Tyler, Tex.: Reconstruction, 1985), p. 25.

[16] Bahnsen and Gentry speak of the world "culturally Christianized" (p. 199), "conversion of all nations" (p. 210). It is noted that there will be some tares, but "when the Lord returns, He will return to a wheat field with tares in it—not to a tare field with wheat in it (Matt. 13:24-30)" (p. 196).

[17] Bahnsen and Gentry, p. 3.

[18] *Ibid.,* p. 218.

[19] David Chilton, p. 75.

[20] George Grant, *The Changing of the Guard: Biblical Principles for Political Action* (Fort Worth, Tex.: Dominion, 1987), p. 51.

[21] David Chilton, *Days of Vengeance* (Fort Worth, Tex.: Dominion, 1987), p. 503.

[22] David Chilton, *Paradise Restored,* p. 224.

[23] Bahnsen and Gentry, pp. 183, 184.

[24] *Ibid.,* pp. 186, 187.

[25] David Chilton, *Paradise Restored,* p. 221.

[26] Cf. House and Ice, p. 239.

[27] Bahnsen and Gentry, p. 198.

[28] House and Ice, pp. 77-80. This agrees with the Christianization concept.

[29] Dave Hunt, *Whatever Happened to Heaven?* p. 72.

[30] *Ibid.,* pp. 169-171.

[31] *Ibid.,* pp. 171-176.

[32] *Ibid.,* p. 179. Kenneth Gentry says he is a Presbyterian, and Reformed (following Calvin) in his confessional life *(House Divided,* p. 1).

[33] *Ibid.,* p. 183.

[34] Gary North, *Healer of the Nations: Biblical Principles for International Relations* (Fort Worth, Tex.: Dominion, 1987), pp. 56, 57.

[35] House and Ice, p. 210.

[36] *Ibid.,* pp. 210, 211.

[37] Augustus H. Strong, *Systematic Theology* (Philadelphia: Judson, 1907, 1949), p. 1008.

The Millennium

[38] *Ibid.,* p. 1011.

[39] Louis Berkhof, *Systematic Theology* (London: Banner of Truth Trust, 1969), p. 708.

[40] J. Rodman Williams, *Renewal Theology,* vol. 3, pp. 421-425.

[41] *Ibid.,* pp. 425-430.

[42] Herman A. Hoyt, *The Meaning of the Millennium: Four Views,* p. 65.

[43] Berkhof, p. 713.

[44] Herman A. Hoyt, "Dispensational Premillennialism," *The Meaning of the Millennium: Four Views,* pp. 63-92. George Ladd points out that the difference between the mediatorial and universal kingdom is not the usual dispensational distinctive *(The Blessed Hope,* p. 93).

[45] Charles Hodge, *Systematic Theology* (Grand Rapids: Eerdmans, n.p.d.), vol. 3, p. 862.

[46] *Ibid.,* pp. 863-866.

[47] George Ladd, "Historic Premillennialism," *The Meaning of the Millennium: Four Views,* p. 21.

[48] *Ibid.,* pp. 39, 40.

[49] Wayne Grudem, *Systematic Theology* (Grand Rapids: Zondervan, 1994), p. 1114.

[50] *Ibid.,* p. 1118.

[51] This is one Adventist view among other options (see *The Seventh-day Adventist Bible Commentary,* vol. 7, pp. 767, 768), and so is a tentative conclusion.

[52] George Ladd, "Historic Premillennialism," in *The Meaning of the Millennium: Four Views,* p. 40.

[53] Grudem, p. 1121.

Chapter 37

How to Have Assurance

In a 1996 survey of Seventh-day Adventist college students 77 percent said they did not know if they would be saved if Jesus came that day.[1] This was an even higher percentage than previous surveys. We have come to the last chapter before we take our journey through end-time events. It is imperative to know how to gain confidence in our salvation. How can we face the coming crisis if we lack assurance today during a comparative calm?

In the survey mentioned above, 37 percent thought that they had to do something in order to be saved. Such a position echoes that of Catholicism. Catholic theology teaches that Calvary forgave only past sins. We must atone for present sins through the Mass. But even that is insufficient. Purgatory comes after death, for Catholics, to continue their preparation for heaven. It can be a long process, and it depends in part on the prayers and offerings of those still on earth. Prayers to saints and to Mary make their contribution. For charismatics, speaking in tongues is a prerequisite to salvation. All are added works to that of Christ.

What Catholics and charismatics unwittingly say is that Christ isn't sufficient for human salvation; Christ plus human works save. But that is totally false. "God credits righteousness apart from works" (Rom. 4:6). Faith in Christ's works for us, trust in Him as our Saviour—that is the work that brings assurance. Once we are in a relationship with Him, then works do follow (John 14:15). I do things to make my wife happy, not to earn her love. She already loves me. I do these things because I love her. So it is with Christ. Overwhelmed by His great gift—His death, the payment for our sins—we find ourselves filled with gratitude and joy. We revel in His presence and have assurance.

Sinners naturally want to earn salvation, and thus assurance. They feel they should; and if they somehow think it is possible (which it isn't), it makes them feel good. Working for salvation is the basis of every non-Christian religion. And that is why it is so tragic to see Seventh-day Adventist university students caught up in this trap. Sincere and wanting to be in heaven, they hope they'll be worthy. In the meantime they claim they know Christ as a personal friend. Actually they're caught up in a quest to be freed from their burden of guilt. Christ may be in view—but He's still only at a distance. Like Christian, the pilgrim in *The Pilgrim's Progress,* they need to find Calvary and let the burden roll off their back. That is why many lack assurance. Calvary hasn't freed them yet. They work toward heaven, but one can get there only through the cross. If reaching to heaven depends upon their works—upon what they can do—they struggle under an unnecessary load. What's the use of going through the final-events journey so weighed down when Calvary can release us from such burdens?

The Good News

It is true that all human beings are sinners (Rom. 3:9). "There is no one who does good, not even one" (verse 12). So all the good works we do don't amount to anything when it comes to earning salvation. God is in heaven, and we're on earth. No matter how high we jump, we can't make it there. The gulf is too great. Heaven is totally out of reach.

Christ saw our predicament. He knew we couldn't cross from our side to His, that even our best attempts at living a good life wouldn't save. So He came to us, became a fellow human, and lived and died to bridge the gulf. When in His last hours He carried our sins and became sin for us, in our place (2 Cor. 5:21), He died for our sins so that we don't have to die for them. He let them crush out His life so we won't have to carry the load. Paul compares the rebellion in Eden with Christ's death on Calvary. "Just as the result of one trespass was condemnation for all men, so also the result of one act of righteousness was justification that brings life for all men" (Rom. 5:18). Christ really did take our place at the cross. We can go free.

Not only what Christ did, but what He's still doing assures us of salvation. Paul declares: "Since we have now been justified by his blood, how much more shall we be saved from God's wrath through him! For if, when we were God's enemies, we were reconciled to him through the death of his Son, how much more, having been reconciled, shall we be saved through his life!" (Rom. 5:9, 10). Christ paid for our salvation on the cross and now ministers to apply that gift to our experience. He intercedes for us at God's throne (Rom. 8:34). "He is able to save completely those who come to God through him, because he always lives to intercede for them" (Heb. 7:25).

God loves us, not because we are good, for compared to Him we are definitely not. Rather, He loves us because He is good. Human salvation is His work through and through. The Father gave His Son (John 3:16). The Son gave His life (Luke 22:42). The Holy Spirit brings that salvation within each person who accepts it. "If God is for us, who can be against us? He who did not spare his own Son, but gave him up for us all—how will he not also, along with him, graciously give us all things?" (Rom. 8:31, 32). God wants to give us assurance. How does it happen?

Christ Is Coming!

Assurance comes when we stop looking at ourselves and our own efforts and focus on Christ and Calvary. Then by beholding them, by responding to whom and what He is, the Holy Spirit can then change us (2 Cor. 3:18). What we concentrate on is the key. When people focus within, they lack assurance. But when they look to Christ, He gives them assurance. He died to save us. That means salvation is assured—if we accept it. Not only that, through the Holy Spirit we receive Christ (John 14:15-18). We're not alone.

"Come to me, all you who are weary and burdened [wearied with works and burdened about salvation and assurance]," Jesus pleads, "and I will give you rest" (Matt. 11:28). "Remain in me, and I will remain in you. . . . Apart from me you can do nothing" (John 15:4, 5). Salvation is simply Jesus Christ. Period! Salvation is a gift, a gift that comes with the Giver. We receive salvation through receiving the Saviour. It's "Christ in you, the hope of glory" (Col. 1:27).

Christ in You

"Christ in you" is just as much a gift as Calvary. We can no more work up an experience of His indwelling through sheer grit than we can save ourselves. Without Christ we're ugly inside. And without His transforming presence we have no hope, and therefore no assurance. Assurance comes from Christ—by focusing our lives on Him and Calvary, and by having Him dwell within—and in that order.

Many Christians do all sorts of things to feel good about themselves, such as buying new clothes, getting a new car, working hard to earn more money, pushing themselves for a promotion—all exterior fixes. But no exterior fix brings assurance.

Max Lucado tells a story about leaving with his wife on a trip when they lived in Rio de Janeiro.[2] Unfortunately he unplugged the refrigerator instead of his ham radio. Guess what happened when they got back? The utility room stank. The fridge was putrid. So he got a bucket and soapy water and began cleaning the fridge on the outside. He buffed and polished until it sparkled. The appliance could have passed a Marine boot camp inspection. But that didn't work.

So he tried something else. Every machine needs friends. He filled the apartment with refrigerators, microwaves, and washing machines. "It was a great party. A couple of toasters recognized each other from the appliance store. Everyone played pin the plug on the socket and had a few laughs about limited warranties. The blenders were the hit, though; they really mixed well." But that didn't stop the smell either. The fridge hadn't changed. He continued the story with other imaginary solutions. His point was that all outward changes cannot substitute for a transformed interior. Or, in our present context, only Christ dwelling within can clean up our lives and bring the spiritual assurance for which we long.

Devotion to Christ

Devotions are times we devote ourselves to Christ. More than reading for information, it's a new giving of ourselves daily to the One who has given Himself to us forever. It's time to gaze on Calvary, to see Him hanging there for us. Time to see His death as our forgiveness, acceptance, and assurance. Calvary is concrete, irreversible, irresistible, extravagant evidence that He has paid for our ticket to salvation. All we have to do is to accept. His death makes certain our future, guarantees our destiny. Calvary calls to each one of us. Won't you claim your gift? It's better than any lottery. Accept Jesus as your Saviour, and your salvation is certain. For Christ and Christ alone is our assurance.

[1] Survey of those taking Last Day Events classes at Southern Adventist University.
[2] Max Lucado, *The Applause of Heaven* (Dallas: Word, 1995), pp. 122-125.

Part Two

The Journey

Chapter 38

It's the End-time

Final events are upon us. The journey is about to begin. What we've learned in the previous chapters gives us information, insight, and inspiration for the trip. If you skipped those chapters, and begin reading here, welcome aboard! After you've gone through the journey in these chapters, you'll want to go back and deepen your background from the rest of the book so you'll be ready for the real journey.

A storm burst upon the fishing boat. That's the way storms always come on the lake—without warning. Heavy winds and huge waves battered the vessel. Its passengers feared for their lives. Although seasoned sailors, they had to struggle to survive. Nothing worked. Not until they thought of Jesus—asleep on a ballast sandbag.

"Master, we perish!" they yelled above the shrieking wind. "Save us!"

Christ never turned down such a request. Didn't they realize what His being on board with them meant? How could they be lost with Him there? But they had no time to think. The storm grabbed their attention, absorbed their energies, and fueled their fear.

"Peace, be still!" That's all it took. The elements obeyed His command. The waves quit, and the wind ceased. Water lapped against the hull as it calmly glided across the surface. Peace at last!

No one is ready for the coming storm. And no one knows what it will be like. Not even the most prepared saints have what it takes to go through. As Christ's disciples couldn't quiet the storm on Galilee, so God's saints won't be able to calm the storm around the globe. Only Christ can do that. Christ is in the boat with us. We must know Him, depend upon Him, love Him, trust Him. His presence will make the difference. Without Him we are lost. But with Him we will have peace even in the storm. He can still the storm and quiet our fears.

Rather than look at the storm—look at the Saviour!

Look What's Coming

"There shall be a time of trouble,

such as never was since there was a nation" (Dan. 12:1, KJV). "We are on the very verge of the time of trouble, and perplexities that are scarcely dreamed of are before us."[1]

"The present is a time of overwhelming interest to all living. Rulers and statesmen, men who occupy positions of trust and authority, thinking men and women of all classes, have their attention fixed upon the events taking place about us. They are watching the relations that exist among the nations. They observe the intensity that is taking possession of every earthly element, and they recognize that something great and decisive is about to take place—that the world is on the verge of a stupendous crisis."[2]

Are you scared of the journey ahead? Do you wish you could go to sleep and wake up in heaven? Do you want to skip what's coming? Listen, you're not alone. Many people fear final events. The number is growing as the new millennium crowds in on us—as the storm clouds gather.

Recently a student blurted out to me, "I don't want to go through the great time of trouble." Another exclaimed, "I don't want to run to the mountains. I'd rather die!"

Worried saints are not bad people, just scared people. They love God, and He loves them. They've just never gone through troubles like those coming. Nor have they had time to think through the journey. So often the great time of trouble, Jacob's trouble, or the death decree jump from the pages of the doctrinal books and articles they have been studying and crowd out every other thought. Their enormity blots out the pathway that travels through these events. Let's sit down and look at that passage through final events and not get stuck on the events themselves. It makes a big difference.

Many saints encounter statements about living without an Intercessor during the worst time of trouble. "Help! Count me out," they say. "Why, I can't even live without an Intercessor in good times, let alone then!"

Others hear they have to live a perfect life after the Holy Spirit withdraws from the world. "How can it be?" they exclaim. "How can we be perfect without the Spirit? It's impossible! I'm not perfect now even with the Spirit!"

That's why I want to take you through the journey. Think of it as a practice run. We'll go through final events in the comfort of your reading couch. The material we read in the previous chapters gives us content to refer to on the journey. Yes, there'll be more data to look at too. But information must aid, not hinder, the journey. If you want good news, news that takes away your fears, news that gives you courage to face final events, then read on. It works in the lives of my university students each semester. A tried and true prescription, it can work for you too.

Gathering for the Journey

They crowd into the classroom, eager to learn about last-day events. College students from across America and beyond. Freshmen through seniors, men and women, prelaw, predentistry, premed, nurses, teachers, ministers, business majors, and more. Most sense themselves as a part of the final generation. The class is more than academics—it's training for a final exam beyond the course.

"They should know the things that will come to pass before the closing up of the world's history. These things concern our eternal welfare, and teachers and students should give more attention to them."[3] "In the night season these words were spoken to me," wrote Ellen G. White. "Charge the teachers in our schools to prepare the students for what is coming upon the world."[4]

Church members gather in last-day events seminars. God calls out, "Let the watchmen now lift up their voice and give the message which is present truth for this time. Let us show the people where we are in prophetic history."[5] "I saw that God's people are on the enchanted ground, and that some have lost nearly all sense of the shortness of time and the worth of the soul."[6]

What's coming? "Many of the prophecies are about to be fulfilled in quick succession," reports one who had a sneak preview. "Every element of power is about to be set to work. Past history will be repeated; old controversies will arouse to new life, and peril will beset God's people on every side. Intensity is taking hold of the human family. It is permeating everything upon the earth."[7]

"As we near the close of this world's history, the prophecies relating to the last days especially demand our study."[8] " 'Search the scriptures.' Study your Bible as you have never studied it before. Unless you arise to a higher, holier state in your religious life, you will not be ready for the appearing of our Lord."[9] Tough words. No wonder "Satan employs every possible device to prevent men from obtaining a knowledge of the Bible. . . . None but those who have fortified the mind with the truths of the Bible will stand through the last great conflict."[10]

Take those last two quotes and turn them around. Those who study the Bible diligently will stand in the last great conflict and be ready for Christ's return. It is a wonderful promise! Students, youth, the generation Xers, and the more mature—all need to think positively. They need to see the endgame and want to win.

Where Should We Begin?

To begin right is crucial. Have you ever come to a fork in the road and wondered which one to take? It is horrible if someone has changed the signs and you go barreling down the wrong road for miles! A fork in the road awaits you when you come to the study of last-day events. One says "Coming Crisis," the other, "Coming Christ." The first tells what is coming, the second, who is coming.

"Well, we need both," someone might quip. "How can we study final events without looking at final events, especially the final event—Christ's return?"

True. Then you would go through the events in a step-by-step way, finishing with the final step—His return. Right?

"What's wrong with that?" some might wonder.

Well, let's put it this way. That's taking the "Coming Crisis" fork. We spend all our time on the crisis events and bring in the good news only at the end of the story. That's not good enough. By that time many will be petrified with fear. The problem with many members is that they're up to their necks in their own crises and feel like screaming when they hear things will get worse.

But what about the other fork? If that path is all Christ, you might as well study the life and teachings of Jesus rather than final events. Right?

While that could be true, it doesn't have to be the case. Look at it this way. If you take the "Coming Christ" fork, you keep your eyes focused on that final event and look at all events in light of the return of Christ. The Sunday laws, death decree, great time of trouble, and Jacob's trouble all collapse with Christ's coming. He moves in like a giant steamroller and grinds them in the dust. The joy of His return puts them into perspective.

So Let's Begin

I want you to travel with me on an imaginary journey. It's true to the facts that face us in our real journey. You'll meet three people on this journey; we'll stay, in turn, with each of them, then resume our own journey.

First, let's take the "Coming Crisis" road. Although it promises to be a better road, an easier one to travel, after a few miles down the pike things get hard. Those trudging along the lowlands route through final events often get stuck in the mud, sink down into swamps, and generally eke out a miserable existence.

Notice that attractive billboard at the entrance. "Come this way for an easier journey." "It sure beats climbing," you say to yourself. The gatehouse offers doughnuts and chocolates and handouts for all. Coffee and tea for those who need them. "We do everything for your comfort," the gatekeeper declares. "Have a good journey."

Crowds gather at the gate, gobble doughnuts and chocolates, drink coffee, and talk about exciting things.

"Antichrist is coming. Someone like Hitler. His number is 666. He's going to launch the New World Order."

"Can hardly wait," chimes in another. "That means the secret rapture is just ahead."

"Yep. Think of all those silly Christians who think you have to go through the great time of trouble. Everyone knows that the Lord is coming to whisk us off the planet just in time. We'll be in heaven looking down on those who trudge through the terrors of final events."

"That's why He's coming as a thief in the night. It's the next event. Think of all the drivers yanked out of airplanes, eighteen-wheelers, and cars! What a spectacular mess! Boy, God is sure going to make a mark on the planet!"

"Israel becomes God's instrument again," someone else adds. "They'll rebuild the Temple, offer sacrifices, survive a major invasion, and take the gospel to the world. We'll have front seats in heaven, glued to the universal satellite coverage. How great of Christ to have us tucked away in heaven during the great tribulation on earth!"

Can you imagine the shock coming to those Christians as the tribulation unleashes its storm and they find themselves still here? Will they doubt their Christian experience? At first, yes. But eventually it will dawn on them that no other Christian has left. All remain on the planet. Then they doubt their Christ. Has He let them down? Horrified, hurt, helpless, hopeless, as the storm overwhelms them, they sink into the swamps of despair. The low road is hard and long. Many give up and perish.

Still others mill around the gatehouse. Reconstructionists. Those pushing Dominion theology. "We've got to build the kingdom of God on earth. Bring in the Old Testament laws. Enforce Sunday. Death to the disobedient!" They really mean business. If the secret rapture group hope to escape the great time of trouble, the reconstructionists plan to make it not happen, because they're out to dominate the world.

If trouble is coming, and coming it is, then it will be upon those who don't go along with them.

Sounds like the Christian Coalition could fit in with that crowd. That is, as far as ruling is concerned. Both see Christians taking over governments and mandating a moral agenda. All these types crowd around the gateway to the low road through final events.

Postmillennialists share many characteristics with the reconstructionists. To them, Christ's second advent occurs after the millennium (premillennialists think the Advent comes before). They too must build God's kingdom on earth. With a work to do and ready for action, they know that a lot depends upon what they do to make it happen.

The Other Road

Back at the fork, across from the gatehouse with doughnuts and chocolates, stands a little chapel near the entrance to the road called "Coming Christ." The chapel door has a notice on it. "Come on in." Inside, a picture of Christ hangs on the far wall, a triple picture with the resurrected Christ in the foreground, Calvary dominating the background, and off to the far left corner, in the shadows, the praying Christ of Gethsemane and judgment halls. The caption below simply reads: "Come to me, all you who are weary and burdened, and I will give you rest" (Matt. 11:28). Seems more restful here. No crowds milling around. No one focusing on what humanity can and must do.

The chapel door creaks open. Danny pushes on it and slips inside. Tall and determined, yet gentle and learning, this 20-year-old premed Seventh-day Adventist university student settles into a seat in front of the picture. He longs for Christ's return. "To be ready for Christ's coming is more important than my career," he had told Barry, a friend from academy and a senior prelaw student. "For what if Christ comes before I finish my study?" He had looked at the puzzled face of his ambitious friend that day in the college library.

"Well, I wish you luck," Barry had replied. "But as for me, I'm too busy right now." And out he went. That was two days ago. The memory haunts Danny. "What good will it be for a man if he gains the whole world, yet forfeits his soul?" (Matt. 16:26).

Danny knows where he is going. He had learned about the charismatic and New Age movements in last-day events class. The amazing success of the Christian Coalition had convinced him that Christ's return was imminent. Having investigated the two routes, he had decided to take the journey on the high road.

Christ Is Coming!

Danny gazes at the picture. How could he miss it? Looming as large as life, it dominates everything in the chapel. As he ponders the picture, he wonders why it doesn't show Christ arriving in the Second Advent. For after all, the road is called "Coming Christ." He will have to wait to find out. Gethsemane, judgment halls, Calvary, and the resurrected Christ. What is the picture trying to say? Then it dawns on him. It is the journey Christ took. Not His journey from heaven and through more than 30 years of living, but Christ's journey through last-day events—for Him. The picture shouts, "I took the journey. I know what it's like to go through final events. I understand!"

For us, final events have everything to do with Christ rather than the crisis. To focus on *who* is coming is more important than upon *what* is coming. And it is essential that we think long about Christ's last-day events. For that will give us courage to face our own coming crisis. Think of it—church and state united to catapult Jesus through final events. Hated Romans with treacherous Jews. Secular and religious leaders combined give Him a great time of trouble. It began with the Jewish Coalition (the Christian Coalition of that day). Imagine Sadducees and Pharisees at each other's throats over doctrinal differences, (e.g. resurrection), now joining to crucify Him. True, they had a common day of worship, but their differences made them as bitter enemies as any Catholic-Protestant fight. Yet they were able to get together on a common cause—get rid of Christ. It was even a moral cause—at least in their eyes. Remember the charge from early days? "Because Jesus was doing these things on the Sabbath, the Jews persecuted him" (John 5:16).

Jesus knew Satan's strategy. He knew the story of Ahab and Elijah. Ahab and his cronies, the Baal worshipers, all former Seventh-day Adventists of that day, worked together to destroy Elijah. "Is that you, you troubler of Israel?" Ahab demanded of Elijah (1 Kings 18:17). Back came the reply, "I have not troubled Israel; but thou, and thy father's house, in that ye have forsaken the commandments of the Lord" (verse 18, KJV). False charges fly again in the end-time. The persecutors "will pursue a course toward God's ambassadors very similar to that which apostate Israel pursued toward Elijah."[11]

Church leaders buried their doctrinal differences to go after Christ. So churches in the end-time put aside their doctrinal differences to go after Seventh-day Adventists. But look who join them. Jesus warned, "Then you will be handed over to be persecuted and put to death, and you will be hated by all nations because of me. At that time many will turn away from the faith and will betray and hate each other, and many false prophets will appear and deceive many people" (Matt. 24:9-11). I hate that prediction. Even church members will persecute, just as they cried "Crucify" 2,000 years ago.

So many thoughts crowd into Danny's mind as he thinks about Christ's journey through final events. In Gethsemane Christ cried out, "My soul is overwhelmed with sorrow to the point of death" (Matt. 26:38). " '*Abba,*

Father,' he said, 'everything is possible for you. Take this cup from me. Yet not what I will, but what you will'" (Mark 14:36). This is how the journey begins. Danny whispers, "Not my will, but thine, my Saviour!"

There in the garden Christ suffered for what Adam and Eve did in the other garden. What a long detour from Eden to Gethsemane, and how different the gardens! And how different the two Adams. One chose Eve above God. The Other said, "Not my will." Christ "seemed to be shut out from the light of God's sustaining presence. Now He was numbered with the transgressors. The guilt of fallen humanity He must bear. Upon Him who knew no sin must be laid the iniquity of us all. So dreadful does sin appear to Him, so great is the weight of guilt which He must bear, that He is tempted to fear it will shut Him out forever from His Father's love. Feeling how terrible is the wrath of God against transgression, He exclaims, 'My soul is exceeding sorrowful, even unto death.'"[12]

Get it straight. Romans and Jews didn't nail Him. My sins did. So did yours. Neither did the Romans and Jews cause Him the great time of trouble. Our sins did.

"Never before had they [the disciples] seen Him so utterly sad and silent. As He proceeded, this strange sadness deepened; yet they dared not question Him as to the cause. His form swayed as if He were about to fall. . . . Every step that He now took was with labored effort. He groaned aloud, as if suffering under the pressure of a terrible burden. Twice His companions supported Him, or He would have fallen to the earth. . . . He felt that by sin He was being separated from His Father. The gulf was so broad, so black, so deep, that His spirit shuddered before it. This agony He must not exert His divine power to escape. As man He must suffer the consequences of man's sin. As man He must endure the wrath of God against transgression."[13]

"As Christ felt His unity with the Father broken up, He feared that in His human nature He would be unable to endure the coming conflict with the powers of darkness. In the wilderness of temptation the destiny of the human race had been at stake. Christ was then conqueror. Now the tempter had come for the last fearful struggle. For this he had been preparing during the three years of Christ's ministry. Everything was at stake with him. If he failed here, his hope of mastery was lost; the kingdoms of the world would finally become Christ's; he himself would be overthrown and cast out. But if Christ could be overcome, the earth would become Satan's kingdom, and the human race would be forever in his power. With the issues of the conflict before Him, Christ's soul was filled with dread of separation from God. Satan told Him that if He became the surety for a sinful world, the separation would be eternal. He would be identified with Satan's kingdom, and would nevermore be one with God."[14]

Here Christ plunged into the greatest time of trouble that will ever overtake the planet. Christ felt God-forsaken, alone, crushed by human sins that separated Him from the Father. Danny thinks long about that. Words jump out of the pages of *The Desire of Ages*. "Strong cries." "They hardly knew Him, His face was so changed by anguish." "They saw His face marked with the bloody sweat of agony." "Again the Son of God was seized with superhuman agony, and fainting and exhausted, He staggered back to the place of His former struggle. His suffering was even greater than before." "Now He was like a reed beaten and bent by the angry storm." His voice was "full of human anguish." Jesus "fell prostrate, overcome by the horror of a great darkness. The humanity of the Son of God trembled in that trying hour."[15]

Three times His humanity shrank from the rest of the journey. "But now the history of the human race comes up before the world's Redeemer. He sees that the transgressors of the law, if left to themselves, must perish. He sees the helplessness of man. He sees the power of sin. The woes and lamentations of a doomed world rise before Him. He beholds its impending fate, and His decision is made. He will save man at any cost to Himself."[16]

"Thank God!" Danny sighs. "What a cost to redeem me!" He thinks of how an angel swooped down from heaven and came to Jesus. Strengthening Him, "he pointed Him to the open heavens."[17] *The heavens are always open to God's saints, even when the storm clouds smother close,* he muses. Danny knows that the high road calls him to look to the open heavens. Yes, he will do that.

For a long time he sits and thinks. The next stage of Christ's journey took Him from Pilate to Herod and back to Pilate. One farce of a trial following another. Here church and state united together to persecute Christ. Religious leaders joined with pagan Roman officials. They all combined to mock, deride, and try Him to the uttermost. Unfeeling wretches cursed, the rabble kicked Him and yanked His beard. A thorn-laden crown, with jagged spikes, stabbed into tender flesh. They spat at Him, pulled Him one way and another, as if to rip limbs from His body. Roman soldiers flogged Him twice till blood flowed freely from a mangled back. How could He go through all the agony? How could He stay there when, with a flick of His finger He could be out of there as King of kings and Lord of lords? Being divine made His time of trouble so much greater than any humans could ever go through!

Danny looks up at Calvary. Cruel, unfeeling wretches shoved Him on that wood, drove spikes through ankles and arms, and let the cross thud into the open hole. The jolt ripped His flesh. Blood flowed freely. Even above the pain, the load of sin slowly crushed out His life. *He hung there for me,* Danny thinks. *How could He do it? He must really love all humanity. Jesus loved as none other has. That's why He suffered as no other can.*

Just then the chapel door opens. "Hi, Danny." In walks Barry.

"Wow, what a surprise! What are you doing here? I didn't expect to see you. Remember two days ago . . ."

"I know. I know," Barry interrupts. "I also know you had something that I wanted. So I went to my room after we talked at the library. Well, since then I've been studying about Christ, and read about Calvary. Danny, it changed me. I'm a new man. I want to take the journey too. So here I am." He watches Danny's face crease into a huge smile.

"Fabulous! Praise the Lord!" The two fall into a big embrace, then laugh.

Then Barry notices the huge picture of Christ. "What a picture!" he exclaims.

"Yes," Danny says. "I've just been meditating about it before the journey."

"Good idea, buddy. You know what I learned? Christ knows what it's like to be guilty, to feel the inner pain of sin." Danny nods. "That is a horrible but beautiful thought. Why should He feel guilty in order to free us from guilt?"

"Barry, I've got to tell you about this picture. It's Christ's journey through last-day events." And he proceeds to tell him all he has thought.

"I wish I had taken more time to think about Christ before in my life," Barry says, shaking his head. "But oh, the peace and freedom I have now!" They both study the eyes of Christ as He hung from Calvary. So pensive, forgiving, and longing. Eyes that say, "I understand if you are afraid of final events. I was too. But look, I went through something you will never have to go through. You will never have to carry your guilt. You will never feel crushed by your sins. I carried them for you so that you can go free. It was terrifying to Me. I cried out, 'My God, My God, why have you forsaken me?' (Matt. 27:46). But I promise you, 'Never will I leave you; never will I forsake you'" (Heb. 13:5).

Darkness smothered Calvary. Gloom settled down over it. Jesus "was despised and rejected by men, a man of sorrows, and familiar with suffering. Like one from whom men hide their faces he was despised, and we esteemed him not. Surely he took up our infirmities and carried our sorrows, yet we considered him stricken by God, smitten by him, and afflicted. But he was pierced for our transgressions, he was crushed for our iniquities; the punishment that brought us peace was upon him, and by his wounds we are healed" (Isa. 53:3-5). His life was "a guilt offering" (Isa. 53:10), for "God made him who had no sin to be sin for us, so that in him we might become the righteousness of God" (2 Cor. 5:21).

"Christ went through the worst part of the journey for us, so that we will not have to. Wow! What a Saviour!" Barry bangs the pew in joy. "Awesome! That's what it is. Awesome!"

"The guilt of every descendant of Adam was pressing upon His heart. The wrath of God against sin, the terrible manifestation of His displeasure because of iniquity, filled the soul of His Son with consternation. . . . with the terrible weight of guilt He bears, He cannot see the Father's reconciling face. The withdrawal of the divine countenance from the Saviour in this hour of supreme anguish pierced His heart with a sorrow that can never be fully understood by man. So great was this agony that His physical pain was hardly felt."[18]

Danny shudders.

"How horrible!" Barry agrees.

"Satan with his fierce temptations wrung the heart of Jesus. The Saviour could not see through the portals of the tomb. Hope did not present to Him His coming forth from the grave a conqueror, or tell Him of the Father's acceptance of the sacrifice. He feared that sin was so offensive to God that Their separation was to be eternal. Christ felt the anguish which the sinner will feel when mercy shall no longer plead for the guilty race. It was the sense of sin, bringing the Father's wrath upon Him as man's substitute, that made the cup He drank so bitter, and broke the heart of the Son of God."[19]

Danny looks at Barry. "You know we've been friends since first grade. Would I be willing to die for you, to carry your guilt, and never go to heaven?"

"Nope," Barry quips. "Nor would I for you. But if my death meant your salvation, and we could then be together forever in heaven, that would be different. Then I would."

"Me too," Danny smiles. "But look, it was as if Jesus said, 'Father, if I cannot go to heaven if these humans are to be saved, then I'll die and never live with You again, in order that these humans can be with You in My place.' And with that He plunged into the abyss and perished. That's the incredible climax of Calvary. He took our place fully. He died in our place, our death, with all its eternal consequences, so that we could go free and have a future. That's the important fact about this journey we must take through final events. If He died so that we might live in His place, then you know He will never let us slip out of His hands during the trip. If He paid such a price for our salvation, why should we worry if we'll be saved?"

What Happened Next

Barry notices it first. The picture of Christ fills the whole western wall of the gatehouse. The portion portraying the resurrected Christ leaving the open tomb with outstretched arms—that part is a door. The sepulcher entrance and Christ filling the doorway. The young men eagerly walk to the door. Will it be open or not? Barry touches the small black knob, hardly noticeable until he comes up close. He turns and pulls. It opens.

They walk through. "Wow! Amazing! Awesome! Unbelievable!" they exclaim. Words tumble out. They stand in a round room. Across the ceiling and all the walls stretch the grandest painting of the Second Advent they've ever seen. Lights blaze from the floor to make it come alive. Angels fill the canvas, and there on the opposite wall and ceiling, in triumphant majesty, rides the King of kings on His cloudy chariot (Rev. 14:14). The painting portrays His other journey, the one just ahead. How different it is from His first journey!

Barry and Danny just stand there, taking it in. They feel surrounded by that coming event. The one who had built the chapel had planned it that way. Two rooms. One pointing to the past. The other to the future. The first, reminding travelers that their journey would never be a time of trouble like His; the other, to point them to their future rendezvous with Him.

"Look," Danny nudges Barry. "Look around the circle above the floor lights. Graves broken open, saints coming forth. Translated Christians about to ascend. This is it, the end of our journey shown us before we begin."

Barry nods. "That's why the caption reads, 'We . . . will be caught up together with them in the clouds to meet the Lord in the air' (1 Thess. 4:17). We stand between two pictures, two journeys of Christ. He took the first alone so that we do not have to take it. He takes the second so we can complete the journey together. Do you know what I think this means?" Barry pauses to search his friend's inquisitive face.

"Tell me," Danny says.

"We are about to go through last-day events. We do not know how long the journey will be, but we know how far. Yes, we'll scoot around giving the loud cry message and run to the hills and mountains later, but think of the distance we will travel after that! The journey to heaven is literally 'out of this world'!"

The last time I saw them they were climbing the trail that leads up a narrow path. They began the journey right. It begins with a relationship with Christ, whom to know is life eternal (John 17:3).

---

[1] E. G. White, *Testimonies for the Church,* vol. 9, p. 43.
[2] E. G. White, *Prophets and Kings,* p. 537.
[3] E. G. White, *Testimonies for the Church,* vol. 6, p. 129.
[4] E. G. White, *Fundamentals of Christian Education,* pp. 526, 527.
[5] E. G. White, *Testimonies for the Church,* vol. 5, p. 716.
[6] E. G. White, *Early Writings,* p. 120.
[7] E. G. White, *Testimonies to Ministers,* p. 116.
[8] E. G. White, *Christ's Object Lessons,* p. 133.
[9] E. G. White, *Testimonies for the Church,* vol. 5, p. 717.
[10] E. G. White, *The Great Controversy,* pp. 593, 594.
[11] *Ibid.,* p. 590.
[12] E. G. White, *The Desire of Ages,* p. 685.
[13] *Ibid.,* pp. 685, 686.
[14] *Ibid.,* pp. 686, 687.
[15] *Ibid.,* pp. 688-693.
[16] *Ibid.,* pp. 690-693.
[17] *Ibid.,* p. 693.
[18] *Ibid.,* p. 753.
[19] *Ibid.*

Chapter 39

Satan's Final Push for World Domination

Have you ever had a Bible fall apart? Me too. So I took scissors and cut out the book of Daniel and the book of Revelation and put them together under a common cover. That's the smallest Bible I've ever had. Then I discovered a remarkable statement. "The books of Daniel and Revelation should be bound together and published. A few explanations of certain portions might be added, but I am not sure that these would be needed."[1]

The two books help to interpret each other. They contain marvelous insights into our journey through last-day events. If we could get away sometime and read through just the two books, repeating the process from time to time, I believe it would encourage us for the journey ahead.

Take the book of Revelation, for example. Full of Christ, it views the coming crisis only within the context of the coming Christ. It shouts out, "Look up to Christ! He finished His journey and works for you in heaven. He's in the business of getting you through your journey in last-day events!"

Behold the Lamb

"Then I saw a Lamb, looking as if it had been slain, standing in the center of the throne" (Rev. 5:6). Imagine a slain lamb at heaven's throne. What's this all about? Let's look into the throne-room scene.

"There before me was a door standing open in heaven. And the voice I had first heard speaking to me [Jesus, Rev. 1:10] like a trumpet said, 'Come up here, and I will show you what must take place after this'" (Rev.. 4:1). "At once I was in the Spirit, and there before me was a throne in heaven with someone sitting on it" (verse 2). That was God the Father. Twenty-four thrones circled God's throne. Twenty-four human beings sat on them. Each wore a crown, *stephanoi,* or laurel wreath of victory given to winners of an Olympic game. They are not the same as diadems worn by royalty. God wears a diadem. Human beings wear a *stephanos*. Thus, as we saw in previous chapters, they are humans who gained victory and are already in heaven. All had died as martyrs.[2]

Jesus took them to His throne to witness His work on behalf of the human race. They observed His intercession and coming pre-Advent judgment. That's how fair Christ is! He gives human beings this special privilege. I like to think Christ's cousin, John the Baptist, sits among the them. Just as Moses didn't get into the promised land but went to heaven, so perhaps John the Baptist was not saved from death, but maybe was resurrected to be with Christ.

Did you know this happens again in the end-time? There will be some martyrs before the close of probation. John says, "I saw thrones on which were seated those who had been given authority to judge. And I saw the souls of those who had been beheaded [like John the Baptist] because of their testimony for Jesus and because of the word of God. They had not worshiped the beast or his image [end-time persecution, Rev. 13:12-15] and had not received his mark on their foreheads or their hands [verses 16-18]. They came to life and reigned with Christ a thousand years" (Rev. 20:4-6). Just as the 24 elders sit on thrones now, so will the end-time martyrs sit on thrones during the millennium. Both groups receive a special privilege to do a work with Christ that concerns the issue in the cosmic controversy about God's justice. They don't judge that He is just, but see that His self-revelation of justice is authentic.

"But that's not much of a reward," someone might protest. "I would rather live."

Consider the case of John the Baptist. "God never leads His children otherwise that they would choose to be led," Ellen White writes, "if they could see the end from the beginning, and discern the glory of the purpose which they are fulfilling as coworkers with Him. Not Enoch, who was translated to heaven, not Elijah, who ascended in a chariot of fire, was greater or more honored than John the Baptist, who perished alone in the dungeon. 'Unto you it is given in the behalf of Christ, not only to believe on Him, but also to suffer for His sake.' Phil. 1:29. And of all the gifts that Heaven can bestow upon men, fellowship with Christ in His sufferings is the most weighty trust and the highest honor."[3]

You see, martyrs experience just a little of what Christ went through. By no means as much, of course. But the little they endure apparently gives them a deeper appreciation of Christ's sufferings. And that may give them a deeper understanding of Christ's journey through His great time of trouble. For this they'll be forever grateful.

Martyrs often rejoice as they go to death. Paul died a martyr. He suffered many beatings and imprisonments. Yet he said, "I am convinced that neither death nor life, neither angels nor demons, neither the present nor the future, nor any powers, neither height nor depth, nor anything else in all creation, will be able to separate us from the love of God which is in Christ Jesus our Lord" (Rom. 8:38, 39). Even death cannot separate the Christian from Christ. The persecution of the end-time can take everything else from us, but it cannot rob us of Christ.

Christ Is Coming!

The thought of being a martyr frightens many. Look at this good news, though. "But, now I realize that 'God is faithful, who will not suffer you to be tempted above that ye are able; but will with the temptation also make a way to escape, that ye may be able to bear it'" (1 Cor. 10:13, KJV). Martyr John Huss proved that text. The flames couldn't drown out his singing. He sang until his last breath, as if he didn't even feel the flames.[4] Remember, "You don't get a martyr's faith until you are faced with a martyr's fate."

The book of Revelation pictures Jesus in heaven as a slain Lamb. He has 24 victorious humans there with Him. Yet the only one found worthy to open the sealed scroll is Jesus Himself, because He went through a martyrdom that no one else will ever be asked to suffer. Only One ever felt totally forsaken by God (Matt. 27:46). No one else will (Heb. 13:5).

Do you remember Ellen Harmon's (later White) first vision? She saw God's end-time saints climbing up a narrow way that goes to heaven. Those who kept their eyes upon Jesus made it, while those who didn't failed. They fell to the world below. "If they kept their eyes fixed on Jesus, who was just before them, leading them to the city, they were safe."[5] The book of Revelation tells us to look to Jesus working for us in heaven, and Ellen's first vision urges us to gaze on Jesus, who is with us in the journey, leading us to heaven. Both are inspired insights. And both are right. For Christ is doing both. He does not work for us long distance, although He is in heaven. He walks with us on earth (Matt. 28:20) as He works for us in heaven (Heb. 6:19, 20; 7:23-25).

We need to consider something else when thinking of martyrs. There'll be none after the close of probation. "At our happy, holy state the wicked were enraged, and would rush violently up to lay hands on us to thrust us into prison, when we would stretch forth the hand in the name of the Lord, and they would fall helpless to the ground."[6] "The context is just before the Second Advent. The saints are happy. The wicked are helpless. We must always keep this in mind as we face troubles ahead. A day is coming when there will be no martyrs. Period!

A Gathering Under Way

With cunning craft, knowing his time is short, Satan pushes for world domination. His final thrust is under way. Furious, fiendish fervor energizes his troops. He works through many avenues to accomplish his grand design. Long has he laid plans for this hour. His counterfeit churches gain global power as his spirits work through the New Age and charismatic movements, through channeling and tongues, through supernatural messages and healings. "The agencies of evil are combining their forces and consolidating. They are strengthening for the last great crisis."[7]

Here's a document I downloaded from the Internet, written by Ralph Reed, former executive director of the Christian Coalition. It gives insight into this gathering under way. "An emerging partnership of Catholics and Evangelical Protestants is going to be the most powerful force in the electorate beyond the 1990s, and anybody who tries to ignore that alliance will make a big mistake. America's 58 million Catholics—who make up about one-fourth of the electorate—are speaking out more than ever before on the social ills that affect America. The political shift that has occurred throughout our nation in the last 18 months [written January 1996] could not have happened if not for the unprecedented involvement of Roman Catholics.

"That involvement stems from a growing concern among people of faith about the direction of our nation. If anyone ever doubted that we are standing at a turning point, there could be no question based on the 1995 budget impasse. What was going on was not a debate between Republicans and Democrats. It was not about whose estimates we should use to determine what we're going to spend every year.

"On one side is a group of people who believe we ought to maintain policies advocating birth control distribution in schools without parental permission; the teaching of homosexuality as an accepted alternative lifestyle; and abortion on demand paid for with our tax dollars—making the taking of innocent human life the most common surgical procedure in America today.

"On the other side are those who believe that what we face ultimately is not a fiscal problem, but a moral problem. If Congress eliminates the deficit tomorrow but does not address the moral and spiritual crisis that ails America, we will not be able to turn this country around.

"In Washington, it's called the devolution revolution. The idea of taking powers and responsibilities that have been centered there for the last 50 years and sending them back to state, private charities, churches and synagogues, and private individuals, and allowing them to more effectively meet those needs.

"In an encyclical 60 years ago, Pope Pius XI said it better than any political leader has ever said it: 'It is wrong to withdraw from the individual and to commit to the government and the community at large what private industry, enterprise and charity can accomplish. It is an injustice and it is a grave evil.'

"Winston Churchill, the best friend America ever had, once said, 'The American people always do the right thing, after they have exhausted every other possibility.'

"We've tried the sexual revolution, we've tried 'If it feels good, do it,' we've tried 'I'm OK, you're OK.'

"We've tried materialism and inquisitiveness, we've tried filling our lives with the possessions and the rudiments of success. But we have discovered as a society what every other society has discovered: You cannot fill what Pascal called the God-shaped vacuum that is in every person's soul with anything except a personal relationship with Jesus Christ and His Father.

"So it's not just a political change; it is a spiritual shift that is shaping the American political landscape. And Catholics have been at the very center of that.

"According to exit polls taken on Election Day 1994, for the first time in American history, a majority of Roman Catholics voted Republican in an off-year election. Catholics today are now the swing vote in American politics. National candidates know that without the Catholic vote, they cannot hope to govern in America.

"The Catholic vote holds the key to the future of America. I believe Catholics can unite with Evangelical Protestants who share their views on the sanctity of innocent human life, on the need for religious liberty, on school choice and common sense values.

"Christian Coalition recently launched the Catholic Alliance, which will continue to build bridges [note the word] in our partnership with Roman Catholics. But Catholic Alliance isn't all we're doing. The truth is that already 16 percent of Christian Coalition supporters are Roman Catholics.

"My study of American history made me keenly aware of the differences that have divided Catholics and Evangelicals. That distrust and suspicion will not disappear overnight. Many theological differences never will be resolved. But surely the moral and social crisis our nation faces today is a crisis we can address together.

"United by our love for Christ and a broken heart for a nation in need, we can move forward, arms locked in cooperation."

His statement reminds me of one in *The Great Controversy*. "The Protestants of the United States will be foremost in stretching their hands across the gulf to grasp the hand of spiritualism; they will reach over the abyss to clasp hands with the Roman power; and under the influence of this threefold union, this country will follow in the steps of Rome in trampling on the rights of conscience."[8]

The Christian Coalition is mostly a Protestant organization. Pat Robertson began the movement in 1990. Protestants took the initiative to join with what I believe is one form of spiritualism through welcoming the charismatic movement into its churches during the early 1960s. The charismatic movement spread like wildfire through most denominations. It finally entered the Catholic Church in the late 1960s and within a short time spread to the church in a hundred countries. Few churches remain untouched by the phenomena. Church leaders believe that the charismatic movement is God's Holy Spirit being poured out upon His people. "Why," they say, "should we stand aloof from one another when God is working through both Protestants and Catholics!"

"Through the agency of spiritualism, miracles will be wrought, the sick will be healed, and many undeniable wonders will be performed. And as the spirits will profess faith in the Bible, and manifest respect for the institutions of the church, their work will be accepted as a manifestation of divine power."[9]

Before his trip to America some years ago, Pope John Paul II issued an encyclical calling for unity among believers. "If Christians, despite their divisions, can grow ever more united in common prayer around Christ, they will grow in the awareness of how little divides them in comparison to what unites them."[10]

The Christian Front and Sunday

"Protestantism is now reaching hands across the gulf to clasp hands with the papacy, and a confederacy is being formed to trample out of sight the Sabbath of the fourth commandment; and the man of sin, who, at the instigation of Satan, instituted the spurious Sabbath, this child of papacy, will be exalted to take the place of God."[11]

Catholics and Protestants differ totally in essential doctrines. But they are united against abortion and the separation of church and state. They share Sunday and the state of the dead too. If Protestants believe they protest against the church and its doctrines, they're not protesting against these two fundamental beliefs. Think how fallen spirits will give messages to humanity, appearing as their dead loved ones, urging them to keep Sunday. Protestants will applaud!

But how can Satan take over the world when Christian churches constitute a shrinking percentage of the world's population? How can a mostly non-Christian world ever support a so-called Christian Sunday law?

Put another way, one could ask, Why would Muslims, Buddhists, New Agers, atheists, and liberals fall for Sunday? Why would China and North Korea and pan-Europe ever pass a Sunday law? It just doesn't make sense. I can't see Louis Farrikan or Saddam Hussein urging a so-called "Christian" day of worship. It's an important question.

The Sunday Battleground

It does appear impossible at the moment. So we need to look at the state of the world when this impossible unification happens. Obviously things have to be radically different from the way they are now. Let's list some facts.

1. Right now God's angels are holding back the winds of strife (Rev. 7:1-3).

2. So strife is coming.

3. This strife results from lack of morality. Sundaykeepers will "put forth the claim that the fast-spreading corruption is largely attributable to the desecration of the so-called 'Christian Sabbath,' and that the enforcement of Sunday observance would greatly improve the morals of society."[12]

4. Such strife includes natural disasters, such as floods, earthquakes, and fires. "Satan puts his interpretation upon events, and they think, as he would have them, that the calamities which fill the land are a result of Sundaybreaking. Thinking to appease the wrath of God these influential men make laws enforcing Sunday observance."[13]

5. So far we have looked only at America. Now let's examine the global scene. First, note that the angels hold the winds of strife, not just in America, but across the planet. Natural disasters don't bombard only America but blanket the world. "The people of every country on the globe will be led to follow her [America's] example."[14] "The Sabbath question is to be the issue in the great final conflict in which all the world will act a part."[15]

A number of factors could bring it about. Revelation 13 suggests that America will force the inhabitants of the planet to worship the Catholic system, which includes keeping their Sunday (see Rev. 13:12).

Satan's Final Takeover

As the overmastering delusion to the planet, Satan comes as Christ, not just to take over America, but the whole world (cf. Matt. 24:24; 2 Cor.

11:14). Fallen angels work globally in the grand scheme to seize control of the planet (Rev. 16:12-16). In unprecedented numbers such angels speak to human beings everywhere. Satan's global network is ready to push the importance of Sunday. He has a worldwide web.

Why are the nations so gullible?

The answer appears in Revelation 16:13, 14. "Then I saw three evil spirits that looked like frogs; they came out of the mouth of the dragon, out of the mouth of the beast and out of the mouth of the false prophet. They are spirits of demons performing miraculous signs, and they go out to the kings of the whole world, to gather them for the battle on the great day of God Almighty." Fallen spirits use signs, or miracles, to convince humanity of their message. God allows them to gather the human race for a final battle. Because the deception is global, no nation is safe from the demonic onslaught. The evil spirits are mighty beings whose power proves irresistible in the end-time. Furthermore, Satan appears as Christ.

"Through spiritualism, Satan appears as a benefactor of the race, healing the diseases of the people, and professing to present a new and more exalted system of religious faith; but at the same time he works as a destroyer. His temptations are leading multitudes to ruin."[16] "As spiritualism more closely imitates the nominal Christianity of the day, it has a greater power to deceive and ensnare. Satan himself is converted, after the modern order of things. He will appear in the character of an angel of light. Through the agency of spiritualism, miracles will be wrought, the sick will be healed, and many undeniable wonders will be performed. And as the spirits will profess faith in the Bible and manifest respect for the institutions of the church, their work will be accepted as a manifestation of divine power."[17]

Here is what happens:

1. Spirits perform miracles before world leaders.

2. They present a seemingly more exalted form of religion.

3. The spirits profess faith in the Bible.

4. People consider their miracles as of divine origin.

5. Satan performs miracles

Someone might ask why the spirits profess faith in the Bible and Satan comes as Christ if they want to take over the non-Christian world.

Survival is the bottom line. Troubles pound the planet, peril grips the nations. It doesn't matter who saves the race. Fallen angels could impersonate all religious leaders and form a retinue with Satan. Their message would be simple: "Christ is the highest Master in the next life. Follow him, and the world will be spared final devastation." Buddha, Muhammad, and others, all walking around praising the assumed Christ and all performing miracles would convince almost anyone. It would be the greatest spectacle ever seen in human history. Earth's inhabitants would conclude they have nothing to lose. If these revered religious leaders request that the human race observe Sunday in gratitude for the promised deliverance, who wouldn't comply? Survival may well be the most urgent reason that the world universally accepts Sunday.

"Wonderful scenes, with which Satan will be closely connected, will soon take place. God's Word declares that Satan will work miracles. He will make people sick, and then will suddenly remove from them his satanic power. They will then be regarded as healed. These works of apparent healing will bring Seventh-day Adventists to the test."[18]

How do we know that Ellen White was not telling us about Sunday laws just because they were popular in her time? After all, she thought Christ would return then.

Good question! Some consider Ellen White a product of her times. She was a Victorian nineteenth-century writer, they argue, speaking out of her cultural context. Sunday laws, like the Blair bill debated in 1888, proved only a passing phenomenon. Alonzo T. Jones opposed the Blair bill in Congress. Anyone living in the twentieth century, such critics assert, knows that Sunday laws are pretty dead today! Years ago someone wrote an article saying that Communism was the big threat—not Catholicism. What would he say today? One thing is clear. Ellen White wasn't just a product of her time. God showed her the future. That future is in the Bible. So she wasn't tied to her day. She went back to the time of the biblical writers and saw the future as they did. We'll look at that next.

[1] E. G. White, *Testimonies to Ministers,* p. 117.

[2] E. G. White, *The Desire of Ages,* p. 786.

[3] *Ibid.,* pp. 224, 225.

[4] E. G. White, *The Great Controversy,* pp. 109, 110.

[5] See E. G. White, *Early Writings,* p. 14.

[6] *Ibid.,* p. 15.

[7] E. G. White, *Testimonies for the Church,* vol. 9, p. 11.

[8] E. G. White, *The Great Controversy,* p. 588.

[9] *Ibid.*

[10] Quoted by Carolyn Curtis, "The Crucial Catholic Vote," *Christian America* 6, No. 9 (November-December 1995): 13.

[11] Ellen G. White, "An Appeal to Our Ministers and Conference Committees," *Special Testimonies,* Series A, No. 1, p. 38.

[12] E. G. White, *The Great Controversy,* p. 587.

[13] E. G. White, *Last Day Events,* p. 129.

[14] E. G. White, *Testimonies for the Church,* vol. 6, p. 18.

[15] *Ibid.,* p. 352.

[16] E. G. White, *The Great Controversy,* p. 589.

[17] *Ibid.,* p. 588.

[18] E. G. White, *Selected Messages,* book 2, p. 53.

Chapter 40

All the World Wondered

You remember the dragon in Revelation 12:9 is Satan. When we look at verse 3 we see he has seven heads and 10 horns. With that in mind, let's come to Revelation 13:1. What does the sea beast have? Seven heads and 10 horns.

In the counterfeit trinity, Satan is the Father and the sea beast (Catholic Church) is Christ. John, the author of Revelation, quotes Christ: "Anyone who has seen me has seen the Father" (John 14:9). Just as Christ and the Father are look-alikes, so Satan and his priestly/hierarchial system are look-alikes. Jon Paulien has an excellent chapter on this in his book *What the Bible Says About the End-time.*[1] For those who want to dig further, I highly recommend Dr. Paulien's book and the three volumes produced by the General Conference Daniel and Revelation Committee under the auspices of the Biblical Research Institute.[2]

The Sea Beast

So Satan is a counterfeit for the Father, and both have look-alikes in Christ and the Catholic Church respectively. Revelation 13:2 says: "The dragon gave the beast his power and his throne and great authority." Satan empowers the abuses of distorted Christianity. Compare that with Matthew 28:18, in which Jesus says, "All authority in heaven and on earth has been given to me." Just as the Father gave authority to Christ, so the counterfeit Father (Satan) gives authority to the counterfeit Christ (the Catholic hierarchy with its theology and tradition). In Revelation 13:3 one of the heads of the beast church received a deadly wound, but later it healed, just as Christ had a death and resurrection. Also in verse 5 the sea beast speaks "for forty-two months." Although this is the 1,260 years (538-1798) when it had free reign to persecute, it is of interest that Revelation expresses it as 42 months, the same as three and a half years—the length of Christ's ministry.

The beast comes from the water, rising in a populated area of the world, for water in prophecy represents peoples

(Rev. 17:15). It's a *therion* beast, or a wild beast. You'd expect that, since Satan gave the beast its power and great authority. No wonder it is mad at the true church in the end-time (Rev. 12:17)! How truly this false Christ manifests the spirit of its father (Satan), as Christ displayed the spirit of His Father.

Now move to Revelation 13:11. Here we find another beast mentioned. The word "another" can either be another of a different kind *(heteros)* or another of the same kind *(allos)*. It is the same kind in this verse. Furthermore, the word for beast is the same as the sea beast, a *therion*, or wild beast. So we have a beast that acts like the Catholic Church and Satan.

The new beast is "coming out of the earth" (verse 11), or from a comparatively unpopulated place. Where would that be?

Revelation 12 presents the cosmic controversy in four major battles. Battle one takes place in heaven, battle two at the time of Christ, and battle three during the 1,260 years (verses 6, 14-16). During this time Satan sends a flood of water (great numbers of people) to destroy God's saints (verse 15), but the earth helped the church (verse 16). Earth is the opposite of water and symbolizes a comparatively unpopulated area. That's what happened. A religious group known as the Pilgrims fled from heavily populated Europe to the comparatively unpopulated New World, and hence "the earth helped the woman" (verse 16). They sought to escape state church persecution (both Catholic and English Protestant) by traveling to the New World—to a place eventually to be called the United States.

Jesus spoke of such persecution in Matthew 24:22, saying that it would be "cut short." That meant the predicted 1,260 years of persecution would end before 1798. The *Mayflower* sailed in 1620, but not until 1776 did America declare its independence. For the first time in centuries the world now had a country free from state church persecution—just 22 years short of the 1798 date. So we have several ways to determine that the earth beast is America.

Did you know that the same number of people left the *Mayflower* who had boarded it, even though one died at sea? You guessed it. A baby was born—Peregrene White, direct ancestor of James White, husband of E. G. White. I believe God especially watched over that infant as he came across on the *Mayflower,* knowing the link he would have with the founders of the Seventh-day Adventist Church, launched in 1844, named in 1860, and organized in 1863. Revelation 12:17 describes this church as having two distinguishing characteristics: keeping all God's commandments, including the seventh-day Sabbath, and having the testimony of Jesus, that is, the prophetic gift (Rev. 19:10).

Both doctrines have characterized God's church since its beginning. Old Testament saints kept the seventh-day Sabbath and had prophets (Scripture and living ones). Jesus observed the Sabbath and was a prophet. Christians honored the Sabbath and had the prophetic writings in Scripture. And in the end-time God's people will keep the seventh-day Sabbath and have the prophetic gift in Scripture as well as E. G. White and her writings. But that is not all.

Joel 2:28 speaks of the end-time days just ahead: "And afterward, I will pour out my spirit upon all people. Your sons and daughters will prophesy, your old men will dream dreams, your young men will see visions." The day of Pentecost in Acts 2 was a partial fulfillment, for the Holy Spirit was poured out, but the church did not receive any prophetic gift then, just tongues. God reserves the prophetic gift for the end-time, and He will add it to what the end-time church already has.

Isn't it exciting! God will not leave us alone to travel through final events but will speak to us in visions and dreams.

America in the End-time

By contrast, in the end-time, evil spirits pour out of the mouth of the false prophet (Rev. 16:13). They are not individuals who pretend to be Christ (Matt. 24:4, 24) but a movement that pretends to be Christian. The false prophet of Revelation 16 is apostate Protestantism. Once the prophetic voice of God sounded through the reformers. "Rome is anti-Christ. Get out of Rome and be free. The just shall live by faith!" Now most of Protestantism isn't protesting anymore. The prophetic message changed. Increasingly we hear "Support Catholicism. It's the moral force in the world. The Catholic Alliance, with the Christian Coalition, is the way to change America."

The earth beast (America) is another wild beast as it rises from the earth, and it has been so from its beginning. Adventist commentators look at this lamblike beast that becomes like a dragon and say, "This is a progressive picture. America was more lamblike in its earlier history and will finally become dragonlike in the end-time." That is true. But that is not all. The beast was wild, or dragonlike, in its infancy. It even treated many religious groups badly in the colonies. Persecution occurred in the name of Christianity, and thus the Christian front to clothe the dragonlike acts existed from the beginning! Even though the dragonlike activity becomes more intense in the end-time, it will never be without the Christian mask. That's why we monitor the Christian Coalition. Having the Christian garb but not the gospel, it is more interested in Washington than heaven, in political success more than personal salvation, in "Christian" power than in Christ's presence. Their union with Catholics is not an accident, as their movement against Washington resembles more the Catholic crusades than soul winning, is more secular than religious, and is more about control than Christ.

So what about America in the end-time? You don't have to rely upon a nineteenth-century Victorian prophetess to get to the essence. You find it in Revelation 13. Ellen White's comments are God-given on the basis of what in principle already appears in Scripture. She fills out the picture. Her supplemental details agree with the basic outline in the chapter. We need both. I thank God for both. Remember, those who deny E. White her proper function in portraying final events unwittingly overlook the fact that Satan is angry at the end-time prophetic gift (Rev. 12:17; 19:10). He has every reason to be. It exposes his nefarious scheme. We need all the help we can get and gladly accept all inspired insights, ancient or modern. After all, God sent us the information and inspiration because He knows we need it.

Think about it. Satan hates the church that has the prophetic gift and observes the Sabbath. If he has done everything to make Sunday an issue in the world, will he not do everything to turn Ellen White's prophetic gift into an issue in the church? He has done this. We can ignore him on both counts.

Look how Revelation 13:12-15 puts it. We'll translate the symbols. "America exercised all the authority of the prophetic beast on its behalf, and made the world and its inhabitants worship the prophetic beast, whose fatal wound had been healed. And America performed great and miraculous signs, even causing fire to come down from heaven to earth in full view of men. Because of the signs he was given power to do on behalf of the prophetic beast, he deceived the inhabitants of the world. America ordered them to set up an image in honor to the prophetic beast that was wounded by the sword and yet lived. America was given power to give breath to the image of the prophetic beast, so that it could speak and cause all who refused to worship the image to the prophetic beast to be killed."

Let's make a summary of these verses, with comments.

1. America exercises all the authority of the prophetic beast. This does not speak of its superpower status but rather of an authority that is the same as the prophetic beast; that is, it is religious as well as secular.

2. America employs its religious/secular power on behalf of the prophetic beast.

3. America uses signs to deceive the world in this venture to help the prophetic beast.

4. America causes fire to come from heaven (an allusion to Elijah bringing fire down on the altar on Mount Carmel to demonstrate God's power) to authenticate its mission to cause the world to worship the prophetic beast.

5. America causes an image to be made to the prophetic beast. The prophetic beast is a union of church and state, and so the image will also be a union of church and state. Note that America orders the inhabitants of the world to set up this image. The fact that America is ordering a religious law suggests that the union of church and state is already a fact in America at that time. Now America forces the same thing in other countries. Such a union of church and state results in a Sunday law, beginning first in America, then adopted worldwide.

Clearly America is going to change. Right now it has enormous influence in the world. The United States is the only superpower left. Since the demise of Communism, America stands poised to fulfill these verses. I believe the fall of Communism should tell us that the time is near when we will see this passage become reality. America is about to become more dragonlike than ever before. But it will be dragonlike in a so-called Christian cause, to bring honor and worship to a Christian religious system. This is the lamblike exterior to its crusade.

Strategy of the Christian Coalition

In chapter 3 of his book *One Nation Under God,* Clifford Goldstein exposes the strategy of the Christian Coalition leaders. Getting Christians to think they are victims of persecution will do more to galvanize them than anything else. And it's working. The enemy includes liberal politicians, humanists, and the press.

"Juxtaposing a picture of the fallen Berlin Wall with one of an abortion protestor being arrested, an advertisement by Pat Robertson's American Center for Law and Justice (ACLJ) asks, 'Have we won the cold war . . . only to lose our own freedom?'

"Jerry Falwell warns that 'Bible-believing Christianity' has been 'outlawed' in America.

"Pat Buchanan bemoans the 'Christian-bashing' so prevalent in America today.

"William Bennett reports that it's 'open season' on Christians.

"Tim LaHaye warns about 'the government-inspired religious persecution that is going on in America today in the name of the First Amendment.'

"The Rutherford Institute writes about 'religious apartheid' against Christians.

"Charles Colson says that Christians have become a 'persecuted minority.'

"Even James Dobson has warned: 'I believe that Christian oppression is just around the corner. I really believe that the level of anger rising out of the homosexual community primarily, but the whole humanistic movement that's out there . . . as they gain political power—and they have it now—they're going to continue to oppress us.'

"New Right lawyer Keith Fournier explains: 'Day after day, the news media brings us horrific reports from the Balkans, Africa and other foreign countries of ethnic-based attacks all too reminiscent of the infamous Holocaust. . . . And yet, a similar insanity is being perpetrated before our eyes in our own country. But ethnic origin isn't the target. It's religion and those who embrace it.'"[3]

I agree with Clifford Goldstein's evaluation. His book is must reading! Just think, apartheid, holocaust against Christians in America? Have you seen any such persecutions of Christians anywhere in America? OK, there's some nasty press, and films make fun, and not all go to church, and liberals think Christians are wacky. But that's a long way from the vaunted cries of the Christian Right. Why, Christians have freedom of religion and tax-free churches, can join whichever church they wish, make billions in sales, and enjoy freedom from any state coercion. The ministers leading them have tax-free parsonage allowances. Such individuals sound like spoiled brats who need to grow up. Knowing nothing about persecution, they need to be ashamed of themselves. Read Goldstein's whole chapter. It is a real eye-opener!

The fact of the matter is that I believe these Christians actually lie about persecution to stir up the political troops, to raise money, and to achieve their agenda. They are power hungry, seek control, and when the time comes will do the very thing to others that they scream about now. Often people see in others that which they have within. Prophecy tells us that a so-called

Christian cause in America will lead to the imposition of a day of worship with a death decree to enforce it (Rev. 13:12-15).[4] Then we'll have a holocaust. Then Christians really will be persecuted. And those screaming about it now will be the ones inflicting it then!

Look Out—It Could Happen Again

The First Amendment's protection is only a piece of paper! Yes, it says Congress shall make no law restricting religion. But that can be overridden if deemed in the best interest of the country. Personal freedom takes second place to national freedom. In a state of emergency the president has special emergency powers. In fact, 470 of them!

In his book *One Nation Under God* Rus Walton documents the 1932 use of emergency powers by President Franklin Roosevelt. Roosevelt had campaigned on a drastic reduction of government, on a balanced annual budget, and on a sound currency. But look what the people got. "The number and powers of federal agencies exploded into a nightmare of alphabets (AAA, NRA, NLRB, PWA, WPA)." Also "the federal budget zoomed and the national debt increased (in the first four years of the Roosevelt administration, spending increased 85 percent: the federal debt increased 72 percent; and the number of federal employees rose 48 percent)." America went off the gold standard and devalued the dollar. "All this was done," Rus Walton said, "in the name of emergency, in the name of economic panic and the banking crisis. By Mr. Roosevelt's own admission in his book, *On Our Way*, the banking crisis lasted only one week."[5]

Japanese-Americans lost their freedom after Japan's attack on Pearl Harbor. Not only ships lay sunk, but American dreams, too. Yanked away from their homes, carted off to internment camps, they discovered that the Bill of Rights suddenly meant nothing. The national fear that Japanese-Americans might collude with the enemy fired the roundup. Nothing is secure about the constitutional protections when national interest is at stake. Through the duration of the war these American citizens eked out an existence as prisoners of war. They had no recourse. It didn't matter if they supported Japan or not. Their professed loyalty to America meant nothing. Instead, the color of their ancestral skin meant everything.

If it happened before, it will happen again. When unprecedented natural disasters shake the country, this will throw America into a national emergency. Governments will exercise unusual powers to save the nation. Consider the scenario. "While appearing to the children of men as a great physician who can heal all their maladies, he [Satan] will bring disease and disaster, until populous cities are reduced to ruin and desolation. Even now he is at work. In accident and calamities by sea and by land, in great conflagrations, in fierce tornadoes and terrific hailstorms, in tempests, floods, cyclones, tidal waves, and earthquakes, in every place and in a thousand forms, Satan is exercising his power. He sweeps away the ripening harvest, and famine and distress follow. He imparts to the air a deadly taint, and thousands perish by the pestilence. These visitations are to become more and more frequent and disastrous. . . . And then the great deceiver will persuade men that those who serve God are causing these evils."[6]

"Those who honor the Bible Sabbath will be denounced as enemies of law and order, as breaking down the moral restraints of society, causing anarchy and corruption, and calling down the judgments of God upon the earth." Then "the dignitaries of church and state will unite to bribe, persuade, or compel all classes to honor the Sunday. The lack of divine authority will be supplied by oppressive enactments. Political corruption is destroying love of justice and regard for truth; and even in free America, rulers and legislators, in order to secure public favor, will yield to the popular demand for a law enforcing Sunday observance. Liberty of conscience, which has cost so great a sacrifice, will no longer be respected."[7] Note the popular demand for a Sunday law. Bribery and compulsion will be used to implement it, and religious liberty will be thrown to the winds.

In this context Ellen White quotes Revelation 12:17, in which Satan is angry against the church that keeps the commandments of God and thus wars against it. So we are dealing with more than emergency powers. We are facing Satan's attempt to take over the world through compelling the American government to legislate his false Sabbath. He causes immense problems, both moral and material, then introduces his own solution—keep Sunday. It appears that the Christian Coalition fits into this scenario.

Another Trap

Satan plunged our planet into the Fall through deception. He plans to finish the job the same way. He will appeal to the senses. We live in a sense-drenched society. Because we are glued to TV, MTV, videos, films, and World Wide Web, he'll give them a visual display.

Fire From Heaven

Do you remember when fire fell from heaven?

First Kings 18 tells the familiar story. Elijah worshiped only God, while most of Israel also worshiped Baal. Who was the true God? That issue brought 450 prophets of Baal and 400 prophets of Asherah to Mount Carmel with Elijah (1 Kings 18:19). All day the Baal worshipers begged their god to send fire on their sacrifice. Nothing happened, even though they wailed loud and long and slashed themselves deeply. They carried on all day and fell exhausted.

Elijah soaked his sacrifice with water and filled the ditch around it. He prayed a simple prayer. Fire fell from the heavens, consuming sacrifice and altar. It was a dramatic endorsement of the true God! America will stage the same test. One can imagine reporters flocking in from all over the world. Much is at stake, since it is part of Satan's bid to take over the planet. He will deceive the world through dragon America that appears as a lamb. "We are here to seek your affirmation, O God. Our mission is to get the whole world to worship you and your church and the Sunday law that is sacred. If our cause is holy and just and will save the planet from coming destruction, then answer, we beg you, by fire." Fire falls from heaven, and all rejoice and dash out to implement America's (really Satan's) plan.

In commenting on Revelation 13:13, 14, Ellen White wrote, "No mere impostures are here foretold. Men are deceived by the miracles which Satan's agents have power to do, not which they pretend to do."[8] Besides his agents bringing fire from heaven, look who else gets into the act. "Satan will come in to deceive if possible the very elect. He claims to be Christ, and he is coming in, pretending to be the great medical missionary. He will cause fire to come down from heaven in the sight of men to prove that he is God."[9] It seems there will be multiple "fire falling" demonstrations. America and Satan will use the false Mount Carmel test to prove their authenticity. Satan claims to be God, and his dragon power works through the lamblike facade of America to deceive the world.

Through deceptive miracles America will lead the world to worship false Christianity. Let's paraphrase Revelation 13:3, 4: "The whole world was astonished and followed false Christianity. Men worshiped Satan because he had given authority to the prophetic beast, and they also worshiped it and asked, 'Who is like the prophetic beast? Who can make war against it?' " It is a statement of great confidence. The church seems invulnerable.

Where Are We Now?

How soon will America lead the world to worship Satan and false Christianity? If we could look behind the scenes, we'd be amazed. For a start, the Vatican has diplomats from around the world. It's like a united nations. The power of the church is felt around the world as no other religious institution. Pope John Paul II is the most traveled pope ever to occupy the papal chair. Looked up to by statesmen everywhere, he wields an enormous influence through his journeys and writings.

Often we check where we are in final events by looking at happenings in America. But we need also to consider what is occurring on the global scene. America will not have to start from scratch in leading the world to worship false Christianity. Much groundwork is already in place.

Besides that, the union of church and state in America is not just a future event but something already in process. The sweeping influence of the Christian Coalition in American politics parallels Catholic influence in international politics. The Christian Coalition carries a moral agenda that it expects senators and congressmen to carry out. It believes it has a right to expect them to fight for their agenda, because the Coalition helped them get elected in the first place. The Christian Coalition members work the grass roots to elect their candidates, and they expect a payoff for their efforts. It has become one of the most powerful lobbies on Capital Hill.

While the Christian Coalition has been gaining unprecedented influence in American politics in an unexpectedly short time since its inception, another concurrent movement is also hard at work paving the way for the final success of the Christian Coalition. I speak of the attack on the wall of separation between church and state. Some believe that church and state should be absolutely separate. But that doesn't make sense, because laws against killing and stealing, to name two, appear in God's Ten Commandments as well as in the laws of the land. Religious influence in governing is proper. Many of the early leaders in America were men of faith. So the state can be appropriately influenced by things of the church.

But that's only one side of the debate. The Pilgrim Fathers fled from a Europe for the most part dominated by state churches. Such churches forced their dogmas through the various governments. Papal persecution was one result of a government imposing the wishes of a state church. It was to protect against the illegitimate control of the state by the church that America's founders established the wall of separation in the First Amendment separation clause of the American Constitution. Today, some revisionists try to rewrite history, saying that America was a Christian country from the beginning, as if church and state were united in all the colonies. They claim that the separation of church and state led to humanism in the public schools when the educational system disallowed God and prayer in the public schools. Thus they blame the moral collapse of the country on this wall of separation of church and state. And what they say does have some truth in it.

Just as the Berlin Wall came crashing down, and the wall of Communism too, so some believe the time has arrived to bring down the wall of separation between church and state in America. In a December 9, 1991, cover story, "America's Holy War," *Time* investigated this drive in the country. In 1980 the Supreme Court decided "more religion cases than ever before." The "establishment" and "free exercise" of religion clause in the First Amendment states that "Congress, and by extension, the states, 'shall make no law respecting the establishment of religion, or prohibiting the free exercise thereof.'" In modern times the Supreme Court interprets this clause to mean that government should not do a thing that promotes religion. As *Time* reports: "The backlash was a long time coming, but now it is here with vengeance."[10] And now it works to break down the wall!

"Look," they say, "the separation of church and state has thrown God and religion out of the public school so American kids may as well attend school in China." One has to ask whether a nation claiming "One nation under God" on its coins and dollar bill is really still the same today. Why is it right for Congress to begin each day with prayer when it bans prayer from their children's classrooms? Do the leaders of the land need God more than their children? (Some may say yes.) One has to wonder how the Supreme Court can forbid the Ten Commandments being on display in public school classrooms when in their building hangs the picture of Moses receiving the Ten Commandments. There's a radical inconsistency here. It blatantly exposes the difference between the time when congressional chaplains were instituted and the Supreme Court painting commissioned, and the way some now interpret laws to control public classrooms all across the country today. I sympathize with the Christian

Coalition in their frustration, but not in their solution.

Think of the Pennsylvania Supreme Court that threw out the conviction of a killer who slew a 70-year-old woman with an axe merely because the prosecutor "unlawfully" mentioned a biblical law to the jury in his summation statement asking for the death penalty. Or consider the Decatur, Illinois, primary teacher who ordered her 7-year-olds to strike out the word "God" in a phonetics textbook, saying it was against the law. What about the Oak Park, Illinois, town authorities who refused to allow the Catholic hospital to have a cross erected on its own smokestack because the councilors thought local residents would be offended?[11]

Little wonder that the Christian Coalition has a cause! Or that Christians are irked! The debate does have two sides, though. The separationists point out that America is far more diverse than when the Supreme Court in 1892 said, "This is a Christian nation." Today America has 1,200 different religious bodies, many of them non-Christian, and so "the only way to keep the peace is to keep them all out of the shared public sphere. Too many wars have been fought," they remind us, "too many freedoms crushed in God's name, for a democracy to try to integrate theology into its public life." The accommodationists protest that the wall of separation has grown so thick that instead of freedom of religion, we now have freedom from religion. "A nation's identity is informed by morality, and morality by faith. How can people freely debate issues like nuclear arms or the death penalty, how can children be educated, without any reference to spiritual heritage?"[12]

The horrible fact is God-bashers have had the upper hand for about 40 years. But just as Republicans took control of the Congress for the first time in 40 years, so the accommodationists are winning the separation-of-church-and-state battle after 40 years of defeats. "'The wall of separation between church and state is a metaphor based on bad history,' declared Chief Justice William Rehnquist in 1985. 'It should be frankly and explicitly abandoned.'"[13]

The Bottom Line

Our planet is closer to all the world wondering after the beast than many realize. Some Adventists demand, "Where's there any agitation for Sunday today? Why, entrepreneurs still do a roaring trade on Sunday afternoons. Anyway," they say, "this is a secular society, and many citizens couldn't care less about Sunday." Sunday means football or baseball—not church. Yet behind the scenes Satan lays his plans in stealth. The Christian Coalition has changed everything in American politics, and the Supreme Court is undermining the separation of church and state. America staggers at the edge of a precipice.

Soon—no one knows how soon—disaster will decide America's destiny. There's no way out. The die is cast. National emergency will kick in a national Sunday law. It will come with overwhelming surprise to many. But, then, so do all emergency powers and their implementation.

---

[1] Jon Paulien, *What the Bible Says About the End-time* (Hagerstown, Md.: Review and Herald Pub. Assn., 1994). John F. Walvoord speaks of the "evil trinity." "Satan corresponding to God the Father, the first beast corresponding to Christ, and the second beast corresponding to the Holy Spirit?" *(The Revelation of Jesus Christ* [Chicago: Moody, 1966/1989], p. 211).

[2] *Symposium on Daniel* (Washington, D.C.: Biblical Research Institute, 1986); *Symposium on Revelation* (Washington, D.C.: Biblical Research Institute, 1992), vols. 1 and 2. All three edited by Frank B. Holbrook.

[3] Clifford Goldstein, *One Nation Under God: Bible Prophecy—When the American Experiment Fails* (Boise, Idaho: Pacific Press, 1995), pp. 29, 30.

[4] E. G. White, *Last Day Events,* pp. 123-142.

[5] Rus Walton, *One Nation Under God* (Nashville: Nelson, 1987), pp. 20, 21.

[6] E. G. White, *The Great Controversy,* pp. 589, 590.

[7] *Ibid.,* p. 592.

[8] *Ibid.,* p. 553.

[9] E. G. White, *Medical Ministry* (Mountain View, Calif.: Pacific Press, 1932), pp. 87, 88.

[10] Nancy Gibbs in *Time,* Dec. 9, 1991, p. 61.

[11] *Ibid.*

[12] *Ibid.,* p. 62.

[13] *Ibid.,* p. 63.

Chapter 41

The Early Time of Trouble

Did you know the book of Acts will repeat itself? "Study carefully in the book of Acts the experiences of Paul and the other apostles," urged Ellen White, "for God's people in our day must pass through similar experiences."[1] Just as the book of Acts starts with Pentecost (chapter 2), so the coming Pentecost arrives at the beginning of the journey through final events. There's a wonderful parallel involved. The Holy Spirit comes in both Pentecosts—in the former rain (Acts 2) and the latter rain (Joel 2:28, 29)—to lead and guide the saints. Let's watch His guidance in Acts.

The Holy Spirit in Charge

The book of Acts mentions the Holy Spirit at least 70 times.[2] Although Jesus appeared to Paul (9:3-5, 17), believers received visions (16:9; 18:9), and the angels aided human beings (12:7, 23), the Holy Spirit is the predominant administrator of the early church. Thus Christ gave commands through the Holy Spirit (1:2). The Spirit baptized (verse 5), empowered (verse 8), was poured out (2:17, 33), and fell on believers (10:44-47). He gave utterance (2:4), the church considered Him the Spokesman (1:16; 4:25; 28:25), and He filled Christians (2:4; 4:8, 31; 6:3, 5; 7:55; 11:22-24).

The church recognized the Holy Spirit as its leader. He directed in the ordination of Saul and Barnabas (13:2, 3) and sent them out on a missionary journey (verse 4). The Spirit directed Paul not to enter Asia (16:6, 7) and guided Philip to the eunuch (8:29), then carried him to his next assignment (verse 39). Besides speaking to Peter (10:19; 11:12), the Spirit gave a message to Paul through Agabus (21:10, 11), and told Paul in every city about his future afflictions and imprisonments (20:22, 23). And the Christians at Tyre conveyed a message from the Holy Spirit to Paul not to go to Jerusalem (21:4).

It's interesting to note that Paul sometimes received direct communication from the Holy Spirit, and at other times through other Christians. The Holy Spirit produced a consciousness of His leadership among them all. In fact, in a letter to the church the leaders wrote near its conclusion, "For it has seemed good to the Holy Ghost and to us, to lay upon you no greater burden than these necessary things" (15:28, KJV). They had the right order—the Holy Spirit first, and human leaders next. We find the Spirit opening Lydia's heart to Paul's speaking (16:14), and Peter, John, and Paul laying hands on those yet ignorant of the Holy Spirit that they might receive His leadership (8:15-17; 19:6).

The early church had a burden to follow the Holy Spirit and have all members be filled with His presence. Although imprisonment (4:3; 5:18; 12:4; 16:23, 24; 22:24; 24:27), stoning (14:19), and beatings (5:40; 16:23) plagued Christians, yet the leadership of the Holy Spirit showed itself stronger than Satan's opposition. Tremendous numbers joined the church—3,000 at Pentecost (2:41), a figure that jumped to 5,000 just two chapters later (4:4). The following chapter records "more and more men and women believed in the Lord and were added to their number" (5:14). By the next chapter we read: "And the word of God increased; and the number of the disciples multiplied in Jerusalem greatly; and a great company of the priests were obedient to the faith" (6:7, KJV). Beyond the shores of Palestine the results were the same. Throughout Macedonia "the churches were strengthened in the faith, and they increased in numbers daily" (16:5, RSV).

In Thessalonica furious men shouted, "These that have turned the world upside down are come hither also" (17:6, KJV). The world had been shaken to its roots, not by these men, but by the Holy Spirit through them. He, and not they, had built up the church, for "in the comfort of the Holy Spirit it was multiplied" (9:31, RSV).

And who were these men, anyway? Peter the coward and Paul the persecutor—not very likely candidates for such an unpopular mission. But when the Holy Spirit filled them, He changed them. And what a transformation! The coward became a man of conviction. The persecutor became a proclaimer. That's what the Holy Spirit does. Indeed, Paul knew from experience that the change within a human being "comes from the Lord who is the Spirit" (2 Cor. 3:18, RSV).

All of Christ's disciples let Him down in His greatest hour of need. But not now. Formerly frightened men strode forth fearlessly to turn the world upside down. Bold preaching of the risen Christ shattered the status quo. Signs and miracles, including even resurrections (Acts 20:9-12) called into question the present order. The book of Acts throbs with the life-giving power of the Holy Spirit. Acts proclaims His acts, not those of the disciples. He, the Holy Spirit, made the decisive difference. We could rename the book "Acts of the Holy Spirit," an observation recorded as early as the fourth century by Church Father Chrysostom.[3]

Coming Pentecost

Scared saints, take courage! The coming outpouring of God's Spirit will transform you too! You'll be shocked, amazed, astounded—and you'll rejoice. "As the time comes for it [the message of the third angel] to be given with greatest power, the Lord will work through humble instruments, leading the minds of those who consecrate themselves to His service. The laborers will be qualified rather by the unction of His Spirit than by the training of literary institutions. Men of faith and prayer will be constrained to go forth with holy zeal, declaring the words which God gives them."[4]

God will use trained people too—if they're humble—just as He did Paul. God is willing to use anyone willing to be used. That's the good news. "Many . . . will be seen hurrying hither and thither, constrained by the Spirit of God to bring the light to others. The truth, the Word of God, is as a fire in their bones, filling them with a burning desire to enlighten those who sit in darkness. Many, even among the uneducated, now proclaim the words of the Lord. Children are impelled by the Spirit to go forth and declare the message from heaven. The Spirit is poured out upon all who will yield to its prompting, and, casting off all man's machinery, his binding rules and cautious methods, they will declare the truth with the might of the Spirit's power. Multitudes will receive the faith and join the armies of the Lord."[5]

"Servants of God, with their faces lighted up and shining with holy consecration, will hasten from place to place to proclaim the message from heaven. By thousands of voices, all over the earth, the warning will be given. Miracles will be wrought, the sick will be healed, and signs and wonders will follow the believers. Satan also works with lying wonders, even bringing down fire from heaven in the sight of men. Thus the inhabitants of the earth will be brought to take their stand."[6]

An age of power is coming. God will send miracles and wonders. But so does Satan. That's not business as usual. "At the commencement of the time of trouble, we were filled with the Holy Ghost as we went forth and proclaimed the Sabbath more fully."[7] "'The commencement of that time of trouble,' here mentioned, does not refer to the time when the plagues shall begin to be poured out, but to a short period just before they are poured out, while Christ is in the sanctuary."[8]

Apparently the early time of trouble occurs between the Sunday law and the close of probation. That is the time of the final invitation to the world to join Christ and keep His Sabbath. Messengers proclaim it everywhere.

We need to stop here and make a point. The latter rain does empower the messengers but doesn't prepare them. What do we mean? Put it this way. I cannot say, "Oh, well, I've got plenty of time. No Sunday agitation yet. I'll get ready when the Sunday law and Holy Spirit arrive. Right now I'll do my own thing. The Spirit will get me ready." Unfortunately, that is not a new attitude. Years ago Mrs. White wrote, "I saw that many were neglecting the preparation so needful and were looking to the time of 'refreshing' and the 'latter rain' to fit them to stand in the day of the Lord, and to live in His sight. Oh, how many I saw in the time of trouble, without a shelter! They had neglected the needful preparation."[9]

We shall return to the question of how to get ready shortly. But right now, notice that it will be too late to wait for the Holy Spirit to transform us during the early time of trouble, since the Holy Spirit comes at its beginning and the early time of trouble commences with the Sunday law, for the proclamation during this period is about the Sabbath.

The Stealth Campaign

In the previous chapter we noted that Sunday is not being agitated publicly right now. It suits Satan's plan to work quietly in the background. He knows Seventh-day Adventists expect a national Sunday law as well as an international Sunday law. Satan wants them to be unprepared when Sunday laws break upon the scene. The Sunday laws agitated in the 1880s served as a warning to get ready. Yet God brought a message about Christ, not about Sunday laws, to the delegates at the Minneapolis General Conference session. Knowing Christ is the only way to get ready. Look to Him. Before this time, too many had looked to human leaders. Now it was time to look to Christ.

You remember the old Adventist engraving depicting the spiritual journey from Eden lost to Eden restored? The law filled the center of the picture, with Calvary shunted off to the side. Ellen White ordered a new picture entitled "Christ the Way." It had the law in the background and Calvary placed in the center. The first 40 years of our church history focused on the law, for after all the Sabbath was a new discovery and was important to us; we wanted to share it. But we often did it without giving Christ His proper place, so that believers became, as Ellen White reminded us, as dry as the hills of Gilboa. The new focus looked at the law in the context of Christ. Spiritual floods fell on spiritually dry ground, and life sprang up. Saints revived.

The function of the Holy Spirit is always to bring attention to Christ and Calvary, rather than to human beings and their works. While many wait for a Sunday law, Satan has prepared for one in stealth. It waits around the corner, even though not grabbing the headlines yet. The sudden inbreaking of the early time of trouble and the Sunday law starts the final journey. One has to be ready for the launch, just as much as for a space trip. It's too late to jump aboard the shuttle when countdown has commenced. When the Sunday law and Holy Spirit comes, it will be too late to take the journey. Now is the only time to get aboard.

"I was shown God's people waiting for some change to take place—a compelling power to take hold of them. But they will be disappointed, for they are wrong. They must act, they must take hold of the work themselves and earnestly cry to God for a true knowledge of themselves."[10]

The Thief in the Night

Christ warned that His return will be "like a thief in the night" (Matt. 24:43; Luke 12:39). Paul (1 Thess. 5:2, 4), Peter (2 Peter 3:10), and John (Rev. 3:3) speak of the sudden coming of Christ as a thief. Is it possible for Seventh-day Adventists to experience thief-in-the-night unreadiness for Christ's return? After all, they expect Christ to arrive after the Sunday law, death decree, and plagues. How could surprise ever overtake them? Well, the answer is never if we think of the Second Advent itself. But if the thief-in-the-night experience occurs before His coming—that's a different matter.

Remember the prophetic promise, "I will send you the prophet Elijah before that great and dreadful day of the Lord comes" (Mal. 4:5)? So out come the Old Testament teachers with a chart of final events relative to the First Advent. Before the Advent they place Elijah's coming. So at least they can wait until Elijah arrives. Then they'll know Christ is coming for sure. The chart will be their guide. Right?

One day Christ's disciples asked Him a question about that chart. "'Why then do the teachers of the law say that Elijah must come first?' Jesus replied, 'To be sure, Elijah comes and will restore all things. But I tell you, Elijah has already come, and they did not recognize him, but have done to him everything they wished. In the same way the Son of Man is going to suffer at their hands.' Then the disciples understood that he was talking to them about John the Baptist" (Matt. 17:10-13).

The people of Jesus' time clung to their coming-events charts and missed both events—the advent of Elijah and that of Christ. Now it doesn't come any worse than that! Two events charted—both missed. The chart really wasn't worth very much.

We need to settle something. The thief-in-the-night experience isn't at Christ's return; that will be too late. After the Sunday law, death decree, great time of trouble, plagues, and the launching of Armageddon, we can expect the Second Advent. But what if the thief-in-the-night experience takes place before all those events? That's a different matter.

Remember, some members wait for the latter rain to prepare them for heaven, only to find it's too late. That's the thief-in-the-night experience, to be unready for the latter rain. Now is the time to get ready. Satan keeps Sunday developments hidden, so that passage of the Sunday law will catch Adventists off guard and thus unready for the latter rain. His strategy is not only to take over the world but to do so by controlling the church that keeps him from his goal.

"Wait a minute," someone might complain, "it isn't fair that Adventists have their thief-in-the-night experience back during the latter rain. That's earlier than other Christians, for the period from the Sunday law to the close of probation still allows time for them to accept the Sabbath truth. So it appears that Adventists must be ready at the beginning of the early time of trouble, whereas other Christians can slip in even near the end of that period."

"That's a superficial way to look at it," another might protest. "Think of it this way. The invitation is, 'Come out of her, my people' (Rev. 18:4). These people are already Christ's people, and therefore ready for His coming. They are ready now just as Adventists must be. The only thing they need to do is to see the truth of the Sabbath and accept it. It takes only a few moments for truth to dawn. By contrast, it requires time to get to know Christ. Those who do not know Him, even if they are Adventists, will be lost (John 17:3). There simply isn't sufficient time to get to know Him. That's one reason God permits a long delay before the latter rain begins (cf. Rev. 7:1-4). God doesn't want 'anyone to perish, but everyone to come to repentance. But the day of the Lord will come like a thief. The heavens will disappear with a roar; the elements will be destroyed by fire, and the earth and everything in it will be laid bare' (2 Peter 3:9, 10)."

Clearly, Peter places the thief in the night at the Advent, and not at some time before. But readiness, or unreadiness, occurs before the Advent. Thus, of the ten virgins waiting for the return of Christ five were found unready (Matt. 25:1-13). Scripture links the Second Advent to the thief-in-the-night experience because that is when people find out they're unready. Jesus warned, "Many will say to me on that day, 'Lord, Lord, did we not prophesy in your name, and in your name drive out demons and perform many miracles?' Then I will tell them plainly, 'I never knew you. Away from me, you evildoers'" (Matt. 7:22, 23; cf. Luke 13:26, 27).

Here's the bottom line: To be ready for the second coming of Christ we must be ready for the second coming of the Holy Spirit. But to be unready for the coming of the Holy Spirit is to be unready for the coming of Christ. That's the thief in the night. It appears that God's people receive the Holy Spirit while the others accept counterfeit power that gives them ability to perform miracles. All will be filled with power during the times of trouble. The power will either be from Christ or from Satan. Even in Christ's parable of the ten virgins, the five foolish must have gotten oil (power) for they banged on the door to get in (Matt. 25:8-13).

The Holy Spirit Resisted

Many members never will receive the latter rain. But not only that, they'll resist the latter rain, just as the Jewish leaders fought John the Baptist and Christ (Matt. 17:10-13). "There is to be in the [Seventh-day Adventist] churches a wonderful manifestation of the power of God, but it will not move upon those who have not humbled themselves before the Lord, and opened the door of the heart by confession and repentance. In the manifestation of that power which lightens the earth with the glory of God, they will see only something which in their blindness they think dangerous, something which will arouse their fears, and they will brace themselves to resist it. Because the Lord does not work according to their ideas and expectations they will oppose the work. 'Why,' they say, 'should we not know the Spirit of God, when we have been in the work so many years?'"[11]

Tragically, some church members will oppose the very power of God that will take them through final events. There's no greater blindness than that! For that reason Christ offers Laodicea, the end-time church, eyesalve so it can see. The problem is that Laodicea doesn't think it is blind, doesn't realize it lacks discernment, and concludes it needs nothing (Rev. 3:17-20).

Some Jews resisted Christ because He did not arrive according to their expectations. He came as a humble teacher-Saviour, without any earthly kingdom, but they assumed that He would appear as a conquering king to liberate them from the hated Romans. God warns, "Only those living up to the light they have will receive greater light. Unless we are daily advancing in the exemplification of the active Christian virtues, we shall not recognize the manifestations of the Holy Spirit in the latter rain. It may be falling on hearts all around us, but we shall not discern or receive it."[12] "Every precaution must be taken to prevent spiritual declension, lest the great day of the Lord overtake us as a thief in the night."[13]

How Many Adventists Will Experience the Thief in the Night?

This section may shock you. I hate to write it, since it is the worst part of teaching last-day events. I wish I could gloss over it. But that would not be honest. God revealed the magnitude of the problem to level with us. He did not tell us to scare us but to prepare us, to make us realize we need Him. It's a reality check God gives in love, to lead us away from self-dependence to total dependence upon Him.

Ellen G. White said, "I have tried in the fear of God to set before His people their danger and their sins, and have endeavored, to the best of my feeble powers, to arouse them. I have stated startling things, which if they had been believed, would have caused them distress and terror, and led them to zeal in repenting of their sins and iniquities. I have stated before them that, from what was shown me, but a small number of those now professing to believe the truth would eventually be saved—not because they could not be saved, but because they would not be saved in God's own appointed way."[14]

Wait a minute. Doesn't that apply to back then, rather than to the future?

Yes, it first had in mind 1868 to 1871.[15] But look what comes next.

"As the storm approaches, a large class who have professed faith in the third angel's message, but have not been sanctified through obedience to the truth, abandon their position and join the ranks of opposition."[16] Sounds like an exodus. But how large is it, and does it relate to the end-time? The answer is specific and staggering. "When the law of God is made void [Sunday law], the church will be sifted by fiery trials, and a larger proportion than we now anticipate, will give heed to seducing spirits and doctrines of devils. Instead of being strengthened when brought into strait places, many prove that they are not living branches of the True Vine; they bore no fruit, and the husbandmen taketh them away."[17]

That's a specific prophecy about the effect of the Sunday law upon many Seventh-day Adventists. Fallen spirits and their doctrines will overcome them. They'll give up at precisely the time when they need to be ready to receive the latter rain to take them through final events. It doesn't get any more tragic than that!

But how many capitulate? "When the religion of Christ is most held in contempt, when His law is most despised [Sunday law], then should our zeal be the warmest and our courage and firmness the most unflinching. To stand in defense of truth and righteousness when the majority forsake us, to fight the battles of the Lord when champions are few—this will be our test. At this time we must gather warmth from the coldness of others, courage from their cowardice, and loyalty from their treason."[18]

A majority leave the church. Ellen White has their cowardice and coldness in mind here. "The church may appear as about to fall, but it does not fall. It remains, while the sinners in Zion will be sifted out—the chaff separated from the precious wheat. This is a terrible ordeal, but nevertheless it must take place."[19]

How to Prepare for the Latter Rain

I don't want to be in that majority, do you? Of course you don't. Then how do we get ready for the latter rain? That's the important question. Eternal life hangs on this one. This is the most important part of all in the book. To miss it is to miss everything.

Satan blinded those Seventh-day Adventists in the Old Testament: those who kept the seventh-day Sabbath and believed in Christ's advent. He got them busy in all sorts of things, such as producing many human-made laws for religious purposes. After all, they worked for the church, for God's people. They spun all sorts of theories—religious, of course. No, they weren't downtown painting it red. But they may as well have been. Christ came, and they didn't know it. Many of them may as well have been on the moon when He arrived in Bethlehem.

It worked for Satan then, and it will be successful again. How can we avoid being in the mass exodus from the church when Sunday laws overtake it? When the world, led on by Satan who is mad at us, turns against Seventh-day Adventists, a majority will leave. What will keep us from running too?

One point before we answer the question. Because the thief in the night takes place for Seventh-day Adventists at the coming of the latter rain—it will be the very next event. No event occurs before the latter rain. That's why it happens without any warning. And that is why we must know how to get ready now!

How, then, should we prepare for the Spirit. "'Ask ye of the Lord rain in the time of the latter rain.' Do not rest satisfied that in the ordinary course of the season, rain will fall. Ask for it. The growth and perfection of the seed rests not with the husbandman. God alone can ripen the harvest. But man's cooperation is required. God's work for us demands the action of our mind, the exercise of our faith. We must seek His favors with the whole heart if the showers of grace are to come to us."[20]

This is the shaking and sifting time, the time when God says, "Their only safety was in keeping their eyes directed upward."[21] Now is the time to keep our eyes upon Jesus, praying to Him for His Holy Spirit. He longs to give us this gift, desperately wants us to go through the process of praying to Him in order to become dependent upon Him. Then we can be sealed. The latter rain accomplishes the sealing. The sealing is "a settling into the truth, both intellectually and spiritually, so they cannot be moved."[22]

So now is the time to settle into truth intellectually through Bible reading and to settle into truth spiritually through prayer. The latter means getting to know the One who is the Truth,

Jesus Christ. For He said, "I am the way and the truth and the life. No one comes to the Father except through me" (John 14:6). The way through final events to the Father is through knowing Christ. Indeed, to know Jesus is life eternal (John 17:3). We should be spending far more time contemplating Christ than the crisis. Many will not know much about the crisis but will know Christ and get to heaven. Others will have memorized end-time events, even to producing charts, and yet not know Jesus. What does it profit a person if he or she knows everything about final events, and doesn't know Jesus, and loses eternal life?

I feel my own need for preparation. Who of us is ready? I love to start the day in my study reading from inspired words. Through them I hear God speaking. I've never heard an audible voice of God. But His promises and admonitions communicate to me. I need both.

Do you like to get up early and spend time with Him? I need Him more and more as we near the approaching challenges. The more I listen to His words and pour out mine to Him, the more I realize my dependence upon Him. I have to keep my eyes on Him—not on myself. I pray for the latter rain. I pray for a hunger for God. I pray to be emptied of self so that I can be filled. Do you long for the infilling? He is more willing to fill us than we are to give good gifts to our children (Matt. 7:7-11). That's good news!

I prayed to the same Jesus when I went off to college. You know how it is when away from home for the first time. Only 17, I was lonely. When the lights went out in Binfield Hall, Newbold College, I slipped to my knees at my bedside and thought about His goodness, the way He was leading in my life, and thanked Him, and worshiped Him. I talked to Him as to a friend.

"But that's a two-way conversation," you say. So true. And how? You repeat His promises and thank Him for them. That's how it began for me. Back then, and still today, I try to picture Christ and imagine I'm in His presence as I pray. This has helped make prayer life real for me. I'm glad I met Him when just a boy! I need Him even more now than when a teen. How He longs to reveal Himself to us and banish our fear of final events!

The disciples watched Christ during His hours of communing with His Father. They implored, "Teach us to pray." Andrew Murray was a great nineteenth-century saint. His books *With Christ in the School of Prayer,*[23] *The Prayer Life,*[24] and *The Ministry of Intercession*[25] could be a great blessing to your prayer life.

How the Disciples Prepared for Pentecost

I believe we can learn much from the disciples. How they prepared for the first Pentecost tells us how we can get ready for the second Pentecost. Christ's last words before He ascended out of their sight were, "You will receive power when the Holy Spirit comes on you; and you will be my witnesses in Jerusalem, and in all Judea and Samaria, and to the ends of the earth" (Acts 1:8).

"As the disciples waited for the fulfillment of the promise, they humbled their hearts in true repentance, and confessed their unbelief. . . . As they meditated upon His pure, holy life they felt that no toil would be too hard, no sacrifice too great, if only they could bear witness in their lives to the loveliness of Christ's character. O, if they could but have the past three years to live over, they thought, how differently they would act! If they could only see the Master again, how earnestly they would strive to show Him how deeply they loved Him, and how sincerely they sorrowed for having grieved Him by a word or an act of unbelief! But they were comforted by the thought that they were forgiven."[26]

Notice the Christ-centered focus. As they studied His life they longed to reveal Him and yearned to show their love for Him. That's when the Spirit comes. For "the Spirit is constantly seeking to draw the attention of men to the great offering that was made on the cross of Calvary, to unfold to the world the love of God, and to open to the convicted soul the precious things of the Scriptures."[27] As we explore His life, long to be like Him, yearn to show Him how much we love Him—then we're ready for the latter rain.

That coming Pentecost will be "the bestowal of spiritual grace in extraordinary measure upon God's church." It's time to plead for the outpouring.

Enoch as Mentor

The Ellen G. White CD ROM contains more than 500 references to Enoch. He has been a type of the end-time saints since God translated him. That's their destiny. And he was the first prophet.[28] The end-time saints are the last ones (Joel 2:28). As the wickedness surrounded him just before the end of his world, so it does the saints.

Enoch needed Christ just as much as we do. "'Come unto me, all ye that labor and are heavy-laden, and I will give you rest. Take my yoke upon you, and learn of me; for I am meek and lowly in heart; and ye shall find rest unto your souls. For my yoke is easy, and my burden is light.' What an invitation! It was this invitation that Christ gave to Enoch before the world was destroyed by a flood."[29]

I believe it was his understanding of Christ's love for the rebel race that made all the difference in his life. He didn't keep God's law legalistically to get translated. Rather, he fell in love with Christ and committed himself wholly to Him. "Enoch learned from the lips of Adam the painful story of the fall, and the precious story of God's condescending grace in the gift of His Son as the world's Redeemer."[30]

"It was no easier for Enoch to live a righteous life in his day than it is for us at the present time. The world at that time was no more favorable to growth in grace and holiness than it is now, but Enoch devoted time to prayer and communion with God, and this enabled him to escape the corruption that is in the world through lust. It was his devotion to God that fitted him for translation."[31]

Devotion, not duty, guided his steps. Relationship, not rules, blessed his life. Christ, not a creed, gave him victory. As Paul later said, "For me, to live is Christ" (Phil. 1:21). That's the way it has always been with those in love with the Saviour. He is the only way home. Enoch had a secret that points out the way you'll go through final events too. "He educated his mind and heart to ever feel that he was in the presence of God, and when in perplexity his prayers would ascend to God to keep him."[32]

Enoch sought God. "He chose to be separate from them [the wicked], and spent much of his time in solitude, giving himself to reflection and prayer. He waited before God, and prayed to know His will more perfectly, that he might perform it. God communed with Enoch through His angels, and gave him divine instruction."[33] The patriarch evangelized the cities from his country solitude and fearlessly warned the inhabitants of their wickedness and of the approaching end.

Results of the Coming Pentecost

We've seen what the latter rain will do to liberate its recipients to proclaim the final invitation. But let's take a closer look at the book of Acts and its coming repetition. Just as visions guided Ananias to find Paul and witness to him, so we'll receive visions or dreams (Joel 2:28, 29) to guide us to honest seekers in towns near where we live. The Sunday law robs Sabbathkeepers of the ability to buy or sell (Rev. 13:17). Sundaykeepers can buy and sell. So what happens? God sends dreams and visions to Sabbathkeepers to go to Sundaykeepers' homes. We'll look at one possible scenario. The Sunday observer receives a dream about the person to come, just as happened in Acts. The Sabbathkeeper will visit and share spiritual food about the Sabbath, and the individual will be overjoyed and happy to share physical food with the messenger. Mutual help—that is what it may be.

When the Sunday law goes into force, then will be time to move out to the country and into the cities. Sounds contradictory? Let me explain. We'll head for the country, from where we shall witness to the cities. Moving to the country occurs in two stages: the first at the beginning of the early time of trouble, and the other after its close.

"The time is not far distant, when, like the early disciples, we shall be forced to seek a refuge in desolate and solitary places. As the siege of Jerusalem by the Roman armies was the signal for flight to the Judean Christians, so the assumption of power on the part of our nation in the decree enforcing the papal sabbath will be a warning to us. It will then be time to leave the large cities, preparatory to leaving the smaller ones for retired homes in secluded places among the mountains."[34] The Sunday law serves as the last sign to leave the cities for country places. Out there the saints live and evangelize the cities just as Enoch did.

The latter rain seals God's people, so they are strengthened to stand. "And God is faithful; he will not let you be tempted beyond what you can bear. But when you are tempted, he will also provide a way out so that you can stand up under it" (1 Cor. 10:13). That's true, even when Satan comes as Christ (cf. 2 Cor. 11:14). The latter-rain Holy Spirit comes for two purposes: (1) to seal and empower God's people, and (2) to proclaim the final message through them. That is why Scripture calls it a loud cry (Rev. 18:1, 2). Not loud, meaning noisy, but a powerful presence of God that moves through human messengers, with power that radiates through them, deepens their communion with Christ, and proclaims His Sabbath more fully.

God doesn't give the latter rain to provide eternal life. Everyone throughout the Christian era has been saved under the former rain. The latter rain equips God's end-time people to pass through all final events, and thus triumph in the Second Advent. Jesus has promised, "Never will I leave you, never will I forsake you" (Heb. 13:5), for "Lo, I am with you alway, even unto the end of the world" (Matt. 28:20, KJV). So Christ, through the Holy Spirit, comes to take His people through the early time of trouble. But what's beyond?

---

[1] E. G. White, *Last Day Events,* p. 148.
[2] W. H. Griffith Thomas, *The Holy Spirit of God,* p. 39.
[3] Chrysostom in *The Nicene and Post-Nicene Fathers,* First Series (Grand Rapids: Eerdmans, 1989), vol. 9, p. 7.
[4] E. G. White, *The Great Controversy,* p. 606.
[5] E. G. White, *Evangelism,* p. 700.
[6] E. G. White, *The Great Controversy,* p. 612.
[7] E. G. White, *Early Writings,* p. 33.
[8] *Ibid.,* p. 85.
[9] *Ibid.,* p. 71.
[10] E. G. White, *Testimonies for the Church,* vol. 1, p. 261.
[11] E. G. White, *Last Day Events,* pp. 209, 210.
[12] E. G. White, *Testimonies to Ministers,* p. 507.
[13] *Ibid.,* p. 510.
[14] E. G. White, *Testimonies for the Church,* vol. 2, p. 445.
[15] *Ibid.,* p. 5.
[16] E. G. White, *The Great Controversy,* p. 608.
[17] E. G. White in *General Conference Bulletin,* 1891, p. 257.
[18] E. G. White, *Testimonies for the Church*, vol. 5, p. 136.
[19] E. G. White, *Selected Messages,* book 2, p. 380.
[20] E. G. White, *Testimonies to Ministers,* p. 508.
[21] E. G. White, *Early Writings,* p. 269.
[22] *The Seventh-day Adventist Bible Commentary,* Ellen G. White Comments, vol. 4, p. 1161.
[23] Andrew Murray, *With Christ in the School of Prayer* (Pittsburgh: Whitaker, 1981).
[24] Andrew Murray, *The Prayer Life* (Pittsburgh: Whitaker, 1981).
[25] Andrew Murray, *The Ministry of Intercession* (Pittsburgh: Whitaker, 1982).
[26] E. G. White, *The Acts of the Apostles,* p. 36.
[27] *Ibid.,* p. 52.
[28] *The Seventh-day Adventist Bible Commentary,* Ellen G. White Comments, vol. 1, 1088.
[29] Ellen G. White, "Our Privileges in Christ Jesus," *Signs of the Times,* Oct. 4, 1899.
[30] Ellen G. White, "The Great Controversy: Seth and Enoch," *Signs of the Times,* Feb. 20, 1879.
[31] Ellen G. White, "Lessons From the Life of Enoch," *Review and Herald,* Apr. 15, 1909, p. 12.
[32] E. G. White, *Last Day Events,* p. 71.
[33] Ellen G. White, "The Great Controversy," *Signs of the Times,* Feb. 20, 1879.
[34] E. G. White, *Testimonies for the Church,* vol. 5, pp. 464, 465.

Chapter 42

A Double Gathering Under Way

Today the signs of the times declare that we are standing on the threshold of great and solemn events. Everything in our world is in agitation. Before our eyes is fulfilling the Saviour's prophecy of the events to precede His coming: 'Ye shall hear of wars and rumors of wars. . . . Nation shall rise against nation, and kingdom against kingdom: and there shall be famines, and pestilences, and earthquakes, in divers places' (Matt. 24:6, 7).

"The present is a time of overwhelming interest to all living. Rulers and statesmen, men who occupy positions of trust and authority, thinking men and women of all classes, have their attention fixed upon the events taking place about us. They are watching the relations that exist among the nations. They observe the intensity that is taking possession of every earthly element, and they recognize that something great and decisive is about to take place—that the world is on the verge of a stupendous crisis."[1]

Have you ever seen last-day-events charts? Did you notice the various differences between them? What pitfalls should we avoid in attempting to outline coming events? First, Scripture and E. G. White do give some sequence to coming events, and we can safely stay with what God has revealed. But we are wise not to be more exact than God has been. Second, sequence, but not duration between successive events, is the focus of revelation. For example, we know Sunday laws appear before the close of probation, but we do not know the time length between the two events. The same is true with the gap between the close of probation and the death decree and the time between the death decree and Armageddon.

So we do not know how long any period is, including the early time of trouble, the great time of trouble, Jacob's trouble, the plagues, and Armageddon. Third, we do not know any dates. The setting of dates has been a part of early Adventist history and continues even today. The 6,000 years of human history followed by the millennium, popular for some since the early Church Fathers, is of no value. As Ussher's chronology is four years off, 1998 is nearly 2002. After 1886 Ellen G. White always said more than 6,000 years.[2] We must be prepared to be here even after the year 2000 if God so plans. The problem of the year 2000 is twofold for the church. "What" is coming may motivate many instead of "who" is coming. Second, if we go beyond the year 2000, interest in the Second Advent may diminish.

Jubilee calendars sway some present date-setting members. We'll make only a brief comment on them. The jubilee was the end of seven sabbatical-year cycles (Lev. 25:8-10). It was either the forty-ninth or fiftieth year. Israel was supposed to free slaves (verse 10), give the land rest (verse 11), and revert land to the original owners (verses 24-28). It was a way to let the poor and slaves get ahead and to check the avarice of the rich.

The fact is, though, that no reference in Scripture suggests that Israel ever kept the jubilee.[3] And we have no biblical evidence that this plan of mercy had anything to do with prophecy, let alone end-time events. So Jubilee speculation is whistling in the dark, as human-made as Sunday. And that is not a good position to be in for last-day events study. Fourth, inspired sources present end-time events in broad strokes of the brush across the canvas of time rather than as a detailed depiction of any part of the total picture. I agree with Marvin Moore in this observation. Behind this broad overview is a focus on the two sides forming in preparation for an ultimate showdown in Armageddon.

As noted in the previous chapter, the coming Sunday law will catch most by surprise. So fifth, trends, rather than any specific event or events, tell us where we are on the journey. For example, reading books on last-day events many years after they were published is always interesting. It amazes me what the authors came up with as signs that Christ was about to return. The rise of the Ottoman empire grabbed early Adventist writers, the First and Second World Wars gripped others later. Israel's return to Palestine became the sign of the end for Hal Lindsey's *Great Late Planet Earth.* The Gulf War as a prelude to Armageddon grasped John Walvoord, then president of Dallas Theological Seminary. The list is endless.

In our book thus far we have looked at a number of movements and have seen that they have all been developing concurrently in the end-time. Each moves to a common goal. Fallen angels work through spiritualism to take over our planet. Spiritualism operates like the Marines, who go in and gain a beachhead so the army can attack. Satan's green berets, his spirit troops, storm various religious centers around the world through the New Age, charismatic, and Christian Coalition movements. Each one is a different avenue, dividing into a three-pincer movement to attack on three sides. So spiritualism works through the three movements to seize different parts of the world.

The observer of final events watches the overall trend of Satan's plan to capture the planet. This trend, as it unfolds, is of interest to anyone who wants to be true to Scripture and the added insights of Ellen G. White. We do not focus on any single movement or any particular event, apart from the context of the overall trend. Thus blue law skirmishes aren't in themselves that important. Nor should we overstress local blue laws. They are only secular Sunday laws when compared to the religious end-time Sunday laws that demand Sunday worship and, in effect, worship of Satan (Rev. 13:3, 4, 12-17).

Sixth, the broad strokes across the canvas bring trends into bold relief, giving a general view of the journey. Scripture and Ellen White do not provide a detailed map, with all the side roads, although they do provide some markers along the way. I once saw a coming-events chart that covered a whole wall! Talk about intricate—it resembled a maze.

Too often we add our own speculations to what God has revealed. Scripture and Ellen White present a simple overview, and it is safest to stay within those parameters.

Two Gatherings

Two worldwide gatherings are underway. They represent the two sides of the great controversy. Satan works through his avenues to draw humanity into his camp, and Christ seeks to draw the human race to Him. The mission is the same for both sides, while the message and methods differ totally. The broad sweep across the canvas of end-time events shows two groups assembling for the final showdown in the battle of Armageddon. All details, including different times of trouble and events during those times, fit into this context. We need to interpret everything from within this context, and not from ideas alien to it.

Unfortunately, Seventh-day Adventists have not always done this. For example, some have viewed Armageddon as a military battle in the Middle East over oil rather than the pre-Advent climax of the great controversy between the forces of good and evil. Obviously it makes a great difference which view one accepts. So the political history of the Middle East is not what determines how we interpret Armageddon, but the biblical context of the end-time's double gathering of good and evil.

1. Satan's Final Push for World Domination

"Then I saw three evil spirits that looked like frogs," John said; "they came out of the mouth of the dragon, out of the mouth of the beast and out of the mouth of the false prophet. They are spirits of demons performing miraculous signs, and they go out to the kings of the whole world, to gather them for the battle on the great day of God Almighty" (Rev. 16:13, 14). Demons visit leaders, and devils go to people around the world. Fallen angels gather the masses for Armageddon!

A false triumvirate counterfeits the three angels' messages; that is already happening. That finale doesn't come suddenly at the end. It is already under way.

a. Angel Movement

Angels work busily to this end. Listen to Karen Goldman, contemporary pioneer writer on angels. In collecting angel stories for her book, *Angel Encounters,* she says, "These are stories of friends and friends of friends. I didn't have to look far to find them. Much to my own amazement, I've discovered that rather than few and far between, angel encounters are happening all around us and that very normal people everywhere have been touched by something or someone that has left them with tremendous faith." "Publishers and producers are finding to their amazement that interest in the topic of angels is not waning but increasing in a mind-boggling way. On a world scale, big business, world politics, and mainstream religion are all acknowledging the new wave of angelic influence."[4]

In fact, "angels have received tremendous publicity recently. They have been featured in *Time* magazine, *Newsweek*, *The Wall Street Journal, USA Today,* and many other publications. They have been the topic of recent books and films, newspaper articles, and talk shows, and have even been featured on CNN, with broadcasts to 140 countries worldwide. TV networks are doing a variety of angel projects, from specials to weekly series and interviews. Angel books are being translated and published in numerous countries throughout the world."[5] Eileen Elias Freeman lists 85 different books on angels, five national angel organizations, five angel religious groups, and 67 mail-order and/or retail stores specializing on angels![6] A March 1993 Gallup poll showed that 76 percent of teens believe in the existence of angels.[7]

"It seems that with the millennium approaching," Karen Goldman observes, "the angels have launched a new campaign. They have broken out of the religious stronghold and are merging into public consciousness, between church steeples, temples, and mosques, out in the streets, and in the homes and workplaces and entertainment capitals of the world."[8] Devils leap forth to capture the world. "Humanity stands at the brink of the Era of Angels," Janice T. Connell declares. "A spiritual awakening unlike anything known in the history of the world begins now [1995]."[9]

Many writers on angels claim that the beings act as mediators between humans and God. Catholics have produced some of the angel books, books that portray angels much as they describe Mary and the saints. Thus it is not surprising that they direct people to angels rather than to God. The books speak much about the love of angels rather than the love of the Trinity for humans.

Barbara Mark and Trudy Griswold, in their book *Angelspeake,*[10] for example, teach people how to speak to their angels. They hold seminars across the country and have appeared on *Good Morning America* to talk about their work. Where in the Bible does it urge us, "Learn to speak to your angel"? Nowhere! Jesus taught His disciples to pray to their heavenly Father, never to angels.

Look at the false theology in these angel books: angels are divine,[11] whereas humans reincarnate,[12] angels receive infused grace (a Catholic concept),[13] and are immortal.[14] Also angels tell human beings that "all knowledge is already within you,"[15] that they enter into human bodies,[16] and that they can communicate to humans through "automatic dictation."[17] Angel books claim that God is within humanity,[18] that humanity is evolving,[19] and that God is "The All" (pantheism).[20]

"All the love, nourishment, and guidance," claims one angel, "is sent through us to you because you are not able to understand or comprehend on the Father's frequency yet."[21] No wonder they act as mediators! The trouble is that the Father has already communicated through Jesus and Scripture. So such angels come as counterfeits for both!

This doesn't mean that good angels cannot communicate with humans, but not because of any inability of the Father to reach us. Thus the Griswolds are wrong when they state, "Sometimes I felt vain to want God to listen to me. He is busy! The angels seem more accessible. I'm much more aware of angels and I know I am being heard by them. I believe the angels *take* my prayer to God. It's a more believable and personal system."[22] Life eternal rests upon knowing God, not angels (John 17:3). Nor does Scripture say that God is too busy to hear us. In fact, it shows the whole Trinity seeking the lost (see Luke 15). Again, Jesus teaches us to pray to the Father as one who is ever ready to listen. He is also omniscient.

Satan works through a global network of angels to take possession of humanity. We have seen how he employs the New Age movement, the charismatic movement, Reconstructionism, and spiritualism, and now what we might call an angel movement. The mission is the same—to gain possession of all humanity and thereby take over the planet.

b. Angel Miracles

Demons will perform miracles to convince leaders around the world and bring the masses to Armageddon (Rev. 16:13, 14). This is already underway. Take, for example, the experience of Eileen Freeman. "Several years ago, while preparing to be hospitalized for major surgery, she suffered a violent reaction to a strong antibiotic. After praying to God, she was visited by a wondrous angel who embraced her with light and warmth and peace. Within an hour the mending began. At once, Eileen knew that her visitor had been Raphael, the archangel of healing, and that he had come to open her mind and spirit to the ways in which God works through angels to help us heal." She wrote her book *Angelic Healing,* in which "she relates stirring real-life stories of people who have been healed through the intervention of angels."[23]

Miracles don't mean a thing when they endorse false doctrines (as noted above). The demons merely masquerade as God's angels. "The Bible will never be superseded by miraculous manifestations," Ellen White warns. "The truth must be studied, it must be searched for as hidden treasure."[24] Because "the last great delusion is soon to open before us. Antichrist is to perform his marvelous works in our sight. So closely will the counterfeit resemble the true that it will be impossible to distinguish between them except by the Holy Scriptures. By their testimony every statement and every miracle must be tested."[25]

"If our eyes could be opened to discern the fallen angels at work with those who feel at ease and consider themselves safe, we would not feel so secure. Evil angels are upon our track every moment. We expect a readiness on the part of bad men to act as Satan suggests; but while our minds are unguarded against his invisible agents, they assume new ground and work marvels and miracles in our sight. Are we prepared to resist them by the word of God, the only weapon we can use successfully? Some will be tempted to receive these wonders as from God. The sick will be healed before us. Miracles will be performed in our sight. Are we prepared for the trial which awaits us when the lying wonders of Satan shall be more fully exhibited? . . . Faith in God's word, prayerfully studied and practically applied, will be our shield from Satan's power and will bring us off conquerors through the blood of Christ."[26]

Angelic miracles are taking the world captive. This all leads inexorably to the coming of Satan as Christ. "The time is at hand," Ellen White reminds us, "when Satan will work miracles to confirm minds in the belief that he is God."[27]

c. How the Miracles Are Performed

Some miracles are utter frauds. "Wonderful scenes, with which Satan will be closely connected, will soon take place. God's word declares that Satan will work miracles. He will make people sick, and then will suddenly remove from them his satanic power. They will then be regarded as healed. These works of apparent healing will bring Seventh-day Adventists to the test. Many who have had great light will fail to walk in the light, because they have not become one with Christ."[28] "We have reached the perils of the last days," Ellen White wrote, "when some, yes, many, shall depart from the faith, giving heed to seducing spirits and doctrines of devils."[29]

Some miracle claims are incredible, such as the woman supposedly healed near Riverside, California. She had a steel bar in her back to help her stand up, and a steel screen to hold her internal organs together. After her healing, X-rays reportedly revealed no signs of the steel bar or screen. *Voice* magazine of October 1972 stated that a man named David had a bad eye healed. "He can see now. It doesn't matter if his plastic eye is in or out!"[30]

"The apostles of nearly all forms of spiritism claim to have the power to heal. They attribute this power to electricity, magnetism, the so-called 'sympathetic remedies,' or to latent forces within the mind of man."[31]

Consider Oral Roberts' account of a meeting in Jacksonville, Florida. Note the emotionally charged atmosphere, and the mention of electricity. "As I sat there praying, God's power would strike my hand every few seconds. It stung like fire. Then suddenly it struck with tremendous force, and I screamed at the top of my voice, 'People, something is coming. People, something is coming!'. . . In a moment the power of God struck my hand a second time with such force that I shouted at the top of my voice, 'People, it's here! People, it's here!' It seemed like an earthquake shook the tent. I saw the people as a blur before me. My right hand was vibrating and shaking with the presence of God in it. The people leaped to their feet and started streaming down the aisles toward me.

People began pulling at my clothes. The voice of the crowd was like the roar of mighty waters.

"I leaped off the main platform on to the lower platform and stood waiting. People started thronging it, and I began laying my right hand upon as many as I could and as fast as I could. It seemed like balls of fire were streaming through my hand and everybody I touched felt the healing power of God. The healing virtue of Jesus would strike them the moment I touched them, and they would go leaping and shouting away. I turned to my right to pray for some people, and there sat a man and a woman in two wheelchairs. I reached out my hand, and they both grabbed it. Without a word they both came out of these wheelchairs, and the last I saw of them they were running down the aisles. Right behind me I heard someone scream that he could see. I whirled around, and it was a bind man who was screaming that he could see the lights, he could see the people's faces. Deaf eardrums were opened, crippled and withered legs were made straight, and people all over the tent were feeling the miraculous power to set them free."[32]

The whole atmosphere is different from the quiet work of the master healer Christ. It is more a show than a ministry. Indiscriminate healing without instruction about how to live healthfully doesn't make sense. "It is labor lost to teach people to look to God as the healer of their infirmities," says Ellen White, "unless they are taught also to lay aside unhealthful practices."[33]

d. The Ultimate Angel Miracle

When angels masquerade before humanity as departed loved ones, just as Satan will pretend to be Christ, we have the ultimate deception. Such experiences will overpower the masses.

"The forms of the dead will appear, through the cunning device of Satan, and many will link up with the one who loveth and maketh a lie." Therefore, Ellen White said, "I warn our people that right among us some will turn away from the faith and give heed to seducing spirits and doctrines of devils, and by them the truth will be evil spoken of. A marvelous work shall take place. Ministers, lawyers, doctors, who have permitted these falsehoods to overmaster their spirit of discernment, will be themselves deceivers, united with the deceived. A spiritual darkness will take possession of them."[34]

"Satan as a powerful general has taken the field. . . . He is sweeping the whole world into his ranks, and the few who are faithful to God's requirements are the only ones who can ever withstand him, and even these he is trying to overcome."[35]

Counterfeit angels look down on a broken society. Human beings labor under the heavy load of poverty, fear, divorce, discouragement, disease, and death. Unfulfilled, they long for something better. Angels of deception give them healing and messages. Like struggling waifs swept down a swollen river, they clutch at straws for security, the only hope they know.

2. Christ's Global Mission

By contrast, the words of Christ for the end-time are full of hope. They speak about truth for our time in the context of the everlasting gospel.

Scripture refers to them as angelic messages too. They are the messages of the three angels of Revelation 14:6, 7: "I saw another angel flying in midair, and he had the eternal gospel to proclaim to those who live on the earth—to every nation, tribe, language and people. He said in a loud voice, 'Fear God and give him glory, because the hour of his judgment has come.'" This hour struck on October 22, 1844. Then Christ began His final pre-Advent ministry prior to His return.

The second angel says that Babylon has fallen. Revelation 16:19; 17:5; 18:2, 10, 21 repeat the symbol of Babylon, the city that defied God with its tower of Babel (Gen. 11:1-9). Scripture calls Satan, who fell from heaven (Rev. 12:4-8; Isa. 14:12), the "king of Babylon" (verse 3). In Scripture Jerusalem represents God's side in the great controversy, and Babylon symbolizes Satan's side. Babylon was a synonym for pagan Rome in Peter's day,[36] but is "the great anti-God system of idolatry" in the second angel's message.[37] A true angelic message, it speaks against the fallen angels who lead people astray in the end-time.

Babylon is the name the book of Revelation gives to "a woman sitting on a scarlet beast that was covered with blasphemous names. . . . She held a golden cup in her hand, filled with abominable things. . . . This title was written on her forehead, *'Mystery, Babylon the Great, The Mother of Prostitutes and of the Abominations of the Earth'* " (Rev. 17:3-5). The woman is drunk with the blood of the saints "who bore testimony to Jesus" (verse 6). She is a mother of prostitutes, "for all the nations have drunk the maddening wine of her adulteries" (Rev. 18:3). "With her the kings of the earth committed adultery" (Rev. 17:2). This counterfeit church opposes Christ and unites with earthly kings instead of with Christ, the King of kings (Rev. 19:16). The harlot has committed spiritual adultery. Through this church the fallen angels have worked, just as they have operated through individuals. But all of this is the same scheme of Satan to take over the world.

The second angel announces Babylon's fall. The new focus on the heavenly sanctuary (first angel) brings into question Babylon's (little horn/beast) emphasis on the earthly priestly system. Babylon has fallen in the allegiance of those who look away to Christ.

The third angel refers to those "who worship the beast and his image" (Rev. 14:11, KJV) as receiving "God's fury" (verse 10). Thus the third angel tells us that God will punish all forms of apostate Christianity. Demonic angels working through the three major religious avenues in the end-time will deceive the world by working false miracles and giving erroneous messages. But Christ will unmask the final deception and destroy the agencies used by the demons. We will see how in a later chapter.

Satan's three counterfeit avenues to deceive the world share common ground. All obscure or hide Christ from human view: angels, Mary, saints—all such things take His place. Angel messages or tradition or special gifts, such as tongues, obscure Scripture about Christ. The focus is no longer upward, but inward. The three angels' messages break into this end-time context to restore the proper focus on Christ and the authority of His Word.

Here is how. Christ is the subject of each clause of the first angel's message. It is about the One who made heaven and earth (Christ, John 1:1-3; Col. 1:15, 16; Heb. 1:1-3). The message calls for the human race to fear (or reverence) Him, to give Him glory, for "the hour of His judgment has come." Remember, it shouts, that the everlasting gospel is good news. Some wonder how Scripture can place the good news of the gospel news along with the judgment, which many regard as bad news.

Look at it this way. The good news of the gospel is first Jesus, who is glorified in the first angel's message. But the good news is also about His judgment, for it overcomes the three counterfeit religious avenues used by demons. While they seem to have taken the world captive, the judgment will be worldwide too (Rev. 19:19-21)! The message that Babylon is fallen speaks of that judgment. Before long God will have utterly vanquished the enemy.

That is because the everlasting gospel has to do with Calvary, where Christ defeated Satan and his angels. It is only a matter of time until the whole world recognizes that fact. Then God will implement the judgment, and the results of Calvary will be forever clear.

So in bold, swift, strong strokes across the canvas of final events we see a picture of two roundups—one through fallen angels with their miracles and messages and the other through the three angels' messages. The vast majority fall for the deceptive work of fallen angels. Satan's coming as Christ will almost overpower the saints. At first glance few seem to remain true to Christ; it looks as if they'll perish. But just in time the tables turn. Christ implements the verdict of the pre-Advent judgment and delivers the saints. This broad picture is the only context in which to study end-time events.

Another Vital Context

Final events begin at the shore of the end-time Red Sea, as we noted in greater depth in chapter 30. The way Christ aided ancient Israel is in principle the same as He will intervene for the end-time remnant. The Sunday law passes. The decree goes forth to enforce Sunday observance. Popular opinion moves against those who honor the Sabbath. Fallen angels work through both Christianity and paganism to galvanize the world against the remnant. It is not just a matter of going to church on Sunday; that could be done. It has become a law against the Sabbath. God's saints find themselves surrounded at the shores of the modern Red Sea.

They see no way out—humanly speaking. Helpless, the saints look beyond the crisis to Christ. This is all they can do. With no strength of their own, they have finally come to give up on themselves. They stand at the mercy of the mob. Then the miraculous moving of the water begins. Christ pushes it back and makes a dry path through final events. The crisis does not change, but a way of escape opens up. Christ's work is to get His people across safely. The role of His people is to trust Him to do that.

In total dependence upon Christ, they come to experience the three angels' messages.

1. The first angel's message says, "Behold Christ!" And by beholding Him we become changed (2 Cor. 3:18) from fear to trust.

2. The second angel's message declares that Babylon is self-dependence. Remember the tower of Babel, it reminds the world. Its builders erected Babel to escape the next flood. Babel flaunted God. It yelled, "We can save ourselves." The second angel's message, as an experience, is the fall of Babylon, or the cessation of self-dependence.

3. The third angel's message speaks of an image to the beast, or a union of church and state. Its message warns of using secular power (our own power apart from Christ) to be religious.

At the banks of the final Red Sea, God's people stand sealed. They have become completely loyal to Jesus Christ, just as the rest of humanity has become completely possessed by Satan and his angels. The saints look beyond the world against them and see Christ. Transformed, their self-dependence crumbles, even to the extent that they no longer try to be religious through their own efforts. That is the condition Christ wants to bring to His people. For this He has worked for a long time. Finally they experience the Sabbath by resting in Him alone. Now He can do for them that which they could never do for themselves. For the first time He can open up a way through final events, and they won't take the credit for it. And He can defeat the enemy around the world, because Satan lies defeated in the lives of His saints.

Elijah a Type of the End-time Saints

Elijah is a type of the end-time saints (Mal. 4:5, 6). The prophet had to learn total trust in God. After the dramatic victory against the 450 priests of Baal on Mount Carmel (1 Kings 18:16-40) he fled through the night out of fear of one woman—Jezebel (1 Kings 19:1-3). He ran for his life—into the desert. There he sat down under a broom tree and prayed to die (verse 4). God sent an angel to him, who gave him food and water (verses 5-7). Elijah "now knew that a quiet trust, a firm reliance on God, would ever find for him a present help in time of need."[38]

"Nothing is apparently more helpless, yet really more invincible, than the soul that feels its nothingness and relies wholly on God. . . . Fellow Christian, Satan knows your weakness; therefore cling to Jesus. . . . Christ will never abandon those for whom He has died. . . . Could our spiritual vision be quickened, we should see souls bowed under oppression and burdened with grief, pressed as a cart beneath sheaves, and ready to die in discouragement. We should see angels flying quickly to the aid of these tempted ones, forcing back the hosts of evil that encompass them, and placing their feet on the sure foundation."[39]

Behind the scenes angels are fighting, just as they waged war in heaven (Rev. 12:7, 8). The only difference now is that they battle over human beings. Fallen angels depressed Elijah and made him run for his life until he cried out, "I want to die." God's angel came to strengthen Elijah and encourage him so he would not die. God saved Elijah in a desert. In ancient times "the woman [church] fled into the desert to a place prepared for her by

God, where she might be taken care of" (Rev. 12:6; cf. verse 14). In the end-time, even though the whole world rushes against the saints, God will open up a way through the crisis, for He has a place prepared for them. Looking to that future time, Ellen White said, "Angels provided them food and water, while the wicked were suffering from hunger and thirst."[40]

---

[1] E. G. White, *Prophets and Kings,* pp. 536, 537.

[2] Warren H. Johns, "Ellen G. White and the Age of the World" (unpublished manuscript, Andrews University, 1995).

[3] Siegfried H. Horn, *Seventh-day Adventist Bible Dictionary,* revised edition (Washington, D.C.: Review and Herald, 1979), p. 625.

[4] Karen Goldman, *Angel Encounters: True Stories of Divine Intervention* (New York: Simon and Schuster, 1995), p. 19.

[5] *Ibid.,* p. 18.

[6] Eileen Elias Freeman, *Angelic Healing: Working With Your Angels to Heal Your Life* (New York: Time Warner, 1994), pp. 199-218.

[7] Brad Steiger and Sherry Hansen Steiger, *Angels Over Their Shoulders* (New York: Fawcett Columbine, 1995), p. 7.

[8] Goldman, p. 19.

[9] Janice T. Connell, *Angel Power* (New York: Ballantine, 1995), p. xiii.

[10] Barbara Mark and Trudy Griswold, *Angelspeake: A Guide: How to Talk With Your Angels* (New York: Simon and Schuster, 1995).

[11] *Ibid.,* p. 22.

[12] *Ibid.,* p. 28.

[13] Connell, p. 108.

[14] Freeman, p. xii.

[15] Mark and Griswold, p. 42.

[16] *Ibid.,* p. 47.

[17] *Ibid.,* p. 51.

[18] *Ibid.,* p. 53.

[19] *Ibid.,* p. 87.

[20] *Ibid.,* p. 91.

[21] *Ibid.,* p. 99.

[22] *Ibid.,* p. 102.

[23] Freeman, dust jacket copy.

[24] E. G. White, *Selected Messages,* book 2, p. 48.

[25] E. G. White, *The Great Controversy,* p. 593.

[26] E. G. White, *Testimonies for the Church,* vol. 1, p. 302.

[27] E. G. White, *Review and Herald,* Aug. 9, 1906.

[28] E. G. White, *Selected Messages,* book 2, p. 53. Compare E. G. White, *Medical Ministry,* p. 110.

[29] E. G. White, *Medical Ministry,* pp. 101, 102.

[30] Roland R. Hegstad, *Rattling the Gates* (Washington, D.C.: Review and Herald, 1974), pp. 171-173.

[31] E. G. White, *Prophets and Kings,* pp. 210, 211.

[32] Oral Roberts, *Life Story,* pp. 113-115, quoted in Roland R. Hegstad, *Rattling the Gates,* pp. 175, 176.

[33] Ellen G. White, *The Ministry of Healing* (Mountain View, Calif.: Pacific Press, 1905), pp. 227, 228.

[34] E. G. White, *Last Day Events,* p. 171.

[35] E. G. White, *Selected Messages,* book 3, p. 389.

[36] Edwin A. Blum, *The Expositor's Bible Commentary,* Frank E. Gaebelein, ed., *2 Peter* (Grand Rapids: Zondervan, 1981), pp. 253, 254.

[37] Alan F. Johnson, *The Expositor's Bible Commentary, Revelation,* p. 541.

[38] E. G. White, *Prophets and Kings,* p. 169.

[39] *Ibid.,* pp. 175, 176.

[40] E. G. White, *Early Writings,* p, 282.

Chapter 43

The Great Time of Trouble

The worst time of trouble—that's what it is. Plagues pound the planet. Doom hangs in the air. Death threatens the saints. Jacob's trouble overshadows us. It is closing time. Probation closes for the world, the sanctuary closes for the saints.

What a time to live without a Mediator! What a time to have no Holy Spirit in the world! Satan has full possession of the wicked. This is it—the time that God's people have feared and wanted to skip, the time that many people have misunderstood.

Too Late

"Here I am in the twilight years of my life," Lee Iacocca wrote, "still wondering what it's all about. . . . I can tell you this, fame and fortune is for the birds."[1] While his was an honest confession, during probationary time the masses never find out what life is all about.

Muhammad Ali, the boxing champion of the world, considered himself a self-made man. Remember his bragging, especially before fights? No wonder they dubbed him the Louisville Lip. He thought he was independent. During a flight one day his plane flew into turbulence, and the captain ordered all passengers to fasten their seat belts. All complied, except Ali. A flight attendant noticed, approached him, and said, "Please fasten your seat belt." To which he responded, "Superman don't need no seat belt." Without a pause she answered, "Superman don't need no airplane either."[2]

Too late the final generation discovers that life has no meaning apart from Christ and dependence upon Him. The masses had every opportunity to come to Him during the loud-cry invitation. They marveled at the saints—at their radiant faces and obvious power. The saints urged them to accept Christ. Many wanted to respond but resisted. "We have power too!" they replied angrily, attempting to stifle conscience. The charismatic movement had power for the churched. The New Age movement and spiritualism had power for the unchurched. Miracles and angelic messages and healings seemed to be the answer to an aching void within. Trapped in the counterfeit, they turned down the invitation.

The final invitation was to board the plane for heaven. No passengers can fly there by themselves, no matter how many times they flap their arms at the end of the runway. No saint goes through final events without Christ anymore than eight survivors swam in the Flood in Noah's day. Both ark and plane represent Christ as the only way to go to the heaven (John 14:6). But much of the world sensed no need. Not even during the first part of the end-time. In effect they say to the saints, "Superman don't need no airplane."

Probation Closes

The close of probation isn't arbitrary. It's not "ready or not, this is it." Rather, it concludes only after everyone has made a free, conscious decision for or against Christ. Those for Him have climbed aboard into safety for the flight. Those rejecting Him stay out on the runway.

"And at that time shall Michael stand up, the great prince which standeth for the children of thy people: and there shall be a time of trouble, such as never was since there was a nation" (Dan. 12:1, KJV). Now Michael stands up in heaven, just as at His ascension He sat down (Heb. 1:3). As sitting down indicated the commencement of His work in heaven, so standing up announces its completion. So the intercession for His people, and the pre-Advent judgment, come to an end.

What does this mean—and not mean? This is where many stumble, falling for a cruel falsehood. They assume that being without a mediator in heaven means they have to go it alone through the greatest time of trouble. Naturally they exclaim, "Help! Let me out of here! I want to die before the close of probation." The other hoax concerns the Spirit of God. They believe He will withdraw from the world. That's why the world has plunged into its greatest time of trouble. Again "I want out of here," they cry.

All this they base on just two pages in *The Great Controversy*. "When He leaves the sanctuary, darkness covers the inhabitants of the earth. In that fearful time the righteous must live in the sight of a holy God without an intercessor. The restraint which has been upon the wicked is removed, and Satan has entire control of the finally impenitent."[3] "The forms of religion will be continued by a people from whom the Spirit of God has been finally withdrawn."[4]

But this doesn't mean the saints have to go it alone. That's the mistake of the lost. They thought they could get by without Christ. Sure they had substitutes with demonic power and messages, but they were still without Christ. The saints remain radically different from the wicked because they completely depend upon Christ. They get on board the plane while they can. The wicked remain independent—outside. It was the same in Noah's day. To be alone is the plight of the wicked. But to be alone is never the lot of the saints. This is what separates the two groups. Yes, Christ has finished His work in heaven, but it hasn't ended on earth. Christ opens up a way through the great time of trouble—as He opened up the Red Sea (Ex. 14:13-19; Isa. 63:11;

Ps. 77:15-20; 114:1-8; Zech. 3:1, 2; Acts 7:30-32; 1 Cor. 10:4). Christ will mediate for His people on earth, even though He has finished His mediation for them in heaven.

At first Christ remained in heaven working out the passenger list for the flight. That responsibility has ended. Now He is here with His people. They are on board for the flight. They don't need to work on tickets when they are on the plane.

The saints are sealed, settled into truth, both intellectually and spiritually, so that nothing can move them. In other words, they're no longer on probation. They don't require an intercession for them in heaven. But they desperately need Christ with them on earth. Probation's close doesn't take Christ away from them. He's still with them. "I . . . will keep thee from the hour of temptation, which shall come upon all the world" (Rev. 3:10, KJV). "Never will I leave you; never will I forsake you" (Heb. 13:5), for "Lo, I am with you alway, even unto the end of the world" (Matt. 28:20, KJV).

Well, what about the Spirit withdrawing from the world? Yes, He leaves the world, but never God's people! For where Christ is, there is His Holy Spirit. Besides, the latter rain is the end-time outpouring of the Holy Spirit in unmeasured abundance. Why? Because God's people need the infilling. That is the only way the final message can become a loud cry and the only way the saints go through the great time of trouble. The latter rain comes precisely to equip the saints to go through final events. How like the enemy to take attention away from Christ. He is doing it today through the mass, human priests, the intercession of Mary and saints, and Sunday as the substitute Sabbath. Satan employs the charismatic tongues as an added requirement for heaven beyond Christ to distract us. The counterfeit Christ of New Age bibles and fallen angels thrusts itself between Christ and humans to block us from our Saviour. And he blinds God's people by yanking the "no Mediator" and "Spirit withdrawn" concepts from their context and thrusting them between Christ and the believer in the church. It is all the same. Anything to take attention away from Christ.

Where was Christ when the Babylonian guards flung the three Hebrews into the fiery furnace? Right in their midst. He'll be right there with us in our journey through final events. Christ doesn't say, "I want you to take the journey through final events. I'll watch from heaven. Good luck!" No! He says, "Come unto me all you who are weary and heavy laden from contemplating final events, and I will give you rest. I will be with you on the journey. Let's go through the final fiery furnace together." His presence makes the trip worthwhile. In fact, His presence makes the trip possible. He's the plane for the ride.

"As in the days of Shadrach, Meshach, and Abednego, so in the closing period of earth's history the Lord will work mightily in behalf of those who stand steadfastly for the right. He who walked with the Hebrew worthies in the fiery furnace will be with His followers wherever they are. His abiding presence will comfort and sustain. In the midst of the time of trouble—trouble such as has not been since there was a nation—His chosen ones will stand unmoved. Satan with all the hosts of evil cannot destroy the weakest of God's saints. Angels that excel in strength will protect them, and in their behalf Jehovah will reveal Himself as a 'God of gods,' able to save to the uttermost those who have put their trust in Him."[5]

"The Lord did not forget His own. As His witnesses were cast into the furnace, the Saviour revealed Himself to them in person, and together they walked in the midst of the fire. In the presence of the Lord of heat and cold, the flames lost their power to consume. . . . The presence of their Saviour had guarded them from harm, and only their fetters had been burned."[6]

"We are standing on the threshold of the crisis of the ages. In quick succession the judgments of God will follow one another—fire, and flood, and earthquake, with war and bloodshed. We are not to be surprised at this time by events both great and decisive; for the angel of mercy cannot remain much longer to shelter the impenitent. . . . The righteous alone shall be hid with Christ in God till the desolation be overpast. Let the language of the soul be:

"'Other refuge have I none,
Hangs my helpless soul on Thee;
Leave, O, leave me not alone!
Still support and comfort me.

Hide me, O my Saviour, hide!
Till the storm of life is past;
Safe into the haven guide,
O receive my soul at last!'"[7]

Satan's Final Fling

What makes it the greatest time of trouble ever? Because God withdraws His Spirit. Angels let loose winds of strife (cf. Rev. 7:1-4). "Satan will then plunge the inhabitants of the earth into one great, final trouble. As the angels of God cease to hold in check the fierce winds of human passion, all the elements of strife will be let loose. The whole world will be involved in ruin more terrible than that which came upon Jerusalem of old."

How?

"A single angel destroyed all the first-born of the Egyptians and filled the land with mourning. When David offended against God by numbering the people, one angel caused that terrible destruction by which his sin was punished. The same destructive power exercised by holy angels when God commands, will be exercised by evil angels when He permits. There are forces now ready, and only waiting the divine permission, to spread desolation everywhere."[8] "The angel of mercy is folding her wings, preparing to step down from the throne and leave the world to the control of Satan."[9]

The evil angels pretend that they love human beings, that their love is unconditional, and that they have no desire to force humans. The angel books we looked at in chapter 42 are full of such claims. They contain numerous angel quotes seemingly full of compassion and caring. Fallen angels present themselves as the best friends of human beings (as if there were no Saviour). They claim to bring them healing and happiness. Then, suddenly, after probation's close, when it is forever too late, they rear their ugly heads and let the human race have it!

By utter contrast, Christ comes to His children during this their greatest time of need. He hovers close and carries them through. How different the genuine from the counterfeit! There is only one Saviour, only One who died to save humanity, only One who is selfless. While fallen angels persecute their followers, Christ protects His people from such horrible demons. That is the stark contrast seen by the onlooking universe.

Where Are the Saints?

"Many will be laid away to sleep before the fiery ordeal of the time of trouble shall come upon our world."[10] They will include the aged. "The Lord has often instructed me," Ellen White wrote, "that many little ones are to be laid away before the time of trouble."[11] God in mercy knows who can go through the events. The very old and the very young sleep through the time, and rise in a special resurrection when the trouble is over (Dan. 12:2). "All who have died in the faith of the third angel's message come forth from the tomb glorified to hear God's covenant of peace with those who have kept His law."[12]

Where will the living saints be during the great time of trouble? Some will be in prisons. "Many of all nations and of all classes, high and low, rich and poor, black and white, will be cast into the most unjust and cruel bondage. The beloved of God pass weary days, bound in chains, shut in by prison bars, sentenced to be slain, some apparently left to die of starvation in dark and loathsome dungeons. No human ear is open to hear their moans; no human hand is ready to lend them help."[13] Now that's one side.

But there's more. "Though enemies may thrust them into prison, yet dungeon walls cannot cut off the communication between their souls and Christ. One who sees their every weakness, who is acquainted with every trial, is above all earthly powers; and angels will come to them in lonely cells, bringing light and peace from heaven. The prison will be as a palace; for the rich in faith dwell there, and the gloomy walls will be lighted up with heavenly light as when Paul and Silas prayed and sang praises at midnight in the Philippian dungeon."[14]

The other place where saints will be is out in nature. "Some [will be] hidden in solitary retreats in the forests and the mountains."[15]

Why the Great Time of Trouble?

Why do God's people have to go through the great time of trouble? They are ready for translation and are sealed. Their work for humanity is over. The last invitation has already been given. Why don't they go to heaven at the close of probation? It is as if they look up to Christ and say, "We've finished our work. We're ready to come home. May we?"

"Not yet, My children, not yet," Jesus replies.

But why would a God of love require His translation-ready people, who have completed their mission, to stay on earth to endure the greatest time of trouble ever experienced by humans? Is He really a God of love after all? This is the Christ of Calvary, who never changes (Mal. 3:6). He is a God of love (1 John 4:7-16). There must be a good reason He says "Not yet."

You remember that the great controversy began in heaven and only later reached our planet. Even if Adam and Eve had remained true to Christ, the struggle between good and evil would have continued in the universe. Humanity's fall merely extended the controversy beyond heaven. Now human beings joined angels in rebellion against God. The order is important—it began in heaven, then came to earth. The solution will follow the same order. Before showing you how, let me remind you that in heaven Satan questioned God's justice, making necessary God's vindication. On earth Satan robbed humans of eternal life, calling for Christ's plan to save them.

Let's package these two facts. Heaven's revolt requires the salvation of God's name, while humanity's fall necessitates our salvation. Two different types of salvation, if you please: saving God's name and saving humans for eternal life.

Now to the order of these two: Just as Satan questioned God's justice before humanity's fall, so the vindication of God's justice will occur before He saves humanity at the Second Advent.

"Wait a minute," someone might protest, "that's not fair! Why should humans have to go through the greatest time of trouble just to help God out? Can't He help Himself? Besides that, didn't Jesus already take care of that at the cross? Didn't His death show how just God is and expose how unjust Satan is since he murdered his Creator?"

Excellent questions. Here are the answers. Calvary did answer the question of God's justice as well as save humanity. In a sense you could ask, "Why didn't the Second Advent take place soon after Calvary? Why has time gone on so long?" Calvary was not only a price paid but a revelation made. But what happened there would take time to comprehend. "The angels did not even then understand all that was involved in the great controversy."[16]

Here's why. Have you ever climbed a mountain? At the foot of the mountain you can see only a part of the slope above you, until you reach a ledge, and there looming before you is more of the mountain. The experience may repeat itself many times until finally you get to the top. In other words, when smack up against the mountain, you can see only a little of its immensity. But if you travel a distance from the mountain, you can look back and view it all. As you travel through space, the mountain hasn't changed—only your perspective.

The same with Calvary. With the passage through time, one can look back and see it for what it really is. Calvary hasn't changed, only our appreciation of it. Before Calvary, Satan urged that justice destroys mercy, so that Christ would not die for us. After Calvary, Satan reversed the attack, arguing that mercy destroys justice.[17] So time has gone on beyond the cross to further expose Satan. One day Satan will manifest himself as Christ, which further demonstrates what his scheme has been all along. So a deeper appreciation of Christ's death and a further exposure of Satan is why the Second Advent didn't take place immediately after the Crucifixion.

But back to the great time of trouble. Why do translation-ready saints have to go through it? Because they will be the final evidence to thwart Satan's charge against God. He claims that no created being can keep the law. "God made an unreasonable law," he yells. "He is unjust!" At the close of probation God's people enter the worst time of trouble ever. But they're so dependent upon Christ, settled into truth both intellectually and spiritually, that nothing can change their allegiance to God. They'll live the law from choice, through latter-rain power.

But why? Two reasons make it necessary. 1. If the weakest of the race under the worst time joyfully keep the law, and if they come from all over the world, then you have positive proof to deny Satan's charge. 2. After the millennium, when the wicked of all time will be resurrected for the final judgment, the end-time generation cannot raise their fists, shake them at God, and yell, "It's not fair! We lived during the worst time of trouble! How do You expect us to keep Your law?" Jesus simply points to their contemporaries who did, and discussion ceases. The evidence is convincing. Their relationship with Christ was the secret. That's precisely what their contemporaries turned down. The lost failed because they rejected Christ.

Jesus really answered this charge as no one else has or will. He demonstrated a whole life of law-keeping. By comparison, the end-time saints live for only a short time like Him. But their infinitely smaller demonstration is vital. Human beings can't then shout, "Of course Christ did it. Who couldn't if he were divine? We're not divine. So what do you expect?" When the end-time saints totally depend alone upon Christ, their lives will stand out in stark contrast from the rest of the end-time generation.

Consider still another answer to the question "Why must the saints go through the great time of trouble?" It's this. Just as time continued after Calvary for Satan to further manifest his designs on the planet, so time goes on after the close of probation for the final outworking of his nefarious scheme. After probation's close he will take over the planet and make an utter mess of things. For this moment he has schemed through the ages. Now Christ allows him even to pretend to be Christ and rule the earth. The contrast between those filled with Satan's power and the saints endowed with the latter rain is the ultimate demonstration of the two sides of the controversy before the Second Advent.

Now for the most important answer. Christ will reveal His powerful presence on behalf of His people precisely during the great time of trouble. His presence and works will make it worthwhile to remain on the planet. In fact, as we'll see later, when the saints get to heaven they'll always be grateful they didn't come to heaven before the great climax to the cosmic controversy.

Time of Judgment

We must never study the great time of trouble in a vacuum. So many do and get scared. The great time of trouble has a context. The pre-Advent judgment stands behind it. Armageddon climaxes it. Both events radically change the way we look at the trouble during the period.

THE GREAT TIME OF TROUBLE

Earlier we studied the pre-Advent judgment presented in Daniel 7. Often we concentrate on the coming Sunday law and death decree and overlook the pre-Advent judgment that precedes both. Yet that judgment verdict in heaven dooms all who attack God's people in the great time of trouble. That is the rest of the story we often ignore. No wonder Satan tried to get end-time saints to throw away the pre-Advent judgment. He'd like to keep that under wraps forever!

The closing moments of the judgment in heaven witnesses the international Sunday law on earth. But this utter rebellion against God and His Sabbath will be punished. The verdict is reached, probation closes, and Christ leaves the sanctuary to implement the decision. So the great time of trouble is judgment time. Sure, Satan's confederacy appears strong. The Sunday law and death decree are tough. The whole world opposes God's people. But Christ moves out of the judgment to implement the irrevocable, irreversible, irresistible verdict. That judgment, not the enemy who marshals all the world against Sabbathkeepers, brings the greatest time of trouble.

The real time of trouble is actually for those who hate God's people and seek to eradicate them. Who will have it worse then, those who face the verdict from heaven or those who face the verdict from church and state on earth? Many people study the great time of trouble with the human verdict in mind, as if no divine verdict existed. Contrary to popular opinion, the great time of trouble is for the enemies of God's people and not for God's people. We must grasp this vital difference.

Do you know which verdict Satan wants Seventh-day Adventists to be preoccupied with? It's the same strategy he has always used. Through the Mass he got millions to look to priests on earth instead of to Christ, the Priest in heaven. What worked with them, Satan now tries on the end-time saints. If he can keep them glued to things of earth, to final events that take place here, then he robs them of the larger view, in which final events have already been determined by the pre-Advent judgment verdict.

If other Christians look to a church instead of to Christ, why not make Seventh-day Adventists do the same (in this case out of fear instead of awe or authority)? Adventists should not worry about what any religious force can do or about a union of church and state that will push a Sunday law with a death decree. Instead, look to Christ. Not what the counterfeit will do *to you*, but what Christ will do *for you* counts. Now is the time for us to look at probation's close as the time of Christ's coming to implement the pre-Advent judgment.

Remember that the end of probation means simply the saints are no longer on probation. Any prisoner released into the free world rejoices when the day finally arrives that the probation officer says, "You're no longer on probation." The saints are free in Christ. Nothing can separate them from Him—even the great time of trouble (Rom. 8:38, 39). By utter contrast, those who push the Sunday law and death decree are not free. "Satan has entire control of the finally impenitent."[18] Who would you rather be during that worst time of trouble—free in Christ or imprisoned by Satan? Those persecuted are far more free than the persecutors. The latter think they fight against human beings. Imagine their surprise when they discover too late that their struggle was against God. What they recognize too late we must grasp now. The saints will be delivered—the wicked destroyed. That's the end-game.

When you look to Christ, sunshine breaks through the midnight gloom, light pierces the darkest doom, and you get a spring in your step again.

The Larger View of the Great Time of Trouble

So we look to Christ. What's next? We need to understand Christ's relationship to His people, and then see what He will do to help them.

1. This Is Wedding Day

Did you know that the great time of trouble is a part of the wedding day that precedes the Bridegroom's coming to receive His bride? Who ever feared their wedding? What bridegroom worth his salt wouldn't stand up for his bride, especially on his wedding day? Christ does so magnificently! The bride can say with Paul, "I am convinced that neither death nor life, neither angels nor demons, neither the present nor the future, nor any powers, neither height nor depth, nor anything else in all creation, will be able to separate us from the love of God that is in Christ Jesus our Lord" (Rom. 8:38, 39). Christ the Bridegroom promised His bride, "Never will I leave you; never will I forsake you" (Heb. 13:5), for "I will be with you always, to the very end of the age" (Matt. 28:20).

An intimate relationship exists between Christ and His bride during the great time of trouble. The saints may be in prisons, but "angels will come to them in lonely cells, bringing light and peace from heaven. The prison will be as a palace, for the rich in faith dwell there, and the gloomy walls will be lighted up with heavenly light as when Paul and Silas prayed and sang praises at midnight in the Philippian dungeon."[19]

In fact, "it is impossible to give any idea of the experience of the people of God who shall be alive upon the earth when celestial glory and a repetition of the persecutions of the past are blended. They will walk in the light proceeding from the throne of God. By means of the angels there will be constant communications between heaven and earth. . . . In the midst of the time of trouble that is coming—a time of trouble such as has not been since there was a nation—God's chosen people will stand unmoved. Satan and his host cannot destroy them, for angels that excel in strength will protect them."[20]

So what the counterfeit angels pretend to do for the wicked, the true angels will accomplish for the saints. We will know our angels in the end-time. But they will come to point us to Christ, just as an angel strengthened Jesus in Gethsemane. "The angel came not to take the cup from Christ's hand, but to strengthen Him to drink it, with the assurance of the Father's love. He came to give power to the divine-human suppliant. He pointed Him to the open heavens, telling Him of the souls that would be saved as the result of His sufferings. He assured Him that

His Father is greater and more powerful than Satan."[21]

During the time of Jacob's trouble Christ's people can only cling to Him, just as the patriarch did. Sensing their great need, they cry to Him. "As the wrestling ones urge their petitions before God, the veil separating them from the unseen seems almost withdrawn. The heavens glow with the dawning of eternal day, and like the melody of angel songs the words fall upon the ear: 'Stand fast to your allegiance. Help is coming.' Christ, the almighty Victor, holds out to His weary soldiers a crown of immortal glory; and His voice comes from the gates ajar: 'Lo, I am with you. Be not afraid. I am acquainted with all your sorrows; I have borne your griefs. You are not warring against untried enemies. I have fought the battle in your behalf, and in My name you are more than conquerors.' The precious Saviour will send help just when we need it. The way to heaven is consecrated by His footprints. Every thorn that wounds our feet has wounded His. Every cross that we are called to bear He has borne before us. The Lord permits conflicts, to prepare the soul for peace. The time of trouble is a fearful ordeal for God's people; but it is the time for every true believer to look up, and by faith he may see the bow of promise encircling him."[22]

Did you see the focus—given both to Christ and the saints—to look up to the open heavens? That's the only secret for success in the journey through final events, whether for Christ or for the saints.

As the latter dwell on their Bridegroom, what do they remember? He too faced a union of church and state. Just as crafty Caiaphas said, "It is better for you that one man die for the people than that the whole nation perish" (John 11:50),[23] so in the end-time it will be urged, "It is better for them [God's people] to suffer than for whole nations to be thrown into confusion and lawlessness."[24] God's people realize the parallel. Christ faced a death decree just as they do. But there's a decided difference. He died in place of His bride, crying, "My God, my God, why have you forsaken me?" (Matt. 27:46). The bride does not die, and Christ does not forsake her (Heb. 13:5).

Christ became "sin for us" (2 Cor. 5:21) and went through His final events under the crushing weight of all human sin. He endured it as a guilty man, carrying my guilt and yours. That's why end-time saints go through as forgiven sinners—sealed. There is no comparison between His final events and ours!

2. Plagues

Devastating plagues sweep our planet during the end-time. Thrown from heaven, they form part of the pre-Advent judgment verdict that Christ implements on behalf of His bride and against her enemies.

Plagues fell on ancient Egypt. That country was a union of church and state too. Pharaoh (he considered himself divine, the son of the sun god Ra, Horus incarnate) and other gods took the place of the true God. Egypt put the Israelites through a great time of trouble. They had to gather straw as well as make bricks. Beaten and bruised, they suffered as slaves. Enter the preincarnate Christ as judge. He flung plagues down on the Egyptians. The hour of

His judgment had come—the verdict was implemented.

What happened to the slaves? Where were they? Joseph had instructed his family that Goshen was to be their dwelling place in Egypt (Gen. 45:10). During the plagues God said, "I will deal differently with the land of Goshen, where my people live; no swarms of flies will be there, so that you will know that I, the Lord, am in this land. I will make a distinction between my people and your people" (Ex. 8:22, 23). In that time "ruin and desolation marked the path of the destroying angel. The land of Goshen alone was spared."[25]

Here is a type of the coming plagues. As the plagues implement the pre-Advent verdict against those opposing the saints, Christ will protect His bride. "While the wicked are dying from hunger and pestilence, angels will shield the righteous and supply their wants. To him that 'walketh righteously' is the promise: 'Bread shall be given him; his waters shall be sure.' "[26] That is why the final invitation to those in Babylon is "Come out of her, my people, so that you will not share in her sins, so that you will not receive any of her plagues" (Rev. 18:4).

3. Punishment of Babylon

Babylon's punishment includes the plagues—and more. In Revelation 17 one of the plague angels reveals the judgment of the woman seated on a scarlet beast. She is Babylon, "the mother of prostitutes" (Rev. 17:5), because she united with the kings of the earth (Rev. 16:12-16; cf. Rev. 18:3) instead of joining with Christ, who is the "King of kings and Lord of lords" (Rev. 19:16). The union of church and state is the wrong union. An adulterous union, it denies the marriage of the church to Christ, the only lawful Bridegroom. The Christian Coalition, in its drive to control the houses of Congress, has not recognized this fact.

Let's take a closer look at this adulterous union. To do so, we need to consider the dragon and the beast for a moment. Prophecy describes both as having seven heads and ten horns (Rev. 12:3; 13:1). Compare the texts and see if you notice anything different about them. Do you see where the crowns are on the dragon and where they are on the beast? What's the significance?

The seven heads are crowned in Revelation 12, and the ten horns have crowns in Revelation 13. Revelation 17 holds the key to unlock the meaning. The seven heads are seven kings (verse 9) and the ten horns are ten kings (verse 12). So both heads and horns are kings. Here we have 17 kings with crowns. The crowns represent the time of their ruling.

According to Revelation 17:9-11, the heads rule first. In John's day five had already fallen, one is, and one is yet to come (verse 10). All seven kingdoms are a church-state union (i.e., religious/secular), and all are enemies of God's people. That's why Satan has both heads and horns as he worked through each, and also on the beast, through whom Satan has also worked. What about the five that are gone? Some believe these nations are Egypt, Assyria, Babylon, Medo-Persia, and Greece. The fact that they are "fallen" (verse 10) points to the end-time when spiritual "Babylon is fallen" (Rev.

14:8; 18:2). It is only a matter of time before Babylon receives its just due. That's all. I prefer the five nations as Babylon, Persia, Greece, pagan Rome, and the papacy, as these, unlike Egypt and Assyria, are found in Daniel, the key source to Revelation.[27]

The worldwide joining of church and state, this coming new world order, is doomed to collapse. That happens in the great time of trouble, the time when Babylon, not God's bride, falls. Christ keeps her "from falling" (Jude 24). In fact, He promised, "I also will keep thee from the hour of temptation, which shall come upon all the world" (Rev. 3:10, KJV). Whose side would you rather be on? Some scared saints act as if they are on the wrong side. They need to know the truth about the great time of trouble. Babylon will really be the one frightened. It has it coming. Christ's bride is bound for heaven, and He will protect her.

What about the other two heads? The one "that is" in John's day is pagan Rome; the one to come is papal Rome, or the Catholic system. The whole world unites with her (Rev. 17:5; 13:3, 12-15). The book of Revelation describes the woman as "drunk with the blood of the saints, the blood of those who bore testimony to Jesus" (Rev. 17:6; cf. Rev. 12:17). During the preprobationary end-time the martyrs "had not worshiped the beast or his image and had not received his mark on their foreheads or their hands" (Rev. 20:4; see Rev. 13:12-17).

A new world order looms on the horizon. The entire world will join together in a tenuous global union of church and state. It is the time when "the whole world was astonished and followed the beast. Men worshiped the dragon because he had given authority to the beast, and they worshiped the beast and asked, 'Who is like the beast? Who can make war against him?'" (Rev. 13:3, 4). All the world in league with the counterfeit Christ system. And the boast goes forth—"He's unbeatable!" All the other countries (Egypt, Assyria, Babylon, Medo-Persia, Greece, and pagan Rome) went down to defeat. One after another fell. But now comes the new world order, the veritable kingdom of God on earth. I can imagine Satan, as Christ, will lead the chant, "Who can make war against us?"

The rest of the book of Revelation answers that question. Christ will. And swiftly. But first, look at the tenuous, tentative, and time-bound union. "The ten horns you saw are ten kings who have not yet received a kingdom, but who for *one hour* will receive authority as kings along with the beast. They have one purpose and will give their power and authority to the beast. They will make war against the Lamb, but the Lamb will overcome them because he is Lord of lords and King of kings—and with him will be his called, chosen and faithful followers" (Rev. 17:12-14). The kings' vaunted pride will crumble in the dust.

For after a fleeting hour, a tiny segment of time, the ten horns, or kings, "will hate the prostitute. They will bring her to ruin and leave her naked; they will eat her flesh and burn her with fire. . . . The woman you saw is the great city that rules over the kings of the earth" (verses 16-18). Thus the woman who rules over the kings of the world, the Babylonian conglomerate that hates God's people, will not only receive plagues from God, but a devastating divorce and destruction from her illicit lovers! Enemies will surround her without and within. She'll come to the banks of her Red Sea. But no way opens for her through it.

Revelation looks at both judgments upon Babylon, her plagues and destruction. "Therefore in one day her plagues will overtake her [cf. "one hour," verses 10, 17, 19, signifying a quick judgment]: death, mourning and famine. She will be consumed by fire, for mighty is the Lord God who judges her" (Rev. 18:8). Then the chapter links this double judgment to the way Babylon oppressed the end-time saints. " 'Rejoice over her, O heaven! Rejoice, saints and apostles and prophets! God has judged her for the way she treated you' " (verse 20). Then Revelation 19 records the response in heaven. "After this I heard what sounded like the roar of a great multitude in heaven shouting: 'Hallelujah! Salvation and glory and power belong to our God, for true and just are his judgments. He has condemned the great prostitute who corrupted the earth by her adulteries. He has avenged on her the blood of his servants' " (verses 1, 2). Whereas the illicit union between church and kings ends in utter destruction, the great multitude in heaven shout with great joy, "Hallelujah! For our Lord God Almighty reigns. Let us rejoice and be glad and give him glory! For the wedding of the Lamb has come, and the bride has made herself ready" (verses 6, 7).

Remember the image in Daniel 2? The nations of the world all crumbled, but Christ's coming kingdom is forever. It doesn't matter if they fling a Sunday law in your face, a death decree down your throat. They're doomed! That's the bottom line. The church-state verdict of heaven cannot be changed. It will topple the church-state verdicts on earth. Like a cat pounces on an unsuspecting mouse, it's suddenly over. "The final movements will be rapid ones."[28]

Other Events in the Great Time of Trouble

Now we have a proper perspective on the great time of trouble. We view it from Christ's viewpoint. Holding the damaging verdict against the end-time union opposing His bride, He shifts from the deliberation mode to one of destruction. The wicked have no escape, no place to hide.

But wait a minute. That is the language too many of God's people use to describe their experience in the great time of trouble. They cite statements about running to the mountains and hiding in the innermost recesses. "What's the point?" they ask. "Modern surveillance from satellites makes no place invisible anymore. All is open to the prying scanner across the globe."

Wrong, comes the answer! Christ can fool them.

"In the time of trouble he shall hide me in his pavilion" (Ps. 27:5, KJV). No one, absolutely no one, can penetrate that pavilion! "Fear not little flock. It is your Father's good pleasure to give you the kingdom" (Luke 12:32, KJV).

Now we are ready to consider what's ahead for Christ's bride in the great time of trouble.

The Great Time of Trouble

"Heaven is very near those who suffer for righteousness' sake. Christ identifies with the interests of His faithful people; He suffers in the person of His saints, and whoever touches His chosen ones touches Him. The power that is near to deliver from physical harm or distress is also near to save from the greater evil, making it possible for the servant of God to maintain his integrity under all circumstances, and to triumph through divine grace."[29]

1. Run for the Mountains

Keep the following time-frame in mind. "Probation is ended a *short time* before the appearing of the Lord in the clouds of heaven."[30] No one knows how brief "short" is, but at least it doesn't say it is long. I believe "short" will be ample enough for God to accomplish His purpose for the saints' journey, and fleeting enough for them to still be hanging on.

Keep in mind the exodus through the final Red Sea and the fact that Christ will be with us during the journey.

Also don't forget the airplane metaphor. His people are all aboard with Christ for takeoff. During the great time of trouble they stand on the tarmac waiting for the takeoff in the Second Coming. True, the plane gets buffeted. But the saints are safe inside. No storming of the plane is possible. Christ will not permit any terrorist seizure. All aboard will take off for heaven. It is just a matter of time until Christ's plane receives its clearance for takeoff.

Change the plane metaphor to one of travel to the mountains. Remember that Christ continues to send dreams and visions to His bride (Joel 2:28, 29). He does not leave us to guess when to leave for solitary places. Nor must we figure out for ourselves where to go. Christ will guide us. So we don't have to pick out a place now. Nor do we have to find a cave and stash away Loma Linda Linketts, canned goods, and other things. "The Lord has shown me repeatedly," Ellen White has told us, "that it is contrary to the Bible to make any provision for our temporal wants in the time of trouble. I saw that if the saints had food laid up by them or in the field in the time of trouble, when sword, famine, and pestilence are in the land, it would be taken from them by violent hands and strangers would reap their fields. . . . I saw that our bread and water will be sure at that time, and that we shall not lack or suffer hunger."[31]

"I saw the saints leaving the cities and villages, and associating together in companies, and living in the most solitary places. Angels provided them food and water, while the wicked were suffering from hunger and thirst."[32]

Plagues decimate crops. Tornadoes, fires, and earthquakes of unprecedented magnitude cause massive upheaval. Utter chaos reigns among the world's inhabitants. They remain totally under Satan's control. Not even a speck of goodness remains in them. "Unsheltered by divine grace, they have no protection from the wicked one."[33] He had promised them everything for following him, but when the heavens open up—he jumps out of the way. How different from Christ, who stays with His people and shelters them! The winds of strife hold no longer (Rev. 7:1-4). "Just as fast as God's Spirit is taken away,

Satan's cruel work will be done upon land and sea."[34]

The devil delights in deception. "I'll look after you," says the father of all lies, and when his followers need protection, he's gone. When he returns, he dashes around destroying all he can. For centuries holy angels kept him from devastating the planet and his people. Not now. He's making up for lost time like an escapee from prison.

So the wicked starve while the saints eat. They may not have pizza and strawberry pie, but their bread and water is sure. Bread, reminiscent of angel food, manna, that fed God's people for 40 years. That took place in a desert too. When earthquakes split pipes and mix the septic and the sanitary, the wicked get sludge while saints receive sparkling fresh water from angels! Now, which side would you rather be on? While angels help the saints, we have not even one bit of evidence that fallen angels aid the wicked any more than their leader does.

God's people remember another time. "The woman fled into the desert to a place prepared for her by God, where she might be taken care of" (Rev. 12:6). "The woman was given the two wings of a great eagle, so that she might fly to the place prepared for her in the desert, where she should be taken care of" (verse 14). Christ did it for His church in the Dark Ages in Europe, and He will do it again for His church during the great time of trouble around the world. He knows the place where you will be and can wing you there. Once He took Philip on a flight (Acts 8:39). Whatever the wings are, He'll get you to the place prepared for you. And when you're there, He'll take care of you.

Did the psalmist picture this day as well?

"Even though I walk through the valley of the shadow of death [the great time of trouble], I will fear no evil, for you are with me; your rod and your staff, they comfort me. You prepare a table [our bread and water is sure] before me in the presence of my enemies. You anoint my head with oil [latter rain]; my cup overflows. Surely goodness and love will follow me all the days of my life [through final events], and I will dwell in the house of the Lord forever" (Ps. 23:4-6).

Sure, it speaks to any believer at any time. But I believe it will mean much more to those who go through the great time of trouble.

2. Death Decree

What comes after the first few plagues? "These plagues enraged the wicked against the righteous; they thought that we had brought the judgments of God upon them, and that if they could rid the earth of us, the plagues would then be stayed. A decree went forth to slay the saints, which caused them to cry day and night for deliverance."[35]

Notice that the word plagues is in the plural. So the death decree occurs after at least two plagues. The first two plagues are sores (Rev. 16:2) and sea turned to blood (verse 3). The third one changed rivers and springs to blood (verse 4). "The angel of God declares: 'Thou art righteous, O Lord, . . . because Thou hast judged thus. For they have shed the blood of saints and prophets, and Thou hast given them blood to drink; for they are worthy' (Rev. 16:2-6). By condemning the people of God to death, they have as truly incurred the guilt of their blood as if it had been shed by their hands."[36] So God sends the third plague because the wicked have issued a death decree against His bride. And the wicked passed the death decree in response to the first two plagues.

So the death decree takes place between the second and third plagues. That's good news. No Christian dies from the death decree. Martyrs are useful only when people can become Christians through their sacrifice. That's not possible after the close of probation. So when the decree goes forth, do not worry. That's one verdict that will never be implemented.

3. Jacob's Trouble

It happened before. Caiaphas said it. "It is expedient for us, that one man should die for the people, and that the whole nation perish not" (John 11:50). Two reasons exist for the death decree. (1) The world blames God's people for the plagues. "Get rid of them, and God won't send any more plagues." (2) The world blames the saints for the possibility of "whole nations to be thrown into confusion and lawlessness." "If they don't comply, then confusion will follow around the world. So go and get them!" It plunges God's people into Jacob's trouble.[37]

Esau marched out to meet Jacob with 400 men. It wasn't a welcome-home committee. They had other business. Jacob had "great fear and distress" (Gen. 32:7) and cried out to the preincarnate Christ, "Save me, I pray, from the hand of my brother Esau, for I am afraid he will come and attack me, and also the mothers with their children" (verse 11). But he didn't stop there. Look at what he said next. "But you have said, 'I will surely make you prosper and will make your descendants like the sand of the sea, which cannot be counted' " (verse 12). He relied on a promise of God. How could that have been fulfilled if Esau's death plans had succeeded? It couldn't. So he clung to Christ that night, seeking a blessing, believing the promise.

His own brother came to kill him. Will family members join the mob to implement the death decree (cf. Matt. 24:9-13)? Jesus' disciple Judas led the mob against Him (Luke 22:47, 48). "As Satan influenced Esau to march against Jacob, so he will stir up the wicked to destroy God's people in the time of trouble."[38] Jesus says, "At that time many will turn away from the faith and will betray and hate each other" (Matt. 24:10).

Satan "sees that holy angels are guarding" the saints. He figures that Christ has pardoned their sins, but "he does not know that their cases have been decided in the sanctuary above." As a result he presents their sins before God "in the most exaggerated light" and "claims them as his prey and demands that they be given into his hands to destroy."[39] Satan vents his anger against God's bride.

Many end-time saints hate the thought of Jacob's trouble. Yes, it involves a struggle. But we need to clearly emphasize something. Even Satan sees that God has pardoned their sins. The fact that plagues pound the planet is proof that Christ is implementing the pre-Advent verdict. It occurs only after all cases close. If we remember that when the plagues fall, then we can cling to that fact as Jacob did to Christ's promise about his future.

God's promises will strengthen His people as His earlier promise fortified Jacob. Consider what the following three prophets said about the coming trouble, including Jacob's trouble. Isaiah urged, "Go, my people, enter your rooms and shut the doors behind you; hide yourselves for a little while until his wrath has passed by. See, the Lord is coming out of his dwelling to punish the people of the earth for their sins" (Isa. 26:20, 21). Jeremiah encouraged, "How awful that day will be! None will be like it. It will be a time of trouble for Jacob, but he will be saved out of it" (Jer. 30:7). Daniel concurs: "At that time Michael, the great prince who protects your people, will arise. There will be a time of distress such as has not happened from the beginning of nations until then. But at that time your people—everyone whose name is found written in the book—will be delivered" (Dan. 12:1). No wonder Ellen White said, "Let none be discouraged in view of the severe trials to be met in the time of Jacob's trouble."[40]

Yes, Satan comes to wipe out the saints. "Dangers thicken on every side, as it is difficult to fix the eye of faith upon the promises amidst the certain evidences of immediate destruction. But in the midst of revelry and violence, there falls upon the ear peal upon peal of the loudest thunder. The heavens have gathered blackness and are only illuminated with the blazing light and terrible glory from Heaven. God utters His voice from His holy habitation. The captivity of His people is turned. With sweet and subdued voices they say to one another, God is our friend. We shall be safe from the power of wicked men."[41] Michael comes to the rescue, the same Michael who threw Satan and his angels out of heaven (Rev. 12:7, 8). Christ conquers Satan and his angels again during Jacob's trouble. All this puts the struggle of Jacob's trouble into its proper context.

If you're tempted to skip Jacob's trouble, think of the alternative to those living at the time. The wicked rush to destroy the saints. Suddenly they find themselves interrupted. They hear God speak to the saints from His throne. "The horror of despair seizes them." Turning against their ministers, they shout, "You have preached to us falsehoods. We have believed a lie, and are lost, forever lost."[42] No plea that the work of the church is to take over the government to promote a moral agenda will hold water then! The final Christian (read Babylon) Coalition had jettisoned the gospel—the only gospel that could have brought them salvation.

"Then I was shown a company who were howling in agony. On their garments was written in large characters, 'Thou art weighed in the balance, and found wanting.' I asked who this company were. The angel said, 'These are they who have once kept the Sabbath and have given it up.' I heard them cry with a loud voice, 'We have believed in Thy coming, and taught it with energy.' And while they were speaking, their eyes would fall upon their garments and see the writing, and then they would wail aloud. I saw that they had drunk of the deep waters, and fouled the residue with their feet—trodden the Sabbath underfoot—and that was why they were weighed in the balance and found wanting."[43] Former Seventh-day Adventists had also jettisoned the gospel and its Sabbath rest in Christ.

The Sabbath rest is the key. It's resting in Christ, clinging to Him as Jacob did, pleading, "I will not let you go except you bless me." God's people cry for a closer connection with Christ, yearn to be filled with His love, seek a total commitment to Him alone. Yes, they have mental anguish about sin, but that is more about letting Christ down than anything else. They cling to Christ because they don't want anything else to come between them. As they do, they sense Christ leading them through the final crossing. They travel through final events as Christ holds back the waves of circumstances so they can walk over on dry ground. The coming Christ pulls them through the present crisis.

The Great Time of Trouble as Remembered by Christ's Bride

How will God's people remember the world's greatest time of trouble in eternity? Will it be forgotten? or will it be celebrated? After the Exodus from Egypt, the great deliverance served as a context for all God's dealing in the Old Testament. It was a high point in Israel's music and praise. In a similar way we will forever remember Christ's journey through the greatest time of trouble on our behalf, in our place. He who knew no sin became sin for us and had His Jacob's trouble, but far worse, in Gethsemane. Satan and his fiends showed up with a death decree and killed Him, but only because He allowed Himself to die in our place. Then He came triumphant through the Resurrection. That grand event was our exodus, in Him, from sin to salvation.

That resurrection event became the context for all Christ's works in the New Testament. So exodus and resurrection loom large over both Testaments as the context within which to interpret everything else. Exodus and resurrection were determinative events by which Christ decisively influenced the rest of history after them. The Christ of exodus and resurrection brings His bride through the final exodus in the end-time. Will the final exodus through final events be just as important for eternal aeons to come? I believe it will be. Let's think about that.

Daniel 12:1 talks both about the greatest time of trouble ever and also deliverance. Many seem to remember the first and forget the second. The good news of Daniel 12:1 appears in the great rescue and not in the greatest time of trouble. But how do we know that the deliverance far outweighs the trouble endured? True, the reward of being with Christ in the trouble and in heaven forever far outweigh any fleeting time of trouble. But the bottom line is how do those going through the great time of trouble evaluate their experience? For after all, that's more authoritative than any other estimate.

Revelation holds the answer to this question. Christ stands with His end-time bride on Mount Zion (Rev. 14:1). Interestingly, in the Old Testament Mount Zion was a place of deliverance.

Christ Is Coming!

For example, "everyone who calls on the name of the Lord will be saved: for on Mount Zion and in Jerusalem there will be deliverance" (Joel 2:32; cf. Isa. 11:9-12; Micah 4:6-8). In the New Testament Mount Zion is in heaven. For example, "you have come to Mount Zion, to the heavenly Jerusalem, the city of the living God" (Heb. 12:22). Thus Scripture portrays Christ's end-time bride as standing with Christ in heaven, either during the millennium or in eternity. His bride will "follow the Lamb wherever he goes" (Rev. 14:4). Whichever you choose, it will be a long time after the great time of trouble. Yet notice what the bride is doing. She sings "a new song before the throne," and "no one could learn the song except the 144,000 who had been redeemed from the earth" (Rev. 14:3).

Ellen White tells us that no one else can sing that song, "for it is the song of their experience—an experience such as no other company have ever had."[44] That is because it will be a song about what they went through during the great time of trouble. Revelation 15 records the song. Notice the focus. "Great and marvelous are your deeds, Lord God Almighty. Just and true are your ways, King of the ages. Who will not fear you, O Lord, and bring glory to your name? For you alone are holy. All nations will come and worship before you, for your righteous acts have been revealed" (verses 3, 4). It says nothing about the perils of the great time of trouble. The song concentrates solely upon Christ and His mighty deeds during that time!

Now, because God's end-time people sing it in the millennium and beyond, it must tell us something about the experience of the great time of trouble. It declares that *if it's worth singing about so long after it happened, it must be worth going through!*

Surely the song rejoices in the deliverance part of Daniel 12:1, rather than the greatest time of trouble part. Looked at from the perspective of the deliverance, the time of trouble is worth experiencing, because of what Christ does for His bride rather than for what His bride does for Him.

---

[1] Lee Iacocca, from his book *Straight Talk*, quoted by Ravi Zacharias, *Can Man Live Without God?* (Dallas: Word, 1994), p. 58.

[2] *Ibid.*, p. 7.

[3] E. G. White, *The Great Controversy*, p. 614.

[4] *Ibid.*, p. 615.

[5] E. G. White, *Prophets and Kings*, p. 513.

[6] *Ibid.*, pp. 508, 509.

[7] *Ibid.*, p. 278.

[8] E. G. White, *The Great Controversy*, p. 614.

[9] E. G. White, *Last Day Events*, p. 250.

[10] Ellen G. White, *Counsels on Health* (Mountain View, Calif.: Pacific Press, 1923), p. 375.

[11] E. G. White, *The Great Controversy*, p. 556.

[12] E. G. White, *Last Day Events*, pp. 271, 272.

[13] E. G. White, *The Great Controversy*, p. 626.

[14] *Ibid.*, p. 627.

[15] *Ibid.*, p. 635.

The Great Time of Trouble

[16] E. G. White, *The Desire of Ages,* p. 761.
[17] *Ibid.,* pp. 761, 762.
[18] E. G. White, *The Great Controversy,* p. 614.
[19] E. G. White, *Last Day Events,* p. 266.
[20] *Ibid.,* pp. 266, 267.
[21] E. G. White, *The Desire of Ages,* p. 693.
[22] E. G. White, *The Great Controversy,* pp. 632, 633.
[23] Cf. E. G. White, *The Desire of Ages,* pp. 539, 540.
[24] E. G. White, *The Great Controversy,* p. 615.
[25] E. G. White, *Patriarchs and Prophets,* p. 269.
[26] E. G. White, *The Great Controversy,* p. 629; cf. E. G. White, *Patriarchs and Prophets,* p. 256.
[27] There are three views espoused by Adventists. See *The Seventh-day Adventist Bible Commentary,* vol. 7, pp. 856, 857.
[28] E. G. White, *Testimonies for the Church,* vol. 9, p. 11.
[29] E. G. White, *Prophets and Kings,* p. 545.
[30] E. G. White, *The Great Controversy,* p. 490.
[31] E. G. White, *Early Writings,* p. 56.
[32] *Ibid.,* p. 282.
[33] E. G. White, *The Great Controversy,* p. 614.
[34] E. G. White, *Last Day Events,* p. 242.
[35] E. G. White, *Early Writings,* pp. 36, 37.
[36] E. G. White, *The Great Controversy,* p. 628.
[37] *Ibid.,* pp. 615, 616.
[38] Ellen G. White, *The Spirit of Prophecy* (Oakland, Calif.: Pacific Press, 1988), vol. 4, p. 435.
[39] E. G. White, *Maranatha,* p. 272.
[40] Ellen G. White, *Our High Calling,* p. 321.
[41] Ellen G. White, "The Great Controversy: Jacob and the Angel," *Signs of the Times,* Nov. 27, 1879, p. 13.
[42] *Ibid.*
[43] E. G. White, *Early Writings,* p. 37.
[44] E. G. White, *The Great Controversy,* p. 649.

Chapter 44

The Greatest Rescue of All Time

"I'm sorry to tell you Bopsy has leukemia." The doctor choked up as he spoke.

"Oh no!" the 26-year-old mother sobbed.

"How long does he have?" the child's father asked.

"Only a few weeks at best. I'm so sorry. I wish I had better news."

Back at home the boy's mother thought of an idea. "Bopsy, have you ever thought about what you'd like to become when you grow up?"

"A fireman." The child smiled at his mother.

Another thought came to her. She went to visit the local fire department in Phoenix and explained about her son's final wish. "Could you take him for a ride around the block in a fire engine?" she asked.

Fireman Bob had a big heart. "No," he said. "We'll do better than that. Bring him next Wednesday and we'll make him an honorary fireman for the whole day. He can eat with us and go out on calls with all the firemen. If you give me his measurements, we'll special-order him a fireman's outfit, with boots and helmet made to fit. The helmet will not be a toy, but the real thing, with the Phoenix fireman's emblem on it. They're manufactured here in Phoenix, so we'll rush-order them."

Three days later Fireman Bob came to the hospital, dressed Bopsy in his fireman's uniform, and escorted him out to the parking lot. They boarded a hook and ladder truck, and Bopsy got to help steer it on the way to the fire station. He was in heaven! His dream had come true! Three fire calls came that day. Bopsy went out on different trucks to all three. He rode in the paramedic's van and the fire chief's car, and TV stations videotaped him for local news. He had so much fun that he lived three months longer than the doctors expected.

Then "one night all of his vital signs began to drop dramatically, and the head nurse, who believed in the Hospice concept that no one should die alone, began to call the family members to the hospital. Then she remembered the day Bopsy had spent as a fireman, so she called the fire chief and asked if it would be possible to send a fireman in uniform to the hospital to be with Bopsy as he made his transition.

"The chief replied, 'We can do better than that. We'll be there in five minutes. Will you please do me a favor? When you hear the sirens screaming and see the lights flashing, will you announce over the PA system that there is not a fire? It's just the fire department coming to see one of its finest members one more time. And will you open the window to his room? Thanks.'

"About five minutes later a hook and ladder truck arrived at the hospital, extended its ladder up to Bopsy's third-floor open window, and 14 firemen and two fire women climbed up the ladder into Bopsy's room. With his mother's permission, they hugged him and held him and told him how much they loved him.

"With his dying breath, Bopsy looked up at the fire chief and said, 'Chief, am I really a fireman now?'

"'Bopsy, you are,' the chief said.

"With those words, Bopsy smiled and closed his eyes for the last time."[1]

What love poured out to the child from those firefighters! It offers just a little insight into the great love God poured out in Jesus Christ for us all. Jesus didn't come to earth because He wanted to become human, but because humanity needed a Saviour. He came for others and not for Himself. Our Saviour came to die. Now the heartbeat of the New Testament throbs with the glorious fact that He will return again. An average of one verse in every 25 speaks of this future.

The Importance of Calvary

As we stand in the shadows of Calvary, looking up to that wonderful Man hanging from the cross, we hear those words of triumph, "It is finished" (John 19:30). They put history into a completely different perspective. Gone are dreams of human beings as the arbiters of their own destiny—for, if they are, why this Man's death? Vanished are the dreams of unlimited self-fulfillment, because Christ came from outside history to bring to humans that which they do not have in themselves and, therefore, could not work out by themselves. Also disappeared is humanity's ultimate despair. History is not careening off course toward nuclear holocaust. Instead of being under the mushroom cloud, history lies beneath the fallout of Calvary. The end of this Man ushered in the beginning for all other humans.

History moves relentlessly toward its rendezvous with destiny—meeting Christ rather than human improvement or extinction. The fact of *this Man* shatters all possibilities, for good or evil, that human beings can control their own future. Human destiny is grounded in the life and work of the *Man Jesus,* and not in any other human. The world moves inexorably toward the unfolding of what has already been completely realized in the life of Jesus as a Man among humanity. Within His life is wrapped up the decisively determining factor of all human history. He brought humanity in Himself through a glorious resurrection to the other side. It is just a matter of time until all His followers stand within their own resurrection or translation. He's coming for both.

Christ Is Coming!

The future has already been lived in the past—in Jesus Christ. He received the final Pentecost—the unlimited outpouring of the Holy Spirit. That launched Him on a mission that brought the close of probation to the people of His lifetime. Then He plunged into the greatest time of trouble that ended in the holocaust of Calvary. That end shattered all human endeavors to usurp the reins of world destiny. True, many have tried since, but His life and death spoke the final word over our world. It is His planet. He won it back from the hands that had wrenched it from Him in Eden. Love bore long with rebel creatures, both angelic and human. But here at the cross their hellish plan lay fully and forever exposed. The Man Jesus died a conqueror. Paying the price, He earned back the right to ownership of Planet Earth. Soon it will be a new earth. It is just a matter of time, that's all.

And no one can change this fact. No tyrant can reach up and grab the world from His grasp. It remains firmly and forever in the hands of the Crucified One. None can undo Calvary anymore than they can undo their birth. Both are irreversible, irrepealable acts. Thus the goal of human history came at Calvary. There humanity reached into the heights. For there God died for humanity. Could there be any more concrete revelation of God's utter compassion and concern for the race? Since the cross, we live in time filled by the victory of Calvary—time determined by that goal. Hence, whether they know it or not, humanity does not merely advance toward a hoped-for goal in some distant day, with the possibility that it may never come. No! Humanity moves triumphantly from a goal Jesus has already reached.

That is the good news of the cross. It has within its very grasp the Second Advent. Because He died and rose again, He will return. Because He died, His people will live. And because He came to His end, they have a new beginning—in Him.

Can Humans Delay the Advent?

"That's all well and good," someone may protest. "I can see Christ bought back the world at the cross. But why hasn't He come to claim it? If I purchased a new car, I wouldn't wait a day to claim it, would you? How come He has waited nearly 2,000 years?"

Good question. Although we see in the New Testament a development from immanency to delay—for example, between First and Second Thessalonians (2 Thess. 2:1-3)—it's also true that immanency never really fully leaves the New Testament. Even in the last book, Revelation, written toward the end of the first century, John, the last surviving disciple, signed off the biblical canon with the words "Yes, I am coming soon" (Rev. 22:20).

Such focus on the immediacy of the Advent has concerned many Christians. They want to believe the authenticity of such promises, but 1,900 intervening years worry them. Could Jesus have been wrong after all? Was Albert Schweitzer right when he believed that Jesus made His promises to return but died a deluded man? Will He ever really return? Various ideas have developed to answer these questions. The theory of a delayed return is one. Its proponents believe Jesus is waiting for His people to mature, to develop to a particular degree of readiness for His coming to take place.

The deepest problem with such an idea is that God has never waited for such developments before, whether destroying cities such as Sodom and Gomorrah (Gen. 19) or the world at the time of the Flood (Gen. 6, 7). Whether we're ready or not, Jesus will return. That's why He compares the kingdom to ten virgins, half of them foolish who never make it into the wedding (Matt. 25:10-13). Elsewhere He says that one will be taken and another left (Matt. 24:40-44), suggesting that His coming will find some ready and others not. Some even remind Him of the good deeds they performed, to which He replies, "I never knew you" (Matt. 7:22, 23).

Christ's parables mention delay. When the Bridegroom did not arrive immediately, all the virgins slept (Matt. 25:5), and a servant says that his Master delays His coming (Matt. 24:48). Now put with these the Ellen White statement "It was not the will of God that the coming of Christ should be so long delayed and His people remain so many years in this world of sin and sorrow."[2] What do we have? It seems the Lord has postponed His coming. Has He, though?

1. The Date Is Set

Many give dates for the Second Advent. William Miller eventually thought it would be October 22, 1844. Lutheran minister Johann Bengel in Germany set a date within a few years of Miller's.[3] Other suggestions popped up during the early days of the Advent movement. In recent times, as we saw in a previous chapter, Jubilee calendar proponents set dates, ignoring the fact that the annual Jubilee of ancient Israel has nothing to do with prophecy. Aad Verbeek, Jan Westein, and Piet Westein announced the discovery of what they considered an important time prophecy in Revelation 9:1-12. The 150-year period found there, they believe, reaches from 1844 to 1994. They conclude, "It means nothing more or less, than the time of Christ's second coming is apparently recorded in the Bible."[4] But the period has passed and Christ is still not here.

"Many Adventists have felt that unless they could fix their faith upon a definite time for the Lord's coming, they could not be zealous and diligent in the work of preparation . . . ," Ellen White warns. "Those who persist in this error will at last fix upon a date too far in the future for the coming of Christ. Thus they will be led to rest in a false security, and many will not be undeceived until it is too late."[5]

God the Father knows everything (Job 37:16; Ps. 139:1-18; 147:5; 1 John 3:20), including the Second Advent date (Matt. 24:36). He could have revealed it to humanity, but He didn't. He realizes that if we knew the time, we'd probably wait until just before the event to get ready. That would be dangerous, because we could die before that date, or if alive, wait too late. More than that, being ready for the Second Advent is the same as fitness for it. It takes time and is not the work of a moment. Exceptions do exist, of course, such as the thief on the cross, but that was for someone who didn't know about Jesus until then, not for a Christian who puts preparation off until the last moment.

The fact that God knows the end from the beginning should not suggest determinism or a type of fatalism. God does not predestinate, or predetermine, human destiny against human volition. Nor does He arbitrarily set the return date. On the other hand, humans cannot—in the ultimate sense—hasten or delay that date either—at least in the absolute sense. Or else Christ may never come.

Yet, it's not fully correct to say, as David J. Bosch did, "mission may never be regarded as precondition or prerequisite for the coming of the end, neither may the church hasten the end through her missionary fervor. Mission is no hand on the clock of the world."[6] The fact is, both divine determinism and human delay are too one-sided.

2. The Balanced Position

Neither God nor human beings have the sole input into the Second Advent date decision. Rather, God's foreknowledge took into consideration all of human hastening and delaying and simply fed all the data into His computer (to use an anthropomorphic illustration) to get the appropriate printout date. His advent will, therefore, take place at the best time, in which He takes into consideration both His foreknowledge and human hastening and delaying. Neither solely determines the date, operating in a vacuum as if the other did not exist.

If humans could really hasten the Advent by themselves, Christians would face the greatest salvation-by-works emphasis ever—in spite of the gospel. On the other hand, if humanity could really delay the Advent by themselves, then the present generation on our planet must represent the terrible lack of preparation and delaying that previous generations experienced. So, in heaven, the final generation will need to thank those prior generations for the miserable lives they lived to delay the Advent and which gave them a chance at birth—and heaven. And if such a thing were true, then the final generation would be an unexpected or unplanned-for one—there merely due to human delaying and not to God's planning. Such thinking posits a second-class status to God's end-time people.

The fact of the matter is that God planned for everyone who enters heaven. Indeed, He loves the world (John 3:16). All come within His divine will, and He loves all equally. The fact that time lingers does not oppose His will, and therefore His love for all humanity. He simply longs for all to be saved and gives time for the work of salvation to reach its logical conclusion. "The Lord is not slow in keeping his promise, as some understand slowness. He is patient with you, not wanting anyone to perish, but everyone to come to repentance. But the day of the Lord will come like a thief" (2 Peter 3:9, 10). Note the balance between (1) divine forbearance and (2) human unexpectedness of the Advent.

Threefold Dimension of Last-Day Events

Eschatology, or final events, are not unidimensional, that is, having to do solely with the future. In the light of the cross they are three-dimensional. We can speak of the end that has already arrived, an end that is present, and an end to come. No vacuum exists between the promise to come and the delay to fulfill it. The coming Christ fills present time. He is on His way.

Early one morning at the Skogsborg Sanitarium in Sweden I awoke surprised to see it light at about 2:00 a.m. It was the morning I wanted to take a picture of a sunrise above the sea. So, dressing quickly, I rushed out to set up the tripod and prepare my camera. Then came the longest wait I've ever had in picture taking. The light from the east began to spread across the horizon until finally, after about an hour, the sun rose above the horizon. In Manila I've seen the sun pop up in a few moments by comparison. Not in Sweden. I took the picture and went back to bed.

Years later I awoke in the night with a thought. Have you ever done that? At such times I've said, "Oh, I'll remember that in the morning," only to find that I didn't have a clue what it was when I woke. Have you also done that? So that night I wrote down the idea, then went back to sleep. The next morning I began to write it out. It became an article published by *These Times.*[7] Here's a synopsis of it.

Just as every day has a sunrise that precedes it, so the coming eternal day has a sunrise too. The light of that sunrise began to show in the eastern horizon when Jesus rose from the grave on Resurrection Sunday. It continued to cast light across the horizon as Jesus returned as the Spirit of Christ at Pentecost (John 14:15-18; Acts 2) and its extension through history ever since. The dawn is getting brighter as we move closer to Christ's appearance—when we will see the Son (1 Thess. 4:16-18). In this way the whole New Testament is the dawn of the eternal day. It means, in a qualified sense, that Christ is already on His way.

No one can stop Christ's coming anymore than anyone can prevent a sunrise. Have you ever tried to stop a boulder pounding down the mountain toward you? Or have you ever tried to jump out of a roller coaster and halt it before it plunges down the big one? "Never," you say. So it is with the Second Advent. No one can block Christ's coming! For, properly understood, it has three dimensions: past, present, and future. To look solely to the future dimension is to lose the full picture.

Scholars have not always recognized this fact. C. H. Dodd emphasized the past dimension in his "realized eschatology," and Rudolph Bultmann focused on the present with his "timeless eschatology," or "existential eschatology." Jürgen Moltmann zeroes in on the future with his "proleptic eschatology." But what is the biblical scenario?

Patently the New Testament documents have a shifting emphasis. The earliest writings, such as 1 Thessalonians, speak of Jesus as almost here (1 Thess. 4:13-18; 5:4, 23). Paul undoubtedly believed then that he would be alive to see Jesus return. But the Lord showed him otherwise, so in his second letter he corrected his earlier optimism. There must pass enough time for a counterfeit anti-Christ system to develop (2 Thess. 2:1-8).

We do not move toward the end, delaying or hastening it, as if humans have a great contribution to make or as if the reins are really dangling from heaven and fall into our hands. Ordinary human hands were not the ones nailed to the cross. His hands were. He alone earned the right to control world events. And He unfolds all others precisely out of that past event. For, in one sense and in a very determinative way, what was enfolded within that pivotal event is what is being unfolded now in time.

All last-day end events issue out of that Calvary end event.

"Well," some might question, "if that is so, was Pentecost or the sending of the Holy Spirit an end event? Isn't this, after all, the fulfillment of His promise to return? Doesn't this explain the supposed delay much better? Isn't it a fact that the immediacy of Pentecost maintained the immediacy of the return? He came through the Spirit 50 days after He left."

But this overlooks the fact that the Bible never equates the two. In fact, it separates them. The Old Testament looked forward to the coming of both members of the Godhead—the Messiah (Isa. 7:4; cf. Matt. 11:3), and the outpouring of the Spirit (Joel 2:28, 29). The New Testament speaks of the advent of both the Spirit (John 14:15-18 and Christ (Matt. 24:30). We mustn't confuse the two.

Bultmann's timeless eschatology subsumed all future reality within the present moment of encounter with the Spirit. He considered it personal, repeatable, and timeless. Thus the Second Advent promises receive their fulfillment every day the Spirit comes to a person, and it will always continue without any change. There is no future Advent day. It is just another day, like today, with endless ones to follow. Here the cross becomes meaningless. After all, could not God have come to us without sending His Son to live and die? Didn't He encounter people in the Old Testament? Doesn't the life and work of Christ make a difference after all? The fact that He came and died gives specificity to His return.

Moltmann's proleptic eschatology focuses on the future to the detriment of the past and present. In fact, he proposes that Christ can do the unexpected, the startling new—cut off from His promises in the Bible. He takes this position in a supposed defense of God's sovereignty—God can do as He chooses. Yet any quest supporting God's future exercise of sovereignty will, if severed from His past demonstration of sovereignty, prove no defense at all. It destroys what it sets out to defend.

Scripture is balanced, recognizing all three dimensions. It roots the return of Christ in a past event of Christ. The end came when Jesus cried out, "It is finished" (John 19:30). That is why Scripture repeatedly speaks of the end as already come. For example, "Now once in the *end* of the world hath he [Christ] appeared to put away sin by the sacrifice of himself" (Heb. 9:26, KJV); "the *ends* of the world are come" (1 Cor. 10:11, KJV); hence, "God . . . hath in these *last days* spoken unto us by his Son" (Heb. 1:2, KJV); and "we know that it is the *last time*" (1 John 2:18, KJV).

Two Pictures of the Second Advent

There are five major passages on

the Second Advent in Revelation. We will consider two of them. In Revelation 14 He arrives on a white cloud as a "Son of man" with a crown on His head. The crown is a *stephanos* in the Greek, that is, a laurel wreath of victory worn by the winner of an Olympic game. Three angels accompany Christ. I call them the other three angels of Revelation 14. The first three angels have a message (Rev. 14:6-13). These three angels have a mission (verses 15-20). Christ and an angel have a sickle. They come to implement the double verdict (deliverance/destruction) of the pre-Advent judgment. The first angel calls for Christ to "take the sickle and reap" (verse 15). Christ reaps the harvest of the righteous (verse 16). Then Revelation introduces the second angel, the one who has a sharp sickle (verse 17). The third angel calls "in a loud voice to him who has the sharp sickle, 'Take your sharp sickle and gather the clusters of grapes from the earth's vine'" (verse 18). To whom does the third angel speak—Christ or the second angel? For both have a sickle. Here is the answer. "The angel swung his sickle on the earth, gathered its grapes and threw them into the great winepress of God's wrath" (verse 19).

The vision pictures Christ as delivering His people and the angel as destroying the wicked. It is significant that Revelation does not present Christ as eradicating the wicked in this scene. Rather, He comes as the Son of man, as a fellow human, with a laurel wreath reminiscent of His human victory for His bride.

In stark contrast, Revelation 19:11 shows Christ arriving on a white horse, leading an army to make war. He wears many diadem crowns on His head, crowns worn only by those of royal heritage. Here Christ returns as King of kings (verse 16), and as such He comes to destroy the enemies of His bride. Thus Revelation presents the Second Advent from two different perspectives. In one, Christ returns as a fellow human being who has been through the greatest time of trouble, worse than any other ever endured by humans. He understands His people in their future great time of trouble and returns to take them home. Christ also arrives as God to defeat the world conglomerate moving to annihilate His bride in the greatest rescue mission of all time, an experience that the redeemed will never forget. Christ delivers His people and destroys their enemies, and He actively implements the double verdict of the pre-Advent judgment in His second advent. We are now ready to study the background to this event and all that is involved: Armageddon.

Armageddon

1. More Than a Middle East Confrontation

Many Christians believe in the battle of Armageddon but hold numerous interpretations. Most look for a Middle East conflict in Palestine's Megiddo region. Multitudes nervously watch Israeli-Arab relations as the trigger to ignite world destruction. After all, the oil stakes are high. But the Bible gives a totally different picture. Scripture speaks of Armageddon as the ultimate climax—not between nations squabbling over oil, but between the two sides of the cosmic controversy. It's a religious struggle, not economic or political.

Before the demise of Russian Communism, historian Arnold J. Toynbee exposed the root crisis of today when he affirmed, "The fundamental conflict is not political but religious; and the dividing line between the two religious camps is not the present world-encompassing political boundary between Russian and an American sphere of political influence. The line cuts across the inward spiritual world within every living soul today—whatever label of political citizenship may have been stamped on its body by the accident of birth."[8] Seventh-day Adventists believe the world is fast polarizing into two groups—those against God and those for Him.

The global nature of the battle is clear from two passages. Revelation 14:14-20 mentions the word "earth" four times. Revelation 16:12-16 tells how spirits of devils go to "the kings of the whole world" to gather people to their side in the battle. Three counterfeit messages call humanity to join Satan's side. The three angels' messages go to the whole world (Rev. 14:6-12) to summon people to join Christ's side in the battle. Here we have two global missions. Three spirits of devils and the three angelic messengers gather the world for the same battle in the end-time.

2. Presentation of the Battle in Revelation

When John has something important to say, he repeats the point, and the repetition expands his thinking. That is true in his presentation of Armageddon. The first mention of the end-time battle occurs in one verse (Rev. 12:17). Satan is angry against the church and goes to wage war against her. This passage focuses on his anger at the end-time church. He is out to destroy end-time saints. Chapter 13 describes his battle against it. Chapters 15-19 continue to add details.

3. The Roots of Armageddon

The well-used Armageddon passage (Rev. 16:12-16) didn't arise in a vacuum. Its roots go back through at least seventeen biblical books clear to Genesis. After all, the book of Revelation comprises a veritable mosaic of Old Testament allusions and references—some 600 of them. Without a thorough knowledge of the Old Testament we will lose much of the meaning of the book, including that of Armageddon.

The Reformers' principle of the Bible interpreting the Bible *(sola scriptura)* is the key to unlock Revelation. We should go to the Bible and not to passing political history, for the interpretation of Armageddon. To look beyond Scripture is to step outside of the canon.

As we approach the Bible we ask it to reveal its own inner rationality rather than superimposing on it any alien presupposition of the researcher. The Bible is a book that operates according to definite laws of interpretation, just as nature does. To discover and apply them will unlock the mystery of Armageddon and help us understand what is happening to the nations today.

A root passage for Armageddon is Joel 3. There God warns, "I will gather all nations and bring them down to the Valley of Jehoshaphat. . . . For there I will sit to judge all the nations on every side. Swing the sickle, for the harvest is ripe. Come, trample the grapes, for the winepress is full and the vats overflow—so great is their wickedness" (Joel 3:2-13). The passage finds its fulfillment in Revelation 14:19, in which "the angel swung his sickle on the earth, gathered its grapes and threw them into the great winepress of God's wrath" (Rev. 14:19). That's part of Armageddon. The past tense emphasizes its certainty. The event happens at the Second Advent.

4. Types of Armageddon in the Old Testament

One principle that emerges from Bible study is that a local happening often typifies something worldwide in scope. For example, Jerusalem's destruction is a type of the coming world destruction (Matt. 24). The same is true of Armageddon. We'll consider a few examples. The local root reference to Megiddo appears in Judges 4 and 5. Israel languished during 20 years of oppression (Judges 4:3). God promised deliverance (verses 6-9), and every enemy soldier perished (verse 16). The Lord avenged Israel (Judges 5:2) at the battle of Megiddo (verse 19), and the land had rest for 40 years (verse 31).

Here we find that Israel—as God's people and not as a political entity—is the focus of attack and of deliverance. Many years later history repeated itself. God's people faced another local battle as a type of Armageddon (not in Megiddo). A number of nations surrounded Israel (2 Chron. 20:1, 2). Judah, under Jehoshaphat, sought God in utter helplessness (verses 3, 12). And the Lord said, "'Fear not, and be not dismayed at this great multitude; for the battle is not yours but God's'" (verse 15, RSV). "'Fear not, and be not dismayed; tomorrow go out against them, and the Lord will be with you'" (verse 17, RSV). The next day strong soldiers sang a doxology—they didn't fight—and God won the battle. Not one of the enemy escaped (verses 21-24).

The river of Kishon (Judges 4:7, 19-21) is a synonym for Megiddo, or Armageddon. The third local Armageddon battle takes place on Mount Carmel between the priests of Baal and Elijah (1 Kings 18:40). Elijah is a type of the end-time church (Mal. 4:5). Just as false worship surrounded Elijah, the world will encompass God's people in Armageddon. Though outnumbered, Elijah triumphed. All the prophets of Baal perished at the river of Kishon, or Megiddo.

In all three local Armageddon examples we find (1) God's people totally outnumbered, (2) the enemy totally destroyed, and (3) God's people totally delivered. Interestingly, each episode involved a prophet: Deborah (Judges 4:4), Jahazeel (2 Chron. 20:14), and Elijah. But far more important, God brought the destruction/deliverance. So it will be in the end-time. God's people will be totally outnumbered—the whole world against a remnant. You can't get any more outnumbered than that! But God will stand up and fight for His people, annihilating the wicked and delivering the saints. And throughout the end-time the prophetic voice will be in the midst of the saints (Joel 2:28, 29).

Leaving these three types of Armageddon, we come to consider one more. Time passed, and so did Israel—into captivity to Babylon. But God was ready for the emergency. More than a century before He had prophesied that Cyrus would be His instrument to deliver Israel from Babylon (Isa. 45-47). Babylon would be overthrown in "a single day" (Isa. 47:9), the same language used of spiritual Babylon in Armageddon's battle (Rev. 18:8). Just as literal Israel triumphed over literal Babylon, so will spiritual Israel (the church) be victorious over spiritual Babylon (the enemy of the church). And the arrival of Cyrus to save Israel from Babylon symbolizes Christ's advent to rescue spiritual Israel.

5. Armageddon and the Cosmic Controversy

"How do you know Armageddon has to do with the cosmic controversy? Sure, you have proved it is worldwide, but so what? Couldn't that be true of a secular war?"

Excellent questions. First, the Bible is not a book about secular history. It's about God's people, and nations get into the Bible only if they have something to do with God's people, whether they fight against them or support them. That's why America appears in the Bible. It will play a major role against God's people in the end-time. On the other hand, China, with a fifth of the world's population, has not even one mention in Scripture.

Furthermore, contextual evidence indicates that Armageddon consists of a spiritual, not a secular, battle. In the middle of the Armageddon passage, Christ says, "'Behold, I come like a thief! Blessed is he who stays awake and keeps his clothes with him, so that he may not go naked and be shamefully exposed'" (Rev. 16:15). It's the same message given to the Laodicean church (Rev. 3:18), a repetition of God's appeal to His last church to wear Christ's robe of righteousness. Only those whom Christ delivers from sin can He rescue in Armageddon (Dan. 12:1).

6. The Battle

When is the battle? The final gathering takes place during the sixth plague (Rev. 16:12). That will be toward the end of Jacob's trouble, a fact that should give pause to those in the past who have seen Armageddon written large on any passing event such as the Gulf War. In order to be Armageddon two international events must take place first: that is, the Sunday law (Rev. 13:3, 4, 12-14), and the death decree (verse 15).

a. Step One: Implementation of Death Decree Attempted

Armageddon rages during the seventh plague. It consists of three major steps. The death decree constitutes the opening volley of the war. "With shouts of triumph, jeering, and imprecation, throngs of evil men are about to rush upon their prey, when, lo, a dense blackness, deeper than the darkness of the night, falls upon the earth. Then a rainbow, shining with the glory from the throne of God, spans the heavens and seems to encircle each praying company. The angry multitudes are suddenly arrested. Their mocking cries die away. The objects of their murderous rage are forgotten."[9]

"But none can pass the mighty guardians stationed about every faithful soul. Some are assailed in their flight from the cities and villages; but the swords raised against them break and fall powerless as a straw. Others are defended by angels in the form of men of war."[10]

"The eye of God, looking down the ages, was fixed upon the crisis which His people are to meet, when earthly powers shall be arrayed against them. Like the captive exile, they will be in fear of death by starvation or by violence. But the Holy One who divided the Red Sea before Israel, will manifest His mighty power and turn their captivity."[11] The preincarnate Christ promised His people during their captivity to Egypt, "I am the Lord, and I will bring you out from under the yoke of the Egyptians. I will free you from being slaves to them and will redeem you with an outstretched arm and with mighty acts of judgment" (Ex. 6:6).

b. Step Two: Enemy Killing Themselves

In so many Armageddonlike battles in history, the enemy forces have killed each other (Judges 7:19-23; 1 Sam. 14:19, 20; 2 Chron. 20:22-24; Isa. 19:2; Eze. 38:14-23; and Haggai 2:22). It happens again in Armageddon. When God manifests Himself as with His people, then those who have followed religious leaders and been deceived now turn on their leaders and put them to death.

"After the saints had been delivered by the voice of God, the wicked multitude turned their rage against one another. The earth seemed to be deluged with blood, and dead bodies were from one end to the other."[12] "The people see that they have been deluded. They accuse one another of having led them to destruction; but all unite in heaping their bitterest condemnation upon the ministers. . . . The swords which were to slay God's people are now employed to destroy their enemies. Everywhere there is strife and bloodshed."[13]

We have already studied that the ten kings who unite with the harlot for one hour in the end-time (Rev. 17:12), when all the world wonders and worships the church (Rev. 13:3, 4), will also turn on her. "They will bring her to ruin and leave her naked; they will eat her flesh and burn her with fire" (Rev. 17:16). Evidently it is not a total annihilation, because Christ will throw the beast into the lake of fire (Rev. 19:19, 20) in the Second Advent (Rev. 19:14-19). For our purpose here, we note that this revenge against the harlot church by the conglomerate of nations may also be a part of the battle of Armageddon.

c. Step Three: Angel of Death

Just as "the destroying angel" did his work in the Passover release of Israel from Egypt,[14] so the destroying angel will do his assignment before the release of God's people in the Second Coming (Rev. 14:19, 20). He "goes forth, represented in Ezekiel's vision by the men with the slaughtering weapons, to whom the command is given: 'Slay utterly old and young, both maids, and little children, and women.' "[15]

d. Step Four: Hail

Now is the time for the seventh plague. Christ has said, "It is done!" (Rev. 16:17). Just as God sent "the worst hailstorm ever" to fall on Egypt (Ex. 9:18), so He afflicts on the planet the worst earthquake ever "since man has been on the earth" (Rev. 16:18), with "huge hailstones of about a hundred pounds each," described as "so terrible" (verse 21). In Armageddon God's people do not fight. They stand still as God manifests His presence to protect them, as He causes the enemy to kill each other, as the angel of death does his work on their behalf, and as hail falls from the heavens to destroy the enemy. Throughout the battle God leads the fight. The saints simply rest in Christ and see Him work out their deliverance.

Often in such Armageddonlike battles God rained down hail on those He punishes (Joshua 10:7-14; Job 38:22, 23; Isa. 30:29, 30). Hail is one of His weapons of choice. The seventh plague will decimate the enemy.

e. Step Five: Second Advent

The fullest amplification of Armageddon comes in the Second Advent portrayal in Revelation 19:14-21. Christ rides a white horse, leading an army on white horses. "I saw heaven opened, and behold, a white horse. And He who sat upon him was called Faithful and True, and in righteousness He judges and makes war. . . . And the armies in heaven, clothed in fine linen, white and clean, followed Him on white horses. Now out of His mouth goes a sharp sword, that with it He should strike the nations. And He Himself will rule them with a rod of iron. . . . And He has on His robe and on His thigh a name written: King of kings and Lord of lords. . . . And I saw the beast, the kings of the earth, and their armies, gathered together to make war against Him who sat on the horse and against His army" (verses 14-19, NKJV).

We should note that people still remain alive after the other steps of Armageddon (Rev. 6:12-17). The armies are gathered to make war. In that war "the beast was captured, and with him the false prophet who had performed the miraculous signs on his behalf. With these signs he had deluded those who received the mark of the beast and worshiped his image [see Rev. 16:13, 14]. The two of them were thrown alive into the fiery lake of burning sulfur. The rest of them were killed with the sword that came out of the mouth of the rider on the horse" (Rev. 19:20, 21).

Scripture has still another way to describe this final phase of the battle. The sixth plague speaks about the water of the Euphrates being "dried up to prepare the way for the kings from the East" (Rev. 16:12). The diversion of the water of the Euphrates caused the fall of ancient Babylon, allowing access to the city. Cyrus gained a glorious victory and later liberated Israel from its 70 years of captivity.

Spiritual Babylon will have spiritual Israel in captivity. The kings of the East will dry up the river. Or put another way, waters (river) represent people (Rev. 17:15). With the annihilation of the enemies of God's people (i.e., drying up of the river), they will be delivered. But who are the kings of the East? Some interpreters once considered Japan and China the kings of the East during World War II. Others have suggested Israel and Palestine as candidates in more recent times. But Armageddon is the final battle in the great controversy this side of the millennium and thus not just a secular battle.

Bible writers regarded east as the direction from heaven. Thus the sealing angel from heaven comes from the east (Rev. 7:2). In Revelation 4 and 5 we have a vision of the throne room. There the Father sits on the throne (Rev. 5:1-5), and the Son comes to Him (verses 6, 7). They hold center stage throughout the chapter. At the end of the chapter we find another presentation of Armageddon: an earthquake and signs in the heavens, with islands and mountains removed from their place (Rev. 6:12-14), the same description about islands and mountains given in the seventh plague (Rev. 16:20). "Then the kings of the earth, the princes, the generals, the rich, the mighty, and every slave and every free man hid in caves and among the rocks of the mountains. They called to the mountains and the rocks, 'Fall on us and hide us from the face of him who sits on the throne [the Father] and from the wrath of the Lamb [Christ]! For the great day of their wrath has come, and who can stand?'" (Rev. 6:15-17). Here we see fulfilled the prophecy of Isaiah when human beings will throw away their money they have idolized and run for the rocks to hide (Isa. 2:10-12, 20, 21; 13:6).

So the Kings of the East, the Father and Son, come vaulting through the heavens on the greatest rescue mission ever attempted in history. They complete the destruction of the wicked and deliver God's people. It is the glorious pre-Advent climax called the battle of Armageddon. Jesus predicted this moment. He said, "'I say to all of you: In the future you will see the Son of Man sitting at the right hand of the Mighty One and coming on the clouds of heaven'" (Matt. 26:64). He also speaks of "when he comes in his glory and in the glory of the Father and of the holy angels" (Luke 9:26).

"Then the lawless one will be revealed, whom the Lord will overthrow with the breath of his mouth and destroy by the splendor of his coming" (2 Thess. 2:8). Ellen White describes the event another way: "At the coming of Christ the wicked are blotted from the face of the whole earth—consumed with the spirit of His mouth and destroyed by the brightness of His glory."[16]

The annihilation of all the enemies of God's people repeats the total destruction of such enemies in previous Armageddon battles (Judges 4:16; 1 Kings 18:40; 2 Chron. 20:23, 24). The world's population is decimated. All the enemies of the saints are dead, and God delivers His people and whisks them off to heaven. That's the finale of their journey through last-day events, the end of their exodus through the ultimate Red Sea.

The Book of Esther

The book of Esther is important for understanding final events. In it we see a death decree issued to kill God's people (Esther 3:13). The authorities give the date of execution, just as it will be in the end-time.[17] But God intervenes, just as He will in the battle of Armageddon.

Haman represents those who hate the saints. Mordecai symbolizes God's saints. Although Haman builds a 75-foot gallows on which to hang Mordecai (Esther 5:14), he ends up executed upon it himself (Esther 7:9, 10). So it will be in the coming death decree. With instruments raised to kill the saints, God will manifest His presence around His people. The murderers halt in their track, and kill those leaders who led them astray, as mentioned above.

The stories of Armageddon show that Christ will be with His people in their hour of greatest need. When all the world is against them, He will be for them. He wants us to know that He will have the last word, because He already had the last word at Calvary. Armageddon is the working out in history of what He accomplished at the cross. For there Christ delivered His people and decided the destiny of the devil. Satan is doomed to destruction, and God's people destined for deliverance—all because of Calvary.

[1] Jack Cranfield and Mark Victor Hansen, *Chicken Soup for the Soul* (Deerfield, Fla.: Health Communications, Inc., 1993), pp. 61-63.

[2] E. G. White, *The Great Controversy,* p. 458.

[3] *Ibid.,* pp. 363, 364.

[4] Aad Verbeek, Jan Westein, and Piet Westein, *Time for His Coming.* Sara Van Akker and Ria Westein, trans., from *Tijd voor der Wederkomst* (Aad Verbeek, Netherlands, 1995), p. 7.

[5] E. G. White, *The Great Controversy,* p. 457.

[6] David J. Bosch, *Witness to the World: The Christian Mission in Theological Perfection* (Atlanta: John Knox, 1980), p. 235.

[7] Norman R. Gulley, "1980: The Dawn of a New Era," *These Times,* January 1980, pp. 3-6.

[8] Cited by Francis D. Nichol in *Our Firm Foundation* (Washington, D.C.: Review and Herald Pub. Assn., 1953), vol. 1, p. 612.

[9] E. G. White, *The Great Controversy,* pp. 635, 636.

[10] *Ibid.,* p. 631.

[11] *Ibid.,* p. 634.

[12] E. G. White, *Early Writings,* p. 290.

[13] E. G. White, *The Great Controversy,* pp. 655, 656.

[14] E. G. White, *Patriarchs and Prophets,* p. 279.

[15] E. G. White, *The Great Controversy,* p. 656.

[16] *Ibid.,* p. 657.

[17] *Ibid.,* p. 635.

Chapter 45

The Other Journey

In their darkest hour—when hope seems gone, when instruments of death stare them in the face—deliverance comes.

"Look up," says a melodious voice, "look up."

Black, angry clouds part, and they "see the glory of God and the Son of man seated upon His throne. In His divine form they discern the marks of His humiliation; and from His lips they hear the request presented before His Father and the holy angels: 'I will that they also, whom thou hast given me, be with me where I am' (John 17:24). Again a voice, musical and triumphant, is heard, saying: 'They come! they come! holy, harmless, and undefiled. They have kept the word of My patience; they shall walk among the angels'; and the pale, quivering lips of those who have held fast their faith utter a shout of victory."[1]

These words from Ellen White's book *The Great Controversy* appear in the chapter "God's People Delivered." Then Ellen White quotes Revelation 16:17 in which God says, "It is done." This occurs at the seventh plague. So right at the beginning of the battle of Armageddon, when God delivers His people from the death decree's implementation, the saints shout victory. Who wouldn't if they saw the Father and the Son in heaven on Their throne? Here is the only focus to have in the end-time, and God gives it to the saints when they need it the most.

The Great Divide

Look at the contrast. "The mountains shake like a reed in the wind, and ragged rocks are scattered on every side. There is a roar as of a coming tempest. The sea is lashed into fury. There is heard the shriek of a hurricane like the voice of demons upon a mission of destruction. The whole earth heaves and swells like the waves of the sea. Its surface is breaking up. Its very foundations seem to be giving way. Mountain chains are sinking. Inhabited islands disappear. The seaports that have become like Sodom for wickedness are swallowed up by the angry waters. . . . Great hailstones, every one 'about the weight of a talent,' are doing their work of destruction (Rev. 16:19, 21). The proudest cites of the earth are laid low. The lordly palaces, upon which the world's great men have lavished their wealth in order to glorify themselves, are crumbling to ruin before their eyes. Prison walls are rent asunder, and God's people, who have been held in bondage for their faith, are set free."[2]

Above all this devastating confusion sit the Father and Son on their throne with innumerable angels. Peace, joy, and love fill heaven. Satan knows that very well. He was there once. So were his demons. Their one aim is to keep a view of that harmony and happiness away from haggard humans—particularly during the end-time. They attack with such ferocity that they hope the terrifying tempest will fill their minds and blot out any other view. Where God is, there is heaven. Where fallen angels are, there is hell.

So great are the falling judgments of God that the "demons acknowledge the deity of Christ and tremble before His power, while men are supplicating for mercy and groveling in abject terror."[3] By contrast, the pale, anxious, haggard saints are transformed. "A rift in the clouds" reveals a brilliant star that "speaks hope and joy to the faithful." "Their voices rise in triumphant song: 'God is our refuge and strength, a very present help in trouble. Therefore will not we fear, though the earth be removed, and though the mountains be carried into the midst of the sea; though the waters thereof roar and be troubled, though the mountains shake with the swelling thereof' (Ps. 46:1-3)."[4]

The Mysterious Hand

It happened once in a palace. The mysterious hand scribbled judgment across the king's dining hall wall. "Mene, Mene, Tekel, Parsin," words of judgment against Belshazzar of Babylon (Dan. 5:25). Now across the sky in the sight of modern Babylon comes this mysterious hand once more. But it doesn't write this time. It has words already composed to present. Ancient words. Words that cannot change. Words from God. The hand opens tables of stone, and there, in stark bold relief "God's ten words, brief, comprehensive, and authoritative,"[5] stare down on eyes riveted to them. The Decalogue speaks of the seventh-day Sabbath, not Sunday. In their mad dash to kill Sabbathkeepers, they see they are fighting God.

Many accepted Sunday in order to appease God, thinking it would halt the natural disasters. It was their attempt to survive. Now, too late, they recognize that it was all in vain. The very thing they feared has overtaken them. The seventh-day Sabbathkeepers are the ones who look secure. God's voice announces the day and hour of the Second Advent. That is the only time we can know the date beforehand. Saints "stand listening, with their eyes fixed upward. Their countenances are lighted up with His glory, and shine as did the face of Moses when he came down from Sinai. The wicked cannot look upon them. And when the blessing is pronounced on those who have honored God by keeping His Sabbath holy, there is a mighty shout of victory."[6]

The Second Coming

Above the dark clouds appear the

Kings of the East, the Father and the Son, with innumerable angels, all descending in mighty power. Everything in nature is in confusion, just as the people are in Babylon. Divine beings arrive in majesty, angels eager to do their bidding attending them. Peace and power pervade their presence. They move as one unified army to bring justice. Too long has wrong been on the throne. Now it is judgment time. Confusion below, unity above. Abject terror below, joy above. The vanquished below, victory above. This is the contrast that Satan has always hidden from humanity. Now human beings perceive the difference. They see both the true God and how Satan only pretended to be Christ. Here are the masses ruined and the remnant redeemed.

Although this is the same Second Advent, the same revelation of the true Father and His Son, the God that the masses have said they worship with their Sundaykeeping, one group shouts out in abject fear and the other in utter joy. One group moans "mercy." The other proclaims "This is our God!" One group is petrified, the other glorified. No greater divide than this—all because one group didn't know Him, and the other did.

Yet the presence of divinity overcomes everyone. "The child of God will be terror-stricken at the first sight of the majesty of Jesus Christ. He feels that he cannot live in His holy presence."[7] "The righteous cry with trembling: 'Who shall be able to stand?' The angels' song is hushed, and there is a period of awful silence. Then the voice of Jesus is heard, saying: 'My grace is sufficient for you.' The faces of the righteous are lighted up, and joy fills every heart. And the angels strike a note higher and sing again as they draw still nearer to the earth."[8]

Oh the wondrous good news about Jesus! Salvation is a free gift that was won at a terrible price. Grace is the only way to heaven, and the only way through final events. God's grace is sufficient for all your needs now—and forever!

Homeward Bound

"Oh, Mom and Dad, it's you!" Big hugs and happy voices. Resurrected and alive again. "Angels 'gather together His elect from the four winds, from one end of heaven to the other.' Little children are borne by holy angels to their mothers' arms. Friends long separated by death are united, nevermore to part, and with songs of gladness ascend together to the City of God."[9]

"Wow! I'm changed! I'm young again! Hallelujah! It all happened suddenly, quickly!"

"We're leaving the planet! Wow, I've always wanted to take a space trip."

"Me too. Just think of it. We're all moving out without space suits." Picking up speed, we rise above the trembling earth. Saints ascend from the surface of the planet as far as eyes can see. The brightness of Father and Son radiate the ruined landscape below. "I'm so glad to be free at last!" someone exclaims.

Angels hover close, full of love for human beings. What tales they have to tell! There will be time for those—plenty of time. All the redeemed meet the guardian angel they had throughout life. Saints wonder why they ever feared when such a mighty angel was ever near. Remembering, "the angel of the Lord encamps around those who fear him, and he delivers them" (Ps. 34:7), they bond with their guardian angel as if they've been together and talked before.

Everyone has much to catch up on as grandchildren get introduced to grandparents who passed away before seeing them. The great surprise is that all of them seem to be from the same generation. Everyone looks and feels young. Grandparents seem as young as their grown grandkids.

You know the little cloud that was first seen in the east, half the size of a man's hand—we're headed toward it. "We all entered the cloud together, and were seven days ascending to the sea of glass."[10] That means that the whole human race will observe its first Sabbath together. All Sundaykeepers who didn't know any different but who died loving Christ will get to experience their first Sabbath before entering heaven. So all the redeemed will be Sabbathkeepers before they arrive in heaven.

"And as the chariot rolled upward, the wheels cried, 'Holy,' and the wings, as they moved, cried, 'Holy,' and the retinue of holy angels around the cloud cried, 'Holy, holy, holy, Lord God Almighty!' And the saints in the cloud cried, 'Glory! Alleluia!'"[11]

The saints pass through a great shiny chasm that leads to the throne of God. The mighty passageway is like a grand avenue to the gates of heaven. There stand the gates of heaven. Father, Son and Holy Spirit, angels and redeemed, prepare to go through. They move as one mighty triumphant army. Arriving at the gates, all stop. The redeemed look at the mighty gates, but only for a moment. Then they gaze at the Father, Son, and Holy Spirit. They see in Their eyes immeasurable love and hear Them say, "Welcome home, children! Welcome home, dear children. Here's the kingdom prepared for you."

"With unutterable love, Jesus welcomes His faithful ones to the joy of their Lord. The Saviour's joy is in seeing, in the kingdom of glory, the souls that have been saved by His agony and humiliation."[12]

"Before entering the city of God, the Saviour bestows upon His followers the emblems of victory, and invests them with the insignia of their royal state. The glittering ranks are drawn up in the form of a hollow square about their King. . . . Upon the heads of the overcomers, Jesus with His own right hand places the crown of glory. . . . In every hand are placed the victor's palm and the shining harp. Then, as the commanding angels strike the note, every hand sweeps the harp strings with skillful touch, awaking sweet music in rich, melodious strains. . . . Before the ransomed throng is the holy city. Jesus opens wide the pearly gates, and the nations that have kept the truth enter in."[13]

A mighty wave of love sweeps across the redeemed. They are caught up in a resounding chorus. The music sweeps across the teeming millions as they sing, "How great is the love the Father has lavished on us, that we should be called children of God!" (1 John 3:1). "For God so loved the world that he gave his one and only Son, that whoever believes in him shall not perish but have eternal life" (John 3:16). They keep singing the words, rising on higher notes each time until the very gates of heaven shake with the glad refrains.

Glorious words come to the minds of many of the end-time generation. "Oh, wonderful redemption! long talked of, long hoped for, contemplated with eager anticipation, but never fully understood."[14] "Oh, how glorious it will be to see Him and be welcomed as His redeemed ones! Long have we waited, but our hope is not to grow dim. If we can but see the King in His beauty we shall be forever blessed. I feel as if I must cry aloud, 'Homeward bound!' "[15] They understand now how Ellen White had felt. She had seen Jesus in vision. There He was before them. How they thrilled as He placed the crowns on their heads, and He said, "Well done." *Beautiful Saviour, how could You die for us? How could You leave heaven for the rebel planet? You must really love us!* Such thoughts race through minds as they behold the King in His glory and hear Him say again, "Welcome home, My children. I've longed for this day with all My heart. No more troubles and tears in this place. You will be safe and secure forevermore." And with that we shout "Alleluia, Glory to the Lamb who was slain," as we enter through the gates.

Heaven at Last

"The angels, touching their golden harps, will welcome the King and His trophies of victory—those who have been washed and made white in the blood of the Lamb. A song of triumph will peal forth, filling all heaven. Christ has conquered. He enters the heavenly courts, accompanied by His redeemed ones, the witnesses that His mission of suffering and sacrifice has not been in vain."[16]

"We are homeward bound. He who loved us so much as to die for us hath builded for us a city. The New Jerusalem is our place of rest. There will be no sadness in the city of God. No wail of sorrow, no dirge of crushed hopes and buried affections, will evermore be heard. Soon the garments of heaviness will be changed for the wedding garment. Soon we shall witness the coronation of our King. . . . And in His presence, all the trials and sufferings of this life will be as nothingness."[17]

The redeemed approach to the throne and see the control center of heaven, where God has guided human affairs. They have come "from garrets, from hovels, from dungeons, from scaffolds, from mountains, from deserts, from the caves of the earth, from the caverns of the sea. On earth they were 'destitute, afflicted, tormented.' Millions went down to the grave loaded with infamy because they steadfastly refused to yield to the deceptive claims of Satan. . . . They are no longer feeble, afflicted, scattered, and oppressed. Henceforth they are to be ever with the Lord. They stand before the throne clad in richer robes than the most honored of the earth have ever worn. They are crowned with diadems more glorious than were ever placed upon the brow of earthly monarchs. The days of pain and weeping are forever ended. The King of glory has wiped the tears from all faces; every cause of grief has been removed. Amid the waving of palm branches they pour forth a song of praise, clear, sweet, and harmonious; every voice takes up the strain, until the anthem swells through the vaults of heaven: 'Salvation to our God which sitteth upon the throne, and unto the Lamb.' And all the inhabitants of heaven respond in the ascription: 'Amen: Blessing, and glory, and wisdom, and thanksgiving, and honor, and power, and might, be unto our God for ever and ever' (Rev. 7:10, 12)."[18]

How Could He Do It?

The redeemed take in the scene. How gorgeous is heaven!—far more beautiful than anything they have ever seen! Earth had nothing to compare. How could Satan have ever rebelled? What strange, inexplicable treason! That he would reject Christ who gave him life, who gave him heaven. But there is no way to understand creaturely pride.

They gaze on Jesus, adored and worshiped by all. How could He leave heaven on the most dangerous rescue mission of all eternity, at the risk of failure—to save rebel humans? In disbelief they shake their heads. He created unnumbered worlds. Why bother with the one that went wrong? He who is worshiped as the God of heaven humbled Himself to help humanity. "He bore the guilt and shame of sin, and the hiding of His Father's face, till the woes of a lost world broke His heart and crushed out His life on Calvary's cross. . . . As the nations of the saved look upon their Redeemer and behold the eternal glory of the Father shining in His countenance; as they behold His throne, which is from everlasting to everlasting, and know that His kingdom is to have no end, they break forth in rapturous song: 'Worthy, worthy is the Lamb that was slain, and hath redeemed us to God by His own most precious blood!' "[19]

An Unforgettable Scene

The redeemed gather in a giant amphitheater. Never a General Conference session like this one, they belong to every nation, ancient and modern. They represent biblical history—Joseph, Jacob, and David, as well as Peter, Paul, and John. And many more. Others embody church history—Wycliffe, Huss, William Miller, and countless more. James and Ellen White and Joseph Bates join throngs from denominational history. They consist of those you know, those you invited, belonging to your family and its ancestors. Many are there, but not all. Each has come to watch the two Adams meet.

A door opens at one end of the huge stage. A 15-foot giant emerges, proportionally built. He weighs a ton as he moves out onto the platform. From the other end enters the second Adam, the God-man, Jesus Christ. The Saviour approaches him with outstretched arms. He enfolds the father of the race in His big strong arms and holds him close for a long time. The redeemed shed tears of joy. They know it must be hard for Adam. He let Jesus down, allowing sin to enter the planet.

Jesus holds Adam, then turns to the redeemed multitude, pointing to them, and says, "Here's your family." Adam stands overwhelmed as he stares at the teeming masses. Then he falls at Christ's feet and worships Him. He weeps as he sees the scars on His hands and feet. "Thank You for being my Redeemer and for saving my children," he whispers. Jesus tenderly picks him up, and they walk to the center of the platform to talk to the human family.

That will be a moment we'll never forget.

The 1,000-Year Vacation

It begins with the marriage supper of the Lamb, where the Bridegroom and the bride celebrate. Christ and the redeemed will have a grand celebration of redemption. We shall have stories to hear, providences to learn, and the thrilling triumphs of the cross to tell. I envisage grand testimony meetings, sessions with our guardian angels, and listening to the great biblical characters. Music such as we have never heard will awe and thrill us. Through it all, the redeemed will enter ever closer into union with each other, their guardian angels, and especially with Christ.

Time always whizzes by when you're having fun. It will pass quickly in heaven. Much of humanity will not be present, including relatives, loved ones, and friends of the redeemed. The saints will have opportunity to see why. I don't think they will look at the wrong such individuals did, for by beholding we become changed (2 Cor. 3:18). If that is true in a short life on earth, imagine a thousand years in heaven! I believe the investigative judgment of the lost will focus on what Christ and His angels did to try to save them. It will be a study of the good rather than the evil. The redeemed will marvel at the infinite patience given to all the lost.

I once met a church administrator who blurted out, "I don't want to spend 1,000 years going through people's records!" He is right. I wouldn't either. That would bore me to tears within an hour. But if we study what Christ and His angels did, in so many different ways, to pull them over the line, then the plan of salvation becomes high drama. Now that is worth studying! Maybe God keeps a video library of heaven's efforts for the lost, and all we do is pull out the ones about which we have questions. When all the redeemed have seen enough and are satisfied, then the work will be done.

John put it this way. The martyrs of the end-time are "given authority to judge." "They came to life and reigned with Christ a thousand years" (Rev. 20:4). Reigning with Christ, the King of kings—what a picture!

I imagine we will have time for lots of fun things, such as exploring the universe and meeting other people. In fact, I think the inhabitants of innumerable planets will take a field trip to visit with the redeemed. Who could ever remain at home when the greatest homecoming has just taken place? We will have fun and fellowship with the perfect beings who watched us during final events. They longed to see us make it, and now they rejoice to see us home. It will be Thanksgiving and Christmas rolled into one, and magnified a million times.

Going Home

There comes the day when God announces, "It's time to return to earth." It is a return trip for the redeemed and moving day for heaven. Even God's throne is ready for the journey. Angels take one long last look at their home, for all are bound for earth.

You've read about the New

Jerusalem coming down from heaven. Just imagine real estate that some believe is a 1,400-mile cube descending through the skies. A cube, reminiscent of the Most Holy Place of heaven's sanctuary, where the pre-Advent judgment took place. It isn't the first piece of real estate to travel through space. The Garden of Eden took off into space just before the Flood.[20] No doubt, it too will return to earth again.

Without any parachutes or reverse-thrust engines, the city settles on the Mount of Olives (Zech. 14:4, 9)—the very place from which Christ took off in His ascension.[21] He's back home in Palestine.

Armageddon, Part II

Christ calls the wicked up from their graves. Teeming billions burst forth. Satan and his angels with utter wonderment watch the New Jerusalem descend from space. It seems incredible to them that God would move the center of the universe from heaven to earth. He couldn't understand how the Father and the Holy Spirit, plus the angels, would be willing to come at Christ's request. Once he had fought to become God in heaven. Now even God has vacated that special place. Such a difference between self and selflessness. Shaking his head, he mutters, "There's one thing for sure—God must be stupid. I'd never do such a silly thing!"

But he doesn't have time for more thinking—it is time for action. Seeing the billions rise from graves, Satan rushes around taking credit for their new life. He and his demons work with frenzied speed to galvanize the billions for battle. "We are far more than those in the city," he tells them. "We are more than able to take it by storm, overthrow those within, and set up the kingdom that has been wrenched from me and which rightly is mine." The wicked have no choice. They throw in their lot with him. Some have come up in a different resurrection than they planned. Their only hope now is to follow Satan as he leads them against the city.

Phase two of Armageddon (called Gog and Magog in Rev. 20:7-9) begins, this time actually in what used to be the Middle East. Satan's force includes many great generals of all time. They assemble their troops and manufacture weapons. It takes time. The redeemed watch from the safety of their homes in the city. At last at Satan's signal the trudging feet of billions move across the face of the planet. They prepare to surround and take the city (verse 9), feeling that they are well able to accomplish their design, for their overwhelming numbers suggest an easy victory. As in the beginning of the cosmic controversy on earth, so now again at its end; humans put stock in what they see. But in this act they stand confronted with their problem, self-dependence.

The Final Revelation

Before the final onslaught the presence of God stops them in their tracks. Now they view their lives. God replays the moments when He came as the light to enlighten each of them (cf. John 1:9). They see individually their own lives, the sum total of which the onlookers in the millennial judgment have witnessed. This time the emphasis is not only on what Christ has done to try to save them, although that is primary, but they also note clearly each time they refused His pleas.

At the end of the review of their lives, some taking more time than others perhaps (for some have lived hundreds of years), comes the final moment of truth when each person realizes that God is just. How? Across the screen of the heavens, in full three-dimensional color replay, they witness the final events of Christ. The redeemed, unfallen, and lost are glued to the presentation.

"And now before the swaying multitude are revealed the final scenes—the patient Sufferer treading the path to Calvary; the Prince of heaven hanging upon the cross; the haughty priests and the jeering rabble deriding His expiring agony. . . . The awful spectacle appears just as it was. Satan, his angels, and his subjects have no power to turn from the picture of their own work."[22]

Satan now stands unmasked before the lost humans, just as he was unmasked before the unfallen worlds at Calvary. But at the same time, the panorama fully reveals God as never before. Even Satan and his angels, together with all creatures, unfallen and fallen, saved and lost, bow their knees (Rom. 14:11; Isa. 45:22, 23), and exclaim, "Great and marvelous are your deeds, Lord God Almighty. Just and true are your ways, King of the ages. Who will not fear you, O Lord, and bring glory to your name? For you alone are holy. All nations will come and worship before you, for your righteous acts have been revealed" (Rev. 15:3, 4). It is the time when Paul says, "We will all stand before God's judgment seat. It is written: 'As surely as I live,' says the Lord, 'every knee will bow before me; every tongue will confess to God'" (Rom. 14:10, 11, a quote from Isa. 45:23).

Paul focuses on the fact that it involves fallen angels as well as human nations in Philippians 2:10, 11: "that at the name of Jesus every knee should bow, in heaven and on earth and under the earth, and every tongue confess that Jesus Christ is Lord." The phrase "in heaven and on earth and under the earth" derives from a Hebrew idiom representing the whole creation (Ex. 20:4; cf. its use in Rev. 5:3). Not until this moment will all who have lived understand the truth of the cross. But then it will be so completely revealed that the question of God's justice will be forever solved. Never again will sin or sinners be a part of the universe. The powerful love of Calvary will have won out at last. Every created being will find in the cross the truth about Jesus. God will be seen as fully just: that He could not ignore sin but that Christ had to die for it. No sin has ever been excused, but all sinners can be forgiven. Such love at so terrible cost to Himself reveals that no one had to be lost. Love simply allows created beings the freedom to make the ultimate choice—to accept or reject Calvary.

So ends the third judgment. The pre-Advent one was for the onlooking universe and some translated humans and angels to behold. The redeemed participated in the millennial judgment. The lost watched the postmillennial. Through these three judgments all created beings, unfallen and fallen, have opportunity to see that God is just. They do not judge Him as such. That would be no better than people sitting in judgment of His Word. No, they *see* that God's self-revelation *is* just, that He has dealt equally and fairly with all, and that the only difference between the saved and the lost is whether they accepted Calvary or not. God doesn't force His gift, even His greatest gift, on anyone. Apart from Calvary there is no salvation.

The lost see they are unfitted for heaven. No selfish person would be happy there. They recognize too late that sin is self-destructive, and they perish. Satan is the last to die. Christ stands in the deep recesses of the city and sobs. All are His children. He died for all humans, and would have for fallen angels too. Satan and the angels were among His first children. Christ will miss them forever. Those looking on exclaim, quietly, "He said, 'Love your enemies' (Luke 6:27). He surely did."

An Empty Heaven?

The only time heaven is emptied, as far as human records go, is at the Second Advent. The Father and Son leave heaven to come as the Kings of the East (Rev. 16:12; 6:16, 17; Matt. 26:64; Luke 9:26), and the angels accompany them (Rev. 19:11-14). John says "there was silence in heaven" (Rev. 8:1). It will be for just a short time. After the millennium, when God, His throne, angels, the redeemed, and the New Jerusalem travel to the earth, it would seem that heaven is empty.

If heaven is vacant, I wonder what it will be used for? Once I visited DollyWood at Pigeon Forge, Tennessee. A new section had just opened up—memories of the 50s. It was like stepping back 40 years to see old Studebakers, Oldsmobiles, and winged Chevies; tall gas pumps with round lights on top and 29 cents a gallon on the meter. It had the round, revolving Coca-Cola signs, rock music, and crewcuts. People throng to places like that to relive memories of former days. What about heaven?

I imagine that the heavenly sanctuary will still be there—an important museum to visit, so that human beings can remember what Christ did for their salvation. I believe the archives of heaven will remain, with a full record of Christ's work for humanity. One can visualize a field trip to heaven to see the visual records of Christ's life and death—probably 33½ years' worth of filming to occupy human minds. Also we may find recordings of the sanctuary ministry, showing how Christ defended His people against the accusations of Satan; and much more. You'll enjoy checking out the video just on your own life—how He interceded for you. Heaven would be a great place to visit to gain historical insights into the great plan of redemption.

Perhaps it will have records of the rebellion among the angels and how Christ tried to keep them back from their tragic revolt, how He pleaded with Lucifer to see the wisdom of God and not plunge into the terrible cosmic controversy. Heaven's archives may have other great moments in salvation's plan.

Calvary Forever

Once our own great time of trouble has ended and the memory of sin and sinners is no more, we shall continue to study the great time of trouble that Christ endured for us. For seeing what He went through makes us realize that heaven is cheap enough, that our trials were nothing, that our final events didn't come anywhere near His.

"In this life we can only begin to understand the wonderful theme of redemption. With our finite comprehension we may consider most earnestly the shame and the glory, the life and the death, the justice and the mercy, that meet in the cross; yet with the utmost stretch of our mental powers we fail to grasp its full significance. The length and the breadth, the depth and the height, of redeeming love are but dimly comprehended. The plan of redemption will not be fully understood, even when the ransomed see as they are seen and know as they are known; but through the eternal ages new truth will continually unfold to the wondering and delighted mind. . . . The cross of Christ will be the science and the song of the redeemed through all eternity."[23]

One day you're sitting on the shore. The sea of life stretches before you. You thrill at the cheapness of heaven. Final events were nothing compared to eternity with Christ, the angels, and the redeemed. You have never had such freedom, such joy, such fulfillment. No more lonely days, heartaches, or emptiness. As you look out across the water you notice a shadow. Half turning, you see sandaled feet with crucifixion marks. "I've come to spend time with you," Jesus says softly as He places His arm around your shoulder and sits down with you. Think of the joy you'll have then! Just the two of you. You can ask Him all the questions you wish. He'll tell you how much He loves you, that you matter to Him, that He would have died just for you even if all the rest had turned Him down.

"Let us fix our eyes on Jesus, the author and perfecter of our faith, who for the joy set before him endured the cross" (Heb. 12:2). He focused His gaze on the goal and endured. So can we.

---

[1] E. G. White, *The Great Controversy,* p. 636.
[2] *Ibid.,* p. 637.
[3] *Ibid.,* p. 638.
[4] *Ibid.,* pp. 638, 639.
[5] *Ibid.,* pp. 639, 640.
[6] *Ibid.,* p. 640.
[7] E. G. White, *Last Day Events,* p. 277.
[8] E. G. White, *The Great Controversy,* p. 641.
[9] *Ibid.,* p. 645.
[10] E. G. White, *Early Writings,* p. 16.
[11] *Ibid.,* p. 35.
[12] E. G. White, *The Great Controversy,* p. 647.
[13] E. G. White, *Last Day Events,* p. 282.
[14] E. G. White, *The Great Controversy,* p. 645.
[15] E. G. White, *Testimonies for the Church,* vol. 8, p. 253.
[16] *Ibid.,* vol. 9, pp. 285, 286.
[17] *Ibid.,* p. 287.
[18] E. G. White, *The Great Controversy,* pp. 650, 651.
[19] *Ibid.,* pp. 651, 652.
[20] E. G. White, *Patriarchs and Prophets,* p. 62.

[21] E. G. White, *The Great Controversy,* pp. 662, 663.
[22] *Ibid.,* p. 667.
[23] *Ibid.,* p. 651.

Biblical Index

Biblical Index

Hosea

Joel

Amos

Obadiah

Micah

Habakkuk

Zephaniah

Haggai

Zechariah

Biblical Index

Biblical Index

Biblical Index

Biblical Index

Name Index

D

E

F

G

Name Index

Name Index

Topical Index

Topical Index